ADOBE
DREAMWEAVER CS5

Adobe
Approved Certification Courseware ™

Adobe
CERTIFIED ASSOCIATE
Approved Courseware ™

REVEALED

ADOBE DREAMWEAVER CS5

Adobe | Approved Certification Courseware ™

CERTIFIED ASSOCIATE
Approved Courseware ™

REVEALED

SHERRY BISHOP

DELMAR
CENGAGE Learning™

Australia • Brazil • Japan • Korea • Mexico • Singapore • Spain • United Kingdom • United States

DELMAR
CENGAGE Learning™

Adobe Dreamweaver CS5 Revealed
Sherry Bishop

Vice President, Career and Professional Editorial:
  Dave Garza

Director of Learning Solutions: Sandy Clark

Senior Acquisitions Editor: Jim Gish

Managing Editor: Larry Main

Product Managers: Jane Hosie-Bounar, Meaghan O'Brien

Editorial Assistant: Sarah Timm

Vice President Marketing, Career and Professional:
  Jennifer Baker

Executive Marketing Manager: Deborah S. Yarnell

Marketing Manager: Erin Brennan

Marketing Coordinator: Erin Deangelo

Production Director: Wendy Troeger

Senior Content Project Manager: Kathryn B. Kucharek

Developmental Editor: Barbara Clemens

Technical Editor: John Shanley

Senior Art Director: Joy Kocsis

Cover Design: Joe Villanova

Cover Art: Spitting Images

Cover Photographs:
  © istockphoto.com/Darko Novakovic (referees)
  © istockphoto.com/Acerebel (zebra)

Text Designer: Liz Kingslein

Production House: Integra Software Services Pvt. Ltd.

Proofreader: Harold Johnson

Indexer: Alexandra Nickerson

Technology Project Manager: Christopher Catalina

Printed in China

2 3 4 5 6 7 15 14 13 12 11

For product information and technology assistance, contact us at **Cengage Learning Customer & Sales Support, 1-800-354-9706**

For permission to use material from this text or product, submit all requests online at **www.cengage.com/permissions**

Further permissions questions can be emailed to **permissionrequest@cengage.com**

Adobe® Premiere Pro®, Adobe® After Effects®, Adobe®, Soundbooth®, Adobe® Encore®, Adobe® Photoshop®, Adobe® InDesign®, Adobe® Illustrator®, Adobe® Flash®, Adobe® Dreamweaver®, Adobe® Fireworks®, and Adobe® Creative Suite® are trademarks or registered trademarks of Adobe Systems, Inc. in the United States and/or other countries. Third party products, services, company names, logos, design, titles, words, or phrases within these materials may be trademarks of their respective owners.

Adobe product screenshots reprinted with permission from Adobe Systems Incorporated.

The Adobe Approved Certification Courseware logo is a proprietary trademark of Adobe. All rights reserved. Cengage Learning and Adobe Dreamweaver CS5—Revealed are independent from ProCert Labs, LLC and Adobe Systems Incorporated, and are not affiliated with ProCert Labs and Adobe in any manner. This publication may assist students to prepare for an Adobe Certified Expert exam, however, neither ProCert Labs nor Adobe warrant that use of this material will ensure success in connection with any exam.

The Adobe Certified Associate Approved Courseware logo is a proprietary trademark of Adobe. All rights reserved. Cengage Learning and Adobe Dreamweaver CS5—Revealed are independent from ProCert Labs, LLC and Adobe Systems Incorporated, and are not affiliated with ProCert Labs and Adobe in any manner. This publication may assist students to prepare for an Adobe Certified Associate exam, however, neither ProCert Labs nor Adobe warrant that use of this material will ensure success in connection with any exam.

Library of Congress Control Number: 2010921374

Hardcover edition:
ISBN-13: 978-1-111-13068-8
ISBN-10: 1-111-13068-X

Soft cover edition:
ISBN-13: 978-1-111-13066-4
ISBN-10: 1-111-13066-3

Delmar
Executive Woods
5 Maxwell Drive
Clifton Park, NY 12065
USA

Cengage Learning is a leading provider of customized learning solutions with office locations around the globe, including Singapore, the United Kingdom, Australia, Mexico, Brazil, and Japan. Locate your local office at **www.cengage.com/global**

Cengage Learning products are represented in Canada by Nelson Education, Ltd.

To learn more about Delmar, visit **www.cengage.com/delmar**

Purchase any of our products at your local college store or at our preferred online store **www.cengagebrain.com**

Notice to the Reader

Revealed Series Vision

The Revealed Series is your guide to today's hottest multimedia applications. These comprehensive books teach the skills behind the application, showing you how to apply smart design principles to multimedia products such as dynamic graphics, animation, websites, software authoring tools, and digital video.

A team of design professionals including multimedia instructors, students, authors, and editors worked together to create this series. We recognized the unique learning environment of the multimedia classroom and created a series that:

- Gives you comprehensive step-by-step instructions
- Offers in-depth explanation of the "Why" behind a skill
- Includes creative projects for additional practice
- Explains concepts clearly using full-color visuals

It was our goal to create a book that speaks directly to the multimedia and design community—one of the most rapidly growing computer fields today. We think we've done just that, with a sophisticated and instructive book design.

—The Revealed Series

New to This Edition

The latest edition of Adobe Dreamweaver CS5 Revealed includes many exciting new features, some of which are listed below:

- The new CSS Enable/Disable CSS Property button
- Redesigned CSS layouts
- Live view navigation feature
- Simplified site setup
- Web 2.0 coverage

AUTHOR'S VISION

This book will introduce you to a fascinating program that will hopefully inspire you to create rich and exciting websites. Through the work of many talented and creative individuals, this text was created for you. Our Product Manager, Jane Hosie-Bounar, guided and directed the team from start to finish. She is a talented and tireless individual—the ultimate professional and visionary. She is rock solid—someone I can always count on for sage advice and guidance. Barbara Clemens, my Development Editor, is an example of so many things I value: joy, kindness, patience, and determination. Although we live thousands of miles apart, I always feel a void when our working time together is over.

The copyright content was generously provided by my dear friend Barbara Waxer. Additional information on locating media on the Internet and determining its legal use is available in her Revealed Series book *Internet Surf and Turf Revealed: The Essential Guide to Copyright, Fair Use, and Finding Media.*

John Shanley did double duty this time. As the Dreamweaver Technical Editor for both Mac and PC, he carefully tested each step to make sure that the end product was error-free. He gave exceptional feedback as he reviewed each chapter. This part of the publishing process is what truly sets Delmar Cengage Learning apart from other publishers.

Tintu Thomas, Amrin Sahay, and Kathy Kucharek, our Content Product Managers, worked on the layout and kept the schedule on track. We thank them for keeping up with the many details and deadlines. The work is beautiful.

Brianna Hawes patiently contacted the websites we used as examples to obtain permission for their inclusion. This component adds much to the content of the book and would not have been possible without her good work. Thank you to each of you that allowed us to use images of your websites.

Harold Johnson quietly worked behind the scenes to ensure that my grammatical and punctuation errors were corrected. He also provided valuable insight in regard to the accuracy of content specifics.

Special thanks go to Jim Gish, Senior Acquisitions Editor, and Sandy Clark, the Director of Learning Solutions. They have embraced the Revealed books with enthusiasm and grace and provided us with such excellent resources to produce books that make us all proud. The book covers and interior design features are spectacular! Joe Villanova also did a fantastic job designing new banners and logos for the websites to give them a fresh new look.

The Beach Club in Gulf Shores, Alabama, (*www.beachclubal.com*) generously allowed us to use several photographs of their beautiful property for The Striped Umbrella website. Christie Adams, Executive Assistant, was extremely helpful and gracious.

The Revealed team watched the Deepwater Horizon environmental disaster in the Gulf of Mexico unfold with heavy hearts. We feel a special connection to this area with the inspiration the Beach Club in Gulf Shores, Alabama, has provided for The Striped Umbrella website. We are confident that the people, wildlife, beaches, and Gulf of Mexico itself will overcome the extreme challenges this tragedy has brought. We realize it will be a long process that will require the commitment of both time and money from many. We join the recovery effort by donating a portion of the proceeds from the sales of this book to The Nature Conservancy.

Typically, your family is the last to be thanked. My husband, Don, supports and encourages me every day, as he has for the last forty years. Our travels with our children and grandchildren provide happy memories for us and content for the websites. You will see the faces of my precious grandchildren Jacob, Emma, Thomas, and Caroline peeking out from some of the pages.

—Sherry Bishop

Introduction to Adobe Dreamweaver CS5, Revealed

Welcome to *Adobe Dreamweaver CS5—Revealed*. This book offers complete coverage of basic to intermediate Dreamweaver skills, helping you to create polished, professional-looking websites. Use this book both in the classroom and as your own reference guide.

This text is organized into 13 chapters. In these chapters, you will explore the many options Dreamweaver provides for creating dynamic Dreamweaver websites. You'll also work with many of the exciting features new to this release of the software. New features are marked with a **NEW** in the text.

What You'll Do

A What You'll Do figure begins every lesson. This figure gives you an at-a-glance look at what you'll do in the chapter, either by showing you a file from the current project or a tool you'll be using.

Comprehensive Conceptual Lessons

Before jumping into instructions, in-depth conceptual information tells you "why" skills are applied. This book provides the "how" and "why" through the use of professional examples. Also included in the text are tips and sidebars to help you work more efficiently and creatively, or to teach you a bit about the history or design philosophy behind the skill you are using.

Step-by-Step Instructions

This book combines in-depth conceptual information with concise steps to help you learn CS5. Each set of steps guides you through a lesson where you will create, modify, or enhance a CS5 file. Step references to large colorful images and quick step summaries round out the lessons. The Data Files for the steps are provided on the CD at the back of this book.

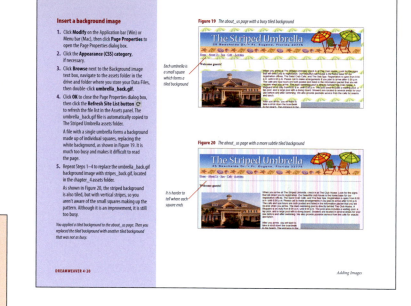

Projects

This book contains a variety of end-of-chapter materials for additional practice and reinforcement. The Skills Review contains hands-on practice exercises that mirror the progressive nature of the lesson material. The chapter concludes with four projects: two Project Builders, one Design Project, and one Portfolio Project. The Project Builders require you to apply the skills you've learned in the chapter. The Design Project incorporates critical thinking skills while evaluating live websites. Portfolio Projects encourage you to address and solve challenges based on the content explored in the chapter in order to create portfolio-quality work.

What Instructor Resources Are Available with This Book?

The Instructor Resources CD-ROM is Delmar's way of putting the resources and information needed to teach and learn effectively into your hands. All the resources are available for both Macintosh and Windows operating systems.

Instructor's Manual

Available as an electronic file, the Instructor's Manual includes chapter overviews and detailed lecture topics for each chapter, with teaching tips. The Instructor's Manual is available on the Instructor Resources CD-ROM.

Sample Syllabus

Available as an electronic file, the Sample Syllabus includes a suggested syllabus for any course that uses this book. The syllabus is available on the Instructor Resources CD-ROM.

PowerPoint Presentations

Each chapter has a corresponding PowerPoint presentation that you can use in lectures, distribute to your students, or customize to suit your course.

Data Files for Students

To complete most of the chapters in this book, your students will need Data Files. The Data Files are available on the CD at the back of this text book. Instruct students to use the Data Files List at the end of this book. This list gives instructions on organizing files.

Solutions to Exercises

Solution Files are Data Files completed with comprehensive sample answers. Use these files to evaluate your students' work. Or distribute them electronically so students can verify their work. Sample solutions to all lessons and end-of-chapter material are provided with the exception of some portfolio projects.

Test Bank and Test Engine

ExamView is a powerful testing software package that allows instructors to create and administer printed and computer (LAN-based) exams. ExamView includes hundreds of questions that correspond to the topics covered in this text, enabling students to generate detailed study guides that include page references for further review. The computer-based and LAN-based/online testing component allows students to take exams using the EV Player, and also saves the instructor time by grading each exam automatically.

Certification

This book covers the objectives necessary for Adobe Dreamweaver ACE and ACA certification. Use the Certification Grids at the back of the book to find out where an objective is covered.

DREAMWEAVER

CONTENTS

CHAPTER 1: GETTING STARTED WITH DREAMWEAVER

CHAPTER 5: WORKING WITH LINKS AND NAVIGATION

CHAPTER 6: POSITIONING OBJECTS WITH CSS AND TABLES

CHAPTER 9: COLLECTING DATA WITH FORMS

CHAPTER 11: ADDING MEDIA AND INTERACTIVITY WITH FLASH AND SPRY

CHAPTER 12: CREATING AND USING TEMPLATES

Intended Audience

This text is designed for the beginner or intermediate user who wants to learn how to use Dreamweaver. The book is designed to provide basic and in-depth material that not only educates, but also encourages you to explore the nuances of this exciting program. Features new to Dreamweaver CS5 and covered in this book are indicated by a New icon.

Approach

The text allows you to work at your own pace through step-by-step tutorials. A concept is presented and the process is explained, followed by the actual steps. To learn the most from the use of the text, you should adopt the following habits:

- Proceed slowly: Accuracy and comprehension are more important than speed.
- Understand what is happening with each step before you continue to the next step.
- After finishing a skill, ask yourself if you could do it on your own, without referring to the steps. If the answer is no, review the steps.

General

Throughout the initial chapters, students are given precise instructions regarding saving their work. Students should feel that they can save their work at any time, not just when instructed to do so.

Icons, Buttons, and Pointers

Symbols for icons, buttons, and pointers are shown in the step each time they are used. Icons may look different in the files panel depending on the file association settings on your computer. Once an icon, button, or pointer has been used on a page, the symbol will be shown for subsequent uses on that page *without* showing its name.

Skills Reference

As a bonus, a Power User Shortcuts table is included at the end of chapters. This table contains the quickest method of completing tasks covered in the chapter. It is meant for the more experienced user, or for the user who wants to become more experienced.

Fonts

The Data Files contain a variety of commonly used fonts, but there is no guarantee that these fonts will be available on your computer. In a few cases, fonts other than those common to a PC or a Macintosh are used. If any of the fonts in use is not available on your computer, you can make a substitution, realizing that the results may vary from those in the book.

Windows and Macintosh

Adobe Dreamweaver CS5 works virtually the same on Windows and Macintosh operating systems. In those cases where there is a significant difference, the abbreviations (Win) and (Mac) are used.

Data Files

To complete the lessons in this book, you need the Data Files on the CD in the back of this book. Your instructor will tell you where to store the files as you work, such as the hard drive, a network server, or a USB storage device. The instructions in the lessons will refer to "the drive and folder where you store your Data Files" when referring to the Data Files for the book.

When you copy the Data Files to your computer, you may see lock icons that indicate that the files are read-only when you view them in the Dreamweaver Files panel. To unlock the files, right-click on the locked file name in the Files panel, then click Turn off Read Only.

Images vs. Graphics

Many times these terms seem to be used interchangeably. For the purposes of this book, the term images is used when referring to pictures on a web page. The term graphics is used as a more encompassing term that refers to non-text items on a web page such as photographs, logos, navigation bars, Flash animations, graphs, background images, and drawings. You may define these terms in a slightly different way, depending on your professional background or business environment.

Preference Settings

The learning process will be much easier if you can see the file extensions for the files you will use in the lessons. To do this in Windows, open Windows Explorer, click Organize, Folder and Search Options, click the View tab, then uncheck the box Hide Extensions for Known File Types. To do this for a Mac, go to the Finder, click the Finder menu, and then click Preferences. Click the Advanced tab, then select the Show all file extensions check box.

Creating a Portfolio

The Portfolio Project and Project Builders allow students to use their creativity to come up with original Dreamweaver designs. You might suggest that students create a portfolio in which they can store their original work.

System Requirements

For a Windows operating system:

- Intel Pentium® 4 AMD Athlon® 64 processor
- Microsoft Windows® XP with Service Pack 2 (Service Pack 3 recommended); Windows Vista® Home Premium, Business, Ultimate, or Enterprise with Service Pack 1; or Windows 7
- 512 MB of RAM
- 1 GB of available hard-disk space for installation; additional free space required during installation (cannot install on removable flash-based storage devices)
- 1,280 × 800 display with 16-bit video card
- DVD-ROM drive
- Broadband Internet connection required for online services

For a Macintosh operating system:

- Multicore Intel® processor
- Mac OS X v10.5.7 or v10.6
- 512 MB of RAM or more recommended
- 1.8 GB of available hard-disk space for installation; additional hard-disk space required during installation (cannot install on a volume that uses a case-sensitive file system or on removable flash-based storage devices)
- 1,280 × 800 display with 16-bit video card
- DVD-ROM drive
- Broadband Internet connection required for online services*

Memory Challenges

If, instead of seeing an image on an open page, you see an image placeholder with a large X across it, your RAM is running low. Try closing any other applications that are running to free up memory.

Building a Website

You will create and develop several websites named The Striped Umbrella, Blooms & Bulbs, TripSmart, and Carolyne's Creations in the lesson material and end of unit exercises in this book. Because each chapter builds off of the previous chapter, it is recommended that you work through the chapters in consecutive order.

Websites Used in Figures

Each time a website is used for illustration purposes in a lesson, where necessary, a statement acknowledging that we obtained permission to use the website is included, along with the URL of the website. Sites whose content is in the public domain, such as federal government websites, are acknowledged as a courtesy.

CHAPTER

GETTING STARTED WITH
DREAMWEAVER

1. Explore the Dreamweaver workspace

2. View a web page and use Help

3. Plan and set up a website

4. Add a folder and pages

CHAPTER 1

GETTING STARTED WITH
DREAMWEAVER

Introduction

Adobe Dreamweaver CS5 is a web development tool that lets you create dynamic web pages containing text, images, hyperlinks, animation, sounds, video, and interactive elements. You can use Dreamweaver to create individual web pages or complex websites consisting of many web pages. A **website** is a group of related web pages that are linked together and share a common interface and design. Dreamweaver lets you create design elements such as text, tables, rollover images, and interactive buttons, or import elements from other software programs. You can also save Dreamweaver files in many different file formats, including XHTML, HTML, JavaScript, CSS, or XML, to name a few. **XHTML** is the acronym for eXtensible HyperText Markup Language, the current standard language used to create web pages. You can still use **HTML** (HyperText Markup Language) in Dreamweaver; however, it is no longer considered the standard language. You use a web browser to view your web pages on the Internet. A **web browser** is a program, such as Microsoft Internet Explorer, Google Chrome, Safari, or Mozilla Firefox, which lets you display web pages.

Using Dreamweaver Tools

Creating an excellent website is a complex task. Fortunately, Dreamweaver has an impressive number of tools that can help. Using Dreamweaver design tools, you can create dynamic and interactive web pages without writing a word of code. However, if you prefer to write code, Dreamweaver makes it easy to enter and edit the code directly and see the visual results of the code instantly. Dreamweaver also contains organizational tools that help you work with a team of people to create a website. You can also use the Dreamweaver management tools to help you manage a website. For instance, you can use the **Files panel** to create folders to organize and store the various files for your website, and to add pages to your website.

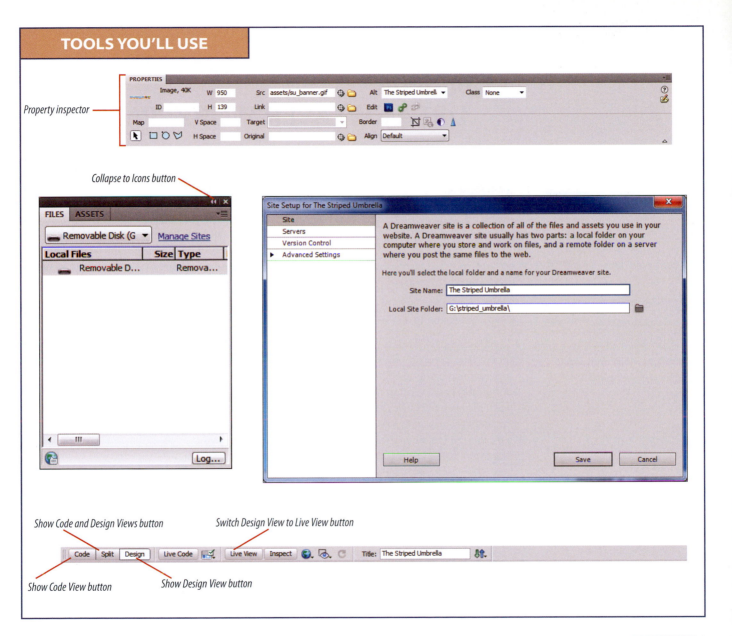

Property inspector

Collapse to Icons button

Show Code and Design Views button

Switch Design View to Live View button

Show Code View button

Show Design View button

Explore the
DREAMWEAVER WORKSPACE

What You'll Do

In this lesson, you will start Dreamweaver, examine the components that make up the Dreamweaver workspace, and change views.

Examining the Dreamweaver Workspace

After you start Dreamweaver, you see the **Dreamweaver workspace**, the screen that includes all of the menus, panels, buttons, inspectors, and panes that you use to create and maintain websites. It is designed to give you easy access to all the tools you need to create web pages. Refer to Figure 1 as you locate the components described below.

The **Document window** is the large area in the Dreamweaver program window where you create and edit web pages. The **Application bar** (Win) or **Menu bar** (Mac), located above the Document window, includes menu names, a Workspace switcher, and other application commands. The Application bar appears on either one bar or two bars, depending on your screen size and resolution. To choose a menu command, click the menu name to open the menu, then click the menu command. The Insert panel appears at the top of the Dreamweaver workspace on the right side of the screen. The **Insert panel**, sometimes called the Insert bar, includes eight categories of buttons displayed through a drop-down menu: Common, Layout,

Forms, Data, Spry, InContext Editing, Text, and Favorites. Clicking a category in the Insert panel displays the buttons and menus for inserting objects associated with that category. For example, if you click the Layout category, you find buttons for using div tags, used for creating blocks of content on pages; Spry buttons for inserting interactive page elements such as buttons or drop-down menus; Table buttons, used for inserting and editing tables; and the Frames button, used for selecting one of 13 different frame layouts.

QUICK TIP

Two additional options are available through the Insert panel drop-down menu. To display the icons in color, click Color Icons, or right-click the Insert panel, then click Color Icons. To hide the button labels, click Hide Labels.

The **Document toolbar** contains buttons and drop-down menus you can use to change the current work mode, check browser compatibility, preview web pages, debug web pages, choose visual aids, and view file-management options.

NEW The **Browser Navigation toolbar**, a new toolbar in Dreamweaver CS5, contains navigation buttons you use when you are

Getting Started with Dreamweaver

following links on your pages in Live view. **Live view** displays an open document as if you were viewing it in a browser, with interactive elements active and functioning.

Two additional toolbars do not appear by default: the Standard toolbar and the Style Rendering toolbar. The **Standard toolbar** contains buttons you can use to execute frequently used commands that are also available on the File and Edit menus. The **Style Rendering toolbar** contains buttons that you can use to display data for different platforms, such as a cell phone. To display or hide the Document, Standard, Browser Navigation, and Style Rendering toolbars, right-click an empty area of an open toolbar, then click the toolbar name you wish to display or hide. You can also use the View, Toolbars menu.

The **Related Files toolbar** is located below an open document's filename tab and displays the names of any related files. **Related files** are files that are linked to a document and are necessary for the document to display and function correctly. An external style sheet, which contains formatting rules that control the appearance of a document, is a good example of a related file. The **Coding toolbar** contains buttons you can use when working

Figure 1 *Dreamweaver CS5 workspace*

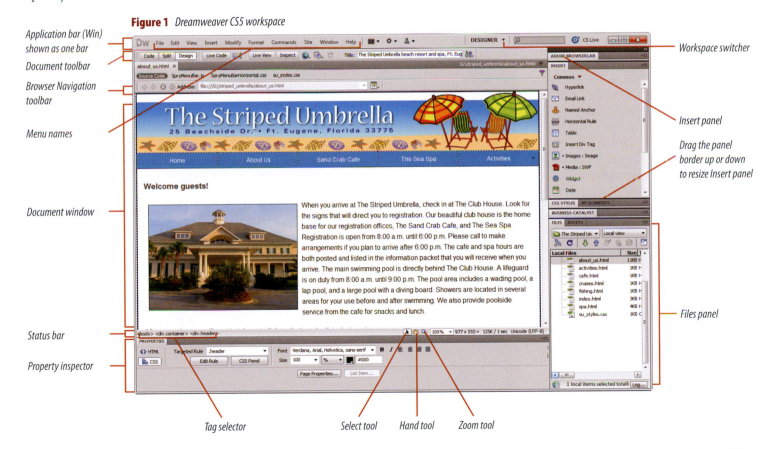

Application bar (Win) shown as one bar

Document toolbar

Browser Navigation toolbar

Menu names

Document window

Status bar

Property inspector

Workspace switcher

Insert panel

Drag the panel border up or down to resize Insert panel

Files panel

Tag selector

Select tool

Hand tool

Zoom tool

directly in the code and is not visible unless you are in Code view. When visible, it appears on the left side of the Document window.

The **Property inspector**, sometimes referred to as the **Properties pane**, located at the bottom of the Dreamweaver window, lets you view and change the properties (characteristics) of a selected object. The Property inspector is context sensitive, which means it changes according to what is selected in the Document window. The **status bar** is located below the Document window. The left side of the status bar displays the **tag selector**, which shows the HTML tags used at the insertion point location. The right side displays the Select tool, used for page editing; the Hand tool, used for panning; the Zoom tool, used for magnifying; and the Set Magnification menu, used to change the percentage of magnification. It also displays the window size and estimated download time for the current page.

A **panel** is a tabbed window that displays information on a particular topic or contains related commands. **Panel groups** are sets of related panels that are grouped together. A collection of panels or panel groups is called a **dock**. To view the contents of a panel in a panel group, click the panel's tab. Panels are docked by default on the right side of the screen. You can undock or "float" them by dragging the panel tab to another screen location. To collapse or expand a panel group, double-click the panel tab or the blank area in the panel title bar, as shown in Figure 2.

NEW When you first start Dreamweaver, the Insert, CSS Styles, AP Elements, Business Catalyst, Files, and Assets panels appear by default. You can open panels using the Window menu commands or the corresponding shortcut keys.

QUICK TIP

The Collapse to Icons button ▶▶ above the top panel lets you collapse all open panels to icons to enlarge the workspace.

Working with Dreamweaver Views

A **view** is a particular way of displaying page content. Dreamweaver has three working views. **Design view** shows the page as it would appear in a browser and is primarily used for designing and creating a web page. **Code view** shows the underlying HTML code for the page; use this view to read or edit the underlying code.

QUICK TIP

You can also split Code view to enable you to work on two different sections of code at once. To change to Split Code view, click View on the Application bar (Win) or Menu bar (Mac), then click Split Code.

Show Code and Design views is a combination of Code view and Design view. Show Code and Design views is the best view for **debugging** or correcting errors because you can immediately see how code modifications change the appearance of the page. The view buttons are located on the Document toolbar.

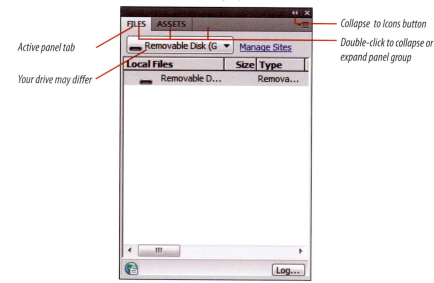

Figure 2 *Panels in panel group*

Active panel tab

Your drive may differ

Collapse to Icons button

Double-click to collapse or expand panel group

Figure 3 *Starting Dreamweaver CS5 (Windows)*

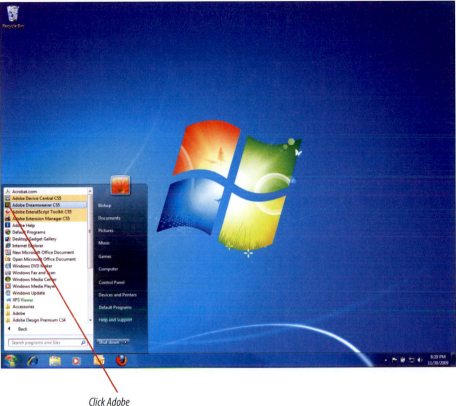

*Click Adobe
Dreamweaver CS5*

Start Dreamweaver (Windows)

1. Click the **Start button** 🟠 on the taskbar.
2. Point to **All Programs**, then click **Adobe Dreamweaver CS5**, as shown in Figure 3.
3. If the Default Editor dialog box opens, click **OK**.

You started Dreamweaver CS5 for Windows.

Hiding and Displaying Toolbars

To hide or display the Style Rendering, Document, Standard, or Browser Navigation toolbars, click View on the Application bar (Win) or Menu bar (Mac), point to Toolbars, then click Style Rendering, Document, Standard, or Browser Navigation. The Coding toolbar is available only in Code view and the Code window in Split view, and appears vertically in the Document window. By default, the Document and Browser Navigation toolbars appear in the workspace.

Start Dreamweaver (Macintosh)

1. Click **Finder** in the Dock, then click **Applications**.

2. Click the **Adobe Dreamweaver CS5 folder**, then double-click the **Adobe Dreamweaver CS5 application**, as shown in Figure 4.

TIP Once Dreamweaver is running, you can add it to the Dock permanently by [control]-clicking the Dreamweaver icon, clicking Options, then clicking Keep In Dock.

You started Dreamweaver CS5 for Macintosh.

Figure 4 *Starting Dreamweaver CS5 (Macintosh)*

Using Two Monitors for Optimum Workspace Layout

One option you have for workspace layout is Dual Screen layout. **Dual Screen layout** is the layout you would choose when you are using two monitors while working with Dreamweaver. The Document window and Property inspector appear on the first monitor and the panels appear on the second monitor. It is seamless to work between the two monitors and optimizes your workspace by allowing you to have multiple panels open without compromising your Document window space.

Figure 5 *Code view for new document*

Show Code
View button

Show Code and
Design Views button

Show Design
View button

Switch Design View
to Live View button

Application bar may be
displayed as two bars

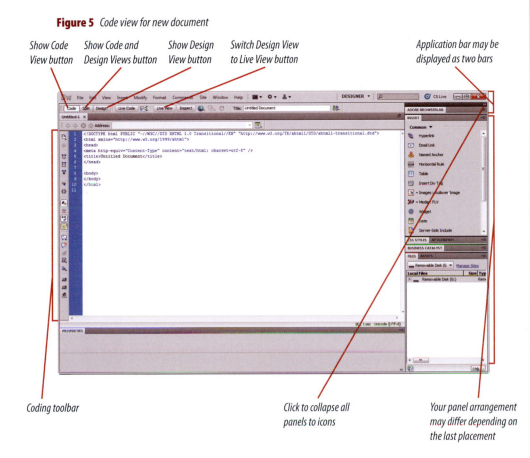

Coding toolbar

Click to collapse all
panels to icons

Your panel arrangement
may differ depending on
the last placement

1. Click **HTML** in the Create New category on the Dreamweaver Welcome Screen.

   The Dreamweaver Welcome Screen provides shortcuts for opening files and for creating new files or websites.

   TIP If you do not want the Dreamweaver Welcome Screen to appear each time you start Dreamweaver, click the Don't show again check box on the Welcome Screen or remove the check mark next to Show Welcome Screen in the General category in the Preferences dialog box.

2. Click the **Show Code View button** `Code` on the Document toolbar.

   The default code for a new document appears in the Document window, as shown in Figure 5.

   TIP The Coding toolbar is available only in Code view and in the Code window in Split view.

3. Click the **Show Code and Design Views button** `Split` on the Document toolbar.

4. Click the **Show Design View button** `Design` on the Document toolbar.

   TIP If your icons appear in black-and-white and you would like to display them in color, click the Insert panel drop-down menu, then click Color Icons.

   (continued)

5. Click the **Assets panel tab**, then compare your screen to Figure 6.

   TIP If the Assets panel is not visible, click Window on the Application bar (Win) or Menu bar (Mac), then click Assets.

6. Click the **Files panel tab** to display the contents of the Files panel.

7. Double-click **Assets** to collapse the panel group.

8. View the contents of the CSS Styles and AP Elements panels.

9. Click and drag the **blank area** next to the AP Elements tab to the middle of the document window.

   The panel group is now in a floating window.

   (continued)

Figure 6 *Displaying a panel group*

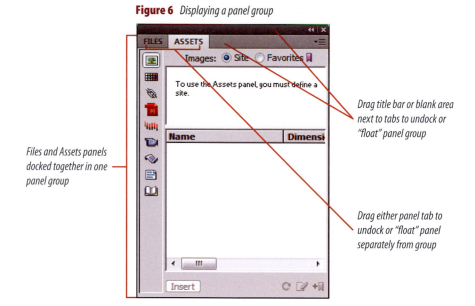

Files and Assets panels docked together in one panel group

Drag title bar or blank area next to tabs to undock or "float" panel group

Drag either panel tab to undock or "float" panel separately from group

Choosing a Workspace Layout

The Dreamweaver interface is an integrated workspace, which means that all of the document windows and panels appear in a single application window. Each open document appears as a tab below the document toolbar. (In the Mac OS, documents can either be tabbed together in a single window or displayed in separate windows.) To view a tabbed document, click the tab with the document's filename. The **Workspace switcher**, a drop-down menu in the top right corner on the Application bar, lets you change the workspace layout. The default layout is the Designer workspace layout, where the panels are docked on the right side of the screen and Split view is the default view. Other workplace layouts include App Developer, App Developer Plus, Classic, Coder, Coder Plus, Designer Compact, and Dual Screen. To change the workspace layout, click the Workspace switcher, then click the desired layout. You can also rearrange the workspace using your own choices for panel placement and save the workspace with a unique name using the "New Workspace" and "Manage Workspaces" commands on the Workspace switcher. The Reset 'Current view' option resets the workspace layout to return to the default positions on the screen for the selected view.

Getting Started with Dreamweaver

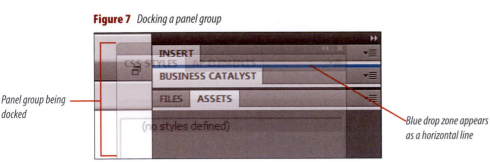

Figure 7 *Docking a panel group*

Panel group being docked

Blue drop zone appears as a horizontal line

10. Click and drag the **panel title bar** back to its original position, then drop it to dock the panel group below the Insert panel.

    Release the mouse only when you see the blue drop zone. The **blue drop zone** is a heavy blue line that appears when the panel is in the correct position to be docked. See Figure 7. If the blue drop zone appears as a box, releasing the button adds the panel to the boxed panel group.

TIP If you have rearranged the panels from their original positions and want to reset them back to their default positions, click the Workspace switcher drop-down menu, then click Reset 'Designer'. You will also have to reset the Color Icons, as color icons are not part of the default Designer workspace.

11. Click **File** on the Application bar (Win) or Menu bar (Mac), then click **Close** to close the open document.

You viewed a new web page using three views, opened panel groups, viewed their contents, then closed panel groups.

Viewing Your Page in Live View

When you view your web pages in Dreamweaver, the page elements appear similar to the way they will appear on the web, but not exactly. To get a better idea of how it will look, you can use the Switch Design View to Live View button on the Document toolbar. This button causes the open document to appear as it would in a browser, with interactive elements active and functioning. Next to the Live View button is the Shows the Live View source in code view button, which displays the code as read-only and cannot be modified without exiting "Shows the Live View source in code view." The code is highlighted in yellow and allows you to see the dynamic changes in the code while you interact with the dynamic content on the page. When the Switch Design View to Live View button is active, the Shows the Live View source in code view button can be toggled on or off. If Live View is not active, selecting the Shows the Live View source in code view button will turn it on. When you click the Live View button the first time, you may see a message that you need to install the Flash plug-in from the Adobe website, www.adobe.com. Download the plug-in and your page can then be viewed using Live View.

View a Web Page
AND USE HELP

What You'll Do

In this lesson, you will open a web page, view several page elements, and access the Help system.

Opening a Web Page

After starting Dreamweaver, you can create a new website, create a new web page, or open an existing website or web page. The first web page that appears when viewers go to a website is called the **home page**. The home page sets the look and feel of the website and directs viewers to the rest of the pages in the site.

Viewing Basic Web Page Elements

There are many elements that make up web pages. Web pages can be very simple and designed primarily with text, or they can be media-rich with images, sound, and movies, creating an enhanced interactive web experience. Figure 8 shows a web page with text and graphics that work together to create a simple and attractive page.

Most information on a web page is presented in the form of text. You can type text directly onto a web page in Dreamweaver or import text created in other programs. You can then use the Property inspector to format text so that it is attractive and easy to read. Text should be short and to the point to engage viewers and prevent them from losing interest and leaving your site.

Hyperlinks, also known as **links**, are images or text elements on a web page that users click to display another location on the page, another web page on the same website, or a web page on a different website.

Images add visual interest to a web page. The saying that "less is more" is certainly true with images, though. Too many images cause the page to load slowly and discourage viewers from waiting for the page to download. Many pages have **banners**, which are images that appear across the top or down the side of the screen that can incorporate a company's logo, contact information, and links to the other pages in the site.

Menu bars, also called navigation bars, are bars that contain multiple links that are usually organized in rows or columns. Sometimes menu bars are used with an image map. An **image map** is an image that has been divided into sections, each of which serves as a link. The way that menu bars and other internal links are used on your pages is referred to as the **navigation structure** of the site.

Rich media content is a comprehensive term that refers to attractive and engaging images, interactive elements, video, or animations.

Some of this content can be created in Dreamweaver, but much of it is created with other programs such as Adobe Flash, Fireworks, Photoshop, or Illustrator.

Getting Help

Dreamweaver has an excellent Help feature that is both comprehensive and easy to use.

When questions or problems arise, you can use the commands on the Help menu to find the answers you need. Clicking the Dreamweaver Help command opens the Dreamweaver Help page that contains a list of topics and subtopics by category. The Help feature in Dreamweaver CS5 **NEW** is now based on Adobe AIR technology. **Adobe AIR** is an Adobe product used for

developing content that can be delivered with a browser or as a desktop application.

The Search text box at the top of the window lets you enter a keyword to search for a specific topic. Context-specific help can be accessed by clicking the Help button on the Property inspector.

Figure 8 *Common web page elements*

National Endowment for the Arts website – www.arts.endow.gov

Open a web page and view basic page elements

1. Click **File** on the Application bar (Win) or Menu bar (Mac), then click **Open**.

2. Click the **Look in list arrow** (Win), or **navigation list arrow** (Mac), locate the drive and folder where you store your Data Files, then double-click the **chapter_1 folder** (Win), or click the **chapter_1 folder** (Mac).

3. Click **dw1_1.html**, then click **Open**. You may not see the .html file extension if the option for hiding file extensions for known file types is selected on your operating system.

TIP If you want your screen to match the figures in this book, make sure the Document window is maximized.

4. Click **Window** on the Application bar (Win) or Menu bar (Mac), then click **Hide Panels** to temporarily hide the panels.

   Hiding the panels gives you a larger viewing area for your web pages. You can also press [F4] to show or hide the panels. Note to Mac users: On the newest Mac OS, the F-keys are assigned to system functions. (F1=monitor brightness and F4=widgets) You can change this in your system preferences. Newer keyboards have an "FN" or "fn" key that can be used in conjunction with the F-keys so that they function "normally."

5. Locate each of the web page elements shown in Figure 9.

TIP Because you are opening a single page that is not in a website with access to the other pages, the links will not work.

(continued)

Figure 9 *Viewing web page elements (Win)*

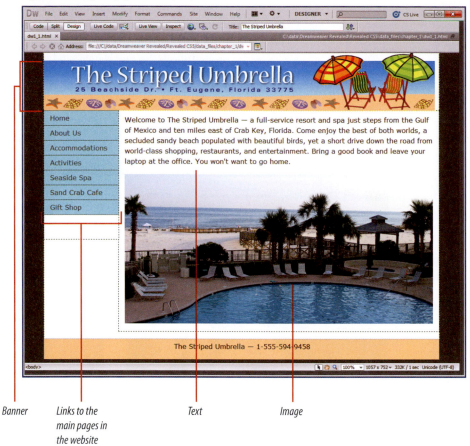

Banner   Links to the main pages in the website   Text   Image

Figure 9 *Viewing web page elements (Mac)*

Banner   Text   Image

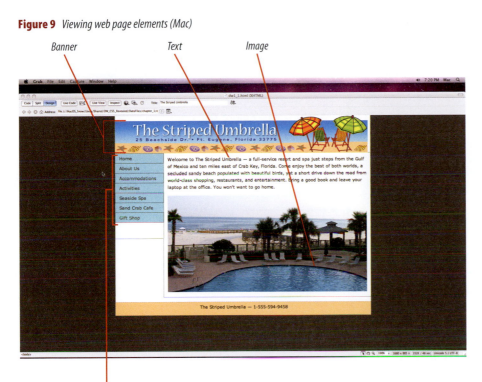

Links to the
main pages in
the website

6. Press **[F4]** to show the panels.

7. Click the **Show Code View button** `Code` to view the code for the page.

8. Scroll down to view all the code, if necessary, then click the **Show Design View button** `Design` to return to Design view.

TIP To show and highlight the code for a particular page element, select the page element in Design view, then click the Show Code View button.

9. Click **File** on the Application bar (Win) or Menu bar (Mac), then click **Close** to close the open page without saving it.

TIP You can also click the X on the filename tab to close the page.

You opened a web page, located several page elements, viewed the code for the page, then closed the page without saving it.

Use Dreamweaver Help

1. Click **Help** on the Application bar (Win) or Menu bar (Mac), then click **Dreamweaver Help**.

   The Adobe Community Help window opens.

TIP You can also open the Help feature by pressing [F1].

2. Click the **View Help PDF** link in the top right corner of the Adobe Dreamweaver CS5 pane as shown in Figure 10.

TIP If you don't see the link, enlarge or maximize the window.

3. Click the **plus sign** next to Chapter 2: Workspace in the left column, click the **plus sign** next to Working in the Document window, then click **Switch between views in the Document window**.

   The topic opens on the right side of the Help window, as shown in Figure 11.

4. Read the text in the content side of the Help window, then click the **Back button** to return to the opening Help screen.

(continued)

Figure 10 *Dreamweaver Help window*

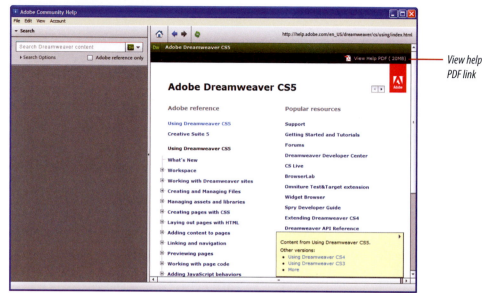

View help PDF link

Figure 11 *Displaying Help content*

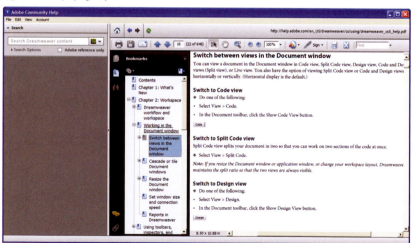

Getting Started with Dreamweaver

Figure 12 *Searching for a topic in Help*

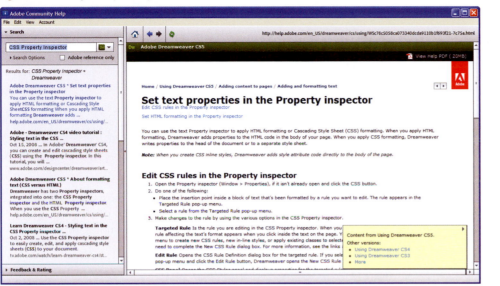

5. In the Search pane, type **CSS Property inspector** in the search text box, then press **[Enter]** (Win) or **[Return]** (Mac).

   A list of topics related to the search terms opens in the Search pane, as shown in Figure 12.

6. Click one of the links to read information about one of the topics of your choice.

7. Close the Adobe Community Help window.

You used Adobe Community Help to read information in the Adobe Dreamweaver CS5 documentation and in the Community Help files.

Using Adobe Community Help

When you access the Help feature in Dreamweaver, you have a choice of using offline help (which is similar to searching in a Dreamweaver manual) or using online help. The online help feature is called Adobe Community Help. **Adobe Community Help** is a collection of materials such as tutorials, published articles, or blogs, in addition to the regular help content. All content is monitored and approved by the Adobe Community Expert program.

Plan and Set Up
A WEBSITE

What You'll Do

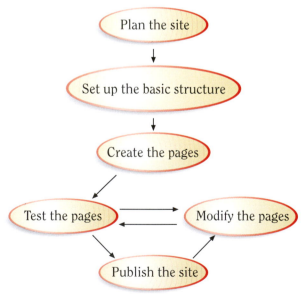

In this lesson, you will review a website plan for The Striped Umbrella, a beach resort and spa. You will also create a local site folder for The Striped Umbrella website, and then set up the website.

Understanding the Website Development Process

Creating a website is a complex process. It can often involve a large team of people working in various roles to ensure that the website contains accurate information, looks good, and works smoothly. Figure 13 illustrates the phases in a website development project.

Planning a Website

Planning is probably the most important part of any successful project. Planning is an essential part of creating a website, and

Figure 13 *Phases of a website development project*

Plan the site

↓

Set up the basic structure

↓

Create the pages

Test the pages ⇄ Modify the pages

Publish the site

is a continuous process that overlaps the subsequent phases. To start planning your website, you need to create a checklist of questions and answers about the site. For example, what are your goals for the site? Who is the audience you want to target? Teenagers? Children? Sports enthusiasts? Senior citizens? How can you design the site to appeal to the target audience? What content is appropriate for the target audience? What content is relevant to the purpose of the website? The more questions you can answer about the site, the more prepared you will be when you begin the developmental phase. Because of the public demand for up-to-date information, your plan should include not just how to get the site up and running, but how to keep it current.

Table 1 lists some of the basic questions you need to answer during the planning phase for almost any type of website. From your checklist, you should create a statement of purpose and scope, a timeline for all due dates, a budget, a task list with work assignments, and a list of resources needed. You should also include a list of deliverables, such as page prototypes and art for approval. The due dates for each deliverable should be included in the timeline.

Plan the Basic Structure

Once you complete the planning phase, you need to determine the structure of the site by creating a wireframe. A **wireframe**, sometimes referred to as a storyboard, is an illustration that represents every page

in a website. Like a flowchart, a wireframe shows the relationship of each page in the site to all the other pages. Wireframes also show how each page element is to be placed on each page. Wireframes are helpful when planning a website, because they allow you to visualize how each page in the site links to others. They are also an important tool to help the client see how the pages will look and work together. Make sure that the client and all other interested stakeholders approve the wireframe before the site construction actually begins. Wireframes range from very simple (known as low-fidelity wireframes) to interactive and multidimensional (known as high-fidelity wireframes). You can create a simple wireframe by using a pencil and

TABLE 1: WEBSITE PLANNING CHECKLIST	
Question	**Examples**
1. Who is the target audience?	Seniors, teens, children
2. How can I tailor the site to reach that audience?	Specify an appropriate reading level, decide the optimal amount of media content, use formal or casual language
3. What are the goals for the site?	Sell a product, provide information
4. How will I gather the information?	Recruit other employees, write it myself, use content from in-house documents
5. What are my sources for media content?	Internal production department, outside production company, my own photographs
6. What is my budget?	Very limited, well financed
7. What is the timeline?	Two weeks, one month, six months
8. Who is on my project team?	Just me, a complete staff of designers
9. How often should the site be updated?	Every 10 minutes, once a month
10. Who will update the site?	Me, other team members

paper or by using a graphics program on a computer, such as Adobe Illustrator, Adobe Fireworks, or Microsoft PowerPoint. To create more complex wireframes that simulate the site navigation and user interaction, use a high-fidelity wireframe program such as OverSite, ProtoShare, Microsoft Visio, or Adobe Flash Catalyst. The basic wireframe shown in Figure 14 shows all the The Striped Umbrella website pages that you will create in this book. The home page appears at the top of the wireframe, and it has four pages linked to it. The home page is called the **parent page**, because it is at a higher level in the web hierarchy and has pages linked to it. The pages linked below it are called **child pages**. The Activities page, which is a child page to the home page, is also a parent page to the Cruises and Fishing pages. You can refer to this wireframe as you create the actual links in Dreamweaver.

More detailed wireframes also include all document names, images, text files, and link information. Use your wireframe as your guide as you develop the site to make sure you follow the planned site structure.

In addition to creating a wireframe for your site, you should also create a folder hierarchy on your computer for all of the files that will be used in the site. Start by creating a folder for the site with a descriptive name, such as the name of the company. This folder, known as the **local site folder**, will store all the pages or HTML files for the site. Traditionally, this folder has been called the **root folder** and many people still use this term; in this book we will call it the local site folder. Then create a subfolder, often called **assets** or **images**, in which you store all of the files that are not pages, such as images and sound files.

After you create the local site folder, you need to set up your site. When you **set up** a site, you use the Dreamweaver Site Setup dialog box to assign your site a name and specify the local site folder. After you have set up your site, the site name and any folders and files it contains appear in the **Files panel**, the panel you use to manage your website's files and folders. Using the Files panel to manage your files ensures that the site links work correctly when the website is published. You also use the Files panel to add or delete pages.

Creating the Web Pages and Collecting the Page Content

This is the fun part! After you create your wireframe, obtain approvals, and set up your site, you need to gather the files you'll need to create the pages, including text, images, buttons, video, and animations. You will import some of these pages from other software programs, and some you will create in Dreamweaver. For example, you can create text in a word-processing program and import or paste it into Dreamweaver, or you can create and format text in Dreamweaver.

Images, tables, colors, and horizontal rules all contribute to making a page attractive and interesting, but they can increase file size. In choosing your page elements, carefully

Figure 14 *The Striped Umbrella website wireframe*

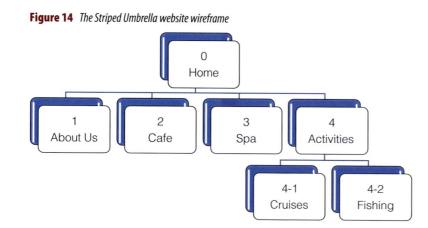

Getting Started with Dreamweaver

consider the file size of each page. A page with too many graphic elements might take a long time to load, which could cause visitors to leave your site.

Testing the Pages

Once all your pages are completed, you need to test the site to make sure all the links work and that everything looks good. It is important to test your web pages using different browser software. The four most common browsers are Microsoft Internet Explorer, Mozilla Firefox, Google Chrome, and Safari. Test your site using different versions of each browser, because older versions may not support the latest web technology. You should also test your site using a variety of screen sizes. Some viewers may have small monitors, while others may have large, high-resolution monitors. Also consider connection download time. Although

more people use cable modems or DSL (digital subscriber line), some still use slower dial-up modems. Testing is a continuous process, for which you should allocate plenty of time.

Modifying the Pages

After you create a website, you'll probably find that you need to keep making changes to it, especially when information on the site needs to be updated. Each time you make a change, such as adding a new button or image to a page, you should test the site again. Modifying and testing pages in a website is an ongoing process.

Publishing the Site

Publishing a website refers to the process of transferring all the files for the site to a **web server**, a computer that is connected

to the Internet with an IP (Internet Protocol) address, so that it is available for viewing on the Internet. A website must be published so that Internet users can view it. There are several options for publishing a website. For instance, many **Internet Service Providers (ISPs)** provide space on their servers for customers to publish websites, and some commercial websites provide limited free space for their viewers. Although publishing happens at the end of the process, it's a good idea to set up web server access in the planning phase. Use the Files panel to transfer your files using the Dreamweaver FTP capability. **FTP (File Transfer Protocol)** is the process of uploading and downloading files to and from a remote site.

Managing a Project with a Team

When working with a team, it is essential that you define clear goals for the project and a list of objectives to accomplish those goals. You plan should be finalized after conferring with both the clients and other team members to make sure that the purpose, scope, and objectives are clear to everyone. Establish the **deliverables**, or products that will be provided to the client at the product completion such as new pages or graphic elements created, and a timeline for their delivery. You should present the web pages at strategic times in the development process to your team members and to your clients for feedback and evaluation. Analyze all feedback objectively, incorporating both the positive and the negative comments to help you make improvements to the site and meet the clients' expectations and goals. A common pitfall in team management is **scope creep**. Scope creep means making impromptu changes or additions to a project without corresponding increases in the schedule or budget. Proper project control and communication between team members and clients can minimize scope creep and achieve the successful and timely completion of a project.

Select the location for your website

1. Open or expand the Files panel if necessary to view the contents.
2. Click the **drive or folder** that is currently displayed in the pop-up menu in the Files panel. See Figure 15.
3. Click to select the **drive or folder** (or subfolder) in the list where you will store your folders and files for your websites.

   Dreamweaver will store all of the folders and files you create inside this drive or folder.

You selected the drive or folder where you will create your website.

Figure 15 *Selecting a drive in the Files panel*

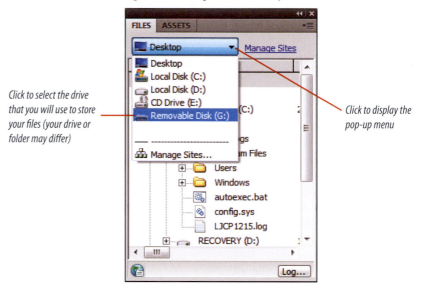

Click to select the drive that you will use to store your files (your drive or folder may differ)

Click to display the pop-up menu

Understanding IP Addresses and Domain Names

To be accessible over the Internet, a website must be published to a web server with a permanent IP address. An **IP address** is an assigned series of numbers, separated by periods, that designates an address on the Internet. To access a web page, you can enter either an IP address or a domain name in the address text box of your browser window. A **domain name** is a web address that is expressed in letters instead of numbers and usually reflects the name of the business represented by the website. For example, the domain name of the Adobe website is www.adobe.com, but the IP address is 192.150.18.200. Because domain names use descriptive text instead of numbers, they are much easier to remember. Compare an IP address to your Social Security number and a domain name to your name. Both your Social Security number and your name are used to refer to you as a person, but your name is much easier for your friends and family to use than your Social Security number. You can type the IP address or the domain name in the address text box of the browser window to access a website. The domain name is also referred to as a **URL** or Uniform Resource Locator.

Figure 16 *Creating a local site folder using the Files panel*

Your drive or folder may differ

striped_umbrella folder will become the local site folder after the site is defined (the folder is yellow (Win) or blue (Mac)

If you just see a drive or folder name here, you do not currently have a website open

Figure 17 *Viewing an open website in the Files panel*

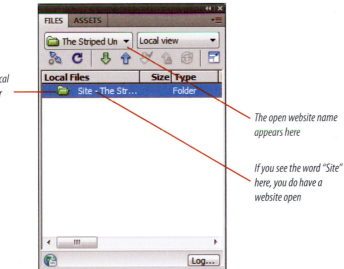

striped_umbrella local site folder (the folder is green)

The open website name appears here

If you see the word "Site" here, you do have a website open

Create a local site folder

1. Verify that the drive or folder where you want to store your site is selected in the Files panel, right-click (Windows) or control-click (Macintosh) the **drive or folder**, then click **New Folder**.

2. Type **striped_umbrella** to rename the folder, then press **[Enter]**.

   The folder is renamed striped_umbrella, as shown in Figure 16. You have not created a website yet. You have just created the folder that will serve as the local site folder after you set up the site.

   The folder color is currently yellow (Mac users will see blue folders), but after you set up the site in the next section, it will change to green. Notice the difference between Figure 16 and Figure 17. In Figure 16, you have only created the local site folder, not the website, and the color of the folder is yellow. In Figure 17, The Striped Umbrella website has been created and is open, so the local site folder is green.

   You created a new folder to serve as the local site folder for The Striped Umbrella website.

Set up a website

1. Click **Site** on the Application bar (Win) or Menu bar (Mac), then click **New Site**.

2. Click **Site** in the category list in the Site Setup for Unnamed Site dialog box (if necessary), then type **The Striped Umbrella** in the Site name text box.

TIP You can use uppercase letters and spaces in the site name because it is not the name of a folder or a file.

3. Click the **Browse for folder icon** 📁 next to the Local Site Folder text box, click the **Select list arrow** (Win) or the **navigation list arrow** (Mac) in the Choose Root folder dialog box, navigate to and click the **drive and folder** where your website files will be stored, then click the **striped_umbrella folder**.

4. Click **Open** (Win) or **Choose** (Mac), then click **Select** (Win). See Figure 18.

You created a website and set it up with the name The Striped Umbrella. You then told Dreamweaver the folder name and location to use for the local site folder.

Figure 18 *Site Setup for The Striped Umbrella dialog box*

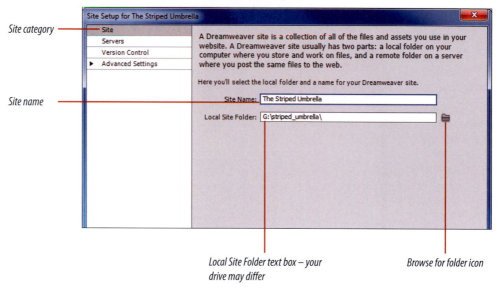

Site category

Site name

Local Site Folder text box – your drive may differ

Browse for folder icon

Understanding the Process of Publishing a Website

Before publishing a website so that web viewers can access it, you should first create a **local site folder**, called the **local root folder**, to house all the files for your website, as you did on page 1-23. This folder usually resides on your hard drive. Next, you need to gain access to a remote server. A **remote server** is a web server that hosts websites and is not directly connected to the computer housing the local site. Many Internet Service Providers, or ISPs, provide space for publishing websites on their servers. Once you have access to a remote server, you can then use the Servers category in the Site Setup dialog box to enter information such as the FTP host, host directory, login, and password. After entering this information, you can then use the Put File(s) button in the Files panel to transfer the files to the designated remote server. Once the site is published to a remote server, it is called a **remote site**.

Figure 19 *Adding a server for Remote Access for the Striped Umbrella website*

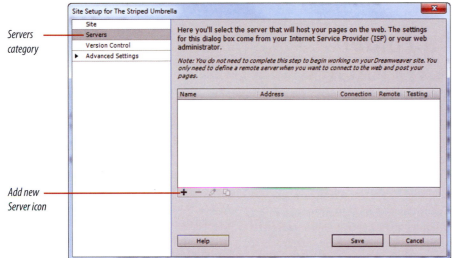

Servers category

Add new Server icon

Figure 20 *Entering publishing information for The Striped Umbrella website*

Enter server name here

Choices for publishing a website

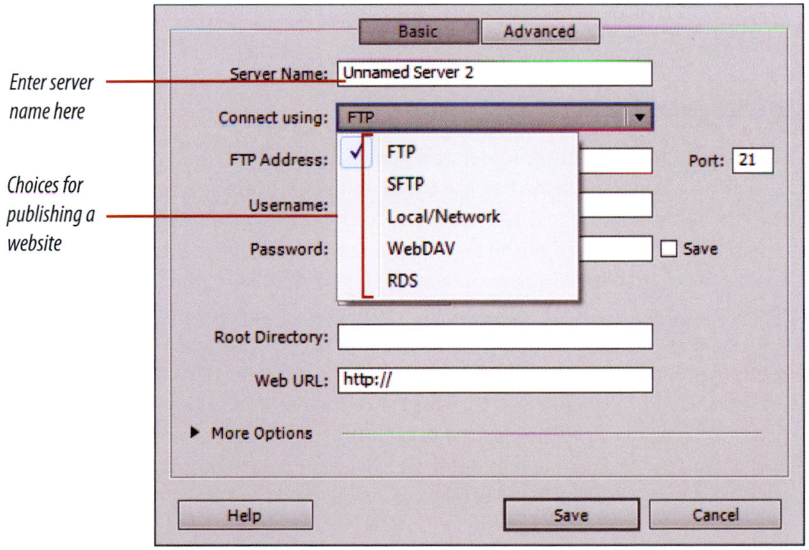

Set up web server access

1. Click **Servers** in the Category list, then click the **Add new Server icon** ✚, as shown in Figure 19.

TIP If you do not have the information to publish your website, skip step 2 and continue to step 3. You can specify this information later.

2. Click the **Connect using: list arrow**, choose the method you will use to publish your website, as shown in Figure 20, enter any necessary information in the Site Setup for The Striped Umbrella dialog box based on the setting you chose, then click **Save**.

TIP Your network administrator or web hosting service will give you the necessary information to publish your website.

3. Click **Save** to close the Site Setup dialog box.

You set up the remote access information to prepare you for publishing your website.

Add a Folder
AND PAGES

What You'll Do

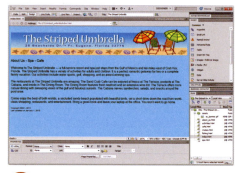

In this lesson, you will use the Files panel to create a new folder and new pages for the website.

Adding a Folder to a Website

After setting up a website, you need to create folders to organize the files that will make up the site. Creating a folder called **assets** is a good beginning. There is nothing magic about the word "assets," though. You can name your folder anything that makes sense to you, as long as you follow proper folder naming conventions such as avoiding the use of spaces. You can use the assets folder to store all non-HTML files, such as images or sound files. Many designers name this folder "images" and use additional folders to store other types of supporting files. After you create the assets folder, it is a good idea to set it as the default location to store the website images. This saves a step when you import new images into the website.

DESIGN**TIP**

Creating An Effective Navigation Structure

When you create a website, it's important to consider how your viewers will navigate from page to page within the site. A menu bar, or navigation bar, is a critical tool for moving around a website, so it's important that all text, buttons, and icons used in a menu bar have a consistent look across all pages. If you use a complex menu bar, such as one that incorporates JavaScript or Flash, it's a good idea to include plain text links in another location on the page for accessibility. Otherwise, viewers might become confused or lost within the site. A navigation structure can include more links than those included in a menu bar, however. For instance, it can contain other sets of links that relate to the content of a specific page and which are placed at the bottom or sides of a page in a different format. No matter which navigation structure you use, make sure that every page includes a link back to the home page. Don't make viewers rely on the Back button on the browser toolbar to find their way back to the home page. It's possible that the viewer's current page might have opened as a result of a search and clicking the Back button will take the viewer out of the website.

Creating the Home Page

The **home page** of a website is the first page that viewers see when they visit your site. Most websites contain many other pages that all connect back to the home page. The home page filename usually has the name index.html (.htm), or default.html (.htm).

Adding Pages to a Website

Websites might be as simple as one page or might contain hundreds of pages. When you create a website, you can add all the pages and specify where they should be placed in the website folder structure in the local site folder. Once you add and name all the pages in the website, you can then add the content, such as text and graphics, to each page. One method is to add as many blank pages as you think you will need in the beginning, rather than adding them one at a time with all the content in place. This enables you to set up the navigation structure of the website at the beginning of the development process and view how each page is linked to others. When you are satisfied with the overall structure, you can then add the content to each page. This is strictly a personal preference, however.

You can also choose to add and link pages as you create them, and that will work just fine, too.

You have a choice of several default document types you can generate when you create new HTML pages. The default document type is designated in the Preferences dialog box. XHTML 1.0 Transitional is the default document type when you install Dreamweaver and will be used throughout this book. It's important to understand the terminology—the pages are still called HTML pages and the file extension is still HTML, but the document type will be XHTML 1.0 Transitional.

Using the Files Panel for File Management

You should use the Files panel to add, delete, move, or rename files and folders in a website. It is very important that you perform these file-maintenance tasks in the Files panel rather than in Windows Explorer (Win) or in the Finder (Mac). Working outside of Dreamweaver, such as in Windows Explorer, can cause linking errors. You cannot take advantage of the simple, yet powerful, Dreamweaver site-management features unless you use the Files panel for all file-management activities. You might choose to use Windows Explorer (Win) or the Finder (Mac) only to create the local site folder or to move or copy the local site folder of a website to another location. If you move or copy the local site folder to a new location, you will have to set up the site again in the Files panel, as you did in Lesson 3 of this chapter. Setting up a site is not difficult and will become routine for you after you practice a bit. If you are using Dreamweaver on multiple computers, such as in labs or at home, you will have to set up your sites the first time you change to a different computer.

Add a folder to a website (Windows)

1. Right-click **Site - The Striped Umbrella** in the Files panel, then click **New Folder**.

2. Type **assets** in the folder text box, then press **[Enter]**.

TIP To rename a folder, click the folder name once, pause, click again, then type the new name.

3. Compare your screen to Figure 21.

You used the Files panel to create a new folder in the striped_umbrella folder and named it "assets".

Add a folder to a website (Macintosh)

1. Press and hold **[control]**, click the **striped_umbrella folder**, then click **New Folder**.

2. Type **assets** in the new folder name text box, then press **[return]**.

TIP To rename a folder, click the folder name text box, type the new name, then press **[return]**.

3. Compare your screen to Figure 22.

You used the Files panel to create a new folder in the striped_umbrella folder and named it "assets".

Figure 21 *The Striped Umbrella site in Files panel with assets folder created (Windows)*

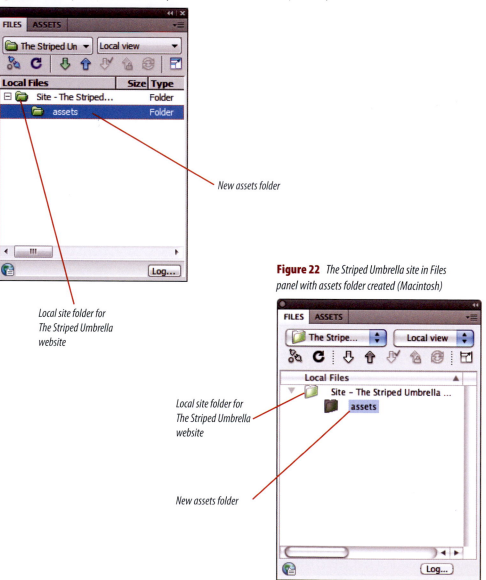

New assets folder

Local site folder for The Striped Umbrella website

Figure 22 *The Striped Umbrella site in Files panel with assets folder created (Macintosh)*

Local site folder for The Striped Umbrella website

New assets folder

Getting Started with Dreamweaver

Figure 23 *Site Setup for The Striped Umbrella dialog box with the assets folder set as the default images folder*

Advanced Settings category

Default Images folder text box

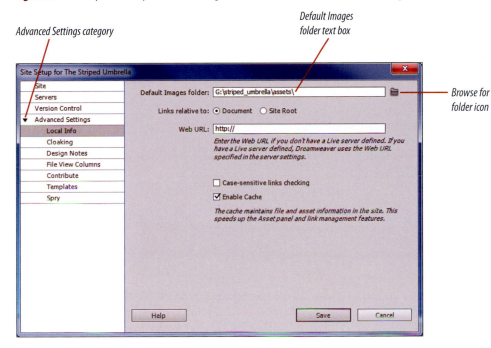

Browse for folder icon

Set the default images folder

1. Click the Site pop-up menu in the Files panel, click **Manage Sites**, then click **Edit**.

2. Click **Advanced Settings** in the category list in the Site Setup dialog box, then click **Local Info** if necessary.

3. Click the **Browse for folder icon** 📁 next to the Default Images folder text box.

4. If necessary, navigate to your striped_umbrella folder, double-click the **assets folder** (Win) or click the **assets folder** (Mac) in the Choose Image Folder dialog box, then click **Select** (Win) or **Choose** (Mac).

   Compare your screen to Figure 23.

5. Click **Save**, then click **Done**.

You set the assets folder as the default images folder so that imported images will be automatically saved in it.

Create the home page

1. Open **dw1_2.html** from the drive and folder where you store your Data Files.

   The file has several elements in it, including a banner image.

2. Click **File** on the Application bar (Win) or Menu bar (Mac), click **Save As**, click the **Save in list arrow** (Win) or the **Where list arrow** (Mac), navigate to the striped_umbrella folder, select **dw1_2.html** in the File name text box (Win) or select **dw1_2** in the Save As text box (Mac), then type **index.html**.

   Windows users do not have to type the file extension. It will be added automatically.

3. Click **Save**, then click **No** when asked to update links.

   As shown in Figure 24, the drive where the local site folder is stored, the local site folder name, and the page's filename are displayed to the right of the document tab and in the Address text box in the Browser Navigation toolbar. This information is called the **path**, or location of the open file in relation to other folders in the website.

   The banner image is no longer visible and a gray broken link placeholder appears in its place. This is because although you saved the .html file under a new name in the website's local site folder, you have not yet copied the image file into the website's assets folder. The banner image is still linked to the Data Files folder. You will fix this in the next set of steps.

   You opened a file, then saved it with the filename index.

Figure 24 *index.html placed in the striped_umbrella local site folder*

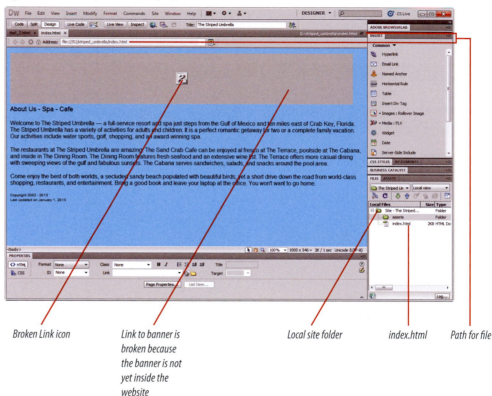

Broken Link icon

Link to banner is broken because the banner is not yet inside the website

Local site folder

index.html

Path for file

Figure 25 *Property inspector showing properties of The Striped Umbrella banner*

The Striped
Umbrella banner

Selection handles

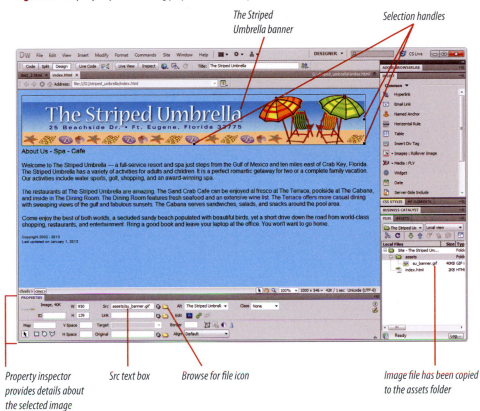

Property inspector
provides details about
the selected image

Src text box

Browse for file icon

Image file has been copied
to the assets folder

Save an image file in the assets folder

1. Click the **broken link placeholder** to select it.

   Small, black selection handles appear around the broken link. To correct the broken link, you must copy the image file from the Data Files folder into the assets folder of your website.

2. Click the **Browse for File icon** ☐ next to the Src text box in the Property inspector, navigate to the assets folder in your Data Files folder for this chapter, click **su_banner.gif**, click **OK** (Win) or **Choose** (Mac), then click in a blank part of the page. (Click the banner placeholder image again if the banner still doesn't appear.)

   The file for The Striped Umbrella banner, su_banner.gif, is automatically copied to the assets folder of The Striped Umbrella website, the folder that you designated as the default images folder. When the image is selected, the Src text box shows the path of the banner to the assets folder in the website, and the banner image is visible on the page.

TIP If you do not see the su_banner.gif file listed in the Files panel, click the Refresh button ⟳ on the Files panel toolbar.

3. Select the banner to view the banner properties in the Property inspector, then compare your screen to Figure 25.

TIP Until you copy an image from an outside folder to your website, the image is not part of the website and will appear as a broken link.

You saved The Striped Umbrella banner in the assets folder.

Add pages to a website (Windows)

1. Click the **plus sign** to the left of the assets folder (if necessary) to open the folder and view its contents, su_banner.gif.

TIP If you do not see a file listed in the assets folder, click the Refresh button  on the Files panel toolbar.

2. Right-click the **striped_umbrella local site folder**, click **New File**, type **about_us.html** to replace untitled.html, then press **[Enter]**.

   Each new file is a page in the website. This page does not have page content or a page title yet.

TIP If you create a new file in the Files panel, use care to make sure the .html file extension is not deleted or that the file does not end up with a double file extension.

3. Repeat Step 2 to add five more blank pages to The Striped Umbrella website, naming the new files **spa.html**, **cafe.html**, **activities.html**, **cruises.html**, and **fishing.html**.

TIP Make sure to add the new files to the site folder, not the assets folder. If you accidentally add them to the assets folder, just drag them to the site folder.

4. Click the **Refresh button** on the Files panel to list the files alphabetically, then compare your screen to Figure 26.

5. Click **File**, **Save**, to save the index.html file, if necessary, close both open files, click **File** on the Application bar then click **Exit**.

TIP If you are prompted to save changes to the dw1_1.html file, click No.

You added the following six pages to The Striped Umbrella website: about_us, activities, cafe, cruises, fishing, and spa.

Figure 26 *New pages added to The Striped Umbrella website (Windows)*

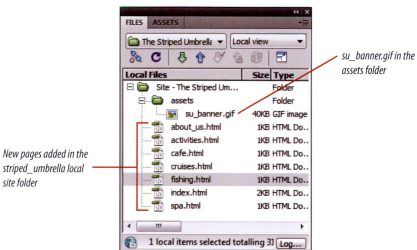

su_banner.gif in the assets folder

New pages added in the striped_umbrella local site folder

DESIGN**TIP**

Adding Page Titles

When you view a web page in a browser, its page title appears in the browser window title bar. (The page title is different from the filename, the name used to save the page on a computer.) The page title reflects the page content and sets the tone for the page. It is especially important to use words in your page title that are likely to match keywords viewers might enter when using a search engine. Search engines compare the text in page titles to the keywords typed into the search engine. When a title bar displays "Untitled Document," the designer has neglected to give the page a title. This is like giving up free "billboard space" and looks unprofessional.

Getting Started with Dreamweaver

Figure 27 *New pages added to The Striped Umbrella website (Macintosh)*

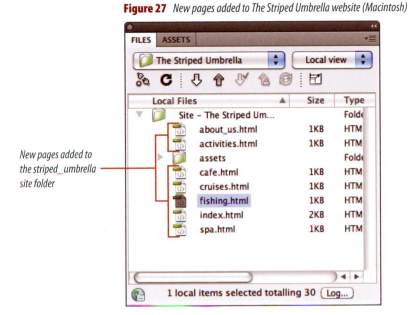

New pages added to the striped_umbrella site folder

Add pages to a website (Macintosh)

1. Click the **triangle** to the left of the assets folder to open the folder and view its contents.

   TIP If you do not see a file listed in the assets folder, click the Refresh button on the Files panel.

2. [control]-click the **striped_umbrella local site folder**, click **New File**, type **about_us.html** to replace untitled.html, then press **[return]**.

   TIP If you create a new file in the Files panel, use care to make sure the .html file extension is not deleted or that the file does not end up with a double file extension.

3. Repeat Step 2 to add five more blank pages to The Striped Umbrella website, naming the new files **spa.html**, **cafe.html**, **activities.html**, **cruises.html**, and **fishing.html**.

   TIP Make sure to add the new files to the site folder, not the assets folder. If you accidentally add them to the assets folder, just drag them to the site folder.

4. Click the **Refresh button** to list the files alphabetically, then compare your screen to Figure 27.

5. Click **File**, **Save**, to save the index.html file, then close both open files.

6. Click **Dreamweaver** on the Menu bar, and then click **Quit Dreamweaver**.

   TIP If you are prompted to save changes, click No.

You added six pages to The Striped Umbrella website: about_us, activities, cafe, cruises, fishing, spa.

POWER USER SHORTCUTS	
To do this:	**Use this shortcut:**
Open a file	[Ctrl][O] (Win) or ⌘ [O] (Mac)
Close a file	[Ctrl][W] (Win) or ⌘ [W] (Mac)
Create a new file	[Ctrl][N] (Win) or ⌘ [N] (Mac)
Save a file	[Ctrl][S] (Win) or ⌘ [S] (Mac)
Get Dreamweaver Help	[F1]
Show/Hide panels	[F4]
Switch between Code view and Design view	[Ctrl][`] (Win) or [control] [`] (Mac)

Explore the Dreamweaver workspace.

1. Start Dreamweaver.
2. Create a new HTML document.
3. Change the view to Code view.
4. Change the view to Code and Design views.
5. Change the view to Design view.
6. Collapse the panels to icons.
7. Expand the panels.
8. Undock the Files panel and float it to the middle of the document window. Dock the Files panel back to its original position.
9. View the Assets panel.
10. Close the page without saving it.

View a web page and use Help.

1. Open the file dw1_3.html from where you store your Data Files.
2. Locate the following page elements: a banner, an image, and text.
3. Change the view to Code view.
4. Change the view to Design view.
5. Use the Dreamweaver Help command to search for information on docking panels.
6. Display and read one of the topics you find.
7. Close the Dreamweaver Help window.
8. Close the page without saving it.

Plan and set up a website.

1. Use the Files panel to select the drive and folder where you store your website files.
2. Create a new local site folder in this folder or drive called **blooms**.
3. Create a new site called **Blooms & Bulbs**.
4. Specify the blooms folder as the local site folder.
5. Use the Remote Info category in the Site Setup for Blooms & Bulbs dialog box to set up web server access. (*Hint*: Skip this step if you do not have the necessary information to set up web server access.)
6. Click Save to close the Site Setup dialog box.

Add a folder and pages.

1. Create a new folder in the blooms local site folder called **assets**.
2. Edit the site to set the assets folder as the default location for the website images.
3. Open the file dw1_4.html from where you store your Data Files, save this file in the blooms local site folder as **index.html**, then click No to updating the links.
4. Select the broken image for the Blooms & Bulbs banner on the page.
5. Use the Property inspector to browse for blooms_banner.jpg, then select it to automatically save it in the assets folder of the Blooms & Bulbs website. (Remember to click off of the banner anywhere else on the page to show the banner as it replaces the broken image if necessary.)
6. Create seven new pages in the Files panel, and name them: **plants.html**, **workshops.html**, **newsletter.html**, **annuals.html**, **perennials.html**, **water_plants.html**, and **tips.html**.
7. Refresh the view to list the new files alphabetically, then compare your screen to Figure 28.
8. Close all open pages.

Figure 28 *Completed Skills Review*

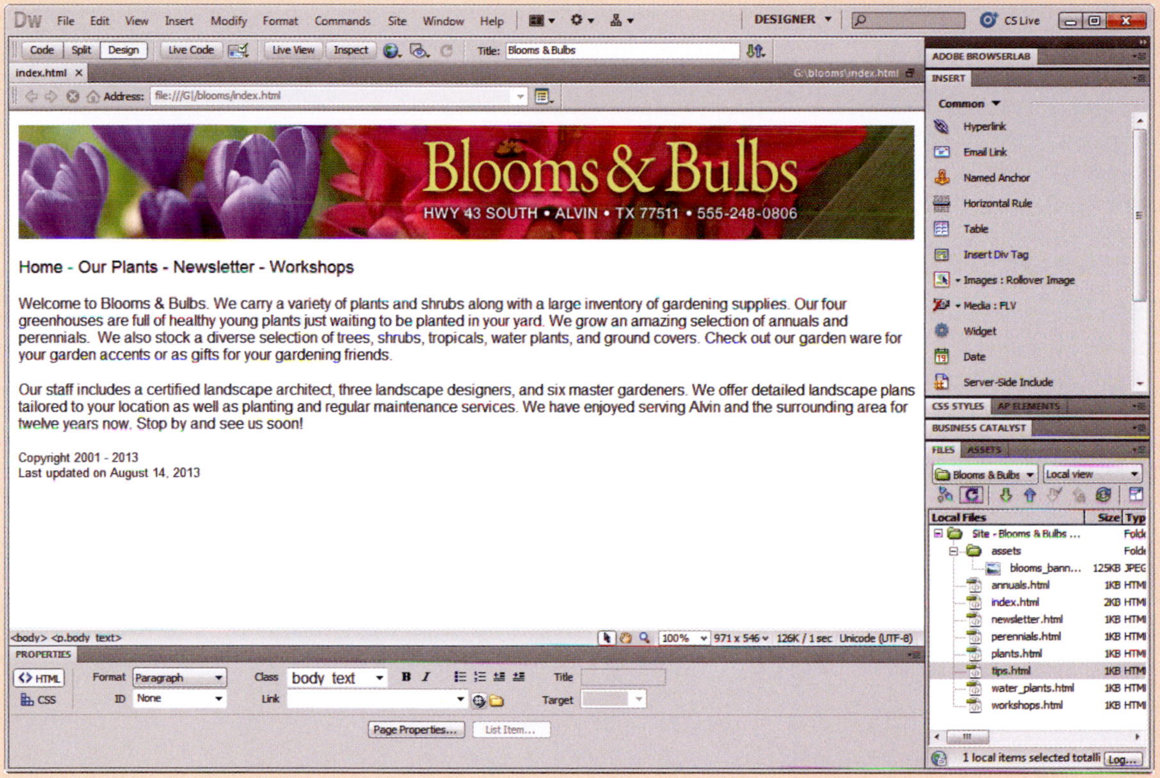

You have been hired to create a website for a travel outfitter called TripSmart. TripSmart specializes in travel products and services. In addition to selling travel products, such as luggage and accessories, they organize trips and offer travel advice. Their clients range from college students to families to vacationing professionals. The owner, Thomas Howard, has requested a dynamic website that conveys the excitement of traveling.

1. Using the information in the preceding paragraph, create a wireframe for this website, using either a pencil and paper or a program such as Microsoft Word. Include the home page with links to four child pages named **catalog.html**, **newsletter.html**, **services.html**, and **tours.html**. Include two child pages under the tours page named **china.html** and **spain.html**.

2. Create a new local site folder named **tripsmart** in the drive and folder where you store your website files.

3. Start Dreamweaver, then create a site with the name **TripSmart**. Set the tripsmart folder as the local site folder for the site.

4. Create an assets folder and set it as the default location for images.

5. Open the file dw1_5.html from where you store your Data Files, then save it in the tripsmart local site folder as **index.html**. (Remember not to update links.)

6. Correct the path for the banner by selecting the banner on the page, browsing to the original source in the Data Files folder, then selecting the file to copy it automatically to your TripSmart assets folder.

7. Create six additional pages for the site, and name them as follows: **catalog.html**, **newsletter.html**, **services.html**, **tours.html**, **china.html**, and **spain.html**. Use your wireframe and Figure 29 as a guide.

8. Refresh the Files panel.

9. Close all open pages.

Figure 29 *Completed Project Builder 1*

Your company has been selected to design a website for a catering business called Carolyne's Creations. In addition to catering, Carolyne's services include cooking classes and daily specials available as take-out meals. She also has a retail shop that stocks gourmet treats and kitchen items.

1. Create a wireframe for this website that includes a home page and child pages named **shop.html,** **classes.html, catering.html,** and **recipes.html**. Create two more child pages under the classes.html page called **children.html** and **adults.html**.

2. Create a new local site folder for the site in the drive and folder where you save your website files, then name it **cc**.

3. Create a website with the name **Carolyne's Creations**, using the cc folder for the local site folder.

4. Create an assets folder for the site and set the assets folder as the default location for images.

5. Open dw1_6.html from the where you store your Data Files then save it as **index.html** in the cc folder.

6. Reset the source for the banner to automatically save the cc_banner.jpg file in the assets folder.

7. Using Figure 30 and your wireframe as guides, create the additional pages shown for the website.

8. Refresh the Files panel to sort the files alphabetically.

9. Close all open pages.

Figure 30 *Completed Project Builder 2*

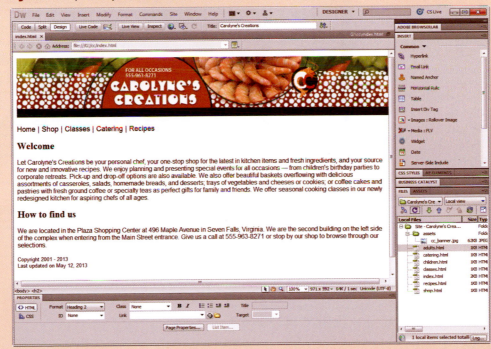

Figure 31 shows the Department of Defense website, a past selection for the Adobe Site of the Day. To visit the current Department of Defense website, connect to the Internet, then go to www.defense.gov. The current page might differ from the figure because dynamic websites are updated frequently to reflect current information. The main navigation structure is under the banner. The page title is The Official Home of the Department of Defense.

Go to the Adobe website at www.adobe.com, click the Customer Showcase link under the Company menu, then click the current Site of the Day. Explore the site and answer the following questions:

1. Do you see page titles for each page you visit?
2. Do the page titles accurately reflect the page content?
3. Is the navigation structure clear?
4. How is the navigation structure organized?
5. Why do you think this site was chosen as a Site of the Day?

Figure 31 *Design Project*

United State Department of Defense website – www.defense.gov

Getting Started with Dreamweaver

The Portfolio Project will be an ongoing project throughout the book, in which you will plan and create an original website without any Data Files supplied. The focus of the site can be on any topic, organization, sports team, club, or company that you would like. You will build on this site from chapter to chapter, so you must do each Portfolio Project assignment in each chapter to complete your website. When you finish this book, you should have a completed site that would be an excellent addition to a professional portfolio.

1. Decide what type of site you would like to create. It can be a personal site about you, a business site that promotes a fictitious or real company, or an informational site that provides information about a topic, cause, or organization.
2. Write a list of questions and answers about the site you have decided to create.
3. Create a wireframe for your site to include at least four pages. The wireframe should include the home page with at least three child pages under it.
4. Create a local site folder and an assets folder to house the assets, then set up your site using the local site folder as the website local site folder and the assets folder as the default images folder.
5. Create a blank page named **index.html** as a placeholder for the home page.
6. Begin collecting content, such as pictures or text to use in your website. You can use a digital camera to take photos, use a scanner to scan pictures, or create your own graphics using a program such as Adobe Fireworks or Adobe Illustrator. Gather the content in a central location that will be accessible to you as you develop your site.

CHAPTER  **2** DEVELOPING A
WEB PAGE

1. Create head content and set page properties
2. Create, import, and format text
3. Add links to web pages
4. Use the History panel and edit code
5. Modify and test web pages

CHAPTER 2 DEVELOPING A WEB PAGE

Introduction

The process of developing a web page requires a lot of thought and planning. If the page is a home page, you need to spend some time crafting the head content. The head content contains information search engines use to help viewers find your website. Next, choose the colors for the page background and text. You then need to add the page content, format it attractively, and add links to other pages in the site or to other websites. Finally, to ensure that all links work correctly and are current, you must test them regularly.

Understanding Page Layout

Before you add content to a page, consider the following guidelines for laying out pages:

Use white space effectively. A living room crammed with too much furniture makes it difficult to appreciate the individual pieces. The same is true of a web page. Too many text blocks, links, animations, and images can be distracting. Consider leaving some white space on each page. **White space**, which is not necessarily white, is the area on a page that contains no text or graphics.

Limit media elements. Too many media elements, such as images, video clips, or sounds, can result in a page that takes too long to load. Viewers might leave your site before the entire page finishes loading. Use media elements only if you have a good reason.

Keep it simple. Often the simplest websites are the most appealing and are also the easiest to create and maintain. A simple, well-designed site that works well is far superior to a complex one that contains errors.

Use an intuitive navigation structure. Make sure your site's navigation structure is easy to use. Viewers should always know where they are in the site and be able to easily find their way back to the home page. If viewers get "lost," they might leave the site rather than struggle to find their way around.

Apply a consistent theme. To help give pages in your website a consistent appearance, consider designing your pages using elements that relate to a common theme. Consistency in the use of color and fonts, the placement of the navigation links, and the overall page design gives a website a unified look and promotes greater ease of use and accessibility. Style sheets and pre-developed page layouts called **templates** can make this task much easier.

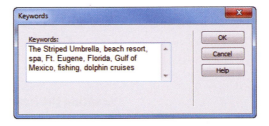

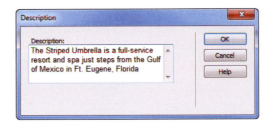

Create Head Content and
SET PAGE PROPERTIES

What You'll Do

In this lesson, you will learn how to enter titles, keywords, and descriptions in the head content section of a web page. You will also change the background color for a web page.

Creating the Head Content

A web page is composed of two distinct sections: the head content and the body. The **head content** includes the page title that appears in the title bar of the browser and some important page elements, called meta tags, that are not visible in the browser.

Meta tags are HTML codes that include information about the page, such as keywords and descriptions. Meta tags are read by screen readers for viewers who have visual impairments. **Keywords** are words that relate to the content of the website. A **description** is a short paragraph that describes the content and features of the website. For instance, the words "beach" and "resort" would be appropriate keywords for The Striped Umbrella website. Search engines find web pages by matching the title, keywords, and description in the head content of web pages with keywords that viewers enter in search engine text boxes. Therefore, it is important to include concise, useful information in the head content. The **body** is the part of the page that appears in a browser window. It contains all the page content that is visible to viewers, such as text, images, and links.

QUICK TIP

Don't confuse page titles with filenames, the name used to store each file on the server.

Setting Web Page Properties

When you create a web page, one of the first design decisions that you should make is to choose properties that control the way the page appears in a browser, such as the **background color**, the color that fills the entire page. The background color should complement the colors used for text, links, and images on the page. Often, backgrounds consist of images for either the entire page or a part of the page, such as a table background or Cascading Style Sheet (CSS) layout block. A **CSS layout block** is a section of a web page that is defined and formatted using a Cascading Style Sheet, a set of formatting characteristics you can apply to text, tables, and other page objects. You will learn more about CSS layout blocks in Chapter 6. When you use the Page Properties dialog box to set page properties such as the background color, Dreamweaver automatically creates a style that modifies the body tag to include the properties you added.

A strong contrast between the text color and the background color makes it easier for viewers to read your text. One of the Web Content Accessibility Guidelines (WCAG), Version 2.0, from the World Wide Web Consortium (W3C) states that contrast will "make it easier for users to see content including separating foreground from background." You can choose a light background color with dark text, or a dark background color with light text. A white background with dark text, though not terribly exciting, provides good contrast and is easiest to read for most viewers. Another design decision you need to make is whether to change the **default font** and **default link colors**, which are the colors used by the browser to display text, links, and visited links. The default color for **unvisited links**, or links that the viewer has not clicked yet, is blue. Unvisited links are usually simply called **links**. The default color for **visited links**, or links that have been previously clicked, is purple. You change the background color, text, and link colors using the color picker in the Page Properties dialog box. You can choose colors from one of the five Dreamweaver color palettes, as shown in Figure 1.

Choosing Colors to Convey Information

Before 1994, colors appeared differently on different types of computers. In 1994, Netscape developed the first web-safe color palette, a set of colors that appears consistently in all browsers and on Macintosh, Windows, and UNIX platforms. The evolution of video cards has made this

less relevant today, but use of appropriate colors is an important factor in creating accessible pages. So always consider both web-safe and non-web-safe colors you have used to make sure they are providing good contrast on your pages. Dreamweaver has two web-safe color palettes, Color Cubes and Continuous Tone, each of which contains 216 web-safe colors. Color Cubes is the

default color palette. To choose a different color palette, open the color picker. You can find the color picker on the CSS Property inspector, in various dialog boxes, and in various panels. Click the color picker list arrow, then click the color palette you want. Another WCAG guideline states that color should never be the only visual means of conveying information.

Figure 1 *Color picker showing color palettes*

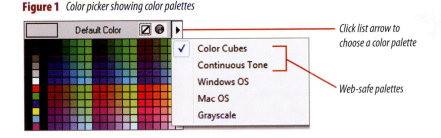

Click list arrow to choose a color palette

Web-safe palettes

Edit a page title

1. Start Dreamweaver, click the **Site list arrow** on the Files panel, then click **The Striped Umbrella** if necessary.

2. Double-click **index.html** in the Files panel to open The Striped Umbrella home page, click **View** on the Application bar (Win) or Menu bar (Mac), then click **Head Content**.

   The Meta icon , Title icon , and CSS icon are now visible in the head content section. See Figure 2.

3. Click the **Title icon** in the head content section.

   The page title The Striped Umbrella appears in the Title text box in the Property inspector.

4. Click after the end of The Striped Umbrella text in the Title text box in the Property inspector, press **[Spacebar]**, type **beach resort and spa, Ft. Eugene, Florida,** press **[Enter]** (Win) or **[return]** (Mac), then click in the title text box.

   Compare your screen with Figure 3. The new title is better, because it incorporates the words "beach resort" and "spa" and the location of the resort—words that potential customers might use as keywords when using a search engine.

   TIP You can also change the page title using the Title text box on the Document toolbar. To view hidden text in the Title box, click in the title and scroll using the left and right keyboard arrow keys.

You opened The Striped Umbrella website, opened the home page, viewed the head content section, and changed the page title.

Figure 2 *Viewing the head content*

Meta icon   Title icon   CSS icon

Head content section

Title text box on Document toolbar

Figure 3 *Property inspector displaying new page title*

PROPERTIES
Title
Title triped Umbrella beach resort and spa, Ft. Eugene, Florida

Click in the title and scroll with arrow key to see the rest of the title

DESIGN**TIP**

Designing Appropriate Content For Your Target Audience

When you begin developing the content for your website, you need to decide what content to include and how to arrange each element on each page. You must design the content with the target audience in mind. What is the age group of your audience? What reading level is appropriate? Should you use a formal or informal tone? Should the pages be simple, consisting mostly of text, or rich with images and media files? Evaluate the font sizes, the number and size of images and animations, the reading level, and the amount of technical expertise necessary to navigate your site, and make sure they fit your audience. Usually, the first page that your audience will see when they visit your site is the home page. Design the home page so that viewers will understand your site's purpose and feel comfortable finding their way around your site's pages.

To ensure that viewers do not get "lost" in your site, design all the pages with a consistent look and feel. You can use templates and Cascading Style Sheets to maintain a common look for each page. **Templates** are web pages that contain the basic layout for each page in the site, including the location of a company logo or a menu of buttons. You'll learn more about Cascading Style Sheets in Lesson 2 and templates in Chapter 12.

Developing a Web Page

Figure 4 *Insert panel displaying the Common category*

Figure 5 *Keywords dialog box*

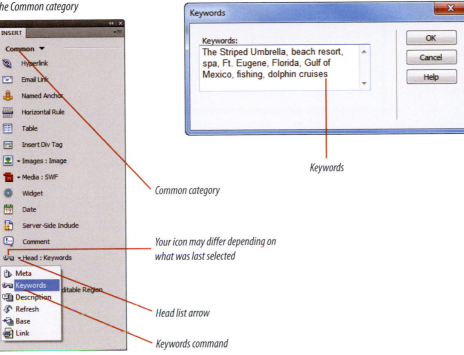

Keywords

Common category

Your icon may differ depending on what was last selected

Head list arrow

Keywords command

Enter keywords

1. Click the **Insert panel list arrow**, then on the dropdown menu, click the **Common category** (if it is not already selected).

2. Click the **Head list arrow**, as shown in Figure 4, then click **Keywords**.

TIP Some buttons on the Insert panel include a list arrow indicating that there is a menu of choices available. The button that you select last will appear on the Insert panel until you select another.

3. Type **The Striped Umbrella**, **beach resort**, **spa**, **Ft. Eugene**, **Florida**, **Gulf of Mexico**, **fishing**, **dolphin cruises** in the Keywords text box, as shown in Figure 5, then click **OK**

   The Keywords icon appears in the head content section, indicating that there are keywords associated with this page. When you click the icon to select it, the keywords appear in the Keywords text box in the Property inspector.

You added keywords relating to the resort to the head content of The Striped Umbrella home page.

DESIGNTIP

Entering Keywords and Descriptions

Search engines use keywords, descriptions, and titles to find pages based on search terms a user enters. Therefore, it is very important to anticipate the search terms your potential customers would use and include these words in the keywords, description, and title. Many search engines display page titles and descriptions in their search results. Some search engines limit the number of keywords that they will index, so make sure you list the most important keywords first. Keep your keywords and descriptions short and concise to ensure that all search engines will include your site. To choose effective keywords, many designers use focus groups to learn which words potential customers or clients might use. A **focus group** is a marketing tool that asks a group of people for feedback about a product, such as the impact of a television ad or the effectiveness of a website design.

Enter a description

1. Click the **Head list arrow** on the Insert panel, then click **Description**.

2. In the Description text box, type **The Striped Umbrella is a full-service resort and spa just steps from the Gulf of Mexico in Ft. Eugene, Florida**.

   Your screen should resemble Figure 6.

3. Click **OK**.

   The description appears in the Description text box in the Property inspector.

4. Click the **Show Code view button** [Code] on the Document toolbar.

   The title, keywords, and description tags appear in the HTML code in the document window, as shown in Figure 7.

TIP Your head content line numbers may differ. Also, you can enter and edit the title tag and the meta tags directly in the code in Code view.

5. Click the **Show Design view button** [Design] to return to Design view.

6. Click **View** on the Application bar (Win) or Menu bar (Mac), then click **Head Content** to close the head content section.

You added a description of The Striped Umbrella resort to the head content of the home page. You then viewed the page in Code view and the head content in the HTML code.

Figure 6 *Description dialog box*

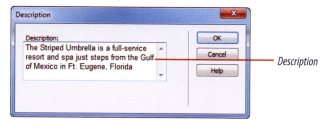

Description

Figure 7 *Head Content displayed in Code view*

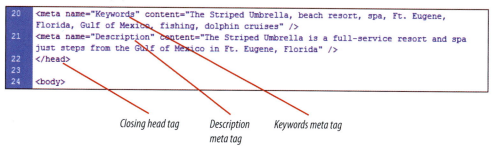

```
20  <meta name="Keywords" content="The Striped Umbrella, beach resort, spa, Ft. Eugene,
    Florida, Gulf of Mexico, fishing, dolphin cruises" />
21  <meta name="Description" content="The Striped Umbrella is a full-service resort and spa
    just steps from the Gulf of Mexico in Ft. Eugene, Florida" />
22  </head>
23
24  <body>
```

Closing head tag   Description   Keywords meta tag
                        meta tag

Using Descriptions for POWDER Authentication

A website description can be stored in an XML file to provide POWDER authentication. **XML** stands for Extensible Markup Language, a type of file that is used to develop customized tags to store information. **POWDER** is the acronym for **Protocol for Web Description Resources**. This is an evaluation system for web pages developed with the World Wide Web Consortium (W3C) that provides summary information about a website. Examples include the date the site was created, the name of the person or company responsible for the content on the site, and a description of the content. It is designed to help users determine if a site would be considered a trustworthy resource of value and interest. It replaces the previous system called PICS, or Platform for Internet Content Selection.

Figure 8 *Page Properties dialog box*

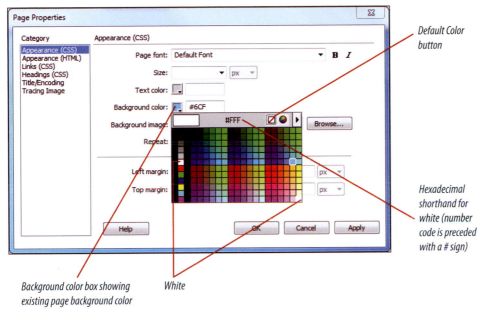

Default Color button

Hexadecimal shorthand for white (number code is preceded with a # sign)

Background color box showing existing page background color

White

Set the page background color

1. Click **Modify** on the Application bar (Win) or Menu bar (Mac), then click **Page Properties** to open the Page Properties dialog box.

2. Click the **Background color box** to open the color picker, as shown in Figure 8.

   The background color box in the Page Properties dialog box changes color based on the currently selected color. It is now blue, reflecting the current page background color, rather than the default icon color shown in the step instructions.

3. Click the rightmost color in the bottom row (white).

4. Click **Apply**, then click **OK**.

   Clicking Apply lets you see the changes you made to the web page without closing the Page Properties dialog box.

TIP If you don't like the color you chose, either click the Default Color button ✎ in the color picker to switch to the default color or click a different color. The default page background color is usually white for most browsers. The default text color is usually black.

   The background color of the web page is now white. The black text against the white background provides a nice contrast and makes the text easy to read.

5. Save your work.

You used the Page Properties dialog box to change the background color to white.

Understanding Hexadecimal Values

Each color is assigned a **hexadecimal RGB value**, a value that represents the amount of red, green, and blue present in the color. For example, white, which is made of equal parts of red, green, and blue, has a hexadecimal value of FFFFFF. This is also called an RGB triplet in hexadecimal format (or a **hex triplet**). Each pair of characters in the hexadecimal value represents the red, green, and blue values. The hexadecimal number system is based on 16, rather than 10 in the decimal number system. Because the hexadecimal number system includes only numbers up to 9, values after 9 use the letters of the alphabet. "A" represents the number 10 in the hexadecimal number system. "F" represents the number 15. The hexadecimal values can be entered in the code using a form of shorthand that shortens the six characters to three characters. For instance: FFFFFF become FFF; 0066CC becomes 06C. The number value for a color is preceded by a pound sign (#) in HTML code.

Create, Import,
AND FORMAT TEXT

What You'll Do

In this lesson, you will enter and format text, import text, set text properties, and check the spelling on the Striped Umbrella home page.

Creating and Importing Text

Most information in web pages is presented in the form of text. You can type text directly on a page in Dreamweaver, import, or copy and paste it from another software program. (Macintosh users do not have the option to import text. They must open a text file, copy the text, then paste it into an HTML document.) When using a Windows computer to import text from a Microsoft Word file, it's best to use the Import Word Document command. Not only will the formatting be preserved, but Dreamweaver will generate clean HTML code. **Clean HTML code** is code that does what it is supposed to do without using unnecessary instructions, which take up memory.

When you format text, it is important to keep in mind that visitors to your site must have the same fonts installed on their computers as the fonts you use. Otherwise, the text might appear incorrectly.

QUICK TIP

Some software programs can also convert text into images so that the text retains the same appearance, no matter which fonts are installed. However, text converted into images is no longer editable.

If text does not have a font specified, the default font on the user's computer will be used to display the text. Keep in mind that some fonts might not appear the same on both a Windows and a Macintosh computer. The way fonts are **rendered** (drawn) on the screen differs because Windows and Macintosh computers use different technologies to render them. It is wise to stick to the standard fonts that work well with both systems. Test your pages using both operating systems.

Formatting Text Two Ways: HTML vs. CSS

Because text is more difficult and tiring to read on a computer screen than on a printed page, you should make the text in your website attractive and easy to read. One way to do this is to format text by changing its font, size, and color. Previously web designers used the Property inspector to apply formatting attributes, such as font type, size, color, alignment, and indents. This created HTML tags in the code that directed the way the fonts would appear in a browser. **Tags** are the parts of the code that specify the appearance for all page content when viewed in a browser.

The more accepted method now is to create Cascading Style Sheets (CSS) to format and place web page elements. **Cascading Style Sheets** are sets of formatting attributes that you use to format web pages to provide a consistent presentation for content across the site. Cascading Style Sheets make it easy to separate page content from the page design. The content is placed in the body section on web pages, and the formatting styles are placed in either an external style sheet file or in the page head content. Separating content from design is preferable because editing content and formatting content are really two separate tasks. Since page content is separate from formatting styles, you can update or change the page content without disturbing the page formatting.

You can apply some formatting, without creating styles, using the Bold and Italic HTML tags. You can also use HTML heading tags, which determine the relative size and boldness of text, and which help to show the importance of text relative to the rest of the text on the page.

To apply CSS or HTML formatting, you use the Property inspector, which has a panel for each method: the CSS Property inspector and the HTML Property inspector. You display them by clicking the CSS or the HTML button on the left side of the Property inspector. Some coding options are unique to each one and some coding options are available on both. For instance, HTML heading tags are only available on the HTML Property inspector. Font tags are only available on the CSS Property inspector. The Bold tag is available on both. Regardless of

which Property inspector you use, CSS styles will be created when you format page objects.

Because CSS is a lot to learn when you are just beginning, we are going to begin by using HTML tags for formatting. Although they are not the currently preferred formatting method, it's still a good idea to know about HTML tags because you might "inherit" a web page that contains them. Then in Chapter 3, we will use the preferred method, CSS.

QUICK TIP

Even if you use the Property inspector to format text with HTML tags, Dreamweaver automatically creates styles when you apply most formatting attributes.

Changing Fonts

You can format your text with different fonts by choosing a font combination, or Font-family, from the Font list in the CSS Property inspector. A **Font-family** is a set of font choices that specify which fonts a browser should use to display the text on your web page. Font-families ensure that if one font is not available, the browser will use the next one specified in the font combination. For example, if text is formatted with the font combination Arial, Helvetica, sans serif, the browser will first look on the viewer's system for Arial. If Arial is not available, then it will look for Helvetica. If Helvetica is not available, then it will look for a sans-serif font to apply to the text. Using fonts within the default settings is wise, because fonts set outside the

default settings might not be available on all viewers' computers.

Changing Font Sizes

There are two ways to change the size of text using the Property inspector. When the CSS option is selected, you can select a numerical value for the size from 9 to 36 pixels (or type a smaller or larger number). Or you can use a size expressed in words from xx-small to larger, which sets the size of selected text relative to other text on the page. On the HTML Property inspector, you do not have font sizes available.

Formatting Paragraphs

The HTML Property inspector displays options to format blocks of text as paragraphs or as different sizes of headings. To format a paragraph as a heading, click anywhere in the paragraph, and then select the heading size you want from the Format list in the HTML Property inspector. The Format list contains six different heading formats. Heading 1 is the largest size, and Heading 6 is the smallest size. Browsers display text formatted as headings in bold, setting them off from paragraphs of text. You can also align paragraphs with the alignment buttons on the CSS Property inspector and indent paragraphs using the Blockquote and Remove Blockquote buttons on the HTML Property inspector.

QUICK TIP

Mixing too many different fonts and formatting attributes on a web page can result in pages that are visually confusing or difficult to read.

Enter text

1. Position the insertion point directly after "want to go home." at the end of the paragraph, press **[Enter]** (Win) or **[return]** (Mac), then type **The Striped Umbrella**.

   Pressing [Enter] (Win) or [return] (Mac) creates a new paragraph.

   TIP If the new text does not assume the formatting attributes as the paragraph above it, click the Show Code and Design views button  Split , position the cursor right after the period after "home", then go back to the page in Design view and insert a new paragraph.

2. Press and hold **[Shift]**, press **[Enter]** (Win) or **[return]** (Mac), then type **25 Beachside Drive**.

   Pressing and holding [Shift] while you press [Enter] (Win) or [return] (Mac) creates a line break. A **line break** places a new line of text on the next line down without creating a new paragraph. Line breaks are useful when you want to add a new line of text directly below the current line of text and keep the same formatting.

3. Add the following text below the 25 Beachside Drive text, using line breaks after each line:

   Ft. Eugene, Florida 33775

   555-594-9458

4. Compare your screen with Figure 9.

   You entered text for the address and telephone number on the home page.

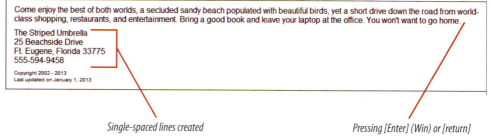

Single-spaced lines created by using line breaks

Pressing [Enter] (Win) or [return] (Mac) creates a new paragraph

TABLE 1: HTML FORMATTING TAGS	
HTML tag	**Represents**
<p> </p>	Opening and closing paragraph tag
 	Line break tag (does not require a closing tag)
<em> </em>	Opening and closing italic (emphasis) tag
<strong> </strong>	Opening and closing bold tag
<u> </u>	Opening and closing underline tag

Using Keyboard Shortcuts

When working with text, the keyboard shortcuts for Cut, Copy, and Paste are very useful. These are [Ctrl][X] (Win) or ⌘ [X] (Mac) for Cut, [Ctrl][C] (Win) or ⌘ [C] (Mac) for Copy, and [Ctrl][V] (Win) or ⌘ [V] (Mac) for Paste. You can view all Dreamweaver keyboard shortcuts using the Keyboard Shortcuts dialog box, which lets you view existing shortcuts for menu commands, tools, or miscellaneous functions, such as copying HTML or inserting an image. You can also create your own shortcuts or assign shortcuts that you are familiar with from using them in other software programs. To view or modify keyboard shortcuts, click the Keyboard Shortcuts command on the Edit menu (Win) or Dreamweaver menu (Mac), then select the shortcut key set you want. Each chapter in this book includes Power User shortcuts, a list of keyboard shortcuts relevant to that chapter.

Figure 10 *Formatting the address on The Striped Umbrella home page*

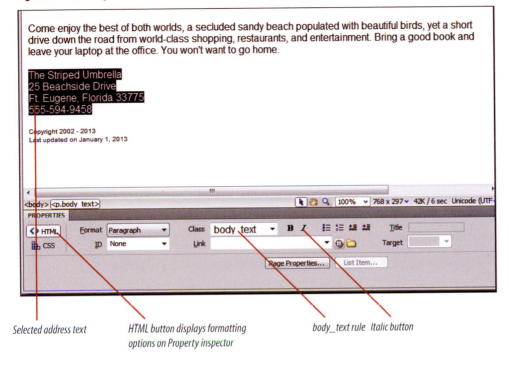

Come enjoy the best of both worlds, a secluded sandy beach populated with beautiful birds, yet a short drive down the road from world-class shopping, restaurants, and entertainment. Bring a good book and leave your laptop at the office. You won't want to go home.

The Striped Umbrella
25 Beachside Drive
Ft. Eugene, Florida 33775
555-594-9458

Copyright 2002 - 2013
Last updated on January 1, 2013

Selected address text

HTML button displays formatting options on Property inspector

body_text rule Italic button

Figure 11 *Viewing the HTML code for the address and phone number*

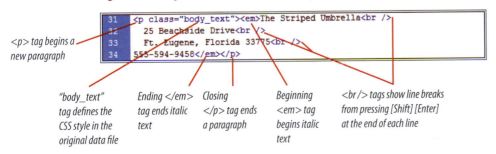

```
31   <p class="body_text"><em>The Striped Umbrella<br />
32      25 Beachside Drive<br />
33      Ft. Eugene, Florida 33775<br />
34   555-594-9458</em></p>
```

<p> tag begins a new paragraph

"body_text" tag defines the CSS style in the original data file

Ending </em> tag ends italic text

Closing </p> tag ends a paragraph

Beginning <em> tag begins italic text

*
 tags show line breaks from pressing [Shift] [Enter] at the end of each line*

Format text

1. Select the entire address and telephone number, then click the **HTML button** `<> HTML` in the Property inspector (if it is not already selected) to change to the HTML Property inspector, as shown in Figure 10.

2. Click the **Italic button** *I* in the Property inspector to italicize the text, then click after the text to deselect it.

3. Click the **Show Code view button** `Code` to view the HTML code, as shown in Figure 11.

   It is always helpful to learn what the HTML code means. Refer to Table 1 to locate some basic HTML formatting tags. As you edit and format your pages, read the code to see how it appears for each element. The more familiar you are with the code, the more comfortable you will feel with Dreamweaver and web design. A strong knowledge of HTML is a necessary skill for professional web designers.

4. Click the **Show Design view button** `Design` to return to Design view.

5. Save your work, then close the page.

You changed the Property inspector options from CSS to HTML, then formatted the address and phone number for The Striped Umbrella by changing the font style to italic.

Save an image file in the assets folder

1. Open dw2_1.html from where you store your Data Files, save it as **spa.html** in the striped_umbrella folder, overwriting the existing file, then click **No** in the Update Links dialog box.

2. Select **The Striped Umbrella** banner.

   Updating links ties the image or hyperlink to the Data Files folder. Because you already copied su_banner.gif to the website, the banner image is visible. Notice that the Src text box shows the link is to the website assets folder, not to the Data Files folder.

3. Click the **sea_spa_logo image broken link placeholder** to select it, click the **Browse for File icon** 🗀 in the Property inspector next to the Src text box, navigate to the chapter_2 assets folder, click **sea_spa_logo.jpg**, then click **OK** (Win) or **Choose** (Mac).

   Because this image was not in the website, it appeared as a broken link. Using the Browse for File icon 🗀 selects the source of the original image file. Dreamweaver automatically copies the file to the assets folder of the website and it is visible on the page. You might have to deselect the new image to see it replace the broken link.

4. Click the **plus sign** (Win) or **expander arrow** (Mac) next to the assets folder in the Files panel, then click the **Refresh button** ↻ on the Files panel toolbar if you don't see sea_spa_logo.jpg listed.

   A copy of sea_spa_logo.jpg file appears in the assets folder, as shown in Figure 12.

You opened a new file, saved it as the new spa page, and fixed a broken link by copying the image to the assets folder.

Figure 12 *Image file added to Striped Umbrella assets folder*

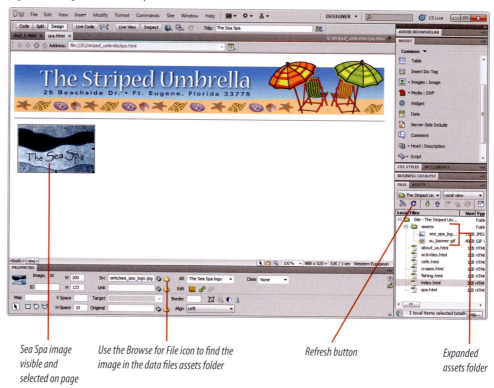

Sea Spa image visible and selected on page

Use the Browse for File icon to find the image in the data files assets folder

Refresh button

Expanded assets folder

Figure 13 *Clean Up Word HTML dialog box*

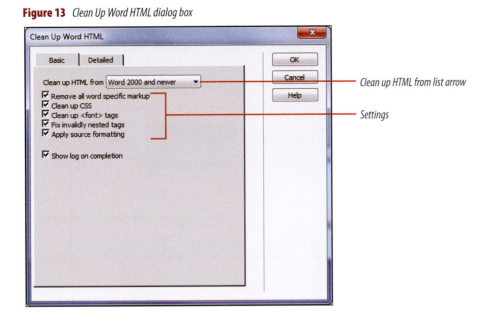

Clean up HTML from list arrow

Settings

Import text

1. Click to place the insertion point to the right of the spa graphic on the spa.html page.

2. Click **File** on the Application bar, point to **Import**, click **Word Document**, double-click the **chapter_2 folder** from where you store your Data Files, then double-click **spa.doc** (Win); or double-click **spa.doc** from where you store your Data Files, select all, copy, close spa.doc, then paste the copied text on the spa page in Dreamweaver (Mac).

3. Click **Commands** on the Application bar (Win) or Menu bar (Mac), then click **Clean Up Word HTML**.

   TIP If a dialog box appears stating that Dreamweaver was unable to determine the version of Word used to generate this document, click OK, click the Clean up HTML from list arrow, then choose the Word 2000 and newer version of Word if it isn't already selected.

4. Make sure each check box in the Clean Up Word HTML dialog box is checked, as shown in Figure 13, click **OK**, then click **OK** again to close the results window.

You imported a Word document, then used the Clean Up Word HTML command.

Choosing Filenames for Web Pages

When you choose a name for a web page, you should use a short, simple descriptive name that reflects the contents of the page. For example, if the page is about your company's products, you could name it products.html. You should also follow some general rules for naming web pages, such as naming the home page index.html. Most file servers look for the file named index.html or default.html to use as the initial page for a website. Do not use spaces, special characters, or punctuation in filenames for files or folders that will you will use in your site. Use underscores rather than spaces for readability; for example: use sea_spa_logo.jpg rather than sea spa logo.jpg. Just to be totally safe for all file servers, use only letters, numbers, or underscores in file or folder names. Many designers also avoid the use of uppercase letters.

Set text properties

1. Select the Common category on the Insert panel if necessary, then scroll up and place the insertion point anywhere within the words "The Sea Spa Services."

2. Click the **Format list arrow** in the HTML Property inspector, then click **Heading 2**.

   The Heading 2 format is applied to the paragraph. Even a single word is considered a paragraph if there is a hard return or paragraph break after it. The HTML code for a Heading 2 tag is <h2>. The tag is then closed with </h2>. For headings, the level of the heading tag follows the h, so the code for a Heading 1 tag is <h1>.

3. Select the text **Massages**, **Facials**, and **Body Treatments**, click the **Format list arrow** in the HTML Property inspector, click **Heading 4**, then click outside the heading to deselect the text.

4. Click after the word "Treatments", insert a line break, click the **Show Code and Design views button** `Split` on the Document toolbar, then compare your screen to Figure 14.

   The word "Massages" after the words "Body Treatments" may be in a different position on your screen. Figure 14 was sized down, so your page will be much wider than the figure shows.

   You applied two heading formats, then viewed the HTML code.

Figure 14 *Viewing the heading tags in Show Code and Design views*

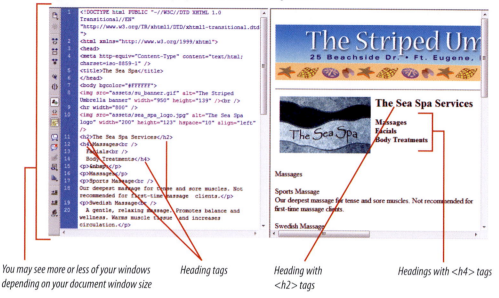

You may see more or less of your windows depending on your document window size   *Heading tags*   *Heading with <h2> tags*   *Headings with <h4> tags*

Importing and Linking Microsoft Office Documents (Windows)

Adobe makes it easy to transfer data between Microsoft Office documents and Dreamweaver web pages. When importing a Word or Excel document, click File on the Application bar, point to Import, then click either Word Document or Excel Document. Select the file you want to import, then click the Formatting list arrow to choose among importing Text only; Text with structure (paragraphs, lists, and tables); Text, structure, basic formatting (bold, italic); or Text, structure, full formatting (bold, italic, styles) before you click Open. The option you choose depends on the importance of the original structure and formatting. Always use the Clean Up Word HTML command after importing a Word file.

You can also create a link to a Word or Excel document on your web page. To do so, browse to locate the Word or Excel document you want to add as a link, then drag the file name to the location on the page where you would like the link to appear. (If the document is located outside the site, you can browse for it using the Site list arrow on the Files panel, Windows Explorer, or Mac Finder.) Next, select the Create a link option button in the Insert Document dialog box, then save the file in your site root folder so it will be uploaded when you publish your site. If it is not uploaded, the link will be broken.

Figure 15 *Check Spelling dialog box*

Facials

Revitalizing Facial
A light massage with a customized essential oil blend that moisturizes the skin and restores circulation.

Gentlemen's Facial
A cleansing facial that restores a healthy glow. Includes a neck and shoulder masage.

Milk Mask
A soothing mask that softens and moisturizes the face. Leaves your skin looking

Body Treatments

Salt Glow
Imported sea salts are massaged into the skin, exfoliating and cleansing the pores

Herbal Wrap
Organic lavender blooms create a detoxifying and calming treatment to relieve ac

Seaweed Body Wrap
Seaweed is a natural detoxifying agent that also helps improve circulation.

Call The Sea Spa desk for prices and reservations. Any of our services can be p
until 9:00 p.m. Call 555-594-9458, extension 39.

Check Spelling

Word not found in dictionary:

masage.   Add to Personal

Change to: massage.

Suggestions: mas age.   Ignore
               massage.
               manage.   Change
               message.
               masses.   Ignore All
               massed.
               maser.   Change All
               messed.

                                     Close   Help

Misspelled word   *Click "Change" to*
                                                  correct spelling

Checking for Spelling Errors

It is very important to check for spelling and grammatical errors before publishing a page. A page that is published with errors will cause the user to immediately judge the site as unprofessional and carelessly made, and the accuracy of the page content will be in question. If you have text in a word processing file that you plan to import into Dreamweaver, check the spelling in the word processor first. Then check the spelling in the imported text again in Dreamweaver. This allows you to add words such as proper names to the Dreamweaver dictionary so the program will not flag them again. Click the Add to Personal button in the Check Spelling dialog box to add a new word to the dictionary. Even though you might have checked a page using the Check Spelling feature, you still must proofread the content yourself to catch usage errors such as "to," "too," and "two." Accuracy in both content and delivery is critical.

Check spelling

1. Click the **Show Design view button** Design to return to Design view.

2. Place the insertion point in front of the text "The Sea Spa Services".

   It is a good idea to start a spelling check at the top of the document because Dreamweaver searches from the insertion point down. If your insertion point is in the middle of the document, you will receive a message asking if you want to check the rest of the document. Starting from the beginning saves time.

3. Click **Commands** on the Application bar (Win) or Menu bar (Mac), then click **Check Spelling**.

   The word "masage" is highlighted on the page as a misspelled word and suggestions are listed to correct it in the Check Spelling dialog box, as shown in Figure 15.

4. Click **massage**. in the Suggestions list if necessary, then click **Change**.

   The word is corrected on the page.

5. Click **OK** to close the Dreamweaver dialog box stating that the Spelling Check is completed.

6. Save and close the spa page, then close the dw2_1.html page.

You checked the page for spelling errors.

Add Links
TO WEB PAGES

What You'll Do

 In this lesson, you will open the home page and add links to the menu bar that link to the About Us, Spa, Cafe, and Activities pages. You will then insert an email link at the bottom of the page.

Adding Links to Web Pages

Links, or hyperlinks, provide the real power for web pages. Links make it possible for viewers to navigate all the pages in a website and to connect to other pages anywhere on the web. Users are more likely to return to websites that have a user-friendly navigation structure. Users also enjoy websites that have interesting links to other web pages or other websites.

To add links to a web page, first select the text or image that you want to serve as a link, and then, in the Link text box in the Property inspector, specify a path to the page to which you want to link.

When you create links on a web page, it is important to avoid **broken links**, or links that cannot find their intended destinations. You can accidentally cause a broken link by typing the incorrect address for the link in the Link text box. Broken links can be caused by companies merging, going out of business, or simply moving their website addresses.

In addition to adding links to your pages, you should provide a **point of contact**, or a place on a web page that provides users with a means of contacting the company. A common point of contact is a **mailto: link**, which is an email address that users with questions or problems can use to contact someone at the company's headquarters.

Using Menu Bars

A **menu bar**, or **navigation bar**, is an area on a web page that contains links to the main pages of a website. Menu bars are usually located at the top or side of the main pages of a website and can be created with text, images, or a combination of the two. Menu bars are the backbone of a website's navigation structure, which includes all navigation aids for moving around a website. You can, however, include additional links to the main pages of the website elsewhere on the page. To make navigating a website as easy as possible, you should place menu bars in the same position on each page. The web page in Figure 16 shows a menu bar that contains a set of main links with additional links that appear as the mouse rolls over each main link. You can create a simple menu bar by typing the names of your website's pages at the top of your web page, formatting the text, and then adding links to each page name. It is always a good idea to provide plain text links for accessibility, regardless of the type of navigation structure you choose to use. For example, if you use Flash for your navigation links, it is a good idea to include a duplicate set of text with links to the same pages.

Following WCAG Accessibility for Navigation

The WCAG Guideline 2.4 lists ways to ensure that all viewers can successfully and easily navigate a website. It states: "Provide ways to help users navigate, find content, and determine where they are." Suggestions include limiting the number of links on a page, using techniques to allow users to quickly access different sections of a page, and making sure that links are readable and easily distinguishable.

Figure 16 *The CIA website*

Central Intelligence Agency website – www.cia.gov

Create a menu bar

1. Open **index.html**.

2. Position the insertion point to the left of "A" in About Us, then drag to select **About Us - Spa - Cafe**.

3. Type **Home - About Us - Spa - Cafe - Activities**, as shown in Figure 17.

   These five text labels will serve as a menu bar. You will add the links later.

You created a new menu bar using text, replacing the original menu bar.

Insert a horizontal rule

1. Click in front of the word "Welcome".

2. Click **Horizontal Rule** in the Common category on the Insert panel to insert a horizontal rule between the menu bar and the first paragraph.

   A horizontal rule is a line used to separate page elements or to organize information on a page.

3. Compare your screen to Figure 18, then save your work.

TIP An asterisk after the filename in the title bar indicates that you have altered the page since you last saved it. After you save your work, the asterisk does not appear.

You added a horizontal rule to separate the menu bar from the page content.

Figure 17 *Viewing the new menu bar*

Figure 18 *Inserting a horizontal rule*

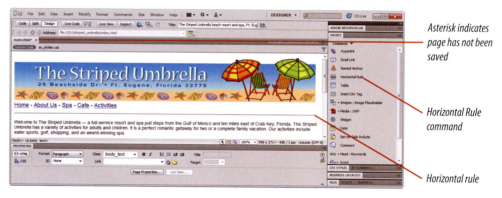

Asterisk indicates page has not been saved

Horizontal Rule command

Horizontal rule

Preventing Data Loss

It is always a good idea to save your files frequently. A good practice is to save a file after you have completed a successful edit, before you attempt a difficult edit, and when you have finished working on an open file. It is also a good idea to close a file when you are not working on it. Having unnecessary files open can be a distraction to your work flow. Do not open files from a different website other than the open site in the Files panel, or you might accidentally save them in the wrong folder!

Figure 19 *Selecting text for the Home link*

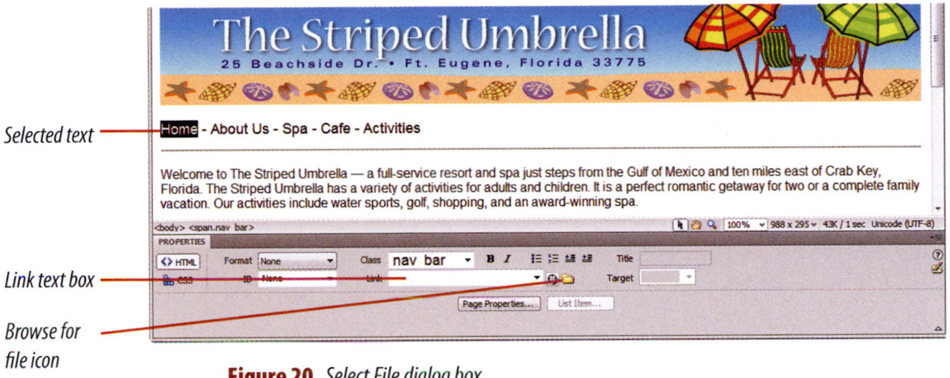

Selected text

Link text box

Browse for file icon

Figure 20 *Select File dialog box*

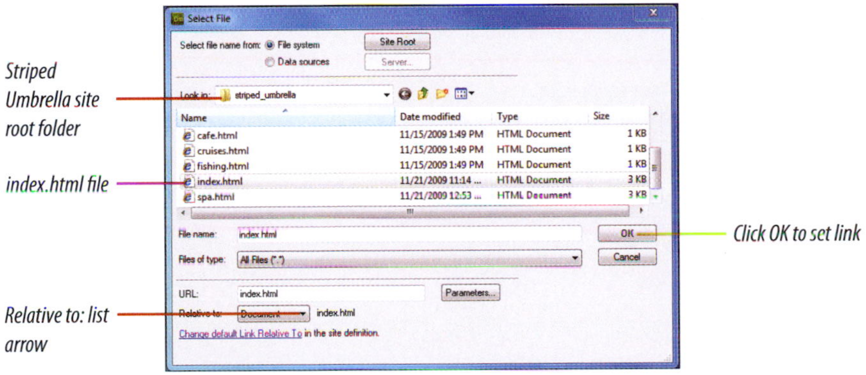

Striped Umbrella site root folder

index.html file

Click OK to set link

Relative to: list arrow

Figure 21 *Links added to menu bar*

Menu bar with links added

Add links to web pages

1. Double-click **Home** to select it, as shown in Figure 19.

2. Click the **Browse for File icon** 📁 next to the Link text box in the HTML Property inspector, then navigate to the striped_umbrella local site folder if necessary.

3. Verify that the link is set Relative to Document in the Relative to: list.

4. Click **index.html** as shown in Figure 20, click **OK** (Win) or **Choose** (Mac), then click anywhere on the page to deselect Home.

TIP Your file listing might differ depending on your view settings.

Home now appears in blue with an underline, indicating it is a link. If users click the Home link, a new page will not open, because the link is on the home page. It might seem odd to create a link to the same page on which the link appears, but this will be helpful when you copy the menu bar to other pages in the site. Always provide viewers a link to the home page.

5. Repeat Steps 1–4 to create links for About Us, Spa, Cafe, and Activities to their corresponding pages in the striped_umbrella site folder.

6. When you finish adding the links to the other four pages, deselect all, then compare your screen to Figure 21.

You created a link for each of the five menu bar elements to their respective web pages in The Striped Umbrella website.

Create an email link

1. Place the insertion point after the last digit in the telephone number, then insert a line break.

2. Click **Email Link** in the Common category on the Insert panel to insert an email link.

3. Type **Club Manager** in the Text text box, type **manager@stripedumbrella.com** in the Email text box, as shown in Figure 22, then click **OK** to close the Email Link dialog box.

TIP If the text does not retain the formatting from the previous line use the Edit, Undo command to undo Steps 1–3. Switch to Code view and place the insertion point immediately to the right of the telephone number, then repeat the steps again in Design view.

4. Save your work.

The text "mailto:manager@stripedumbrella.com" appears in the Link text box in the HTML Property inspector. When a viewer clicks this link, a blank email message window opens in the user's default email software, where the user can type a message. See Figure 23.

TIP You must enter the correct email address in the Email text box for the link to work. However, you can enter any descriptive name, such as customer service or Bob Smith in the Text text box. You can also enter the email address as the text if you want to show the actual email address on the web page.

You inserted an email link to serve as a point of contact for The Striped Umbrella.

Figure 22 *Email Link dialog box*

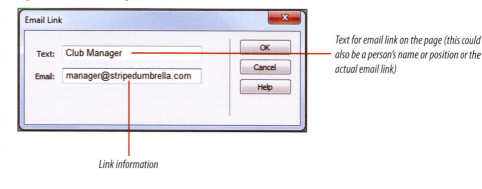

Text for email link on the page (this could also be a person's name or position or the actual email link)

Link information

Figure 23 *mailto: link on the Property inspector*

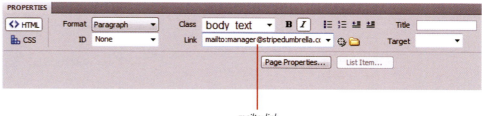

mailto: link

Figure 24 *The Assets panel URL category*

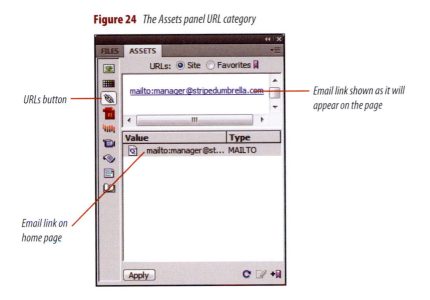

URLs button

Email link shown as it will appear on the page

Email link on home page

View the email link in the Assets panel

1. Click the **Assets panel tab** to view the Assets panel.

2. Click the **URLs button** to display the URLs in the website.

3. Click the **Refresh button** at the bottom of the Assets panel, if necessary, to view the link, then compare your screen to Figure 24.

   URL stands for **Uniform Resource Locator**. The URLs listed in the Assets panel show all of the **external links**, or links pointing outside of the website. An email link is outside the website, so it is an external link. You will learn more about URLs and links in Chapter 5. The links you created to the site pages are internal links (inside the website), and are not listed in the Assets panel.

4. Click the **Files panel tab** to view the Files panel.

You viewed the email link on the home page in the Assets panel.

Use the History
PANEL AND EDIT CODE

What You'll Do

 In this lesson, you will use the History panel to undo formatting changes you make to a horizontal rule. You will then use the Code Inspector to view the HTML code for the horizontal rule. You will also insert a date object and then view its code in the Code Inspector.

Using the History Panel

Throughout the process of creating a web page, it's likely that you will make mistakes along the way. Fortunately, you have a tool named the History panel to undo your mistakes. The **History panel** records each editing and formatting task you perform and displays them in a list in the order in which you completed them. Each task listed in the History panel is called a **step**. You can drag the **slider** on the left side of the History panel to undo or redo steps, as shown in Figure 25. You can also click in the bar to the left of a step to undo all steps below it. You click the step to select it. By default, the History panel records 50 steps. You can change the number of steps the History panel records in the General category of the Preferences dialog

box. However, keep in mind that setting this number too high might require additional memory and could affect Dreamweaver's performance.

Viewing HTML Code in the Code Inspector

If you enjoy writing code, you occasionally might want to make changes to web pages by entering the code rather than using the panels and tools in Design view. Often it is actually easier to make editing or formatting corrections in the code. You can view the code in Dreamweaver using Code view, Code and Design views, or the Code Inspector. The **Code Inspector**, shown in Figure 26, is a separate window that displays the current page in Code view.

Understanding Other History Panel Features

Dragging the slider up and down in the History panel is a quick way to undo or redo steps. However, the History panel offers much more. It has the capability to "memorize" certain tasks and consolidate them into one command. This is a useful feature for steps that you perform repetitively on web pages. Some Dreamweaver features, such as drag and drop, cannot be recorded in the History panel and are noted by a red "x" placed next to them in the panel. The History panel does not show steps performed in the Files panel.

The advantage of using the Code Inspector is that you can see a full-screen view of your page in Design view while viewing the underlying code in a floating window that you can resize and position wherever you want.

You can add advanced features, such as JavaScript functions, to web pages by copying and pasting code from one page to another in the Code Inspector. A **JavaScript** function is a block of code that adds dynamic content such as rollovers or interactive forms to a web page. A **rollover** is a special effect that changes the appearance of an object when the mouse moves over it.

QUICK TIP

If you are new to HTML, you can use the Reference panel to find answers to your HTML questions. The Reference panel contains many resources besides HTML help, such as JavaScript help. You can open the Reference panel from the Code Inspector or the Results panel.

Figure 25 *The History panel*

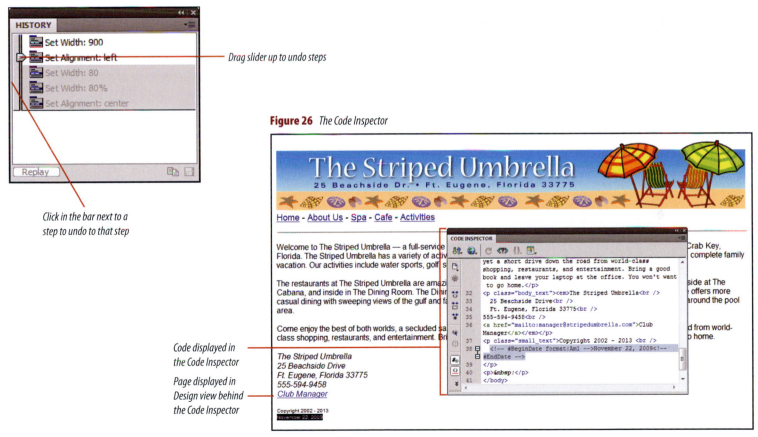

Drag slider up to undo steps

Click in the bar next to a step to undo to that step

Figure 26 *The Code Inspector*

Code displayed in the Code Inspector

Page displayed in Design view behind the Code Inspector

Use the History panel

1. Click **Window** on the Application bar (Win) or Menu bar (Mac), then click **History**.

   The History panel opens and displays steps you have recently performed.

2. Click the **History panel options button**, 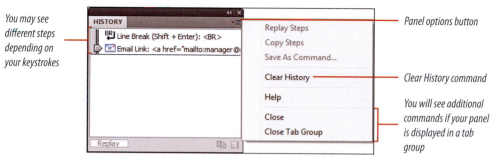 click **Clear History**, as shown in Figure 27, then click **Yes** to close the warning box.

3. Select the **horizontal rule** on the home page.

   The Property inspector shows the properties of the selected horizontal rule.

4. Click the W text box in the Property inspector, type **900**, click the **Align list arrow**, click **Left**, then compare your Property inspector to Figure 28.

   Horizontal rule widths can be set in pixels or as a percent of the width of the window. If the width is expressed in pixels, the code will only show the number, without the word "pixels". Pixels is understood as the default width setting.

5. Using the Property inspector, change the W text box value to **80**, change the measurement unit to **%**, click the **Align list arrow**, then click **Center**.

6. Drag the **slider** on the History panel up to Set Alignment: left, as shown in Figure 29.

   The bottom three steps in the History panel appear gray, indicating that these steps have been undone.

7. Right-click (Win) or Control-click (Mac) the **History panel title bar**, then click **Close** to close the History panel.

You formatted the horizontal rule, made changes to it, then used the History panel to undo some of the changes.

Figure 27 *Clearing the History panel*

You may see different steps depending on your keystrokes

Panel options button

Clear History command

You will see additional commands if your panel is displayed in a tab group

Figure 28 *Property inspector settings for horizontal rule*

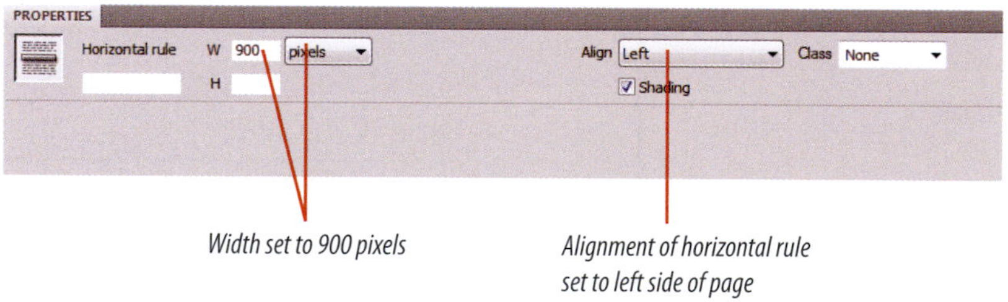

Width set to 900 pixels

Alignment of horizontal rule set to left side of page

Figure 29 *Undoing steps using the History panel*

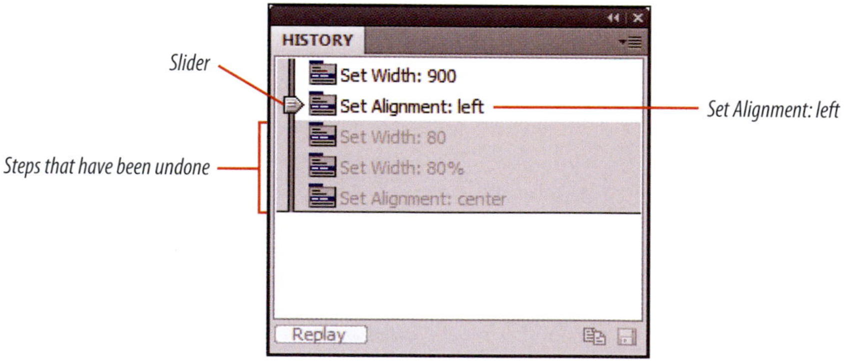

Slider

Set Alignment: left

Steps that have been undone

Figure 30 *Viewing the Options menu in the Code Inspector*

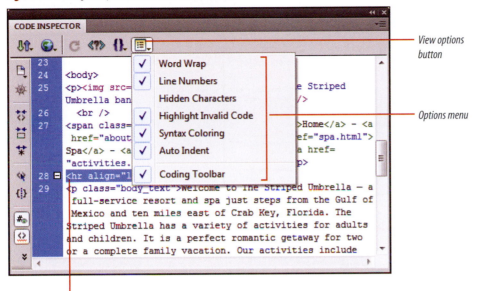

View options button

Options menu

Code for horizontal rule

Use the Code Inspector

1. Click the **horizontal rule** to select it if necessary, click **Window** on the Application bar (Win) or Menu bar (Mac), then click **Code Inspector**.

   Because the horizontal rule on the page is selected, the corresponding code is highlighted in the Code Inspector.

   TIP You can also press [F10](Win) or [fn][option][F10] (Mac) to display the Code Inspector.

2. Click the **View Options button** 📋 on the Code Inspector toolbar to display the View Options menu, then if **Word Wrap** is unchecked, click it once to activate it.

   The Word Wrap feature forces text to stay within the confines of the Code Inspector window, allowing you to read without scrolling sideways.

3. Click the **View Options button** 📋, then verify that the Word Wrap, Line Numbers, Highlight Invalid Code, Syntax Coloring, Auto Indent, and Coding Toolbar menu items are checked, as shown in Figure 30. If they are not checked, check them.

4. Select **900** in the horizontal rule width code, type **950**, then click the Refresh button [🔁 Refresh] in the Property inspector.

You changed the width of the horizontal rule by changing the code in the Code Inspector.

POWER USER SHORTCUTS	
To do this:	**Use this shortcut:**
Select All	[Ctrl][A] (Win) or ⌘[A] (Mac)
Copy	[Ctrl][C] (Win) or ⌘[C] (Mac)
Cut	[Ctrl][X] (Win) or ⌘[X] (Mac)
Paste	[Ctrl][V] (Win) or ⌘[V] (Mac)
Line Break	[Shift][Enter] (Win) or [Shift][return] (Mac)
Show or hide the Code Inspector	[F10] (Win) or [fn][option][F10] (Mac)
Preview in browser	[F12] (Win) or [fn][option][F12] (Mac)
Check spelling	[Shift][F7] (Win) or [fn][Shift][F7] (Mac)

Use the Reference panel

1. With the horizontal rule still selected, click the **Reference button** ⟨?⟩ on the Code Inspector toolbar, as shown in Figure 31, to open the Results Tab Group below the Property inspector, with the Reference panel visible.

TIP If the horizontal rule is not still selected, you will not see the horizontal rule description in the Reference panel.

2. Read the information about horizontal rules in the Reference panel, as shown in Figure 32, right-click in an empty area of the **Results Tab Group title bar**, then click **Close Tab Group** (Win) or click the **Panel options button** ▾☰ then click **Close Tab Group** (Mac and Win) to close the Results Tab Group.

3. Close the Code Inspector.

You read information about horizontal rule settings in the Reference panel.

Figure 31 *Reference button on the Code Inspector toolbar*

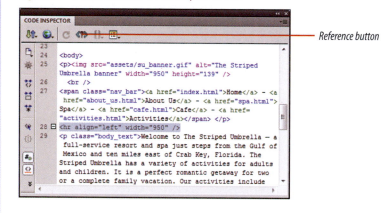

Reference button

Figure 32 *Viewing the Reference panel*

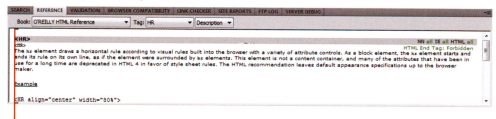

Information on <HR> (horizontal rule tag)

Developing a Web Page

Figure 33 *Insert Date dialog box*

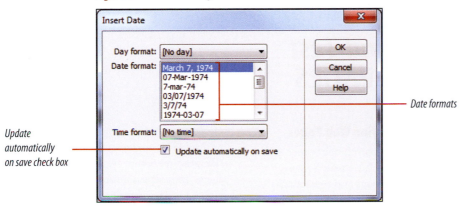

Update automatically on save check box

Date formats

Figure 34 *Viewing the date object code*

Code for date object (your date code may be on a different line number)

```
                >
37  <p class="small_text">Copyright 2002 - 2013 <br />
38  Last updated on
39    <!-- #BeginDate format:Am1 -->May 16, 2010<!-- #EndDate -->
40  </p>
41  <p> </p>
42  </body>
43  </html>
```

Insert a date object

1. Scroll down the page, if necessary, to select **January 1**, **2013**, then press **[Delete]** (Win) or **[delete]** (Mac).

2. Click **Date** in the Common category in the Insert panel, then click **March 7**, **1974** if necessary in the Date format list.

3. Check the **Update automatically on save check box**, as shown in Figure 33, click **OK**, then deselect the text.

4. Change to Code and Design views.

   The code has changed to reflect the date object, which is set to today's date, as shown in Figure 34. (Your date will be different.) The new code is highlighted with a light yellow background, indicating that it is a date object, automatically coded by Dreamweaver, rather than a date that has been manually typed on the page by the designer.

5. Return to Design view, then save the page.

You inserted a date object that will be updated automatically when you open and save the home page.

Inserting Comments

A handy Dreamweaver feature is the ability to insert comments into HTML code. Comments can provide helpful information describing portions of the code, such as a JavaScript function. You can create comments in any Dreamweaver view, but you must turn on Invisible Elements to see them in Design view. Use the Edit (Win) or Dreamweaver (Mac), Preferences, Invisible Elements, Comments option to enable viewing of comments; then use the View, Visual Aids, Invisible Elements menu option to display them on the page. To create a comment, select the Common category on the Insert panel, click Comment, type a comment in the Comment dialog box, and then click OK. Comments are not visible in browser windows. Comments are also not visible in Design view unless you turn them on as a preference. To do this, click View, Visual Aids, Invisible elements.

Modify and Test
WEB PAGES

What You'll Do

 In this lesson, you will preview the home page in the browser to check for typographical errors, grammatical errors, broken links, and overall appearance. After previewing, you will make slight formatting adjustments to the page to improve its appearance.

Testing and Modifying Web Pages

Testing web pages is a continuous process. You never really finish a website, because there are always additions and corrections to make. As you add and modify pages, you must test each page as part of the development process. The best way to test a web page is to preview it in Live view or in a browser window to make sure that all text and image elements appear the way you expect them to. You should also test your links to make sure they work properly. You need to proofread your text to make sure it contains all the necessary information for the page with no typographical or grammatical errors.

Designers typically view a page in a browser, return to Dreamweaver to make necessary changes, and then view the page in a browser again. They repeat this process many times before the page is ready for publishing. In fact, it is sometimes difficult to stop making improvements to a page and move on to another project. You need to strike a balance among quality, creativity, and productivity.

Testing a Web Page Using Different Browsers and Screen Sizes

Because users access the Internet using a wide variety of computer systems, it is important to design your pages so that

---

DESIGNTIP

Using "Under Construction" Or "Come Back Later" Pages

Many people are tempted to insert an unfinished page as a placeholder for a page that they intend to finish later. Rather than have real content, these pages usually contain text or an image that indicates the page is not finished, or "under construction." You should not publish a web page that has a link to an unfinished page. It is frustrating to click a link for a page you want to open only to find an "under construction" note or image displayed. You want to make the best possible impression on your viewing audience. If you cannot complete a page before publishing it, at least provide enough information on it to make it "worth the trip."

all browsers and screen sizes can display them well. You should test your pages using different browsers and a wide variety of screen sizes to ensure the best view of your page by the most people possible. Although the most common screen size that designers use today is 1024 × 768, some viewers restore down (reduce) individual program windows to a size comparable to 800 × 600 to be able to have more windows open simultaneously on their screen. In other words, people use their "screen real estate" according to their personal work style. To view your page using different screen sizes, click the Window Size pop-up menu on the status bar, then choose the setting you want to use. Table 2 lists the Dreamweaver default window screen sizes. To view your pages using several different browsers, click the Preview/Debug in Browser button on the Application bar (Win) Menu bar (Mac), click Edit Browser List, then use the Add icon to add additional browsers of your choice to the list. You can also designate which browser to use as the default browser, the browser which opens when the F12 key is pressed. Remember also to check your pages using Windows and Macintosh platforms. Some page elements such as fonts, colors, table borders, layers, and horizontal rules might not appear consistently in both.

Testing a Web Page as Rendered in a Mobile Device

Dreamweaver has another preview feature that allows you to see what a page would look like if it were viewed on a mobile hand-held device, such as a BlackBerry or iPhone. To use this feature, click the Preview/Debug in Browser button on the Document toolbar, then click Preview in Device Central.

TABLE 2: DREAMWEAVER DEFAULT WINDOW SCREEN SIZES	
Window Size (Inside Dimensions of the Browser Window Without Borders)	Monitor Size
592W	
536 × 196	640 × 480, default
600 × 300	640 × 480, maximized
760 × 420	800 × 600, maximized
795 × 470	832 × 624, maximized
955 × 600	1024 × 768, maximized

Modify a web page

1. Click the **Restore Down button** 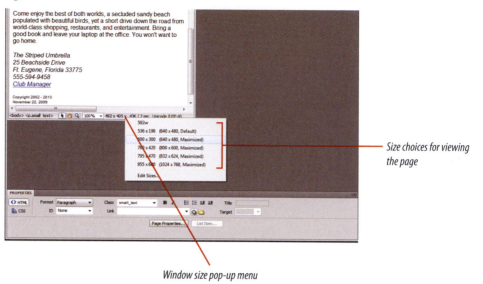 on the index.html title bar to decrease the size of the home page window (Win) or skip to Step 2 (Mac).

   TIP You cannot use the Window Size options if your Document window is maximized (Win).

2. Click the current window size on the status bar, as shown in Figure 35, then click **600 × 300 (640 × 480, Maximized)**, if necessary.

   A viewer using this setting will be forced to use the horizontal scroll bar to view the entire page.

3. Click the current window size on the status bar, then click **955 × 600 (1024 × 768, Maximized)**.

4. Replace the period after the last sentence, "You won't want to go home." with an exclamation point.

5. Click the **Maximize button** ☐ on the index.html title bar to maximize the home page window.

   TIP If you don't see the Maximize button, collapse your panels temporarily.

6. Save your work.

You viewed the home page using two different window sizes and you made simple formatting changes to the page.

Figure 35 *Window screen sizes*

Size choices for viewing the page

Window size pop-up menu

Using Smart Design Principles in Web Page Layout

As you view your pages in the browser, take a critical look at the symmetry of the page. Is it balanced? Are there too many images compared to text, or vice versa? Does everything "heavy" seem to be on the top or bottom of the page, or do the page elements seem to balance with the weight evenly distributed between the top, bottom, and sides? Use design principles to create a site-wide consistency for your pages. Horizontal symmetry means that the elements are balanced across the page. Vertical symmetry means that they are balanced down the page. Diagonal symmetry balances page elements along the invisible diagonal line of the page. Radial symmetry runs from the center of the page outward, like the petals of a flower. These principles all deal with balance; however, too much balance is not good, either. Sometimes it adds interest to place page elements a little off center or to have an asymmetric layout. Color, white space, text, and images should all complement each other and provide a natural flow across and down the page. The **rule of thirds**—dividing a page into nine squares like a tic-tac-toe grid—states that interest is increased when your focus is on one of the intersections in the grid. The most important information should be at the top of the page where it is visible without scrolling, or "above the fold," as they say in the newspaper business.

Figure 36 *Viewing The Striped Umbrella home page in the Firefox browser*

Visited links

Edited text

Test web pages by viewing them in a browser

1. Click the **Preview/Debug in browser button** on the Document toolbar, then choose your browser from the menu that opens.

   The Striped Umbrella home page opens in your default browser.

   TIP If previewing the page in Internet Explorer 7, click the Information bar when prompted, click Allow Blocked Content, then click Yes to close the Security Warning dialog box.

2. Click each link on the menu bar, then after each click, use the Back button on the browser toolbar to return to the home page.

   Pages with no content at this point will appear as blank pages. Compare your screen to Figure 36.

3. Close your browser window, then close all open pages in Dreamweaver.

You viewed The Striped Umbrella home page in your browser and tested each link on the menu bar.

DESIGN**TIP**

Choosing a Window Size

Today, the majority of viewers use a screen resolution of 1024 × 768 or higher. Because of this, more content can be displayed at one time on a computer monitor. Some people might use their whole screen to view pages on the Internet. Others might choose to allocate a smaller area of their screen to the browser window. In other words, people tend to use their "screen real estate" in different ways. The ideal web page will not be so small that it tries to spread out over a larger screen size or so large that the viewer has to use horizontal scroll bars to read the page content. The WCAG guideline 1.4.8 states that " … Text can be resized without assistive technology up to 200 percent in a way that does not require the user to scroll horizontally to read a line of text on a full-screen window." Achieving the best balance and meeting accessibility guidelines is one of the design decisions that you must make during the planning process.

Create head content and set page properties.

1. Open the Blooms & Bulbs website.
2. Open the index page and view the head content.
3. Edit the page title so it reads **Blooms & Bulbs - your complete garden center**.
4. Insert the following keywords: **garden, plants, nursery, flowers, landscape, bulbs, Blooms & Bulbs, Alvin, Texas**.
5. Insert the following description: **Blooms & Bulbs is a premier supplier of plants, trees, and shrubs for both professional and home gardeners**.
6. Switch to Code view to view the HTML code for the head content, then switch back to Design view.
7. Open the Page Properties dialog box to view the current page properties.
8. Change the background color to a color of your choice.
9. Change the background color to white, then save your work.

Create, import, and format text.

1. Create a new paragraph after the second paragraph of text and type the following text, inserting a line break after each line.
   Blooms & Bulbs
   Highway 43 South
   Alvin, Texas 77511
   555-248-0806
2. Verify that the HTML button is selected in the Property inspector, and select it if it is not.
3. Italicize the address and phone number lines.
4. Change to Code view to view the formatting code for the italicized text.

5. Return to Design view, save your work, hide the head content, then close the home page.
6. Open dw2_2.html and save it as **tips.html** in the Blooms & Bulbs website, overwriting the existing file, but not updating links.
7. Click the broken image link below the Blooms & Bulbs banner, use the Property inspector to browse to the chapter_2 assets folder where you store your Data Files, select the file butterfly.jpg in the assets folder, then click OK to save a copy of it in the Blooms & Bulbs website.
8. Place the insertion point to the right of the butterfly image, then insert a paragraph break.
9. Import gardening_tips.doc from where you store your Data Files, using the Import Word Document command (Win) or copy and paste the text (Mac).
10. Use the Clean Up Word HTML command to correct or remove any unnecessary code.
11. Click inside the Seasonal Gardening Checklist heading, then use the Property inspector to apply a Heading 3 format.
12. Click inside the Basic Gardening Tips heading, then use the Property inspector to format the selected text with a Heading 3 format.
13. Place the insertion point at the top of the document, then check the page for spelling errors by using the Check Spelling command, and make any necessary corrections.
14. Save your work and close the tips page and the data file.

Add links to web pages.

1. Open the index page, then select the current menu bar and replace it with **Home - Featured Plants -**

Garden Tips - Workshops - Newsletter. Use a hyphen with a space on either side to separate the items.
2. Add a horizontal rule between the menu bar and the first paragraph of text.
3. Use the Property inspector to link Home on the menu bar to the index.html page in the Blooms & Bulbs website.
4. Link Featured Plants on the menu bar to the plants.html page.
5. Link Garden Tips on the menu bar to the tips.html page.
6. Link Workshops on the menu bar to the workshops.html page.
7. Link Newsletter on the menu bar to the newsletter.html page.
8. Create a line break after the telephone number and then use the Insert panel to create an email link, with **Customer Service** as the text and **mailbox@ blooms.com** as the email address.
9. Save your work.
10. View the email link in the Assets panel, refreshing it if necessary, then view the Files panel.

Use the History panel and edit code.

1. Open the History panel, then clear its contents.
2. Select the horizontal rule under the menu bar, then change the width to 900 pixels and the alignment to Left.
3. Change the width to 70% and the alignment to Center.
4. Use the History panel to restore the horizontal rule settings to 900 pixels wide, left aligned.

5. Close the History panel.

6. Open the Code Inspector and verify that Word Wrap is selected.

7. Edit the code in the Code Inspector to change the width of the horizontal rule to 950 pixels.

8. Open the Reference panel and scan the information about horizontal rules.

9. Close the Code Inspector and close the Reference panel tab group.

10. Delete the current date in the Last updated on statement on the home page and replace it with a date using the March 7, 1974 format that will update automatically when the file is saved.

11. Examine the code for the date at the bottom of the page to verify that the code that forces it to update on save is included in the code. (*Hint*: The code should be highlighted with a light yellow background.)

12. Return to Design view, then save your work.

Modify and test web pages.

1. Restore down the document window if necessary, use the Window Size pop-up menu to view the home page at 600 × 300 (640 × 480, Maximized) and 760 × 420 (800 × 600, Maximized), then maximize the Document window.

2. View the page in your browser. (*Hint*: If previewing the page in Internet Explorer 7, click the Information bar when prompted to allow blocked content.)

3. Verify that all links work correctly, then close the browser.

4. On the home page, add the text "We are happy to deliver or ship your purchases." to the end of the first paragraph.

5. Save your work, then view the pages in your browser, comparing your pages to Figure 37 and Figure 38.

6. Close your browser, then save and close all open pages.

Figures 37 & 38   *Completed Skills Review, home page and tips page*

You have been hired to create a website for TripSmart, a travel outfitter. You have created the basic framework for the website and are now ready to format and edit the home page to improve the content and appearance.

1. Open the TripSmart website, then open the home page.
2. Enter the following keywords: **TripSmart, travel, trips, vacations,** and **tours.**
3. Enter the following description: **TripSmart is a comprehensive travel store. We can help you plan trips, make travel arrangements, and supply you with travel gear.**
4. Change the page title to **TripSmart - serving all your travel needs.**
5. Replace the existing menu bar with the following text: **Home, Catalog, Services, Tours,** and **Newsletter.** Between each item, use a hyphen with a space on either side to separate the items.
6. Replace the date in the last updated statement with a date that will update automatically on save.
7. Add a paragraph break after the last paragraph, then type the following address, using line breaks after each line:
   TripSmart
   1106 Beechwood
   Fayetteville, AR 72704
   555-848-0807

8. Insert an email link in the line below the telephone number, using **Contact Us** for the text and **mailbox@tripsmart.com** for the email link.
9. Italicize TripSmart, the address, phone number, and email link.
10. Link the menu bar entries to index.html, catalog.html, services.html, tours.html, and newsletter.html.
11. View the HTML code for the page, then return to Design view.
12. Insert a horizontal rule above the address.

13. Change the horizontal rule width to 950 pixels and align it to the left side of the page.
14. Save your work.
15. View the page using two different window sizes, then test the links in your browser window.
16. Compare your page to Figure 39, close the browser, then close all open pages.

Figure 39 *Completed Project Builder 1*

Developing a Web Page

Your company has been selected to design a website for a catering business named Carolyne's Creations. You are now ready to add content to the home page and apply formatting options to improve the page's appearance, using Figure 40 as a guide.

1. Open the Carolyne's Creations website, then open the home page.
2. Edit the page title to read **Carolyne's Creations - Premier Gourmet Food Shop**.
3. Add the description **Carolyne's Creations is a full-service gourmet food shop. We offer cooking classes, take-out meals, and catering services. We also have a retail shop that stocks gourmet items and kitchen accessories.**
4. Add the keywords **Carolyne's Creations, gourmet, catering, cooking classes, kitchen accessories, take-out**.
5. Place the insertion point in front of the sentence in the second paragraph beginning "Give us a call" and type **We also have a pick-up window on the right side of the building for take-out orders**.
6. Add the following address below the second paragraph using line breaks after each line:
   Carolyne's Creations
   496 Maple Avenue
   Seven Falls, Virginia 52404
   555-963-8271
7. Enter another line break after the telephone number and type **Email**, add a space, then add an email link using Carolyne Kate for the text and carolyne@carolynescreations.com for the email address.

8. Create links from each menu bar element to its corresponding web page.
9. Replace the date that follows the text "Last updated on" with a date object that will automatically update on save, then save your work.
10. Insert a horizontal rule between the menu bar and the Welcome heading.
11. Set the width of the horizontal rule to 400 pixels, then left-align the horizontal rule.

12. Save your work, view the completed page in your default browser, then test each link. (*Hint*: If previewing the page in Internet Explorer 7, click the Information bar when prompted to allow blocked content.)
13. Close your browser.
14. Close all open pages.

Figure 40 *Completed Project Builder 2*

Copyright 2001 - 2013
Last updated on December 10, 2009

Albert Iris is looking for a durable laptop case that he can use for the frequent trips he takes with his laptop computer. He is searching the Internet looking for one that is attractive, strong, and that provides quick access for removing the laptop for airport security. He knows that websites use keywords and descriptions in order to receive "hits" with search engines. He is curious about how they work. Follow the steps below and write your answers to the questions.

1. Connect to the Internet, then go to **www.sfbags.com** to view the Waterfield Designs website's home page, as shown in Figure 41.
2. View the page source by clicking View on the Application bar, then clicking Source (Internet Explorer) or Page Source (Mozilla Firefox).
3. Can you locate a description and keywords? If so, what are they?

4. How many keyword terms do you find?
5. Is the description appropriate for the website? Why or why not?
6. Look at the numbers of keyword terms and words in the description. Is there an appropriate number?

7. Use a search engine such as Google at www.google.com, then type the words **laptop bag** in the Search text box.
8. Click a link in the list of results and view the source code for that page. Do you see keywords and a description? Do any of them match the words you used in the search?

Figure 41 *Design Project*

Waterfield Designs website used with permission from Waterfield Designs – www.sfbags.com

Developing a Web Page

In this assignment, you will continue to work on the website you defined in Chapter 1. In Chapter 1, you created a wireframe for your website with at least four pages. You also created a local site folder for your site and an assets folder to store the site asset files. You set the assets folder as the default storage location for your images. You began to collect information and resources for your site and started working on the home page.

1. Think about the head content for the home page. Add the title, keywords, and a description.

2. Create the main page content for the home page.
3. Add the address and other contact information to the home page, including an email address.
4. Consult your wireframe and design the menu bar.
5. Link the menu bar items to the appropriate pages.
6. Add a last updated on statement to the home page with a date that will automatically update when the page is saved.
7. Edit the page content until you are satisfied with the results. You will format the content after you have learned to use Cascading Style Sheets in the next chapter.

8. Verify that all links, including the email link, work correctly.
9. When you are satisfied with the home page, review the checklist questions shown in Figure 42, then make any necessary changes.
10. Save your work.

Figure 42 *Portfolio Project*

Website Checklist

1. Does the home page have a page title?
2. Does the home page have a description and keywords?
3. Does the home page contain contact information, including an email address?
4. Does the home page have a menu bar that includes a link to itself?
5. Does the home page have a "last updated on" statement that will automatically update when the page is saved?
6. Do all paths for links and images work correctly?
7. Does the home page look good using at least two different browsers and screen resolutions?

CHAPTER 3

WORKING WITH TEXT AND
CASCADING STYLE SHEETS

1. Create unordered and ordered lists
2. Create, apply, and edit Cascading Style Sheets
3. Add rules and attach Cascading Style Sheets
4. Use coding tools to view and edit rules

WORKING WITH TEXT AND
CASCADING STYLE SHEETS

Introduction

Most web pages depend largely on text to convey information. Dreamweaver provides many tools for working with text that you can use to make your web pages attractive and easy to read. These tools can help you format text quickly and make sure your text has a consistent look across all your web pages.

Formatting Text as Lists

If a web page contains a large amount of text, it can be difficult for viewers to digest it all. You can break up the monotony of large blocks of text by dividing them into smaller paragraphs or by organizing them as lists. You can create three types of lists in Dreamweaver: unordered lists, ordered lists, and definition lists.

Using Cascading Style Sheets

You can save time and ensure that all your page elements have a consistent appearance by using **Cascading Style Sheets (CSS)**. CSS are sets of formatting instructions, usually stored in a separate file, that control the appearance and position of text and graphics on a web page or throughout a website. CSS are a great way to define consistent formatting attributes for page elements such as paragraph text, lists, and table data throughout your website. You can then apply the formatting attributes to any element in a single document or to all of the pages in a website. This chapter will focus on using Cascading Style Sheets to format text.

PROPERTIES

<> HTML	Format None ▼	Class None ▼	**B** *I*	Title
CSS	ID None ▼	Link ▼		Target ▼

Page Properties... | List Item...

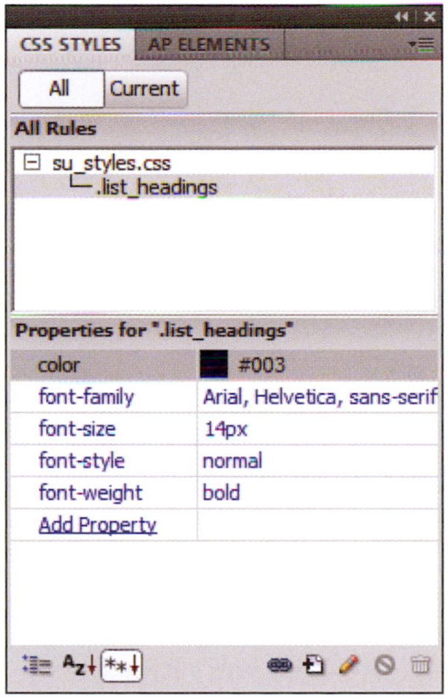

CSS STYLES | AP ELEMENTS

All | Current

All Rules

⊟ su_styles.css
  └ .list_headings

Properties for ".list_headings"

color	■ #003
font-family	Arial, Helvetica, sans-serif
font-size	14px
font-style	normal
font-weight	bold
Add Property	

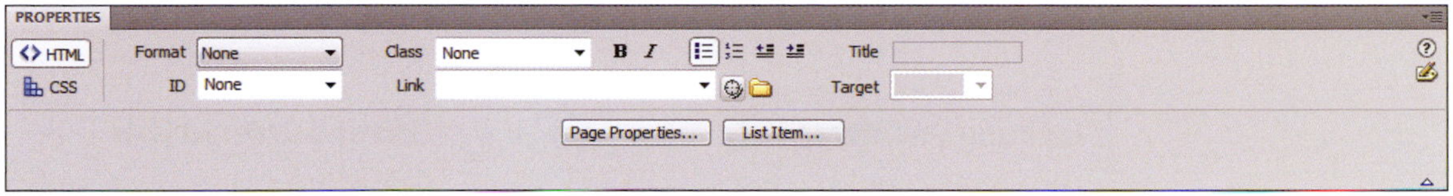

Create Unordered AND ORDERED LISTS

What You'll Do

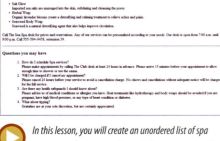

- Salt Glow
  Imported sea salts are massaged into the skin, exfoliating and cleansing the pores.
- Herbal Wrap
  Organic lavender blooms create a detoxifying and calming treatment to relieve aches and pains.
- Seaweed Body Wrap
  Seaweed is a natural detoxifying agent that also helps improve circulation.

Call The Sea Spa desk for prices and reservations. Any of our services can be personalized according to your needs. Our desk is open from 7:00 a.m. until 9:00 p.m. Call 555-594-9458, extension 39.

Questions you may have

1. How do I schedule Spa services?
   Please make appointments by calling The Club desk at least 24 hours in advance. Please arrive 15 minutes before your appointment to allow enough time to shower or use the sauna.
2. Will I be charged if I cancel my appointment?
   Please cancel 24 hours before your service to avoid a cancellation charge. No-shows and cancellations without adequate notice will be charged for the full service.
3. Are there any health safeguards I should know about?
   Please advise us of medical conditions or allergies you have. Heat treatments like hydrotherapy and body wraps should be avoided if you are pregnant, have high blood pressure, or any type of heart condition or diabetes.
4. What about tipping?
   Gratuities are at your sole discretion, but are certainly appreciated.

In this lesson, you will create an unordered list of spa services on the spa page. You will also import text with questions and format them as an ordered list.

Creating Unordered Lists

Unordered lists are lists of items that do not need to appear in a specific sequence, such as a grocery list, which often lists items in a random order. Items in unordered lists are usually preceded by a **bullet**, a small dot or similar icon. Unordered lists that contain bullets are sometimes called **bulleted lists**. Although you can use paragraph indentations to create an unordered list, bullets can often make lists easier to read. To create an unordered list, first select the text you want to format as an unordered list, then use the Unordered List button in the HTML Property inspector to insert bullets at the beginning of each paragraph of the selected text.

Formatting Unordered Lists

In Dreamweaver, the default bullet style is a round dot. To change the bullet style to a square, click inside a bulleted item, expand the HTML Property inspector to its full size, as shown in Figure 1, click the List Item button in the Property inspector to open the List Properties dialog box, as shown in Figure 2, then set the style for bulleted lists to Square. Be aware, however, that not all browsers display square bullets correctly, in which case the bullets will appear differently.

Creating Ordered Lists

Ordered lists, which are sometimes called **numbered lists**, are lists of items that are presented in a specific sequence and that are preceded by sequential numbers or letters. An ordered list is appropriate for a list in which each item must be executed according to its specified order. A list that provides numbered directions for driving from Point A to Point B or a list that provides instructions for assembling a bicycle are both examples of ordered lists.

Formatting Ordered Lists

You can format an ordered list to show different styles of numbers or letters by using the List Properties dialog box, as shown in Figure 3. You can apply numbers, Roman numerals, lowercase letters, or uppercase letters to an ordered list.

Creating Definition Lists

Definition lists are similar to unordered lists but are displayed with a hanging indent and are not preceded by bullets. They are often used with terms and definitions, such as in a dictionary or glossary. To create a definition list, select the text to use for the list, click Format on the Application bar (Win) or Menu bar (Mac), point to List, and then click Definition List.

Figure 1 *Expanded HTML Property inspector*

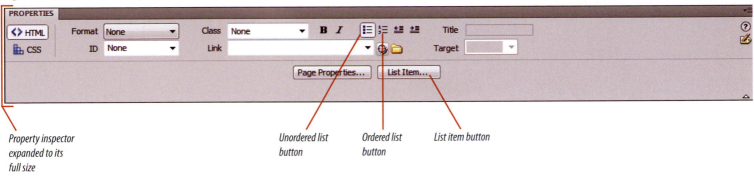

Property inspector
expanded to its
full size

Unordered list
button

Ordered list
button

List item button

Figure 2 *Choosing a bulleted list style in the List Properties dialog box*

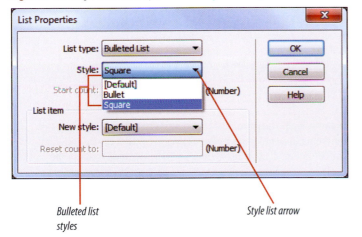

Bulleted list
styles

Style list arrow

Figure 3 *Choosing a numbered list style in the List Properties dialog box*

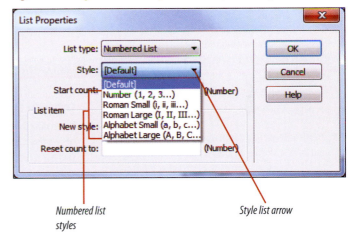

Numbered list
styles

Style list arrow

Create an unordered list

1. Open the spa page in The Striped Umbrella website.

2. Select the three items and their descriptions under the Massages heading.

3. Click the **HTML button** <> HTML in the Property inspector to switch to the HTML Property inspector if necessary, click the **Unordered List button** to format the selected text as an unordered list, click anywhere to deselect the text, then compare your screen to Figure 4.

   Each spa service item and its description are separated by a line break. That is why each description is indented under its corresponding item, rather than formatted as a new list item. You must enter a paragraph break to create a new list item.

4. Repeat Step 3 to create unordered lists of the three items under the Facials and Body Treatments headings, being careful not to include the contact information in the last paragraph on the page as part of your last list.

TIP Pressing [Enter] (Win) or [return] (Mac) once at the end of an unordered list creates another bulleted item. To end an unordered list, press [Enter] (Win) or [return] (Mac) twice.

You opened the spa page in Design view and formatted three spa services lists as unordered lists.

Figure 4 *Creating an unordered list*

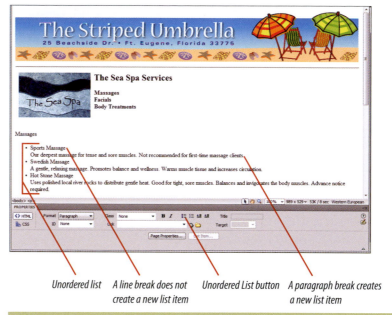

Unordered list   A line break does not   Unordered List button   A paragraph break creates
create a new list item   a new list item

DESIGN TIP

Coding for the Semantic Web

You may have heard the term "semantic web." The word "semantics" refers to the study of meanings of words or sentences. So the term "semantic web" refers to the way page content can be coded to convey meaning to other computer programs such as search engines. One example is to use the <em> tag which means "emphasis" rather than the <i> tag which means "italic" to show emphasis. Another example would be to use font size attributes such as <small> or <medium> rather than using font size attributes expressed in pixels. Cascading Style Sheets are used to define the appearance of semantic tags. For instance, you can specify the attributes of the <h1> heading tag by choosing the Selector Type: Tag (redefines an HTML element) rules in the New CSS Rules dialog box. CSS and semantic coding work together to enhance the meaning of the page content and provide well-designed pages that are attractive and consistent throughout the site. An ideal website would incorporate semantic coding with external style sheets to format all website content. This approach will enable "Semantic Web" programs to interpret the content presented, make it easier for web designers to write and edit, and enhance the overall experience for site visitors.

Figure 5 *List Properties dialog box*

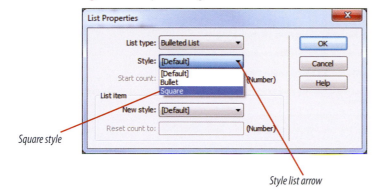

Square style

Style list arrow

Figure 6 *HTML tags in Code view for unordered list*

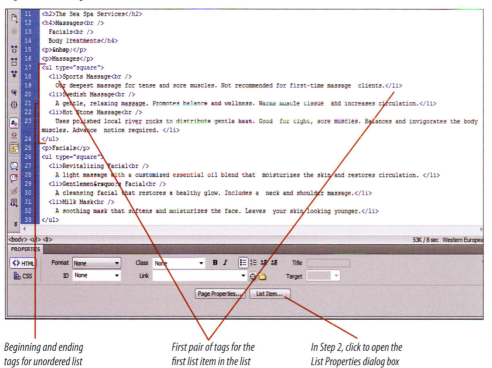

Beginning and ending tags for unordered list

First pair of tags for the first list item in the list

In Step 2, click to open the List Properties dialog box

Format an unordered list

1. Click any of the items in the first unordered list to place the insertion point in the list.

2. Expand the Property inspector if necessary, click **List Item** in the HTML Property inspector to open the List Properties dialog box, click the **Style list arrow**, click **Square**, as shown in Figure 5, then click **OK**.

    The bullets in the unordered list now have a square shape.

3. Repeat Step 2 to format the next two unordered lists.

4. Position the insertion point to the left of the first item in the first unordered list, then click the **Show Code view button** `Code` on the Document toolbar to view the code for the unordered list, as shown in Figure 6.

    A pair of HTML tags surrounds each type of element on the page. The first tag in each pair begins the code for a particular element, and the last tag ends the code for the element. For instance, the tag <ul> begins the unordered list, and the </ul> tag ends it. The tags <li> and </li> surround each item in the list.

5. Click the **Show Design view button** `Design` on the Document toolbar.

6. Save your work.

You used the List Properties dialog box to apply the Square bullet style to the unordered lists. You then viewed the HTML code for the unordered lists in Code view.

Create an ordered list

1. Place the insertion point at the end of the page, after the words "extension 39."

2. Use the File, Import, Word Document command to import **questions.doc** from where you store your Data Files (Win) or open **questions.doc** from where you store your Data Files, select all, copy, then paste the copied text on the page (Mac).

The inserted text appears on the same line as the existing text.

3. Use the Clean Up Word HTML command, place the insertion point to the left of the text "Questions you may have," then click **Horizontal Rule** in the Common category on the Insert panel.

A horizontal rule appears and separates the unordered list from the text you just imported.

4. Select the text beginning with "How do I schedule" and ending with the last sentence on the page.

5. Click the **Ordered List button** in the HTML Property inspector to format the selected text as an ordered list.

6. Deselect the text, then compare your screen to Figure 7.

You imported text on the spa page. You also added a horizontal rule to help organize the page. Finally, you formatted selected text as an ordered list.

Figure 7 *Creating an ordered list*

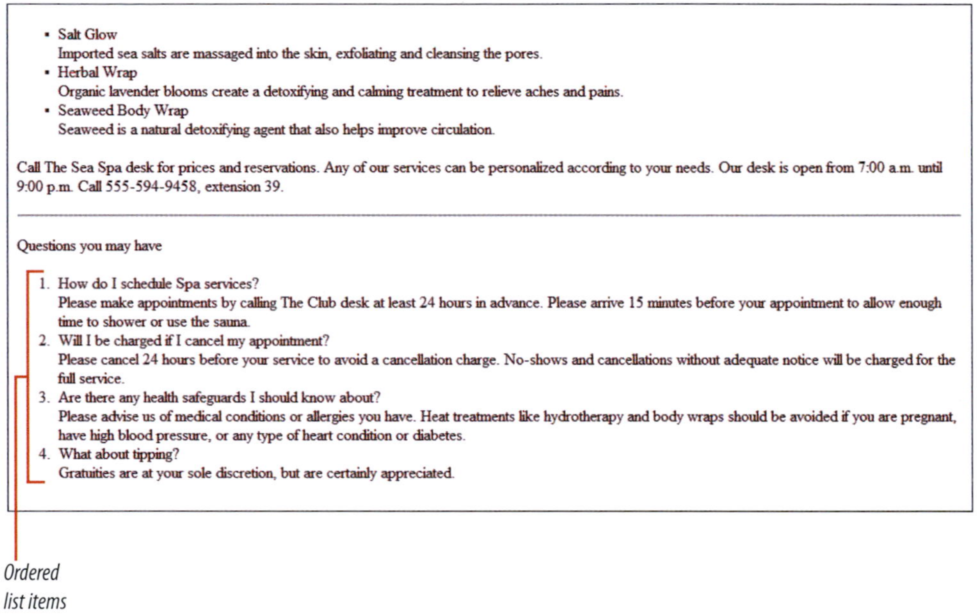

- Salt Glow
  Imported sea salts are massaged into the skin, exfoliating and cleansing the pores.
- Herbal Wrap
  Organic lavender blooms create a detoxifying and calming treatment to relieve aches and pains.
- Seaweed Body Wrap
  Seaweed is a natural detoxifying agent that also helps improve circulation.

Call The Sea Spa desk for prices and reservations. Any of our services can be personalized according to your needs. Our desk is open from 7:00 a.m. until 9:00 p.m. Call 555-594-9458, extension 39.

Questions you may have

1. How do I schedule Spa services?
   Please make appointments by calling The Club desk at least 24 hours in advance. Please arrive 15 minutes before your appointment to allow enough time to shower or use the sauna.
2. Will I be charged if I cancel my appointment?
   Please cancel 24 hours before your service to avoid a cancellation charge. No-shows and cancellations without adequate notice will be charged for the full service.
3. Are there any health safeguards I should know about?
   Please advise us of medical conditions or allergies you have. Heat treatments like hydrotherapy and body wraps should be avoided if you are pregnant, have high blood pressure, or any type of heart condition or diabetes.
4. What about tipping?
   Gratuities are at your sole discretion, but are certainly appreciated.

Ordered list items

Working with Text and Cascading Style Sheets

Figure 8 *Spa page with ordered list*

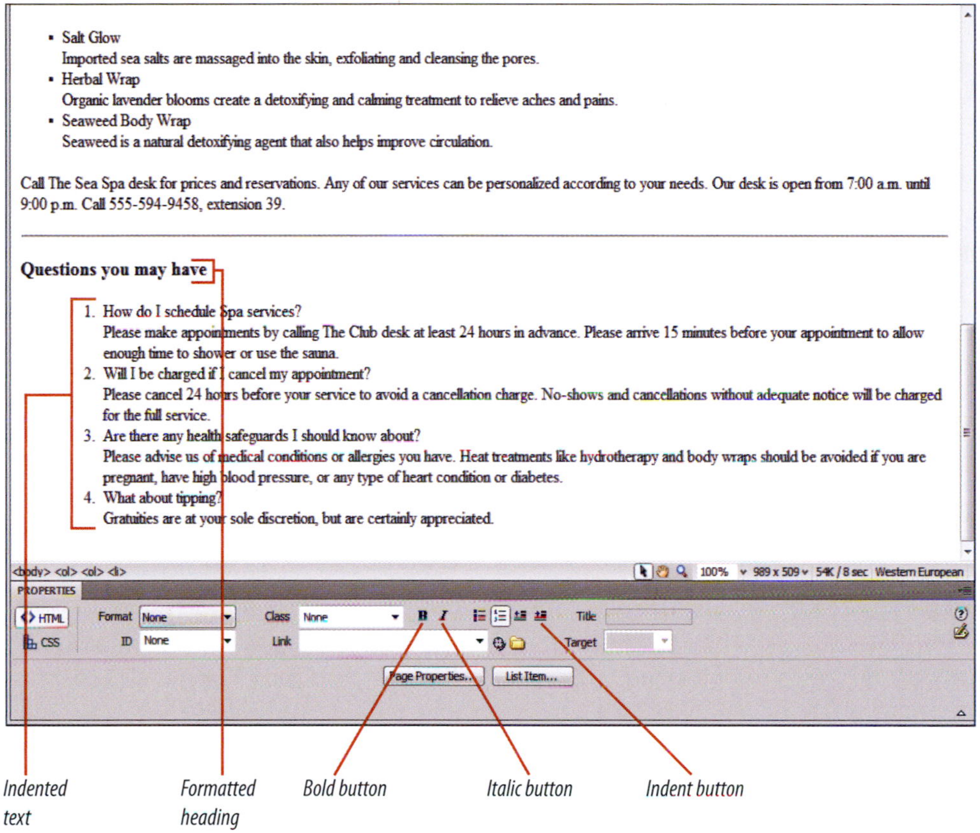

Salt Glow
Imported sea salts are massaged into the skin, exfoliating and cleansing the pores.
Herbal Wrap
Organic lavender blooms create a detoxifying and calming treatment to relieve aches and pains.
Seaweed Body Wrap
Seaweed is a natural detoxifying agent that also helps improve circulation.
Call The Sea Spa desk for prices and reservations. Any of our services can be personalized according to your needs. Our desk is open from 7:00 a.m. until 9:00 p.m. Call 555-594-9458, extension 39.
Questions you may have
1. How do I schedule Spa services?
Please make appointments by calling The Club desk at least 24 hours in advance. Please arrive 15 minutes before your appointment to allow enough time to shower or use the sauna.
2. Will I be charged if I cancel my appointment?
Please cancel 24 hours before your service to avoid a cancellation charge. No-shows and cancellations without adequate notice will be charged for the full service.
3. Are there any health safeguards I should know about?
Please advise us of medical conditions or allergies you have. Heat treatments like hydrotherapy and body wraps should be avoided if you are pregnant, have high blood pressure, or any type of heart condition or diabetes.
4. What about tipping?
Gratuities are at your sole discretion, but are certainly appreciated.
<body> <ol> <ol> <li>
100%
989 x 509
54K / 8 sec
Western European
PROPERTIES
HTML
CSS
Format
None
ID
None
Class
None
Link
Title
Target
Page Properties...
List Item...
Indented text
Formatted heading
Bold button
Italic button
Indent button

Format an ordered list

1. Click to place the insertion point in the heading "Questions you may have," then use the HTML Property inspector to apply the **Heading 3** format.

   TIP You could show emphasis by using the Bold button **B** or the Italic button *I* on the HTML Property inspector, as shown in Figure 8, but the heading code shows the significance (semantics) of the phrase more clearly. It shows that the phrase is a heading related to the text that follows it.

2. Select the four questions and answers, click the **Indent button** in the HTML Property inspector, deselect the text, then compare your screen to Figure 8.

   When a list item is selected, the Blockquote and Remove Blockquote button names change to Indent and Outdent. The Indent and Outdent buttons are used to indent selected text or remove an indent from selected text.

   TIP If you want to see more of your web page in the Document window, you can collapse the Property inspector.

3. Save your work.

You formatted the "Questions you may have" heading. You also indented the four questions and answers text.

Create, Apply, and
EDIT CASCADING STYLE SHEETS

What You'll Do

In this lesson, you will create a Cascading Style Sheet file for The Striped Umbrella website. You will also create a rule named list_headings and apply it to the list item headings on the spa page.

Understanding Cascading Style Sheets

Cascading Style Sheets (CSS) are made up of sets of formatting attributes called **rules**, which define the formatting attributes for page content. Rules are also referred to as styles. Style sheets are classified by where the code is stored. The code can be saved in a separate file (**external style sheet**), as part of the head content of an individual web page (**internal or embedded styles**), or as part of the body of the HTML code (**inline styles**). External CSS are saved as files with the .css extension and are stored in the website's directory structure. Figure 9 shows an external style sheet named su_styles.css listed in the Files panel. External style sheets are the preferred method for creating and using styles.

CSS are also classified by their type. A **Class type** can be used to format any page element. An **ID type** and a **Tag type** are used to redefine an HTML tag. A **Compound** type is used to format a selection. In this chapter, we will use the class type stored in an external style sheet file.

Using the CSS Styles Panel

You use buttons on the CSS Styles panel to create, edit, and apply rules. To add a rule, use the New CSS Rule dialog box to name the rule and specify whether to add it to a new or existing style sheet. You then use the CSS Rule definition dialog box to set the formatting attributes for the rule. Once you add a new rule to a style sheet, it appears in a list in the CSS Styles panel. To apply a rule, you select the text to which you want to apply the rule, and then choose a rule from the Targeted Rule list in the CSS Property inspector. You can apply CSS rules to elements on a single web page or to all of the pages in a website. When you edit a rule, such as changing the font size it specifies, all page elements formatted with that rule are automatically updated. Once you create an external CSS, you can attach it to the remaining pages in your website.

Use the CSS Styles panel to manage your styles. The Properties pane displays properties for a selected rule at the bottom of the panel. You can easily change a property's value by clicking an option from a drop-down menu.

Comparing the Advantages of Using Style Sheets

You can use CSS styles to save an enormous amount of time. Being able to define a rule and then apply it to page elements on all the pages of your website means that you can make hundreds of formatting changes in a few minutes. In addition, style sheets create a more uniform look from page to page and they generate cleaner code. Using style sheets separates the development of content from the way the content is presented. Pages formatted with CSS styles are much more compliant with current accessibility standards than those with manual formatting.

QUICK TIP

For more information about Cascading Style Sheets, visit www.w3.org/Style.

Understanding CSS Code

You can see the properties for a CSS rule by looking at the style sheet code. A CSS rule consists of two parts: the selector and the declaration. The **selector** is the name of the tag to which the style declarations have been assigned. The **declaration** consists of a property (such as font-size or font-weight) and a value (such as 14 px or bold). For example, Figure 10 shows the code for an internal style that sets the background color for a page. In this example, the selector is the body tag. The only property assigned to this selector is background-color. The value for this property is #FFF, or white. The property and value together comprise the declaration. When there is more than one property, each additional property and value are separated by a semicolon.

When you create a new CSS external file, you will see it as a related files document in the Document window. Save this file as you make changes to it.

Figure 9 *Cascading Style Sheet file created in striped_umbrella site root folder*

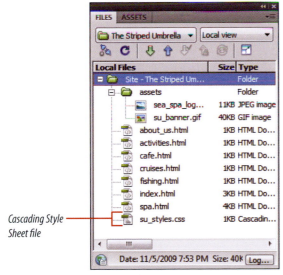

Cascading Style Sheet file

Figure 10 *Viewing CSS code*

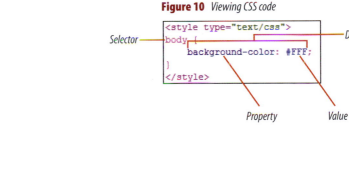

Selector

Declaration

Property

Value

Create a Cascading Style Sheet and add a rule

1. Click the **CSS button** 📇 CSS in the Property inspector to switch to the CSS Property inspector, as shown in Figure 11.

2. If the CSS Styles panel is not open, click **Window** on the Application bar (Win) or Menu bar (Mac), then click **CSS Styles** to open the CSS Styles panel.

3. Click the **Switch to All (Document) Mode button** [All] on the CSS Styles panel if it's not already active, then click the **New CSS Rule button** 🔂 in the CSS Styles panel to open the New CSS Rule dialog box.

4. Verify that Class (can apply to any HTML element) is selected under Selector Type, then type **list_headings** in the Selector Name text box.

TIP Class selector names are preceded by a period in the code and in the CSS panel. If you don't enter a period when you type the name, Dreamweaver will add the period for you when the rule is created.

5. Click the **Rule Definition list arrow**, click **(New Style Sheet File)**, compare your screen with Figure 12, then click **OK**.

This indicates that you want to create a new style sheet file, which will contain your list_headings rule and any other rules you may create for this site. The Save Style Sheet Files As dialog box opens.

(continued)

Figure 11 *CSS Property inspector*

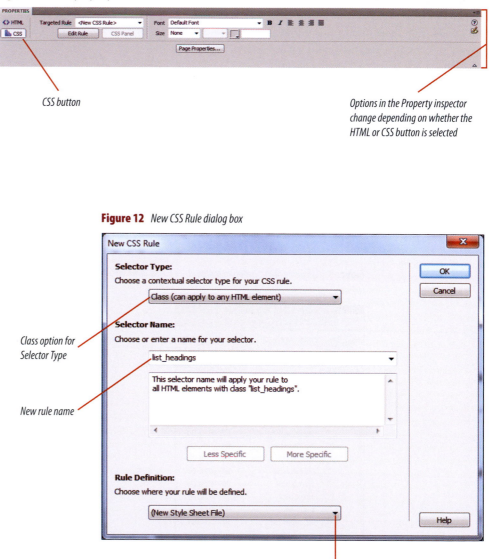

CSS button

Options in the Property inspector change depending on whether the HTML or CSS button is selected

Figure 12 *New CSS Rule dialog box*

Class option for Selector Type

New rule name

Rule Definition list arrow

Working with Text and Cascading Style Sheets

Figure 13 *CSS Rule Definition for .list_headings in su_styles.css dialog box*

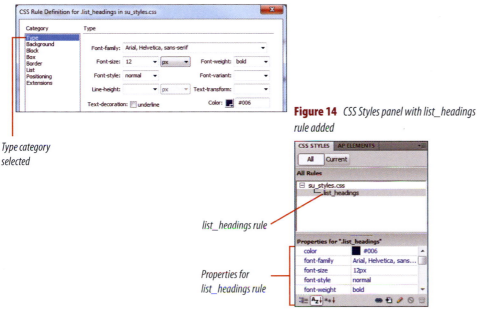

Type category selected

Figure 14 *CSS Styles panel with list_headings rule added*

list_headings rule

Properties for list_headings rule

6. Type **su_styles** in the File name text box (Win) or the Save As text box (Mac), verify that the striped_umbrella folder appears in the Save in box, then click **Save** to open the CSS Rule Definition for .list_headings in su_styles.css dialog box.

   The .list_headings rule will be stored within the su_styles.css file in the Striped Umbrella local site folder. Next, you define the formatting properties of the rule.

7. Verify that Type is selected in the Category list, set the Font-family to **Arial**, **Helvetica**, **sans-serif**, set the Font-size to **12 px**, set the Font-weight to **bold**, set the Font-style to **normal**, set the Color to **#006**, compare your screen to Figure 13, then click **OK**.

TIP You can modify the font combinations in the Font-family list by clicking Format on the Application bar (Win) or Menu bar (Mac), pointing to Font, then clicking Edit Font List.

Other interesting type options that are available in the CSS Rule Definition dialog box are Line-height, which changes the height of each line measured in pixels; Text-decoration, which adds text effects, Font-variant, which allows you to change the text to small caps, and Text-transform, which has options to change text to all upper-case or all lower-case.

8. Click the **plus sign** (Win) or the **expander arrow** (Mac) next to su_styles.css in the CSS Styles panel and expand the panel, if necessary, to see the list_headings rule displayed, then select the **list_headings rule**.

   The CSS rule named .list_headings and its properties appear in the CSS Styles panel, as shown in Figure 14.

You created a Cascading Style Sheet file named su_styles.css and a rule called .list_heading within the style sheet.

Choosing Fonts

There are two classifications of fonts: sans-serif and serif. **Sans-serif** fonts are block-style characters that are often used for headings and subheadings. The headings in this book and the text you are reading now use a sans-serif font. Examples of sans-serif fonts include Arial, Verdana, and Helvetica. **Serif** fonts are more ornate and contain small extra strokes at the beginning and end of the characters. Serif fonts are considered easier to read in printed material, because the extra strokes lead your eye from one character to the next. Examples of serif fonts include Times New Roman, Times, and Georgia. The paragraph text on the first page of each chapter is in a serif font. Many designers feel that a sans-serif font is preferable when the content of a website is primarily intended to be read on the screen, but that a serif font is preferable if the content will be printed. When you choose fonts, you need to keep in mind the amount of text each page will contain and whether most viewers will read the text on-screen or print it. A good rule of thumb is to limit each website to no more than three font variations.

Apply a rule in a Cascading Style Sheet

1. Click **View** on the Application bar (Win) or Menu bar (Mac), point to **Toolbars**, then click **Style Rendering**.

TIP You can also right-click on an empty area on an open toolbar to see the displayed and hidden toolbars listed in a drop-down menu. The displayed toolbars have a check next to them. To display or hide a toolbar, click its name on the menu.

2. Verify that the Toggle Displaying of CSS Styles button 🔲 on the Style Rendering toolbar is active, as shown in Figure 15.

TIP You can determine if the Toggle Displaying of CSS Styles button is active if it has a dark outline around the button. As long as this button is active, you do not have to display the toolbar on the screen.

You use the Toggle Displaying of CSS Styles button to see how styles affect your page. If it is not active, you will not see the effects of your styles and the default browser settings will be used to display the content.

3. Select the paragraph heading "Massages," click the **Targeted Rule list arrow** in the Property inspector, then click **list_headings**, as shown in Figure 16.

4. Repeat Step 3 to apply the list_headings rule to each of the spa services unordered list headings, click anywhere in the document to deselect the text, then compare your screen to Figure 17.

TIP You can use the keyboard shortcut [Ctrl][Y] (Win) or [Command][Y] (Mac) to repeat the previous action.

You applied the list_headings rule to each of the Spa Services category headings.

Figure 15 *Style Rendering toolbar*

Toggle Displaying of CSS Styles button

Figure 16 *Applying a CSS rule to selected text*

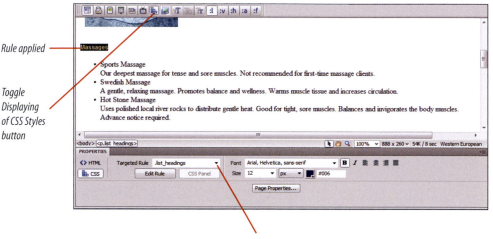

Rule applied

Toggle Displaying of CSS Styles button

Targeted Rule list arrow

Figure 17 *Unordered list with list_headings rule applied*

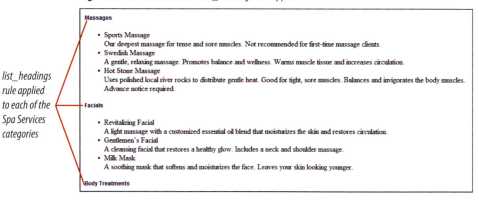

list_headings rule applied to each of the Spa Services categories

Figure 18 *Editing a rule*

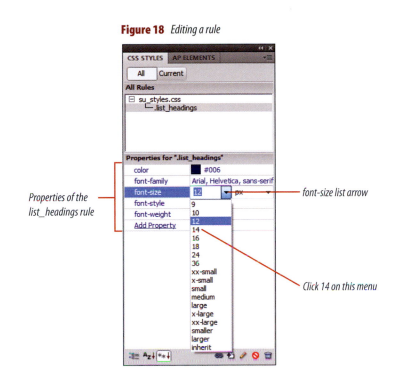

Properties of the
list_headings rule

font-size list arrow

Click 14 on this menu

Figure 19 *Viewing the changes made to the list_headings rule*

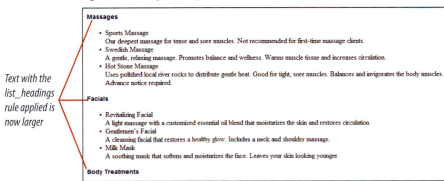

Text with the
list_headings
rule applied is
now larger

Massages

- Sports Massage
  Our deepest massage for tense and sore muscles. Not recommended for first-time massage clients.
- Swedish Massage
  A gentle, relaxing massage. Promotes balance and wellness. Warms muscle tissue and increases circulation.
- Hot Stone Massage
  Uses polished local river rocks to distribute gentle heat. Good for tight, sore muscles. Balances and invigorates the body muscles.
  Advance notice required.

Facials

- Revitalizing Facial
  A light massage with a customized essential oil blend that moisturizes the skin and restores circulation.
- Gentlemen's Facial
  A cleansing facial that restores a healthy glow. Includes a neck and shoulder massage.
- Milk Mask
  A soothing mask that softens and moisturizes the face. Leaves your skin looking younger.

Body Treatments

Edit a rule in a Cascading Style Sheet

1. Click **.list_headings** in the CSS Styles panel.

   The rule's properties and values appear in the Properties pane, the bottom part of the CSS Styles panel.

TIP Click the plus sign (Win) or expander arrow (Mac) to the left of su_styles.css in the CSS Styles panel if you do not see .list_headings. Click the plus sign (Win) or expander arrow (Mac) to the left of <style> if you do not see su_styles.css.

2. Click **12 px** in the CSS Styles panel, click the **font-size list arrow**, click **14** as shown in Figure 18, then compare your screen to Figure 19.

   All of the text to which you applied the list_headings rule is larger, reflecting the changes you made to the list_headings rule. You can also click the **Edit Rule button** in the CSS Styles panel to open the CSS Rule Definition for .list_headings dialog box.

TIP If you position the insertion point in text that has a CSS rule applied to it, that rule is displayed in the Targeted Rule text box in the CSS Property inspector or the Class text box in the HTML Property inspector.

3. Use the File, Save All command to save the spa page and the style sheet file.

4. Hide the Style Rendering toolbar.

You edited the list_headings rule to change the font size to 14 pixels. You then viewed the results of the edited rule in the unordered list.

View code with the Code Navigator

1. Click in the paragraph heading "Massages" and hover until the **Click indicator to bring up the Code Navigator** icon ⚙ appears, as shown in Figure 20.

2. Click the **Click indicator to bring up the Code Navigator icon** ⚙ .

   A window opens, as shown in Figure 21, with the name of the style sheet that is linked to this page (su_styles.css) and the name of the rule in the style sheet that has been applied to this text (list_headings).

   (continued)

Figure 20 *Viewing the Click indicator to bring up the Code Navigator icon*

Click indicator
to bring up the
Code Navigator icon

Figure 21 *Viewing the Code Navigator*

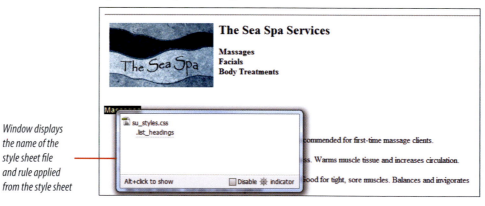

Window displays
the name of the
style sheet file
and rule applied
from the style sheet

Figure 22 *Viewing the Code Navigator*

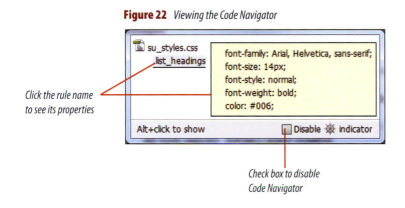

Click the rule name
to see its properties

Check box to disable
Code Navigator

TIP You can also [Alt]-click (Win) or [Command] [Option]-click (Mac) the text on the page to display the Code Navigator.

3. Position your cursor over the list_headings rule name until you see a box with the rule's properties, as shown in Figure 22.

TIP You can disable the Code Navigator by clicking the Disable check box as shown in Figure 22.

You displayed the Code Navigator to view the properties of the list_headings rule.

Using the Style Rendering Toolbar

The Style Rendering toolbar allows you to display your page as it would appear for different media types, such as print, TV, or handheld. To display it when a page is open, click View on the Application bar (Win); or Menu bar (Mac), point to Toolbars, and then click Style Rendering. The buttons on the Style Rendering toolbar allow you to see how your page will look as you select different media types. The seventh button on the toolbar is the Toggle Displaying of CSS Styles button, which you can use to view how a page looks with styles applied. It works independently of the other buttons. The next button to the right is the Design-time Style Sheets button, which you can use to show or hide particular combinations of styles while you are working in the Document window.

NEW The Style Rendering toolbar in Dreamweaver CS5 has several additional buttons on the right side of the toolbar that can be used to change the text size or show the link properties for links in the active document.

Lesson 2   Create, Apply, and Edit Cascading Style Sheets

Use the Code Navigator to edit a rule

1. Click **.list_headings** in the Code Navigator.

   The document window splits into two panes. The left pane displays the code for the CSS file and the right section displays the HTML page in Design view, as shown in Figure 23.

   TIP The default setting for Show Code and Design views in Dreamweaver CS5 splits the two windows vertically, rather than horizontally. To view the two windows split horizontally on the screen, click View on the Application bar (Win) or Menu bar (Mac), then click Split Vertically to uncheck the option and split the screens horizontally.

   (continued)

Figure 23 *Using Code and Design views to view rule properties*

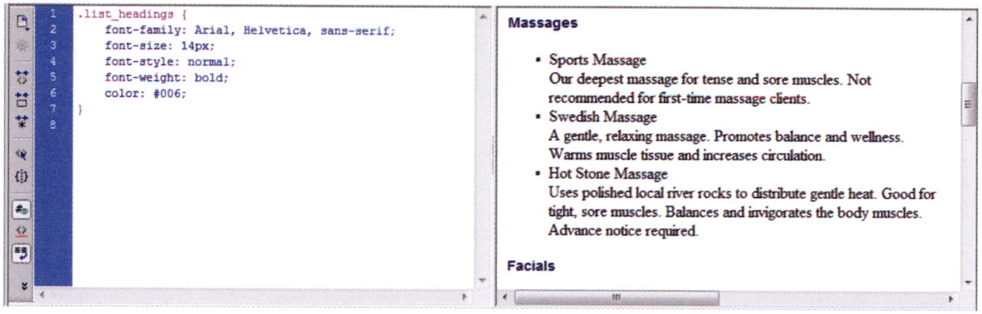

Transitioning to a Real-World Work Process

As you learn Dreamweaver throughout the chapters in this book, you practice its many features in a logical learning sequence. You will develop an understanding of both current concepts like CSS and older, but still used, features such as HTML formatting and embedded styles. Once you learn Dreamweaver and start using it to create your own websites, you would ideally format all pages with rules from one external style sheet. You would move all of the embedded styles in the predesigned CSS layouts to the external style sheet because the embedded styles on each page would be redundant. After you have worked through this book, you should have the skills and understanding to design sites built entirely and efficiently with CSS.

Working with Text and Cascading Style Sheets

Figure 24 *Using Code and Design views to edit a rule*

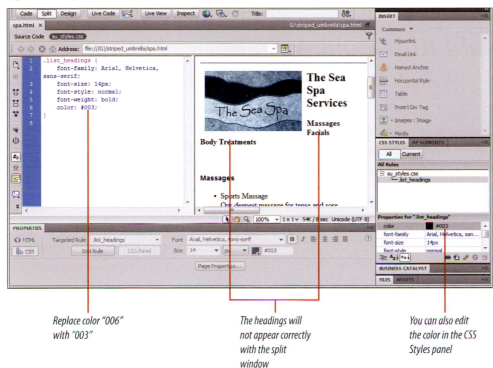

Replace color "006"
with "003"

The headings will
not appear correctly
with the split
window

You can also edit
the color in the CSS
Styles panel

2. Type directly in the code to replace the color "006" with the color "**003**" as shown in Figure 24. The page subheadings to the right of the logo will not wrap correctly in Split view if the document window is too small. When you return to Design view, they will wrap correctly.

TIP You can also edit the rule properties in the CSS Styles panel.

3. Save all files.

4. Click the **Show Design view button** [Design].

The font color has changed in Design view to reflect the new shade of blue in the rule.

You changed the color property in the .list_headings rule.

Add Rules and Attach
CASCADING STYLE SHEETS

What You'll Do

In this lesson, you will add a rule to a Cascading Style Sheet. You will then attach the style sheet file to the index page and apply one of the rules to text on the page.

Understanding External and Embedded Style Sheets

When you are first learning about CSS, the terminology can be confusing. In the last lesson, you learned that external style sheets are separate files in a website, saved with the .css file extension. You also learned that CSS can be part of an HTML file, rather than a separate file. These are called internal, or embedded, style sheets. External CSS files are created by the web designer. Embedded style sheets are created automatically in Dreamweaver if the designer does not create them, using default names for the rules. The code for these rules resides in the head content for that page. These rules are automatically named style1, style2, and so on. You can rename the rules as they are created to make them more recognizable for you to use, for example, paragraph_text, subheading, or address. Embedded style sheets apply only to a single page, although you can copy them into the code in other pages or move them to an external style sheet. Remember that style sheets can be used to format much more than text objects. They can be used to set the page background, link properties, or determine the appearance of almost any object on the page. Figure 25 shows the code for some embedded rules and a link to an external style sheet. The code resides in the head content of the web page.

When you have several pages in a website, you will probably want to use the same CSS for each page to ensure that all your elements have a consistent appearance. To attach a style sheet to another document, click the Attach Style Sheet button on the CSS Styles panel to open the Attach External Style Sheet dialog box, make sure the Add as Link option is selected, browse to locate the file you want to attach, and then click OK. The rules contained in the attached style sheet will appear in the CSS Styles panel, and you can use them to apply rules to text on the page. External style sheets can be attached, or linked, to any page. This is an extremely powerful tool. If you decide to edit a rule, the changes will automatically be made to every object that it formats.

Understanding Related Page Files

When an HTML file is linked to other files necessary to display the page content, these files are called **related files.** When a file that has related files is open in the Document window, each related file name is displayed in the Related Files toolbar above the Document window. A Cascading Style Sheet file is an example of a related file. When an HTML document has an attached CSS file, the page file will display in the browser without the CSS file, but will not be formatted correctly. It takes both the HTML file and the CSS file working together to display the content properly. When HTML files are uploaded, it is important to remember to upload all related page files. Other examples of related page files are Flash player, video files and JavaScript files.

When an HTML file with a linked CSS file is open in Dreamweaver, the name of the CSS filename appears below the page tab. When you click on the CSS filename, the screen changes to Split view, with the right side displaying the open HTML page in Design view and the left side displaying the CSS file. If you click Source Code next to the related page filename, the code for the top level document (open HTML file) will appear on the left side. You can edit both Code view windows by typing directly in the code.

Figure 25 *Code for embedded rules and a link to an external style sheet*

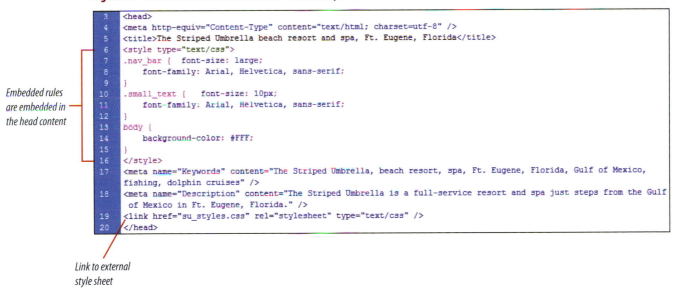

Embedded rules are embedded in the head content

```
3   <head>
4   <meta http-equiv="Content-Type" content="text/html; charset=utf-8" />
5   <title>The Striped Umbrella beach resort and spa, Ft. Eugene, Florida</title>
6   <style type="text/css">
7   .nav_bar {  font-size: large;
8       font-family: Arial, Helvetica, sans-serif;
9   }
10  .small_text {   font-size: 10px;
11      font-family: Arial, Helvetica, sans-serif;
12  }
13  body {
14      background-color: #FFF;
15  }
16  </style>
17  <meta name="Keywords" content="The Striped Umbrella, beach resort, spa, Ft. Eugene, Florida, Gulf of Mexico,
    fishing, dolphin cruises" />
18  <meta name="Description" content="The Striped Umbrella is a full-service resort and spa just steps from the Gulf
     of Mexico in Ft. Eugene, Florida." />
19  <link href="su_styles.css" rel="stylesheet" type="text/css" />
20  </head>
```

Link to external style sheet

Add a rule to a Cascading Style Sheet

1. Click the **New CSS Rule button** 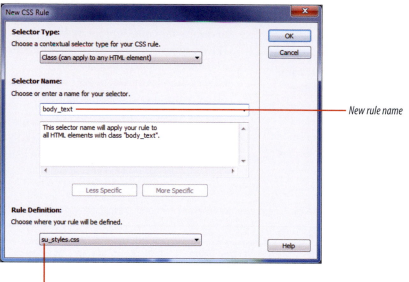 in the CSS Styles panel.

2. Type **body_text** in the Selector Name text box, verify that su_styles.css appears in the Rule Definition text box, as shown in Figure 26, then click **OK**.

   The new rule will be saved in the su_styles.css file as an external style.

3. Set the Font-family to **Arial**, **Helvetica**, **sans-serif**, set the Font-size to **12**, set the set the Color to **#000**, compare your screen to Figure 27, then click **OK**.

4. Select the three list items and their descriptions under the Massages heading, click the **Targeted Rule list arrow** in the CSS Property inspector, then click **body_text** to apply it to the three massage names and descriptions.

   The rule is applied to the text, but the text would be easier to read if it were a little larger.

5. Click the **Edit Rule button** ✏ in the CSS Styles panel.

6. Change the font size to **14** in the Type category of the CSS Rule Definition for body_text in su_styles.css dialog box, as shown in Figure 28, then click **OK**.

   (continued)

Figure 26 *Adding a rule to a CSS*

New rule name

su_styles.css is displayed in the Rule Definition text box

Figure 27 *Formatting options for body_text rule*

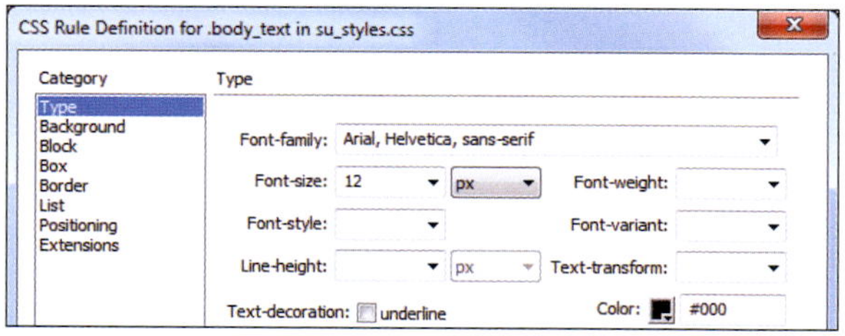

Figure 28 *Editing the body_text rule*

Change the Font-size to 14

Figure 29 *Spa page with style sheet applied to rest of text on page*

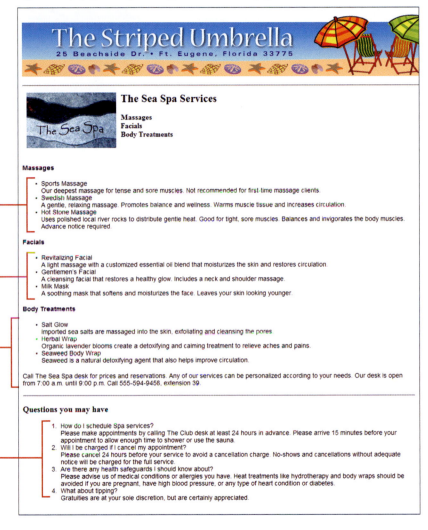

Text formatted with the body_text rule

7. Repeat Step 4 to apply the body_text rule to the rest of the text on the page except for the text that has already been formatted with the list_headings rule or heading tags, as shown in Figure 29.

8. Click **File** on the Application bar (Win) or Menu bar (Mac), then click **Save All**, to save both the spa page and the su_styles.css file.

    The rule is saved in the style sheet file and applied to the text in the HTML file.

TIP You must save the open su_styles.css file after editing it, or you will lose your changes.

You added a new rule called body_text to the su_styles.css file. You then applied the rule to selected text.

Attach a style sheet

1. Close the spa page and open the index page.

2. Click the **Attach Style Sheet button** 🔗 on the CSS Styles panel.

3. Click **Browse** then navigate to the file su_styles.css, if necessary, click the **su_styles.css** file, click **OK** (Win) or click **Choose** (Mac), verify that the **Link option button** is selected, as shown in Figure 30, then click **OK**.

   There are now two rules named body_text. One is an internal style that was in the data file when we brought it into the website and one is in the external style sheet. Since these rules have duplicate names, it would be better to delete the internal style and let the external style format the text.

4. Select the **body_text rule** under the <style> section of the CSS Styles panel, as shown in Figure 31, then click the **Delete CSS Rule button** 🗑 on the CSS Styles panel.

5. Click the **Show Code view button** `Code` and view the code that links the su_styles.css file to the index page, as shown in Figure 32.

6. Click the **Show Design view button** `Design`, then save your work.

You attached the su_styles.css file to the index.html page and deleted the body_text internal style, allowing the body_text external style to format the page text.

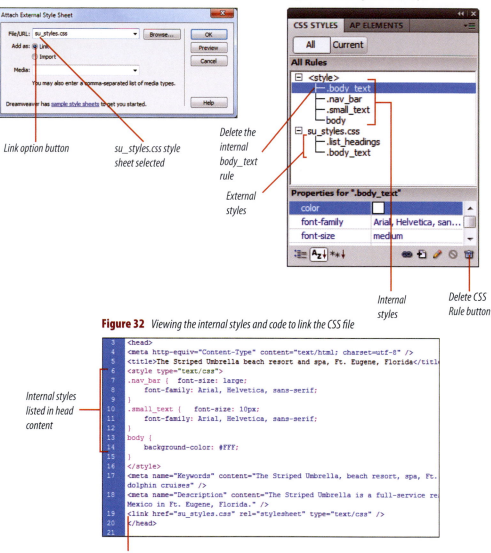

Figure 30 *Attaching a style sheet to a file*

Link option button

su_styles.css style sheet selected

Figure 31 *Deleting an internal style*

Delete the internal body_text rule

External styles

Internal styles

Delete CSS Rule button

Figure 32 *Viewing the internal styles and code to link the CSS file*

Internal styles listed in head content

```
3   <head>
4   <meta http-equiv="Content-Type" content="text/html; charset=utf-8" />
5   <title>The Striped Umbrella beach resort and spa, Ft. Eugene, Florida</titl
6   <style type="text/css">
7   .nav_bar {  font-size: large;
8        font-family: Arial, Helvetica, sans-serif;
9   }
10  .small_text {   font-size: 10px;
11       font-family: Arial, Helvetica, sans-serif;
12  }
13  body {
14       background-color: #FFF;
15  }
16  </style>
17  <meta name="Keywords" content="The Striped Umbrella, beach resort, spa, Ft.
    dolphin cruises" />
18  <meta name="Description" content="The Striped Umbrella is a full-service re
    Mexico in Ft. Eugene, Florida." />
19  <link href="su_styles.css" rel="stylesheet" type="text/css" />
20  </head>
21
```

Code linking external style sheet file to the index page in head content

Figure 33 *Using the Related Files toolbar to view an external style sheet file*

Click su_styles.css to view external style sheet file

Left pane displays code for external style sheet

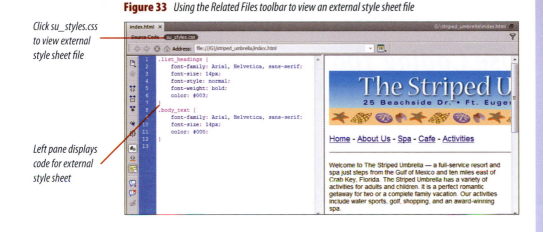

Use the Related Files toolbar to view styles

1. Click **su_styles.css** on the Related Files toolbar.

   The document window changes to Show Code and Design views with the external CSS file in the left pane and the HTML page in Design view in the right pane, as shown in Figure 33.

2. Click **Source Code** on the Related Files toolbar.

   The code for the HTML file appears on the left with the code for the embedded styles as shown in Figure 34.

3. Click the **Show Design view button** | Design | to return to Design view.

You viewed the external and embedded styles using the Related Files toolbar.

Figure 34 *Using the Related Files toolbar to view embedded styles*

Click Source Code to view embedded styles

Left pane displays code for embedded styles

Use Coding Tools to
VIEW AND EDIT RULES

What You'll Do

In this lesson, you will collapse, then expand the code for the index page to view the code for the embedded and external styles. You will then move embedded styles to the external style sheet file.

Coding Tools in Dreamweaver

In Code view, you can see the Coding toolbar, shown in Figure 35. It contains a number of handy tools that help you navigate your code and let you view your code in different ways. It has buttons that expand or collapse code, buttons for changing the way the code is displayed, and buttons for inserting and removing comments. The Coding toolbar appears on the left side of the Document window. Although you cannot move it, you can hide it, using the Toolbars command on the View menu in Code view.

As you learned in Chapter 2, you can customize the way your page code appears in Code view. You can wrap the lines of code, display or hide line numbers and hidden characters, or highlight invalid code so you can fix it. You can also have different code types appear in different colors, indent lines of code, and display syntax error alerts. In Chapter 2, you viewed these options using the View Options button on the Code Inspector toolbar. You can also view and change them on the Code View options menu under the View menu on the Document toolbar.

Figure 35 *Coding toolbar*

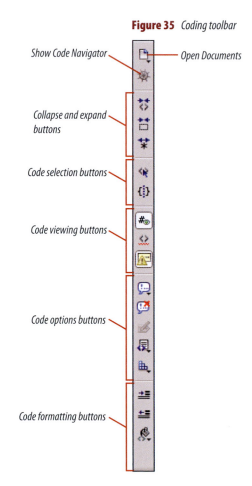

Show Code Navigator

Open Documents

Collapse and expand buttons

Code selection buttons

Code viewing buttons

Code options buttons

Code formatting buttons

Working with Text and Cascading Style Sheets

Using Coding Tools to Navigate Code

As your pages get longer and the code more complex, it is helpful to collapse sections of code, much as you can collapse and expand panels, folders, and styles. Collapsing code lets you temporarily hide code between two different sections of code that you would like to read together. To collapse selected lines of code, you can click the minus sign (Win) or the triangle (Mac) next to the line number. You can also use the Collapse Full Tag or Collapse Selection buttons on the Coding toolbar. This will allow you to look at two different sections of code that are not adjacent to each other.

Adding comments is an easy way to add documentation to your code, which is especially helpful when you are working in a team environment and other team members will be working on pages with you. For example, you might use comments to communicate instructions like "Do not alter code below this line." or "Add final schedule here when it becomes available." Comments are not visible in the browser.

Using Code Hints to Streamline Coding

If you are typing code directly into Code view, Dreamweaver can speed your work by offering you code hints. **Code hints** are lists of tags that appear as you type, similar to other auto-complete features that you have probably used in other software applications. As you are typing code, Dreamweaver will recognize the tag name and offer you choices to complete the tag simply by double-clicking a tag choice in the menu, as shown in Figure 36. You can also add your own code hints to the list using JavaScript. Code hints are stored in the file CodeHints.xml.

Converting Styles

You can also convert one type of style to another. For instance, you can move an embedded style to an external style sheet or an inline style to either an embedded style or a style in an external style sheet. To do this, select the style in Code view, right-click the code, point to CSS Styles, then click Move CSS Rules. You can also move styles in the CSS Styles panel by selecting the style, right-clicking the style, and choosing the action you want from the shortcut menu.

Figure 36 *Using code hints*

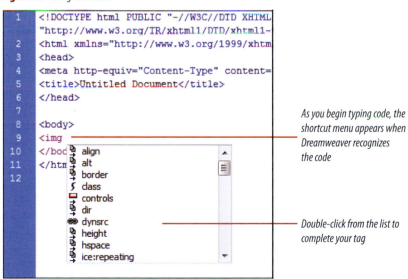

As you begin typing code, the shortcut menu appears when Dreamweaver recognizes the code

Double-click from the list to complete your tag

Collapse code

1. Verify that the index page is open, then change to Code view.

2. Scroll up the page, if necessary, to display the code that ends the embedded styles (</style>).

   The code will probably be on or close to line 16 in the head section.

3. Select the line of code under the line ending the embedded style code (it begins with <meta name = "Keywords"), then drag down to select all of the code above the line of code that links the external style sheet, as shown in Figure 37.

TIP If your code is in a slightly different order, scroll to find the meta data code to select it.

4. Click the **minus sign** (Win) or **vertical triangle** (Mac) in the last line of selected code to collapse all of the selected code.

   You can now see both code fragments—before and after the collapsed code section—as shown in Figure 38. The plus sign (Win) or horizontal triangle (Mac) next to the line of code indicates that there is hidden code. You also see a gap in the line numbers where the hidden code resides.

You collapsed a block of code in Code view to be able to see two non-adjacent sections of the code at the same time.

Figure 37 *Selecting lines of code on the index page to collapse*

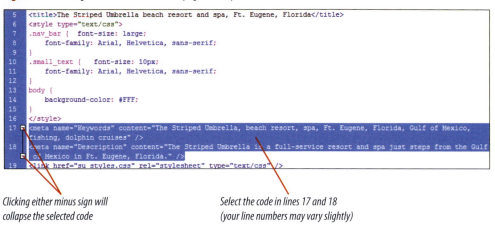

Clicking either minus sign will collapse the selected code

Select the code in lines 17 and 18 (your line numbers may vary slightly)

Figure 38 *Collapsed code in Code view*

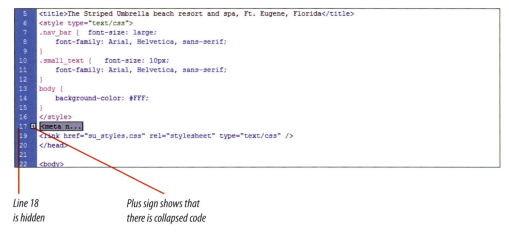

Line 18 is hidden

Plus sign shows that there is collapsed code

Figure 39 *Expanded code for index page*

```
5   <title>The Striped Umbrella beach resort and spa, Ft. Eugene, Florida</title>
6   <style type="text/css">
7   .nav_bar {  font-size: large;
8       font-family: Arial, Helvetica, sans-serif;
9   }
10  .small_text {   font-size: 10px;
11      font-family: Arial, Helvetica, sans-serif;
12  }
13  body {
14      background-color: #FFF;
15  }
16  </style>
17  <meta name="Keywords" content="The Striped Umbrella, beach resort, spa, Ft. Eugene, Florida, Gulf of Mexico,
    fishing, dolphin cruises" />
18  <meta name="Description" content="The Striped Umbrella is a full-service resort and spa just steps from the Gulf
    of Mexico in Ft. Eugene, Florida." />
19  <link href="su_styles.css" rel="stylesheet" type="text/css" />
```

Code is expanded again

Expand code

1. Click the **plus sign** (Win) or **horizontal triangle** (Mac) on line 17 to expand the code.

2. Compare your screen to Figure 39, then click in the page to deselect the code.

   All line numbers are visible again.

You expanded the code to display all lines of the code again.

POWER USER SHORTCUTS	
To do this:	**Use this shortcut:**
Switch views	[Ctrl][`] (Win) or [control][`] (Mac)
Indent text	[Ctrl][Alt][]] (Win) or ⌘ [option][]] (Mac)
Outdent text	[Ctrl][Alt][[] (Win) or ⌘ [option][[] (Mac)
Align Left	[Ctrl][Alt][Shift][L] (Win) or ⌘ [option][shift][L] (Mac)
Align Center	[Ctrl][Alt][Shift][C] (Win) or ⌘ [option][shift][C] (Mac)
Align Right	[Ctrl][Alt][Shift][R] (Win) or ⌘ [option][shift][R] (Mac)
Align Justify	[Ctrl][Alt][Shift][J] (Win) or ⌘ [option][shift][J] (Mac)
Bold	[Ctrl][B] (Win) or ⌘ [B] (Mac)
Italic	[Ctrl][I] (Win) or ⌘ [I] (Mac)
Refresh	[F5]

Move an embedded style to an external CSS

1. Select the lines of code in the head section with the properties of the small_text rule (including the closing bracket) on the index page.

   The code will be on or close to lines 10 and 12.

2. Right-click (Win) or control-click (Mac) the **selected code**, point to **CSS Styles**, then click **Move CSS Rules**, as shown in Figure 40.

   TIP You can also convert a rule in the CSS Styles panel. To do this, right-click the rule name, then click Move CSS Rules.

3. In the Move to External Style Sheet dialog box, verify that su_styles.css appears in the Style Sheet text box, as shown in Figure 41, then click **OK**.

   (continued)

Figure 40 *Moving the embedded small_text rule to the external style sheet file*

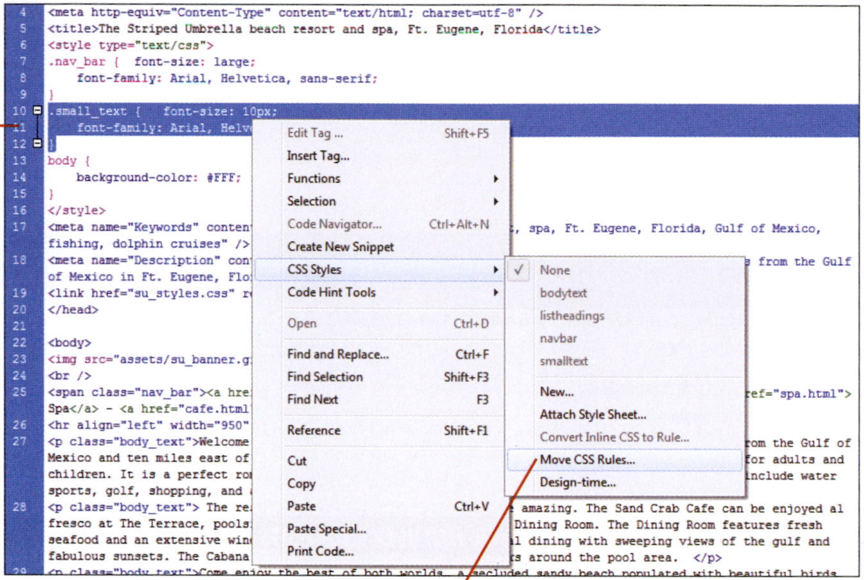

Selected code for small_text rule

Move CSS Rules command

Figure 41 *Moving the embedded style to the external style sheet file*

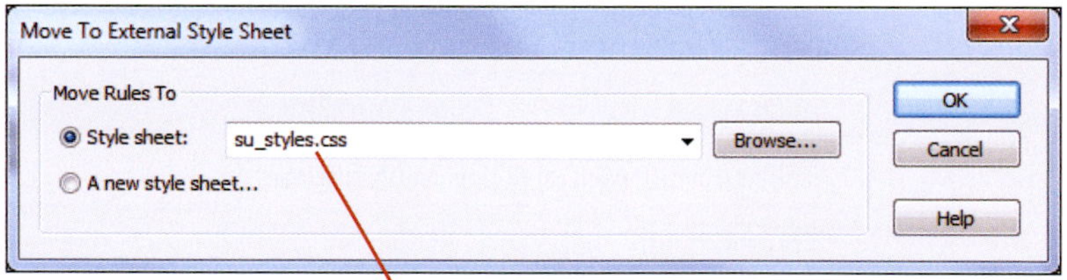

The embedded small_text rule will move to the su_styles file

Working with Text and Cascading Style Sheets

Figure 42 *Viewing the small_text rule in the external style sheet*

small_text rule is now in the su_styles.css file

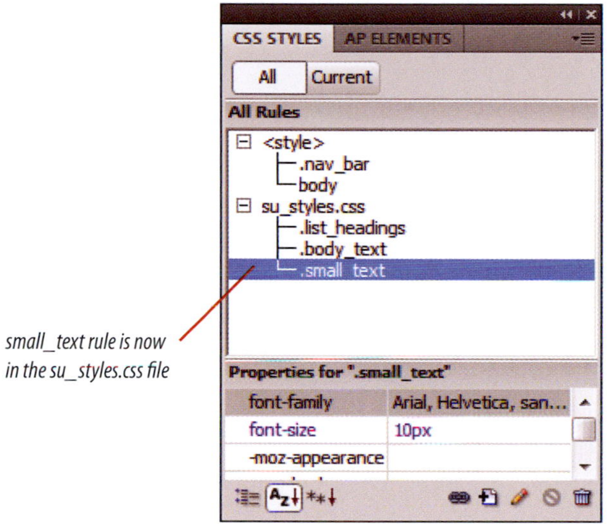

4. Expand the su_styles.css style in the CSS Styles panel, if necessary, to display its rules, then compare your panel with Figure 42 to verify that the style has been moved to the external style sheet file.

5. Return to Design view, then save and close all open files.

You moved an embedded style for the small_text rule to an external CSS.

Create unordered and ordered lists.

1. Open the Blooms & Bulbs website.
2. Open the tips page.
3. Select the text items below the Seasonal Gardening Checklist heading and format them as an unordered list. (*Hint*: There are no paragraph breaks between each item. To correct this, enter a paragraph break between each line, then remove any extra spaces.)
4. Select the lines of text below the Basic Gardening Tips heading and format them as an ordered list. (Refer to the Step 3 hint if each line does not become a separate list item.)
5. Indent the unordered list items one stop, then change the bullet format to square.
6. Add a line break before the Seasonal Gardening checklist heading, then save your work.

Create, apply, and edit Cascading Style Sheets.

1. Create a new CSS rule named **bullet_term**, making sure that the Class option button is selected in the Selector Type section and that the (New Style Sheet File) option button is selected in the Rule Definition section of the New CSS Rule dialog box.
2. Click OK, name the style sheet file **blooms_styles** in the Save Style Sheet File As dialog box, then click Save.

3. Choose the following settings for the bullet_term rule: Font-family = Arial, Helvetica, sans-serif; Font-size = large; Font-style = normal; Font-weight = bold; and Color = #333.
4. Apply the bullet_term rule to the names of the seasons in the Seasonal Gardening Checklist: Fall, Winter, Spring, and Summer.
5. Edit the bullet_term rule by changing the font size to 16 pixels.

Add rules and attach Cascading Style Sheets.

1. Create a new class rule named **paragraph_text** in the blooms_styles.css file with the Arial, Helvetica, sans-serif, size 14 px.
2. Apply the paragraph_text rule to the rest of the text on the page that has not been previously formatted with either an HTML heading or a rule, then save the page. (*Hint*: If the Seasonal Gardening Checklist heading is not under the picture, verify that there's a line break before it, and add one if necessary.)
3. Open the index page and attach the blooms_styles.css file.
4. Select the paragraphs and the contact information and apply the paragraph_text rule.
5. Delete the body_text embedded style.

6. Use the Save All command on the File menu to save both the page and the style sheet, then view both pages in the browser. (*Hint*: If previewing the page in Internet Explorer 7, click the Information bar when prompted to allow blocked content.)
7. Close the browser.

Use coding tools to view and edit rules.

1. Verify that the index page is open, then change to Code view.
2. Display the code that ends the embedded styles.
3. Select the lines of code under the line ending the embedded style code (it begins with <meta name = "Keywords"), then drag down to select all of the code above the line of code that links the external style sheet.
4. Collapse all of the selected code.
5. Expand the code.
6. Select the lines of code that define the small_text rule properties in the head section (including the closing bracket), then move the rule to the blooms_styles external style sheet.
7. Return to Design view, save all open files, compare your pages to Figures 43 and 44, then close all open files.

Figure 43 & 44 *Completed Skills Review*

Home - Featured Plants - Garden Tips - Workshops - Newsletter

Welcome to Blooms & Bulbs. We carry a variety of plants and shrubs along with a large inventory of gardening supplies. Our four greenhouses are full of healthy young plants just waiting to be planted in your yard. We grow an amazing selection of annuals and selection of trees, shrubs, tropicals, water plants, and ground covers. Check out our garden ware for your g friends. We are happy to deliver or ship your purchases.

Our staff includes a certified landscape architect, three landscape designers, and six master gardeners. We your location as well as planting and regular maintenance services. We have enjoyed serving Alvin and the by and see us soon!

Blooms & Bulbs
Highway 43 South
Alvin, Texas 77511
555-248-0806
Customer Service

Copyright 2001 - 2013
Last updated on December 11, 2009

We have lots of tips we would like to share with you as you prepare your gardens this season. Remember, there is always something to be done for your gardens, no matter what the season. Our experienced staff is here to help you plan your gardens, select your plants, prepare your soil, assist you in the planting, and maintain your beds. Check out our calendar for a list of our scheduled workshops. Our next workshop is "Attracting Butterflies to Your Garden." All workshops are free of charge and on a first-come, first-served basis! They fill up quickly, so be sure to reserve your spot early.

Seasonal Gardening Checklist

- **Fall** – The time to plant trees and spring-blooming bulbs. Take the time to clean the leaves and dead foliage from your beds and lawn.
- **Winter** – The time to prune fruit trees and finish planting your bulbs. Don't forget to water young trees when the ground is dry.
- **Spring** – The time to prepare your beds, plant annuals, and apply fertilizer to established plants. Remember to mulch to maintain moisture and prevent weed growth.
- **Summer** – The time to supplement rainfall so that plants get one inch of water per week. Plant your vegetable garden and enjoy bountiful harvests until late fall.

Basic Gardening Tips

1. Select plants according to your climate.
2. In planning your garden, consider the composition, texture, structure, depth, and drainage of your soil.
3. Use compost to improve the structure of your soil.
4. Choose plant foods based on your garden objectives.
5. Generally, plants should receive one inch of water per week.
6. Use mulch to conserve moisture, keep plants cool, and cut down on weeding.

Use Figure 45 as a guide to continue your work on the TripSmart website that you began in Project Builder 1 in Chapter 1, and continued to work on in Chapter 2. You are now ready to create some rules to use for the text on the newsletter and index pages.

1. Open the TripSmart website.
2. Open dw3_1.html from where you store your Data Files and save it in the tripsmart site folder as **newsletter.html**, overwriting the existing newsletter.html file and not updating the links.
3. Verify that the path for the banner is correctly set to the assets folder of the TripSmart website, then type the title **Travel Tidbits** in the Title text box on the Document toolbar.
4. Create an unordered list from the text beginning "Be organized." to the end of the page.
5. Create a new CSS rule called **paragraph_text** making sure that the Class option is selected in the Selector Type section and that the (New Style Sheet File) option is selected in the Rule Definition section of the New CSS Rule dialog box.
6. Save the style sheet file as **tripsmart_styles.css** in the TripSmart website site folder.
7. Choose a font family, size, style, weight, and color of your choice for the paragraph_text style.
8. Apply the paragraph_text rule to all of the text on the page except the "Ten Tips for Stress-Free Travel" heading.
9. Create another class rule in the tripsmart_styles.css file called **list_heading** with a font, size, style, color, and weight of your choice and apply it to the "Ten Tips for Stress-Free Travel" heading.

10. Create another rule in the external style sheet called **list_term** with a font, size, style, color, and weight of your choice and apply it to each of the item names in the list such as "Be organized."
11. Save the newsletter page and the style sheet, then close the dw3_1.html page.
12. Open the index page, then attach the tripsmart_styles style sheet.
13. Select the two paragraphs and contact information, then apply the paragraph_text rule.
14. Delete the body_text embedded rule, then save the index page.
15. Preview the index and newsletter pages in your browser. (*Hint*: If previewing the page in Internet Explorer 7, click the Information bar when prompted to allow blocked content.)
16. Close your browser, then close all open files.

Figure 45 *Sample Project Builder 1*

Our staff recently conducted a contest to determine ten top travel tips for stress-free travel. We compiled over forty great tips, but the following were selected as the winners. We hope you will find them useful for your next trip!

Ten Tips for Stress-Free Travel

- **Be organized.**
  Make a list of what you want to pack in each bag and check it as you pack. Take this inventory with you in the event your bags are lost or delayed. Then use the list again when you repack, to make sure you haven't left anything behind.
- **Carry important information with you.**
  Keep your important travel information in easy reach at all times. Include a list of your flight numbers, confirmation numbers for your travel and hotel reservations, and any car rentals. And don't forget printouts of your itinerary and electronic tickets. Remember to bring your passport, and keep a photocopy of it in another piece of baggage. Be sure to have copies of prescriptions, emergency phone numbers, telephone numbers and addresses of friends and relatives, complete lists of medications, and credit card information. It's not a bad idea to email this information to yourself as a backup if you will have email access.
- **Pack smartly.**
  You know the old saying: lay out everything on your bed you plan to take with you, then remove half of it. Pack the remainder and carry your bags around the block once to make sure you can handle them yourself. If in doubt, leave it out! Use packing cubes or zip-top bags to organize your personal items, such as underwear and socks. Make distinctive-looking luggage tags with your name and address for easy identification, and be sure to include the same information inside your luggage.
- **Include basic medical necessities.**
  Besides your prescription drugs, take a basic first aid kit with the basics: bandages, anti-nausea medications, anti-diarrhea medications, aspirin, antibiotics, and prescription drugs.
- **Wear comfortable shoes.**
  Blisters can ruin a wonderful trip. Wear comfortable shoes and socks. Your priority should be comfortable, dry, warm feet — not fashion. Don't buy new shoes without breaking them in first.

In this exercise, you continue your work on the Carolyne's Creations website that you started in Project Builder 2 in Chapter 1, and continued to build in Chapter 2. You are now ready to add a page to the website that will showcase a recipe. Figure 46 shows a possible solution for this one page in this exercise. Your finished page will look different if you choose different formatting options.

1. Open the Carolyne's Creations website
2. Open dw3_2.html from where you store your Data Files, save it to the website site folder as **recipes. html**, overwriting the existing file and not updating the links. Close the dw3_2.html file.
3. Select the pie image broken link placeholder, then use the Property inspector to browse for the pie.jpg image in the assets folder where you store your Data Files.
4. Format the list of ingredients on the recipes page as an unordered list.
5. Create a CSS rule named **body_text** and save it in a style sheet file named **cc_styles.css** in the website root folder. Use any formatting options that you like, then apply the body_text rule to all text except the menu bar and the text "Caramel Coconut Pie," "Ingredients," and "Directions."
6. Create another rule in the external style sheet called **headings** using appropriate formatting options and apply it to the text "Caramel Coconut Pie," "Ingredients," and "Directions."
7. Save the page.
8. Open the index page, then attach the cc_styles.css to the file.

9. Delete the embedded body_text rule, allowing the body_text rule in the external style sheet to format the text.
10. Convert the nav_bar rule to an external rule in the cc_styles style sheet, then switch back to the recipes page and format the menu bar with the nav_bar rule.
11. Save all open files, then preview both pages in the browser. (*Hint*: If previewing the page in Internet Explorer 7, click the Information bar when prompted to allow blocked content.)
12. Close your browser, then close all open pages.

Figure 46 *Sample Project Builder 2*

Charles Chappell is a new sixth-grade history teacher. He is reviewing educational websites for information he can use in his classroom.

1. Connect to the Internet, then navigate to the Library of Congress website at www.loc.gov. The Library of Congress website is shown in Figure 47.
2. Which fonts are used for the main content on the home page—serif or sans-serif? Are the same fonts used consistently on the other pages in the site?
3. Do you see ordered or unordered lists on any pages in the site? If so, how are they used?
4. Use the Source command on the View menu to view the source code to see if a style sheet was used.
5. Do you see the use of Cascading Style Sheets noted in the source code?

Figure 47 *Design Project*

The Library of congress website – www.loc.gov

In this assignment, you will continue to work on the website that you started in Chapter 1, and continued to build in Chapter 2. No Data Files are supplied. You are building this site from chapter to chapter, so you must do each Portfolio Project assignment in each chapter to complete your website.

You continue building your website by designing and completing a page that contains a list, headings, and paragraph text. During this process, you will develop a style sheet and add several rules to it

1. Consult your wireframe and decide which page to create and develop for this chapter.

2. Plan the page content for the page and make a sketch of the layout. Your sketch should include at least one ordered or unordered list, appropriate headings, and paragraph text. Your sketch should also show where the paragraph text and headings should be placed on the page and what rules should be used for each type of text. You should plan on creating at least two CSS rules.

3. Create the page using your sketch for guidance.

4. Create a Cascading Style Sheet for the site and add to it the rules you decided to use. Apply the rules to the appropriate content.

5. Attach the style sheet to the index page you developed in Chapter 2 and consider converting any existing embedded styles to the external style sheet.

6. Preview the new page in a browser, then check for page layout problems and broken links. Make any necessary corrections in Dreamweaver, then preview the page again in the browser. Repeat this process until you are satisfied with the way the page looks in the browser. (*Hint*: If previewing the page in Internet Explorer 7, click the Information bar when prompted to allow blocked content.)

7. Use the checklist in Figure 48 to check all the pages in your site.

8. Close the browser, then close all open pages.

Figure 48 *Design Project*

Website Checklist

1. Does each page have a page title?
2. Does the home page have a description and keywords?
3. Does the home page contain contact information?
4. Does every completed page in the site have consistent navigation links?
5. Does the home page have a last updated statement that will automatically update when the page is saved?
6. Do all paths for links and images work correctly?
7. Is there a style sheet with at least two rules?
8. Did you apply the rules to all text blocks?
9. Do all pages look good using at least two different browsers?

CHAPTER 4 ADDING IMAGES

1. Insert and align images

2. Enhance an image and use alternate text

3. Insert a background image and perform site maintenance

4. Add graphic enhancements

CHAPTER 4

ADDING IMAGES

Introduction

Most web pages contain a combination of text and images. The majority of web page information appears in the form of text. But pages are much more interesting if they also contain images that enhance or illustrate the information. A well-designed web page usually includes a balanced combination of text and images. Dreamweaver provides many tools for working with images that you can use to make your web pages attractive and easy to understand.

Using Images to Enhance Web Pages

Images make web pages visually stimulating and more exciting than pages that contain only text. However, you should use images sparingly. You should add images to a page just as you would add seasoning to food. A little seasoning enhances the flavor and brings out the quality of the dish. Too much seasoning overwhelms the dish and masks the flavor of the main ingredients. Too little seasoning results in a bland dish. There are many ways to work with images

so that they complement the content of pages in a website. You can use specific file formats used to save images for websites to ensure maximum quality with minimum file size.

Graphics Versus Images

Two terms that designers sometimes use interchangeably are graphics and images. For the purposes of discussion in this text, we will use the term **graphics** to refer to the appearance of most non-text items on a web page, such as photographs, logos, menu bars, Flash animations, charts, background images, and drawings. Files for items such as these are called graphic files. They are referred to by their file type, or graphic file format, such as JPEG (Joint Photographic Experts Group), GIF (Graphics Interchange Format), or PNG (Portable Network Graphics). We will refer to the actual pictures that you see on the pages as images. But don't worry about which term to use. Many people use one term or the other according to habit or region, or use them interchangeably.

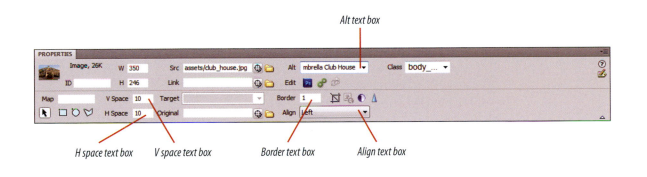

Alt text box

H space text box   V space text box   Border text box   Align text box

Insert and
ALIGN IMAGES

What You'll Do

In this lesson, you will insert three images on the about_us page in The Striped Umbrella website. You will then adjust the alignment of the images on the page to make the page more visually appealing.

Understanding Graphic File Formats

When you choose graphics to add to a web page, it's important to use graphic files in the appropriate file format. The three primary graphic file formats used in web pages are **GIF** (Graphics Interchange Format), **JPEG** or **JPG** (Joint Photographic Experts Group), and **PNG** (Portable Network Graphics). GIF files download very quickly, making them ideal to use on web pages. Though limited in the number of colors they can represent, GIF files have the ability to show transparent areas. JPEG files can display many colors. Because they often contain many shades of the same color, photographs are often saved in JPEG format. Files saved with the PNG format can display many colors and use various degrees of transparency, called **opacity**. However, not all older browsers support the PNG format.

QUICK TIP

The Dreamweaver status bar shows the total download time for the open web page. Each time you add a new graphic to the page, you can see how much additional download time that graphic has added to the total.

Understanding the Assets Panel

When you add a graphic to a website, Dreamweaver automatically adds it to the Assets panel. The **Assets panel**, located in the Files panel group, displays all the assets in a website. The Assets panel contains nine category buttons that you use to view your assets by category. These include Images, Colors, URLs, SWF, Shockwave, Movies, Scripts, Templates, and Library. To view a particular type of asset, click the appropriate category button.

The Assets panel is divided into two panes. When you click the Images button, as shown in Figure 1, the lower pane displays a list of all the images in your site and is divided into five columns. You might need to resize the Assets panel to see all five columns. To resize the Assets panel, undock the Files tab group and drag a side or corner of the panel border.

The top pane displays a thumbnail of the selected image in the list. You can view assets in each category in two ways. You can use the Site option button to view all the assets in a website, or you can use the Favorites option button to view those assets that you have designated as **favorites**, or assets that you expect to use repeatedly while you work on the site.

You can use the Assets panel to add an asset to a web page by dragging the asset from the Assets panel to the page or by using the Insert button on the Assets panel. If you are working on a page layout without final images ready to place, you can insert an image placeholder to hold the image position on the page. An **image placeholder** is a graphic the size of an image you plan to use. You can place it on a page until the actual image is finalized and ready to place on the page. To insert an image placeholder, use the Insert, Image Objects, Image Placeholder command. When the final image is ready, simply replace the image placeholder with the final image.

Inserting Files with Adobe Bridge

You can manage project files, including video and Camera Raw files, with a file-management tool called Adobe Bridge. **Camera Raw** file formats are files that contain unprocessed data and are not yet ready to be printed, similar to a negative from a film camera. **Adobe Bridge** is an image file management program that is used across the Adobe suite applications. Bridge is an easy way to view files in their original locations before bringing them into the website. Bridge is an integrated application, which means you can use it to manage files among other Adobe programs such as Photoshop and Illustrator. You can also use Bridge to add meta tags and search text to your files. To open Bridge, click the Browse in Bridge command on the File menu or click the Browse In Bridge button on the Standard toolbar.

Aligning Images

When you insert an image on a web page, you need to position it in relation to other page elements such as text or other images. Positioning an image is also called **aligning** an image. By default, when you insert an image in a paragraph, its bottom edge aligns with the baseline of the first line of text or any other element in the same paragraph. When you select an image, the Align button in the Property inspector shows the alignment setting for the image. You can change the alignment setting using the options in the Align menu in the Property inspector.

Figure 1 *The Assets panel*

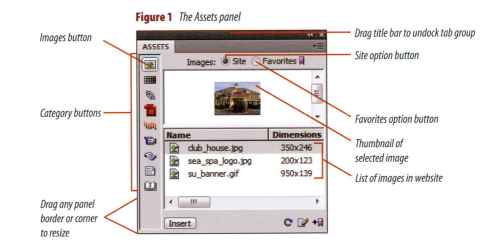

Images button

Category buttons

Drag any panel border or corner to resize

Drag title bar to undock tab group

Site option button

Favorites option button

Thumbnail of selected image

List of images in website

Name	Dimensions
club_house.jpg	350x246
sea_spa_logo.jpg	200x123
su_banner.gif	950x139

Insert an image

1. Open The Striped Umbrella website, open dw4_1.html from the drive and folder where you store your Data Files, then save it as **about_us.html** in the striped_umbrella site root folder.

2. Click **Yes** (Win) or **Replace** (Mac) to overwrite the existing file, click **No** to Update Links, then close dw4_1.html.

3. Click the **Attach Style Sheet button** in the CSS Styles panel, then attach the su_styles.css style sheet to the page.

4. Select the two large paragraphs of text on the page, click the **HTML button** on the Property inspector, verify that the Format is set to Paragraph, click the **CSS button**, then apply the **body_text** rule to the selected text.

5. Click the **HTML button**, then apply the Heading 3 tag to the text "Welcome guests!"

6. Place the insertion point before "When" in the first paragraph, click the **Images list arrow** in the Common category in the Insert panel, then click **Image** to open the Select Image Source dialog box.

7. Navigate to the assets folder in the drive and folder where you store your Data Files, double-click **club_house.jpg**, type the alternate text **Club House** if prompted, click **OK**, open the Files panel if necessary, then verify that the file was copied to your assets folder in the striped_umbrella site root folder.

   Compare your screen to Figure 2.

   (continued)

Figure 2 *The Striped Umbrella about_us page with the inserted image*

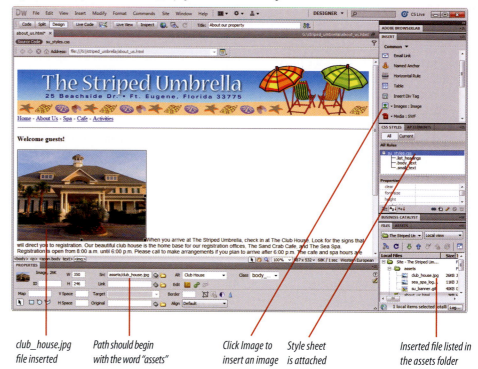

club_house.jpg file inserted

Path should begin with the word "assets"

Click Image to insert an image

Style sheet is attached

Inserted file listed in the assets folder

Figure 3 *Image files for The Striped Umbrella website listed in Assets panel*

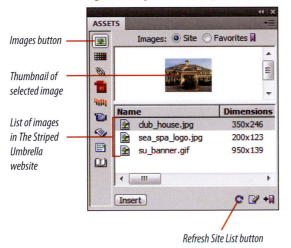

Images button

Thumbnail of selected image

List of images in The Striped Umbrella website

Refresh Site List button

8. Click the **Assets panel tab** in the Files tab group, click the **Images button** in the Assets panel (if necessary), then click the **Refresh Site List button** in the Assets panel to update the list of images in The Striped Umbrella website.

The Assets panel displays a list of all the images in The Striped Umbrella website, as shown in Figure 3. If you don't see the new image listed, press and hold [CTRL] (Win) or [⌘] (Mac) before you click the Refresh Site List button.

You inserted one image on the about_us page and copied it to the assets folder of the website.

Organizing Assets for Quick Access

Your can organize the assets in the Assets panel in two ways, using the Site and Favorites options buttons. The Site option lists all of the assets in the website in the selected category in alphabetical order. But in a complex site, your asset list can grow quite large. To avoid having to scroll to search for frequently used items, you can designate them as Favorites. To add an asset to the Favorites list, right-click (Win) or [control]-click (Mac) the asset name in the Site list, and then click Add to Favorites. When you place an asset in the Favorites list, it still appears in the Site list. To delete an asset from the Favorites list, click the Favorites option button in the Assets panel, select the asset you want to delete, and then press [Delete] or the Remove from Favorites button on the Assets panel. If you delete an asset from the Favorites list, it still remains in the Site list. You can further organize your Favorites list by creating folders for similar assets and grouping them inside the folders.

Insert an image placeholder

1. Click to place the insertion point before the word "After" at the beginning of the second paragraph.
2. Click the **Images list arrow** in the Common category in the Insert panel, then click **Image Placeholder** to open the Image Placeholder dialog box.
3. Type **boardwalk** in the Name text box, **350** in the Width text box, **218** in the Height text box, and **Boardwalk to the beach** in the Alternate text text box, as shown in Figure 4.
4. Click **OK** to accept these settings, then compare your screen to Figure 5.

You inserted an image placeholder on the about_us page to hold the location on the page until the final image is ready to insert.

Figure 4 *Image Placeholder dialog box*

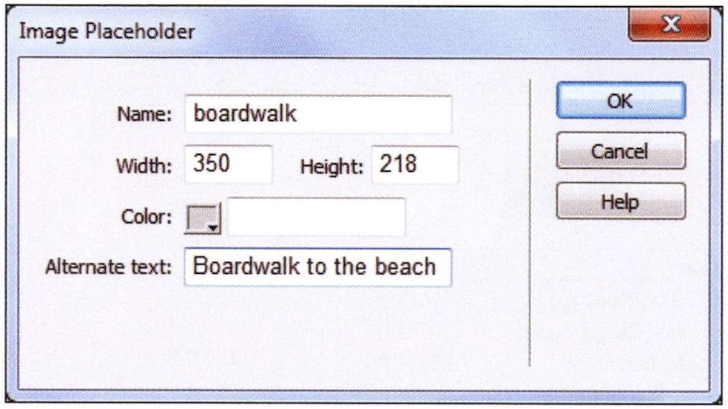

Figure 5 *Image placeholder on the about_us page*

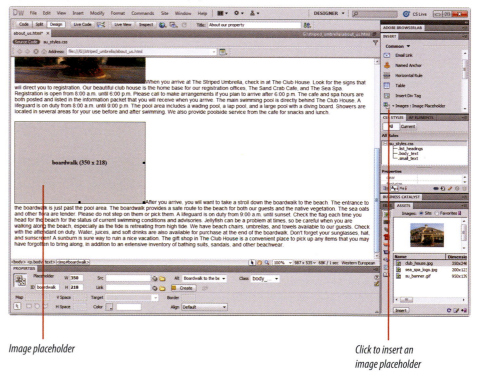

Image placeholder

Click to insert an image placeholder

Figure 6 *The about_us page with the boardwalk image inserted*

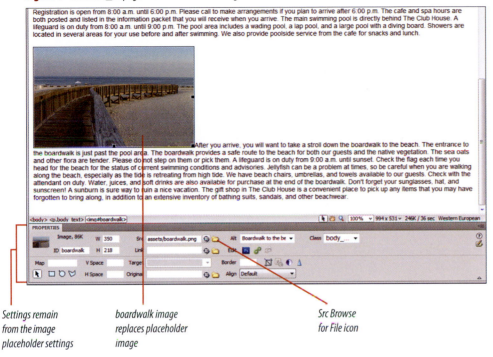

Settings remain
from the image
placeholder settings

boardwalk image
replaces placeholder
image

Src Browse
for File icon

Replace an image placeholder with an image

1. Click to select the **image placeholder** on the about_us page.

2. Click the **Browse for File icon** 📁 next to the Src text box on the Property inspector and browse to the assets folder where you store your Data Files if necessary.

TIP You can also double-click an image placeholder to open the Select Image Source dialog box.

3. Double-click **boardwalk.png** to replace the image placeholder with the boardwalk image.

   The alternate text and the height and width settings on the Property inspector are the same that you entered in the Image Placeholder dialog box, as shown in Figure 6.

4. Save your work.

You replaced an image placeholder on the about_us page with a final image.

Use Adobe Bridge

1. Click to place the insertion point at the end of the last sentence on the page, then enter a paragraph break.

2. Click **File** on the Application bar (Win) or Menu bar (Mac), click **Browse in Bridge**, close the dialog box asking if you want Bridge to start at login by answering Yes or No, (if necessary), click the **Folders tab**, navigate to where you store your Data Files, then click the thumbnail image **su_logo.gif** in the assets folder, as shown in Figure 7.

   The Bridge window is divided into several panels; files and folders are listed in the Folders panel. The files in the selected folder appear in the Content panel. A picture of the file appears in the Preview panel. The Metadata and Keywords panels list any tags that have been added to the file.

3. Click **File** on the Application bar (Win) or Menu bar (Mac), point to **Place**, then click **In Dreamweaver**.

4. Type the alternate text **The Striped Umbrella logo**, if prompted, then click **OK**.

   The image appears on the page.

TIP You can also click the Browse in Bridge button 🗔 on the Standard toolbar to open Bridge.

After refreshing, your Assets panel should resemble Figure 8.

You inserted an image on the about_us page using Adobe Bridge.

Figure 7 *Using Adobe Bridge*

Your path may differ   Folders tab   Folders panel   su_logo.gif image is selected in Content panel

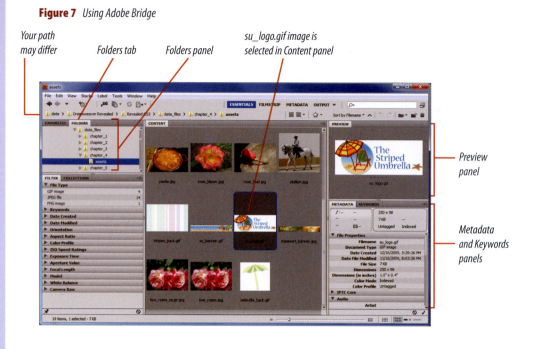

Preview panel

Metadata and Keywords panels

Figure 8 *Assets panel with five images*

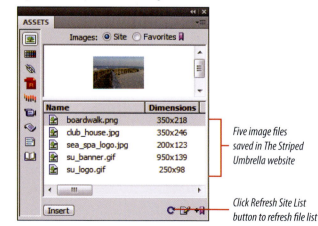

Five image files saved in The Striped Umbrella website

Click Refresh Site List button to refresh file list

Figure 9 *Left-aligned club house image*

Left-aligned
club house
image

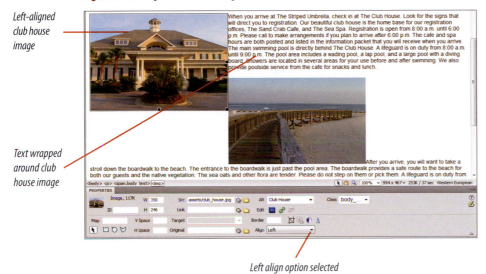

Text wrapped
around club
house image

Left align option selected

Figure 10 *Aligned images on the about_us page*

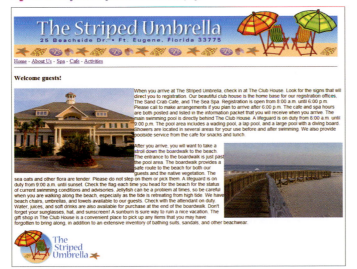

Align an image

1. Scroll to the top of the page, then click the **club house image**.

   Because an image is selected, the Property inspector displays tools for setting the properties of an image.

2. Click the **Align list arrow** in the Property inspector, then click **Left**.

   The club house photo is now left-aligned with the text and the paragraph text flows around its right edge, as shown in Figure 9.

3. Select the boardwalk image, click the **Align list arrow** in the Property inspector, then click **Right**.

   You do not need to set the alignment for the logo because it does not have another object next to it.

4. Save your work.

5. Preview the web page in your browser, compare your screen to Figure 10, then close your browser.

TIP If you are previewing the page in Internet Explorer 7, click the Information bar when prompted to allow blocked content.

6. Close Adobe Bridge.

You used the Property inspector to set the alignment for two of the images. You then previewed the page in your browser.

Enhance an Image and
USE ALTERNATE TEXT

What You'll Do

In this lesson, you will add borders to images, add horizontal and vertical space to set them apart from the text, and then add or edit alternate text to each image on the page.

Enhancing an Image

After you place an image on a web page, you have several options for enhancing it, or improving its appearance. To make changes to the image itself, such as removing scratches from it, or erasing parts of it, you need to use an image editor such as Adobe Fireworks or Adobe Photoshop.

QUICK TIP

You can copy a Photoshop PSD file and paste it directly into Dreamweaver. After inserting the image, Dreamweaver will prompt you to optimize the image for the web.

You can use Dreamweaver to enhance how images appear on a page. For example, you can modify the brightness and contrast, add borders around an image or add horizontal and vertical space. **Borders** are frames that surround an image. Horizontal and vertical space is blank space above, below, and on the sides of an image that separates the image from text or other elements on the page. Adding horizontal or vertical space is the same as adding white space, and helps images stand out on a page. In the web page from the First Federal Bank website shown in Figure 11, the horizontal and vertical space around the images helps make these images more

DESIGN TIP

Resizing Graphics Using an External Editor

Each image on a web page takes a specific number of seconds to download, depending on the size of the file. Larger files (in kilobytes, not width and height) take longer to download than smaller files. It's important to determine the smallest acceptable size for an image on a page. Then, if you need to resize an image to reduce the file size, use an external image editor to do so, instead of resizing it in Dreamweaver. Decreasing the size of an image using the H (height) and W (width) settings in the Property inspector does not reduce the file size or the time it will take the file to download. Ideally you should use images that have the smallest file size and the highest quality possible, so that each page downloads as quickly as possible.

prominent. Adding horizontal or vertical space does not affect the width or height of the image. Spacing around web page objects can also be created by using "spacer" images, or transparent images that act as placeholders.

Using Alternate Text

One of the easiest ways to make your web page viewer-friendly and accessible to people of all abilities is to use alternate text. Alternate text is descriptive text that appears in place of an image while the image is downloading or not displayed. Screen readers, devices used by persons with visual impairments to convert written text on a computer monitor to spoken words, can "read" alternate text and make it possible for viewers to have an image described to them in detail. You should also use alternate text when inserting form objects, text displayed as graphics, buttons, frames, and media files. Without alternate text assigned to these objects, screen readers will not be able to read them.

One of the default preferences in Dreamweaver is to prompt you to enter alternate text whenever you insert an image on a page. You can set alternate text options in the Accessibility category of the Preferences dialog box. You can program some browsers to display only alternate text and to download images manually. Earlier versions of some browsers used to show alternate text when the mouse was placed over an image, such as Internet Explorer versions before version 8.0.

The use of alternate text is the first checkpoint listed in the Web Content Accessibility Guidelines (WCAG), Version 2.0, from the World Wide Web Consortium (W3C). It states that a website should "Provide text alternatives for any non-text content so that it can be changed into other forms people need, such as large print, Braille, speech, symbols, or simpler language." To view the complete set of accessibility guidelines, go to the Web Accessibility Initiative page at www.w3.org/WAI/. You should always strive to meet these criteria for all web pages.

Figure 11 *First Federal Bank website*

First Federal Bank website used with permission from First Federal Bank – www.ffbh.com

Add a border

1. Select the club house image.
2. Type **1** in the Border text box, press **[Tab]** to apply the border to the club house image, then compare your screen to Figure 12.

   The border setting is not visible until you preview the page in a browser.

3. Repeat Step 2 to add a border to the boardwalk image.

You added a 1-pixel border to two images on the about_us page.

Add horizontal and vertical space

1. Select the club house image, type **10** in the V Space text box in the Property inspector, press **[Tab]**, type **10** in the H Space text box, press **[Tab]**, deselect the image, then compare your screen to Figure 13.

   The text is more evenly wrapped around the image and is easier to read, because it is not so close to the edge of the image.

2. Repeat Step 1 to set the V Space and H Space to 10 for the boardwalk image.

   The spacing under each picture differs because of the difference in the lengths of the paragraphs.

You added horizontal spacing and vertical spacing around two images on the about_us page.

Figure 12 *Using the Property inspector to add a border*

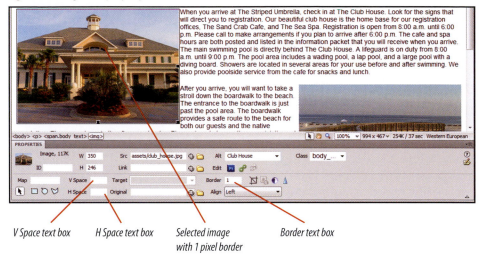

V Space text box   H Space text box   Selected image with 1 pixel border   Border text box

Figure 13 *Comparing images with and without horizontal and vertical space*

Image with horizontal and vertical space   Image without horizontal and vertical space   Horizontal space here resulted from paragraph break

Adding Images

Figure 14 *Viewing the Image Preview dialog box*

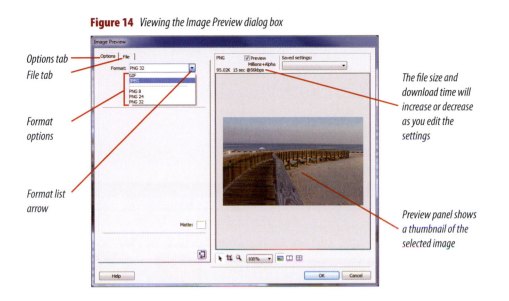

Options tab

File tab

Format
options

Format list
arrow

The file size and
download time will
increase or decrease
as you edit the
settings

Preview panel shows
a thumbnail of the
selected image

Integrating Photoshop CS5 with Dreamweaver

Dreamweaver has many functions integrated with Photoshop CS5. For example, you can copy and paste a Photoshop PSD file directly from Photoshop into Dreamweaver. Dreamweaver will prompt you to optimize the image by choosing a file format and settings for the web. Then it will paste the image on the page. If you want to edit the image later, select the image, then click the Edit button in the Property inspector to open the image in Photoshop. (The appearance of the Edit button will change according to the default image editor you have specified.) Photoshop users can set Photoshop as the default image editor in Dreamweaver for specific image file formats. Click Edit on the Application bar, click Preferences (Win), or click Dreamweaver, click Preferences (Mac), click File Types/Editors, click the Extensions plus sign button, select a file format from the list, click the Editors plus sign button, then use the Select External Editor dialog box to browse to Photoshop (if you don't see it listed already), and then click Make Primary. You can also edit an image in Photoshop and export an updated Smart Object instantly in Dreamweaver. A **Smart Object** is an image layer that stores image data from raster or vector images. Search the Adobe website for a tutorial on Photoshop and Dreamweaver integration. Fireworks is another commonly used default image editor. Use the same steps to select it rather than Photoshop.

Edit image settings

1. Select the **boardwalk image** if necessary.

2. Click the **Edit Image Settings button** 🔧 in the Property inspector, then click the **Format list arrow** on the Options tab, as shown in Figure 14.

   You can use the Image Preview dialog box to save a copy of the image in a different file format. File property options vary depending on which graphics format you choose. When you choose a different file format, then edit and save it, the program creates a copy and does not alter the original file.

3. Choose the JPEG format, then notice that the file size that appears in the Preview panel is much smaller than the PNG image.

4. Click **OK** to save the changes and close the Image Preview dialog box.

TIP In addition to being able to save an image using different file formats on the Options tab, you can also use the File tab to scale or resize an image.

   The Save Web Image dialog box opens. Here you choose the location where you want to save the image with the new file format.

5. Navigate to the website assets folder in the Save Web Image dialog box, then click **Save** to save the boardwalk.jpg image.

   There are now two copies of this image in the assets folder. One is a PNG and one is a JPG. If you don't see the new image, refresh the Files panel.

You experimented with file format settings in the Image Preview dialog box, then saved the image as a JPG file.

Edit alternate text

1. Select the club house image, select **Club House** in the Alt text box in the Property inspector (if necessary), type **The Striped Umbrella Club House** as shown in Figure 15, then press **[Enter]** (Win) or **[return]** (Mac).

2. Select the boardwalk image, type **The boardwalk to the beach** in the Alt text box, then press **[Enter]** (Win) or **[return]** (Mac).

3. Save your work.

4. Preview the page in your browser, compare your screen to Figure 16, then close your browser.

You edited the alternate text for three images on the page.

Figure 15 *Alternate text setting in the Property inspector*

Alt text box

Figure 16 *about_us page viewed in browser*

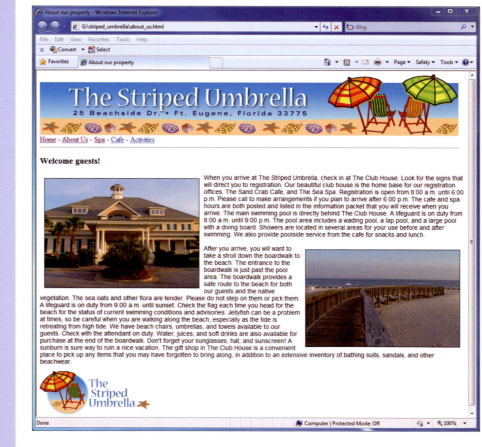

Adding Images

Figure 17 *Preferences dialog box with Accessibility category selected*

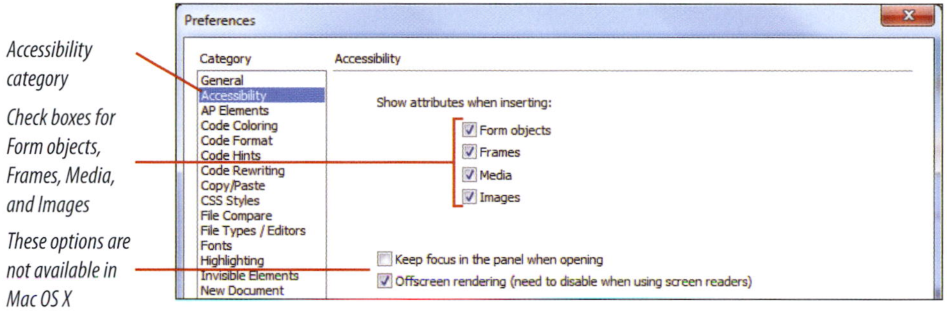

Accessibility category

Check boxes for Form objects, Frames, Media, and Images

These options are not available in Mac OS X

Set the alternate text accessibility option

1. Click **Edit** on the Application bar (Win) or **Dreamweaver** on the Menu bar (Mac), click **Preferences** to open the Preferences dialog box, then click the **Accessibility category**.

2. Verify that the four attributes check boxes are checked, as shown in Figure 17, check them if they are not checked, then click **OK**.

TIP Once you set the Accessibility preferences, they will be in effect for all websites that you develop, not just the one that's open when you set them.

You set the Accessibility preferences to prompt you to enter alternate text each time you insert a form object, frame, media, image, or object on a web page.

POWER USER SHORTCUTS	
To do this:	**Use this shortcut:**
Switch views	[Ctrl][`] (Win) or ⌘ [`] (Mac)
Insert image	[Ctrl][Alt][I] (Win) or ⌘ [option][I] (Mac)
Refresh	[F5]
Browse in Bridge	[Ctrl][Alt][O] (Win) or ⌘ [option][O] (Mac)

Displaying Alternate Text in a Browser

There is a simple method you can use to force alternate text to display in a browser when a mouse is held over an image. To do this, add a title tag to the image properties using the same text as the alt tag. Example: <img src="assets/club_house.jpg" alt="The Striped Umbrella Club House" title="The Striped Umbrella Club House" width="350" height="246" hspace="10" vspace="10" border="1" align="left" /> This method will work in Internet Explorer 8 and later versions and Mozilla Firefox.

Insert a Background Image and
PERFORM SITE MAINTENANCE

What You'll Do

In this lesson, you will insert two types of background images. You will then use the Assets panel to delete them both from the website, along with the boardwalk.png file. You will also check for non-web-safe colors in the Assets panel.

Inserting a Background Image

You can insert a background image on a web page to provide depth and visual interest to the page, or to communicate a message or mood. **Background images** are image files used in place of background colors. Although you can use background images to create a dramatic effect, you should avoid inserting them on web pages where they would not provide the contrast necessary for reading page text. Even though they might seem too plain, standard white backgrounds are usually the best choice for web pages. If you choose to use a background image on a web page, it should be small in file size. You can choose a single image that fills the page background, or you can choose a tiled image. A **tiled image** is a small image that repeats across and down a web page, appearing as individual squares or rectangles. A tiled image will download much faster than a large image.

When you create a web page, you can use either a background color or a background image, unless you want the background color to appear while the background image

finishes downloading. The background in the web page shown in Figure 18 uses an ocean-wave graphic, which ties to the restaurant name "Mermaids" and the ocean theme for the restaurant decor. This image background does not compete with the text on the page, however, because a solid black background is placed behind the text and in front of the image background. This can be done using tables or divs.

Managing Images

As you work on a website, you might find that you accumulate files in your assets folder that you don't use in the website. To avoid accumulating unnecessary files, it's a good idea to look at an image first, before you place it on the page, and copy it to the assets folder. If you inadvertently copy an unwanted file to the assets folder, you should delete it or move it to another location. This is a good website management practice that will prevent the assets folder from filling up with unwanted image files.

Removing an image from a web page does not remove it from the assets folder in the local site root folder of the website. To remove an asset from a website, if you have a lot of files, it is faster to locate the file you want to remove in the Assets panel. You then use the Locate in Site command to open the Files panel with the unwanted file selected. If you don't have many images in your site, it is faster to locate them in the Files panel. You can then use the Delete command to remove the file from the site.

QUICK TIP

You cannot use the Assets panel to delete a file. You must use the Files panel to delete files and perform all file-management tasks.

Removing Colors from a Website

You can use the Assets panel to locate non-web-safe colors in a website. **Non-web-safe** colors are colors that may not appear uniformly across computer platforms. After you replace a non-web-safe color with another color, you should use the Refresh Site List button on the Assets panel to verify that the color has been removed. Sometimes it's necessary to press [Ctrl] (Win) or ⌘ (Mac) while you click the Refresh Site List button. If refreshing the Assets panel does not work, try re-creating the site cache, and then refreshing the Assets panel.

QUICK TIP

To re-create the site cache, click Site on the Application bar (Win) or Menu bar (Mac), point to Advanced, then click Recreate Site Cache.

Figure 18 *Mermaids website*

Mermaids website used with permission from Mermaids Restaurant and Catering – www.mermaids.ws

Insert a background image

1. Click **Modify** on the Application bar (Win) or Menu bar (Mac), then click **Page Properties** to open the Page Properties dialog box.

2. Click the **Appearance (CSS) category**, if necessary.

3. Click **Browse** next to the Background image text box, navigate to the assets folder in the drive and folder where you store your Data Files, then double-click **umbrella_back.gif**.

4. Click **OK** to close the Page Properties dialog box, then click the **Refresh Site List button** ⟳ to refresh the file list in the Assets panel. The umbrella_back.gif file is automatically copied to The Striped Umbrella assets folder.

   A file with a single umbrella forms a background made up of individual squares, replacing the white background, as shown in Figure 19. It is much too busy and makes it difficult to read the page.

5. Repeat Steps 1–4 to replace the umbrella_back.gif background image with stripes_back.gif, located in the chapter_4 assets folder.

   As shown in Figure 20, the striped background is also tiled, but with vertical stripes, so you aren't aware of the small squares making up the pattern. Although it is an improvement, it is still too busy.

You applied a tiled background to the about_us page. Then you replaced the tiled background with another tiled background that was not as busy.

Figure 19 *The about_us page with a busy tiled background*

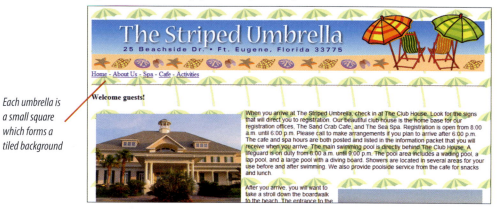

Each umbrella is a small square which forms a tiled background

Figure 20 *The about_us page with a more subtle tiled background*

It is harder to tell where each square ends

Figure 21 *Removing a background image*

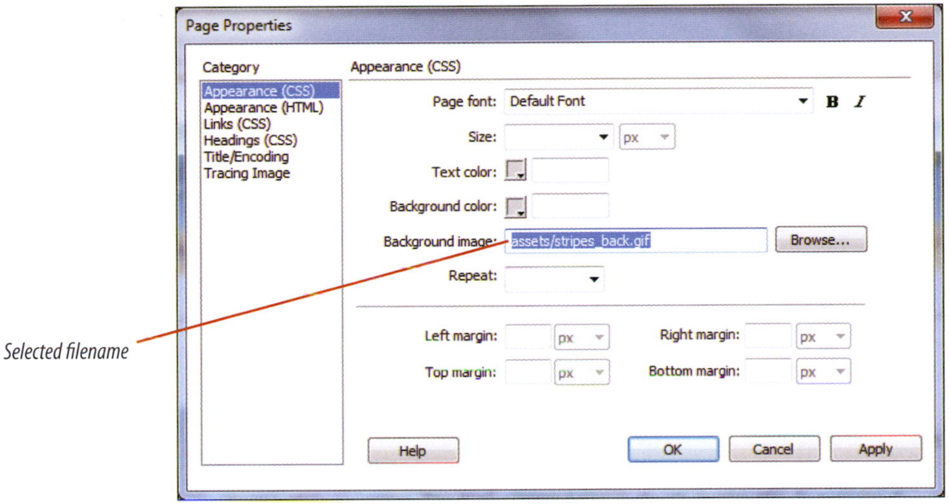

Selected filename

Remove a background image from a page

1. Click **Modify** on the Application bar (Win) or Menu bar (Mac), click **Page Properties**, then click **Appearance (CSS)**.

2. Select the text in the Background image text box, as shown in Figure 21, press **[Delete]**, then click **OK**.

   The background of the about_us page is white again.

3. Save your work.

You deleted the link to the background image file to change the about_us page background back to white.

Understanding HTML Body Tags

When you set page preferences, it is helpful to understand the HTML tags that are being generated. Sometimes it's easier to make changes to the code, rather than use menus and dialog boxes. The code for the page background color is located in the head section. If you want to change the page properties, you add additional codes to the body tag. Adding a color to the background will add a style to the page; for example, "body { background-color: #000; }". If you insert an image for a background, the code will read "body { background-image: url assets/stripes.gif); }".

Delete files from a website

1. Click the **Assets panel tab** if necessary, then click the **Images button** 🖼 if necessary.

2. With the Site option selected, refresh the Assets panel, right-click (Win) or [control]-click (Mac) **stripes_back.gif** in the Assets panel, click **Locate in Site** to open the Files panel, select **stripes_back.gif** on the Files panel, if necessary, press **[Delete]**, then click **Yes** in the dialog box that appears.

   TIP Refresh the Files panel if you don't see the highlighted file; then refresh the Assets panel if you still see the file listed.

3. Click the **Assets panel tab**, then repeat Step 2 to remove umbrella_back.gif and boardwalk.png from the website, open the Assets panel, then refresh the Assets panel.

   TIP If you delete a file on the Files panel that has an active link to it, you will receive a warning message. If you rename a file on the Files panel that has a link to it, the Files panel will update the links to correctly link to the renamed file. To rename a file, right-click (Win) or [control]-click (Mac) the file you want to rename, point to Edit, click Rename, then type the new name.

   Your Assets panel should resemble Figure 22.

   You removed three image files from The Striped Umbrella website, then refreshed the Assets panel.

Figure 22 *Images listed in Assets panel*

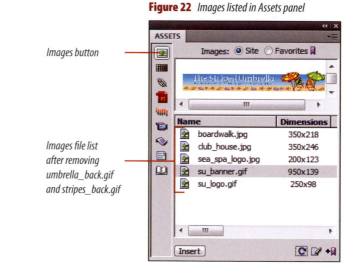

Images button

Images file list after removing umbrella_back.gif and stripes_back.gif

Managing Image Files

It is a good idea to store original unedited copies of your website image files in a separate folder, outside the assets folder of your website. If you edit the original files, resave them using different names. Doing this ensures that you will be able to find a file in its original, unaltered state. You may have files on your computer that you are currently not using at all; however, you may need to use them in the future. Storing currently unused files also helps keep your assets folder free of clutter. Storing copies of original website image files in a separate location also ensures that you have back-up copies in the event that you accidentally delete a file from the website.

Adding Images

Figure 23 *Colors listed in Assets panel*

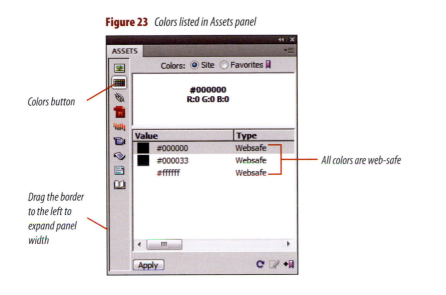

Colors button

Drag the border
to the left to
expand panel
width

All colors are web-safe

Check for non-web-safe colors

1. Click the **Colors button** ▦ in the Assets panel to display the colors used in the website, then drag the left border of the Assets panel to display the second column, if necessary, as shown in Figure 23.

Colors listed may either be on pages or in style sheet files. The Assets panel does not list any non-web-safe colors for The Striped Umbrella website.

TIP If you see a non-web-safe color listed, click Site on the Application bar (Win) or Menu bar (Mac), point to Advanced, then click Recreate Site Cache. The non-web-safe color should then be removed from the Assets panel. This should also remove any colors you have experimented with, unless you have saved a page with a color left on it. If you see an extra color, use the Find and Replace command to locate it, then remove it from the page and refresh the Assets panel again.

2. Save your work, preview the page in your browser, then close your browser.

You checked for non-web-safe colors in the Assets panel list of colors.

Using Color in Compliance with Accessibility Guidelines

Web Content Accessibility Guidelines (WCAG), Version 2.0, from the World Wide Web Consortium (W3C), states that a website should not rely on the use of color alone. This means that if your website content depends on your viewer correctly seeing a color, then you are not providing for those people who cannot distinguish between certain colors or do not have monitors that display color. Be especially careful when choosing color used with text, so you provide a good contrast between the text and the background.

If you are typing in the code or in a text box, it is better to reference colors as numbers, rather than names. For example, use "#FFF" instead of "white." Using style sheets for specifying color formats is the preferred method for coding. For more information, see the complete list of accessibility guidelines listed on the W3C website, www.w3.org.

Add Graphic
ENHANCEMENTS

What You'll Do

▶ In this lesson, you will use a small image to link to a larger image and add a favicon to a page.

Adding a Link to a Larger Image

Sometimes designers want to display a small image on a page with an option for the viewer to click on the image to display a larger image. You frequently see this practice on retail sites with multiple items for sale. It is done both to conserve space and to keep the page size as small as possible. These sites will display a **thumbnail image**, or small version of a larger image, so that more images will fit on the page. Another technique is to link from one image to a second image that incorporates the first image. For example, a furniture site may create a link from an image of a chair to an image of the chair in a furnished room. An additional enhancement is often added to allow viewers to click on the larger image to magnify it even more.

To accomplish this, you need two versions of the same image using an image editor such as Photoshop: one that is small (in dimensions and in file size) and one that is large (in dimensions and in file size.) After you have both images ready, place the small image on your page, select it, then link it to the large image. When a user clicks the small image

in a browser, the large image will open. Another option is to place the large image on a new web page so you can also include additional descriptive text about the image or a link back to the previous page.

Adding Favicons

In most browsers today, when you add a web page to your favorites list or bookmarks, the page title will appear with a small icon that represents your site, similar to a logo, called a **favicon** (short for favorites icon). This feature was introduced in Microsoft Internet Explorer 5. Most browsers will now also display favicons in the browser address bar. Favicons are a nice way to add branding, or recognition, for your site. To create a favicon, first create an icon that is 16 pixels by 16 pixels. Second, save the file as an icon file with the .ico file extension in your site root folder. Do not save it in a subfolder such as an assets or images folder.

> **QUICK TIP**
>
> There are plug-ins available for Photoshop that will save files with an icon file format, or you can search the Internet for programs that will generate icons.

Third, add HTML code to the head section of your page to link the icon file. The browser will then find the icon and load it in the address bar when the page loads.

QUICK TIP

The Firefox and Opera browsers can read a .jpg or a .png file, in addition to an .ico file.

Figure 24 shows a favicon in the Snapfish by HP website. Notice that the favicon is displayed both on the address bar and on the page tab. The design of the favicon ties in with the name of the company and other images of fish that are used in the page content. This is a nice touch to complete a well-designed site.

Adding a No Right-Click Script

On most websites, viewers are able to save an image on a page by right-clicking an image, then clicking Save on the shortcut menu. If you would like to prevent viewers from having this option, you can add a **no right-click script**, or JavaScript code that will not allow users to display the shortcut menu by right-clicking an image. To do this, locate JavaScript code that will add this option and copy and paste it into the head content of your page. To locate JavaScript code, use a search engine to search the Internet with a term such as "no right-click script." You will find scripts that prevent viewers from saving any image on the page, or all content of any kind on the page. Some scripts return a message in the browser such as "This function is disabled," and some do not return a message at all. These scripts will keep many viewers from saving your images, but they will not stop the most serious and knowledgeable perpetrators.

You can also protect website images by inserting the image as a table, cell, or CSS block background and then placing a transparent image on top of it. When a viewer attempts to save it with the shortcut menu, they will only save the transparent image.

Figure 24 *Snapfish website*

Favicon displayed in the address bar and on the page tab

Favicon is similar in appearance to other images on the page

© 2009 The Snapfish by HP website used with permission from Snapfish by HP – www.snapfish.com

Use an image to link to another image

1. Click to place the insertion point to the right of the su_logo image, insert the image **map_small.jpg** from the assets folder where you store your Data Files, type **Map to The Striped Umbrella** in the Image Tag Accessibility Attributes dialog box, then click **OK**.

2. Select the **map_small image**, then type **30** in the H Space text box, then press **[Tab]**.

3. With the map_small image selected, click the **Browse for File icon** next to the Link text box, navigate to the assets folder in the drive and folder where you store your Data Files, click **map_large.jpg**, then click **OK**.

   The small map image now links to the large map image, so viewers can click the small version to view the large version.

4. Click to place the insertion point after the last paragraph, insert a paragraph break, type **Click the map below to view a larger size image**, then compare your screen to Figure 25.

5. Save your work, then preview the page in your browser.

6. Click the **small map image** to view the large map image in a separate window, use the Back button to return to the about_us page, then close the browser.

You inserted a small image on the page and linked it to a larger image.

Figure 25 *The about_us page with an image linking to a larger image*

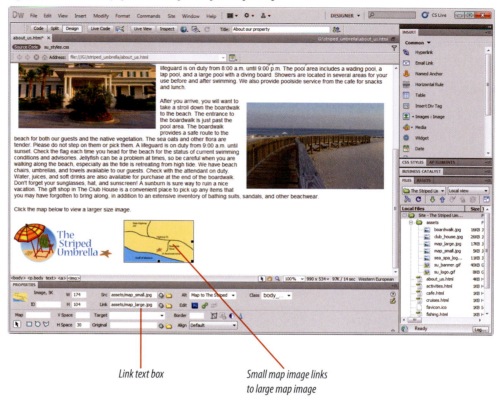

Link text box

Small map image links to large map image

Figure 26 *Copying the favicon.ico file to the site root folder*

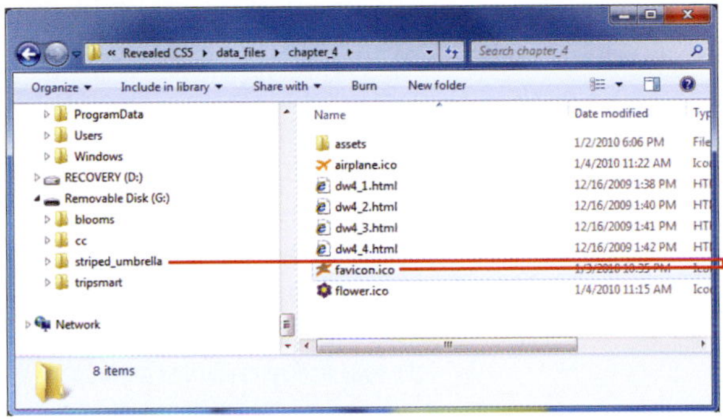

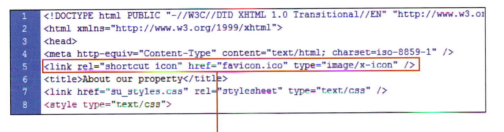

Copy the favicon.ico file
to the striped_umbrella
site root folder

Figure 27 *Adding code to link the favicon*

```
1  <!DOCTYPE html PUBLIC "-//W3C//DTD XHTML 1.0 Transitional//EN" "http://www.w3.or
2  <html xmlns="http://www.w3.org/1999/xhtml">
3  <head>
4  <meta http-equiv="Content-Type" content="text/html; charset=iso-8859-1" />
5  <link rel="shortcut icon" href="favicon.ico" type="image/x-icon" />
6  <title>About our property</title>
7  <link href="su_styles.css" rel="stylesheet" type="text/css" />
8  <style type="text/css">
```

Type this code above the <title> tag

Figure 28 *Viewing a favicon in the Firefox browser*

Starfish favicon

Insert a favicon on a page

1. Open Windows Explorer (Win) or Finder (Mac), then browse to the chapter_4 folder in the drive and folder where your Data Files are stored.

2. Right-click the file **favicon.ico**, copy it, browse to your site root folder, then paste the **favicon.ico** file into the site root folder, as shown in Figure 26, then close Windows Explorer (Win) or Finder (Mac).

3. Switch to Code view in Dreamweaver, insert a blank line above the line of code for the page title, then insert this code directly above the <title> tag: **<link rel = "shortcut icon" href = "favicon.ico" type = "image/x-icon" />** as shown in Figure 27.

4. Save your work, then preview the about_us page in the browser.

   The favicon will appear in the address bar right before the page title and on the page tab in browsers that use tabbed pages, as shown in Figure 28.

TIP Internet Explorer may not display the favicon until the website is published to a server.

5. Copy the code for the favicon link, then paste it into the code for the index and spa pages.

6. Save your work, close all open pages, then exit Dreamweaver.

You copied a favicon to the site root folder, then added code to the About Us page to direct browsers to display the favicon in the title bar when the page is viewed in a browser.

Insert and align images.

1. Open the Blooms & Bulbs website, open dw4_2.html from the drive and folder where you store your Data Files, then save it as **plants.html** in the Blooms & Bulbs website, overwriting the existing plants.html file. Do not update links.
2. Verify that the path of the Blooms & Bulbs banner is set correctly to the assets folder in the blooms site root folder.
3. Verify that the Accessibility preferences will prompt you to add alternate text to images is set.
4. Insert an image placeholder to the left of the words "Who can resist" with the following settings: Name: **rose_bud**; Width: **300 pixels**; Height: **207 pixels**; Alternate text: **Rose bud on bird bath**.
5. Use the Browse for file button next to the Src text box on the Property inspector to replace the image placeholder with the rose_bud.jpg file from the assets folder in the drive and folder where you store your Data Files
6. Use Bridge to insert the rose_bloom.jpg file, from the assets folder in the drive and folder where you store your Data Files, in front of the words "For ease of growing" and add **Rose bloom** as alternate text.
7. Insert the two_roses.jpg file from the assets folder in the drive and folder where you store your Data Files in front of the words "The Candy Cane" and add **Candy Cane Floribunda** as alternate text.
8. Refresh the Files panel to verify that all three images were copied to the assets folder.
9. Left-align the rose_bud image.
10. Right-align the rose_bloom image.
11. Left-align the two_roses image.
12. Save your work.

Enhance an image and use alternate text.

1. Apply a 1-pixel border, vertical spacing of 10 pixels, and horizontal spacing of 20 pixels around the rose_bud image.
2. Apply a 1-pixel border, vertical spacing of 10 pixels, and horizontal spacing of 20 pixels around the rose_bloom image.
3. Apply a 1-pixel border, vertical spacing of 10 pixels, and horizontal spacing of 20 pixels around the two_roses image.
4. Attach the blooms_styles.css file to the page, then use the HTML Property inspector to apply the Heading 3 format to the heading at the top of the page and the paragraph_text rule to the rest of the text on the page. (*Hint*: Use the Class text box to select the paragraph_text rule from the list.)
5. Save your work, preview it in the browser, then compare your screen to Figure 29. (*Hint*: If previewing the page in Internet Explorer 7, click the Information bar when prompted to allow blocked content.)

Figure 29 *Completed Skills Review*

Insert a background image and perform site maintenance.

1. Insert the daisies.jpg file as a background image from the assets folder where you store your Data Files.
2. Save your work.
3. Preview the web page in your browser, then close your browser.
4. Remove the daisies.jpg file from the background.
5. Open the Assets panel, then refresh the Files list.
6. Use the Files panel to delete the daisies.jpg file from the list of images.
7. Refresh the Assets panel, then verify that the daisies.jpg file has been removed from the website.
8. View the colors used in the site in the Assets panel, then verify that all are web-safe.
9. Save your work.

Add graphic enhancements.

1. Select the two_roses image on the plants page.
2. Use the Link text box on the Property inspector to link the two_roses image to the two_roses_large.jpg file in the assets folder where you store your Data Files.
3. Add the sentences **You must see a close-up of these beauties! Click the image on the left to enlarge them**. at the end of the last paragraph.
4. Save your work, preview the page in the browser, then click the two_roses image to view the larger version of the image.
5. Use the Back button to return to the plants page, then close the dw4_2.html data file.

6. Open Windows Explorer (Win) or Finder (Mac), browse to the folder where you store your Data Files, then copy the file flower.ico.
7. Paste the file flower.ico in the blooms site root folder, then rename it **favicon.ico.**
8. Close Windows Explorer (Win) or Finder (Mac), then switch to Code view for the plants page.
9. Insert a blank line above the title tag, then type this code directly above the <title> tag:
   <link rel = "shortcut icon" href = "favicon.ico" type = "image/x-icon" />

10. Verify that you entered the code correctly, copy the new line of code, then switch back to Design view.
11. Copy the same code you typed in step 9 to the index and tips pages, then save all files.
12. Preview the page in the browser, compare your screen to Figure 30, then close all open page.

Figure 30 *Completed Skills Review*

Use Figure 31 as a guide to continue your work on the TripSmart website that you began in Project Builder 1 in Chapter 1, and continued to work on in Chapters 2 and 3. You are now ready to begin work on the destinations page that showcases one of the featured tours to Spain. You want to include some colorful pictures on the page.

1. Open the TripSmart website.
2. Open dw4_3.html from the drive and folder where you store your Data Files and save it in the tripsmart site root folder as **tours.html**, overwriting the existing tours.html file and not updating the links.
3. Verify that the path for the banner is correctly set to the assets folder of the TripSmart website.
4. Attach the tripsmart_styles.css file, then apply the paragraph_text rule to all of the text on the page except the "Destination: Spain" heading.
5. Apply the Heading 2 format to the "Destination: Spain" heading.
6. Insert bull_fighter.jpg from the assets folder in the drive and folder where you store your Data Files to the left of the sentence beginning "Our next trip to Spain", then add appropriate alternate text.
7. Insert stallion.jpg from the assets folder in the drive and folder where you store your Data Files to the left of the sentence beginning "We will also visit Jerez", then add appropriate alternate text.
8. Align both images using the Align button in the Property inspector with alignments of your choice, then add horizontal spacing, vertical spacing, or borders if desired.

9. Apply any additional formatting to enhance the page appearance if you would like to, then add the page title **Destination: Spain**.
10. Check the site for non-web-safe colors and remove them if you find any.
11. Copy the file airplane.ico from the folder where you store your data files to your site root folder, then rename it **favicon.ico**.
12. Add appropriate code to the head content to link the favicon to the page, then copy the code to the index and newsletter pages.
13. Save your work, then preview the tours, index, and newsletter pages in your browser. (*Hint*: If previewing the page in Internet Explorer 7, click the Information bar when prompted to allow blocked content.)
14. Close your browser, then close all open files.

Figure 31 *Sample Project Builder 1*

In this exercise, you continue your work on the Carolyne's Creations website that you started in Project Builder 2 in Chapter 1, and continued to build in Chapters 2 and 3. You are now ready to add a new page to the website that will display featured items in the kitchen shop. Figure 32 shows a possible solution for this exercise. Your finished page will look different if you choose different formatting options.

1. Open the Carolyne's Creations website.
2. Open dw4_4.html from the drive and folder where you store your Data Files, save it to the site root folder as **shop.html**, overwriting the existing file and not updating the links.
3. Insert paella_pan.jpg from the assets folder in the drive and folder where you store your Data Files, on the page, add alternate text and your choice of alignment, horizontal space, and vertical space settings. (*Hint*: In Figure 32 the align setting is set to right, and the H space is set to 30.)
4. Attach the cc_styles.css file to the page.
5. Apply the nav_bar rule to the navigation links, the headings rule to the page heading "January Special: Paella Pans" and the body_text rule to the paragraphs of text.
6. Link the paella_pan image to the file paella.jpg from the assets folder where you store your Data Files, then enter some descriptive text on the page to prompt viewers to click on the paella_pan image.

7. Save the shop page, then preview it in the browser. (*Hint*: If previewing the page in Internet Explorer 7, click the Information bar when prompted to allow blocked content.)
8. Close your browser, then close all open pages.

Figure 32 *Sample Project Builder 2*

Home | Shop | Classes | Catering | Recipes

January Special: Paella Pans

We try to feature special items each month and love to promote local foods. This month features paella pans in three sizes: 12 inches, 18 inches, and 24 inches.

This pan is made of polished stainless steel with red baked enamel handles for easy transfer from stove top to table. Paella is a traditional Spanish dish with rice as the basic ingredient. Caroline found these wonderful pans during a recent trip to Valencia, Spain. Although it looks a little similar in appearance to a wok, you do not stir paella while it is cooking! The secret to the perfect paella is to cook it until it is almost burned, forming a crunchy crust on the bottom, called soccarat. To view some of Chef Carolyne's tempting paella, click on the image on the right.

Patsy Broers is working on a team project to design a website for her high school drama department. She has been assigned the task of gathering images to add interest and color.

1. Connect to the Internet, then navigate to the William J. Clinton Presidential Center website at www.clintonpresidentialcenter.org, shown in Figure 33.
2. Do you see a favicon used on the page?
3. Are any of the images on the page used as links to other images or pages?
4. Is a background image used for any of the page objects?
5. How do the images, horizontal and vertical spacing, color, and text work together to create an attractive and interesting experience for viewers?

Figure 33 *Design Project*

The William J. Clinton Presidential Center website used with permission from the William J. Clinton Presidential Center www.clintonpresidentialcenter.org

In this assignment, you will continue to work on the website that you started in Chapter 1, and continued to build in Chapters 2 and 3. No Data Files are supplied. You are building this site from chapter to chapter, so you must do each Portfolio Project assignment in each chapter to complete your website.

You continue building your website by inserting appropriate images on a page and enhancing them for maximum effect. You will also check for non-web-safe colors and remove any that you find.

1. Consult your wireframe and decide which page to create and develop for this chapter.
2. Plan the page content and make a sketch of the layout. Your sketch should include several images and a background color or image.
3. Create the page using your sketch for guidance.
4. Access the images you gathered, and place them on the page so that the page matches the sketch you created in Step 2. Add a background image if you want, and appropriate alternate text for each image.
5. Remove any non-web-safe colors.
6. Identify any files in the Assets panel that are currently not used in the site. Decide which of these assets should be removed, then delete these files.

7. Preview the new page in a browser, then check for page layout problems and broken links. (*Hint*: If previewing the page in Internet Explorer 7, click the Information bar when prompted to allow blocked content.) Make any necessary corrections in Dreamweaver, then preview the page again in the browser. Repeat this process until you are satisfied with the way the page looks in the browser.
8. Use the checklist in Figure 34 to check all the pages in your site.
9. Close the browser, then close the open pages.

Figure 34 *Portfolio Project checklist*

Website Checklist

1. Does each page have a page title?
2. Does the home page have a description and keywords?
3. Does the home page contain contact information?
4. Does the home page have a last updated statement that will automatically update when the page is saved?
5. Do all paths for links and images work correctly?
6. Do all images have alternate text?
7. Are all colors web-safe?
8. Are there any unnecessary files you can delete from the assets folder?
9. Is there a style sheet with at least two rules?
10. Did you apply the rules to all text?
11. Do all pages look good using at least two different browsers?

CHAPTER 5 **WORKING WITH LINKS**
AND NAVIGATION

1. Create external and internal links
2. Create internal links to named anchors
3. Create, modify, and copy a Spry menu bar
4. Create an image map
5. Manage website links
6. Incorporate Web 2.0 technology

CHAPTER 5

WORKING WITH LINKS
AND NAVIGATION

Introduction

What makes websites so powerful are the links, or hyperlinks, that connect one page to another within a website or to any page on the web. Although you can enhance a website with graphics, animations, movies, and other features to make it visually attractive, the links you include are often a site's most essential components. Links that connect the pages within a site are important because they help viewers navigate between the pages of the site. If it's important to keep viewers within your site, link only to pages within your website and avoid including links to external sites. For example, most e-commerce sites only link to other pages in their own site to discourage shoppers from leaving.

In this chapter, you will create links to other pages in The Striped Umbrella website and to other sites on the web. You will insert a Spry menu bar, and check the site links to make sure they all work correctly. You will also learn about Web 2.0 and social networking, an area of the Internet that has exploded in recent years. **Social networking** refers to the grouping of individual web users who connect and interact with other users in online communities. **Online communities**, or virtual communities, are social websites you can join, such as Facebook and Twitter, where you can communicate with others by posting messages or media content such as images or videos. You will learn about how you can connect your website to these communities.

Understanding Internal and External Links

Web pages contain two types of links: internal links and external links. **Internal links** are links to web pages within the same website, and **external links** are links to web pages in other websites or to email addresses. Both internal and external links have two important parts that work together. The first part of a link is displayed on a web page, for example, text, an image, or a button that is used for a link. The second part of a link is the **path**, or the name and location of the web page or file that will open when viewers click the element. Setting and maintaining the correct paths for all of your links is essential to avoid having broken links in your site, which can cause a visitor to click away immediately.

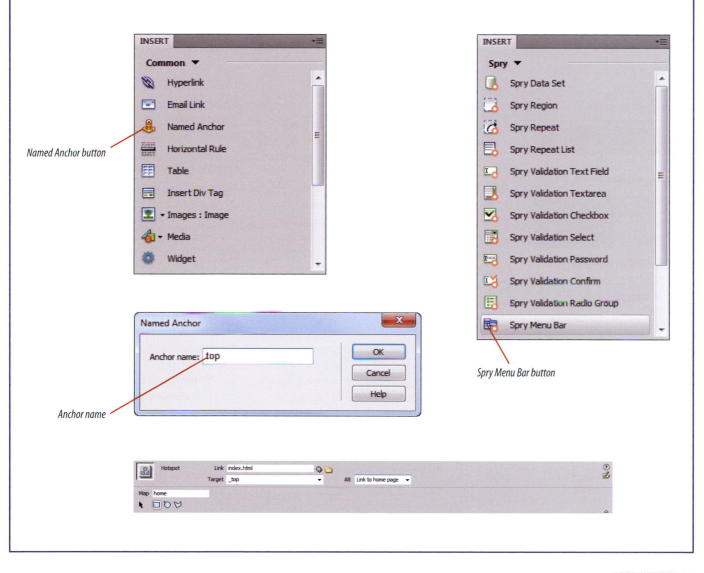

Named Anchor button

Anchor name

Spry Menu Bar button

Create External and
INTERNAL LINKS

What You'll Do

 In this lesson, you will create external links on The Striped Umbrella activities page that link to websites related to area attractions. You will also create internal links to other pages within The Striped Umbrella website.

Creating External Links

A good website often includes a variety of external links to other related websites so that viewers can get more information on a particular topic. To create an external link, you first select the text or object that you want to serve as a link, then you type the absolute path to the destination web page in the Link text box in the Property inspector. An **absolute path** is a path used for external links that includes the complete address for the destination page, including the protocol (such as http://) and the complete **URL** (Uniform Resource Locator), or address, of the destination page. When necessary, the web page filename and folder hierarchy are also part of an absolute path. Figure 1 shows an example of an absolute path showing the protocol, URL, and filename. An example

for the code for an external link would be <a href="http://www.adobe.com"> Adobe website</a>.

Creating Internal Links

Each page in a website usually focuses on an individual information category or topic. You should make sure that the home page provides links to each major page in the site, and that all pages in the site contain numerous internal links so that viewers can move easily from page to page. To create an internal link, you first select the text element or image that you want to use to make a link, and then use the Browse for File icon next to the Link text box in the HTML Property inspector to specify the relative path to the destination page. A **relative path** is a type of path that

Figure 1 *An example of an absolute path*

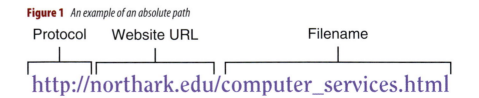

Protocol   Website URL   Filename

http://northark.edu/computer_services.html

references web pages and image files within the same website. Relative paths include the filename and folder location of a file. An example for the code for a relative internal link would be <a href="activities.html">Activities</a>. Figure 2 shows an example of a relative path. Table 1 describes absolute and relative paths. Relative paths can either be site-root relative or document-relative. The internal links that you will create in this lesson will be document-relative. You can also use the Point to File icon in the HTML Property inspector to select the file you want to link to, or drag the file you want to use for the link from the Files panel into the Link text box in the Property inspector.

You should take great care in managing your internal links to make sure they work correctly and are timely and relevant to the page content. Design the navigation structure of your website so that viewers are never more than three or four clicks away from the page they are seeking.

Figure 2 *An example of a relative path*

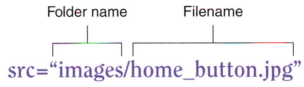

Folder name   Filename

src="images/home_button.jpg"

TABLE 1: DESCRIPTION OF ABSOLUTE AND RELATIVE PATHS		
Type of path	**Description**	**Examples**
Absolute path	Used for external links and specifies protocol, URL, and filename of destination page	http://www.yahoo.com/recreation
Relative path	Used for internal links and specifies location of file relative to the current page	spa.html or assets/heron.gif
Root-relative path	Used for internal links when publishing to a server that contains many websites or where the website is so large it requires more than one server	/striped_umbrella/activities.html
Document- relative path	Used in most cases for internal links and specifies the location of file relative to current page	cafe.html or assets/heron.gif

Create an external link

1. Open The Striped Umbrella website, open dw5_1.html from the drive and folder where you store your Chapter 5 Data Files, then save it as **activities.html** in the striped_umbrella site root folder, overwriting the existing activities page, but not updating links.

2. Attach the **su_styles.css** file, then apply the **body_text rule** to the paragraphs of text on the page (not to the menu bar).

3. Select the first broken image link, click the **Browse for File icon** next to the Src text box, then select heron_waiting_small.jpg in the Data Files assets folder to save the image in your assets folder.

4. Click on the page next to the broken image link to see the heron_waiting_small image, then click to select the image, as shown in Figure 3.

5. Repeat Step 3 for the second image, two_dolphins_small.jpg, then refresh the Assets panel if necessary.

   The two new files are copied into the assets folder, as shown in Figure 4.

6. Scroll down, then select the text "Blue Angels" in the first line of the second to last paragraph.

(continued)

Figure 3 *Saving an image file in assets folder*

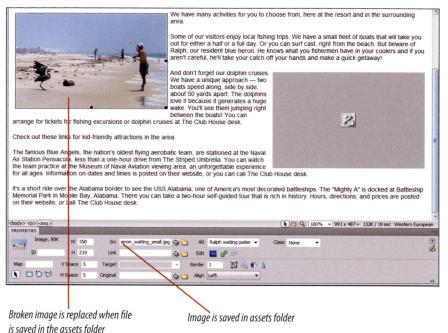

Broken image is replaced when file is saved in the assets folder

Image is saved in assets folder

Figure 4 *Assets panel with two new images added*

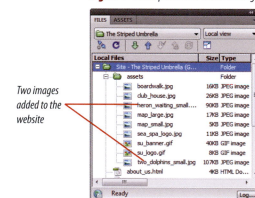

Two images added to the website

Working with Links and Navigation

Figure 5 *Creating an external link to the Blue Angels website*

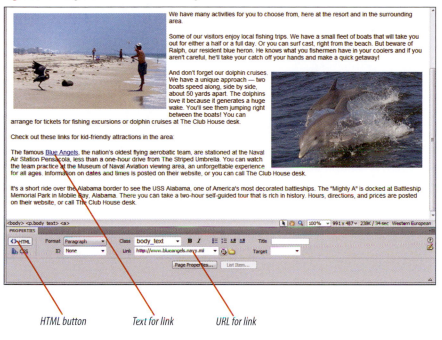

HTML button   Text for link   URL for link

7. Click the **HTML button** `<> HTML` in the Property inspector to switch to the HTML Property inspector if necessary, click in the Link text box, type **http://www.blueangels.navy.mil**, press [**Enter**] (Win) or [**return**] (Mac), click on the page to deselect the link, then compare your screen to Figure 5.

8. Repeat Steps 6 and 7 to create a link for the USS Alabama site in the next paragraph: **http://www.ussalabama.com**.

9. Save your work, preview the page in your browser, test all the links to make sure they work, then close your browser.

TIP You must have an active Internet connection to test the external links. If clicking a link does not open a page, make sure you typed the URL correctly in the Link text box.

You opened The Striped Umbrella website, replaced the existing activities page, attached the su_styles.css.file, applied the paragraph_text style to the text, then imported images into the site. You added two external links to other sites, then tested each link in your browser.

Typing URLs

Typing URLs in the Link text box in the Property inspector can be tedious. When you need to type a long and complex URL, it is easy to make mistakes and create a broken link. You can avoid such mistakes by copying and pasting the URL from the Address text box (Internet Explorer) or Location bar (Mozilla Firefox) to the Link text box in the Property inspector. Copying and pasting a URL ensures that the URL is entered correctly.

Create an internal link

1. Select the text "fishing excursions" in the third paragraph.

2. Click the **Browse for File icon**  next to the Link text box in the HTML Property inspector, then double-click **fishing.html** in the Select File dialog box to set the relative path to the fishing page.

   The filename fishing.html appears in the Link text box in the Property inspector, as shown in Figure 6 (The link is deselected in the figure for readability.)

TIP Pressing [F4] will hide or redisplay all panels, including the Property inspector and the panels on the right side of the screen.

3. Select the text "dolphin cruises" in the same sentence.

4. Click the **Browse for File icon**  next to the Link text box in the HTML Property inspector, then double-click **cruises.html** in the Select File dialog box to specify the relative path to the cruises page.

   The words "dolphin cruises" are now a link to the cruises page.

5. Save your work, preview the page in your browser, verify that the internal links work correctly, then close your browser.

   The fishing and cruises pages do not have page content yet, but serve as placeholders until they do.

You created two internal links on the activities page, then tested the links in your browser.

Figure 6 *Creating an internal link on the activities page*

Text to be used for link   *Relative link to fishing.html*   *Browse for File icon*

Using Case-Sensitive Links

When you hear that text is "case sensitive," it means that the text will be treated differently when it is typed using uppercase letters rather than lowercase letters, or vice-versa. With some operating systems, such as Windows, it doesn't matter which case you use when you enter URLs. However, with other systems, such as UNIX, it does matter. To be sure that your links will work with all systems, use lowercase letters for all URLs. This is another good reason to select and copy a URL from the browser address bar, and then paste it in the Link text box or Dreamweaver code when creating an external link. You won't have to worry about missing a case change.

Figure 7 *Assets panel with three external links*

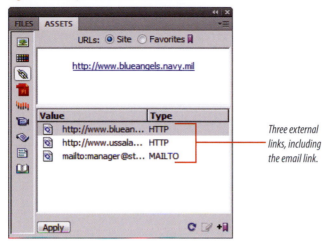

Three external links, including the email link.

View links in the Assets panel

1. Click the Assets panel tab if necessary to view the Assets panel.

2. Click the **URLs button** in the Assets panel.

3. Click the **Refresh Site List button** .

   Three links appear in the Assets panel: one external link for the email link on the home page and two external links, to the Blue Angels and USS Alabama websites on the activities page, as shown in Figure 7. Notice that the internal links do not appear in the Assets panel. The Assets panel shows the links for the entire site, not just for the open page.

4. Click the **Files panel tab** to view the Files panel.

5. Close the activities page and the dw5_1.html page.

You viewed the external links on the activities page in the Assets panel.

Create Internal Links
TO NAMED ANCHORS

What You'll Do

In this lesson, you will insert four named anchors on the spa page: one for the top of the page and three for each of the spa services lists. You will then create internal links to each named anchor.

Inserting Named Anchors

Some web pages have so much content that users must scroll repeatedly to get to the bottom of the page and then back up to the top of the page. To make it easier for users to navigate to specific areas of a page without scrolling, you can use a combination of internal links and named anchors. A **named anchor** is a specific location on a web page that has a descriptive name. Named anchors act as targets for internal links and make it easy for users to jump to a particular place on the same page quickly. A **target** is the location on a web page that a browser displays when users click an internal link. For example, you can insert a named anchor called "top" at the top of a web page, and then create a link to it from the bottom of the page.

You can also insert named anchors in strategic places on a web page, such as at the beginning of paragraph headings. The Ozark Arts Council website shown in Figure 8 uses named anchors on their About Us page to divide the content about the organization

into separate sections on the page. Text links at the top of the page link to the respective section headers with named anchors.

You insert a named anchor using the Named Anchor button in the Common category on the Insert panel. You then enter the name of the anchor in the Named Anchor dialog box. You should choose short names that describe the named anchor location on the page. Named anchors appear on a web page as yellow anchor icons in Design view. Selected anchors appear as blue icons. You can show or hide named anchor icons by clicking View on the Application bar (Win) or Menu bar (Mac), bar, pointing to Visual Aids, and then clicking Invisible Elements.

Creating Internal Links to Named Anchors

Once you create a named anchor, you can create an internal link to it using one of two methods. You can select the text or image on the page that you want to use to make a link, and then drag the Point to File icon from the Property inspector to the named anchor icon on the page. Or, you can select the text or image to which you want to use to make a link, then type # followed by the named anchor name (such as "#top") in the Link text box in the Property inspector.

QUICK **TIP**

To avoid possible errors, you should create a named anchor before you create a link to it.

Figure 8 *Ozark Arts Council website with named anchors*

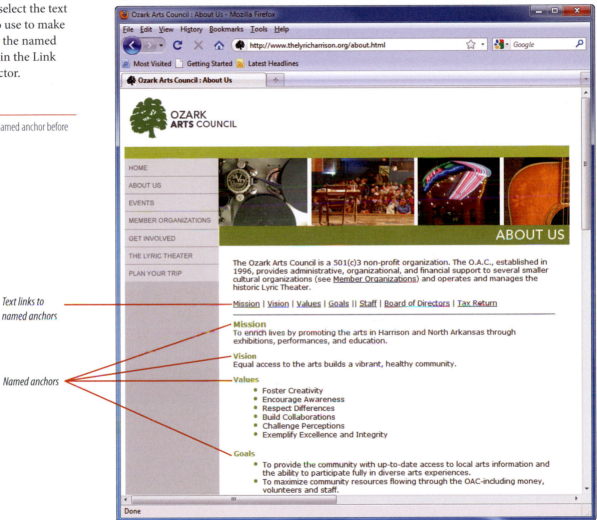

Text links to named anchors

Named anchors

Ozark Arts Council website used with permission from the Ozark Arts Council – www.thelyricharrison.org

Insert a named anchor

1. Open the spa page, click the **banner image** to select it, then press [←] to place the insertion point to the left of the banner.

2. Click **View** on the Application bar (Win) or Menu bar (Mac), point to **Visual Aids,** then verify that Invisible Elements is checked.

TIP If there is no check mark next to Invisible Elements, this feature is turned off. Click Invisible Elements to turn this feature on.

3. Select the Common category on the Insert panel if necessary.

4. Click **Named Anchor** on the Insert panel to open the Named Anchor dialog box, type **top** in the Anchor name text box, compare your screen with Figure 9, then click **OK**.

   An anchor icon now appears before The Striped Umbrella banner. Depending on your window size, the anchor icon might appear above the banner or to the left of the banner.

TIP Use lowercase letters, no spaces, and no special characters in named anchor names. You should also avoid using a number as the first character in a named anchor name.

(continued)

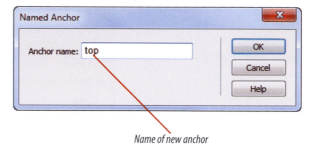

Figure 9 *Named Anchor dialog box*

Name of new anchor

Using Visual Aids

The Visual Aids submenu on the View menu gives you several choices for displaying page elements in Design View, such as named anchor icons. Named anchor icons are considered invisible elements. When you check the Invisible Elements option, you will see the named anchor icons on the page. The icons do not appear when the page is viewed in a browser. Turning on visual aids makes it easier to edit the page. Other options in the Visual Aids menu are CSS Layout Backgrounds, CSS Layout Box Model, CSS Layout Outlines, AP Element Outlines, Table Widths, Table Borders, Frame Borders, and Image Maps. The Hide All option hides all of these page elements. In later chapters, as you work with each page object that these refer to, you will see the advantages of displaying them. The CSS options allow you to see the formatting properties for CSS layout blocks such as the outline, background color, and margins.

Figure 10 *Named anchors on the spa page*

Named anchor icons

Selected named anchor icon

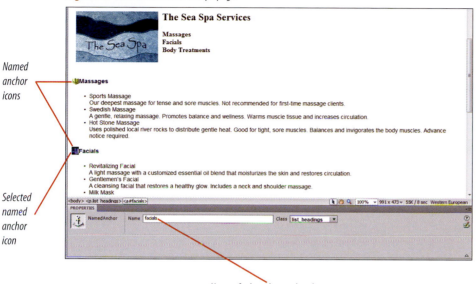

Name of selected named anchor

5. Scroll down to the list of massages, click to the left of the Massages heading, then insert a named anchor named **massages**.

6. Insert named anchors to the left of the Facials and Body Treatments headings using the following names: **facials** and **body_treatments**.

   Your screen should resemble Figure 10.

You created four named anchors on the activities page, one at top of the page, and three that will help viewers quickly access the Spa Services headings on the page.

Create an internal link to a named anchor

1. Select the word "Massages" to the right of The Sea Spa logo, then drag the **Point to File icon** ⊕ from the Property inspector to the anchor next to the massages heading, as shown in Figure 11.

   The word "Massages" is now linked to the Massages named anchor. When viewers click the word "Massages" at the top of the page, the browser will display the Massages heading at the top of the browser window. The Link text box on the Property inspector now reads #massages.

TIP The name of a named anchor is always preceded by a pound (#) sign in the Link text box in the Property inspector.

2. Create internal links for Facials and Body Treatments to the right of The Sea Spa logo by first selecting each of these words or phrases, then dragging the **Point to File icon** ⊕ to the appropriate named anchor icon.

   The words "Facials" and "Body Treatments" are now links that connect to the Facials and Body Treatments headings.

TIP Once you select the text on the page you want to link, you might need to scroll down to view the named anchor on the screen. Once you see the named anchor on your screen, you can drag the Point to File icon on top of it. You can also move the pointer to the edge of the page window (still in the white area of the page) to scroll the page.

(continued)

Figure 11 *Dragging the Point to File icon to a named anchor*

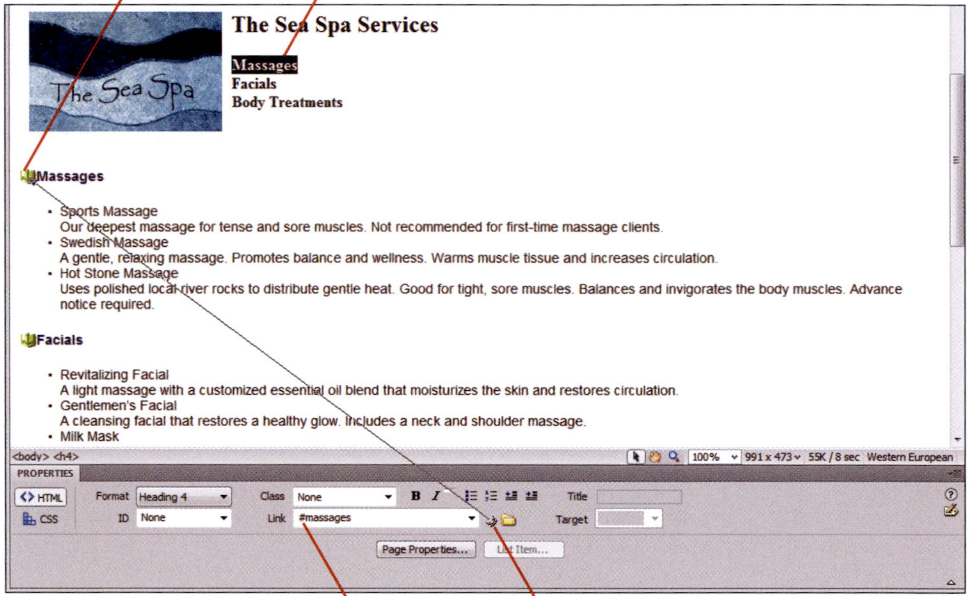

Point to File icon dragged to named anchor

Text to link to named anchor

Named anchor name preceded by # sign

Point to File icon

Figure 12 *Spa page with internal links to named anchors*

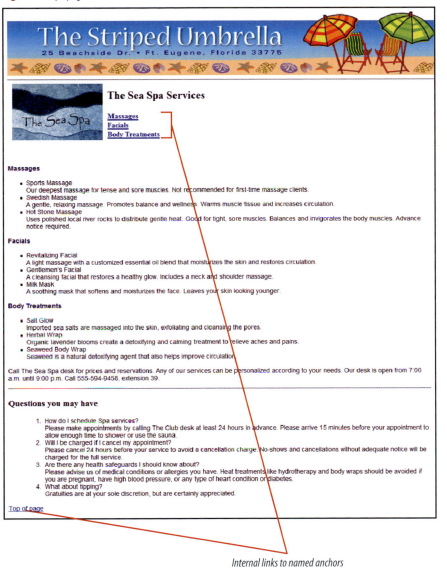

Internal links to named anchors

3. Scroll down to the bottom of the page, then place the insertion point at the end of the last sentence on the page.

4. Press **[Enter]** (Win) or **[return]** (Mac) twice to insert two paragraph breaks, then type **Top of page**.

5. Place the insertion point to the left of the text "Top of page," then click the **Remove Blockquote button** ≛ to move the text to the left margin.

6. Apply the body_text rule to "Top of page" if necessary.

7. Select the text "Top of page", scroll to the top of the page, then use the Point to File icon on the HTML Property inspector to link the text to the anchor named top.

8. Save your work, preview the page in your browser, as shown in Figure 12, then test the links to each named anchor, using the Back button to return to the links.

   When you click the spa packages link in the browser, the associated named anchor may appear in the middle of the page instead of at the top. This happens because the spa page is not long enough to position this named anchor at the top of the page.

9. Close your browser.

You created internal links to the named anchors next to the Spa Services headings and to the top of the spa page. You then previewed the page in your browser and tested each link.

Create, Modify, and
COPY A SPRY MENU BAR

What You'll Do

▶ In this lesson, you will create a menu bar on the spa page that can be used to link to each main page in the website. The menu bar will have five elements: Home, About Us, Cafe, Spa, and Activities. You will also copy the new menu bar to other pages in the website. On each page you will modify the appropriate element state to reflect the current page.

Creating a Spry Menu Bar

To make your website more visually appealing, you can add special effects. For example, you can create a menu bar with rollover images rather than plain text links. One way to do this is to insert a Spry menu bar. A **Spry menu bar** is one of the pre-set widgets available in Dreamweaver that creates a dynamic, user-friendly menu bar that is easy to insert and customize. A **widget** is a piece of code that allows a user to interact with a program, such as clicking a menu item to open a page. Other examples of widgets are interactive buttons, pop-up windows, and progress indicators. **Spry**, or **Spry framework**, is open source code developed by Adobe Systems to help designers quickly incorporate dynamic content on their web pages. To insert a Spry menu bar, click Insert on the Application bar (Win) or Menu bar (Mac), point to Layout Objects, then click Spry Menu Bar. The Insert Spry Menu Bar dialog box appears. You use this dialog box to specify the appearance of the menu bar and each link, called an **item**. When you first insert a Spry menu bar, Dreamweaver automatically assigns it four menu items, some of which have submenu items. If you want your menu

bar to display a different number of menu items and submenu items, you can add new ones and delete the ones you do not need.

You can add special effects for menu bar items by changing the characteristics for each item's state. A **state** is the condition of the item relative to the mouse pointer. You can create a rollover effect for each menu item by using different background and text colors for each state, to represent how the menu item appears when the users move their mouse over it or away from it. You can also create special effects for web page links. The NASA website shown in Figure 13 contains a menu bar that uses rollovers and also contains images that link to featured items in the website.

When you insert a menu bar on a web page using the Insert Spry Menu Bar command, Dreamweaver automatically adds JavaScript code and CSS styles to the page to make the interaction work with the menu bar items. Dreamweaver also creates a SpryAssets folder and adds it to the site root folder. The SpryAssets folder stores the newly created files that make the menu function correctly in the browser. When a viewer views a web page with one of these menu bars, the files that run the menu functions are stored on the user's, or client's, computer.

There are other methods that you can use to create a menu bar with images, such as an image map. You will learn about image maps in Lesson 4.

Copying and Modifying a Menu Bar

After you create a menu bar, you can save time by copying and pasting it to the other main pages in your site. Make sure you place the menu bar in the same position on each page. This practice ensures that the menu

bar will look the same on each page, making it much easier for viewers to navigate to all the pages in your website. If you are even one line or one pixel off, the menu bar will appear to "jump" as it changes position from page to page.

Figure 13 *NASA website*

Menu bar with rollovers

Navigation links with rollovers

Images serving as links

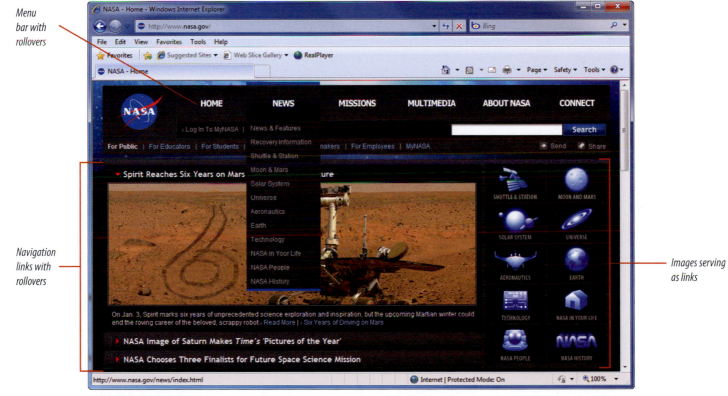

NASA website – www.nasa.gov

Create a Spry menu bar

1. Select the banner on the spa page, press the **right arrow key,** then press **[Shift][Enter]** (Win) or **[Shift][return]** (Mac) to enter a line break after the banner.

    The insertion point is now positioned between the banner and the horizontal rule.

2. Click the **Spry** category on the Insert panel, then click **Spry Menu Bar**.

    TIP The Spry Menu Bar button is also in the Layout category on the Insert panel.

3. Click to select the **Horizontal** layout on the Spry Menu Bar dialog box to specify that the menu bar be placed horizontally on the page, if necessary, as shown in Figure 14, then click **OK**.

    Your new menu bar containing four items appears under the banner. The menu bar is selected and the Property inspector shows its properties. Each button contains placeholder text, such as Item 1.

    TIP If your horizontal rule is not below the menu bar, click to the right of the menu bar, then press [Shift] [Enter] (Win) or [Shift] [return] (Mac) to create another line break, then point to the menu bar and click its Spry MenuBar: MenuBar1 label to select it again. If your menu bar wraps to two lines, this will correct itself when viewed in the browser. Your screen size may not be quite large enough to see all page elements in the Dreamweaver workspace.

4. Type **Menu** in the Menu Bar text box on the Property inspector, then notice that Item 1 is selected in the Item column (first column on the left) in the Property inspector.

    (continued)

Figure 14 *Spry Menu Bar dialog box*

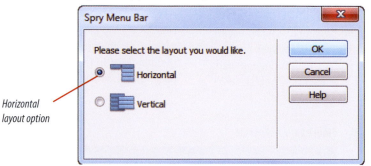

Horizontal
layout option

Inserting a Fireworks Menu Bar

Another option for adding a menu bar to your page is to create a menu bar in Fireworks and import it onto an open page in Dreamweaver. To do this you first create a menu bar in Fireworks and export the file to a Dreamweaver site folder. This file contains the HTML code that defines the menu bar properties. Next, open the page you want to insert it on in Dreamweaver, then use the Insert, Image objects, Fireworks HTML command to place the HTML code on the page. You can also use Dreamweaver to import rollover images and buttons created in Fireworks.

Figure 15 *Property inspector with Menu Bar properties*

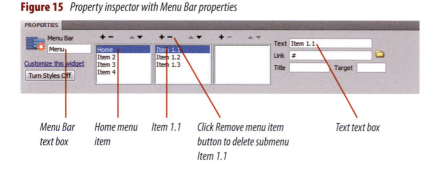

Menu Bar text box   Home menu item   Item 1.1   Click Remove menu item button to delete submenu Item 1.1   Text text box

Figure 16 *Home item on the Menu Bar*

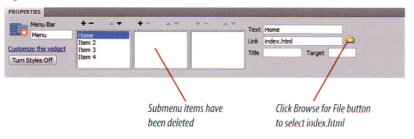

Submenu items have been deleted   Click Browse for File button to select index.html

Figure 17 *The Spry Menu Bar on the spa page*

Spry Menu Bar label   Item 1 is renamed "Home"

Now you are ready to rename the first item, delete its submenu items, and choose the file you want this item to link to.

5. Select Item 1 in the Text text box on the right side of the Property inspector, type **Home**, select Item 1.1 in the first submenu column (second column) in the Property inspector, as shown in Figure 15, then click the **Remove menu item** button ➖ above the first submenu column to delete the submenu item 1.1.

6. Click the **Remove menu item button** ➖ two more times to delete the submenu Item 1.2 and Item 1.3.

   The three submenu items would have appeared as a drop-down menu under the Home menu, but the Home link does not require a submenu, so they can be deleted.

TIP You can add submenu items by clicking the Add menu item button ➕.

7. Click the **Browse for File** button 🗁 next to the Link text box on the Property inspector, then double-click the file **index.html**.

   The Home item is now linked to the index page.

8. Click to place the insertion point to the right of the menu bar, enter a line break, compare your screen to Figures 16 and 17, save your file, then click **OK** to close the Copy Dependent Files dialog box.

   A SpryAssets folder and six files are copied to the site root folder. These are dependent files necessary for the SpryMenu bar. If you don't see them listed, refresh the Files panel.

You used the Insert Spry Menu Bar dialog box to create a menu bar for the spa page and renamed the first item "Home." You deleted the placeholder submenu items under the Home menu item.

Add items to a menu bar

1. Click the Spry Menu Bar tab to select it, click **Item 2** in the first column under the Home item in the Property inspector, then replace the text "Item 2" in the Text text box with **About Us**.

2. Click the **Browse for File button** 📁 next to the Link text box, then double-click **about_us.html** in the site folder to link the About Us menu item to the about_us page.

3. Repeat Steps 1 and 2 to rename Item 3 **Sand Crab Cafe** and link it to the cafe.html page.

4. Delete each submenu item under the Sand Crab Cafe item, clicking **OK** to close the warning box that asks if you want to also remove the submenus, or children menus, under the submenu item.

5. Repeat Steps 1 and 2 to rename Item 4 **The Sea Spa** and link it to the spa.html page.

6. With The Sea Spa menu item selected in the Property inspector, click the **Add menu item button** ➕ above the first column to add an additional menu item, then name it **Activities** and link it to the activities.html page.

7. With the Activities menu item selected, click the **Add menu item button** ➕ above the *second* column to add a submenu item named **Cruises** and link it to the cruises.html page.

8. Repeat Step 7 to add another submenu item named **Fishing** that is linked to the fishing.html page.

9. Save your work, then compare your screen to Figure 18.

TIP If you accidentally created menus, instead of submenus, for Cruises and Fishing, delete them and try again, selecting Activities and adding the items to the second column.

You completed The Striped Umbrella menu bar by adding four more elements to it, each of which contains links to four pages in the site. You then added two submenus under the Activities menu item.

Figure 18 *Menu bar with all menu and submenu items in place*

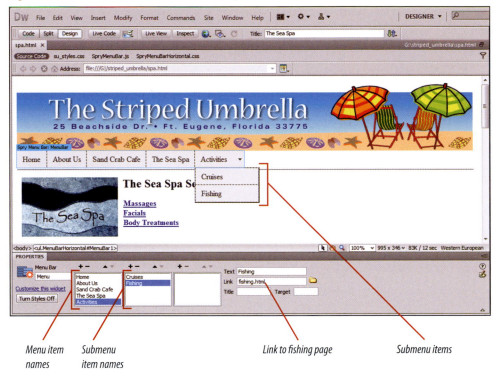

Menu item names

Submenu item names

Link to fishing page

Submenu items

Figure 19 *Settings for .ulMenuBarHorizontal rule*

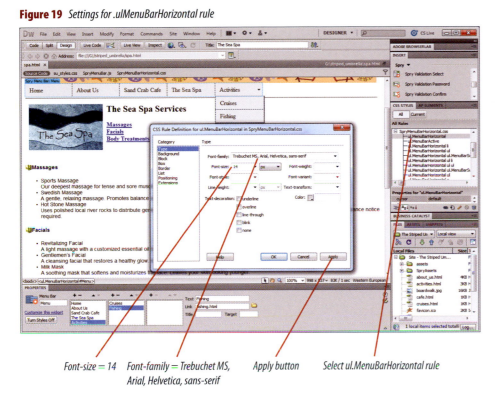

Font-size = 14   Font-family = Trebuchet MS,   Apply button   Select ul.MenuBarHorizontal rule
                  Arial, Helvetica, sans-serif

1. Click the **All button** [All] in the CSS Styles panel if necessary, click the **plus sign** next to SpryMenuBarHorizontal.css in the CSS Styles panel, select the rule ul.MenuBarHorizontal, then click the **Edit Rule** button to open the CSS Rule Definition for ul.MenuBarHorizontal in SpryMenuBarHorizontal.css dialog box.

   The SpryMenuBarHorizontal.css style sheet, which was automatically created when you inserted the Spry menu bar, contains properties for the way the menu items will appear in the browser. In that style sheet, the ul.MenuBarHorizontal rule determines the global settings, including the font family, font size, and font alignment, for all the menu and submenu items, regardless of whether the mouse is placed over them.

   TIP You can also use the Properties pane in the CSS Styles panel to modify style properties.

2. Click the **Type** Category, click the **Font-family** list arrow, then click **Trebuchet MS, Arial, Helvetica, sans-serif.**

3. Click the **Font-size** list arrow, click **14**, click the **Font size unit of measure list arrow**, then click **px** as shown in Figure 19, then click **OK**.

   Next, you set the width and height for each menu item button by modifying the ul.MenuBarHorizontal li rule. Recall that the <li> tag is HTML code for list item. The Spry menu bar is built using unordered list items for each menu item. This rule sets the properties that determine the appearance of the menu items.

   (continued)

4. Select the rule **ul.MenuBarHorizontal li** in the CSS Styles panel, then click the **Edit Rule** button ✎ to open the CSS Rule Definition for ul.MenuBarHorizontal li in SpryMenuBarHorizontal.css dialog box

5. Click the **Box** Category, click the **Width** text box, replace the current value with **190**, click the **Width unit of measure list arrow,** then click **px** if necessary.

TIP To calculate the width for each menu item, divide the number of pixels of the banner width by the number of menu items.

6. Click the **Height** text box, type **25**, click the **Height unit of measure list arrow**, click **px** if necessary, then compare your screen to Figure 20.

   The menu bar items are now spread across the page to equal the width of the banner. Next, you'll edit the rule that defines the properties, and therefore the appearance, of each menu item button when the mouse is not positioned over them.

7. In the Block category, change the Text-align value to **center**, then click **OK**.

8. Click the **ul.MenuBarHorizontal a** rule in the CSS Styles panel, then click the **Edit Rule** button ✎ to open the CSS Rule Definition for ul.MenuBarHorizontal a in SpryMenuBarHorizontal.css dialog box

TIP If you want to understand the function of each rule in the SpryMenuBarHorizontal.css style sheet, click the SpryMenuBarHorizontal.css button in the Related files toolbar and take a few minutes to read the comments for each rule. Click the Show Design View button to return to Design view.

(continued)

Figure 20 *Add properties to the ul.MenuBarHorizontal li rule*

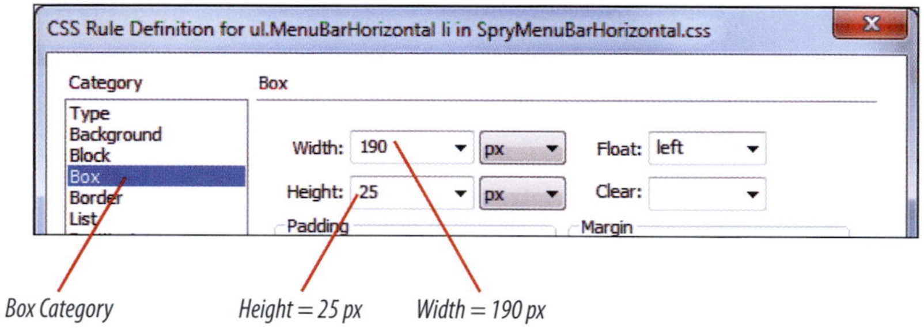

Box Category   Height = 25 px   Width = 190 px

Working with Links and Navigation

Figure 21 *Setting the menu item appearance when the mouse will not be over them*

The named anchor icon may keep the menu bar from lining up right under the banner, but will appear correctly in the browser

9. Click the **Type** Category, type **#FFF** in the Color text box, click the **Background** Category, type **#09C** in the Background-color text box, then click **OK**

   The menu items will have a blue background with white text when the mouse is not positioned over them, as shown in Figure 21. Now you are ready to set the colors the menu bar items will be when users point to (hover their mouse over) a menu item that has submenus (in this case, the Activities button). This rule is the longest one in the style sheet, because it includes properties that determine the appearance of menu items with submenus open. It determines their appearance when the mouse is hovering over them and when the mouse is not hovering over them.

10. Click the longest rule name, **ul.MenuBarHorizontal a.MenuBarItemHover, ul.MenuBarHorizontal a.MenuBarItemSubmenuHover, ul.MenuBarHorizontal a.MenuBarSubmenuVisible** in the CSS Styles panel, then click the **Edit Rule** button 🖉 to open the rule definition dialog box, click the **Type** Category, type **#630** in the Color text box, click the **Background** category, type **#FC9** in the Background-color text box, then click **OK**.

   The menu and submenu items will have a sand background with brown text when the mouse is positioned over them in the browser.

TIP To locate the longest rule, place your mouse over each rule name to see the extended names. You will quickly spot the longest name!

(continued)

11. Save all files, preview your page in the browser, compare your screen to Figure 22, test each link to ensure that each works correctly, then close the browser.

The cafe, cruises, and fishing pages are still blank. You will have to use your Back button after you click these links to return to pages with content.

TIP If you see a message asking if you want to allow blocked content, click yes. The code from the Spry menu bar is being flagged by your Internet security settings.

As you roll the mouse over each menu and submenu item, the background and text colors change.

You edited the properties of four rules in the style sheet that sets the appearance of the menu bar on the page. The appearance of each menu and submenu item changes when the mouse is placed over it.

Figure 22 *Spa page in the browser with the mouse over the About Us item*

Menu item appearance when the mouse is placed over it

Figure 23   *Selecting the menu bar on the spa page*

Click tab to select the menu bar

Figure 24   *The activities page with the completed menu bar*

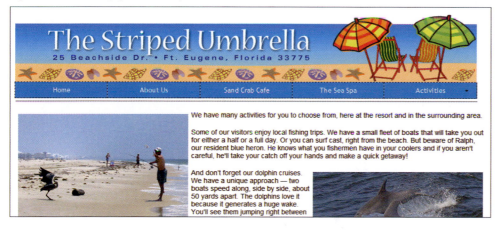

Copy and paste a menu bar

1. Click the **Spry Menu Bar: Menu tab** above the top left corner of the menu bar, as shown in Figure 23.

2. Click **Edit** on the Application bar (Win) or Menu bar (Mac), then click **Copy**.

3. Double-click **activities.html** on the Files panel to open the activities page.

4. Select the original menu bar on the page, click **Edit** on the Application bar (Win) or Menu bar (Mac), click **Paste**, click to the right of the menu bar, enter a line break, compare your screen to Figure 24, then save the page.

5. Open the index page, delete the existing menu bar, paste the new menu bar, add 2 line breaks between the menu bar and horizontal rule if necessary, then save and close the index page.

6. Open the about_us page, replace the existing menu bar with the new menu bar, add 2 line breaks between the menu bar and horizontal rule if necessary, then save your work.

7. Preview the about_us page in your browser, test the menu bar on the home, about_us, spa, and activities pages, then close your browser.

    The cafe, cruises, and fishing pages are blank at this point, so use the Back button when you test those links to return to the page you were viewing previously.

8. Close all open pages except the activities page.

You copied the menu bar on the spa page to three additional pages in The Striped Umbrella website.

Create an
IMAGE MAP

What You'll Do

In this lesson, you will create an image map by placing a hotspot on The Striped Umbrella banner on the activities page that will link to the home page.

Another way to create links for web pages is to combine them with images by creating an image map. An **image map** is an image that has one or more hotspots placed on top of it. A **hotspot** is a clickable area on an image that, when the user clicks it, links to a different location on the page or to another web page. For example, see the National Park Service website shown in Figure 25. When you click a state, you link to information about national parks in that state. You can create hotspots by first selecting the image on which you want to place a hotspot, and then using one of the hotspot tools in the Property inspector to define its shape.

There are several ways to create image maps to make them user-friendly and accessible. One way is to be sure to include alternate text for each hotspot. Another is to draw the hotspot boundaries a little larger than they need to be to cover the area you want to set as a link. This allows viewers a little leeway when they place their mouse over the hotspot by creating a larger target area for them. Always assign a unique name for each image map.

Dreamweaver hotspot tools make creating image maps a snap. In addition to the Rectangle Hotspot Tool, you can create any shape you need using the Circle Hotspot Tool and the Polygon Hotspot Tool. For instance, on a map of the United States, you can draw an outline around each state with the Polygon Hotspot Tool and then make each state "clickable." You can easily change and rearrange hotspots on the image. Use the Pointer Hotspot Tool to select the hotspot you would like to edit. You can drag one of the hotspot selector handles to change its size or shape. You can also move the hotspot by dragging it to a new position on the image. It is a good idea to limit the number of complex hotspots in an image because the code can become too lengthy for the page to download in a reasonable length of time.

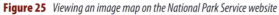

Figure 25 *Viewing an image map on the National Park Service website*

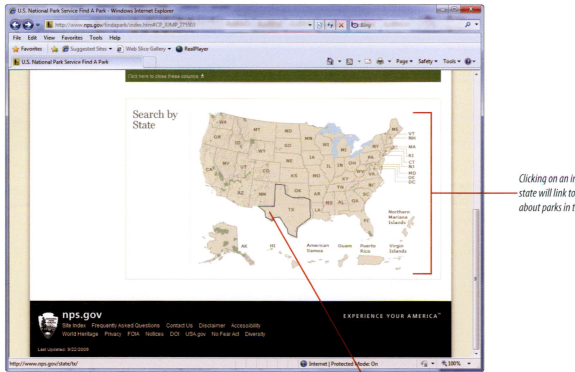

Clicking on an individual state will link to information about parks in that state

National Park Service website – www.nps.gov

Pointing to the Texas image and holding down the mouse button causes the hotspot border to be visible.

Create an image map

1. Select the banner on the activities page, then click the **Rectangle Hotspot Tool** ☐ in the Property inspector.

2. Drag the **pointer** to create a rectangle over the text "The Striped Umbrella" in the banner, as shown in Figure 26, then click **OK** to close the dialog box that reminds you to supply alternate text for the hotspot.

TIP To adjust the shape of a hotspot, click the Pointer Hotspot Tool ▸ in the Property inspector, then drag a sizing handle on the hotspot.

3. Drag the **Point to File icon** ⊕ next to the Link text box in the Property inspector to the index.html file on the Files panel to link the hotspot to the index page.

4. Replace the default text "Map" with **home** in the Map text box in the Property inspector to give the image map a unique name.

5. Click the **Target list arrow** in the Property inspector, then click **_top**.

   When the hotspot is clicked, the _top option causes the home page to open in the same window. See Table 2 for an explanation of the four target options.

   (continued)

Figure 26 *Properties of the hotspot on the banner*

Hotspot

Rectangle Hotspot Tool

TABLE 2: OPTIONS IN THE TARGET LIST	
Target	**Result**
_blank	Displays the destination page in a separate browser window
_parent	Displays the destination page in the parent frameset (replaces the frameset)
_self	Displays the destination page in the same frame or window
_top	Displays the destination page in the whole browser window

Working with Links and Navigation

Figure 27 *Hotspot properties*

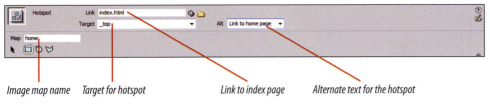

Image map name   Target for hotspot   Link to index page   Alternate text for the hotspot

Figure 28 *Preview of the image map on the activities page in the browser*

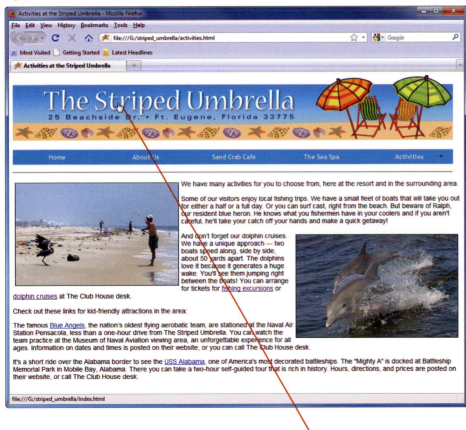

Pointing finger indicates pointer is over the link hotspot

6. Type **Link to home page** in the Alt text box in the Property inspector, as shown in Figure 27, then press **[Enter]** (Win) or **[return]** (Mac).

 You may see a small space between the banner and the menu bar, but it will display correctly in the browser.

7. Save your work, preview the page in your browser, then place the pointer over the image map.

 As you place the pointer over the hotspot, the pointer turns to a pointing finger, indicating that it is a link, as shown in Figure 28.

8. Click the link to test it, close the browser, then close all open pages.

You created an image map on the banner of the activities page using the Rectangle Hotspot Tool. You then linked the hotspot to the home page.

Manage WEBSITE LINKS

▶ *In this lesson, you will use some Dreamweaver reporting features to check The Striped Umbrella website for broken links and orphaned files.*

Managing Website Links

Because the World Wide Web changes constantly, websites might be up one day and down the next. If a website changes server locations or goes down due to technical difficulties or a power failure, the links to it become broken. Broken links, like misspelled words on a web page, indicate that a website is not being maintained diligently.

Checking links to make sure they work is an ongoing and crucial task you need to perform on a regular basis. You must check external links manually by reviewing your website in a browser and clicking each link to make sure it works correctly. The Check Links Sitewide feature is a helpful tool for managing internal links. You can use it to check your entire website for the total number of links and the number of links that are broken, external, or orphaned, and then view the results in the Link Checker panel. **Orphaned files** are files that are not linked to any pages in the website.

DESIGN**TIP**

Using Good Navigation Design

As you work on the navigation structure for a website, you should try to limit the number of links on each page to no more than is necessary. Too many links may confuse visitors to your website. You should also design links so that viewers can reach the information they want within a few clicks. If finding information takes more than three or four clicks, the viewer may become discouraged or "lost" in the site. It's a good idea to provide visual clues on each page to let viewers know where they are, much like a "You are here" marker on a store directory at the mall, or a breadcrumbs trail. A **breadcrumbs trail** is a list of links that provides a path from the initial page you opened in a website to the page that you are currently viewing. Many websites provide a list of all the site's pages, called a **site map**. A site map is similar to an index. It lets viewers see how the information is divided between the pages and helps them locate the information they need quickly.

Figure 29 *Link Checker panel displaying external links*

List of external links   Show list arrow

Figure 30 *Link Checker panel displaying no orphaned files*

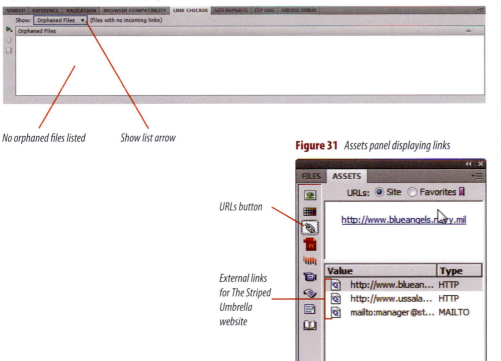

No orphaned files listed   Show list arrow

Figure 31 *Assets panel displaying links*

URLs button

External links for The Striped Umbrella website

Manage website links

1. Click **Site** on the Application bar (Win) or Menu bar (Mac), point to **Advanced**, then click **Recreate Site Cache**.

2. Click **Site** on the Application bar (Win) or Menu bar (Mac), then click **Check Links Sitewide**.

    The Results tab group opens, with the Link Checker panel in front. By default, the Link Checker panel initially lists any broken internal links found in the website. The Striped Umbrella website has no broken links.

3. Click the **Show list arrow** in the Link Checker panel, click **External Links**, then compare your screen to Figure 29.

4. Click the **Show list arrow**, then click **Orphaned Files** to view the orphaned files in the Link Checker panel, as shown in Figure 30.

    The Striped Umbrella website has no orphaned files.

5. Right-click (Win) or Control-click (Mac) in an empty area of the Results tab group title bar, then click **Close tab group**.

6. Display the Assets panel if necessary, then click the **URLs button** 🗋 in the Assets panel if necessary to display the list of links in the website.

    The Assets panel displays the external links used in the website, as shown in Figure 31.

You used the Link Checker panel to check for broken links, external links, and orphaned files in The Striped Umbrella website. You also viewed the external links in the Assets panel.

Update a page

1. Open dw5_2.html from the drive and folder where you store your Data Files, then save it as **fishing.html** in the striped_umbrella site root folder, overwriting the existing fishing page, but not updating the links.

2. Click the broken link image placeholder, click the **Browse for File icon**  next to the Src text box in the Property inspector, then browse to the drive and folder where you store your Data Files, open the assets folder, then select the file heron_small.jpg to copy the file to the striped_umbrella assets folder.

3. Deselect the image placeholder and the image appears, as shown in Figure 32.

    The text is automatically updated with the body_text style. The code was already in place on the page linking su_styles.css to the file. The Spry menu bar was also updated with the internal styles already in place for the menu bar.

4. Save and close the fishing page, then close the dw5_2.html page.

5. Open dw5_3.html from the drive and folder where you store your Data Files, then save it as **cruises.html** in the striped_umbrella site root folder, overwriting the existing cruises page, but not updating the links.

6. Click the broken link graphic placeholder, click the **Browse for File icon** next to the Src text box in the Property inspector, then browse to the drive and folder where you store your Data Files, open the assets folder, then select the file boats.jpg to copy the file to the striped_umbrella assets folder.

(continued)

Figure 32 *Fishing page updated*

As you can see, Ralph scores occasionally. We certainly don't encourage you to feed Ralph. We feel it is important to intrude as little as possible with our wild friends and their diets. Just don't be surprised if you see him roaming the beach trying to blend in with the other fishermen.

Testing Your Website Against the Wireframe

Another test you should be running regularly is a comparison of how your developing website pages are meeting the specifications of your wireframe prototype. Compare each completed page against its corresponding wireframe to make sure that all page elements have been placed in their proper locations on the page. Verify that all specified links have been included and test them to make sure that they work correctly. You might also consider hiring site-usability testers to test your site navigation. A site usability test provides impartial feedback on how intuitive and user-friendly your site is to use.

Figure 33 *Cruises page updated*

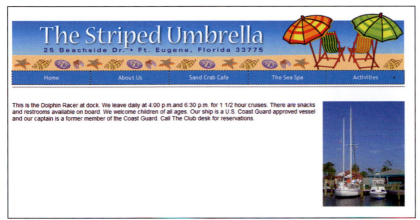

7. Deselect the image placeholder and the image will appear as shown in Figure 33.

   The text is automatically updated with the body_text style. The code was already in place on the page linking su_styles.css to the file. The Spry menu bar was also updated as the internal styles were applied.

8. Save your work if necessary.

9. Preview each page in the browser, close the browser, then close all open pages.

You added content to two previously blank pages in the website and previewed each page to check for consistent layout.

POWER USER SHORTCUTS	
To do this:	**Use this shortcut:**
Close a file	[Ctrl][W] (Win) or ⌘ [W] (Mac)
Close all files	[Ctrl][Shift][W] (Win) or ⌘ [Shift][W] (Mac)
Print code	[Ctrl][P] (Win) or ⌘ [P] (Mac)
Check page links	[Shift][F8] (Win) or [fn][shift][F8] (Mac)
Undo	[Ctrl][Z], [Alt][BkSp] (Win) or ⌘ [Z], [option][delete] (Mac)
Redo	[Ctrl][Y], [Ctrl][Shift][Z] (Win) or ⌘ [Y], ⌘ [Shift][Z] (Mac)
Refresh Design view	[F5]
Hide all visual aids	[Ctrl][Shift][I] (Win) or ⌘ [Shift][I] (Mac)
Insert a named anchor	[Ctrl][Alt][A] (Win) or ⌘ [option][A] (Mac)
Make a link	[Ctrl][L] (Win) or ⌘ [L] (Mac)
Remove a link	[Ctrl][Shift][L] (Win) or ⌘ [Shift][L] (Mac)
Check links sitewide	[Ctrl][F8] (Win) or [fn] ⌘ [F8] (Mac)
Show Files tab group	[F8] (Win) or ⌘ [Shift][F] (Mac)

Incorporate Web 2.0
TECHNOLOGY

What You'll Do

In this lesson, you will explore some of the Web 2.0 applications that can be used to engage website viewers.

What Exactly is Web 2.0?

The term **Web 2.0** describes the recent evolution of web applications that facilitate and promote information sharing among Internet users. These applications not only reside on computers, but on cell phones, in cars, on portable GPS devices, and in game devices. **GPS (Global Positioning System)** devices are used to track your position through a global satellite navigation system, and are popular to use for driving directions, hiking, and map making. Web 2.0 applications do not simply display information for viewers to read passively; they allow viewers to actively contribute to the content.

RSS feeds are another easy way to share information with viewers. **RSS** stands for **Really Simple Syndication**. Websites use **RSS feeds** to distribute news stories, information about upcoming events, and announcements. Web users can subscribe to RSS feeds to receive regular releases of information from a site. Users can download and play these digitally broadcasted files called **podcasts (Programming On Demand)** using devices such as computers or MP3 players. Many news organizations and educational institutions publish both audio

and video podcasts. Video podcasts are referred to as **vodcasts** or **vidcasts**.

Web 2.0 also includes the ever-increasing use of social networking. **Social networking** refers to any web-based service that facilitates social interaction among users. Examples of social networking sites include **Facebook** and **MySpace**. These sites allow users to set up profile pages and post information on them for others to view. Facebook and MySpace pages often contain lots of text, images, and videos. To fully view and post to an individual's page, you must be accepted by that person as a "friend," which lets you control who has access to your page content.

A wiki is another example of a Web 2.0 application. The term **wiki** (named for the Hawaiian word for "quick") refers to a site where a user can use simple editing tools to contribute and edit the page content in a site. A good example is **Wikipedia**, an online encyclopedia. Wikipedia allows viewers to post new information and edit existing information on any topic. Although people have different opinions about the academic integrity of the information on Wikipedia, Wikipedia is still a rich source of information. Proponents argue that its many active and vigilant users maintain its information integrity.

Blogs (web logs) are another example of a Web 2.0 application. **Blogs** are websites where the website owner regularly posts commentaries and opinions on various topics. Content can consist of text, video, or images. Viewers can respond to the postings and read postings by other viewers. **Twitter** is a website where viewers can post short messages, called **tweets**. Twitter is considered a blog or a micro blog, because you cannot enter more than 140 characters in each post. To use Twitter, you must first join by creating a free account. Then you can post messages about yourself, "follow" other people's tweets, and invite others to "follow" you. It is a quick and easy way to exchange short bits of information and keep in touch with friends.

There are many video sharing applications such as Skype, Google Video Chat, and YouTube. **Skype** and **Google Video Chat** are free applications that you use to communicate live with other people through video conferencing, using a high-speed Internet connection and a web camera, called a **web cam**. You can also use Skype or Google Chat to make regular telephone calls over the Internet. **YouTube** is a website where you can upload and share videos. To upload videos, you need to register with the site. But you don't need to register if you only want to view videos others have posted.

So how do these various Web 2.0 components relate to the process of creating websites? Most websites today engage their viewers or "users" of their site in one or more of these applications. The Peace Corps website, shown in Figure 34, has links to Facebook, Twitter, YouTube, and RSS Feeds. When you are designing a site, one of the decisions you must make is not if, but how you will incorporate Web 2.0 technology to fully engage your viewers. To incorporate one of these applications into your website, first register to set up an account on the social networking site, then place a link on one of your site's web pages (usually the home page) that links to the social networking site and opens your page. For example, if your Twitter account is located at www.twitter.com/your_name, add this link to your home page using the Twitter logo as a graphic link. You can download social networking sites' logos from their websites. You can also enter plain text links if you prefer. Some applications specify how you should refer to and link to their site.

Using the applications that are a part of Web 2.0 with your website can bring your site from simply presenting information on pages for viewers to read to facilitating a compelling dialog with your viewers. They will no longer be just "viewers," but active participants.

Figure 34 *Viewing social networking links on the Peace Corps website*

Links to Facebook, Twitter, YouTube, RSS Feeds

Peace Corps website – www.peacecorps.gov

Create external and internal links.

1. Open the Blooms & Bulbs website.
2. Open dw5_4.html from the drive and folder where you store your Data Files, then save it as **newsletter.html** in the Blooms & Bulbs website, overwriting the existing file without updating the links. Close dw5_4.html.
3. Verify that the banner path is set correctly to the assets folder in the website and correct it, if it is not, then browse to the drive and folder where you store your Chapter 5 Data Files assets folder and copy the grass, trees, and plants broken images to the site assets folder.
4. Scroll to the bottom of the page, then link the National Gardening Association text to http://www.garden.org.
5. Link the Organic Gardening text to http://www.organicgardening.com.
6. Link the Southern Living text to http://www.southernliving.com/southern.
7. Save the file, then preview the page in your browser, verifying that each link works correctly.
8. Close your browser, then return to the newsletter page in Dreamweaver.
9. Scroll to the paragraph about gardening issues, select the gardening tips text in the last sentence, then link the selected text to the tips.html file in the blooms site root folder.
10. Enter the page title **Gardening Matters,** then save your work.
11. Open the plants page and add a new paragraph to the bottom of the page: **In addition to these marvelous roses, we have many annuals, perennials, and water plants that have just arrived**.

12. Apply the paragraph_text rule to the new paragraph if necessary.
13. Link the "annuals" text to the annuals.html file, link the "perennials" text to the perennials.html file, and the "water plants" text to the water_plants.html file.
14. Save your work, test the links in your browser, then close your browser. (*Hint*: These pages do not have content yet, but are serving as placeholders.)

Create internal links to named anchors.

1. Show Invisible Elements, if necessary.
2. Click the Common category in the Insert panel.
3. Switch to the newsletter page, then insert a named anchor in front of the Grass heading named **grass**.
4. Insert a named anchor in front of the Trees heading named **trees**.
5. Insert a named anchor in front of the Plants heading named **plants**.
6. Use the Point to File icon in the Property inspector to create a link from the word "grass" in the Gardening Issues paragraph to the anchor named "grass."
7. Create a link from the word "trees" in the Gardening Issues paragraph to the anchor named "trees."
8. Create a link from the word "plants" in the Gardening Issues paragraph to the anchor named "plants."
9. Save your work, view the page in your browser, test all the links to make sure they work, then close your browser.

Create, modify, and copy a Spry menu bar.

1. Select the banner, press the right arrow key, enter a line break, click the Spry category on the Insert panel, then click Spry Menu Bar to insert a horizontal Spry menu bar at the top of the newsletter page below the banner and

above the horizontal rule. Add two paragraph breaks to separate the menu bar from the horizontal rule.
2. Select Item 1 in the Property inspector if necessary, remove the three submenu items under Item 1, type **Home** in the Text text box, then browse to link the Home menu item to the **index.html** file.
3. Select Item 2, then replace the text name with **Newsletter** and link it to the **newsletter.html** file.
4. Repeat Step 3 to rename Item 3 **Plants** and link it to the **plants.html** file.
5. Select the submenu Item 3.1, rename it **Annuals**, link it to the **annuals.html** file, then delete the submenu items under the Annuals submenu item.
6. Repeat Step 5 to rename Item 3.2 **Perennials**, then link it to the **perennials.html** file.
7. Repeat Step 5 to rename Item 3.3 **Water Plants**, then link it to the **water_plants.html** file.
8. Select the Item 4 menu item, rename it **Tips**, then link it to the **tips.html** file.
9. Add a new menu item named **Workshops**, then link it to the **workshops.html** file.
10. Edit the ul.MenuBarHorizontal rule to change the Font-family to **Verdana, Geneva, sans-serif**, and the Font-size to **14 px**.
11. Edit the u.MenuBarHorizontal li to set the Text-align to **Center**, the Box width to **190 px** and the Box height to **25 px**.
12. Edit the ul.MenuBarHorizontal a rule to change the Type color to **#030** and the background color to **#99F**.
13. Edit the ul.MenuBarHorizontal a.MenuBarItemHover, ul.MenuBarHorizontal a.MenuBarItemSubmenuHover, ul.MenuBarHorizontal a.MenuBarSubmenuVisible

rule to change the Type color to **#FFC** and the background color to **#030**.

14. Save all files, copying dependent files, test each link in the browser to make sure the links work correctly, then close the browser.

15. Select and copy the menu bar, then open the home page.

16. Delete the current menu bar on the home page, and paste the new menu bar under the banner, but above the horizontal rule. Remove any space between the banner and menu bar if necessary. (*Hint*: If you see space between the banner and the menu bar, go to Code view and check to make sure that you used a <br /> tag between the banner and the menu bar.)

17. Save and close the page, switch to the plants page, then copy the menu bar to the page in the same position under the banner.

18. Add a horizontal rule under the banner, then save and close the page. (*Hint*: Make sure the spacing between the banner and the horizontal rule is the same as on the index and newsletter pages. Use Code view to check for any differences and correct them.)

19. Open the tips page and repeat Steps 17 and 18 to add the menu bar and horizontal rule to the page.

20. Save and close the tips page.

21. Save your work, preview all the pages in your browser, compare your newsletter page to Figure 35, test all the links, then close your browser.

Figure 35 *Completed Skills Review*

Blooms & Bulbs
HWY 43 SOUTH • ALVIN • TX 77511 • 555-248-0806

Home   Newsletter   Plants   •   Tips   Workshops

Gardening Matters

Welcome, fellow gardeners. My name is Cosie Simmons, the owner of blooms & bulbs. My passion has always been my gardens. Ever since I was a small child, I was drawn to my back yard where all varieties of beautiful plants flourished. A lush carpet of thick grass bordered with graceful beds is truly a haven for all living creatures. With proper planning and care, your gardens will draw a variety of birds and butterflies and become a great pleasure to you.

Gardening Issues

There are several areas to concentrate on when formulating your landscaping plans. One is your grass. Another is the number and variety of trees you plant. The third is the combination of plants you select. All of these decisions should be considered in relation to the climate in your area. Be sure and check out our gardening tips before you begin work.

Grass

Lawn experts classify grass into two categories: cool-climate and warm-climate. The northern half of the United States would be considered cool-climate. Examples of cool-climate grass are Kentucky bluegrass and ryegrass. Bermuda grass is a warm-climate grass. Before planting grass, whether by seeding, sodding, sprigging, or plugging, the ground must be properly prepared. The soil should be tested for any nutritional deficiencies and cultivated. Come by or call to make arrangements to have your soil tested. When selecting a lawn, avoid letting personal preferences and the cost of establishment be the overriding factors. Ask yourself these questions: What type of lawn are you expecting? What level of maintenance are you willing to provide? What are the site limitations?

Trees

Before you plant trees, you should evaluate your purpose. Are you interested in shade, privacy, or color? Do you want to attract wildlife? Attract birds? Create a shady play area? Your purpose will determine what variety of tree you should plant. Of course, you also need to consider your climate and available space. Shape is especially important in selecting trees for ornamental and shade purposes. Abundant shade comes from tall trees with long spreading or weeping branches. Ornamental trees will not provide abundant shade. We carry many varieties of trees and are happy to help you make your selections to fit your purpose.

Plants

There are so many types of plants available that it can become overwhelming. Do you want border plants, shrubs, ground covers, annuals, perennials, vegetables, fruits, vines, or bulbs? In reality, a combination of several of these works well. Design aspects such as balance, flow, definition of space and focalization should be considered. Annuals provide brilliant bursts of color in the garden. By selecting flowers carefully to fit the conditions of the site, it is possible to have a beautiful display without an unnecessary amount of work. Annuals are also great as fresh and dry cut flowers. Perennials can greatly improve the quality of your landscape. Perennials have come and gone in popularity, but today are as popular as ever. Water plants are also quite popular now. We will be happy to help you sort out your preferences and select a harmonious combination of plants for you.

Further Research

These are some of my favorite gardening links. Take the time to browse through some of the information they offer, then give me a call at (555) 248-0806 or e-mail me at cosie@blooms&bulbs.com.

National Gardening Association
Organic Gardening
Southern Living

Create an image map.

1. Use the Rectangle Hotspot Tool to draw an image map across the name "Blooms & Bulbs", on the banner on the newsletter page that will link to the home page.
2. Name the image map **home** and set the target to _top.
3. Add the alternate text **Link to home page**, save the page, then preview it in the browser to test the link. (*Hint*: You might see a small space between the banner and menu bar, but it will display correctly in the browser.)
4. Close the page.

Manage website links.

1. Use the Link Checker panel to view and fix broken links and orphaned files in the blooms & bulbs website. (*Hint*: Remember to recreate your site cache if you see any. That usually fixes them.)
2. Open dw5_5.html from the drive and folder where you store your Data Files, then save it as **annuals.html**, replacing the original file. Do not update links, but save the file coleus.jpg from the Chapter 5 Data Files assets folder in the assets folder of the website. Close dw5_5.html.
3. Repeat Step 2 using dw5_6.html to replace perennials.html, saving the ruby_grass.jpg file in the assets folder and using dw5_7.html to replace water_plants.html, saving the water_lily.jpg file in the assets folder.
4. Save your work, then close all open pages.

Use Figure 36 as a guide to continue your work on the TripSmart website, which you began in Project Builder 1 in Chapter 1 and developed in the previous chapters. You have been asked to create a new page for the website that lists helpful links for customers. You will also add content to the destinations, china, and spain pages.

1. Open the TripSmart website.
2. Open dw5_8.html from the drive and folder where you store your Data Files, then save it as **services.html** in the TripSmart website root folder, replacing the existing file and not updating links. Close dw5_8.html.
3. Verify that the TripSmart banner is in the assets folder of the site root folder.
4. Apply the paragraph_text rule to the paragraphs of text and the list_heading rule to the four main paragraph headings.

5. Create named anchors named **reservations**, **outfitters**, **tours**, and **links** in front of the respective headings on the page, then link each named anchor to "Reservations," "Travel Outfitters," "Escorted Tours," and "Helpful Links in Travel Planning" in the first paragraph.
6. Link the text "on-line catalog" in the Travel Outfitters paragraph to the catalog.html page.
7. Link the text "CNN Travel Channel" under the heading Helpful Links in Travel Planning to http://www.cnn.com/TRAVEL.
8. Repeat Step 7 to create links for the rest of the websites listed:
   U.S. Department of State: http://travel.state.gov
   Yahoo! Currency Converter:
   http://finance.yahoo.com/currency-converter
   The Weather Channel: http://www.weather.com

9. Save the services page, preview the page in the browser to test each link, then open the index page.
10. Replace the menu bar on the home page with a horizontal Spry menu bar, using formatting of your choice. The menu bar should contain the following elements: **Home**, **Catalog**, **Services**, **Tours**, and **Newsletter**. Figure 36 shows one example of a possible menu bar. Create two submenu items for the china and spain pages under the tours menu item, then delete all other submenu items.
11. Test the menu bar links in the browser, then close the browser and correct any errors you find.
12. Copy the menu bar, then place it on each completed page of the website.
13. Save each page, then check for broken links and orphaned files.

14. Open the tours.html file in your site root folder and save it as **spain.html**, overwriting the existing file, then close the file.

15. Open dw5_9.html from the drive and folder where you store your Data Files, then save it as **china.html**, overwriting the existing file. Do not update links, but save the warriors.jpg and great_wall.jpg files from the data files folder in the assets folder of the website, then save and close the file. Close dw5_9.html.

16. Open dw5_10.html from the driver and folder where you store your Data Files, then save the file as **tours.html**, overwriting the existing file. Do not update links, but save the panda.jpg and gaudi_dragon.jpg files from the data files folder in the assets folder of the website. Close dw5_10.html.

17. Link the text "Spain" in the second sentence of the first paragraph on the tours page to the spain.html file.

18. Link the text "China" in the first sentence in the second paragraph on the tours page to the china.html file.

19. Save all files and preview them in the browser, checking to see that all links work and all pages have a consistent look.

20. Compare your tours page to Figure 36, close your browser, then close all open pages.

Figure 36 *Sample Project Builder 1*

You are continuing your work on the Carolyne's Creations website, which you started in Project Builder 2 in Chapter 1 and developed in the previous chapters. Chef Carolyne has asked you to create a page describing her cooking classes offered every month. You will create the content for that page and individual pages describing the children's classes and the adult classes. Refer to Figures 37, 38, and 39 for possible solutions.

1. Open the Carolyne's Creations website.
2. Open dw5_11.html from the drive and folder where you store your Data Files, save it as **classes.html** in the site root folder of the Carolyne's Creations website, overwriting the existing file and not updating the links. Close dw5_11.html.
3. Select the broken banner image, browse to the data files folder, then select the new banner, cc_banner_with_text.jpg, then verify that it was saved to the site assets folder. Notice that styles have already been applied to the page text, the data file included a relative link to the style sheet.
4. Select the text "adults' class" in the last paragraph, then link it to the adults.html page. (*Hint*: This page has not been developed yet.)
5. Select the text "children's class" in the last paragraph and link it to the children.html page. (*Hint*: This page has not been developed yet.)
6. Create an e-mail link from the text "Sign me up!" that links to **carolyne@carolynescreations.com**
7. Insert the image file fish.jpg from the assets folder where you store your Data Files at the beginning of the second paragraph, add appropriate alternate text, then choose your own alignment and formatting settings.
8. Add the image file children_cooking.jpg from the assets folder where you store your Data Files at the beginning of the third paragraph, then choose your own alignment and formatting settings.
9. Create hot spots on the black bar at the bottom of the new banner that was imported with the data file, cc_banner_with_text.jpg, that link each menu item with its corresponding page. (*Hint*: Remember to include alternate text and a target for each menu item.)
10. Compare your work to Figure 37 for a possible solution, copy the new banner, then save and close the file.
11. Open dw5_12.html from the drive and folder where you store your Data Files, then save it as **children.html,** overwriting the existing file and not updating links. Save the image cookies_oven.jpg from the assets folder where you store your Data Files to the website assets folder. Close dw5_12.html.

Figure 37 *Completed Project Builder 2*

Cooking Classes are fun!

Chef Carolyne loves to offer a fun and relaxing cooking school each month in her newly refurbished kitchen. She teaches an **adult class** on the fourth Saturday of each month from 6:00 to 8:00 pm. Each class will learn to cook a complete dinner and then enjoy the meal at the end of the class with a wonderful wine pairing. This is a great chance to get together with friends for a fun evening.

Chef Caroline also teaches a **children's class** on the second Tuesday of each month from 4:00 to 5:30 pm. Our young chefs will learn to cook two dishes that will accompany a full meal served at 5:30 pm. Kids aged 5–8 years accompanied by an adult are welcome. We also host small birthday parties where we put the guests to work baking and decorating the cake! Call for times and prices.

We offer several special adult classes throughout the year. The **Valentine Chocolate Extravaganza** is a particular favorite. You will learn to dip strawberries, make truffles, and bake a sinful Triple Chocolate Dare You Torte. We also host the **Not So Traditional Thanksgiving** class and the **Super Bowl Snacks** class each year with rave reviews. Watch the Web site for details!

Prices are $40.00 for each adults' class and $15.00 for each children's class. Sign up for classes by calling 555-963-8271 or by emailing us: Sign me up!

See what's cooking this month for the adults' class and children's class.

12. Paste your new banner on the children.html page, replacing the previous banner, compare your work to Figure 38 for a possible solution, then save and close the file.

13. Repeat Steps 11 and 12 to open the dw5_13.html file and save it as **adults.html**, overwriting the existing file and saving the files dumplings1.jpg, dumplings2.jpg, and dumplings3.jpg from the folder where you save your data files in the assets folder, then use alignment settings of your choice. Replace the banner with your new banner, compare your work to Figure 39 for a possible solution, then save and close the files.

14. Open the index page and delete the menu bar and horizontal rule.

15. Replace the banner with your new banner.

16. Copy the new banner with the menu bar to each completed page, deleting existing menu bars and banners.

17. Save all the pages, then check for broken links and orphaned files. You will see one orphaned file, the original version of the banner. Delete this file.

18. Apply a rule from the style sheet to any text that is not formatted with a style.

19. Preview all the pages in your browser, check to make sure the links work correctly, close your browser, then close all open pages.

Figure 38 *Completed Project Builder 2*

Children's Cooking Class for March: Oven Chicken Fingers, Chocolate Chip Cookies

This month we will be baking oven chicken fingers that are dipped in a milk and egg mixture, then coated with breadcrumbs. The chocolate chip cookies are based on a famous recipe that includes chocolate chips, M&Ms, oatmeal, and pecans. Yummy! We will be learning some of the basics like how to cream butter and crack eggs without dropping shells into the batter.

We will provide French fries, green beans, fruit salad, and a beverage to accompany the chicken fingers.

Figure 39 *Completed Project Builder 2*

Adult Cooking Class for March: Chinese Cuisine

The class in March will be cooking several traditional Chinese dishes: Peking dumplings, wonton soup, fried rice, Chinese vegetables, and shrimp with lobster sauce. For dessert: banana spring rolls.

This looks easier than it is! Chef Carolyne is demonstrating the first steps in making Chinese dumplings, known as *jiaozi* (pronounced geeow dz). Notice that she is using a traditional wooden rolling pin to roll out the dough. These dumplings were stuffed with pork and then steamed, although other popular fillings are made with chicken and leeks or vegetables with spiced tofu and cellophane noodles. Dumplings can be steamed, boiled, or fried, and have unique names depending on the preparation method.

Sherrill Simmons is a university English instructor. She would like to find new ways to engage her students through her university website. She decided to explore incorporating podcasts, FaceBook, and Twitter. She spends several hours looking at other websites to help her get started.

1. Connect to the Internet, then navigate to the Shiloh Museum website pictured in Figure 40 at www.springdalear.gov/shiloh. This site won the Media & Technology Committee of the American Association of Museums 2008 Bronze MUSE Award for one of their vodcasts. There have been over 25,000 downloads since they began offering podcasting in May of 2006. Their iTunes U content has been downloaded over 14,000 times since June of 2008.

2. How do you think podcasting has enhanced the museum website?

Figure 40 *Design Project*

Shiloh Museum website used with permission from the Shiloh Museum of Ozark History, Springdale, Arkansas – www.springdalear.gov/shiloh

3. Navigate to the U.S. Navy website at www.navy.mil, as shown in Figure 41.
4. Describe how the Navy is using Web 2.0 technology. What do you think their purpose might be for incorporating each application?
5. Which Web 2.0 applications would you include on your website if you were Sherrill?
6. Describe how you would use each one of them to engage her students.

Figure 41 *Design Project*

U.S. Navy website – www.navy.mil

In this assignment, you will continue to work on the website that you started in Chapter 1 and developed in the previous chapters.

You will continue building your website by designing and completing a page with a menu bar. After creating the menu bar, you will copy it to each completed page in the website. In addition to the menu bar, you will add several external links and several internal links to other pages as well as to named anchors. You will also link text to a named anchor. After you complete this work, you will check for broken links and orphaned files.

1. Consult your wireframe to decide which page or pages you would like to develop in this chapter. Decide how to design and where to place the menu bar, named anchors, and any additional page elements you decide to use. Decide which reports should be run on the website to check for accuracy.

2. Research websites that could be included on one or more of your pages as external links of interest to your viewers. Create a list of the external links you want to use. Using your wireframe as a guide, decide where each external link should be placed in the site.

3. Add the external links to existing pages or create any additional pages that contain external links.

4. Create named anchors for key locations on the page, such as the top of the page, then link appropriate text on the page to them.

5. Decide on a design for a menu bar that will be used on all pages of the website.

6. Create the menu bar and copy it to all finished pages on the website.

7. Think of a good place to incorporate an image map, then add it to a page.

8. Decide on at least one Web 2.0 application that you might like to incorporate and determine how and on what page they would be included.

9. Use the Link Checker panel to check for broken links and orphaned files.

10. Use the checklist in Figure 42 to make sure your website is complete, save your work, then close all open pages.

Figure 42 *Portfilio Project checklist*

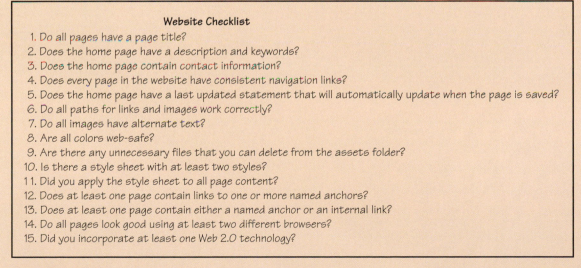

Website Checklist

1. Do all pages have a page title?
2. Does the home page have a description and keywords?
3. Does the home page contain contact information?
4. Does every page in the website have consistent navigation links?
5. Does the home page have a last updated statement that will automatically update when the page is saved?
6. Do all paths for links and images work correctly?
7. Do all images have alternate text?
8. Are all colors web-safe?
9. Are there any unnecessary files that you can delete from the assets folder?
10. Is there a style sheet with at least two styles?
11. Did you apply the style sheet to all page content?
12. Does at least one page contain links to one or more named anchors?
13. Does at least one page contain either a named anchor or an internal link?
14. Do all pages look good using at least two different browsers?
15. Did you incorporate at least one Web 2.0 technology?

CHAPTER 6

POSITIONING OBJECTS
WITH CSS AND TABLES

1. Create a page using CSS layouts
2. Add content to CSS layout blocks
3. Edit content in CSS layout blocks
4. Create a table
5. Resize, split, and merge cells
6. Insert and align images in table cells
7. Insert text and format cell content

6 POSITIONING OBJECTS WITH CSS AND TABLES

Introduction

To create an organized, attractive web page, you need precise control of the position of page elements. CSS page layouts can provide this control. **CSS page layouts** consist of containers formatted with CSS into which you place web page content. These containers can accommodate images, blocks of text, Flash movies, or any other page element. The appearance and position of the containers are set through the use of HTML tags known as **div tags**. Using div tags, you can position elements next to each other as well as on top of each other.

Another option for controlling the placement of page elements is through the use of tables. **Tables** are placeholders made up of small boxes called **cells**, into which you can insert text and graphics. Cells in a table are arranged horizontally in **rows** and vertically in **columns**. Using tables on a web page gives you control over the placement of each object on the page, similar to the way CSS blocks control placement. In this chapter, you use a predesigned CSS page layout with div tags to place text and graphics on a page. You then add a table to one of the CSS blocks on the page.

Using Div Tags Versus Tables for Page Layout

Div tags and tables both enable you to control the appearance of content in your web pages. Unlike tables, div tags allow you to stack your information, allowing for one piece of information to be visible at a time. Tables are static, which makes it difficult to change them quickly as need arises. Div tags can be dynamic, changing in response to variables such as a mouse click. You can create dynamic div tags using JavaScript **behaviors**, simple action scripts that let you incorporate interactivity by modifying content based on variables like user actions. For example, you could add a JavaScript behavior to text in a div tag to make it become larger or smaller when the pointer is over it.

There has been much discussion since the inception of CSS about which tool is better—CSS layouts or table layouts. Both have advantages and disadvantages, but designers tend to prefer CSS layouts for page design and tables for placing lists of data. In practice, many designers use a combination of both tools, choosing the tool that is the better suited to the current design challenge.

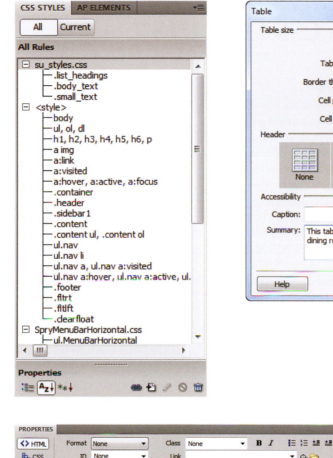

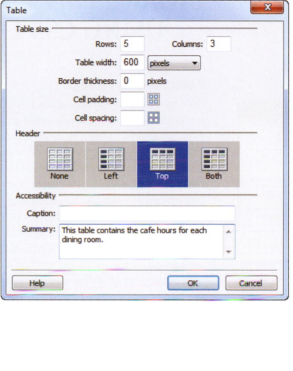

Create a Page
USING CSS LAYOUTS

What You'll Do

Insert_logo (180 x 90)	
Link one	**Instructions**
Link two	
Link three	Be aware that the CSS for these layouts is heavily commented. If you do most of your work in Design view, have a peek at the code to get tips on working with the CSS for the fixed layouts.
Link four	
The above links demonstrate a basic navigational structure using an unordered list styled with CSS. Use this as a starting point and modify the properties to produce your own unique look. If	**Clearing Method**
	Because all the columns are floated, this layout uses a clear:both declaration in the .footer rule. This clearing technique forces the .container to understand where the columns end in order to show any borders or background colors you place on the .container. If your design requires you to remove the .footer from the .container, you'll need to use a different clearing method. The most reliable will be to add a <br class="clearfloat" /> or <div class="clearfloat"></div> after your final floated column (but before the .container closes). This will have the same clearing effect.
	Logo Replacement

In this lesson, you will create a new page based on a predesigned CSS layout to become the new cafe page for the website.

Understanding Div Tags

Div tags are HTML tags that define how areas of content are formatted or positioned on a web page. For example, when you center an image on a page or inside a table cell, Dreamweaver automatically inserts a div tag in the HTML code. In addition to using div tags to align page elements, designers also use them to assign background colors or borders to content blocks, CSS styles to text, and many other properties to page elements. One type of div tag is an AP div tag. AP stands for absolutely positioned, so an **AP div tag** creates a container that has a specified, fixed position on a web page. The resulting container that an AP div tag creates on a page is called an **AP element**.

NEW Using CSS Page Layouts

Because building a web page using div tags can be tedious for beginning designers, Dreamweaver CS5 provides 16 predesigned layouts that are available in the New Document dialog box, as shown in Figure 1. This is a change from CS4, which offered 32 predesigned layouts. Although there are fewer choices, the layouts are better designed with more helpful information for the designer in the placeholder text. You can use these layouts to create web pages with attractive and consistent layouts. There are two types of CSS layouts: fixed and liquid. A **fixed layout** expresses all widths in pixels and remains the same size regardless of the size of the browser window. A **liquid layout** expresses all widths in percents and changes size depending on the size of the browser window.

Predesigned CSS layouts contain div tags that control the placement of page content using placeholders. Each div tag container has placeholder text that appears until you replace it with your own content. Because div tags use CSS for formatting and positioning, designers prefer them for building web page content. When you use the Dreamweaver predesigned layouts, you can be sure that your pages will appear with a consistent design when viewed in all browsers. Once you become more comfortable using the predesigned layouts, you will begin to build your own CSS-based pages from scratch.

QUICK TIP

The Browser Compatibility Check feature flags code that might present a CSS rendering issue in some browsers by underlining code in green. To see this feature, switch to Code view and browse through the code.

Viewing CSS Layout Blocks

As you design your page layouts using div tags, you can use Design view to see and adjust CSS content blocks. In Design view, text or images that have been aligned or positioned using div tags have a dotted border, as shown in Figure 2. In the Visual Aids list on the View menu, you can display selected features of div tag elements, such as CSS Layout Backgrounds, CSS Layout Box Model, CSS Layout Outlines, and AP Element Outlines. The CSS Layout Box Model displays the padding and margins of a block element.

Figure 1 *New Document dialog box*

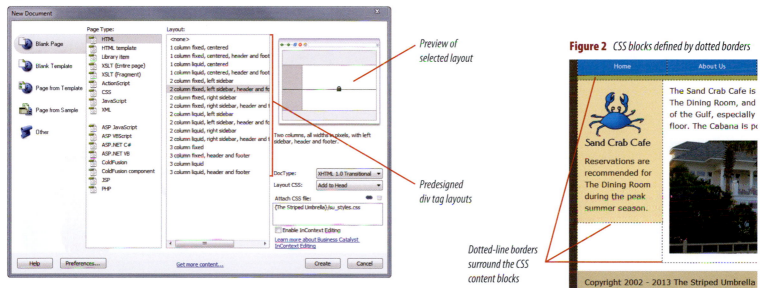

Preview of selected layout

Predesigned div tag layouts

Figure 2 *CSS blocks defined by dotted borders*

Dotted-line borders surround the CSS content blocks

Using Tracing Images for Page Design

Another design option for creating a page layout is the use of a tracing image. A **tracing image** is an image that is placed in the background of a document. By adjusting the transparency (opacity) of the image, you can then use it to create page elements on top of it, similar to the way you would place a piece of tracing paper on top of a drawing and trace over it. To insert a tracing image, Use the Modify, Page Properties, Tracing Image dialog box or the View, Tracing Image, Load command. Browse to select the image you want to use for the tracing image, then adjust the transparency as desired. The tracing image serves as a guide or pattern, and is not needed after you complete your design.

Create a page with a CSS layout

1. Open The Striped Umbrella website.

2. Click **File** on the Application bar (Win) or Menu bar (Mac), click **New**, verify that Blank Page is highlighted in the first column of the New Document dialog box, click **HTML** in the Page Type column if necessary, then click **2 column fixed, left sidebar, header and footer** in the Layout column, as shown in Figure 3.

   A fixed layout remains the same size regardless of the size of the browser window.

3. Click the **Attach Style Sheet button**  in the bottom-right corner of the dialog box, then click **Browse** in the Attach External Style Sheet dialog box.

   The Select Style Sheet File dialog box opens.

4. Select the su_styles.css external style sheet in the Select Style Sheet File dialog box, then click **OK** to close the Select Style Sheet File dialog box.

   If a dialog box opens reminding you to save your file before a document-relative path can be created, click OK to close the dialog box.

   NEW Dreamweaver CS5 also has a new option in the New Document dialog box to enable **InContext Editing**, or **ICE**. This feature sets up editable regions on web pages that users can make changes to while the page is being viewed in a browser.

5. Verify that the Link option is selected in the Attach External Style Sheet dialog box, then click **OK** to close the Attach External Style Sheet dialog box.

   (continued)

Figure 3 *Predesigned CSS layout selected for new page*

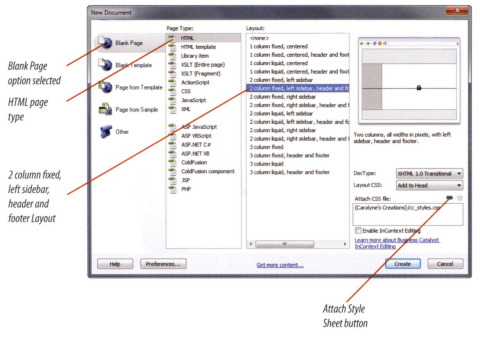

Blank Page option selected

HTML page type

2 column fixed, left sidebar, header and footer Layout

Attach Style Sheet button

Using XML and XSL to Create and Format Web Page Content

You can also create information containers on your web pages using XML, Extensible Markup Language, and XSL, Extensible Stylesheet Language. **XML** is a language that you use to structure blocks of information, similar to HTML. It uses similar opening and closing tags and the nested tag structure that HTML documents use. However, XML tags do not determine how the information is formatted, which is handled using XSL. **XSL** is similar to CSS; the XSL stylesheet information formats the containers created by XML. Once the XML structure and XSL styles are in place, **XSLT**, **Extensible Stylesheet Language Transformations**, interprets the code in the XSL file to transform an XML document, much like style sheet files transform HTML files from an unformatted file to a formatted file. XSL transformations can be written as client-side or server-side transformations. To create XML documents, use the XML page type in the New Document dialog box.

Figure 4 *The su_styles.css file is attached to the new page*

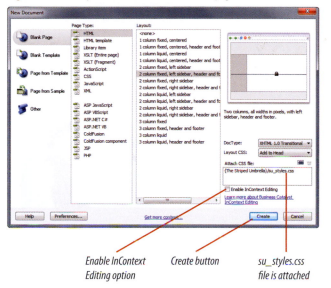

Enable InContext
Editing option

Create button

su_styles.css
file is attached

Figure 5 *New page based on CSS layout*

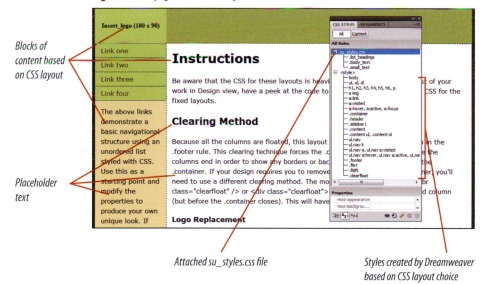

Blocks of
content based
on CSS layout

Placeholder
text

Attached su_styles.css file

Styles created by Dreamweaver
based on CSS layout choice

The su_styles.css file is attached to the new page, as shown in Figure 4. The next time you create a new page, the style sheet will be selected automatically.

6. Click **Create** in the New Document dialog box, open the CSS Styles panel if necessary, then expand the style sheets if necessary.

A new two-column HTML page opens based on the predesigned CSS layout you chose. It has CSS content blocks arranged in two columns, one as a sidebar on the left side, as well as a header and footer. Placeholder text appears in each of the blocks, as shown in Figure 5. You will replace the text with content for The Striped Umbrella website. The CSS blocks each have a different color background to help you see how the blocks are arranged on the page. This new page will replace the blank cafe page.

Notice that you have two sets of styles now: the external style sheet su_styles.css; and the internal style sheet <style> containing the styles that define the CSS blocks on the page.

You created a new page based on a predesigned CSS layout with the attached style sheet for The Striped Umbrella website.

Add Content to CSS
LAYOUT BLOCKS

What You'll Do

In this lesson, you will copy the menu bar and banner from the index page and paste it into the new page. You will then overwrite the old cafe page with this new one.

Understanding Div Tag Content

As you learned in Lesson 1, a div tag is a container that formats blocks of information on a web page, such as background colors, images, links, tables, and text. Once you have created a layout using div tags, you are ready to insert and format text. As with formatting text on a web page, you should use CSS styles to format text in div tags. You can also add all other properties such as text indents, padding, margins, and background color using CSS styles.

In this lesson, you use a CSS layout to create a new cafe page that arranges the content into defined areas on the page.

Using Dreamweaver New Page Options

You can use either the Welcome Screen or the New command on the File menu to create several different types of pages. The predesigned CSS page layouts make it easy to design accessible web pages based on Cascading Style Sheets, without an advanced level of expertise in writing HTML code. Predesigned templates are another time-saving feature that promotes consistency across a website. Framesets, CSS Style Sheets, and Sample Pages are a few of the other options. It is worth the time to explore each category to understand what is available to you as a designer. Once you have selected a page layout, you can customize it to suit your client's content and design needs.

Understanding CSS Code

When you view a page based on a predesigned CSS layout in Code view, you see helpful comments that explain sections of the code, as shown in Figure 6. The comments are in gray to differentiate them from the rest of the code. The CSS rules reside in the Head section. The code for a CSS container begins with the class, or name of the rule, and is followed by rule properties. For example, in Figure 6, the container described on line 45 begins with the class name .container, which is followed by three properties and values: width: 960 px; background: #FFF; and margin: 0 auto. The code that links the rules to the content is located in the body section.

Figure 6 *Code view for CSS in head content*

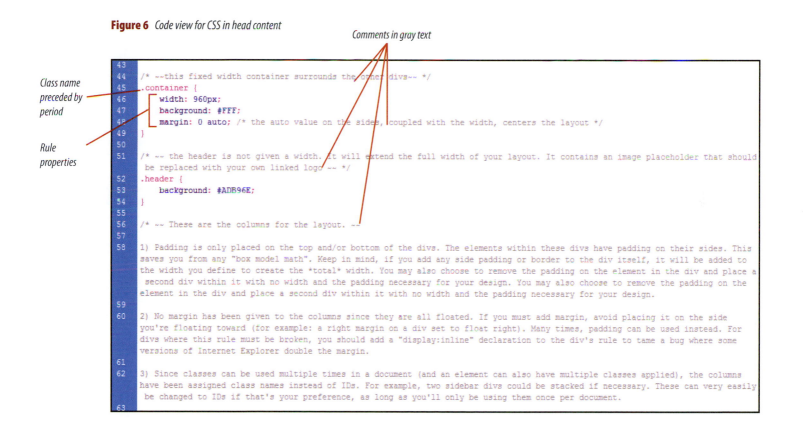

Comments in gray text

Class name preceded by period

Rule properties

```
43
44    /* --this fixed width container surrounds the other divs~~ */
45    .container {
46        width: 960px;
47        background: #FFF;
48        margin: 0 auto; /* the auto value on the sides, coupled with the width, centers the layout */
49    }
50
51    /* ~~ the header is not given a width. It will extend the full width of your layout. It contains an image placeholder that should
        be replaced with your own linked logo ~~ */
52    .header {
53        background: #ADB96E;
54    }
55
56    /* ~~ These are the columns for the layout. ~~
57
58    1) Padding is only placed on the top and/or bottom of the divs. The elements within these divs have padding on their sides. This
       saves you from any "box model math". Keep in mind, if you add any side padding or border to the div itself, it will be added to
       the width you define to create the *total* width. You may also choose to remove the padding on the element in the div and place a
       second div within it with no width and the padding necessary for your design. You may also choose to remove the padding on the
       element in the div and place a second div within it with no width and the padding necessary for your design.
59
60    2) No margin has been given to the columns since they are all floated. If you must add margin, avoid placing it on the side
       you're floating toward (for example: a right margin on a div set to float right). Many times, padding can be used instead. For
       divs where this rule must be broken, you should add a "display:inline" declaration to the div's rule to tame a bug where some
       versions of Internet Explorer double the margin.
61
62    3) Since classes can be used multiple times in a document (and an element can also have multiple classes applied), the columns
       have been assigned class names instead of IDs. For example, two sidebar divs could be stacked if necessary. These can very easily
       be changed to IDs if that's your preference, as long as you'll only be using them once per document.
63
```

Add text to a CSS container

1. Select all content between the Header and Footer in the main section (content block) of the page through the last paragraph describing the backgrounds, as shown in Figure 7, then press **[Delete]**.

TIP Before you delete placeholder text, it is a good idea to read it. The placeholder text has helpful information that helps you to understand the way the page is designed. It gives you pointers for the best way to replace the placeholder text with your text.

2. Change to the HTML Property inspector, click the **Format list arrow**, then click **Paragraph** if necessary.

   If you had a remaining H1 tag in the block, this removes it.

3. Import the file cafe.doc from the drive and folder where you store your Data Files (Win) or copy and paste it (Mac) in the blank container, then delete any extra space after the paragraph.

(continued)

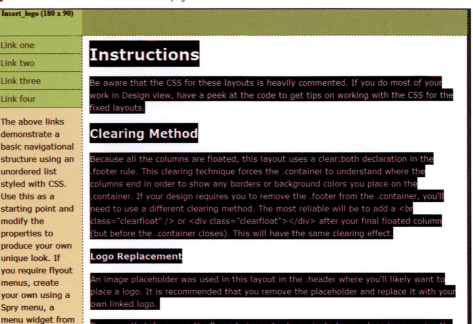

Figure 7 *Text selected in content block of new page*

Positioning Objects with CSS and Tables

Figure 8 *Text selected in sidebar1 block in Code view*

Beginning tag for
sidebar1 block

Ending tag for
sidebar1 block

Figure 9 *Text pasted into Content block and typed into sidebar1 block and footer block of new page*

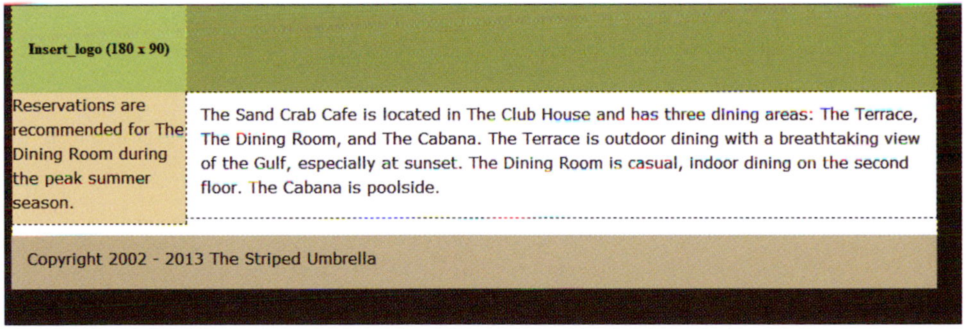

4. Switch to Code view, select the code between the beginning and end of the <div class="sidebar1"> tag, as shown in Figure 8, then press **[Delete]** to delete the placeholder text.

   Be careful not to delete the beginning and ending div tags.

5. Return to Design view, then type **Reservations are recommended for The Dining Room during the peak summer season.** at the insertion point.

6. Delete all of the text in the footer block, then type **Copyright 2002 - 2013 The Striped Umbrella** as shown in Figure 9.

7. Save the page as **cafe.html** in The Striped Umbrella website, overwriting the existing file.

You imported text and typed text in the CSS blocks, replacing the placeholder text, then saved the page as the new cafe.html page.

Add images to a CSS block

1. Open the Striped Umbrella index page and copy both the banner and the menu bar.

TIP You might find it easier to copy the banner and menu bar separately. If you copy them together, you can use Code view to make sure you have selected all the necessary code.

2. Switch back to the cafe page, click the **placeholder logo image**, then paste the banner and menu bar into the header section of the page.

TIP Press [Ctrl][Tab] (Win) or ⌘ ['] (Mac) to switch between two open pages.

3. Close the index page.

4. Place the insertion point immediately in front of the word "Reservations", insert a paragraph break, press [↑], insert **cafe_logo.gif** from the drive and folder where you store your Data Files, then type **Sand Crab Cafe logo** as the alternate text in the Image Tag Accessibility Attributes dialog box.

5. Select the **crab logo** if necessary, press [←], then enter a line break in front of the logo.

6. Place the insertion point after the period after the word "poolside", insert a paragraph break, insert **cafe_photo.jpg** from the drive and folder where you store your Data Files, as shown in Figure 10, then type **Sand Crab Cafe photo** as the alternate text.

(continued)

Figure 10 *Images added to header, sidebar 1, and content blocks*

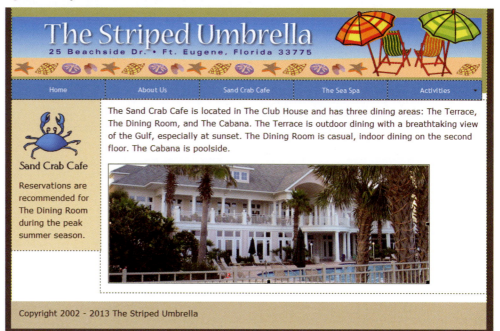

Positioning Objects with CSS and Tables

Figure 11 *Images placed on page*

7. Deselect the image, click the **HTML Property inspector button** `<> HTML` if necessary to switch to the HTML Property inspector, then click to place the insertion point in the content CSS block above the cafe_photo image.

   Notice that the Class text box in the HTML Property inspector shows the class to be "content."

8. Click to place the insertion point in the sidebar1 and header blocks.

   The Property inspector displays the class rule assigned to each block.

TIP If you have difficulty placing the insertion point in the header block, select the banner, then press [←].

9. Select the menu bar, press [→], then enter two line breaks.

10. Save your file, not updating links if prompted, then compare your screen to Figure 11.

You copied the banner and menu bar from the index page, pasted it onto the new cafe page, then added the cafe logo and photo to the page.

Edit Content in CSS
LAYOUT BLOCKS

What You'll Do

In this lesson, you will center the two images you have added to the page. You will then view the div tag properties and edit the background colors. You will also change the body background color.

Editing Content in CSS Layout Blocks

It is unlikely that you will find a predesigned CSS page layout that is exactly what you have in mind for your website. However, once you have created a page with a predesigned CSS layout, it is easy to modify the individual style properties to change content formatting or placement to better fit your needs. For example, you can easily change the properties to fit the color scheme of your website.

If your CSS layout has both external and internal style sheets, you can change the rule properties the same way. Click the plus sign next to the style sheet name, if necessary, to see the rules listed in each section, as shown in Figure 12, and then select the rule you

want to modify. The properties and values for the selected rule appear in the Properties pane, where you can modify them. You can use either style sheet or a combination of both style sheets to format the page content.

Figure 12 *Viewing the CSS Styles panel*

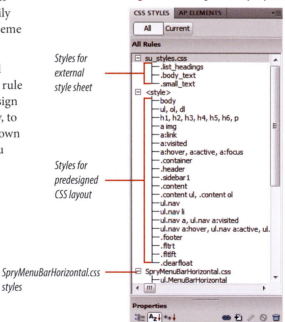

Styles for external style sheet

Styles for predesigned CSS layout

SpryMenuBarHorizontal.css styles

Figure 13 *Centering content in layout blocks*

Logo and text are centered within CSS blocks

1. Place the insertion point in front of the cafe logo.

   Notice that the class rule for this block is named .sidebar1.

2. Click the **.sidebar1 rule** in the CSS Styles panel, click the **Edit Rule button** , click the **Block category** in the CSS Rule definition for .sidebar1 dialog box, click the **Text-align list arrow**, click **center**, then click **OK**.

   The logo and text are now centered in the left sidebar.

3. Click to place the insertion point in the footer block at the bottom of the page.

   The class rule for this block is .footer.

4. Click the **.footer rule** in the CSS Styles panel, click the **Edit Rule button** , click the **Block category** in the CSS Rule definition for .footer dialog box, click the **Text-align list arrow**, click **center**, then click **OK**.

5. Compare your screen to Figure 13. The content in both blocks should be centered within each block.

(continued)

Using the Adobe CSS Advisor for Cross-Browser Rendering Issues

You can use the **Browser Compatibility Check (BCC)** feature to check for problems in the HTML code for CSS features that may render differently in multiple browsers. It flags and rates code on three levels: an error that could cause a serious display problem; an error that probably won't cause a serious display problem; or a warning that it has found code that is unsupported, but won't cause a serious display problem. Each bug is linked to the CSS Advisor, a part of the Adobe website, that offers solutions for that particular bug and other helpful information for resolving any issues with your pages. To check for browser compatibility, click File, point to Check Page, and then click Browser Compatibility or click the Check browser compatibility button on the Document toolbar.

6. Move the pointer over the top of the content block (the block containing the cafe description and picture), click the **red border** to select the block (the border turns blue after it is selected), then move the pointer inside the block and hover until the floating window shown in Figure 14 appears.

The properties of the div tag are displayed in a floating window. The Property inspector displays the div tag class name.

TIP You can change the border color of div tags when the mouse is positioned over them in the Preferences dialog box. Select the Highlighting category, then click the Mouse-Over color box and select a different color. You can also disable highlighting by deselecting the Show check box for Mouse-Over.

7. Save your work.

You centered the logo, reservations text, and copyright statement. You also viewed the properties of the div tag.

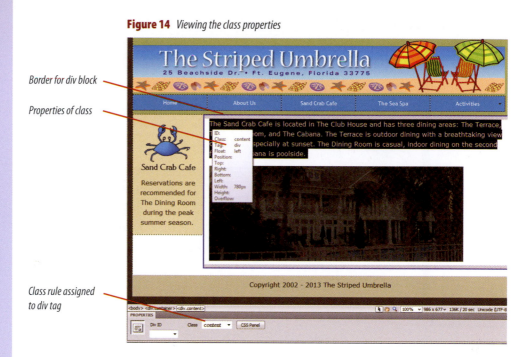

Figure 14 *Viewing the class properties*

Border for div block

Properties of class

Class rule assigned to div tag

Viewing Options for CSS Layout Blocks

You can view your layout blocks in Design view in several ways. You can choose to show or hide outlines, temporarily assign different background colors to each individual layout block, or view the **CSS Layout Box Model** (padding, margins, borders, etc.) of a selected layout. To change these options, use the View/Visual Aids menu, and then select or deselect the CSS Layout Backgrounds, CSS Layout Box Model, or CSS Layout Outlines menu choice. You can also use the Visual Aids button on the Document toolbar.

Figure 15 *Setting the body Font-family value*

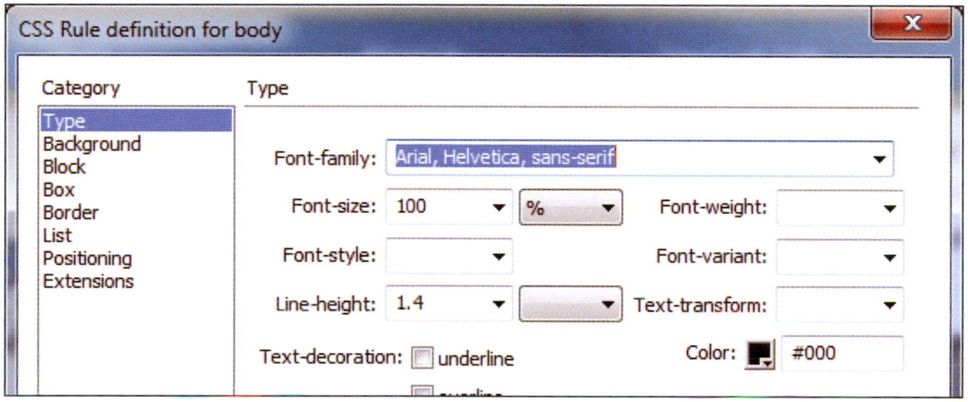

Figure 16 *The cafe page with edited body Font-family property*

Edit type properties in CSS layout blocks

1. Select the **body rule** in the CSS Styles panel, click the **Edit Rule button** , then click the **Type category** in the CSS Rule definition for body dialog box.

2. Click the **Font-family list arrow** in the CSS Rule definition for body dialog box, then click **Arial, Helvetica, sans-serif,** as shown in Figure 15.

3. Click **OK** to close the dialog box, compare your screen to Figure 16, then save your work.

    The new font family property is applied to the text on the page. The Font-family property in the body rule determines the font family for all text on the page unless another one is specified for a different container, such as the footer, with an external style or a different internal style. The body is a **parent container**, a container with other tags falling between its opening and closing tags. **Child containers** are containers whose code resides inside a parent container. All HTML tags for page content are inside the body tags. So unless a different font is specified in a different container, each child container inherits the properties from the parent container.

    You leave the rest of the type properties with the default CSS settings.

You changed the font-family property in the body that determines the font family for all text on the page.

Edit CSS layout block properties

1. Click the **header rule** in the CSS Styles panel to select it, then click the **Show only set properties button** ✴✴↓ .

   The value for the background property is displayed in the Properties pane. The header block has background color of #ADB96E, a muted green color.

2. Click the **background text box** to place the insertion point, replace #ADB96E with **#FFF**, press **[Enter]** (Win) or **[return]** (Mac) and compare your screen to Figure 17.

   TIP You may have to adjust the size of your CSS Styles panel to view both panes.

   The header background color changes to white.

3. With the header rule still selected, click the **Edit Rule button** 🖉 , click the **Box category**, type **5** in the Top Margin text box, verify that the Same for all check box is checked, as shown in Figure 18, then click **OK**.

   You can edit rule properties in either the CSS Styles Properties pane or by opening the CSS Rule definition dialog box. With block margins set, the banner now appears more centered on the page.

   (continued)

Figure 17 *Editing the properties of the header rule*

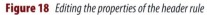

Select the header rule

Change the background color to #FFF

Show only set properties button

Figure 18 *Editing the properties of the header rule*

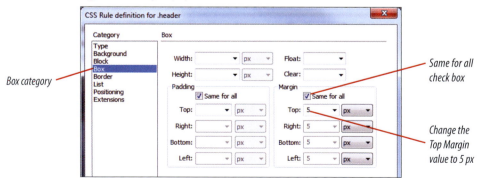

Box category

Same for all check box

Change the Top Margin value to 5 px

Figure 19 *The four layout blocks now have a white background*

The four blocks have the same background color

4. Select the cafe photo image, click the **H space text box** in the Property inspector, type **40** to indent the image in the block, then press **[Tab]**.

5. Repeat Step 2 to change the background color in the footer rule to #FFF and the background color in the sidebar1 rule to #FFF.

   The header, footer, and sidebar1 background colors are now white.

TIP You only need to use the abbreviated hexadecimal color code, such as #FFF, when specifying colors. However, in the Dreamweaver predesigned CSS layouts, the color codes are shown with the full 6-character codes. Either code works. You can also specify colors by their names. For example, the color magenta can be specified as "magenta", #FF00FF or #F0F

6. Save your work, then compare your screen to Figure 19.

You changed the margin width of a CSS layout block, indented the cafe photo, then changed the background color of three CSS layout blocks to white.

Edit page properties

1. Select the **container rule** in the CSS Styles panel.

2. Open the CSS Rule definition for .container dialog box, then click the **Border category**.

   A border around the page sets it off from the extra space around it when it is viewed in a browser.

3. Click the **Top list arrow** in the Style column, then click **solid**.

4. Click the **Width list arrow** in the first text box in the Width column, then click **thin**.

5. Click the first **Color text box** in the Color column, type **#033**, press **Tab**, compare your screen to Figure 20, then click **OK**.

6. Click the **body rule** in the CSS Styles panel, then open the CSS Rule definition for body dialog box.

7. Click the **Background category**, change the Background-color text box to **#FFF**, then click **OK**.

   (continued)

Figure 20 *Adding a border to the container*

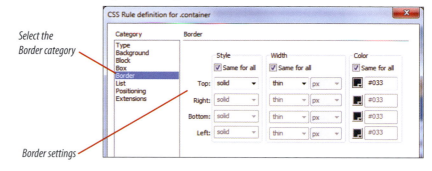

Select the Border category

Border settings

Positioning Objects with CSS and Tables

Figure 21 *Viewing the cafe page in the browser*

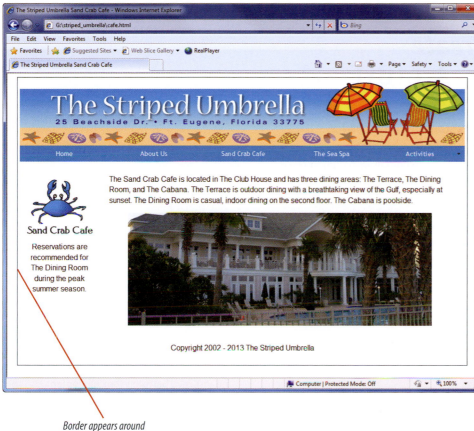

Border appears around
page in browser

8. Use the Document toolbar to add the page title **The Striped Umbrella Sand Crab Cafe** to the page.

9. Save your work, preview the page in your browser, compare your screen to Figure 21, then close the browser.

TIP If you are using Internet Explorer and receive a warning message about the page being restricted from running scripts, click the yellow bar above the page, click Allow Blocked Content, then click Yes to close the dialog box.

You added a border to the page.

Create
A TABLE

What You'll Do

In this lesson, you will create a table for the cafe page in The Striped Umbrella website to provide a grid for the cafe hours.

Understanding Table Modes

Now that you have learned how CSS can act as containers to hold information in place on web pages, let's look at tables as another layout tool. Tables are great when you need a grid layout on a page, such as a list of items and prices. Some web pages are based entirely on tables for their page layouts and some pages contain tables inside CSS layout blocks. To create a table, click the Table button on the Insert panel. When the Layout category of the Insert panel is displayed, you can choose between two modes that give you different ways to view your table: Standard mode or Expanded Tables mode. Expanded Tables mode adds extra space between cells, which makes it easier to select small cells. Click the appropriate button on the Insert panel after selecting a table on the page.

Creating a Table

To create a table in Standard mode, click the Table button on the Insert panel to open the Table dialog box. Enter values for the number of rows and columns, the border thickness, table width, cell padding, and cell spacing. The **border** is the outline or frame around the table and the individual cells

and is measured in pixels. The table width can be specified in pixels or as a percentage. When the table width is specified as a percentage, the table width expands to fill up its container (the browser window, a CSS container, or another table). A table placed inside another table is called a **nested table**. Figure 22 shows a table set to 100% width of a CSS container. The content spreads across the entire width of the container. When the table width is specified in pixels, the table width stays the same, regardless of the size of the container. The table in Figure 23 is an example of the same table with a fixed width. Regardless of the size of the container, the table width remains constant. **Cell padding** is the distance between the cell content and the **cell walls**, the lines inside the cell borders. **Cell spacing** is the distance between cells.

Before you create a table, you should include in your wireframe a plan for it that shows its location on the page and the placement of text and graphics in its cells. You should also decide whether to include borders around the tables and cells. Setting the border value to 0 causes the table borders to appear invisible. Viewers will not realize that you used a table for the layout unless they look at the code. Figure 24 shows a sketch of the table you will create on The Striped Umbrella cafe page to organize the cafe hours.

Using Expanded Tables Mode

Expanded Tables mode is a feature that allows you to change to a table view with expanded table borders and temporary cell padding and cell spacing. This mode makes it easier to actually see how many rows and columns you have in your table. Often, especially after splitting empty cells, it is difficult to place the insertion point precisely in a table cell. Expanded Tables mode allows you to see each cell clearly. However, most of the time, you will want to work in Standard mode to maintain the WYSIWYG environment. **WYSIWYG** is the acronym for What You See Is What You Get, and means that your page should look the same in the browser as it does in the web editor.

Setting Table Accessibility Preferences

You can make a table more accessible to visually disabled viewers by adding a table caption and a table summary that screen readers can read. The table caption appears on the screen; the table summary does not. The table summary is added to the page code and is used by screen readers. Captions and summaries are especially useful for tables that are used for tabular data, rather than for page layout. **Table headers** are another way to provide accessibility. Table headers can be placed at the top or sides of a table containing data. They are automatically centered and bold and are used by screen readers to help viewers identify the table content. Table captions, summaries, and headers are all created in the Table dialog box.

Figure 22 *Table based on a 100% width spreads across the page*

Content spreads across the available space

Figure 23 *Same table shown with a fixed-width*

Table displayed with fixed width; leftover white space displayed outside table borders

Figure 24 *Sketch of table on cafe page*

Cafe Hours

Photo | Hours listed by room

Create a table

1. Click to place the insertion point to the right of the cafe photo.

2. Click **Table** in the Common category on the Insert panel.

   The Table dialog box opens.

3. Type **5** in the Rows text box, type **3** in the Columns text box, type **600** in the Table width text box, click the **Table width list arrow**, click **pixels** if necessary, type **0** in the Border thickness text box, then click the **Top** Header.

TIP It is better to add more rows than you think you need when you create your table. After they are filled with content, it is easier to delete rows than to add rows if you decide later to split or merge cells in the table.

4. In the Summary text box, type **This table contains the cafe hours for each dining room.**, then compare your screen to Figure 25.

5. Click **OK**.

   The table appears on the page, but the table summary is not visible. The summary does not appear in the browser, but is read by screen readers.

TIP To edit accessibility preferences for a table, switch to Code view to edit the code directly.

(continued)

Figure 25 *Table dialog box*

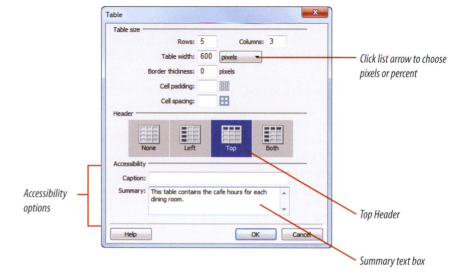

Click list arrow to choose pixels or percent

Accessibility options

Top Header

Summary text box

Figure 26 *Expanded Tables mode*

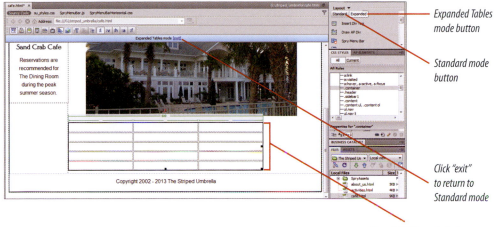

Expanded Tables mode button

Standard mode button

Click "exit" to return to Standard mode

Expanded Tables mode displays more space between cells for easier editing

Figure 27 *Property inspector showing properties of selected table*

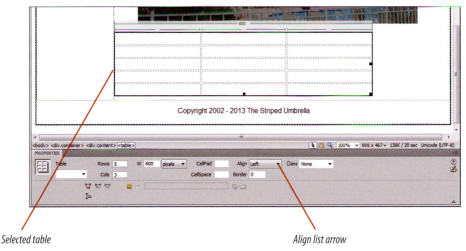

Selected table

Align list arrow

6. Click the **Insert panel list arrow**, click **Layout**, click the **Expanded Tables mode button** Expanded , click **OK** in the Getting Started in Expanded Tables Mode dialog box if necessary, then compare your screen to Figure 26.

   The Expanded Tables mode makes it easier to select and edit tables.

7. Click the **Standard mode button** Standard to return to Standard mode.

TIP You can also return to Standard mode by clicking [exit] in the blue bar below the Document toolbar.

You created a table on the cafe page that will display the cafe hours with five rows and three columns and a width of 600 pixels. You used a top header and added a table summary that will be read by screen readers.

Set table properties

1. Select the table by clicking the **<table> tag** on the tag selector.

TIP You can also select a table by moving the pointer slowly to the top or bottom edge of the table until you see the pointer change to a Table pointer then clicking the table border.

2. Expand the Property inspector (if necessary) to display the current properties of the new table.

   The Property inspector displays information about the table only when the table is selected.

3. Click the **Align list arrow** in the Property inspector, then click **Left** to left-align the table in the content block on the page, as shown in Figure 27.

   The left-alignment formatting left-aligns the table inside the CSS container.

You selected and left-aligned the table.

Resize, Split,
AND MERGE CELLS

What You'll Do

In this lesson, you will set the width of the table cells to be split across the table in predetermined widths. You will then split one cell. You will also merge some cells to provide space for the table header.

Resizing Table Elements

You can resize the rows or columns of a table by dragging. To resize a table, row, or column, you must first select the table, then drag one of the table's three selection handles. To change all the columns in a table so that they are the same size, drag the middle-right selection handle. To resize the height of all rows simultaneously, drag the middle-bottom selection handle. To resize the entire table, drag the right-corner selection handle. To resize a row or column individually, drag the interior cell borders up, down, to the left, or to the right. You can also resize selected columns, rows, or individual cells by entering specific measurements in the W and H text boxes in the Property inspector specified either in pixels or as a percentage. Cells whose width or height is specified as a percentage maintain that percentage in relation to the width or height of the entire table if the table is resized.

Adding or Deleting a Row

As you add new content to your table, you might find that you have too many or too few rows or columns. You can add or delete one row or column at a time or several at once. You use commands on the Modify menu to add and delete table rows and columns. When you add a new column or row, you must first select the existing column or row to which the new column or row will be adjacent. The Insert Rows or Columns dialog box lets you choose how many rows or columns you want to insert or delete, and where you want them placed in relation to the selected row or column. The new column or row will have the same formatting and number of cells as the selected column or row. After you have split and merged cells, it can be challenging to add or delete rows.

Using the Table button creates a new table with evenly-spaced columns and rows. Sometimes you want to adjust the cells in a table by splitting or merging them. To **split** a cell means to divide it into multiple rows or columns. To **merge** cells means to combine multiple cells into one cell. Using split and merged cells gives you more flexibility and control in placing page elements in a table and can help you create a more visually exciting layout. When you merge cells, the HTML tag used to describe the merged cell changes from a width size tag to a column span or row span tag. For example, <td colspan="2"> is the code for two cells that have been merged into one cell that spans two columns.

QUICK TIP

You can split merged cells and merge split cells.

DESIGNTIP

Using Nested Tables

A nested table is a table inside a table. To create a nested table, you place the insertion point in the cell where you want to insert the nested table, then click the Table button on the Insert panel. A nested table is a separate table that can be formatted differently from the table in which it is placed. Nested tables are useful when you want part of your table data to have visible borders and part to have invisible borders. For example, you can nest a table with red borders inside a table with invisible borders. You need to plan carefully when you insert nested tables. It is easy to get carried away and insert too many nested tables, which makes it more difficult to apply formatting and rearrange table elements. Before you insert a nested table, consider whether you could achieve the same result by adding rows and columns or by splitting cells.

Resize columns

1. Click inside the **first cell** in the bottom row.

2. Type **30%** in the W text box in the Property inspector, then press **[Enter]** (Win) or **[return]** (Mac) to change the width of the cell to 30 percent of the table width.

   Notice that the column width is shown as a percentage at the top of the first column in the table, along with the table width of 600 pixels.

TIP   You need to type the % sign next to the number you type in the W text box. Otherwise, the width is expressed in pixels.

3. Repeat Steps 1 and 2 for the next two cells in the last row, using **30%** for the middle cell and **40%** for the last cell, then compare your screen to Figure 28.

   The combined widths of the three cells add up to 100 percent. As you add content to the table, the columns remain in this proportion unless you insert an image that is larger than the table cell. If a larger image is inserted, the cell width expands to display it.

TIP   Changing the width of a single cell changes the width of the entire column.

You set the width of each of the three cells in the bottom row to set the column sizes for the table. This will keep the table from resizing when you add content.

Figure 28 *Setting a cell width*

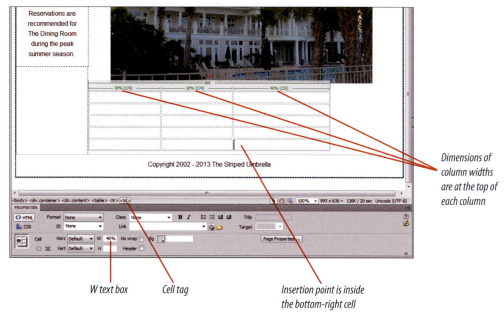

Dimensions of column widths are at the top of each column

W text box   *Cell tag*   *Insertion point is inside the bottom-right cell*

Resetting Table Widths and Heights

After resizing columns and rows in a table, you might want to change the sizes of the columns and rows back to their previous sizes. To reset columns and rows to their previous widths and heights, select the table, click Modify on the Application bar (Win) or Menu bar (Mac), point to Table, then click Clear Cell Heights or Clear Cell Widths. Using the Clear Cell Heights command also forces the cell border to snap to the bottom of any inserted graphics, so you can also use this command to tighten up extra white space in a cell. This menu also has choices for converting table widths and heights from pixels to percents and vice versa.

Figure 29 *Resizing the height of a row*

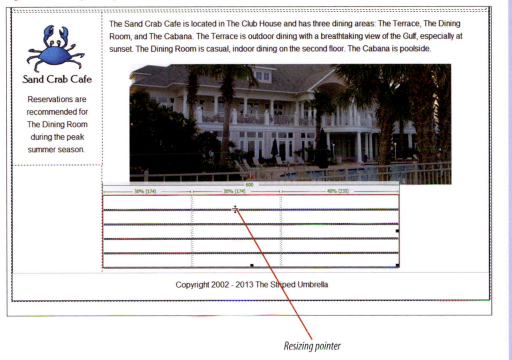

Resizing pointer

1. Place the pointer over the bottom border of the first row until it changes to a resizing pointer ⊥, as shown in Figure 29, then click and drag down about 1/4 of an inch to increase the height of the row.

   The border turns darker when you select and drag it.

2. Click **Window** on the menu bar, click **History**, then drag the **slider** in the History panel up one line to the **Set Width: 40%** mark to return the row to its original height.

3. Close the History panel.

You changed the height of the top row, then used the History panel to change it back to its original height.

Understanding HTML Table Tags

When formatting a table, it is important to understand the basic HTML table tags. The tags for creating a table are <table> </table>. The tags to create table rows are <tr></tr>. The tags used to create table cells are <td></td>. Dreamweaver places the   code into each empty table cell at the time you create it. The   code represents a nonbreaking space, or a space that a browser will display on the page. Some browsers collapse an empty cell, which can ruin the look of a table. The nonbreaking space holds the cell until you place content in it, when it is automatically removed.

Split cells

1. Click inside the first cell in the fifth row, then click the **<td>** in the tag selector.

TIP You can click the cell tag <td> (the HTML tag for that cell) on the tag selector to select the corresponding cell in the table.

2. Click the **Splits cell into rows or columns button** in the Property inspector.

3. Click the **Split cell into Rows option button** (if necessary), type **2** in the Number of rows text box (if necessary), as shown in Figure 30, click **OK**, then click in the cell to deselect it.

   The cell is split, as shown in Figure 31.

TIP To create a new row identical to the one above it at the end of a table, place the insertion point in the last cell, then press [Tab].

You split a cell into two rows.

Figure 30 *Splitting a cell into two rows*

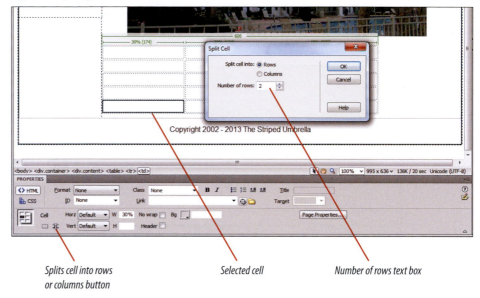

Splits cell into rows or columns button

Selected cell

Number of rows text box

Figure 31 *Splitting one cell into two rows*

Two cells split from one cell

Positioning Objects with CSS and Tables

Figure 32 *Merging selected cells into one cell*

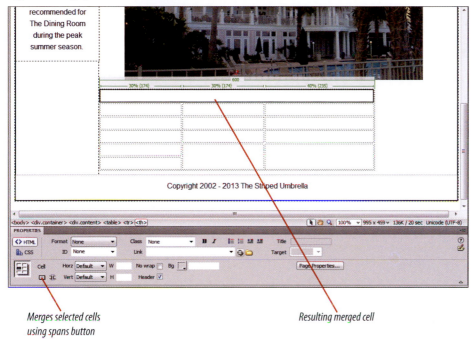

Merges selected cells
using spans button

Resulting merged cell

Figure 33 *Code for merged cells*

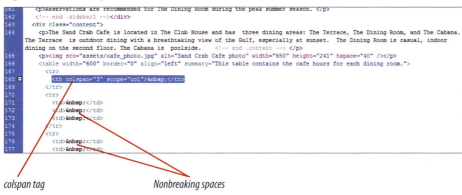

colspan tag   Nonbreaking spaces

Merge cells

1. Click to set the insertion point in the first cell in the top row, then drag to the right to select the three cells in the top row.

2. Click the **Merges selected cells using spans button** in the Property inspector.

   The three cells are merged into one cell, as shown in Figure 32. Merged cells are good placeholders for banners or headings.

   TIP You can only merge cells that are adjacent to each other.

3. Click the **Show Code view button** Code , then view the code for the merged cells, as shown in Figure 33.

   Notice the table tags denoting the column span (th colspan="3") and the nonbreaking spaces ( ) inserted in the empty cells.

4. Click the **Show Design view button** Design , select and merge the first cells in rows 2, 3, 4, and 5 in the left column, then save your work.

You merged three cells in the first row to make room for the table header. You then merged four cells in the left column to make room for an image.

Insert and Align
IMAGES IN TABLE CELLS

What You'll Do

In this lesson, you will insert an image of a chocolate cake in the left column of the table. After placing the image, you will align it within the cell.

Inserting Images in Table Cells

You can insert images in the cells of a table using the Image command in the Images menu on the Insert panel. If you already have images saved in your website that you would like to insert in a table, you can drag them from the Assets panel into the table cells. When you add a large image to a cell, the cell expands to accommodate the inserted image. If you select the Show attributes when inserting Images check box in the Accessibility category of the Preferences dialog box, the Image Tag Accessibility Attributes dialog box opens after you insert an image, prompting you to enter alternate text. Figure 34 shows the John Deere website, which uses several tables for page layout and contains images in its table cells. Notice that some images appear in cells by themselves, and some appear in cells containing text or other graphics. Some cells have a white background, and some have a green background.

Aligning Images in Table Cells

You can align images both horizontally and vertically within a cell. You can align an image horizontally using the Horz (horizontal) alignment options in the Property inspector, as shown in Figure 35. This option is used to align the entire contents of the cell, whether there is one object or several. You can also align an image vertically by the top, middle, bottom, or baseline of a cell. To align an image vertically within a cell, use the Vert (vertical) Align list arrow in the Property inspector, then choose an alignment option.

To control spacing between cells, you can use cell padding and cell spacing. **Cell padding** is the space between a cell's border and its contents. **Cell spacing** is the distance between adjacent cells.

Figure 34 *Deere & Company website*

© 2009 Deere & Company website used with permission from Deere & Company – www.johndeere.com

Figure 35 *Horizontally aligning cell contents*

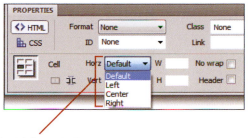

Horizontal alignment options

Insert images in table cells

1. Click in the merged cells in the left column of the table (under the merged cell in the top row) to place the insertion point.
2. Insert **chocolate_cake.jpg** from the drive and folder where you store your Data Files, then type **Chocolate Grand Marnier Cake** for the alternate text.

TIP You may have to click out of the cell if you see extra space around the image.

3. Compare your screen to Figure 36.
4. Refresh the Files panel and verify that the new image was copied to The Striped Umbrella website assets folder.
5. Save your work, then preview the page in your browser.
6. Close your browser.

You inserted an image into a table cell on the cafe page.

Figure 36 *Image inserted into table cell*

chocolate_cake.jpg image

Using Rulers, Grids, and Guides for Positioning Page Content

To help you position your page content, the View menu offers grids and guides. **Grids** provide a graph paper-like view of a page. Horizontal and vertical lines fill the page when this option is turned on. You can edit the line colors, the distance between them, whether they are composed of lines or dots, and whether or not objects "snap" to them. **Guides** are horizontal or vertical lines that you drag onto the page from the rulers. You can edit both the colors of the guides and the color of the distance, a feature that shows you the distance between two guides. You can lock the guides so you don't accidentally move them and you can set them either to snap to page elements or have page elements snap to them. To display grids or guides, click View on the Application bar (Win) or Menu bar (Mac), point to Grid, then click Show Grid or point to Guides and then click Show Guides.

Figure 37 *Aligning image in cell*

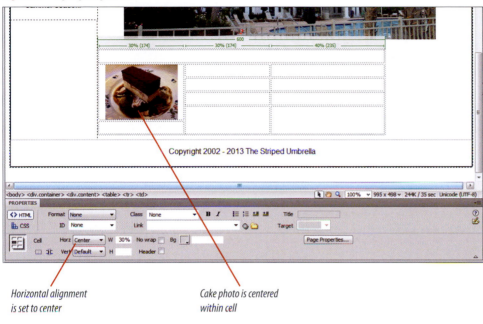

*Horizontal alignment
is set to center*

*Cake photo is centered
within cell*

Align graphics in table cells

1. Click to the right side of the **chocolate_cake image** in the same cell to place the insertion point.

2. Click the **Horz list arrow** in the Property inspector, then click **Center**. (Both the HTML and CSS Property inspectors have the alignment options.)

   The chocolate cake image is centered in the cell. The alignment applies to all content inserted into this cell. The effect of the alignment, however, may not be apparent until you add more content to the table.

3. Compare your screen to Figure 37.

4. Save your work.

5. Preview the page in your browser, view the aligned image, then close your browser.

You center-aligned cell content.

Working with Div Tags

Div tags are used to format blocks of content, similar to the way P tags are used to format paragraphs of text. However, div tags are more flexible because they can act as containers for any type of block content. They are convenient for centering content on a page or applying color to an area of a web page. Div tags combine easily with Cascading Style Sheets for formatting and positioning. When you align a page element Dreamweaver automatically adds a div tag. Div tags are frequently used in style sheets to specify formatting attributes.

Insert Text and Format
CELL CONTENT

What You'll Do

In this lesson, you will type the cafe hours in the table. You will also format the text to enhance its appearance on the page. Last, you will add formatting to some of the cells and cell content.

Inserting Text in a Table

You can enter text in a table either by typing it in a cell, copying it from another source and pasting it into a cell, or importing it from another program. Once you place text in a table cell, you can format it to make it more readable and more visually appealing on the page.

Formatting Cell Content

To format the contents of a cell, select the cell contents, then apply formatting to it. For example, you can select an image in a cell and center it, add a border, or add V space. Or, you can select text in a cell and apply a style or use the Blockquote or Remove Blockquote buttons in the HTML Property inspector to move the text farther away from or closer to the cell walls.

If a cell contains multiple objects of the same type, such as text, you can either format each item individually or select the entire cell and apply formatting that applies identically to all items. You can tell whether you have selected the cell contents or the cell itself by looking at the options showing in the Property inspector. Figure 38 shows a selected image in a cell. Because the image is selected, the Property inspector displays options for formatting the object, rather than options for formatting the cell.

Formatting Cells

Formatting a cell is different from formatting a cell's contents. Formatting a cell can include setting properties that visually enhance the cell's appearance, such as setting a cell width and assigning a background color.

You can also set global alignment properties for the cell content, using the Horz or Vert list arrows on the Property inspector. These options align the cell content horizontally or vertically. To format a cell, you need to either select the cell or place the insertion point inside the cell you want to format, then choose the cell formatting options you want in the Property inspector. For example, to choose a fill color for a selected cell, click the Background Color button in the Property inspector, then choose a color from the color picker. To format a cell, expand the Property inspector to display the cell formatting options.

QUICK TIP

You can also set cell and table formatting using rules in a Cascading Style Sheet. Some options, such as using an image for a cell background, cannot be set using the Property inspector and must be set using CSS.

In Figure 39, the insertion point is positioned in the chocolate cake cell, but the image is not selected. The Property inspector displays the formatting options for cells.

Figure 38 *Property inspector showing properties for selected image*

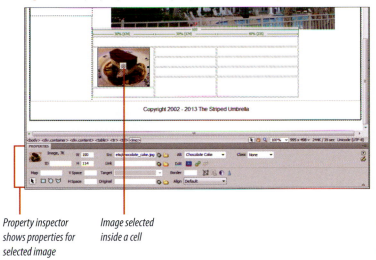

Property inspector shows properties for selected image

Image selected inside a cell

Figure 39 *Property inspector showing options for formatting a cell*

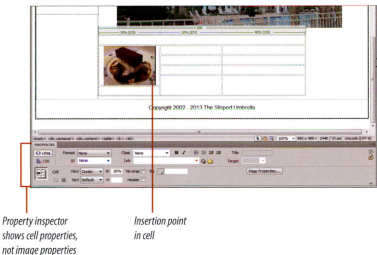

Property inspector shows cell properties, not image properties

Insertion point in cell

Insert text

1. Click in the cell below the chocolate cake photo, type **Chocolate**, press **[Shift][Enter]** (Win) or **[shift][return]** (Mac), type **Grand Marnier**, press **[Shift][Enter]** (Win) or **[shift][return]** (Mac), then type **Cake**.

   TIP If you can't see the last lines you typed, click the <div.container> tag on the Tag selector to refresh the container size on the screen, or resize your screen to refresh the screen.

2. Click in the top row of the table to place the insertion point, then type **Sand Crab Cafe Hours**.

   The text is automatically bolded because you selected the top row header when you created the table. A table's header row is bold by default.

3. Merge the two bottom-right cells in the last row, then enter the cafe dining area names, hours, and room service information as shown in Figure 40. Use a line break after the first line of text in the last cell.

   The type in the table has inherited the Font-family property from the body tag properties.

   TIP If your table cells seem to have extra space in them, click the <table> tag to tighten it up.

You entered text in the table to provide information about the dining room hours.

Figure 40 *Typing text into cells*

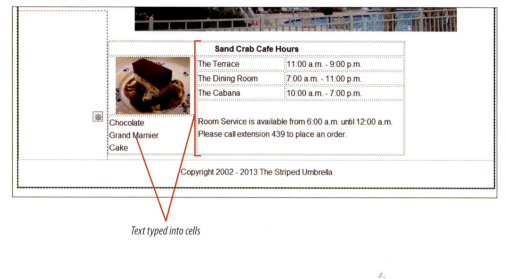

Text typed into cells

Importing and Exporting Data from Tables

You can import and export tabular data into and out of Dreamweaver. Tabular data is data that is arranged in columns and rows and separated by a **delimiter**: a comma, tab, colon, semicolon, or similar character. **Importing** means to bring data created in another software program into Dreamweaver, and **exporting** means to save data created in Dreamweaver in a special file format that can be opened by other programs. Files that are imported into Dreamweaver must be saved as delimited files. **Delimited files** are database, word processing, or spreadsheet files that have been saved as text files with delimiters such as tabs or commas separating the data. Programs such as Microsoft Access and Microsoft Excel offer many file formats for saving files. To import a delimited file, click File on the Application bar (Win) or Menu bar (Mac), point to Import, then click Tabular Data. The Import Tabular Data dialog box opens, offering you formatting options for the imported table. To export a table that you created in Dreamweaver, click File on the Application bar (Win) or Menu bar (Mac), point to Export, then click Table. The Export Table dialog box opens, letting you choose the type of delimiter you want for the delimited file.

Positioning Objects with CSS and Tables

Figure 41 *Formatting text using a Cascading Style Sheet*

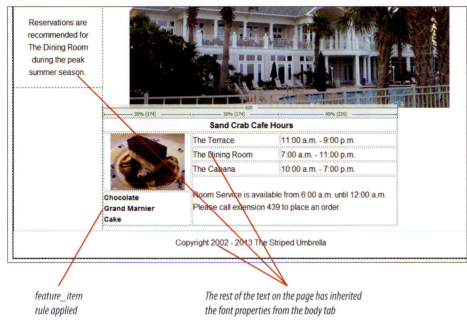

feature_item rule applied

The rest of the text on the page has inherited the font properties from the body tab

POWER USER SHORTCUTS	
To do this:	**Use this shortcut:**
Insert table	[Ctrl][Alt][T] (Win) or ⌘ [option][T] (Mac)
Select a cell	[Ctrl][A] (Win) or ⌘ [A] (Mac)
Merge cells	[Ctrl][Alt][M] (Win) or ⌘ [option][M] (Mac)
Split cell	[Ctrl][Alt][S] (Win) or ⌘ [option][S] (Mac)
Insert row	[Ctrl][M] (Win) or ⌘ [M] (Mac)
Insert column	[Ctrl][Shift][A] (Win) or ⌘ [Shift][A] (Mac)
Delete row	[Ctrl][Shift][M] (Win) or ⌘ [Shift][M] (Mac)
Delete column	[Ctrl][Shift][-] (Win) or ⌘ [Shift][-] (Mac)
Increase column span	[Ctrl][Shift][]] (Win) or ⌘ [Shift][]] (Mac)
Decrease column span	[Ctrl][Shift][[] (Win) or ⌘ [Shift][[] (Mac)

Format cell content

1. Click the **New CSS Rule button** to create a new class style called **feature_item** in the su_styles.css style sheet file.

   The CSS Rule Definition for .feature_item in su_styles.css dialog box opens.

2. In the Type category, set the Font-size to **14**, the Font-weight to **bold**, the Color to **#003**, then click **OK** to close the CSS Rule Definition for .feature_item in su_styles.css dialog box.

   You use this rule to format the name of the featured dessert.

3. Select **Chocolate Grand Marnier Cake** under the cake image, click the **CSS button** on the Property inspector, then apply the **feature_item rule** to the text.

   Your screen should resemble Figure 41. Because the only property values you set for the feature_item rule were for the font size, font weight, and color, the font family value was inherited from the parent body tag and is the same as the rest of the text on the page.

You created a new rule in the su_styles.css style sheet and used it to format text in a table cell.

Format cells

1. Click to place the insertion point in the cell with the cake text.

2. Click the **Horz list arrow** in the Property inspector, then click **Center** to center the cell contents.

   You do not need to select the text because you are setting the alignment for all contents in the cell.

3. Repeat Steps 1 and 2 for the cell with the room service information.

4. With the insertion point in the room service text, click the **Vert list arrow**, then click **Bottom**, as shown in Figure 42.

5. Save your work.

You formatted table cells by adding horizontal and vertical alignment.

Modify cell content

1. Click after the word "cake" in the bottom left cell, then press **[Tab]**.

   Pressing the Tab key while the insertion point is in the last cell of the table creates a new row. Even though it looks like the cell with the room service information is the last cell, it is not because of the merged cells.

2. Merge the cells in the new row, click in the merged cells, click **Insert** on the Application bar (Win) or Menu bar (Mac), point to **HTML**, then click **Horizontal Rule**.

3. Click in front of the table header, insert another horizontal rule, then save your work.

You added two horizontal rules to the table to set the table off from the rest of the page.

Figure 42 *Formatting cells using horizontal and vertical alignment*

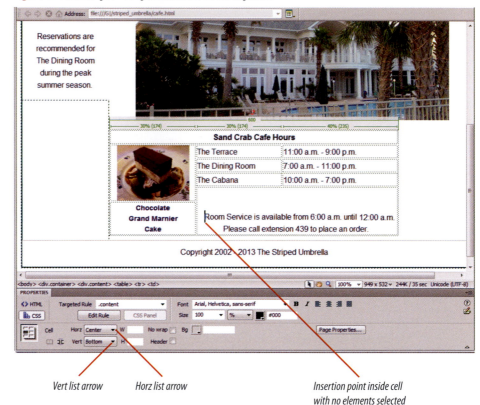

Vert list arrow   Horz list arrow

Insertion point inside cell with no elements selected

Using Inherited Properties to Format Cell Content

If a table is inside a CSS layout, you can simply let the properties from the existing CSS rules format the content, rather than applying additional rules. This is called **inheritance**. When a tag is placed, or **nested**, inside another tag (the parent tag), the properties from the parent tag are inherited by any tags nested within that tag. For example, if you set the Font-family property in the body tag, all content on the page inherits and displays that same font family unless you specify otherwise.

Figure 43 *Hiding visual aids*

Dotted lines showing
borders are hidden

Live View button

Visual aids button

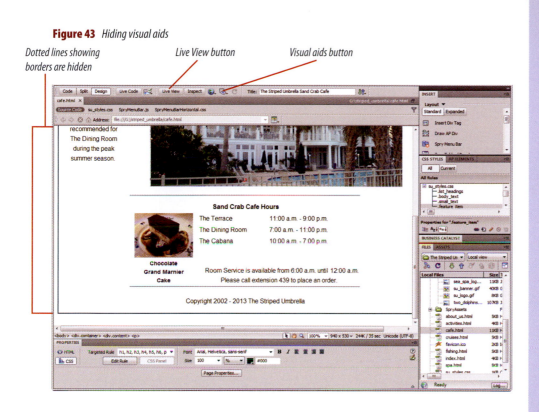

Check layout

1. Click the **Visual Aids button** on the Document toolbar, then click **Hide All Visual Aids**.

   As shown in Figure 43, the borders around the table, table cells, and CSS blocks are all hidden, allowing you to see more clearly how the table will look in the browser. Visual aids are helpful while you are editing and formatting a page. However, turning them off is a quick way to see how the page will appear in the browser without having to open it in the browser window.

2. Repeat Step 1 to show the visual aids again.

TIP You can also click the Live View button on the Document toolbar to see how the page will look in the browser. Turn Live View off by clicking it again.

3. Save your work, preview the cafe page in the browser, close the browser, then close Dreamweaver.

You used the Hide All Visual Aids command to hide the table borders and layout block outlines, then showed them again.

Create a page using CSS layouts.

1. Open the Blooms & Bulbs website, then create a new blank HTML page with the 2 column fixed, left sidebar, header and footer style, linking the blooms_styles.css file to the page.
2. Save the file as **workshops.html**, overwriting the existing workshops page.

Add content to CSS layout blocks.

1. Open the index page, then copy the banner and menu bar. (*Hint*: Select the banner, hold down your Shift key, then click the SpryMenuBar tab to select the menu bar and the banner together.)
2. Close the index page, then on the workshops page, delete the logo placeholder in the header, then paste the banner and menu bar in the header block. (*Hint*: If you have trouble copying and pasting the banner and menu bar together, try copying and pasting them separately.)
3. Delete the footer placeholder text, then type **Copyright 2001 - 2013 Blooms & Bulbs** in the footer Block.
4. Delete the placeholder content from the content block.
5. Type **New Composting Workshop!**, enter a paragraph break, then import the text composting.doc from the drive and folder where you store you Data Files.
6. Enter a paragraph break, then insert the chives.jpg from the drive and folder where you store your Data Files. Add the alternate text **Even chives can be beautiful** to the image when prompted.

7. Select the chives image and add a 40 pixel H space.
8. Save your work.

Edit content in CSS layout blocks.

1. Select the footer rule in the Styles panel, then edit its Text-align property in the Block category to center the content.
2. Select the heading "New Composting Workshop!" and format it using the H3 tag.
3. Select the header rule in the CSS Styles panel and change its background color to **#FFF**.
4. Repeat Step 3 to change the background color of the sidebar1 rule to **#FFF**.
5. Edit the header rule so that the header has a 5-pixel margin on all sides.
6. Edit the body rule to change the Font-size to 14 pixels.
7. Save your work.

Create a table.

1. Delete the placeholder text, including the <H1> tag, in the sidebar, then insert a table with the following settings: Rows: **8**, Columns: **2**, Table width: **175 pixels**, Border thickness: **0**, Cell padding: **5**, Cell spacing: **5**, and Header: **Top**. In the Summary text box, enter the text **This table is used to list the workshop names and dates**.
2. Edit the sidebar1 rule to center-align the contents.
3. Add the page title **Blooms & Bulbs scheduled workshops** then save your work.

Resize, split, and merge cells.

1. Select the first cell in the second row of the table, then set the cell width to **60%**.
2. Select the second cell in the second row, then set the cell width to **40%**.
3. Merge the two cells in the first row.
4. Merge the two cells in the last row.
5. Save your work.

Insert and align images in table cells.

1. Use the Insert panel to insert gardening_gloves.gif in the last row of the table. You can find this image in the assets folder where you store your Data Files. Add the alternate text **Gardening gloves** to the image when prompted, then center the image in the merged cell.
2. Save your work.

Insert text and format cell content.

1. Type **Scheduled Workshops** in the merged cell in the first row.
2. Go to Code View, locate the .sidebar1 style around line 75, verify that the text alignment is set to center, then return to Design view.
3. Type the names and dates for the workshops from Figure 44 in each row of the table.
4. Save your work, preview the page in your browser, then close your browser.
5. Close all open pages.

Figure 44 *Completed Skills Review*

Blooms & Bulbs

HWY 43 SOUTH • ALVIN • TX 77511 • 555-248-0806

| Home | Newsletter | Plants ▾ | Tips | Workshops |

Scheduled Workshops

Composting	8/1/13
Irrigation Basics	8/8/13
Pruning	8/15/13
Water Gardening	8/22/13
Mulching	8/29/13
Green Gardening	9/4/13

New Composting Workshop!

Our next workshop is entitled "Everything You Need to Know About Composting." This informative workshop will be great for any gardener, whether you plan to invest in a commercial compost bin or simply start a compost pile in a corner of your garden. You will be amazed at how quickly you can produce rich, nutrient-filled compost with only a little effort. Use this black gold to amend your soil naturally, to encourage the growth of healthy plants. Not only will you create rich soil and save water—you will also reduce trash at the landfill by recycling your kitchen scraps and garden materials.

We offer this free workshop on a first-come, first-served basis. All workshop participants will receive a packet of bacteria to kick-start their composting process. Our speaker will be Ann Porter from the County Extension Office. Ann recently completed her Master Composter Certification and is eager to share her knowledge. She is an engaging speaker you will be sure to enjoy. Call 555-248-0806 today to reserve your spot!

Copyright 2001 - 2013 Blooms & Bulbs

In this exercise, you continue your work on the TripSmart website that you began in Project Builder 1 in Chapter 1 and developed in the previous chapters. You are ready to begin work on a page featuring catalog items. You plan to use a CSS layout with a table to place the information on the page.

1. Open the TripSmart website.
2. Create a new page based on the 1 column fixed, centered, header and footer CSS page layout, attaching the tripsmart_styles.css file, then save the file as **catalog.html**, replacing the placeholder catalog page in the website.
3. Open the index page, copy the banner and menu bar, then close the index page.
4. Delete the logo image placeholder in the header, then paste the banner and menu bar in the header block. (*Hint*: Check the code to make sure you did not copy any break tags after the menu bar or you will have extra space on the page after the menu bar.)
5. Edit the embedded footer rule to center align the content, remove the top and bottom padding, and set the background color to #FFF.
6. Edit the header rule so its background is #FFF and all margins to 5 px.
7. Edit the embedded body style to change the Font-family to Arial, Helvetica, sans-serif, the Font-size to 14 pixels, and the background color to white.
8. Save your work.
9. Delete the placeholder content in the content block, use the Format list arrow in the HTML Property inspector to change the formatting to Paragraph, then enter a line break after the menu bar.
10. Insert a table into the content block with the following settings: Rows: **5**, Columns: **3**, Table width: **950 pixels**, Border thickness: **0**, Header: **Top**. Delete any value, if necessary, in the cell padding text box, enter an appropriate table summary, then center-align the table.
11. Set the cell widths in the bottom row to **33%**, **33%**, and **34%**.
12. Merge the three cells in the first row, enter a line break in the merged cell, then type **Our products are backed with a 100% guarantee**.
13. In the three cells in the second row, type **Protection from UV rays; Cool, light-weight, versatile;** and **Pockets for everything** then center the text in each cell.
14. Place the files hat.jpg, pants.jpg, and vest.jpg from the assets folder where you store your Data Files in the three cells in the third row, adding the following alternate text to the images: **Safari hat**, **Kenya convertible pants**, and **Photographer's vest**; center the three images.
15. Type **Safari Hat**, **Kenya Convertible Pants**, and **Photographer's Vest** in the three cells in the fourth row, then center each label.
16. Type **Item number 50501** and **$29.00** with a line break between them in the first cell in the fifth row.
17. Repeat Step 16 to type **Item number 62495** and **$39.50** in the second cell in the fifth row.
18. Repeat Step 16 to type **Item number 52301** and **$54.95** in the third cell in the fifth row, then center each item number and price in the cells.
19. Create a new class rule in the tripsmart_styles.css style sheet named **reverse_text** with the following settings: Font-family, Arial, Helvetica, sans-serif; Font-size, 14 px; Font-style, normal; Font-weight, bold; Color, #FFF. (*Hint*: Be sure to choose Class under Selector Type.)
20. Apply the reverse_text rule to the three item names under the images, then change the cell background color to #666633.
21. Create a new class rule called **item_numbers** with the following settings: Font: Arial, Helvetica, sans-serif; Size: 12 px; Style: normal; Weight: bold.
22. Apply the item_numbers rule to the three items' numbers and prices.
23. Delete the footer placeholder text, then type **TripSmart Copyright 2002 – 2013**.
24. Edit the footer style to change the Font-size property to 12 pixels and remove any padding if necessary.
25. Edit the container style properties to include a solid, thin border, color #030.
26. Save your work, view the page in your browser, then close the browser.
27. Add the page title **TripSmart featured catalog items**.
28. Open the index page and copy the line of code that inserts the favicon on the page, then paste it in the code on the catalog page right above the code for the title.
29. Save your work, preview the page in the browser and compare your screen to Figure 45, close the browser, then close all open pages.

Figure 45 *Sample Project Builder 1*

Use Figure 46 as a guide to continue your work on the Carolyne's Creations website that you started in Chapter 1 and developed in the previous chapters. You are now ready to begin work on a page showcasing the company's catering services. You decide to use CSS with a table for page layout.

1. Open the Carolyne's Creations website, then create a new page based on the 1 column fixed, centered, header and footer layout, attach the cc_styles.css file, and save the page as **catering.html**, overwriting the existing page.
2. Copy the banner that includes the menu bar from one of the other pages, then paste it on the page, replacing the logo placeholder.
3. Delete the container placeholder text, then edit the container rule properties with values of your choice to format the page to blend with the existing pages in the website.
4. Insert a table in the content block to showcase the catering services, with the following settings: Rows: 9, Columns: 3, Table width: 925 pixels, Border thickness: 0, Cell padding: 3, Cell spacing: 0, Header: Top, then add an appropriate table summary.
5. Center-align the table and set the width of the three cells to 33%, 33%, and 34%.
6. Merge the cells in the top row, then type **Catering for All Occasions** in the merged cells.
7. Merge the cells in the 5th row, type **Dinner to Go**, apply the H4 format, then center-align it.
8. Merge the cells in the 4th and 8th rows, then insert horizontal rules in the resulting merged cells. (*Hint*: Change the view to Expanded Tables mode to be able to see the cells more easily.)
9. Type **Lunch Boxes**, **Brunch Boxes**, and **Gift Baskets** in the three cells in the second row.
10. Type **Soups**, **Entrees**, and **Desserts** in the three cells in the sixth row.
11. Apply the headings rule to the text you typed in Steps 9 and 10, then center each of the labels.
12. Use a color of your choice for the background for each cell in the second and sixth rows.
13. In the first cell of the last row, enter the following text on three lines, using a line break between each sentence: **Call/fax by 9:00 a.m. for lunch orders.**

Call/fax by 1:00 p.m. for dinner orders. Fax number: 555-963-5938.

14. Apply the body_text rule to the text you typed in Step 13.
15. Use your word processor to open the file **menu items.doc** from the drive and folder where you store your Data Files. Copy and paste each text block into the cells in the third and seventh rows, apply the body_text rule to each text block, then center align each text block in the cells, using Figure 46 as a guide.
16. Merge the last two cells in the last row, then insert the image muffins.jpg with alternate text and any additional formatting of your choice.
17. Edit the footer properties with values of your choice, then type **Carolyne's Creations Copyright 2001 – 2013**.
18. Add the page title **Carolyne's Creations Catering Services**.
19. Modify the properties for the header block to blend in with the page color scheme.
20. Save your work, preview the page in your browser, make any adjustments that you feel would improve the page appearance, then close all open files.

Figure 46 *Sample Project Builder 2*

Jon Bishop is opening a new restaurant and wants to launch his restaurant website two weeks before his opening. He has hired you to create the site and has asked for several design proposals. You begin by looking at some restaurant sites with pleasing designs.

1. Connect to the Internet, then go to www.jamesatthemill.com, as shown in Figure 47.
2. How are CSS styles used in this site?
3. How are CSS styles used to prevent an overload of information in one area of the screen?
4. View the source code for the page and locate the html tags that control the CSS layout on the page.
5. Use the Reference panel in Dreamweaver to look up the code used in this site to place the content on the page. (*Hint*: To do this, make note of a tag that you don't understand, then open the Reference panel and find that tag in the Tag list in the Reference panel. Select it from the list and read the description in the Reference panel.)
6. Do you see any tables on the page? If so, how are they used?

Figure 47 *Design Project*

James at the Mill website used with permission from Miles James — www.jamesatthemill.com

For this assignment, you continue to work on the portfolio project that you have been developing since Chapter 1. No Data Files are supplied. You are building this website from chapter to chapter, so you must do each Portfolio Project assignment in each chapter to complete your website.

You continue building your website by designing and completing a page that uses a CSS layout for page design.

1. Consult your wireframe to decide which page to create and develop for this chapter. Draw a sketch of the page to show how you plan to use CSS to lay out the content.
2. Create the new page for the site using one of the predesigned CSS layouts.
3. Add text, background images, and background colors to each container.
4. Create the navigation links that will allow you to add this page to your site.
5. Update the other pages of your site so that each page includes a link to this new page.
6. Add images in the containers (where appropriate), making sure to align them attractively.
7. Review the checklist in Figure 48 and make any necessary changes.
8. Save your work, preview the page in your browser, make any necessary modifications to improve the page appearance, close your browser, then close all open pages.

Figure 48 *Portfolio Project checklist*

```
                    Website Checklist
1. Do all pages have page titles?
2. Do all navigation links work correctly?
3. Are all colors in the site web-safe?
4. Did you use a predesigned CSS page layout for at least one page?
5. Do your pages look the same in at least two current browsers?
6. Does all content in your CSS containers appear correctly?
```

CHAPTER **7**

MANAGING A WEB
SERVER AND FILES

1. Perform website maintenance

2. Publish a website and transfer files

3. Check files out and in

4. Cloak files

5. Import and export a site definition

6. Evaluate web content for legal use

7. Present a website to a client

CHAPTER 7

MANAGING A WEB
SERVER AND FILES

Once you have created all the pages of your website, finalized all the content, and performed site maintenance, you are ready to publish your site to a remote server so the rest of the world can access it. In this chapter, you start by running some reports to make sure the links in your site work properly and that any orphaned files are removed. Next, you set up a connection to the remote site for The Striped Umbrella website. You then transfer files to the remote site and learn how to keep them up to date. You also check out a file so that it is not available to other team members while you are editing it and you learn how to cloak files. When a file is **cloaked**, it is excluded from certain processes, such as being transferred to the remote site. Next, you export the site definition file from The Striped Umbrella website so that other designers can import the site. Finally, you research important copyright issues that affect all websites, and learn how to present your work to a client.

Preparing to Publish a Site

Before you publish a site, it is extremely important that you test it to make sure the content is accurate and up to date and that everything is functioning properly. When viewing pages over the Internet, users find it frustrating to click a link that doesn't work or to wait for pages that load slowly because of large graphics and animations. Remember that the typical user has a short attention span and limited patience.

Before you publish your site, be sure to use the Link Checker panel to check for broken links and orphaned files. Make sure that all image paths are correct and that all images load quickly and have alternate text. Verify that all pages have titles, and remove all non-websafe colors that could present a problem. View the pages in at least two different browsers and different versions of the same browser to ensure that everything works correctly. The more frequently you test, the better the chance that your users will have a positive experience at your site and want to return. Finally, before you publish your pages, verify that all content is original to the website, has been obtained legally, and is used properly without violating the copyright of someone else's work.

TOOLS YOU'LL USE

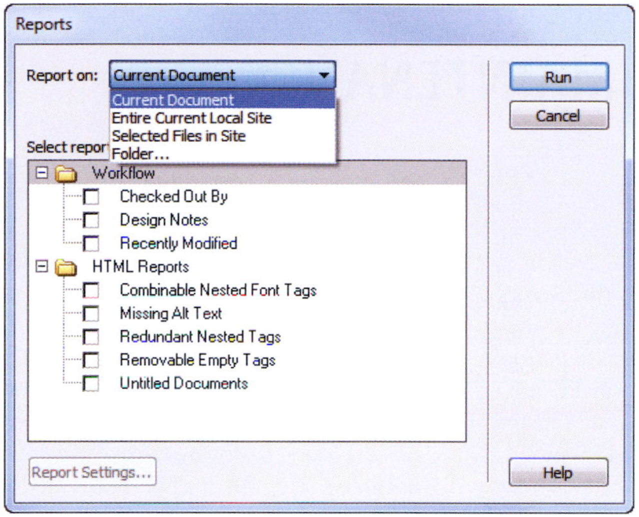

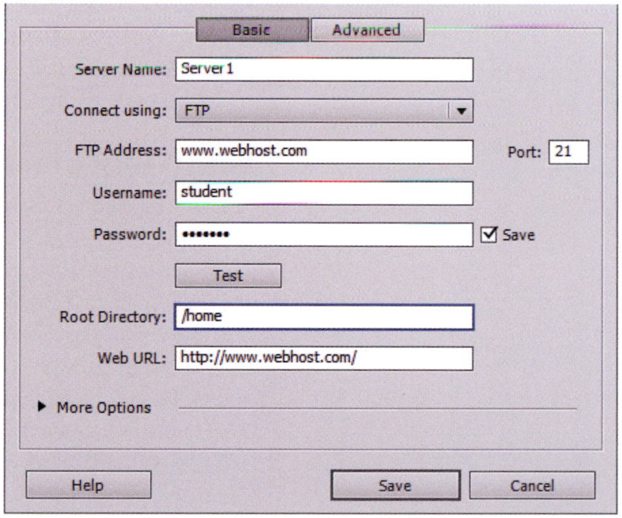

Reports

Report on: Current Document ▼

- Current Document
- Entire Current Local Site
- Selected Files in Site
- Folder...

Run

Cancel

Select report

☐ 📁 Workflow
- ☐ Checked Out By
- ☐ Design Notes
- ☐ Recently Modified

☐ 📁 HTML Reports
- ☐ Combinable Nested Font Tags
- ☐ Missing Alt Text
- ☐ Redundant Nested Tags
- ☐ Removable Empty Tags
- ☐ Untitled Documents

Report Settings...

Help

Basic | Advanced

Server Name: Server1

Connect using: FTP ▼

FTP Address: www.webhost.com   Port: 21

Username: student

Password: ●●●●●●   ☑ Save

Test

Root Directory: /home

Web URL: http://www.webhost.com/

▶ More Options

Help   Save   Cancel

Perform
WEBSITE MAINTENANCE

What You'll Do

In this lesson, you will use some Dreamweaver site management tools to check for broken links, orphaned files, and missing alternate text. You will also verify that all colors are websafe. You will then evaluate and correct any problems that you find.

Maintaining a Website

As you add pages, links, and content to a website, it can quickly become difficult to manage. It's easier to find and correct errors as you go, rather than waiting until the end of the design phase. It's important to perform maintenance tasks frequently to make sure your website operates smoothly and remains "clean." You have already learned about some of the tools described in the following paragraphs. Although it is important to use them as you create and modify your pages, it is also important to run them at periodic intervals after publishing your website to make sure it is always error-free.

Using the Assets Panel

You should use the Assets panel to check the list of images and colors used in your website. If you see images listed that are not being used, you should move them to a storage folder outside the website until you need them. You should also make note of any non-websafe colors. This is much less of an issue today than in the past, but it doesn't hurt to evaluate any non-websafe colors you find to evaluate whether slight variations in the way the colors are rendered could cause contrast problems.

Checking Links Sitewide

Before and after you publish your website, you should use the Link Checker panel to make sure all internal links are working. If the Link Checker panel displays any broken links, you should repair them. If the Link Checker panel displays any orphaned files, you should evaluate whether to delete them or link them with existing pages. To delete a file that you decide not to use, select it in the Files panel, then press [Delete] or right-click the file, click Edit, then click Delete. You should also check all external links by testing them in a browser to make sure that all links find the intended website.

Using Site Reports

You can use the Reports command in the Site menu to generate five different HTML reports that can help you maintain your website. You choose the type of report you want to run in the Reports dialog box, shown in Figure 1. You can specify whether to generate the report for the current document, the entire current local site, selected files in the site, or a selected folder. You can also generate workflow reports to see files that have been checked out by others or recently modified or you can view the Design Notes attached to files.

Design Notes are separate files in a website that contain additional information about a page file or a graphic file. If several designers are working collaboratively to design a site, they can record notes to exchange information with other design team members about the status of a file. Design Notes are also a good place to store information about the source files for graphics, such as Flash or Fireworks files.

Validating Markup

Because web development can now use multiple languages, it's important to ensure that the various language versions are compatible. To address this need, Dreamweaver can validate markup. To **validate markup**, Dreamweaver searches through the code to look for errors that could occur with different language versions, such as XHTML or XML. To validate code for a page, click File on the Application bar (Win) or Menu bar (Mac) point to Validate, and then click ColdFusion or As XML. The Results tab group displaying the Validation panel opens and lists any pages with errors, the line numbers where the errors occur, and an explanation of the errors.

Testing Pages

Finally, you should test your website using many different types and versions of browsers, platforms, and screen resolutions. You can use the Check browser compatibility button on the Document toolbar to check for issues with your site pages that might cause problems when they are viewed using certain browsers. Examples can include the rendering of square bullets, table borders, horizontal rules, or CSS AP elements. If you find such issues, you can choose to change your pages to eliminate the problems. The Results Tab group's Browser Compatibility panel includes a URL that you can visit to find the solutions to identified problems. You should test every link to make sure it connects to a valid, active website.

NEW Adobe has an application called **Adobe BrowserLab** that is a useful tool for cross-browser and cross-platform compatibility testing. Adobe BrowserLab is an online service, so you can access it from any computer with an Internet connection. There are two MXP extensions that you can download to enable this service to be used with Dreamweaver. Go to http://browserlab.adobe.com to learn more about using Adobe BrowserLab.

If, in your testing, you find any pages that download slowly, reduce their size to improve performance. Consider optimizing graphics by cropping or resizing images, reducing the number of Flash files, or streamlining the page code.

As part of your ongoing site testing, you should present the web pages at strategic times in the development process to your team members and to your clients for feedback and evaluation. Analyze all feedback on the website objectively, incorporating both the positive and the negative comments to help you make improvements to the site and meet the clients' expectations and goals.

Figure 1 *Reports dialog box*

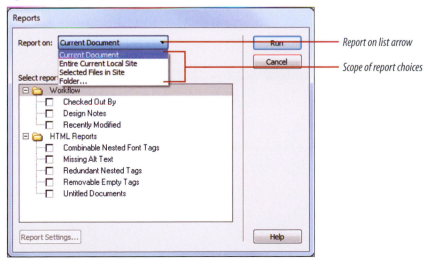

Check for broken links

1. Open The Striped Umbrella website.

2. Show the Files panel, if necessary.

3. Click **Site** on the Application bar (Win) or Menu bar (Mac), point to **Advanced**, then click **Recreate Site Cache**.

   It is a good idea to recreate the site cache to force Dreamweaver to refresh the file listing before running reports.

4. Click **Site** on the Application bar (Win) or Menu bar (Mac), then click **Check Links Sitewide**.

   No broken links are listed in the Link Checker panel of the Results Tab Group, as shown in Figure 2.

You verified that there are no broken links in the website.

Check for orphaned files

1. On the Link Checker panel, click the **Show list arrow**, then click **Orphaned Files**.

   There are no orphaned files, as shown in Figure 3.

2. Close the Results Tab Group.

You verified that there are no orphaned files in the website.

Figure 2 *Link Checker panel displaying no broken links*

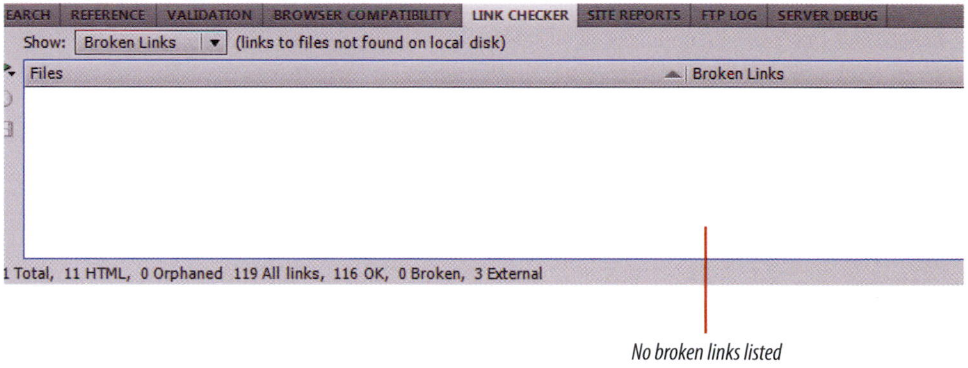

No broken links listed

Figure 3 *Link Checker panel displaying no orphaned files*

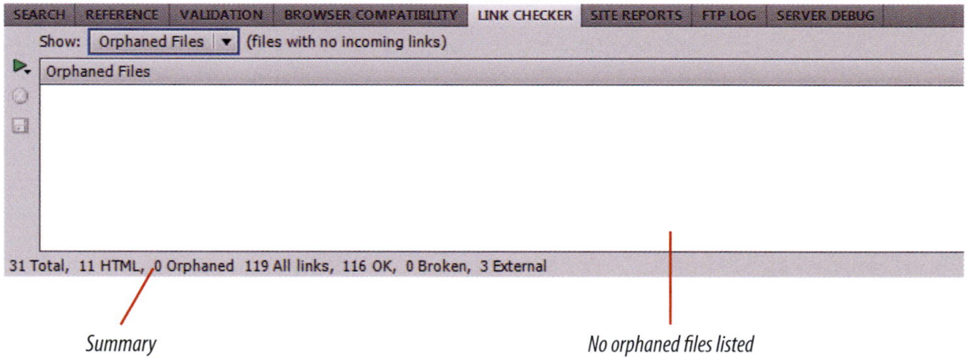

Summary

No orphaned files listed

Figure 4 *Assets panel displaying websafe and non-websafe colors*

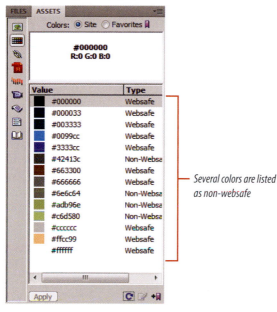

Several colors are listed as non-websafe

Figure 5 *Locating a non-websafe color*

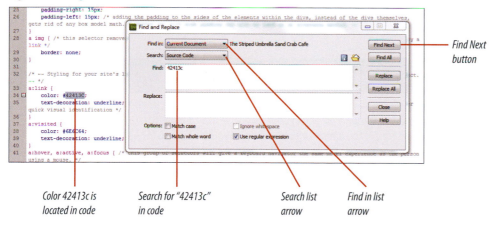

Color 42413c is located in code

Search for "42413c" in code

Search list arrow

Find in list arrow

Find Next button

Search for non-websafe colors

1. Click the **Assets panel tab**, then click the **Colors button** to view the website colors, as shown in Figure 4.

   The Assets panel shows that all but four colors listed are websafe. It is a good idea to look at any non-websafe colors listed and decide whether they could affect the appearance of any page elements. If they do, you might consider replacing them with websafe colors.

2. Open the **cafe page**, switch to Code view, click **Edit** on the Application bar (Win) or Menu bar (Mac), click **Find and Replace**, verify that Current Document is selected next to Find in, verify that Source Code is selected next to Search, type **42413c** in the Find text box, then click **Find Next**.

   The text "42413c" is a search string. A **string** is a series of characters or words. You use strings each time you enter terms in a search text box. The string "42413c" is located and selected in the cafe page code, as shown in Figure 5. This color is in one of the styles from the predesigned page layout and is not used on this page, so it is not a problem.

3. Click **Find Next**.

   There are no more occurrences of this search string. The bottom of the Find and Replace dialog box shows that the search is done, with one item found in the current document.

4. Close the Find and Replace dialog box, then close the cafe page.

   (continued)

5. Click **Edit** on the Application bar (Win) or Menu bar (Mac), click **Find and Replace**, click the **Find in list arrow**, click **Entire Current Local Site**, click the **Search list arrow**, click **Source Code**, type **6e6c64** in the Find text box, then click **Find Next**.

The cafe page opens in Code view with the non-websafe color selected. This color is in another style from the predesigned page layout that is not used on this page, so it is not a problem. Any unopened page with this code will be opened in Code view with the code selected after you click Find Next.

6. Search for the rest of the non-websafe colors, then close the Find and Replace dialog box.

None of these colors affect the page elements on the cafe page, so no changes need to be made at this time.

You viewed the websafe and non-websafe colors in the website and decided that the non-websafe colors were not a problem.

Check for untitled documents

1. Click **Site** on the Application bar (Win) or Menu bar (Mac), then click **Reports** to open the Reports dialog box.

2. Click the **Report on list arrow**, click **Entire Current Local Site**, click the **Untitled Documents check box**, as shown in Figure 6, then click **Run**.

The Site Reports panel opens in the Results Tab Group, and shows that all pages have page titles, as shown in Figure 7.

You ran a report for untitled documents, and verified that all pages have page titles.

Figure 6 *Reports dialog box with Untitled Documents option selected*

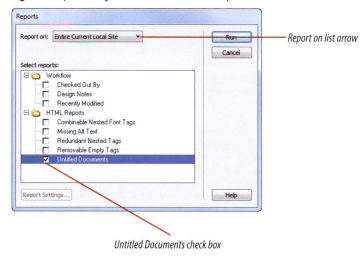

Report on list arrow

Untitled Documents check box

Figure 7 *Reports dialog box showing no pages without page titles*

No pages are listed without page titles

Using Find and Replace to Locate Non-Websafe Colors

As with many software applications, Dreamweaver has a Find and Replace feature on the Edit menu that you can use both in Design view and in Code view. Use this command to search the current document, selected files, or the entire current local site. If you are looking for a particular non-websafe color, you can save time by using the Find and Replace feature to locate the hexadecimal color code in Code view. If a site has many pages, this is the fastest way to locate it. The Find and Replace feature can also be used to locate other character strings, such as a phrase that begins or ends with a particular word or tag. These patterns of character strings are referred to as **regular expressions**. To find out more, search for "regular expressions" in Dreamweaver Help.

Figure 8 *Reports dialog box with Missing Alt Text option selected*

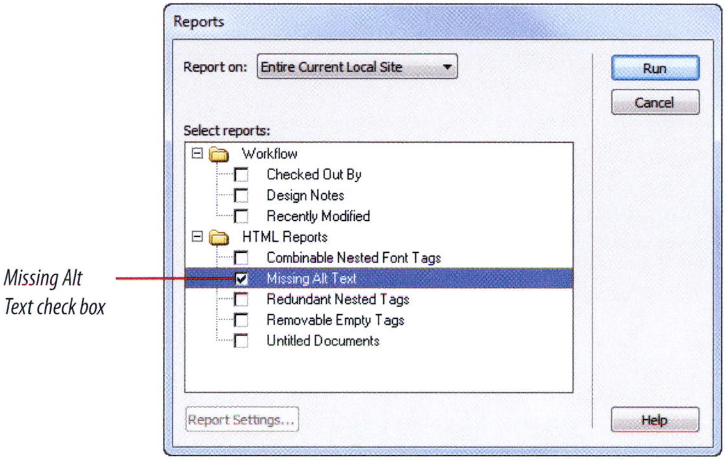

Missing Alt
Text check box

Check for missing alternate text

1. Using Figure 8 as a guide, run another report that checks the entire current local site for missing alternate text.

   There are no images with missing alternate text, as shown in Figure 9.

2. Close the Results Tab Group, then close all open pages.

You ran a report to check for missing alternate text in the entire site.

Figure 9 *Site Reports panel displaying missing "alt" tag*

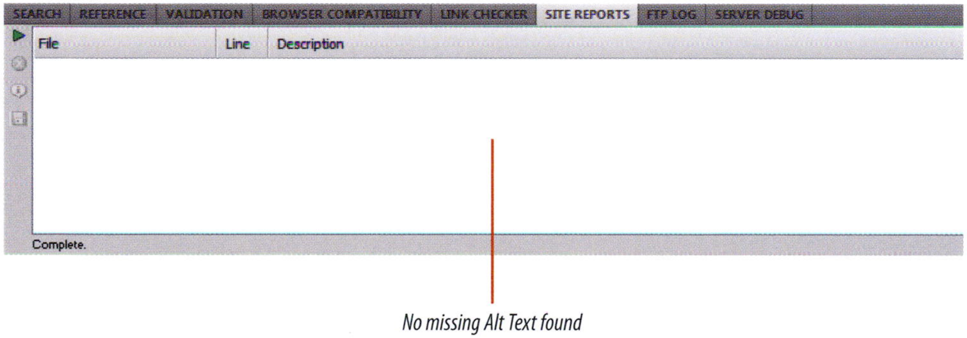

No missing Alt Text found

Validating Accessibility Standards

There are many accessibility issues to consider to ensure that your website conforms to current accessibility standards. HTML Reports provide an easy way to check for missing alternate text, missing page titles, and improper markup. You can run HTML Reports on the current document, selected files, or the entire local site.

Enable Design Notes

1. Click **Site** on the Application bar (Win) or Menu bar (Mac), click **Manage Sites**, verify that The Striped Umbrella site is selected, click **Edit**, click **Advanced Settings**, then click **Design Notes**.

2. Click the **Maintain Design Notes check box**, to select it, if necessary, as shown in Figure 10.

    When this option is selected, designers can record notes about a page in a separate file linked to the page. For instance, a Design Note for the index.html file would be saved in a file named index.html.mno. Dreamweaver creates a folder named _notes and saves all Design Notes in that folder. This folder does not appear in the Files panel, but it is visible in the site root folder in Windows Explorer (Win) or Finder (Mac).

3. Click **File View Columns**, then click **Notes** in the Name column.

4. Click the **Edit existing Column button** ✎, click the **Options: Show check box** to select it, if necessary, then click **Save**.

    The Notes column now displays the word "Show" in the Show column, as shown in Figure 11, indicating that the Notes column will be visible in the Files panel.

5. Click **Save** to close the Site Setup for The Striped Umbrella dialog box, then click **Done** in the Manage Sites dialog box.

    You set the preference to use Design Notes in the website. You also set the option to display the Notes column in the Files panel.

Figure 10   *Design Notes setting in the Site Setup for The Striped Umbrella*

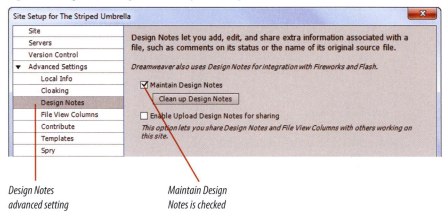

Design Notes
advanced setting

Maintain Design
Notes is checked

Figure 11   *Site Setup for The Striped Umbrella*

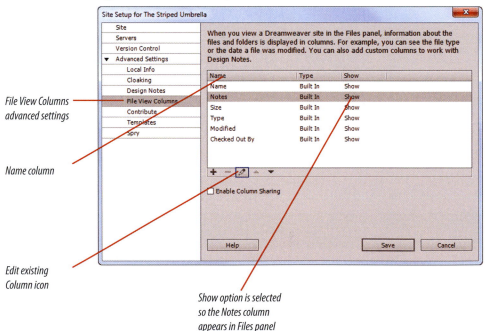

File View Columns
advanced settings

Name column

Edit existing
Column icon

Show option is selected
so the Notes column
appears in Files panel

Figure 12 *Design Notes dialog box*

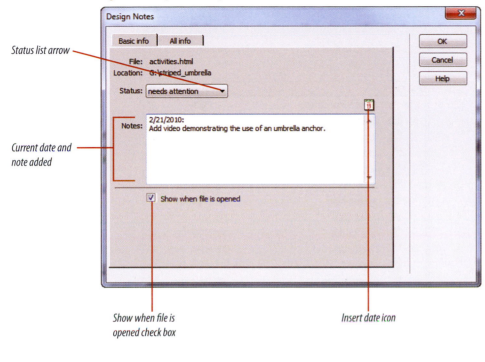

Status list arrow

Current date and note added

Show when file is opened check box

Insert date icon

1. Open the activities page, click **File** on the Application bar (Win) or Menu bar (Mac), click **Design Notes**, then click the **Basic info tab**, if necessary.

   The Design Notes dialog box opens. You can enter a note related to the open file in the text box. You can also assign the note a status, insert today's date, and indicate if the note appears whenever the file is opened.

2. Click the **Insert date icon** above the Notes text box on the right.

   The current date is added to the Notes text box.

3. Click under the date, then type **Add video demonstrating the use of an umbrella anchor**. in the Notes text box.

4. Click the **Status list arrow**, then click **needs attention**.

5. Click the **Show when file is opened** check box to select it, as shown in Figure 12, then click **OK**.

6. Click the **Refresh button** on the Files panel.

   An icon appears next to the activities page in the Notes column in the Files panel, indicating that there is a Design Note attached to the file.

You added a design note to the activities page with the current date and a status indicator. The note opens each time the file is opened.

Using Version Cue to Manage Assets

Another way to collaborate with team members is through Adobe Version Cue, a workgroup collaboration system that is included in Adobe Creative Suite 5. You can manage security, back up data, and use metadata to search files. **Metadata** includes information about a file such as keywords, descriptions, and copyright information. Adobe Bridge also organizes files with metadata.

Edit a Design Note

1. Click **File** on the Application bar (Win) or Menu bar (Mac), then click **Design Notes** to open the Design Note associated with the activities page.

TIP You can also right-click (Win) or [control]-click (Mac) the filename in the Files panel, as shown in Figure 13, then click Design Notes to open the Design Note.

2. Edit the note by adding the sentence **Ask Sue Geren to send the file**. after the existing text in the Notes section, then click **OK** to close it.

   Dreamweaver created a file named activities.html.mno in a new folder called _notes in the site root folder. This folder and file do not appear in the Files panel unless you have selected the option to show hidden files and folders. To show hidden files, click the Files Panel options button, then click View, Show hidden files. However, you can switch to Windows Explorer (Win) or Finder (Mac) to see them without selecting this option. When you select the option to Enable Upload Design Notes for sharing, you can share the notes with team members working with you on the site.

3. Right-click (Win) or [control]-click (Mac) **activities.html** in the Files panel, then click **Explore** (Win) or **Reveal in Finder** (Mac).

(continued)

Figure 13 *Files panel with Notes icon displayed*

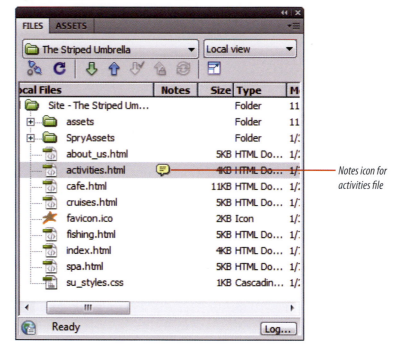

Notes icon for *activities file*

Deleting a Design Note

There are two steps to deleting a Design Note that you don't need anymore. The first step is to delete the Design Note file. To delete a Design Note, right-click the filename in the Files panel that is associated with the Design Note you want to delete, and then click Explore (Win) or Reveal in Finder (Mac) to open your file management system. Open the _notes folder, delete the .mno file in the files list, and then close Explorer (Win) or Finder (Mac). The second step is done in Dreamweaver. Leave Maintain Design Notes selected in the Site Setup dialog box, then click Site on the Application bar (Win) or Menu bar (Mac), click Manage Sites, click Edit, click Advanced Settings, then select the Design Notes category. Click the Clean Up button. (*Note*: Don't do this if you deselect Maintain Design Notes first or it will delete all of your Design Notes!) The Design Notes icon will be removed from the Notes column in the Files panel.

Figure 14 *Windows Explorer displaying the _notes file and folder*

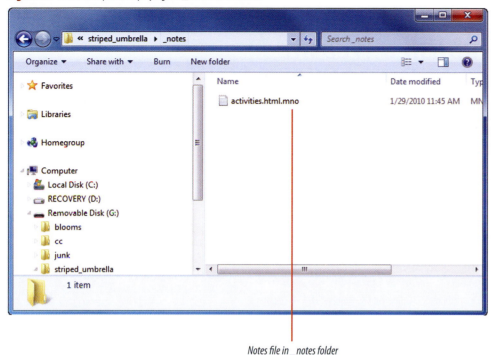

Notes file in _notes folder

4. Double-click the **_notes** folder to open it, then double-click the file **activities.html.mno**, shown in Figure 14, to open the file in Dreamweaver.

The notes file opens in Code view in Dreamweaver, as shown in Figure 15.

5. Read the file, close it, close Explorer (Win) or Finder (Mac), then close the activities page.

You opened the Design Notes dialog box and edited the note in the Notes text box. Next, you viewed the .mno file that Dreamweaver created when you added the Design Note.

Figure 15 *Code for the activities.html.mno file*

```
1  <?xml version="1.0" encoding="utf-8" ?>
2  <info>
3     <infoitem key="notes" value="1/29/2010: &#xD;Add video demonstrating the use of an umbrella anchor. Ask Sue Geren to send
   the file." />
4     <infoitem key="status" value="needs attention" />
5     <infoitem key="showOnOpen" value="true" />
6  </info>
7
```

Publish a Website
AND TRANSFER FILES

What You'll Do

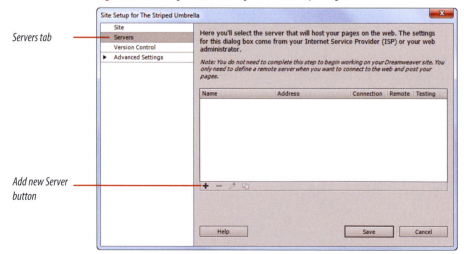

In this lesson, you will set up remote access to either an FTP folder or a local/network folder for The Striped Umbrella website. You will also view a website on a remote server, upload files to it, and synchronize the files.

Defining a Remote Site

As you learned in Chapter 1, publishing a site means transferring a copy of all the site's files to a web server. A **web server** is a computer with software that enables it to host websites and is connected to the Internet with an IP (Internet Protocol) address so that it is available on the Internet. Before you can publish a site to a web server, you must first define the remote site by specifying the Servers settings in the

Site Setup dialog box as shown in Figure 16. You can specify remote settings when you first create a new site and define the site root folder (as you did in Chapter 1 when you defined the remote access settings for The Striped Umbrella website). Or you can do it after you have completed all of your pages and are confident that your site is ready for public viewing. To specify the remote settings for a site, click the Add new Server button in the Site Setup

Figure 16 *Accessing the server settings in the Site Setup dialog box*

Servers tab

Add new Server button

dialog box, then add your server name, and choose a connection setting, which specifies the type of server you will use.

NEW Dreamweaver CS5 allows you to set up multiple servers. You can set up a server for testing purposes only and a server for the live website. The most common connection setting is FTP (File Transfer Protocol). If you choose FTP, you need to specify a server address and folder name on the FTP site where you want to store your site root folder. You can also use **Secure FTP (SFTP)**, an FTP option, which lets you encrypt file transfers to protect your files, user names, and passwords. To use SFTP, check the Use Secure FTP (SFTP) check box in the Site Setup dialog box. You also need to enter login and password information. Figure 17 shows an example of FTP settings in the Add new server dialog box.

QUICK TIP

If you do not have access to an FTP site, you can publish a site to a local/network folder. This is referred to as a **LAN**, or a Local Area Network. Use the alternate steps provided in this lesson to publish your site to a local/network folder.

Viewing a Remote Site

Once you have set up a remote server, you can then view the remote folder in the Files panel by choosing Remote view from the View list. If your remote site is located on an FTP server, Dreamweaver will connect to it. You will see the File Activity dialog box showing the progress of the connection. You can also use the Connects to remote host button on the Files panel toolbar to connect to the remote site. If you defined your site on a local/network folder, then you don't need to use the Connects to remote host button; the site root folder and

any files and folders it contains appear in the Files panel when you switch to Remote view.

Transferring Files to and from a Remote Site

After you set up a remote site, you need to **upload**, or copy, your files from the local version of your site to the remote host. To do this, view the site in Local view, select the files you want to upload, and then click the Put File(s) button on the Files panel toolbar.

NEW In Dreamweaver CS5, the Put File(s) button now includes the name of the server in the tooltip. Once you click this button, a copy of the files is transferred to the remote site. To view the uploaded files, switch to Remote server in the Files panel. Or, you can expand the Files panel to view both the Remote Site and the Local Site panes by clicking the Expand to show local and remote sites button in the Files panel.

If a file you select for uploading requires additional files, such as graphics, a dialog box opens after you click the Put File(s) button and asks if you want those files (known as **dependent files**) to be uploaded. By clicking Yes, all dependent files for the selected page will be uploaded to the appropriate folder in the remote site. If a file that you want to upload is located in a folder in the local site, the folder will automatically be transferred to the remote site.

QUICK TIP

To upload an entire site to a remote host, select the site root folder, then click the Put File(s) button.

Figure 17 *Viewing remote server settings in the Add new server dialog box*

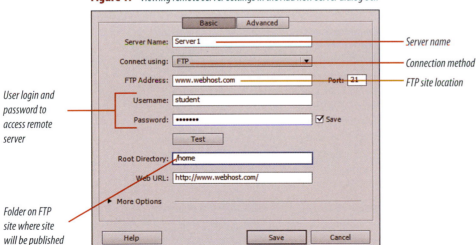

Server name

Connection method

FTP site location

User login and password to access remote server

Folder on FTP site where site will be published

If you are developing or maintaining a website in a group environment, there might be times when you want to transfer or **download** files that other team members have created from the remote site to your local site. To do this, switch to Remote Server in the Files panel, select the files you want to download, then click the Get File(s) button on the Files panel toolbar.

NEW In Dreamweaver CS5, the Get File(s) button now includes the name of the server in the tooltip.

Synchronizing Files

To keep a website up to date—especially one that contains several pages and involves several team members—you need to update and replace files. Team members might make changes to pages on the local version of the site or make additions to the remote site. If many people are involved in maintaining a

site, or if you are constantly making changes to the pages, ensuring that both the local and remote sites have the most up-to-date files could get confusing. Luckily, you can use the Synchronize command to keep things straight. The **Synchronize command** instructs Dreamweaver to compare the dates of the saved files in both versions of

the site, then transfers only copies of files that have changed. To synchronize files, use the Synchronize Files dialog box, shown in Figure 18. You can synchronize an entire site or only selected files. You can also specify whether to upload newer files to the remote site, download newer files from the remote site, or both.

Figure 18 *Synchronize Files dialog box*

Instructs Dreamweaver to synchronize all files in the site

Understanding Dreamweaver Connection Options for Transferring Files

The connection types with which you are probably the most familiar are FTP and Local/Network. Other connection types that you can use with Dreamweaver include Microsoft Visual SafeSource (VSS), WebDav, and RDS. **VSS** is used only with the Windows operating system with Microsoft Visual SafeSource Client version 6. **WebDav** stands for Web-based Distributed Authoring and Versioning. This type of connection is used with the WebDav protocol. An example would be a website residing on an Apache web server. The **Apache web server** is a public domain, open source web server that is available using several different operating systems including UNIX and Windows. **RDS** stands for Remote Development Services, and is used with web servers using Cold Fusion.

Figure 19 *FTP settings specified in the Site Setup for The Striped Umbrella dialog box*

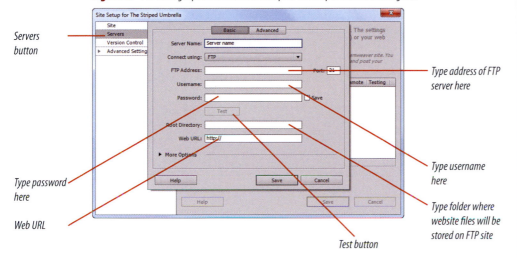

Servers button

Type password here

Web URL

Type address of FTP server here

Type username here

Type folder where website files will be stored on FTP site

Test button

Set up a web server connection on an FTP site

NOTE: Complete these steps only if you know you can store The Striped Umbrella files on an FTP site and you know the login and password information. If you do not have access to an FTP site, complete the exercise called Set up web server access on a local or network folder on Page 7-18.

1. Click **Site** on the Application bar (Win) or Menu bar (Mac), then click **Manage Sites**.

2. Click **The Striped Umbrella** in the Manage Sites dialog box, if necessary, then click **Edit**.

3. Click **Servers** in the Site Setup dialog box, click the **Add new Server** button ✚, type your server name, click the **Connect using list arrow**, click **FTP** if necessary, then compare your screen to Figure 19.

4. Enter the FTP Address, Username, Password, Root Directory, and Web URL information in the dialog box.

TIP You must have file and folder permissions to use FTP. The server administrator can give you this and also tell you the folder name and location you should use to publish your files.

5. Click the **Test button** to test the connection to the remote site.

6. If the connection is successful, click **Save** to close the dialog box; if it is not successful, verify that you have the correct settings, then repeat Step 5.

7. Click **Save** to close the open dialog box, click **Save** to close the Site Setup dialog box, then click **Done** to close the Manage Sites dialog box.

You set up remote access information for The Striped Umbrella website using FTP settings.

Comparing Two Files for Differences in Content

There are situations where it would be helpful to be able to compare the contents of two files, such as a local file and the remote version of the same file; or an original file and the same file that has been saved with a different name. Once the two files are compared and differences are detected, you can merge the information in the files. A good time to compare files is before you upload them to a remote server to prevent accidentally writing over a file with more recent information. To compare files, you must first locate and install a third-party file comparison utility, or "dif" tool, such as Araxis Merge or Beyond Compare. (Dreamweaver does not have a file comparison tool included as part of the software, so you need to download one. If you are not familiar with these tools, find one using your favorite search engine.)

After installing the file comparison utility, use the Preferences command on the Edit menu to open the Preferences dialog box, then select the File Compare category. Next, browse to select the application you want to use to compare files. After you have set your Preferences, click the Compare with Remote Server command on the File menu to compare an open file with the remote version.

Set up a web server connection to a local or network folder

NOTE: Complete these steps if you do not have the ability to post files to an FTP site and could not complete the previous lesson.

1. Using Windows Explorer (Win) or Finder (Mac), create a new folder on your hard drive or on a shared drive named **su_yourlastname** (e.g., if your last name is Jones, name the folder **su_jones**).

2. Switch back to Dreamweaver, open The Striped Umbrella website, then open the Manage Sites dialog box.

3. Click **The Striped Umbrella**, then click **Edit** to open the Site Setup for The Striped Umbrella dialog box.

TIP You can also double-click the site name in the Site Name box in the Files panel to open the Site Setup dialog box.

4. Click **Servers**, then click the **Add new Server button** ➕.

5. Type **SU Remote** for the Server Name, click the **Connect using list arrow**, then click **Local/Network**.

6. Click the **Browse icon** 📁 next to the Server Folder text box to open the Browse For Folder dialog box, navigate to and double-click the folder you created in Step 1, then click **Select**.

7. Compare your screen to Figure 20, click **Save**, click **Save** to close the Site Setup dialog box, then click **Done**.

You created a new folder and specified it as the remote location for The Striped Umbrella website, then set up remote access to a local or network folder.

Figure 20 *Local/Network settings in the Site Setup for The Striped Umbrella dialog box*

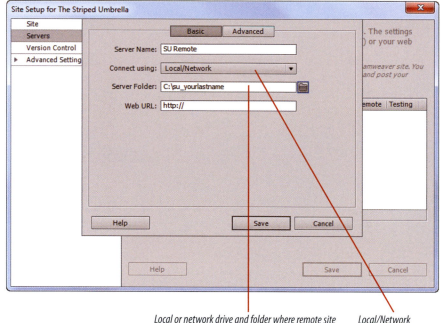

Local or network drive and folder where remote site will be published (your drive may differ and the folder name should end with your last name)

Local/Network setting selected

Testing Your Site's Usability

Once you have at least a prototype of the website ready to evaluate, it is a good idea to conduct a site usability test. This is a process that involves asking unbiased people, who are not connected to the design process, to use and evaluate the site. A comprehensive usability test includes pre-test questions, participant tasks, a post-test interview, and a post-test survey. This provides much-needed information as to how usable the site is to those unfamiliar with it. Typical questions include: "What are your overall impressions?"; "What do you like the best and the least about the site?"; and "How easy is it to navigate inside the site?" For more information, go to www.w3.org and search for "site usability test."

Figure 21 *Connecting to the remote site*

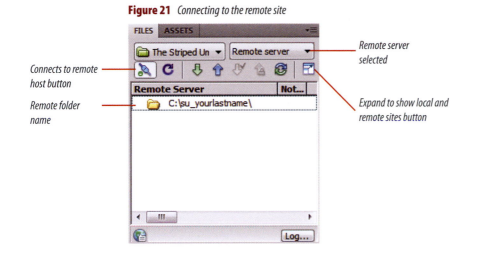

Connects to remote host button

Remote folder name

Remote server selected

Expand to show local and remote sites button

Figure 22 *Viewing the local and remote site folders*

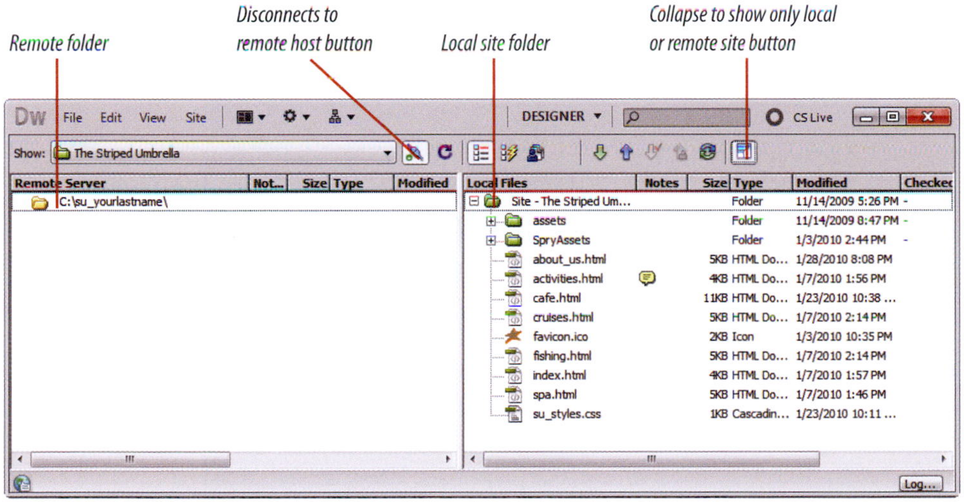

Remote folder

Disconnects to remote host button

Local site folder

Collapse to show only local or remote site button

View a website on a remote server

1. Click the **View list arrow** in the Files panel, then click **Remote Server**, then compare your screen to Figure 21.

   If you set your remote access to be a local or network folder, then the su_yourlastname folder appears in the Files panel. If your remote access is set to an FTP site, Dreamweaver connects to the host server and displays the remote folders and file.

2. Click the **Expand to show local and remote sites button** ⊞ on the Files panel to view both the Remote Site and Local Files panes. The su_yourlastname folder appears in the Remote Site portion of the expanded Files panel, as shown in Figure 22.

TIP If you don't see your remote site files, click the Connects to remote host button 🔌 or the Refresh button ⟳. If you don't see two panes, one with the remote site files and one with the local files, drag the panel border to enlarge the panel.

When the Files panel is expanded to show both the local and remote sites, the Expand to show local and remote sites button ⊞ becomes the Collapse to show only local or remote site button. ⊞ and the Connects to remote host button 🔌 becomes the Disconnects from remote host button 🔌.

You used the Files panel to set the view for The Striped Umbrella site to Remote view. You then connected to the remote server to view the remote folder you created earlier.

Upload files to a remote server

1. Click the **about_us.html file**, then click the **Put file(s) button** ⬆ on the Files panel toolbar.

   Notice that the Put File(s) button tooltip includes the name of the remote server you are using. The Dependent Files dialog box opens, asking if you want to include dependent files.

2. Click **Yes**.

   The about_us file, the style sheet files, the Spry assets files, and the image files used in the about_us page are copied to the remote server. The Background File Activity dialog box appears and flashes the names of each file as they are uploaded.

3. Expand the assets folder and the SpryAssets folder in the remote site if necessary, then compare your screen to Figure 23.

   The remote site now contains the about_us page as well as the Spry files, the image files, and the external style sheet files, all of which are needed by the about_us page.

TIP You might need to expand the su_yourlastname folder in order to view the assets folder.

You used the Put File(s) button to upload the about_us file and all files that are dependent files of the about_us page.

Figure 23 *Remote view of the site after uploading the about_us page*

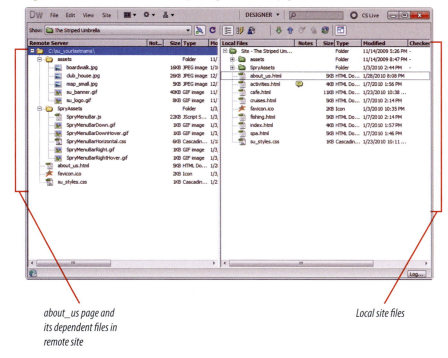

about_us page and its dependent files in remote site

Local site files

Continuing to Work While Transferring Files to a Remote Server

During the process of uploading files to a remote server, there are many Dreamweaver functions that you can continue to use while you wait. For example, you can create a new site, create a new page, edit a page, add files and folders, and run reports. However, there are some functions that you cannot use while transferring files, many of which involve accessing files on the remote server or using Check In/Check Out.

Figure 24 *Synchronize Files dialog box*

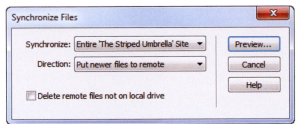

Figure 25 *Files that need to be uploaded to the remote site*

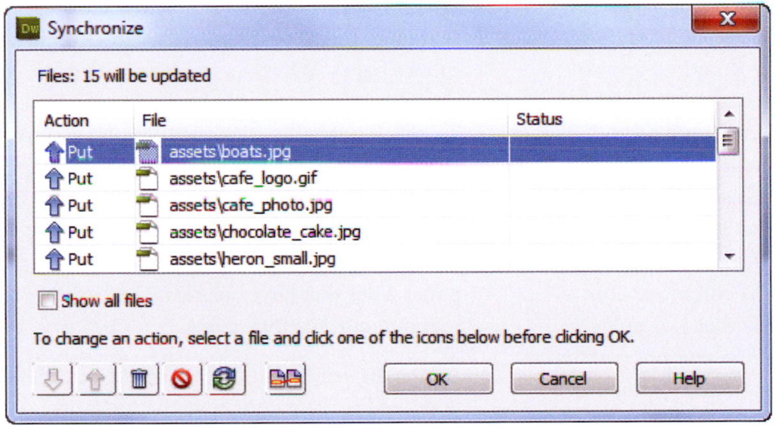

Synchronize files

1. Click the **Collapse to show only local or remote site button** ⊡, change to Local view, then open each page in the website in Code view and locate those that are missing the link to the website favicon in the line above the code for the page title.

2. Open the index page, then copy the code in the head content that links the favicon to the page.

3. Copy the favicon link to each of the pages you identified in Step 1, then save each page.

4. Click the **Synchronize button** ⟳ on the Files panel toolbar to open the Synchronize Files dialog box.

5. Click the **Synchronize list arrow**, then click **Entire 'The Striped Umbrella' Site**.

6. Click the **Direction list arrow**, click **Put newer files to remote** if necessary, then compare your screen to Figure 24.

7. Click **Preview**.

   The Background File Activity dialog box might appear and flash the names of all the files from the local version of the site that need to be uploaded to the remote site. The Synchronize dialog box, shown in Figure 25, opens and lists all the files that need to be uploaded to the remote site.

8. Click **OK**.

   All the files from the local The Striped Umbrella site are copied to the remote version of the site. If you open the Files panel, you will notice that the remote folders are yellow (Win) or blue (Mac) and the local folders are green.

You synchronized The Striped Umbrella website files to copy all remaining files from the local root folder to the remote root folder.

Check Files
OUT AND IN

What You'll Do

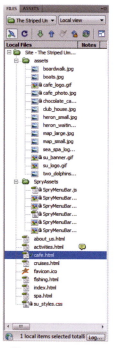

In this lesson, you will use the Site Setup dialog box to enable the Check Out feature. You will then check out the cafe page, make a change to it, and then check it back in.

Managing a Website with a Team

When you work on a large website, chances are that many people will be involved in keeping the site up to date. Different individuals will need to make changes or additions to different pages of the site by adding or deleting content, changing graphics, updating information, and so on. If everyone had access to the pages at the same time, problems could arise. For instance, what if you and another team member both made edits to the same page at the same time? If you post your edited version of the file to the site after the other team member posts his edited version of the same file, the file that you upload will overwrite his version and none of his changes will be incorporated. Not good! Fortunately, you can avoid this scenario by using Dreamweaver's collaboration tools.

Checking Out and Checking In Files

Checking files in and out is similar to checking library books in and out or video/DVD rentals. No one else can read the same copy that you have checked out. Using Dreamweaver's Check Out feature ensures that team members cannot overwrite each other's pages. When this feature is enabled, only one person can work on a file at a time. To check out a file, click the file you want to work on in the Files panel, and then click the Check Out File(s) button on the Files panel toolbar. Files that you have checked out are marked with green check marks in the Files panel. Files that have been checked in are marked with padlock icons.

After you finish editing a checked-out file, you need to save and close the file, and then click the Check in button to check the file back in and make it available to other users. When a file is checked in, you cannot make edits to it unless you check it out again. Figure 26 shows the Check Out File(s) and Check in buttons on the Files panel toolbar.

Enabling the Check out Feature

To use the Check out feature with a team of people, you must first enable it. To turn on this feature, check the Enable file check-out check box in the Remote Info settings of the Site Setup dialog box. If you do not want to use this feature, you should turn it off so you won't have to check files out every time you open them.

Using Subversion control

Another file management tool is Subversion control. A remote SVN (Apache Subversion) repository is used to maintain current and historical versions of your website files. It is used in a team environment to move, copy, and delete shared files. You can protect files from being accessed using the svn:ignore property to create a list of files that are to be ignored in a directory.

Figure 26 *Check Out File(s) and Check in buttons on the Files Panel toolbar*

Check Out File(s) button   Check In button

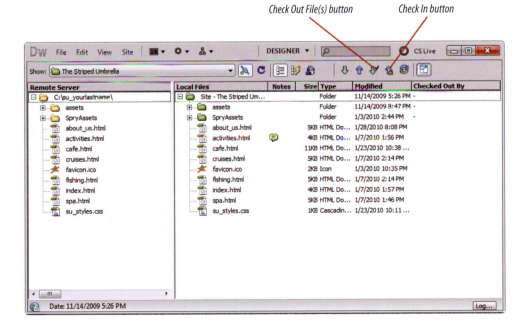

Activate the Enable file Check-out feature

1. Change to expanded view in the Files panel, click **Site** on the Application bar (Win) or Menu bar (Mac), click **Manage Sites** to open the Manage Sites dialog box, click **The Striped Umbrella** in the list, then click **Edit** to open the Site Setup for The Striped Umbrella dialog box.

2. Click **Servers**, select your remote server, click the **Edit existing Server button** 🖉 , click the **Advanced tab**, then click the **Enable file check-out check box** to select it.

3. Check the **Check out files when opening check box** to select it, if necessary.

4. Type your name using all lowercase letters and no spaces in the Check-out Name text box.

5. Type your email address in the Email Address text box.

6. Compare your screen to Figure 27, click **Save** to close the open dialog box, click **Save** to close the Site Setup for The Striped Umbrella dialog box, then click **Done** to close the Manage Sites dialog box. Your dialog box will differ from the figure if you are using FTP access.

You used the Site Definition for The Striped Umbrella dialog box to enable the Check out feature, which tells team members when you are working with a site file.

Figure 27 *Enabling the Check-out feature*

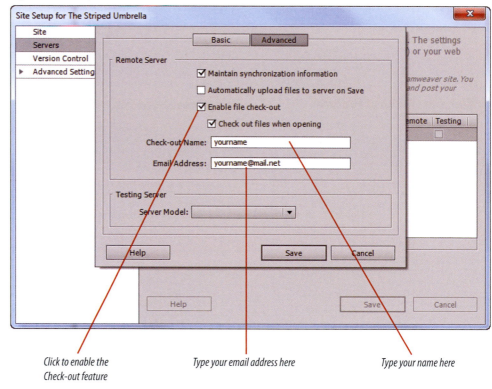

Click to enable the Check-out feature

Type your email address here

Type your name here

Figure 28 *Files panel in Local view after checking out cafe page*

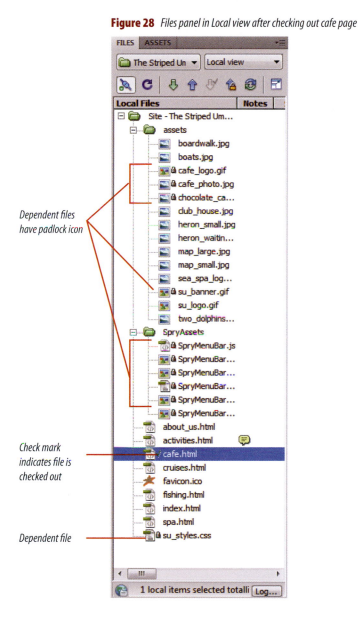

Dependent files have padlock icon

Check mark indicates file is checked out

Dependent file

Check out a file

1. Click the **cafe page** in the Local Files list in the Files panel to select it.

2. Click the **Check Out File(s) button** on the Files panel toolbar.

   The Dependent Files dialog box appears, asking if you want to include all files that are needed for the cafe page.

3. Click **Yes**, expand the assets and SpryAssets folders if necessary in the local site files, collapse the Files panel, click the **View list arrow**, click **Local view**, then compare your screen to Figure 28.

   The cafe file has a check mark next to it indicating you have checked it out. The dependent files have a padlock icon, indicating that they cannot be changed as long as the cafe file is checked out.

You checked out the cafe page so that no one else can use it while you work on it.

Check in a file

1. Open the cafe page, change the closing hour for The Cabana in the table to **8:00 p.m.**, then save your changes.

2. Close the cafe page, then click the **cafe page** in the Files panel to select it.

3. Click the **Check In button** 🔒 on the Files panel toolbar.

   The Dependent Files dialog box opens, asking if you want to include dependent files.

4. Click **Yes**, click another file in the Files panel to deselect the cafe page, then compare your screen to Figure 29.

   A padlock icon appears instead of a green check mark next to the cafe page on the Files panel. The padlock icon indicated that the file is read-only now and cannot be edited unless it is checked out.

   You made a content change on the cafe page, then checked in the cafe page, making it available for others to check it out.

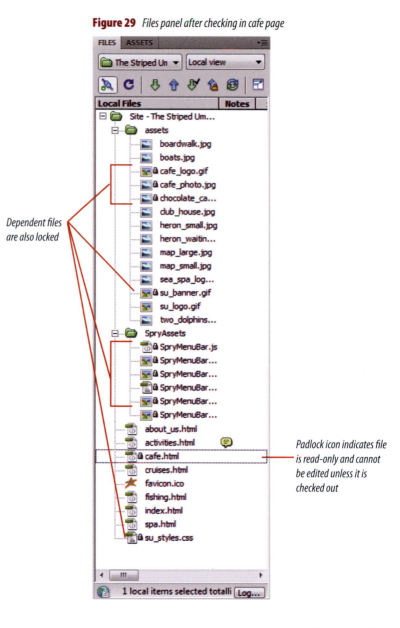

Figure 29 *Files panel after checking in cafe page*

Dependent files are also locked

Padlock icon indicates file is read-only and cannot be edited unless it is checked out

Figure 30 *Files panel after turning off the read-only feature*

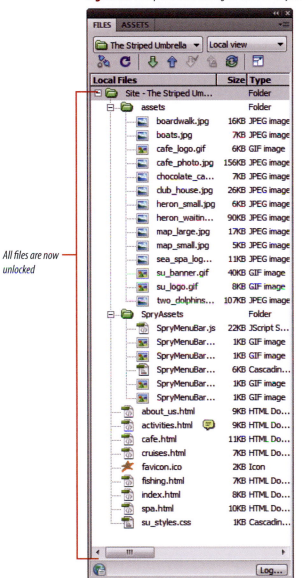

All files are now unlocked

Edit site preferences

1. Click **Site** on the Application bar (Win) or Menu bar (Mac), click **Manage Sites** to open the Manage Sites dialog box, click **The Striped Umbrella** in the list, then click **Edit** to open the Site Setup for The Striped Umbrella dialog box.

2. Click **Servers**, select your remote server, click the **Edit existing Server button** , click the **Advanced tab**, then click the **Enable file check-out check box** to deselect it.

   Now that you understand how to use this feature, it will be easier to have this option turned off so that each time you open a page you will not have to check it out the next time you use it.

3. Click **Save** to close the open dialog box, click **Save** to close the Site Setup dialog box, then click **Done** to close the Manage Sites dialog box.

4. Right-click the **site root folder** in the Files panel, then click **Turn off Read Only** (Win) or **Unlock** (Mac).

   All files are writeable now and the padlock icons have disappeared, as shown in Figure 30.

You disabled the Enable file check-out feature and then turned off the Read-only feature for all site files.

Cloak FILES

What You'll Do

In this lesson, you will cloak the assets folder so that it is excluded from various operations, such as the Put, Get, Check In, and Check Out commands. You will also use the Site Setup dialog box to cloak all .gif files in the site.

Understanding Cloaking Files

There may be times when you want to exclude a particular file or files from being uploaded to a server. For instance, suppose you have a page that is not quite finished and needs more work before it is ready to be viewed by others. You can exclude such files by **cloaking** them, which marks them for exclusion from several commands, including Put, Get, Synchronize, Check In, and Check Out. Cloaked files are also excluded from site-wide operations, such as checking for links or updating a template or library item. You can cloak a folder or specify a type of file to cloak throughout the site.

Cloaking a Folder

In addition to cloaking a file or group of files, you might also want to cloak an entire folder. For example, if you are not concerned with replacing outdated image files, you might want to cloak the assets folder of a website to save time when synchronizing files. To cloak a folder, select the folder, click the Files panel Options button, point to Site, point to Cloaking, and then click Cloak. The folder you cloaked and all the files it contains appear with red slashes across them, as shown in Figure 31. To uncloak a folder, click the Panel options button on the Files panel, point to Site, point to Cloaking, and then click Uncloak.

QUICK TIP

To uncloak all files in a site, click the Files Panel options button, point to Site, point to Cloaking, then click Uncloak All.

Cloaking Selected File Types

There may be times when you want to cloak a particular type of file, such as a .jpg file.

To cloak a particular file type, open the Site Setup dialog box, click Advanced, click Cloaking, click the Cloak files ending with check box, and then type a file extension in the text box below the check box. All files throughout the site that have the specified file extension will be cloaked.

Figure 31 *Cloaked assets folder in the Files panel*

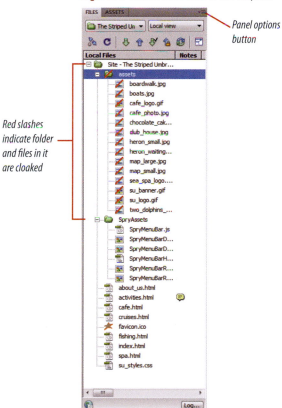

Panel options button

Red slashes indicate folder and files in it are cloaked

Cloak and uncloak a folder

1. Verify that Local view is displayed in the Files panel, then open the Manage Sites dialog box.

2. Click **The Striped Umbrella** if necessary, click **Edit** to open the Site Setup for The Striped Umbrella dialog box, click **Advanced Settings**, click **Cloaking**, verify that the Enable Cloaking check box is checked, click **Save**, then click **Done**.

3. Click the **assets folder** in the Files panel, click the **Files Panel options button** 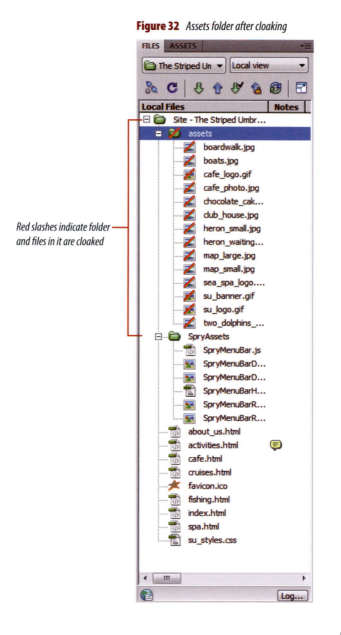, point to **Site**, point to **Cloaking**, click **Cloak**, then compare your screen to Figure 32.

   A red slash now appears on top of the assets folder in the Files panel, indicating that all files in the assets folder are cloaked and will be excluded from putting, getting, checking in, checking out, and many other operations.

TIP You can also cloak a folder by right-clicking (Win) or [control]-clicking (Mac) the folder, pointing to Cloaking, then clicking Cloak.

4. Right-click (Win) or [control]-click (Mac) the **assets folder**, point to **Cloaking**, then click **Uncloak**.

   The assets folder and all the files it contains no longer appear with red slashes across them, indicating they are no longer cloaked.

You cloaked the assets folder so that this folder and all the files it contains would be excluded from many operations, including uploading and downloading files. You then uncloaked the assets folder.

Figure 32 *Assets folder after cloaking*

Red slashes indicate folder and files in it are cloaked

Figure 33 *Specifying a file type to cloak*

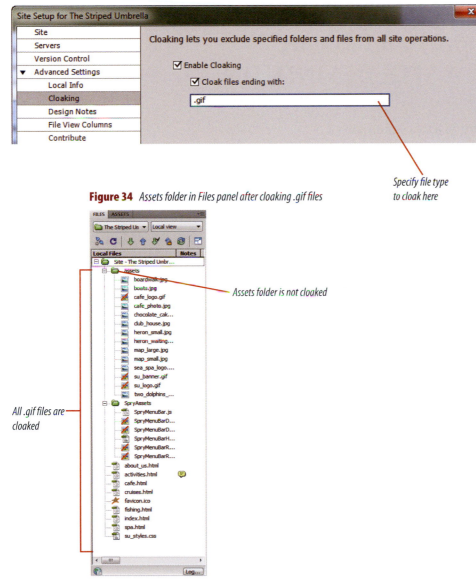

Specify file type
to cloak here

Figure 34 *Assets folder in Files panel after cloaking .gif files*

Assets folder is not cloaked

All .gif files are
cloaked

Cloak selected file types

1. Right-click (Win) or [control]-click (Mac) the **assets folder** in the Files panel, point to **Cloaking**, then click **Settings** to open the Site Setup for The Striped Umbrella dialog box with the Cloaking category selected.

2. Click the **Cloak files ending with check box**, select the text in the text box that appears, type **.gif** in the text box, then compare your screen to Figure 33.

3. Click **Save**.

   A dialog box opens, indicating that the site cache will be recreated.

4. Click **OK**, expand the assets folder if necessary, then compare your screen to Figure 34.

   All of the .gif files in the assets folder appear with red slashes across them, indicating that they are cloaked. Notice that the assets folder is not cloaked.

5. Click the **site root folder** in the Files panel, right-click, point to **Cloaking**, click **Uncloak All**, then click **Yes** to close the warning message.

   All files are uncloaked now and will not be excluded from any site commands.

You cloaked all the .gif files in The Striped Umbrella website. You then uncloaked all files.

Import and Export
A SITE DEFINITION

What You'll Do

▶ In this lesson, you will export the site definition file for The Striped Umbrella website. You will then import The Striped Umbrella website.

Exporting a Site Definition

When you work on a website for a long time, it's likely that at some point you will want to move it to another machine or share it with other collaborators who will help you maintain it. When you move a site, you need to move its site definition. The **site definition** for a website contains important information about the site, including its URL, preferences that you've specified, and other secure information, such as login and password information. You can use the Export command to export the site definition file to another location. The Export command creates a file with an .ste file extension. To do this, open the Manage Sites dialog box, click the site you want to export, and then click Export. Because the site definition file contains password information that you will want to keep secret from other site users, you should never save the site definition file in the website. Instead, save it in an external folder.

Importing a Site Definition

If you want to be able to access the site settings in a website that someone else has created, you can import the site definition file once you have the necessary .ste file. To do this, click Import in the Manage Sites dialog box to open the Import Site dialog box, navigate to the .ste file you want to import, then click Open.

Figure 35 *Saving The Striped Umbrella.ste file in the su_site_definition folder*

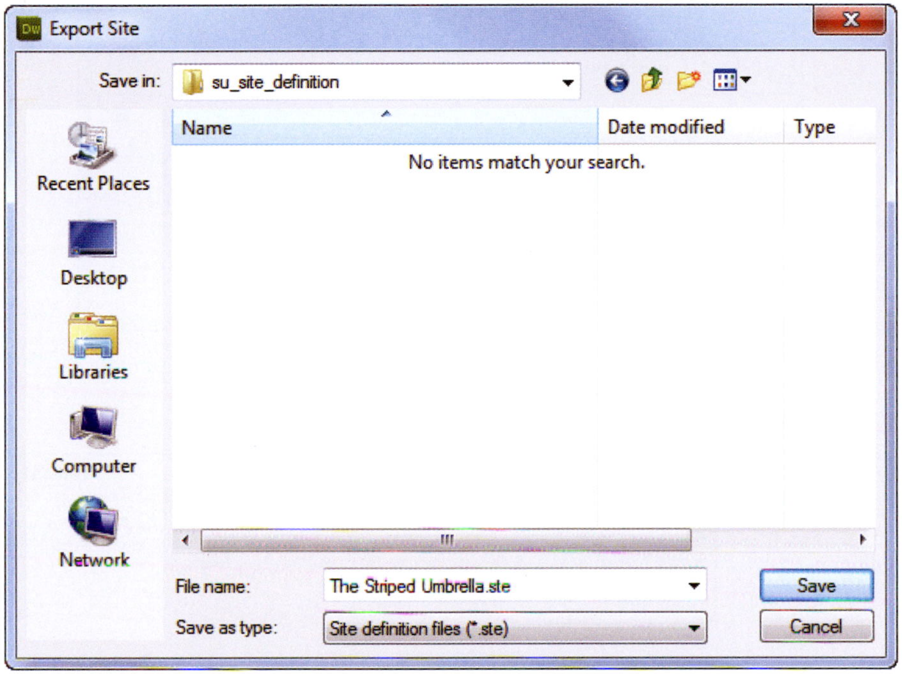

Export a site definition

1. Use Windows Explorer (Win) or Finder (Mac) to create two new folders on your hard drive or external drive named **su_site_definition** and **su_backup_site**

2. Switch back to Dreamweaver, open the Manage Sites dialog box, click **The Striped Umbrella**, then click **Export** to open the Export Site dialog box.

TIP If you see a message asking if you are exporting the site to back up your settings or to share your settings with other users, choose the Back up my settings option, then click **OK**.

3. Navigate to and double-click to open the **su_site_definition folder** that you created in Step 1, as shown in Figure 35, click **Save**, then click **Done**.

You used the Export command to create the site definition file and saved it in the su_site_definition folder.

Import a site definition

1. Open the Manage Sites dialog box, click **The Striped Umbrella**, then click **Import** to open the Import Site dialog box.

2. Navigate to the su_site_definition folder, compare your screen to Figure 36, select **The Striped Umbrella.ste**, then click **Open**.

   A dialog box opens and says that a site named The Striped Umbrella already exists. It will name the imported site The Striped Umbrella 2 so that it has a different name.

3. Click **OK**.

4. Click **The Striped Umbrella 2** if necessary, click **Edit**, then compare your screen to Figure 37.

   The settings show that The Striped Umbrella 2 site has the same site root folder and default images folder as The Striped Umbrella site. Both of these settings are specified in The Striped Umbrella.ste file that you imported. Importing a site in this way makes it possible for multiple users with different computers to work on the same site.

   TIP Make sure you know who is responsible for which files to keep from overwriting the wrong files when they are published. The Synchronize Files and Check In/Check Out features are good procedures to use with multiple designers.

5. Click **Save**, click **OK** to close the warning message, then click **Done**.

   TIP If a dialog box opens warning that the root folder chosen is the same as the folder for the site "The Striped Umbrella," click OK. Remember that you only import the site settings when you import a site definition. You are not importing any of the website files.

   You imported The Striped Umbrella.ste file and created a new site, The Striped Umbrella 2.

Figure 36 *Import Site dialog box*

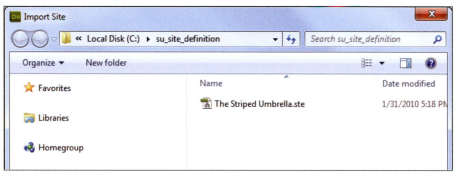

Figure 37 *Site Definition for The Striped Umbrella 2 dialog box*

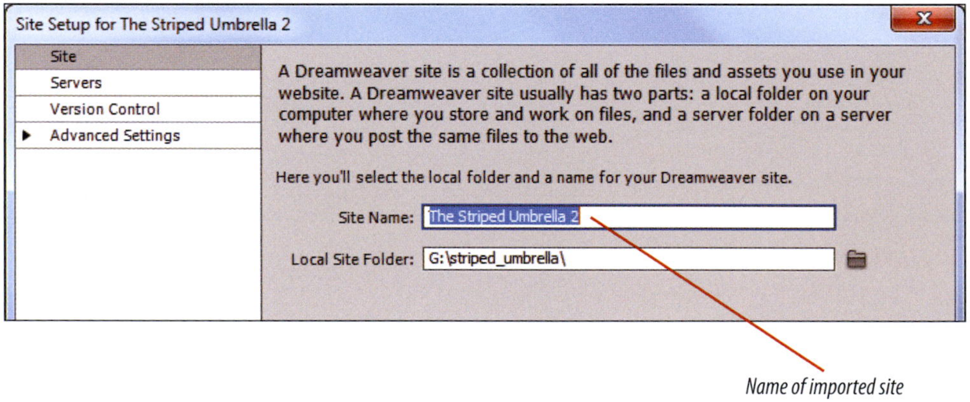

Name of imported site

Managing a Web Server and Files

Figure 38 *Viewing The Striped Umbrella 2 website files*

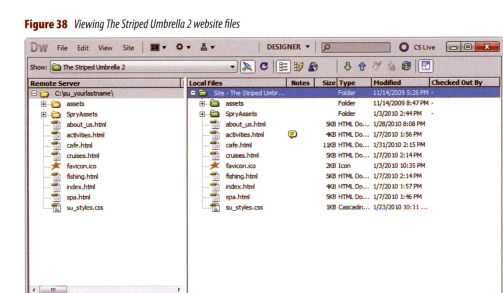

POWER USER SHORTCUTS

To do this:	Use this shortcut:
Get	[Ctrl][Shift][D] (Win) or ⌘ [Shift][D] (Mac)
Check Out	[Ctrl][Alt][Shift][D] (Win) or ⌘ [opt] [Shift][D] (Mac)
Put	[Ctrl][Shift][U] (Win) or ⌘ [Shift][U] (Mac)
Check In	[Ctrl][Alt][Shift][U] (Win) or ⌘ [opt] [Shift][U] (Mac)
Check Links	[Shift][F8] (Win) or [fn][shift][F8] (Mac)
Check Links Sitewide	[Ctrl][F8] (Win) or [fn] ⌘ [F8] (Mac)

View the imported site

1. Click the **Expand to show local and remote sites button** ⊡ on the Files panel toolbar to expand the Files panel.

2. Expand the Site root folder in the Local Files pane to view the contents, if necessary.

3. Click the **Refresh button** ↻ to view the files in the Remote Site pane.

   As shown in Figure 38, the site is identical to the original The Striped Umbrella site, except the name has been changed to The Striped Umbrella 2.

TIP If you don't see your remote site files, click the Connects to remote host button.

4. Click the **Collapse to show only local or remote site button** ⊡ to collapse the Files panel.

5. Open the Manage Sites dialog box, verify that The Striped Umbrella 2 site is selected, click **Remove**, click **Yes** in the warning dialog box, then click **Done** to delete The Striped Umbrella 2 website.

6. Close all open pages, then close Dreamweaver.

You viewed the expanded Files panel for The Striped Umbrella 2 website, then deleted The Striped Umbrella 2 website.

Evaluate Web Content
FOR LEGAL USE

What You'll Do

In this lesson, you will examine copyright issues in the context of using content gathered from sources such as the Internet.

Can I Use Downloaded Media?

The Internet has made it possible to locate compelling and media-rich content to use in websites. A person who has learned to craft searches can locate a multitude of interesting material, such as graphics, animations, sounds, and text. But just because you can find it easily does not mean that you can use it however you want or under any circumstance. Learning about copyright law can help you decide whether or how to use content created and published by someone other than yourself.

Understanding Intellectual Property

Intellectual property is a product resulting from human creativity. It can include inventions, movies, songs, designs, clothing, and so on.

The purpose of copyright law is to promote progress in society, not expressly to protect the rights of copyright owners. However, the vast majority of work you might want to download and use in a project is protected by either copyright or trademark law.

Copyright protects the particular and tangible *expression* of an idea, not the idea itself.

If you wrote a story using the idea of aliens crashing in Roswell, New Mexico, no one could copy or use your story without permission. However, anyone could write a story using a similar plot or characters—the *idea* of aliens crashing in Roswell is not copyright-protected. Generally, copyright lasts for the life of the author plus 70 years.

Trademark protects an image, word, slogan, symbol, or design used to identify goods or services. For example, the Nike swoosh, Disney characters, or the shape of a classic Coca-Cola bottle are works protected by trademark. Trademark protection lasts for 10 years with 10-year renewal terms, lasting indefinitely provided the trademark is in active use.

What Exactly Does the Copyright Owner Own?

Copyright attaches to a work as soon as you create it; you do not have to register it with the U.S. Copyright Office. A copyright owner has a "bundle" of six rights, consisting of:

1) reproduction (including downloading)
2) creation of **derivative works** (for example, a movie version of a book)
3) distribution to the public

4) public performance
5) public display
6) public performance by digital audio transmission of sound recordings

By default, only a copyright holder can create a derivative work of his or her original by transforming or adapting it.

Understanding Fair Use

The law builds in limitations to copyright protection. One limitation to copyright is **fair use**. Fair use allows limited use of copyright-protected work. For example, you could excerpt short passages of a film or song for a class project or parody a television show. Determining if fair use applies to a work depends on the *purpose* of its use, the *nature* of the copyrighted work, *how much* you want to copy, and the *effect* on the market or value of the work. However, there is no clear formula on what constitutes fair use. It is always decided on a case-by-case basis.

How Do I Use Work Properly?

Being a student doesn't mean you can use any amount of any work for class. On the other hand, the very nature of education means you need to be able to use or reference different work in your studies. There are many situations that allow you to use protected work.

In addition to applying a fair use argument, you can obtain permission, pay a fee, use work that does not have copyright protection, or use work that has a flexible copyright

license, where the owner has given the public permission to use the work in certain ways. For more information about open-access licensing, visit www.creativecommons.org. Work that is no longer protected by copyright is in the **public domain**; anyone can use it however they wish for any purpose. In general, the photos and other media on Federal government websites are in the public domain.

Understanding Licensing Agreements

Before you decide whether to use media you find on a website, you must decide whether you can comply with its licensing agreement.

A **licensing agreement** is the permission given by a copyright holder that conveys the right to use the copyright holder's work under certain conditions.

Websites have rules that govern how a user may use its text and media, known as **terms of use**. Figures 39, 40, and 41 are great examples of clear terms of use for the Library of Congress website.

A site's terms of use do not override your right to apply fair use. Also, someone cannot compile public domain images in a website and then claim they own them or dictate

Figure 39 *The Library of Congress home page*

Library of Congress website – www.loc.gov

Link to legal information regarding the use of content on the website

how the images can be used. Conversely, someone can erroneously state in their terms of use that you can use work on the site freely, but they may not know the work's copyright status. The burden is on you to research the veracity of anyone claiming you can use work.

Obtaining Permission or a License

The **permissions process** is specific to what you want to use (text, photographs, music, trademarks, merchandise, and so on) and how you want to use it (school term paper, personal website, fabric pattern). How you want to use the work determines the level and scope of permissions you need to secure. The fundamentals, however, are the same. Your request should contain the following:

- Your full name, address, and complete contact information.
- A specific description of your intended use. Sometimes including a sketch, storyboard, wireframe, or link to a website is helpful.
- A signature line for the copyright holder.

- A target date when you would like the copyright holder to respond. This can be important if you're working under deadline.

Posting a Copyright Notice

The familiar © symbol or "Copyright" is no longer required to indicate copyright, nor does it automatically register your work, but it does serve a useful purpose. When you post or publish it, you are stating clearly to those who may not know anything about copyright

Figure 40 *Library of Congress website legal page*

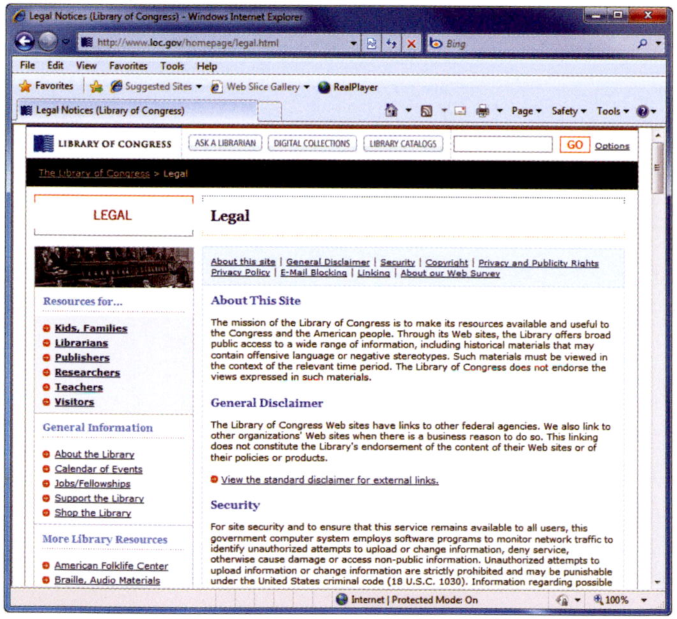

Library of Congress website – www.loc.gov

Figure 41 *Library of Congress website copyright information*

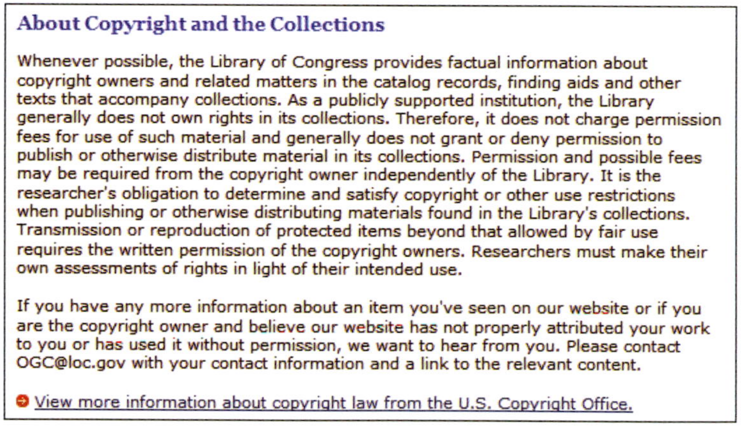

Library of Congress website – www.loc.gov

Managing a Web Server and Files

law that this work is claimed by you and is not in the public domain. Your case is made even stronger if someone violates your copyright and your notice is clearly visible. That way, a violator can never claim ignorance of the law as an excuse for infringing. Common notification styles include:

Copyright 2013
Delmar, Cengage Learning
or
© 2013 Delmar, Cengage Learning

Giving proper attribution for text excerpts is a must; giving attribution for media is excellent practice, but is never a substitute for applying a fair use argument, buying a license, or simply getting permission.

You must provide proper citation for materials you incorporate into your own work, such as the following:

References
Waxer, Barbara M., and Baum, Marsha L. 2006. *Internet Surf and Turf—The Essential Guide to Copyright, Fair Use, and Finding Media*. Boston: Thomson Course Technology.

This expectation applies even to unsigned material and material that does not display the copyright symbol (©). Moreover, the expectation applies just as certainly to ideas you summarize or paraphrase as to words you quote verbatim.

Guidelines have been written by the American Psychological Association (APA) to establish an editorial style to be used to present written material. These guidelines include the way citations are referenced. Here's a list of the elements that make up an APA-style citation of web-based resources:

- Author's name (if known)
- Date of publication or last revision (if known), in parentheses
- Title of document
- Title of complete work or website (if applicable), underlined
- URL
- Date of access, in parentheses

Following is an example of how you would reference the APA Home page on the Reference page of your paper:

APA Style.org. (Retrieved August 22, 2012), from APA Online website: http://www.apastyle.org/electext.html.

There are APA styles that are used for other sources of text such as magazines, journals, newspaper articles, blogs, and email messages. Here's a list of the elements that make up an APA-style citation of images, sounds, or video:

- Name of the researching organization
- Date of publication
- Caption or description
- Brief explanation of what type of data is there and in what form it appears (shown in brackets)
- Project name and retrieval information.

Another set of guidelines used by many schools and university and commercial presses is the Modern Language Association (MLA) style. For more information, go to http://www.mla.org.

Present a WEBSITE TO A CLIENT

What You'll Do

In this lesson, you will explore options for presenting a website to a client at the completion of a project.

Are You Ready to Present Your Work?

Before you present a website to a client as a finished project, you should do a final check on some important items. First, do all your final design and development decisions reflect your client's goals and requirements? Does the website not only fulfill your client's goals and requirements, but those of the intended audience as well? Second, did you follow good web development practices? Did you check your pages against your wireframes as you developed them? Did you check each page against current accessibility standards? Did you run all necessary technical tests, such as validating the code, and searching for missing alternate text or missing page titles? Did you verify that all external and internal links work correctly? Third, did your final delivery date and budget meet the timeframe and budget you originally promised the client?

If you find that you did spend more time on the site than you expected to, determine if it was because you underestimated the amount of work it would take, ran into unforeseen technical problems, or because the client changed the requirements or increased the scope of the project as it went

along. If you underestimated the project or ran into unexpected difficulties from causes other than the client, you usually cannot expect the client to make up the difference without a prior agreement. No client wants surprises at the end of a project, so it's best to communicate frequently and let the client know the status of all site elements as you go.

If the client changes the project scope, make sure you discuss the implication of this with the client. Ideally, you have made the client aware of any schedule or budget changes at the time they began to occur, and the client expects that your estimate will grow by a predictable, agreed-upon amount.

Client communication, both at the beginning of a project and throughout a project, is critical to a successful web design and a solid customer relationship. In building a house, a good architect makes an effort to get to know and understand a new client before beginning a house design. The design must be functional and meet the client's checklist of requirements, but it must also fit the client's personality and taste. The final structure must continue to meet those needs; the same is true of a website.

Some clients have a difficult time looking at architectural drawings and visualizing what the home will look like, so architects use different methods to communicate their design. Some use scale mockups, 3-D renderings, or photos of similarly styled homes to help the client visualize what their home will look like when completed. Web designers use similar strategies. You may be capable of building a great website, but you must communicate with the client from the beginning of the project to set and satisfy client expectations. Without this mutual understanding, the project's successful completion will be at risk. It is much less expensive to make changes and adjustments at the beginning of a project, and as changes occur, rather than close to completion. Communication is key.

What Is the Best Way to Present Your Work?

Ideally, you presented some form of prototype of the website at the beginning of the development process. You may have chosen to use low-fidelity wireframes such as one created in Microsoft PowerPoint or Adobe Photoshop. Or you may have used a high-fidelity wireframe that is interactive and multidimensional such as OverSight, ProtoShare, or Adobe Flash Catalyst, as shown in Figure 42. To communicate with your client and ensure a mutual understanding of the project, you could also use **BaseCamp**, a web-based project collaboration tool that many companies use. There is a monthly fee for using it, based on

the number of projects you are running and your storage needs. You can use BaseCamp throughout the project cycle, not just at the end. To present the final project, consider publishing the site to a server and sending the client a link to view the completed website. Creating PDFs of the site and sending them to the client for approval is another possible method.

Another communication option is to invite the client to your office and do a full walkthrough of the site with them, which offers them a chance to ask questions. This is probably one of the best options if it is feasible. If you have taken the time to build a relationship of trust over the project, neither side should expect unpleasant surprises at the end.

Figure 42 *Adobe Flash Catalyst information on the Adobe website*

Adobe product screen shot reprinted with permission from Adobe Systems Incorporated – www.adobe.com

Perform website maintenance.

1. Open the Blooms & Bulbs website, then re-create the site cache.
2. Use the Link Checker panel to check for broken links, then fix any broken links that appear.
3. Use the Link Checker to check for orphaned files. If any orphaned files appear in the report, take steps to link them to appropriate pages or remove them.
4. Use the Assets panel to check for non-websafe colors. Evaluate any non-websafe colors you find to see if they affect your page content.
5. Run an Untitled Documents report for the entire local site. If the report lists any pages that have no titles, add page titles to the untitled pages. Run the report again to verify that all pages have page titles.
6. Run a report to look for missing alternate text. Add alternate text to any graphics that need it, then run the report again to verify that all images contain alternate text.
7. Verify that the Design Notes preference is enabled and add a Design Note to the workshops page as follows: **Shoot a video of the hanging baskets class to add to the page**. Add the status **needs attention**, add the current date, and check the Show when file is opened option.

Publish a website and transfer files.

1. Set up web server access for the Blooms & Bulbs website on an FTP server or a local/network server (whichever is available to you) using blooms_ yourlastname as the remote folder name.
2. View the Blooms & Bulbs remote site in the Files panel.
3. Upload the water_lily.jpg file to the remote site, then view the remote site.
4. Add the code that links the favicon to the head content of any pages in the site that do not have it.
5. Synchronize all files in the Blooms & Bulbs website, so that all files from the local site are uploaded to the remote site.

Check files out and in.

1. Enable the Enable file check-out feature.
2. Check out the plants page and all dependent pages.
3. Open the plants page, then change the heading to "Featured Spring Plants: Roses!" and the style to Heading 2, then save the file.
4. Check in the plants page and all dependent files.
5. Disable the Enable file check-out feature.
6. Turn off read only (Win) or Unlock (Mac) for the entire site.

Cloak files.

1. Verify that cloaking is enabled in the Blooms & Bulbs website.
2. Cloak the assets folder, then uncloak it.
3. Cloak all the .jpg files in the Blooms & Bulbs website, then expand the assets folder if necessary to view the cloaked files in the Files panel.
4. Uncloak the .jpg files.

Import and export a site definition.

1. Create a new folder named **blooms_site_ definition** on your hard drive or external drive.
2. Export the Blooms & Bulbs site definition to the blooms_site_definition folder.
3. Import the Blooms & Bulbs site definition to create a new site called **Blooms & Bulbs 2**.
4. Make sure that all files from the Blooms & Bulbs website appear in the Files panel for the imported site, then compare your screen to Figure 43.
5. Remove the Blooms & Bulbs 2 site.
6. Close all open files.

Figure 43 *Completed Skills Review*

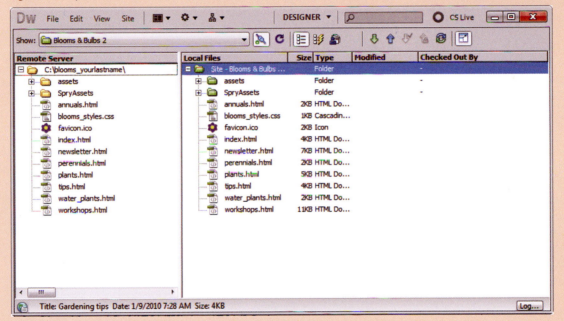

In this Project Builder, you publish the TripSmart website that you have developed throughout this book to a local/network folder. Thomas Howard, the owner, has asked that you publish the site to a local folder as a backup location. You first run several reports on the site, specify the remote settings for the site, upload files to the remote site, check files out and in, and cloak files. Finally, you export and import the site definition.

1. Use the TripSmart website that you began in Project Builder 1 in Chapter 1 and developed in previous chapters.
2. Use the Link Checker panel to check for broken links, then fix any broken links that appear.
3. Use the Link Checker to check for orphaned files. If any orphaned files appear in the report, take steps to link them to appropriate pages or remove them.
4. Use the Assets panel to check for non-websafe colors. If you find any, evaluate whether or not they pose a problem for any of the pages.
5. Run an Untitled Documents report for the entire local site. If the report lists any pages that lack titles, add page titles to the untitled pages. Run the report again to verify that all pages have page titles.
6. Run a report to look for missing alternate text. Add alternate text to any graphics that need it, then run the report again to verify that all images contain alternate text.
7. Enable the Design Notes preference, if necessary, and add a design note to the tours page as follows: **Add content and a Flash video for the San**

Francisco tour. Add the current date, the status **needs attention** and check the Show when file is opened option.
8. If you did not do so in Project Builder 1 in Chapter 1, use the Site Definition dialog box to set up web server access for a remote site using a local or network folder.
9. Upload the index page and all dependent files to the remote site.
10. View the remote site to make sure that all files uploaded correctly.
11. Add the code that links the favicon to the head content of any pages in the site that do not have it.
12. Synchronize the files so that all other files on the local TripSmart site are uploaded to the remote site.
13. Enable the Enable file check-out feature.
14. Check out the index page in the local site and all dependent files.
15. Open the index page, close the index page, then check in the index page and all dependent pages.
16. Disable the Enable file check-out feature, then turn off the read-only status (Win) or unlock (Mac) for the entire site.
17. Cloak all .jpg files in the website.
18. Export the site definition to a new folder named **tripsmart_site_definition**.
19. Import the TripSmart.ste file to create a new site named TripSmart 2.
20. Expand the assets folder in the Files panel if necessary, then compare your screen to Figure 44.
21. Remove the TripSmart 2 site.
22. Uncloak all files in the TripSmart site, then close any open files.

Figure 44 *Sample completed Project Builder 1*

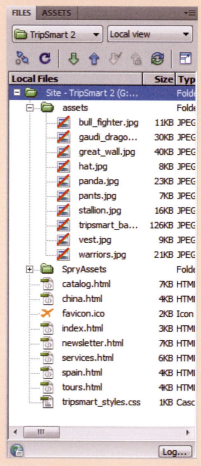

In this Project Builder, you finish your work on the Carolyne's Creations website. You are ready to publish the website to a remote server and transfer all the files from the local site to the remote site. First, you run several reports to make sure the website is in good shape. Next, you enable the Enable file check-out feature so that other staff members may collaborate on the site. Finally, you export and import the site definition file.

1. Use the Carolyne's Creations website that you began in Project Builder 1 in Chapter 1 and developed in previous chapters.
2. If you did not do so in Project Builder 2 in Chapter 1, use the Site Definition dialog box to set up web server access for a remote site using either an FTP site or a local or network folder.
3. Run reports for broken links and orphaned files, correcting any errors that you find.
4. Run reports for untitled documents and missing alt text, correcting any errors that you find.
5. Check for non-web-safe colors. If you find any, evaluate them to see whether or not they pose a problem for any of the pages.
6. Upload the classes.html page and all dependent files to the remote site.
7. View the remote site to make sure that all files uploaded correctly.
8. Synchronize the files so that all other files on the local Carolyne's Creations site are uploaded to the remote site.
9. Enable the Enable file check-out feature.

10. Check out the classes page and all its dependent files.
11. Open the classes page, then change the price of the adult class to **$45.00**.
12. Save your changes, close the page, then check in the classes page and all dependent pages.
13. Disable the Enable file check-out feature, then turn off read only for the entire site.
14. Export the site definition to a new folder named **cc_site_definition**.
15. Import the Carolyne's Creations.ste file to create a new site named Carolyne's Creations 2.
16. Expand the site root folder in the Files panel if necessary, compare your screen to Figure 45, then remove the Carolyne's Creations2 site.

Figure 45 *Sample completed Project Builder 2*

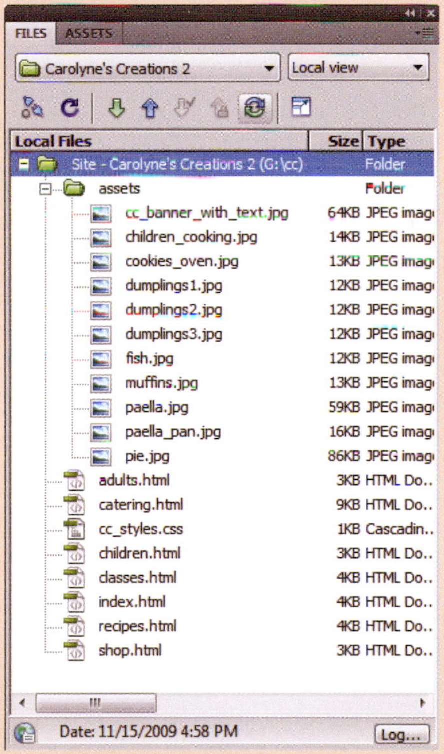

Throughout this book you have used Dreamweaver to create and develop several websites that contain different elements, many of which are found in popular commercial websites. For instance, Figure 46 shows the National Park Service website, which contains photos and information on all the national parks in the United States. This website contains many types of interactive elements, such as image maps and tables—all of which you learned to create in this book.

1. Connect to the Internet, then go to the National Park Service website at www.nps.gov.
2. Spend some time exploring the pages of this site to familiarize yourself with its elements.
3. Type a list of all the elements in this site that you have learned how to create in this book. After each item, write a short description of where and how the element is used in the site.
4. Click the link for the Site Index in the menu bar at the bottom of the page. Describe the information provided with the site index.
5. Click the Text Sizes links and describe how the page appearance changes as you click each option. How do you think this feature adds to the page accessibility?
6. Print the home page and one or two other pages that contain some of the elements you described and attach it to your list.

Figure 46 *Design Project*

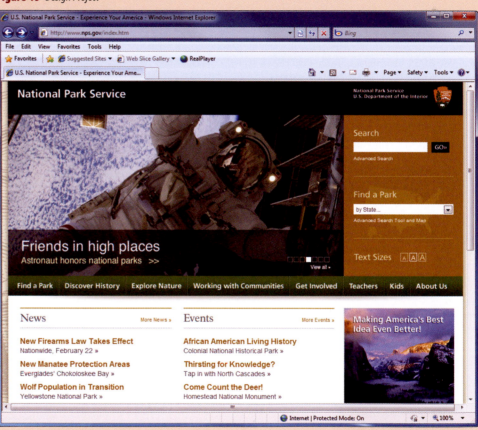

National Park Service website – www.nps.gov

In this project, you will finish your work on the website that you created and developed throughout this book. You publish your site to a remote server or local or network folder.

1. Before you begin the process of publishing your website to a remote server, make sure that it is ready for public viewing. Use Figure 47 to assist you in making sure your website is complete. If you find problems, make the necessary changes to finalize the site.

2. Decide where to publish your site. The folder where you will publish your site can be either an FTP site or a local/network folder. If you are publishing to an FTP site, be sure to write down all the information you will need to publish to the site, including the URL of the FTP host, the directory on the FTP server where you will publish your site root folder, and the login and password information.

3. Use the Site Setup dialog box to specify the remote settings for the site using the information that was decided upon in Step 2.

4. Transfer one of the pages and its dependent files to the remote site, then view the remote site to make sure the appropriate files were transferred.

5. Synchronize the files so that all the remaining local pages and dependent files are uploaded to the remote site.

6. Enable the Enable file check-out feature.

7. Check out one of the pages. Open the checked-out page, make a change to it, save the change, close the page, then check the page back in.

8. Cloak a particular file type.

9. Export the site definition for the site to a new folder on your hard drive or on an external drive.

10. Close any open pages, then exit Dreamweaver.

Figure 47 *Portfolio Project*

Website Checklist

1. Are you satisfied with the content and appearance of every page?
2. Are all paths for all links and images correct?
3. Does each page have a title?
4. Are all colors web-safe?
5. Do all images have appropriate alternate text?
6. Have you eliminated any orphaned files?
7. Have you deleted any unnecessary files?
8. Have you viewed all pages using at least two different browsers?
9. Does the home page have keywords and a description?
10. Is all text based on a CSS style?

CHAPTER 8 USING STYLES AND STYLE SHEETS FOR DESIGN

1. Create and use embedded styles

2. Modify embedded styles

3. Work with external style sheets

4. Work with conflicting styles

CHAPTER 8

USING STYLES AND STYLE SHEETS FOR DESIGN

Introduction

In Chapter 3, you learned how to create, apply, and edit Cascading Style Sheets. Using CSS is the best and most powerful way to ensure that all elements in a website are formatted consistently. The advantage of using CSS is that all of your formatting rules can be kept in a separate or **external style sheet** file, so that you can change the appearance of every page to which the style sheet is attached by modifying the style sheet file. For example, suppose your external style sheet contains a style called headings that is applied to all top-level headings in all your website pages. If you want to change the heading color to blue, you simply change that rule's color value to blue, and all headings in the website are updated instantly. This type of rule that affects all website content is called a **global CSS rule**. Because style sheets separate the formatting from the content, all pages in the site are formatted automatically from the style sheet information without affecting the content itself.

You can also create **embedded styles**, which are internal styles whose code is located within the head section of the HTML code of a web page. The advantage of embedded

styles is that you can use them to override an external style. For instance, if all headings in your website are blue because the external style applied to them specifies blue as the color value, you could change the color of one of those headings to a different color by creating and applying an embedded style that specifies a different color as the color attribute. Embedded styles are used in the Dreamweaver CSS predesigned layouts to format the div tags on each page. However, in general, you should use embedded styles for small formatting changes or for content that needs specific formatting, rather than to format all the pages of a website. Keeping formatting rules in a separate file from the web page content reduces the overall file sizes of your pages. In practice, you will find that most formatting code can be stored in a single file, rather than in individual page files.

In this chapter, you back up your site files, and then import a redesigned Striped Umbrella website. Each page has been redesigned using CSS for page layout to provide consistency. You will use this new site for the rest of the book. You then create and apply embedded styles and work with external style sheets to format the pages in the site.

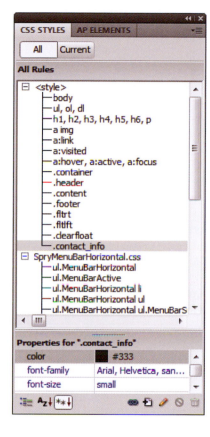

New CSS Rule

Selector Type:

Choose a contextual selector type for your CSS rule.

Class (can apply to any HTML element) ▾

Selector Name:

Choose or enter a name for your selector.

contact_info ▾

This selector name will apply your rule to
all HTML elements with class "contact_info".

◀ ▶

Less Specific   More Specific

Rule Definition:

Choose where your rule will be defined.

(This document only) ▾

OK

Cancel

Help

Create and Use
EMBEDDED STYLES

What You'll Do

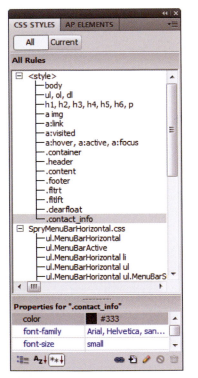

In this lesson, you will replace your Striped Umbrella files by importing a revised website. Next, you will create and apply an embedded style to the home page.

Understanding Embedded Styles

In Chapter 3, you learned how to create and use an external style sheet to apply consistent formatting to website elements. Recall that an external style sheet is a separate file with a .css extension that contains a collection of rules that create styles to format web page elements. Because you can apply external style sheets to multiple pages, they are a great tool to help ensure consistent formatting globally, across all pages of a website. For instance, you can set link properties, background colors, and text properties to appear uniformly on all pages. However, you might want to create a rule that is used only on a single page in your site. You can do this using an **embedded style**, a style whose code is embedded in the code of an individual page. Embedded styles do not format website content globally. Rather, they format elements on a single page. If both an external style and embedded style are applied to a single element, the embedded style overrides the external style.

There is also a type of style similar to an embedded style called an inline style. Like an embedded style, the **inline style** is part of the individual page code, but it is written in the body section, rather than the head section. Inline styles refer to a specific instance of a tag. The ID selector type creates an inline style. ID selector types (as opposed to class, tag, or compound types) can only be used once on each page. For example, <p id="footer"> would apply the footer style to one paragraph. Inline style rule names are preceded by a # sign. To apply an inline style to a page element, use the ID list arrow on the HTML Property inspector.

Creating and Applying Embedded Styles

To create an embedded style, you use the New CSS Rule button in the CSS Styles panel to open the New CSS Rule dialog box, as shown in Figure 1. You use this dialog box to create both embedded styles as well as styles that are added to external style sheets. To specify the new style as an embedded style, click the (This document only) option in the Rule Definition section. If you click the (New Style Sheet File) option, you need to name and save a new CSS external style sheet file using the Save Style Sheet File As dialog box. You also have the choice of creating a new style in an existing style sheet, such as the one you have already created for The Striped Umbrella website. So you can create a new style that is an embedded style, an external style saved in a new external style sheet file, or an external style added to an existing external style sheet file.

You use the New CSS Rule dialog box to create a **class style** (also known as a **custom style**), which contains a combination of formatting attributes that can be applied to a block of text or other page elements. When you name a class style, you begin the name with a period (.).

QUICK TIP

If you don't type a period at the beginning of a class style name, Dreamweaver automatically adds it for you.

After you name the rule and click OK, the CSS Rule definition dialog box opens with settings for the Type category displayed, as shown in Figure 2. This dialog box contains eight different categories whose settings you can define. To specify the settings for a category, click the category, then enter the settings. When you finish specifying settings for all of the desired categories, click OK.

Once you create a class style, it appears in the CSS Styles panel. It also appears as a choice in the Class list in the HTML Property inspector or in the Targeted Rule list in the CSS Property inspector. To apply a class style to a web page element, select the element, then click the style from the Class list in the HTML Property inspector or the Targeted Rule list in the CSS Property inspector.

QUICK TIP

Most browsers read style sheets. A browser that cannot read style sheets ignores the styles and renders the affected page elements with default settings.

Figure 1 *New CSS Rule dialog box*

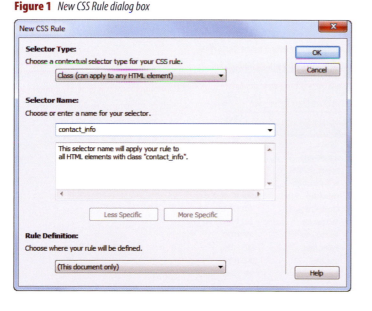

Figure 2 *CSS Rule Definition for .contact_info style*

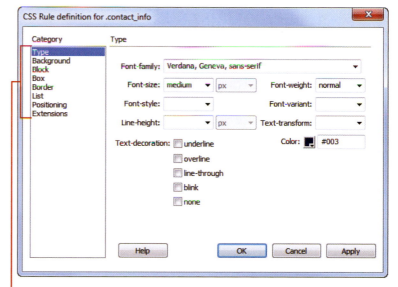

Choose a category to see property options for that category

Replace the folder for The Striped Umbrella website (Win)

1. Open Windows Explorer, navigate to the drive and folder where you store your striped_umbrella website, select the striped_umbrella folder, click **Organize**, then click **Copy**.

2. Navigate to a folder where you would like to store your original files, click **Organize**, then click **Paste**.

TIP It is a good practice to make a backup copy of files in an offsite location before you delete them.

3. Navigate to the drive and folder where you store your Data Files for this chapter, so that the files appear in the right pane, select the striped_umbrella folder in the chapter_8 data_files folder as shown in Figure 3, click **Organize** on the toolbar, then click **Copy**.

4. Navigate to the drive and folder where you store your website files, select the original striped_umbrella folder, click **Organize**, click **Delete**, confirm the deletion when the confirmation dialog box opens, click **Organize**, then click **Paste**.

   The redesigned pages in the new folder replace the original folder. While your old files were useful for learning, you now know how to use many of the tools in Dreamweaver to create attractive, accessible pages. The new site files use CSS styles consistently for page formatting and more accurately reflect optimal site design principles.

5. Close Windows Explorer, then start Dreamweaver.

6. Open The Striped Umbrella website, and view the new files in the Files panel, as shown in Figure 4.

You copied your original files to a different folder as a backup before you replaced the folder with new redesigned files for The Striped Umbrella website.

Figure 3 *Copying the striped_umbrella folder from the Data Files (Win)*

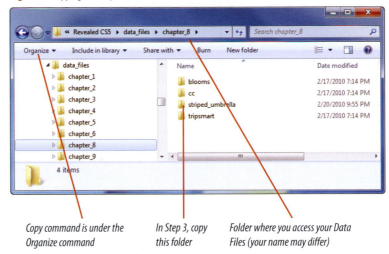

Copy command is under the Organize command

In Step 3, copy this folder

Folder where you access your Data Files (your name may differ)

Figure 4 *The Files panel with the new files (Win)*

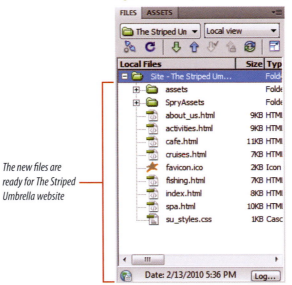

The new files are ready for The Striped Umbrella website

Using Styles and Style Sheets for Design

Figure 5 *Copying the striped_umbrella folder from the Data Files (Mac)*

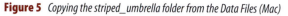

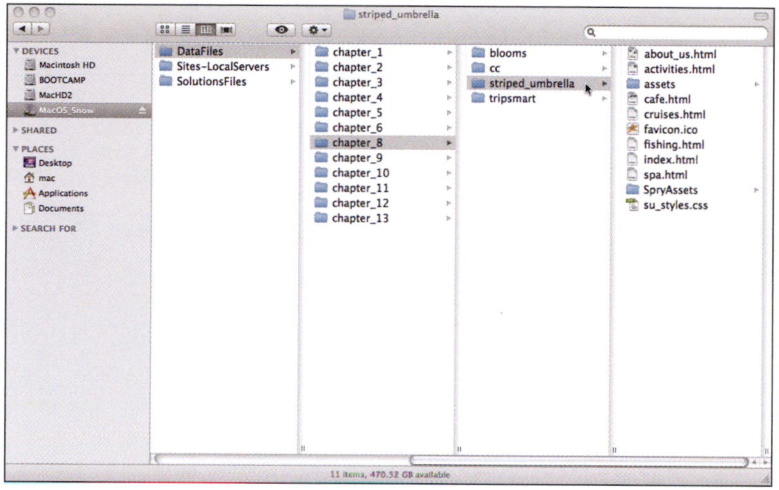

Figure 6 *The Files panel with the new files (Mac)*

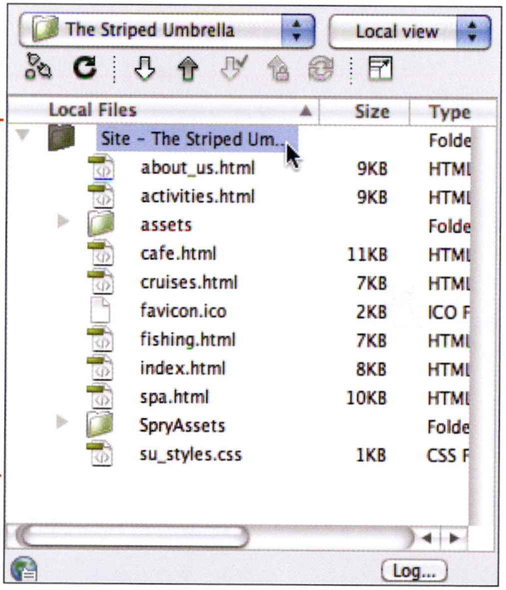

The new files are ready for The Striped Umbrella website

Replace the folder for The Striped Umbrella website (Mac)

1. Open Finder, navigate to the drive and folder where you store your striped_umbrella website, select the striped_umbrella folder, click **Edit** on the menu bar, then click **Copy striped_umbrella**.

2. Click **File** on the Menu bar, click **New Finder Window** to open another instance of Finder, navigate to a folder where you would like to store your original files, click **Edit** on the menu bar, then click **Paste Item**.

   It is a good practice to make a backup copy of files in an offsite location before you delete them.

3. Navigate to the drive and folder where you store your Data Files for this chapter, select the striped_umbrella folder in the chapter_8 data_files folder as shown in Figure 5, click **Edit** on the menu bar, then click **Copy striped_umbrella**.

4. Navigate to the drive and folder where you store your website files, select the original striped_umbrella folder, click **Move to Trash**, click **Edit**, then click **Paste Item**.

   The redesigned pages in the new folder replace the original folder.

5. Close Finder, then start Dreamweaver.

6. Open The Striped Umbrella website, then verify that the new files are displayed in the Files panel, as shown in Figure 6.

TIP If you do not see the files listed in the Files panel, click the plus sign next to the site root folder.

You copied your original files to a different folder as a backup before you replaced the folder with new redesigned files for The Striped Umbrella website.

Create a class style

1. Open the index page in The Striped Umbrella website, expand the CSS Styles panel, then click the **Switch to All (Document) Mode button** ⬚ All (if necessary).

   The new, redesigned home page is now based on a CSS layout. The CSS block elements are outlined with dotted borders.

2. Click the **New CSS Rule button** 🔁 in the CSS Styles panel to open the New CSS Rule dialog box.

3. Click the **Selector Type list arrow**, click **Class (can apply to any HTML element)**, click in the **Selector Name text box**, type **contact_info**, click the **Rule Definition list arrow**, click **(This document only)**, then compare your screen to Figure 7.

4. Click **OK** to open the CSS Rule definition for .contact_info dialog box, and verify that the Type category is selected.

5. Set the Font-family to **Arial, Helvetica, sans-serif**; set the Font-size to **small**; set the Font-style to **italic**; set the Color to **#003**, then compare your screen to Figure 8.

6. Click **OK**.

   The contact_info style appears in the CSS Styles panel.

TIP If you do not see the contact_info style, click the plus sign (Win) or the triangle (Mac) next to <style> in the CSS Styles panel.

You created a new custom style named contact_info and set the rule properties for it.

Figure 7 *New CSS Rule dialog box with settings for contact_info style*

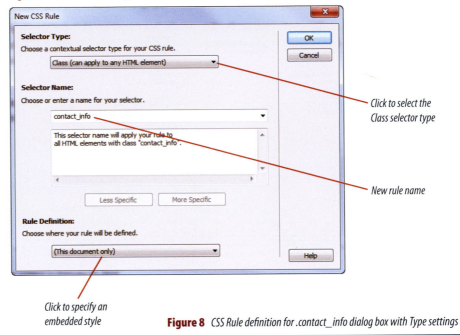

Click to select the Class selector type

New rule name

Click to specify an embedded style

Figure 8 *CSS Rule definition for .contact_info dialog box with Type settings*

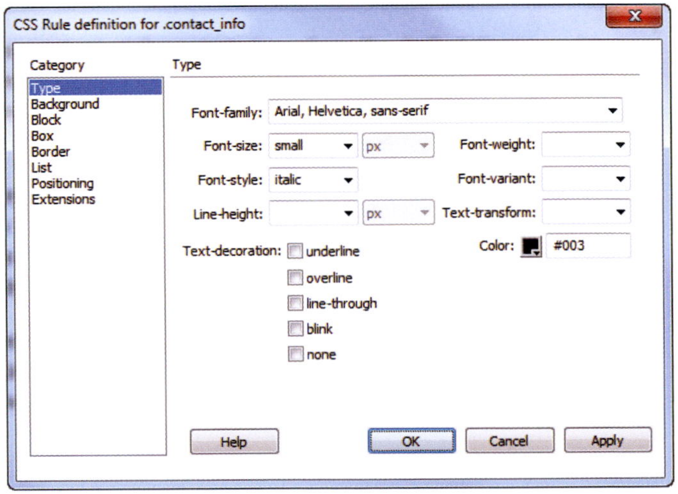

Using Styles and Style Sheets for Design

Figure 9 *Applying the contact_info style using the Property inspector*

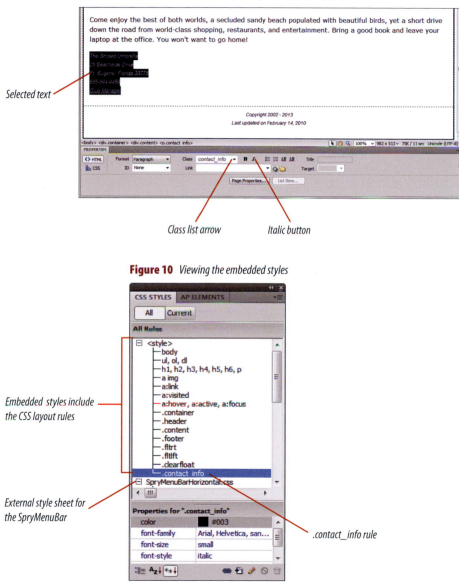

Selected text

Class list arrow   Italic button

Figure 10 *Viewing the embedded styles*

Embedded styles include
the CSS layout rules

External style sheet for
the SpryMenuBar

.contact_info rule

Apply a class style

1. Select the paragraph with The Striped Umbrella contact information.

2. Click the **Italic button** *I* in the HTML Property inspector to remove the italic formatting.

   You must remove manual formatting before applying a CSS style.

3. Click the **Class list arrow** in the Property inspector, click **None**, click the **Class list arrow**, click **contact_info**, compare your results to Figure 9, then deselect the text.

   Before applying a new style, you should remove any existing syles. The selected text is now smaller and gray, as specified by the contact_info rule.

4. Scroll down in the CSS Styles panel if necessary to view the contact_info rule, as shown in Figure 10.

   The contact_info rule appears in the CSS Styles panel, but not as a part of the su_styles.css style sheet. The contact_info rule is an embedded rule, along with the rules that are used to define the CSS layout and the SpryMenuBar.

5. Save your work.

You used the Property inspector to apply the contact_info rule to the contact information.

Modify EMBEDDED STYLES

What You'll Do

In this lesson, you will modify the contact_info style, redefine an HTML tag, edit an embedded style, and then delete an embedded style.

Editing Embedded Styles

To edit a style, click the rule you want to edit in the CSS Styles panel, click the Edit Rule button in the CSS Styles panel, then use the CSS Rule Definition dialog box to change the settings as you wish, or simply enter the new settings in the CSS properties panel. Any changes that you make to the rule are automatically reflected on the page; all elements to which the style is applied update to reflect the change.

Redefining HTML Tags

When you use the Property inspector to format a web page element, a predefined HTML tag is added to that element. You might want to change the definition of an HTML tag to add more "pizzazz" to elements that have that tag. For instance, perhaps you want all text that has the <em> tag, which is the tag used for italic formatting, to appear in bold purple. To change the definition of an HTML tag, click the Tag (redefines an HTML element) selector type in the New CSS Rule

dialog box, click the Selector Name list arrow to view all available HTML tags, click the tag you want to redefine, then click OK to open the CSS Rule definition dialog box, where you specify the desired formatting settings. Once you save the rule and apply it, the tags you target will be formatted according to the altered settings you specified.

Using the CSS Styles Panel

There are two modes in the CSS Styles panel: All mode and Current mode. When All mode is selected, style sheet rules appear in the top half of the panel, which is called the **All Rules pane**. When you click one of the rules, the bottom half, which is called the **Properties pane**, lists that rule's properties, as shown in Figure 11.

When Current mode is selected, the top half of the panel is called the **Summary for Selection pane**. When an object with a style is selected on an open web page, the Summary for Selection pane displays the properties for that style, as shown in Figure 12. The bottom half of the CSS Styles panel is called the Properties pane in either mode. The small pane between the Summary for Selection pane and the Properties pane in Current mode is called the Rules pane. The **Rules pane** displays the location of the current selected rule in the open document.

QUICK TIP

To delete an embedded rule, click the rule you wish to delete, then click the Delete CSS Rule button in the CSS Styles panel.

Figure 11 *CSS Styles panel in All mode*

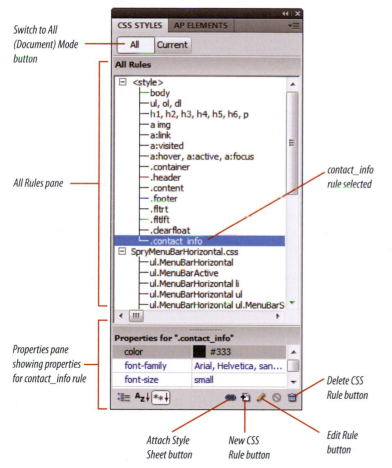

Switch to All (Document) Mode button

All Rules pane

Properties pane showing properties for contact_info rule

contact_info rule selected

Attach Style Sheet button

New CSS Rule button

Delete CSS Rule button

Edit Rule button

Figure 12 *CSS Styles panel in Current mode*

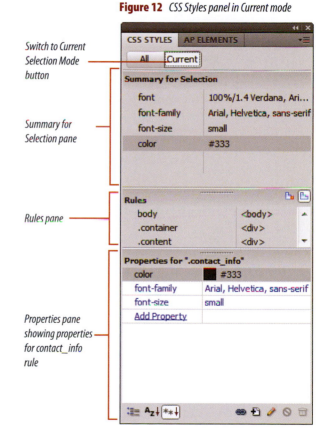

Switch to Current Selection Mode button

Summary for Selection pane

Rules pane

Properties pane showing properties for contact_info rule

Modify a class style

1. Click the **contact_info rule** in the CSS Styles panel, then click the **Edit Rule button** 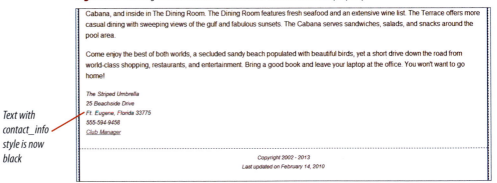.

2. Change the Color to **#000**, click **Apply**, then compare your screen to Figure 13.

3. Click **OK**, compare your screen to Figure 14, then save and close the index page.

   The text with the contact_info style applied to it automatically changed to reflect the changes that you made to the rule.

You made a formatting change in the Type category of the contact_info rule. You then saw this change reflected in text with the contact_info style applied to it.

Figure 13 *CSS Rule definition for .contact_info dialog box with modified type setting*

CSS Rule definition for .contact_info

Category | Type
Type
Background
Block
Box
Border
List
Positioning
Extensions

Font-family: Arial, Helvetica, sans-serif

Font-size: small px   Font-weight:

Font-style: italic   Font-variant:

Line-height: px   Text-transform:

Text-decoration: ☐ underline   Color: ☐ #000

☐ overline
☐ line-through
☐ blink
☐ none

Help   OK   Cancel   Apply

Modified setting

Figure 14 *Viewing the contact information with the modified rule property*

Cabana, and inside in The Dining Room. The Dining Room features fresh seafood and an extensive wine list. The Terrace offers more casual dining with sweeping views of the gulf and fabulous sunsets. The Cabana serves sandwiches, salads, and snacks around the pool area.

Come enjoy the best of both worlds, a secluded sandy beach populated with beautiful birds, yet a short drive down the road from world-class shopping, restaurants, and entertainment. Bring a good book and leave your laptop at the office. You won't want to go home!

The Striped Umbrella
25 Beachside Drive
Ft. Eugene, Florida 33775
555-594-9458
Club Manager

Copyright 2002 - 2013
Last updated on February 14, 2010

Text with contact_info style is now black

Figure 15 *Creating a new CSS Rule to redefine the hr HTML tag*

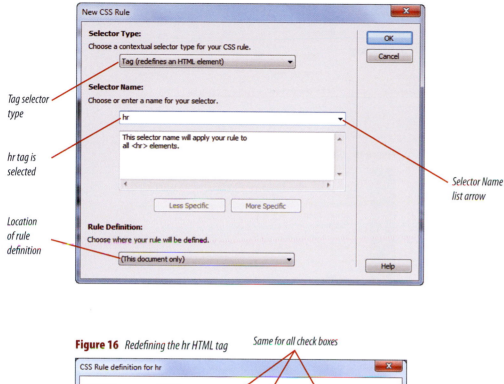

Tag selector type

hr tag is selected

Location of rule definition

Selector Name list arrow

Figure 16 *Redefining the hr HTML tag*

Same for all check boxes

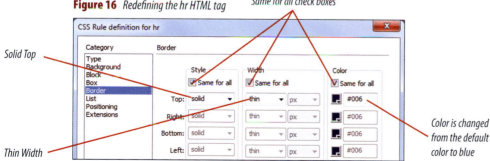

Solid Top

Thin Width

Color is changed from the default color to blue

Redefine an HTML tag

1. Open the cafe page, then click the **New CSS Rule button** in the CSS Styles panel to open the New CSS Rule dialog box.

2. Click the **Selector Type list arrow**, click the **Tag (redefines an HTML element)**, click the **Selector Name list arrow**, scroll down, click **hr**, click the **Rule Definition list arrow**, then click **(This document only)** if necessary, as shown in Figure 15.

   The hr tag is the tag that creates a horizontal rule.

   TIP To scroll quickly to the tags that begin with the letter h, type h after you click the Selector Name list arrow.

3. Click **OK** to open the CSS Rule definition for hr dialog box, click the **Border category**, set the Top style to **solid**, set the Width to **thin**, set the Color to **#006**, press **[Tab]**, compare your screen to Figure 16, make sure that each Same for all check box above each column is checked, then click **OK**.

   The horizontal rules on the page have changed to blue because the rule definition has changed the way a horizontal rule is rendered. The rules will look much better in the browser than they do in Design view.

4. Click the **Switch Design View to Live View button** Live View on the Document toolbar, see the horizontal rules as they will appear in the browser, then click Live View to return to Design view.

   (continued)

5. Using Steps 1 through 3 as a guide, create a new embedded CSS rule that redefines the body HTML tag, by using the Background category rather than the Type category to set the page Background color to **#033**, as shown in Figure 17, then click **OK**.

The page now has a dark gray background. (The page background is behind the CSS container with all of the page content. You may need to collapse your panels and scroll to see it.)

6. Switch to Code view, then scroll through the head section to view the code that changes the properties for the horizontal rule and the body tags, as shown in Figure 18.

Because these are embedded styles, the code for the styles is embedded into the page in the head section of the code. The style changing the background page color to dark gray overrode the white page background color that you defined earlier by using the Page Properties dialog box.

7. Scroll up or down in the code, if necessary, to find the code that links the external style sheet file, as shown in Figure 19.

You cannot see the individual rule properties, because the file is linked, not embedded. If you open the su_styles.css file, however, you see the rules and properties listed.

TIP If you have two embedded styles, you can tell which style takes precedence by its position in the tag selector. Tags with greater precedence are positioned to the right of other tags in the tag selector.

You used the New CSS Rule dialog box to redefine the hr and body HTML tags. You also viewed the code for the new embedded styles and the code that links the external style sheet file.

Figure 17 *Redefining the body HTML tag*

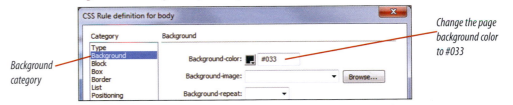

Background category

Change the page background color to #033

Figure 18 *Viewing the code for embedded styles*

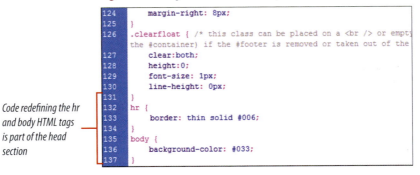

Code redefining the hr and body HTML tags is part of the head section

```
124        margin-right: 8px;
125    }
126    .clearfloat { /* this class can be placed on a <br /> or empt;
       the #container) if the #footer is removed or taken out of the
127        clear:both;
128        height:0;
129        font-size: 1px;
130        line-height: 0px;
131    }
132    hr {
133        border: thin solid #006;
134    }
135    body {
136        background-color: #033;
137    }
```

Figure 19 *Viewing the code linking two external style sheet files*

Code linking the SpryMenuBar and the su_styles style sheet files to the cafe page

The code linking the two files resides in the head section of the code

```
135    body {
136        background-color: #033;
137    }
138    -->
139    </style>
140    <script src="SpryAssets/SpryMenuBar.js" type="text/javascript"></script>
141    <link href="SpryAssets/SpryMenuBarHorizontal.css" rel="stylesheet" type="text/css" />
142    <link href="su_styles.css" rel="stylesheet" type="text/css" />
143    </head>
144
145    <body>
146
147    <div class="container">
148      <div class="header"><!-- end .header --><img src="assets/su_banner.gif" width="950" height=
       banner" /><br />
```

Using Styles and Style Sheets for Design

Figure 20 *Changing the border color property of the hr tag*

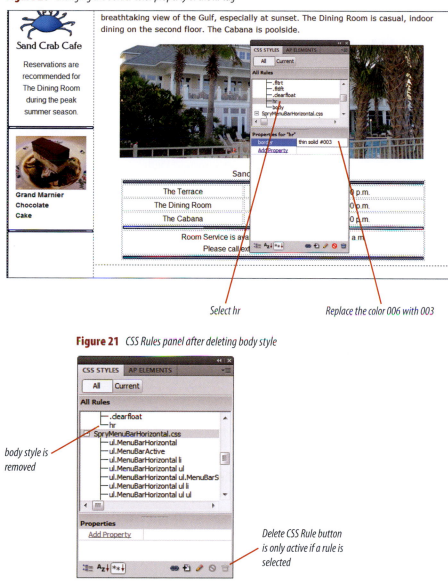

Select hr   Replace the color 006 with 003

Figure 21 *CSS Rules panel after deleting body style*

body style is removed

Delete CSS Rule button is only active if a rule is selected

Edit an embedded style in the Properties pane

1. Switch to Design view, then view the external and embedded styles for the cafe page in the CSS Styles panel.

2. Click the **hr style** in the CSS Styles panel.

   The properties of the hr rule are displayed in the Properties pane.

3. Click to place the insertion point beside the border color number in the Properties pane, then replace color #006 with color **#003** to change the horizontal rule to a darker blue, press **[Tab]**, then compare your screen to Figure 20.

   TIP You may have to resize your CSS Styles panel to see the contents of the Properties pane.

   You used the CSS Styles panel to change the color settings for the hr embedded style.

Delete an embedded style

1. Click the **body rule** at the bottom of the embedded rules list in the CSS Styles panel to select it.

2. Click the **Delete CSS Rule button** 🗑 , then compare your screen to Figure 21.

   The body rule is removed from the CSS Styles panel. The page background changes back to white.

   TIP You can also delete an embedded style by right-clicking (Win) or [control]-clicking (Mac) the rule in the CSS Styles panel, then clicking Delete.

3. Save your changes, then close the cafe page.

   You used the CSS Styles panel to delete the body rule.

Work with External
STYLE SHEETS

What You'll Do

In this lesson, you will make formatting changes in the style sheet and see those changes reflected on pages. You will also add hyperlink styles and custom code to the su_styles style sheet. Finally, you will delete a style from the su_styles style sheet.

Using External Style Sheets

If you want to ensure consistent formatting across all elements of a website, it's a good idea to use external style sheets instead of HTML styles or embedded styles. Most web developers prefer to use external style sheets so they can make global changes to the appearance of a website without opening each page. Using embedded styles requires you to make changes to the styles on each page, which takes more time and leaves room for error and inconsistency.

Attaching an External Style Sheet to a Page or Template

One of the big advantages of using external style sheets is that you can attach them to pages that you've already created. When you do this, all of the rules specified in the style sheet are applied to the HTML tags on the page. So for example, if your external style sheet specifies that all first-level headings are formatted in Arial 14-point bold blue, then all text in your web page that has the <h1> tag will change to reflect these settings when you attach the style sheet to the page. To attach an external style sheet to a page, open the page, and then use the Attach Style

Sheet button in the CSS Styles panel to open the Attach External Style Sheet dialog box, as shown in Figure 22. Use this dialog box to browse for the external style sheet file you want to attach and to specify whether to link or import the file. In most cases, you should choose to link the file so that the content of the page is kept separate from the style sheet file.

If all the pages in your site are based on a template, you can save an enormous amount of time and development effort by attaching an external style sheet to the template. Doing this saves you from having to attach the style sheet to every page in the site; you have to attach it only to the template file. Then, when you make changes to the style sheet, those changes are reflected in the template and are updated in every page based on the template, when you save the template.

Adding Hyperlink Rules to a Style Sheet

You can use an external style sheet to create rules for all links in a website. To do this, click the New CSS Rule button in the CSS Styles panel to open the New CSS Rule dialog box. Click the Selector Type list arrow, click Compound (based on your selection) and then choose one of the selectors from the Selector Name list, as shown in Figure 23. After you choose a selector and click OK, the CSS Rule Definition dialog box opens, where you can specify the formatting of the selected link. In addition to adding hyperlink rules, you can also create rules for other types of tags using the Compound selector type. By default, the Selector Name text box displays the name of the tag at the insertion point on an open page. In Figure 23, the insertion point was in the body tag, so the body tag is listed in the Selector Name text box as a choice. But you can type any tag name in the text box to modify any tag other than the one that is selected.

Adding Custom Code to a Style Sheet

You can make changes to a style sheet by editing the code in the style sheet file rather than through the CSS Styles panel. To do this, open the style sheet file so that it appears in the document window, click to place the insertion point where you want to add code, and then type the code you want. For instance, you can add code to the body tag of the style sheet that changes the colors of a viewer's scroll bar to match the colors of your website.

Figure 22 *Attach External Style Sheet dialog box*

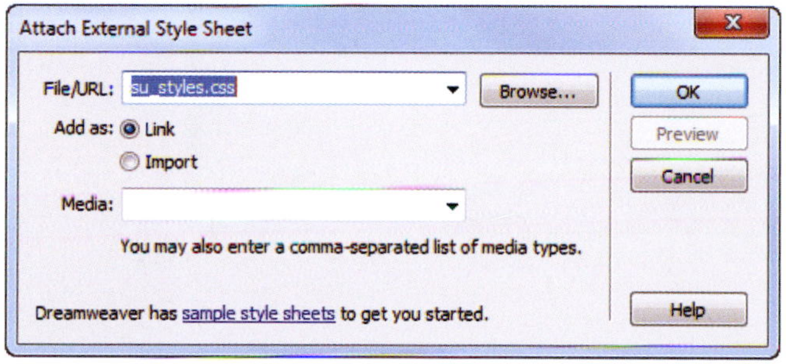

Figure 23 *New CSS Rule dialog box with Compound selector type displayed*

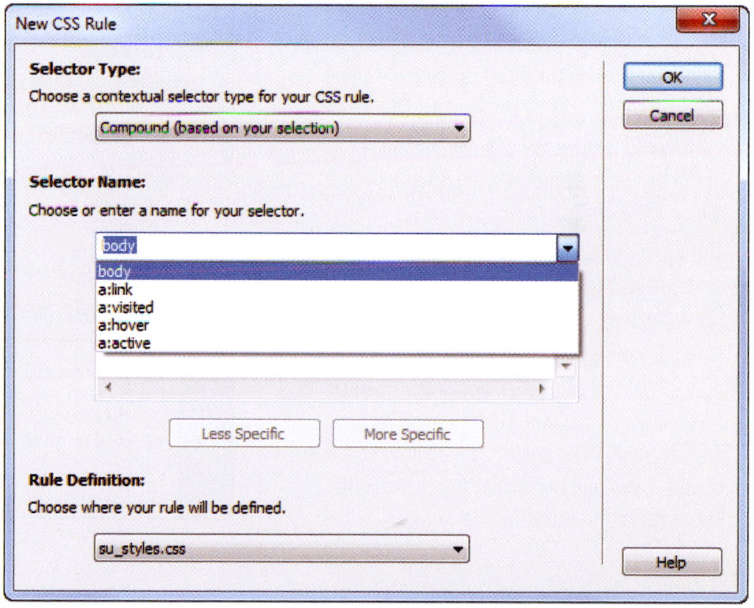

Modify an external style sheet

1. Open the activities page.

2. Double-click the **su_styles.css file** in the site root folder in the Files panel.

   The su_styles.css file opens in Code view in the Document window.

3. Switch back to the activities page, then click the **New CSS Rule button** ⊞ in the CSS Styles panel to open the New CSS Rule dialog box.

4. Click the **Selector Type list arrow**, then click **Compound (based on your selection)**.

5. Click the **Selector Name list arrow**, click **a:link**, click the **Rule Definition list arrow**, click **su_styles.css** if necessary, as shown in Figure 24, then click **OK**.

6. Set the Font-family to **Arial, Helvetica, sans-serif**; set the Font-size to **small**; set the Font-weight to **bold**; set the Color to **#036**; then click **OK**.

7. Click the **su_styles.css tab** to view the file in the Document window, then compare your screen to Figure 25.

   The su_styles.css page now contains new code that reflects the font settings you specified for the a:link style.

8. Save your changes, switch to the activities page, scroll down the page, then notice that the fishing excursions and dolphin cruises page links now appear smaller and bolder with a different shade of blue, reflecting the formatting changes that you made to the a:link rule.

You opened the su_styles.css file, made modifications to the a:link rule using the CSS Rule Definition dialog box and viewed the results of the change in the activities page.

Figure 24 *Adding the a:link rule to the style sheet*

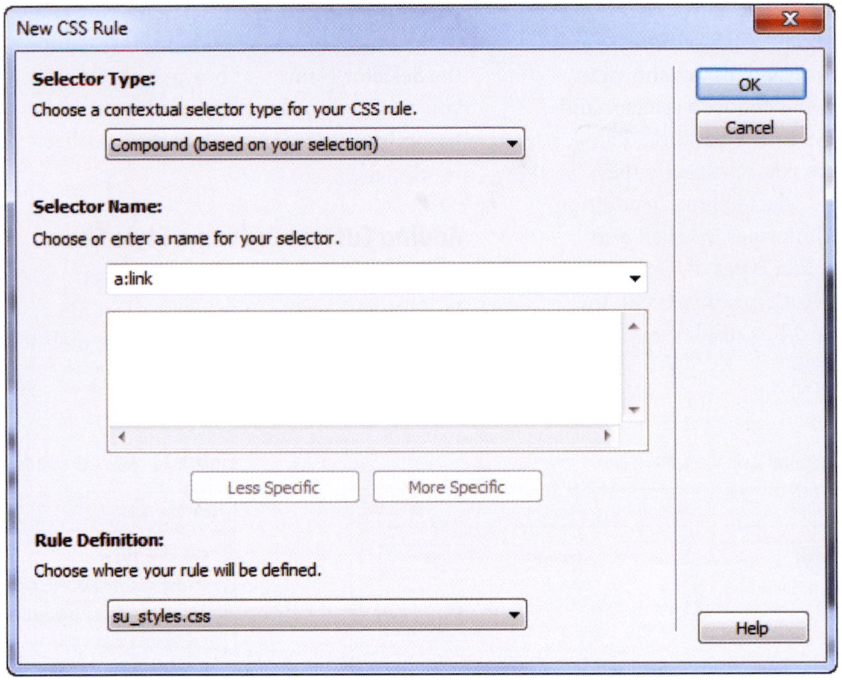

Figure 25 *Modifying the a:link rule*

```
40   a:link {
41       font-family: Arial, Helvetica, sans-serif;
42       font-size: small;
43       font-weight: bold;
44       color: #036;
45   }
46
```

Figure 26 *about_us page after redefining the h4 HTML tag*

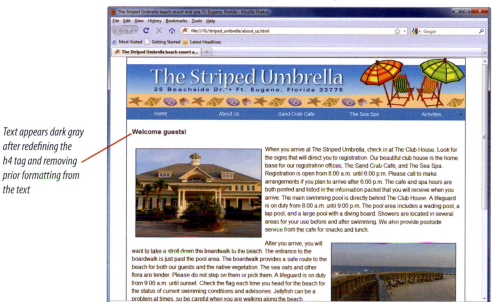

Text appears dark gray after redefining the h4 tag and removing prior formatting from the text

Designing Media-Dependent Style Sheets

One challenge web designers have is to provide alternate versions of web pages that will display attractively on hand-held devices. Because of the vast difference in screen sizes, a page designed for viewing on a computer screen will not work well when viewed on a hand-held device, such as a smartphone. **Media-dependent style sheets** are tools for identifying the device being used and formatting the page appropriately. You can use one of two methods to identify a specific type of media that will be used to open a page: You can add code to an external style sheet such as "@media handheld" or "@media print," or you can add code to the head section of a document that specifies the target medium within the document language. For more information, go to www.w3.org and search for "media-dependent style sheets."

Add heading styles

1. Close the activities page, open the about_us page, then click the **New CSS Rule button** in the CSS Styles panel to open the New CSS Rule dialog box.

2. Click the **Selector Type list arrow**, click **Tag (redefines an HTML element)**, click the **Selector Name list arrow**, then click **h4**.

3. Click the **Rule Definition list arrow**, click **su_styles.css** if necessary, then click **OK** to open the CSS Rule definition for h4 in su_styles.css dialog box.

4. Set the Font-family to **Arial, Helvetica, sans-serif**; set the Font-size to **large**; set the Font-weight to **bold**; set the Color to **#333**; then click **OK**.

5. Select **Welcome Guests** at the top of the page, click the **Class list arrow** in the HTML Property inspector, click **none**, then click on the page.

   Clicking None in the Class list removes the body_text style from the heading, and the properties you set for the h4 tag are now used to format the text.

6. Click **File** on the Application bar (Win) or Menu bar (Mac), click **Save All** to save all pages, preview the about_us page in your browser, then compare your screen to Figure 26.

   The text with the h4 tag appears dark gray, reflecting the formatting changes that you made to the h4 tag.

7. Close your browser, close the about_us page, then save the su_styles.css file. Leave the su_styles.css file open.

You redefined the h4 tag using the CSS Rule definition dialog box.

Add custom code to a style sheet

1. Open the spa page, then switch to the su_styles.css file.

2. Locate the .list_headings style code in the style sheet, then replace the color with **#333**, as shown in Figure 27.

3. Switch to the spa page, then compare your screen to Figure 28.

   The text with the .list_headings style is the same color as other styles and promotes better consistency across the site.

4. Close the spa page, then save the su_styles.css file.

You opened the su_styles.css file, made changes to the list_headings rule directly in the code, and observed the results on the spa page.

Figure 27 *su_styles.css file after changing the color for the list_headings rule*

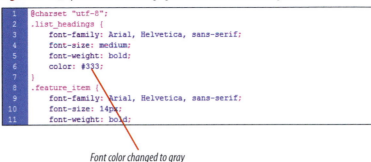

```
1   @charset "utf-8";
2   .list_headings {
3       font-family: Arial, Helvetica, sans-serif;
4       font-size: medium;
5       font-weight: bold;
6       color: #333;
7   }
8   .feature_item {
9       font-family: Arial, Helvetica, sans-serif;
10      font-size: 14px;
11      font-weight: bold;
```

Font color changed to gray

Figure 28 *spa page after rule has been modified*

Text with list_headings rule is a different color

Figure 29 *Selected a:link code in su_styles.css file*

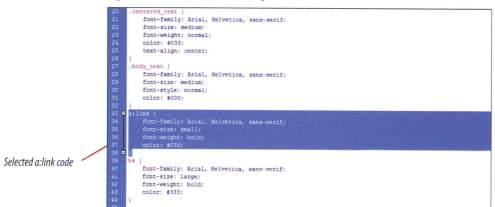

```
20    .centered_text {
21        font-family: Arial, Helvetica, sans-serif;
22        font-size: medium;
23        font-weight: normal;
24        color: #033;
25        text-align: center;
26    }
27    .body_text {
28        font-family: Arial, Helvetica, sans-serif;
29        font-size: medium;
30        font-style: normal;
31        color: #000;
32    }
33  ▢ a:link {
34        font-family: Arial, Helvetica, sans-serif;
35        font-size: small;
36        font-weight: bold;
37        color: #036;
38  ▢ }
39    h4 {
40        font-family: Arial, Helvetica, sans-serif;
41        font-size: large;
42        font-weight: bold;
43        color: #333;
44    }
45
```

Selected a:link code

POWER USER SHORTCUTS

To do this:	Use this shortcut:
Collapse selection of code	[Ctrl][Shift][C] (Win) or ⌘ [shift][C] (Mac)
Collapse outside selection of code	[Ctrl][Alt][C] (Win) or ⌘ [option][C] (Mac)
Expand selection of code	[Ctrl[Shift][E] (Win) or ⌘ [shift][E] (Mac)
Collapse full tag	[Ctrl][Shift][J] (Win) or ⌘ [shift][J] (Mac)
Collapse outside full tag	[Ctrl][Alt][J] (Win) or ⌘ [option][J] (Mac)
Expand all (code)	[Ctrl][Alt][E] (Win) or ⌘ [option][E] (Mac)
Indent code	[Ctrl][Shift][>] (Win) or ⌘ [shift][>] (Mac)
Outdent code	[Ctrl][Shift][<] (Win) or ⌘ [shift][<] (Mac)
Balance braces	[Ctrl]['] (Win) or ⌘ ['] (Mac)
Go to line (of code)	[Ctrl][G] (Win) or ⌘ [,] (Mac)
Show code hints	[Ctrl][Spacebar] (Win) or [control][spacebar] (Mac)
Refresh code hints	[Ctrl][.] (Win) or [control][.] (Mac)

Use Code view to delete external styles from a style sheet

1. In the su_styles.css file, select the a:link tag and the five lines of code below it, then compare your screen to Figure 29.

2. Press **[Delete]** (Win) or **[delete]** (Mac), then save your changes and refresh the CSS Styles panel.

   The a:link style no longer appears in the CSS Styles panel.

3. Open the activities page, then preview the page in your browser.

   The activities page text links no longer appear blue, indicating that the a:link style has been deleted from the style sheet.

TIP You can detach a style sheet from a template or web page by clicking the style sheet file in the CSS Styles panel, then clicking the Unlink CSS Stylesheet button. When you do this, the file is no longer linked to the web page, but it is not deleted; it remains in its original location on your computer.

4. Close the browser.

You deleted the a:link style from the su_styles.css file and then saved your changes.

Work with CONFLICTING STYLES

Understanding the Order of Precedence

When you have a mixture of embedded styles, external styles, and styles redefining HTML tags, you need to understand what happens when these styles conflict. First, you must understand the term "cascading" as applied to style sheets. **Cascading** refers to the way styles are ranked in order of precedence as they are applied to page elements. Style sheets originate from three sources: the author, or creator of the page and style sheet; the user, or person who is viewing the page; and the user agent, the software through which the page is delivered, such as a browser or a mobile device. All user agents have default style sheets that are used to read and display web pages.

The first order of precedence is to find declarations that specify and match the media type being used, such as a computer screen. For instance, if you are designing a page for a cell phone, you would use the rule "@media handheld" in the style sheet. For a page being viewed on a computer screen, you would use "@media screen" in the style sheet.

The second order of precedence is by importance and origin as follows:

1. user important declarations
2. author important declarations
3. author normal declarations
4. user normal declarations
5. user agent declarations

To be classified as an important declaration, the word "important" is included in the rule. For example: "p {font-size: 14 px ! important }" would take precedence over a p font-size tag without the important designation.

The third order of precedence is by specificity of the selector. More specific rules are applied when they are on an equal importance and origin with more general rules. The fourth and final order of precedence is by order specified in the code. Imported, or external style sheets, are considered to be before any internal styles.

When discussing the order of precedence of style types, pseudo-class styles are considered as normal class styles. **Pseudo class styles** refer to styles that determine the appearance of a page element when a certain condition resulting from information external to the HTML source is met. For instance, a rule that sets the appearance of a link that has previously been clicked by a user might be:

a:visited {

    color: #999;

    text-decoration: underline

}

The color of the visited link in this example is specified as gray and underlined. The most common pseudo-class selectors are a:link, a:visited, a:hover, and a:active. For more information on cascading style sheets go to the W3C website at www.w3.org/TR/CSS1.

Using Tools to Manage Your Styles

There are several tools available to assist you in defining, modifying, and checking CSS rules. You have learned to use some of them such as the Code Navigator and Live View. The Browser Compatibility

Check feature flags issues on a page that may present a problem when viewed in a particular browser. To use the Browser Compatibility Check feature, open a page you want to check, then use the File, Check Page, Browser Compatibility command to locate issues that may be a problem. Any issues Dreamweaver finds are listed in the Browser Compatibility Panel in the Results Panel Group with the line number and issue listed for each item it finds. You can modify the settings to add additional versions of browsers by clicking the arrow menu in the top left corner of the panel, then clicking Settings, as shown in Figure 30.

 Another tool for managing your styles is Inspect mode, a new feature in Dreamweaver CS5. Inspect mode helps you to identify HTML elements and their associated styles. To access Inspect mode, click the Inspect button next to the Live View button in the Document toolbar. The Document window changes to split view with Live view enabled. As you hover over a

page element in Inspect mode, the element is highlighted in Design view in the right pane with the CSS box model attributes displayed in color. Different colors are used for the border, margin, padding, and content. The attributes of the highlighted element are also displayed in Code view in the left pane and in any related open panels, such as the CSS Styles panel.

NEW Another new tool for managing your styles is Disable/Enable CSS. This feature allows you to disable a rule property in Design view so you can compare the effects of the affected page element with and without that property. To use this feature, select a rule property in the Properties pane in the CSS Styles panel, then click to the left of the property. The property will be disabled and an icon will appear beside it. Click the icon to enable the property.

Figure 30 *Using the Browser Compatibility Check*

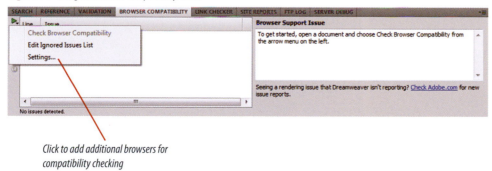

Click to add additional browsers for compatibility checking

Compare conflicting styles

1. On the Activities page, select the first sentence on the page beginning "We have many . . .", click the **CSS button**  on the Property inspector if necessary, click the **Targeted Rule list arrow**, click **<Remove Class>**, then deselect the text.

   When the body_text style in the external style sheet is removed from the sentence, the font style from the body tag in the internal style sheet is applied, as shown in Figure 31. Notice that the targeted rule text box shows all of the heading tags grouped together separated by commas. To help to reduce the size of style sheets, multiple selectors that share common properties and values can be grouped together. These are called **group selectors**.

2. Click **Edit** on the Application bar (Win) or Menu bar (Mac), then click **Undo Apply <span>** (Win) or **Undo** (Mac) to apply the body_text style from the external style sheet again.

   You found that the external body_text style had precedence over the internal body style.

Figure 31 *Text with rule applied from redefined body tag*

The font in the first paragraph is now different from the rest of the page text

Example of group selectors

With no style applied, the font family is applied from the body tag

Using Styles and Style Sheets for Design

Figure 32 *Using the Browser Compatibility Check*

No issues are detected

Panel options button

Figure 33 *Using the Browser Compatibility Check*

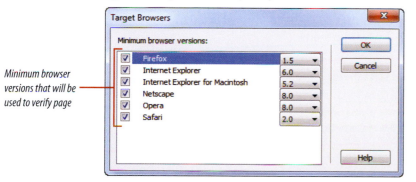

Minimum browser versions that will be used to verify page

Check for errors with Browser Compatibility Check

1. With the activities page open, click **File** on the Application bar (Win) or Menu bar (Mac), point to **Check Page**, then click **Browser Compatibility**.

   The Browser Compatibility panel opens in the Results panel group and shows no compatibility errors, as shown in Figure 32.

2. Click the panel options button ▼≣ in the upper-right corner of the Browser Compatibility panel, then click **Settings**.

   The names and versions of each browser that will be used to check the page for rendering issues are listed, as shown in Figure 33.

3. Close the Target Browsers dialog box, close the Results panel group, close all open files, then close Dreamweaver.

You checked the activities page for errors using the Browser Compatibility panel and found no errors. You then viewed the names and versions of the browsers that are currently set as the target browsers.

DESIGN TIP

Recognizing and Addressing Printing Issues

There are many factors that affect how a page will print compared to how it will appear in a browser window. While a page background color will appear in a browser window, it will not print unless the user selects the print option to print background colors. Although the width of the page in the browser window may fit on the screen, it could actually be too wide to print on a standard printer in portrait orientation. Also, table borders, horizontal rules, and divs may not print exactly how they look in a browser. Printing your pages to see how they actually appear will allow you to address most issues. You can also go to a site such as the World Wide Web Consortium (W3C) at w3.org to find the best solution for any printing problems you identify.

Create and use embedded styles.

1. Copy the Blooms & Bulbs site root folder to a drive and folder where you want to store your original files.
2. Delete your original blooms site root folder, then copy and paste the blooms folder from the chapter_8 Data Files folder to the same location where you stored your original folder.
3. Open Dreamweaver, open the Blooms & Bulbs website, then open the plants page.
4. Create a new embedded style for the plants page that will redefine the horizontal rule tag.
5. In the Border category, set the Top style to solid, set the Top width to thin, set the Top color to #033; and in the Box category, set the Width to 400 px.
6. Insert a horizontal rule right after the third paragraph ending "to enlarge them". (*Hint*: If your horizontal rule is not displayed as centered on the page, view it in Live view or the browser.)

Modify embedded styles.

1. Modify the horizontal rule settings to change the width to 500 px.
2. Modify the footer style on the plants page by setting the font-style to italic.
3. Save your changes, then open each page in the site and modify the footer style to match the footer on the plants page, then save and close each page except the plants page.
4. Preview the plants page in your browser, click each page link to check all footers, then close your browser.

Work with external style sheets.

1. Use the New CSS Rule dialog box to redefine the h3 tag in the blooms_styles.css file. Set the font-family to Arial, Helvetica, sans-serif and the font-size to large.
2. Use the New CSS Rule dialog box to redefine the h4 tag in the blooms_styles.css file. Set the font-family to Arial, Helvetica, sans-serif and the font-size to medium.
3. Save your changes, then preview each page in your browser to make sure that the headings appear according to the settings you specified.
4. Compare your screen to Figure 34, then close the browser and close the plants page.

Work with conflicting styles.

1. Open the index page.
2. Select the paragraphs of text and remove the paragraph_text rule.
3. Reapply the paragraph_text rule.
4. Save and close the index page.

Figure 34 *Completed Skills Review*

Blooms & Bulbs
HWY 43 SOUTH • ALVIN • TX 77511 • 555-248-0806

| Home | Newsletter | Plants ▾ | Tips | Workshops |

Featured Spring Plants: Roses!

Who can resist the romance of roses? Poets have waxed poetically over them throughout the years. Many persons consider the beauty and fragrance of roses to be unmatched in nature. The varieties are endless, ranging from floribunda to hybrid teas to shrub roses to climbing roses. Each variety has its own personality and preference in the garden setting. Pictured on the left is a Summer Breeze Hybrid Tea bud. This variety is fast growing and produces spectacular blooms that are beautiful as cut flowers in arrangements. The enchanting fragrance will fill your home with summer sweetness. They require full sun. Hybrid teas need regular spraying and pruning, but will reward you with classic blooms that will be a focal point in your landscaping and provide you with beautiful arrangements in your home. They are well worth the effort!

For ease of growing, Knock Out® roses are some of our all-time favorites. Even beginners will not fail with these garden delights. They are shrub roses and prefer full sun, but can take partial shade. They are disease resistant and drought tolerant. You do not have to be concerned with either black spot or dead-heading with roses such as the Knock out®, making them an extremely low-maintenance plant. They are also repeat bloomers, blooming into late fall. The shrub can grow quite large, but can be pruned to any size. The one you see on the right is Southern Belle. Check out all our varieties as you will not fail to have great color with these plants.

The Candy Cane Floribunda shown on the left is a beautiful rose with cream, pink, and red stripes and swirls. They have a heavy scent that will remind you of the roses you received on your most special occasions. These blooms are approximately four inches in diameter. They bloom continuously from early summer to early fall. The plants grow up to four feet tall and three feet wide. They are shipped bare root in February. You must see a close-up of these beauties! Click the image on the left to enlarge them.

In addition to these marvelous roses, we have many annuals, perennials, and water plants that have just arrived.

Copyright 2001 - 2013 Blooms & Bulbs

In this Project Builder you will continue your work on the TripSmart website. You have decided to add a few more styles to the style sheet to improve some of the page formatting.

1. Copy your tripsmart folder to a different location for a backup copy, then replace your tripsmart folder with the new tripsmart folder from the drive and folder where you store your Chapter 8 Data Files.
2. Open the TripSmart website, then open catalog page.
3. Create a new embedded rule that redefines the hr HTML tag using settings of your choice.
4. Add a horizontal rule above the copyright statement in the footer, using Figure 35 as a guide (your rule may have different characteristics).
5. Edit the hr style to change the color to a different color or length.
6. Convert the hr style to an external style in the tripsmart_styles.css styles file.
7. Open each page and add a horizontal rule above the copyright information in the footer.
8. Save all files.
9. Preview the each page in your browser.
10. Close your browser, then close all open files.

Figure 35 *Sample Project Builder 1*

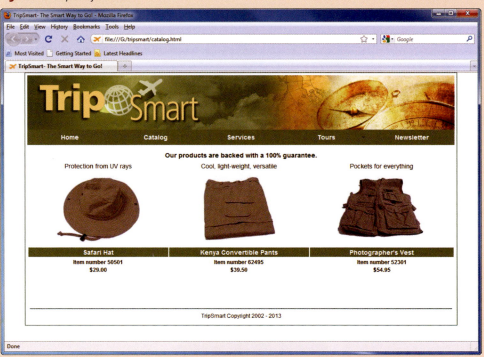

In this Project Builder, you will continue your work on the Carolyne's Creations website that you started in Project Builder 2 in Chapter 1. You will continue to work on the page formatting to include as much formatting as you can with the use of CSS styles.

1. Copy your cc folder to a different location for your backup copy, then replace your cc folder with the new cc folder from the drive and folder where you store your Chapter 8 Data Files.
2. Open the Carolyne's Creations website, then open the shop page.
3. Create a new class style in the cc_styles.css file called **prices**.
4. Refer to Figure 36 for ideas, then select the settings of your choice for the prices style that you will then use to format the prices of the three paella pans on the page. Use the prices style for all formatting for this text.
5. Apply the prices style to each of the three lines with the pricing information.
6. Create a new class style for this page only, named **special_name**, selecting formatting settings of your choice.
7. Apply the special_name style to the January Special: Paella Pans text.
8. Convert the special_name style to an external style in the cc_styles.css file.
9. Save your work, then preview the shop page in your browser. See Figure 36 for a possible solution.
10. Close your browser, then close all open files.

Figure 36 *Sample Project Builder 2*

Using Styles and Style Sheets for Design

Many of today's leading websites use CSS to ensure consistent formatting and positioning of text and other elements. For instance, the United States Department of Justice website uses them. Figure 37 shows the Department of Justice home page.

1. Connect to the Internet, then go to the United States Department of Justice website at www.usdoj.gov.
2. Spend some time exploring the many pages of this site.
3. When you finish exploring all of the different pages, return to the home page. View the source code for the page.
4. Look in the head content area for code relating to the style sheet used. Read through the code and list five class names that you find on the page that are used for formatting page elements.
5. Close the Source window, then look at the home page. List any links that you find for social networking.

Figure 37 *Design Project*

United States Department of Justice website – www.usdoj.gov

In this assignment, you will continue to work on the website that you created in Chapters 1 through 7.

You will continue refining your site by using style sheets and embedded styles to format the text in your site consistently.

1. Write a plan in which you define styles for all of the text elements in your site. Your plan should include how you will use an external style sheet as well as embedded styles. You can use either the external style sheet you created in Chapter 3 or create a new one. Your plan should include at least one class style, one style that redefines an HTML tag, and one style that uses a selector.
2. Attach the completed style sheet to all individual pages in the site.
3. Create and apply the embedded styles you identified in your plan.
4. Create and apply the styles that will be added to the external style sheet.
5. Review the pages and make sure that all text elements appear as they should and look appropriate. Use the checklist in Figure 38 to make sure you have completed everything according to the assignment.
6. Make any necessary changes.
7. Save your work, then close all open pages.

Figure 38 *Portfolio Project*

Website Checklist
1. Do all text elements in the site have a style applied to them?
2. Does your site have at least one embedded style?
3. Is the external style sheet attached to each page in the site?
4. Did you define and apply at least one class style, one style that redefines an HTML tag, and one style that uses a selector?
5. Are you happy with the overall appearance of each page?

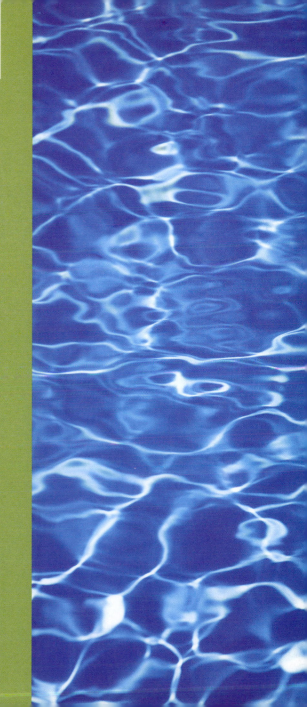

CHAPTER  COLLECTING DATA
WITH FORMS

1. Plan and create a form

2. Edit and format a form

3. Work with form objects

4. Test and process a form

CHAPTER 9 COLLECTING DATA WITH FORMS

Introduction

Many websites have pages designed to collect information from users. You've likely seen such pages when ordering books online from Amazon.com or purchasing airline tickets from an airline website. Adding a form to a web page provides interactivity between your users and your business. To collect information from users, you add forms for them to fill out and send to a web server to be processed. Forms on a web page are no different from other forms you use in everyday life. Your bank checks are simple forms that ask for information: the date, the amount of the check, the name of the check's recipient, and your signature. A form on a web page consists of **form objects** such as text boxes or radio buttons into which users type information or from which they make selections. **Form labels** identify the form object by its function, such as a "First Name" label beside a text box that collects the user's first name.

In this chapter, you add a form to a page that provides a way for interested users to ask for more information about The Striped Umbrella resort. The form will also give them the opportunity to comment on the website and make helpful suggestions. Feedback is a vital part of a website and must be easy for a user to submit.

Using Forms to Collect Information

Forms are just one of the many different tools that web developers use to collect information from users. A simple form can consist of one form object and a button that submits information to a web server, for example, a search text box that you fill out, and a button that you click to start the search. More complex forms can collect contact information, or allow students to take exams online and receive grades instantly. You can use forms to insert information into databases, or to find a specific record in a database. The range of uses for forms is limited only by your imagination.

All forms need to be connected to an application server that will process the information that the form collects. This application can store the form data in a database, or simply send it to you in an email message. You need to specify how you want the information used, stored, and processed.

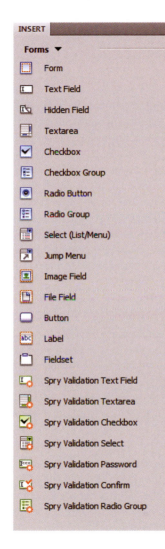

Input Tag Accessibility Attributes

ID: first_name

Label:

⊙ Attach label tag using 'for' attribute

Style: ⊙ Wrap with label tag

⦿ No label tag

Position: ⦿ Before form item

⊙ After form item

Access key: ___   Tab Index: ___

If you don't want to enter this information when inserting objects, change the Accessibility preferences.

[OK] [Cancel] [Help]

Radio Group

Name: newsletters

Radio buttons: [+] [−]   [▲] [▼]

Label	Value
Yes	positive
No	negative

Lay out using: ⦿ Line breaks (
 tags)

⊙ Table

[OK] [Cancel] [Help]

Plan and
CREATE A FORM

What You'll Do

In this lesson you will add a new form to a feedback page in The Striped Umbrella website.

Planning a Form

Before you use Dreamweaver to create a form, it's a good idea to write down the information you want to collect and the order in which you want to collect it. It's also a good idea to make a sketch of the form for your wireframe. Planning your form content at the beginning saves you from spending time organizing the information when you create the form in Dreamweaver. The Striped Umbrella website will contain a form for users to request more information, sign up for an electronic newsletter, and submit their comments about the website. Figure 1 shows a sketch of the form that you create in this chapter.

When planning your form content, you should organize the information in a logical order that will make sense to users. For instance, users expect to fill in their name before their address, because almost all forms, from your birth certificate to your IRS tax forms, request your name before your address, so you should follow this standard. Placing information in a different order will confuse your users.

People on the Internet are notoriously hurried and often provide only information that is required or that is located on the top half of the form. Therefore, it's a good idea to put the most important information at the top of your form. In fact, this is a good rule to follow for web pages in general. The most important information should be "above the fold" or on the part of the page that is visible before you have to scroll to see the rest. As with all pages, your forms should have good contrast between the color of the text and the color of the form background.

Creating Forms

Once you finish planning your form content, you are ready to create the form in Dreamweaver. To create a form object on a web page, you use the Form button in the Forms category on the Insert panel. Clicking the Form button inserts a dashed red outline around the form area. But by itself, a form object can do nothing. To make your form usable, you need to configure it so that it "talks" to the scripts or email server and processes the information users enter. The form must have a script or program running "behind" it to process the information users enter so you can gather and use it.

Collecting Data with Forms

Designers use two methods to process the information collected in a form: server-side scripting and client-side scripting. **Server-side scripting** uses applications that reside on your web server and interact with the form information collected. For example, when you order clothing from a retail website, the host web server stores and processes the item, size, color, price, shipping information, and credit card information. The most common types of server-side applications are **Common Gateway Interface (CGI)** scripts, **Cold Fusion** programs, **Java Server Page (JSP)**, and **Active Server Pages (ASP)** applications. **Client-side scripting** means that the user's computer processes the form. The script resides on the web page, rather than on the server. For example, a mortgage calculator that allows you to enter prices and interest rates to estimate mortgage payments processes the data on the user's computer. The most common types of scripts stored on a web page are created with a scripting language called **JavaScript**, or **Jscript**. Server-side applications and scripts collect the information from the form, process the information, and perform some sort of action depending on the information the form contains.

You can process form information several ways. The easiest and most common way is to have the information collected from the form and emailed to the contact person on the website. You can also have form data stored in a database to use at a later date. You can even have the application both collect the form data in a database and send it in an email message. You can also have the form data processed instead of stored. For instance, you can create a form that calculates item quantities and prices and provides a total cost to the user on the order page, without recording any subtotals in a database or email message. In this example, only the final order total would be stored in the database or sent in an email message.

You can also create forms that make changes to your web page based on information users enter. For example, you could create a form that asks users to select a background color for a web page. In this type of form, the information could be collected and sent to the processor. The processor could then compare the selected background color to the current background color and change the color if it is different from the user's selection.

Setting Form Properties

After you insert a form, use the Property inspector to specify the application that you want to process the form information and how you want it sent to the processing application. The **Action property** in the Property inspector specifies the application or script that will process the form data. Most of the time the Action property is the name and location of a CGI script, such as /cgi-bin/myscript.cgi; a Cold Fusion page, such as mypage.cfm; or an Active Server Page,

Figure 1 *Sketch of the form you will add to the feedback page*

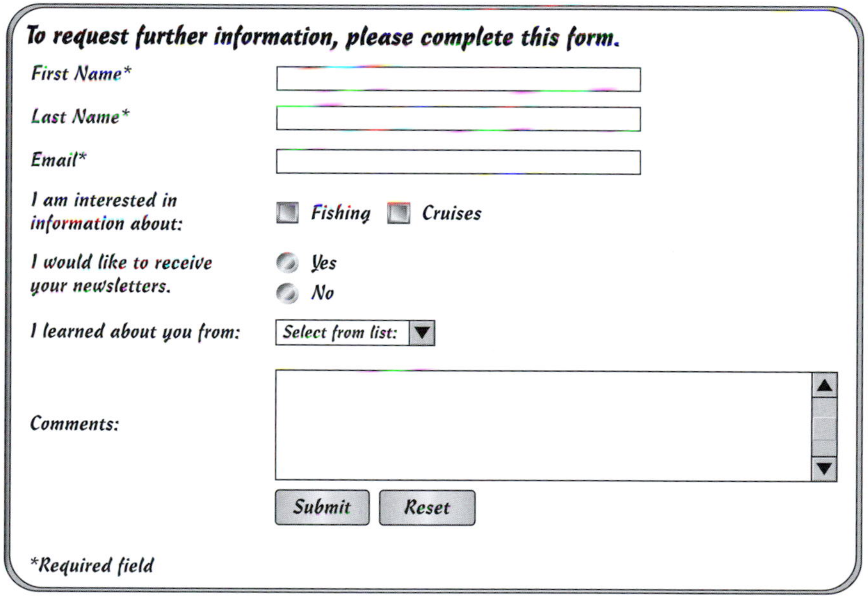

Lesson 1   Plan and Create a Form

such as mypage.asp. Figure 2 shows the properties of a selected form.

The **Method property** specifies the **HyperText Transfer Protocol (HTTP)** used to send the form data to the web server. The **GET method** specifies that ASCII data collected in the form will be sent to the server appended to the URL or the file included in the Action property. For instance, if the Action property is set to /cgi-bin/myscript.cgi, then the data will be sent as a string of characters after the address, as follows: /cgi-bin/ myscript.cgi?a+collection+of+data+collected+by+the+form. Data sent with the GET method is usually limited to 8K or less, depending on the web browser. The **POST method** specifies that the form data should be sent to the processing script as a binary or encrypted file, allowing you to send data securely. When you specify the POST method, there is no limit to the amount of information that can be collected in the form, and the information is secure.

The **Form name property** specifies a unique name for the form. The name can be a string of any alphanumeric characters and cannot include spaces. The **Target property** lets you specify the window in which you want the form data to be processed. For instance, the _blank target will open the form in a separate browser window.

Figure 2 *Form controls in the Property inspector*

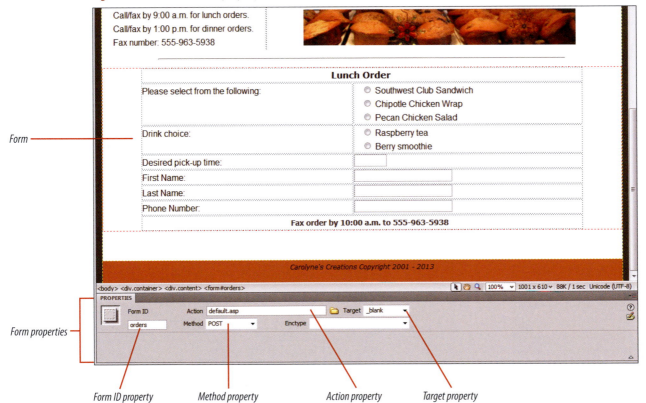

Understanding CGI Scripts

CGI is one of the most popular tools used to collect form data. CGI allows a web browser to work directly with the programs that are running on the server and also makes it possible for a website to change in response to user input. CGI programs can be written in the computer languages Perl or C, depending on the type of server that is hosting your website. When a CGI script collects data from a web form, it passes the data to a program running on a web server, which in turn passes the data back to the user's web browser, which then makes changes to the website in response to the form data. The resulting data is then stored in a database or sent to an email server, which then sends the information in an email message to a designated recipient. Figure 3 illustrates how a CGI script processes information collected by a form.

Figure 3 *Illustration of CGI process on a web server*

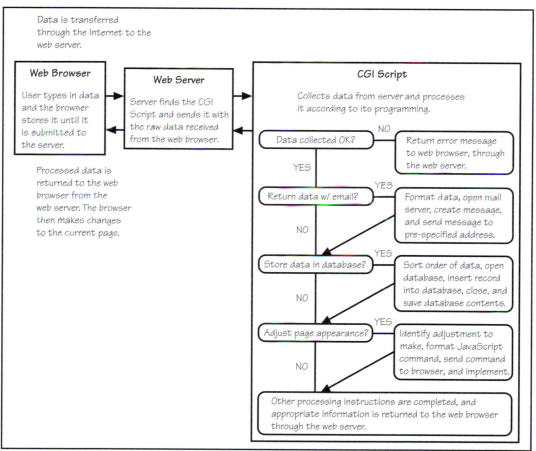

Insert a form

1. Open The Striped Umbrella website, open the file dw9_1.html from the drive and folder where you store your Data Files, then save it as **feedback.html** in The Striped Umbrella website, but do not update links.

2. Close the dw9_1.html file, then click inside the content container on the feedback page to place the insertion point.

    TIP The #content container top border is under the menu bar. Click right under it to place the insertion point in the correct location. To verify that it is the correct location, go to Code view and verify that the insertion point is after the <br> tag, but before the closing div tag for the content container.

3. Select the Forms category on the Insert panel, then click the **Form button** to insert a new form on the page.

    A dashed red rectangular outline appears on the page, as shown in Figure 4. As you add form objects to the form, the form expands.

    TIP You can see the form only if Invisible Elements are turned on. To turn on Invisible Elements, click View on the Application bar (Win) or Menu bar (Mac), point to Visual Aids, then click Invisible Elements.

You inserted a new form on the feedback page of The Striped Umbrella website.

Figure 4 *New form inserted on the feedback page*

Form outline

Form button

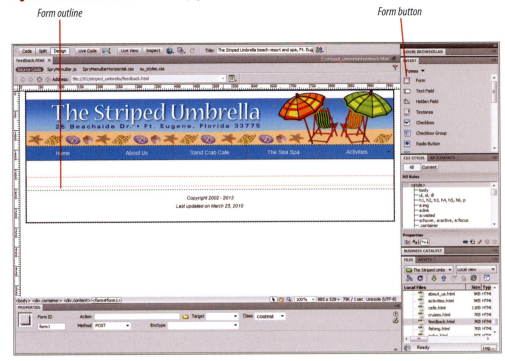

Figure 5 *Property inspector showing properties of selected form*

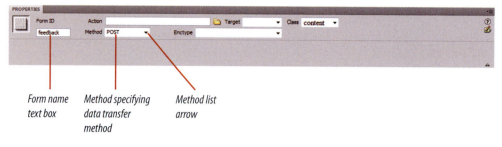

Form name text box

Method specifying data transfer method

Method list arrow

Set form properties

1. Click the **Form tag (<form#form1>)** in the tag selector on the status bar to select the form and display the form properties in the Property inspector.

2. Select form1 in the Form ID box in the Property inspector, then type **feedback**.

3. Click the **Method list arrow** in the Property inspector, then click **POST** if necessary, as shown in Figure 5.

TIP Leave the Action and Target text boxes blank unless you have the information necessary to process the form.

4. Save your work.

You configured the form on the feedback page.

Using CGI scripts

You can use CGI scripts to start and stop external programs or to specify that a page update automatically based on user input. You can also use them to create surveys, site search tools, and games. You can even use CGI to do basic tasks such as record entries to a guest book or count the number of people who have accessed a specific page of your site. CGI also lets you create dynamic web documents "on the fly" so that pages can be generated in response to preferences specified by the user. Although instructions for creating and modifying CGI scripts are not covered in this book, you can probably find a low-priced script by searching on the Internet.

Edit and
FORMAT A FORM

What You'll Do

In this lesson, you will insert a table that will contain the form on the feedback page. You will also add and format form labels.

Using Tables to Lay Out a Form

Just as you can use CSS or tables to help place page elements on a web page, you can also use CSS or tables to help lay out forms. To make sure that your labels and form objects appear in the exact positions you want on a web page, you can place them on the page using layout options such as div tags, tables, and lists. When you use a table to lay out a form, you can place labels in the first column and place form objects in the second column, as shown in Figure 6.

Adding Labels to Form Objects

When you create a form, you need to include form field labels so that users know what information you want them to enter in each field of the form. Because labels play such an important part in identifying the information that the form collects, you need to make sure to use labels that make sense to your users. For example, First Name and Last Name are good form field labels, because users understand clearly what information they should enter. However, a label such as Top 6 Directory Name might confuse users and cause them

Using Fieldsets to Group Form Objects

If you are creating a long form on a web page, you might want to organize your form elements in sections to make it easier for users to fill out the form. You can use fieldsets to group similar form elements together. A **fieldset** is an HTML tag used to group related form elements together. You can have as many fieldsets on a page as you want. To create a fieldset, use the Fieldset button on the Insert panel.

to leave the field blank or enter incorrect information. If creating a simple and obvious label is not possible, then include a short paragraph that describes the information users should enter into the form field.

Figure 7 shows clearly marked labels for each form field, as well as additional text providing directions or examples for the user to follow.

You can add labels to a form using one of two methods. You can simply type a label in the appropriate table cell of your form or use the Label button in the Forms category on the Insert panel to link the label to the form object.

Figure 6 *Website that uses tables to lay out a form*

Federal Bureau of Investigation website – www.fbi.gov

Figure 7 *Website that clearly marks labels for form fields*

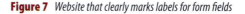

Social Security Administration website – www.ssa.gov

Add a table to a form

1. Click to place the insertion point inside the form outline, as shown in Figure 8.

2. Select the Common category on the Insert panel, then click the **Table button**.

3. In the Table dialog box, set the Rows to **10**, Columns to **2**, Table width to **90 percent**, Border thickness to **0**, Cell padding to **2**, and Cell spacing to **1**, then click the **Top header option** in the Header section.

4. Type **Table used for form layout.** in the Summary text box, compare your screen to Figure 9, then click **OK**.

5. With the table selected, click the **Align list arrow** in the Property inspector, click **Center** to center the table in the form, set the lower-left cell width to **30%**, set the lower-right cell width to **70%**, as shown in Figure 10, then save your work.

   You can set the cell widths by using any of the cells, but if you try to consistently use a specific row to set the cell widths, you can easily find them if you have to change them. It is difficult to correct formatting errors when you have conflicting cell widths set in the same column.

You added a table to the form on the feedback page. You also set the table alignment and cell widths.

Figure 8 *Placing the insertion point inside the form*

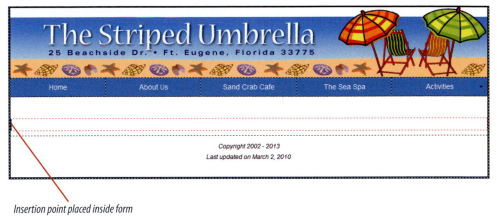

Insertion point placed inside form

Figure 9 *Setting table properties*

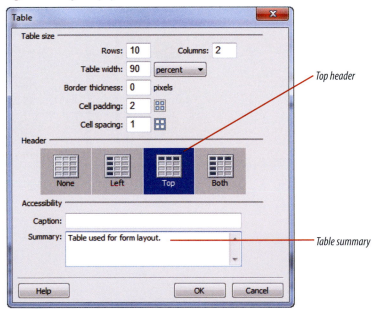

Top header

Table summary

Collecting Data with Forms

Figure 10 *Setting table and cell properties*

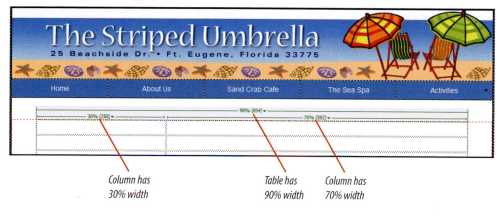

Column has
30% width

Table has
90% width

Column has
70% width

Figure 11 *Typing labels in table cells*

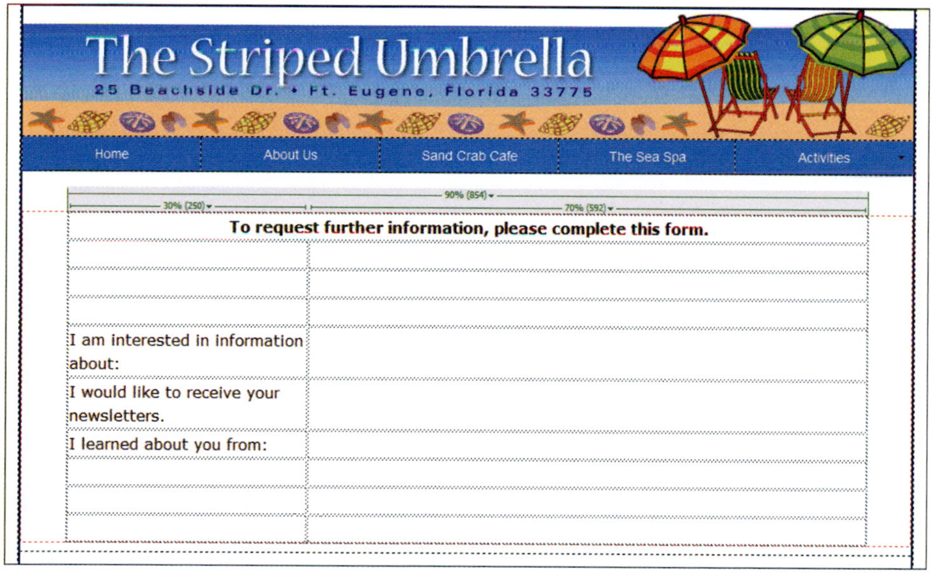

To request further information, please complete this form.

I am interested in information about:

I would like to receive your newsletters.

I learned about you from:

1. Merge the top two cells in the first row of the table, then type **To request further information**, **please complete this form** in the merged cells.

   Because you designated a header for this table, the top row text is automatically centered and bold. Screen readers use the header to assist users who have visual impairments to identify the table.

2. Click in the first cell in the fifth row, then type **I am interested in information about:**.

3. Press [↓], then type **I would like to receive your newsletters**.

4. Press [↓], type **I learned about you from:**, then press [↓].

5. Compare your screen to Figure 11.

   You added a header and three form labels to table cells in the form.

Add form labels using the Label button

1. Verify that the insertion point is in the cell below the one that contains the text "I learned about you from:".

2. Select the Forms category on the Insert panel, then click the **Label button**.

   The view changes to Code and Design view, as shown in Figure 12. The insertion point is positioned in the Code view pane between the tags <label> and </label>, which were added when you clicked the Label button.

TIP You may need to scroll down in the Design pane to see the cell.

(continued)

Figure 12 *Adding a label to a form using the Label button*

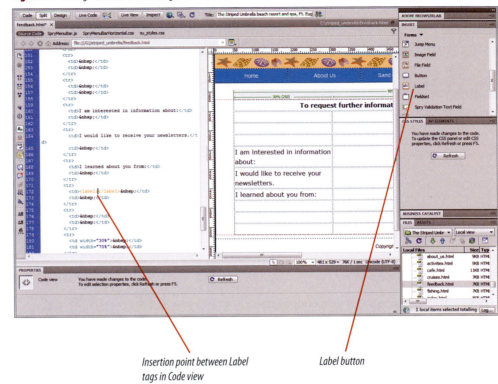

Insertion point between Label tags in Code view

Label button

Collecting Data with Forms

Figure 13 *New label added using the Label button*

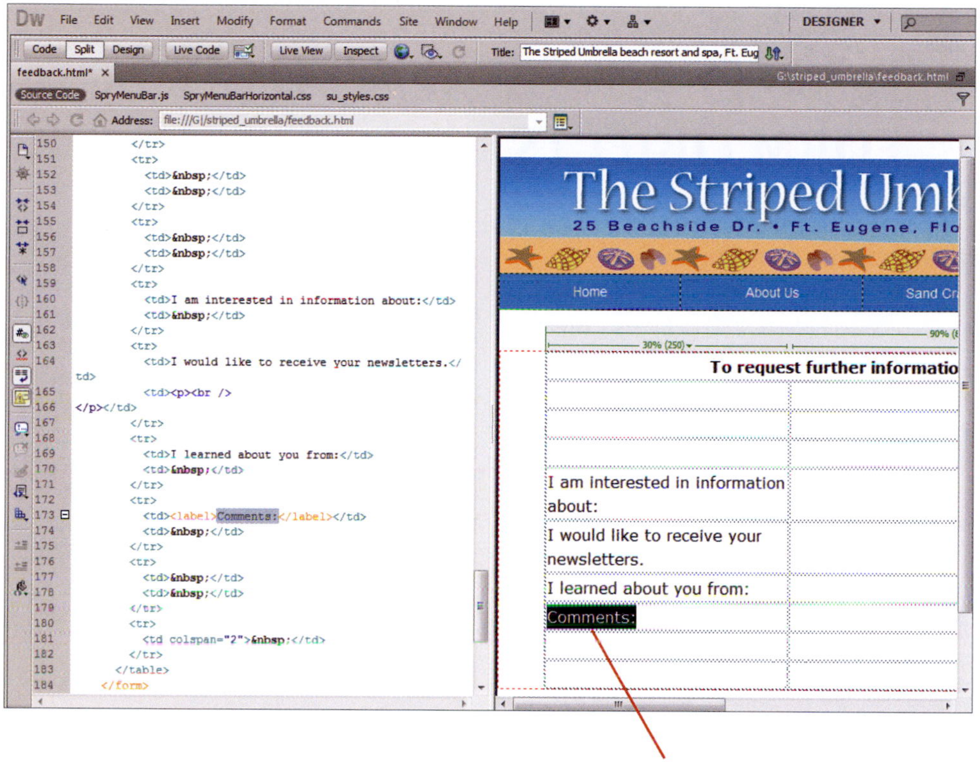

New label

3. Type **Comments:**, then click the **Refresh button** `C Refresh` in the Property inspector.

   The label appears in the table cell in the Design view pane.

4. Compare your screen to Figure 13, click the **Show Design view button** `Design`, then save your work.

You added a new label to the form on the feedback page using the Label button.

Work with
FORM OBJECTS

What You'll Do

In this lesson, you will add form objects to the form on the feedback page.

Understanding Form Objects

A form provides a structure in which you can place form objects. Form objects—which are also called **form elements**, **form controls**, **form inputs**, or **form fields**—are the form components such as check boxes, text boxes, and radio buttons that allow users to provide information and interact with the website. You can use form objects in any combination to collect the information you require. Figure 14 shows a form that contains a variety of form objects.

Text fields are the most common type of form object and are used for collecting a string of characters, such as a name, address, password, or email address. For some text fields, such as those collecting dollar amounts, you might want to set an initial value of 0. Use the Text Field button on the Insert panel to insert a text field. You can specify single-line or multi-line text fields.

A **text area field** is a text field that can store several lines of text. You can use text area fields to collect descriptions of problems, long answers to questions, comments, or even a résumé. Use the Textarea button on the Insert panel to insert a text area.

You can use **check boxes** to create a list of options from which a user can make multiple selections. For instance, you could add a series of check boxes listing hobbies and ask users to select the ones that interest them.

You can use **radio buttons** to provide a list of options from which only one selection can be made. A group of radio buttons is called a **radio group**. Each radio group you create allows only one selection from within that group. You could use radio groups to ask users to select their annual salary range, their age group, or the T-shirt color they want to order. You could also use a radio group for users to answer a yes or no question. To insert a radio group, use the Radio Group button in the Forms category on the Insert panel.

You can insert a **menu** or **list** on a form using the Select(List/Menu) button on the Insert panel. You use menus when you want a user to select a single option from a list of choices. You use lists when you want a viewer to select one or more options from a list of choices. Menus are often used to provide navigation on a website, while lists are commonly used in order forms to let users choose from a list of possibilities.

Menus must be opened to see all of the options they contain, whereas lists display some of their options all of the time. When you create a list, you need to specify the number of lines that will be visible on the screen by setting a value for the Height property in the Property inspector.

Using **hidden fields** makes it possible to provide information to the web server and form-processing script without the user knowing that the information is being sent. For instance, you could add a hidden field that tells the server who should receive an email message and what the subject of the message should be. You can also use hidden fields to collect information that a user does not enter and cannot see on the screen. For instance, you can use a hidden field to send you the user's browser type or IP address.

You can insert an **image field** into a form using the Image Field button on the Insert panel. You can use image fields to create buttons that contain custom graphics.

If you want your users to upload files to your web server, you can insert a **file field**. You could insert a file field to let your users upload sample files to your website or to post photos to your website's photo gallery.

All forms must include a **Submit button**, which users click to transfer the form data to the web server. You can also insert a **Reset button**, which lets users clear data from a form and reset it to its default values, or a **custom button** to trigger an action that you specify on the page. You can insert a Submit,

Reset, or custom button using the Button button on the Insert panel. Place Submit and Reset buttons at the bottom of the form.

Jump menus are navigational menus that let users go quickly to different pages in your site or to different sites on the Internet. You can create jump menus quickly and easily by using the Jump Menu button in the Forms category on the Insert panel.

When you insert a form object in a form, you use the Property inspector to specify a unique

name for it. You can also use the Property inspector to set other appropriate properties for the object, such as the number of lines or characters you want the object to display.

Setting Form Object Attributes

As you place a control on a form, you usually need to add a label. You can place a form label either before or after it by typing it directly on the form. This is a good idea if you need more than a word or two for a form label.

Figure 14 *Website form with several form objects*

Text field

Radio button

Menu

U. S. Department of State – www.travel.state.gov

For instance, "Please explain the problem you are experiencing." would need to be typed on the form next to a text box. If, however, you only need the words "Yes" and "No" beside two check boxes, you can add the labels "Yes" and "No" using a form attribute called a **label tag**. You can add a label tag before or after the form object using the Input Tag Accessibility Attributes dialog box. Label tags provide good accessibility for your form objects, as they clearly identify each form object and are read with screen readers.

Using Dreamweaver Exchange

To obtain form controls designed for creating specific types of forms, such as online tests and surveys, you can visit the Adobe Marketplace & Exchange (www.adobe.com/cfusion/exchange), shown in Figure 15, a central storage location for program extensions, also known as **add-ons**. You can search the site by using keywords in a standard Search text box. You can also search for items featured by their staff, and for the most recent, most popular, and most highly rated.

Figure 15 *Using Adobe Marketplace & Exchange*

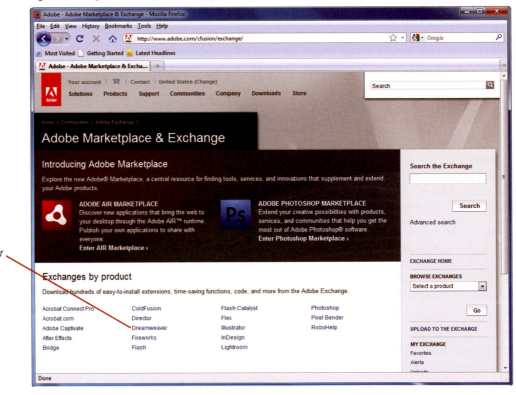

Click to visit Dreamweaver Exchange

Adobe product screen shot reprinted with permission from Adobe Systems Incorporated – www.adobe.com

Figure 16 *Input Tag Accessibility Attributes dialog box*

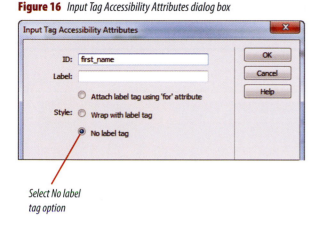

Select No label
tag option

Figure 17 *Property inspector showing properties of selected text field*

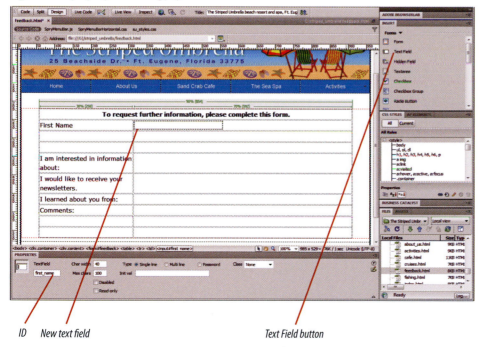

ID   New text field   Text Field button

Insert single-line text fields

1. Place the insertion point in the first cell under the header, then type **First Name**.

2. Press **[Tab]**, then click the **Text Field button** on the Insert panel to open the Input Tag Accessibility Attributes dialog box.

   TIP The Image Tag Accessibility Attributes dialog box does not appear if you do not have the accessibility preference set for adding form objects.

3. Type **first_name** in the ID text box, click the **No label tag option button** in the Style section, as shown in Figure 16, then click **OK**.

   TIP You can also type the text field name in the TextField text box in the Property inspector.

4. Type **40** in the Char width text box in the Property inspector.

   This specifies that 40 characters will be visible inside this text field when displayed in a browser.

5. Type **100** in the Max chars text box in the Property inspector.

   This specifies that a user can type no more than 100 characters in this field.

6. Click the **Single line option button** in the Property inspector if necessary, then compare your screen to Figure 17.

7. Repeat Steps 1 through 6 to create another label and single-line text field under the First Name label and text field, typing **Last Name** as the label in the first column and **last_name** for the text field.

(continued)

8. Repeat Steps 1 through 6 to create another label and single-line text field under the Last Name label and text field, using **Email** for the label and **email** for the TextField name.

9. Click to place the insertion point anywhere in the table, click the **<table>tag** on the Tag Selector, click the **Class list arrow**, then click **body_text** to apply the body_text style to the table.

TIP There are several ways to apply styles in a table. You can apply styles by selecting text, clicking inside a paragraph, selecting a cell and applying a style to it, or applying a style to an HTML tag, such as a table tag. If you want to use the same style throughout the table, this is the most efficient method.

10. Save your changes, preview the page in your browser, compare your screen to Figure 18, then close your browser.

You added three single-line text fields to the form, applied the body-text rule to the entire table, then previewed the page in your browser.

Figure 18 *Form with single-line text fields added*

Collecting Data with Forms

Figure 19 *Property inspector with properties of selected text area displayed*

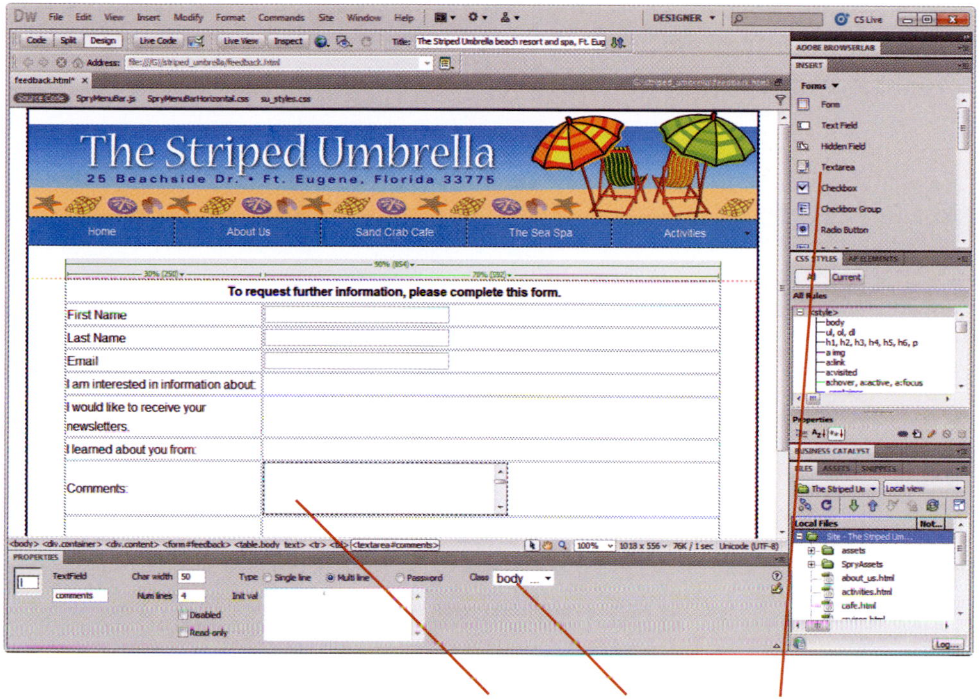

New multiple-
line text field

body_text style
applied to table

Textarea button

Insert a multiple-line text field

1. Click in the cell to the right of the Comments: label.

2. Click the **Textarea button** on the Insert panel, type **comments** in the ID text box, click the **No label tag option button** in the Input Tag Accessibility Attributes dialog box if necessary, then click **OK**.

3. Verify that the Multi line option button is selected in the Property inspector.

4. Type **50** in the Char width text box in the Property inspector.

   This specifies that 50 characters will be visible inside this text field when the page is displayed in a browser.

5. Type **4** in the Num lines text box in the Property inspector, as shown in Figure 19.

   This specifies that the text box will display four lines of text.

You added a multiple-line text field to the form.

Insert check boxes

1. Place the insertion point in the empty table cell to the right of "I am interested in information about:".

   This field will use a form label tag that is added when the form control is added.

2. Click the **Checkbox button** on the Insert panel.

3. Type **fishing** in the ID text box, type **Fishing** in the Label text box, click the **Wrap with label tag option button** in the Style section, click the **After form item option button** in the Position section, as shown in Figure 20, then click **OK**.

   The Wrap with label tag option combined with the After form item option instruct Dreamweaver to insert the check box and the form label together with the label placed after the check box on the form.

4. Select the check box on the form.

5. Type **fish** in the Checked value text box in the Property inspector.

   This is the value that will be sent to your script or program when the form is processed.

6. Click the **Unchecked option button** after Initial state in the Property inspector if necessary, as shown in Figure 21.

   The check box will appear unchecked by default. If the user clicks it, a check mark will appear in the box.

(continued)

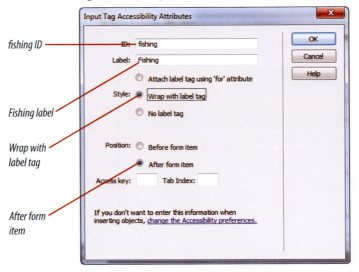

fishing ID

Fishing label

Wrap with label tag

After form item

Figure 21 *Property inspector with check box properties displayed*

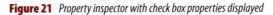

Checkbox name = fishing

Fishing check box

Checked value = fish

Initial state = Unchecked

Figure 22 *Feedback page in browser with check boxes added to the form*

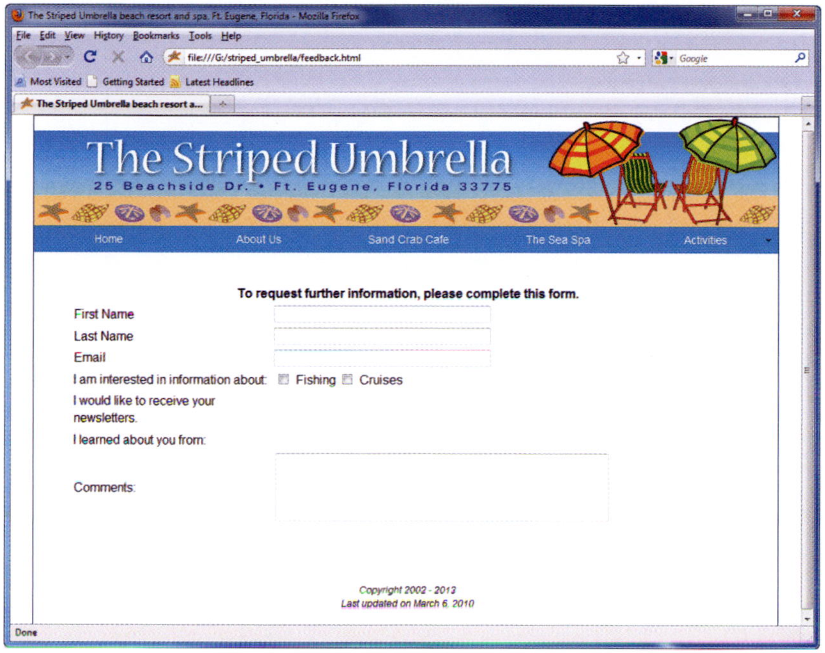

7. Insert a space after the Fishing label, then repeat Steps 2 through 6 to place a check box to the right of the Fishing text box with the check box name (ID) **cruises**, the label **Cruises**, a Checked value of **cruise**, and the Initial state of **Unchecked**.

8. Save your changes, preview the page in your browser, compare your screen to Figure 22, then close your browser.

You added two check boxes to the form that will let users request more information about fishing and cruises.

Add radio groups to a form

1. Click in the empty table cell to the right of "I would like to receive your newsletters."

2. Click the **Radio Group button** on the Insert panel to open the Radio Group dialog box.

3. Type **newsletters** in the Name text box.

4. Click the **first instance of Radio** in the Label column of the Radio Group dialog box to select it, then type **Yes**.

5. Press **[Tab]** or click the **first instance of Radio** in the Value column to select it, then type **positive**.

   You named the first radio button Yes and set positive as the value that will be sent to your script or program when the form is processed when users click this check box.

6. Press **[Tab]** or click the **second instance of Radio** to add another radio button named **No** with a value of **negative**.

7. Click the **Line breaks (
 tags) option button**, if necessary, to select it.

   TIP If the Table option button is selected, then the radio buttons will appear in a separate table within the currently selected table.

8. Compare your screen with Figure 23, then click **OK** to close the Radio Group dialog box.

(continued)

Figure 23 *Radio Group dialog box*

First instance

Second instance

Line breaks (
 tags) option button

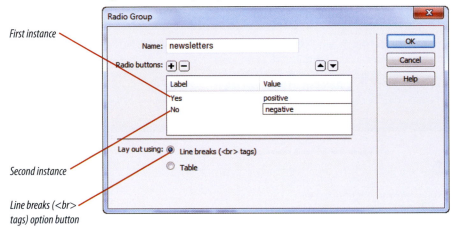

Collecting Data with Forms

Figure 24 *Feedback page with new radio group*

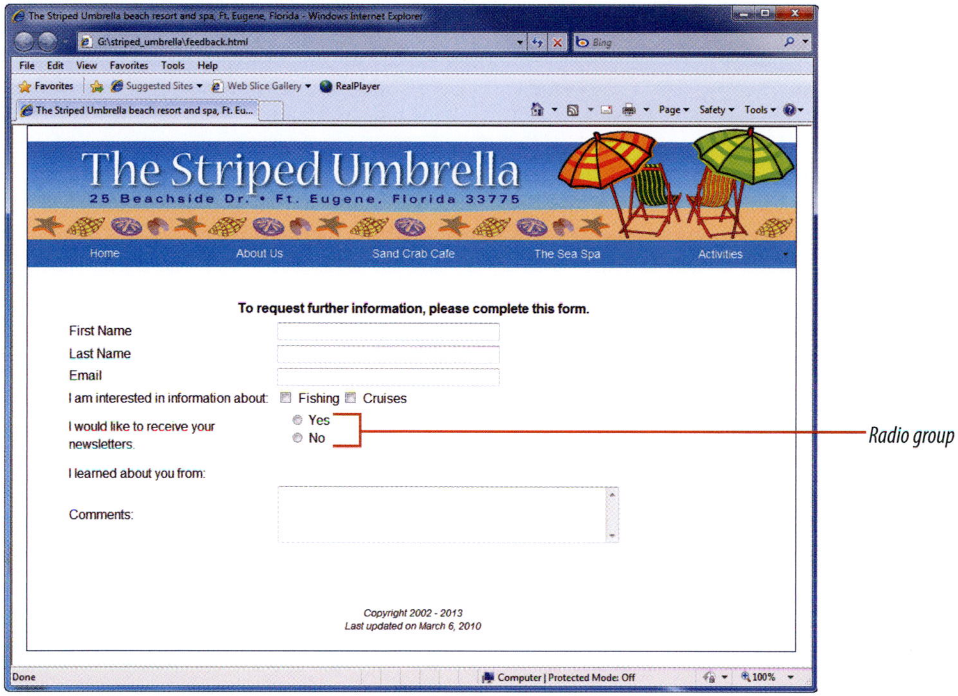

Radio group

9. Save your work, preview the page in your browser, compare your screen to Figure 24, then close your browser.

TIP To create radio buttons that are not part of a radio group, click the Radio Button button on the Insert panel.

You added a radio group that will let users answer whether or not they would like to receive The Striped Umbrella newsletters.

Add a menu

1. Click in the cell to the right of the text "I learned about you from:".

2. Click the **Select (List/Menu) button** on the Insert panel, click the **No label tag option button** in Style section of the Input Tag Accessibility Attributes dialog box, then click **OK**.

3. Type **reference** in the Select text box in the Property inspector.

4. Verify that the Menu option button in the Type section is selected in the Property inspector, as shown in Figure 25, then click **List Values** to open the List Values dialog box.

5. Click below the Item Label column heading if necessary, type **Select from list:**, then press **[Tab]**.

6. Type **none** in the Value column.

   This value will be sent to the processing program when a user accidentally skips this menu. If one of the real choices was in the top position, it might return false positives when users really did not select it, but just skipped it. This is a clue to users that they have not made a choice yet, but will not penalize them if they accidentally skip over this form control.

   (continued)

Figure 25 *Property inspector showing properties of selected List/Menu*

Menu option button

List Values button

Figure 26 *List Values dialog box*

Add button

New item
labels

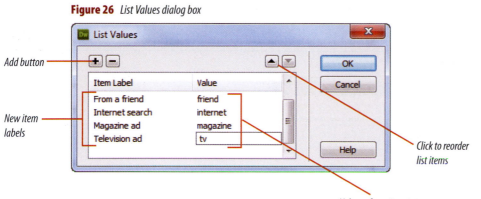

Click to reorder
list items

Values of new items

Figure 27 *Feedback page with menu*

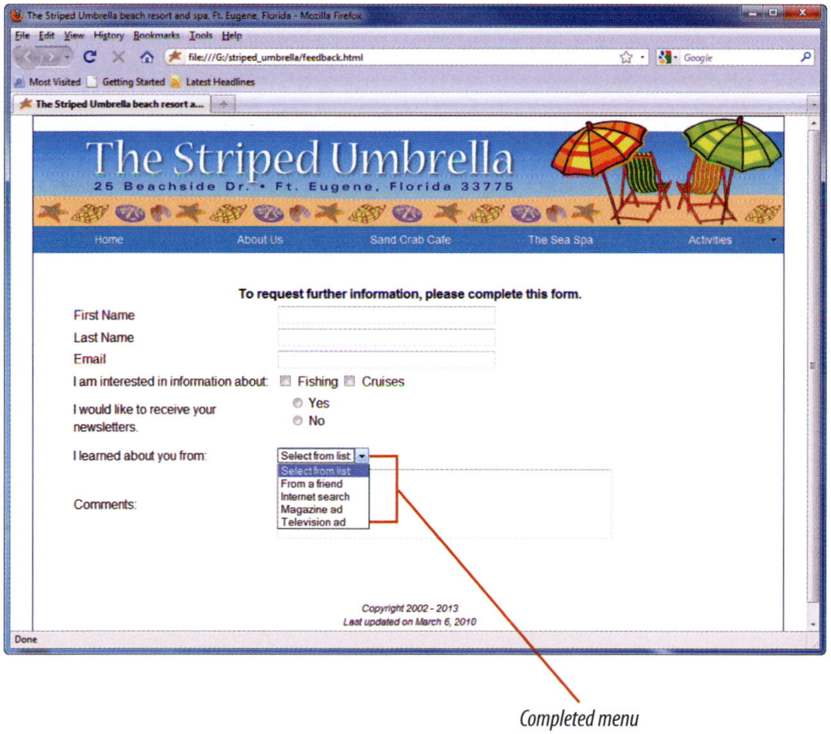

Completed menu

7. Press **[Tab]**, type **From a friend** as a new Item Label, then type **friend** in the Value column.

8. Use the **Add button ✚** to add the following three Item Labels: **Internet search**, **Magazine ad**, and **Television ad**, setting the Values as **internet**, **magazine**, and **tv**.

TIP You can also press [Tab] after entering an entry in the Value column to add a new item label.

9. Compare your screen to Figure 26, then click **OK**.

10. Save your work, preview the page in your browser, click the **list arrow** to view the menu, compare your screen to Figure 27, then close your browser.

You added a menu to the form on the feedback page.

Insert a hidden field

1. Click to the left of the First Name label at the top of the form to place the insertion point.

2. Click the **Hidden Field button** on the Insert panel.

   A Hidden Field icon appears at the insertion point.

TIP If you do not see the Hidden Field icon, click View on the Application bar (Win) or Menu bar (Mac), point to Visual Aids, then click Invisible Elements.

3. Type **required** in the HiddenField text box in the Property inspector, then type **first_name**, **last_name**, **email** in the Value text box, as shown in Figure 28.

   Typing first_name, last_name, email in the Value text box specifies that users must enter text in the First Name, Last Name, and Email fields before the script can process the form. The field names you type in the Value text box must match those in your form exactly.

4. Save your work.

You added a hidden field to the form that will let users know if they neglect to complete the fields for their first name, last name, and email address.

Figure 28 *Property inspector showing properties of selected hidden field*

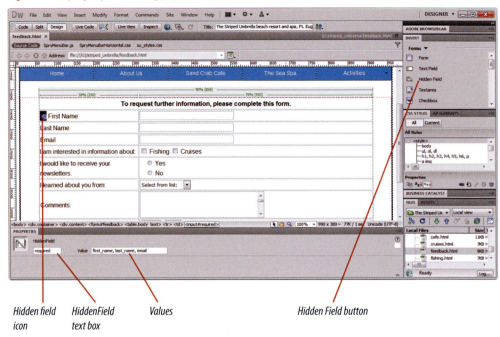

Hidden field icon   HiddenField text box   Values   Hidden Field button

Collecting Data with Forms

Figure 29 *New Submit and Reset buttons added to form*

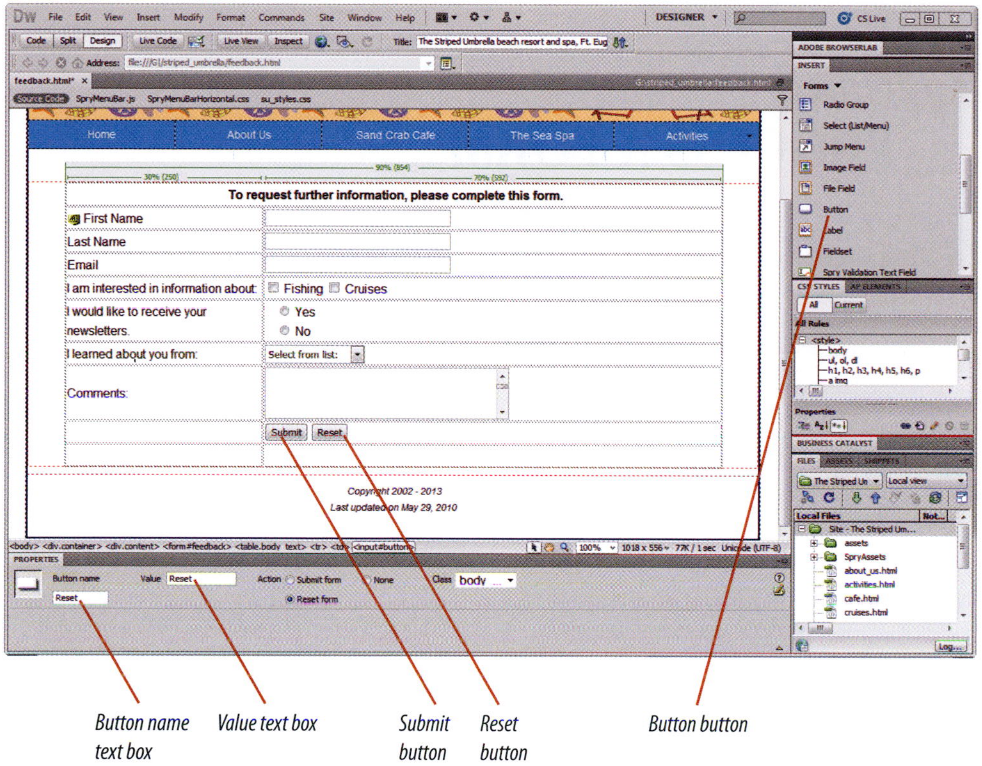

Button name text box   Value text box   Submit button   Reset button   Button button

Add Submit and Reset buttons

1. Click in the **second cell** of the second to last row of the table.

2. Click the **Button button** on the Insert panel, type **Submit** in the ID text box, click the **No label tag option button** in the Input Tag Accessibility Attributes dialog box if necessary, then click **OK**.

3. Verify that the Submit form option button is selected next to Action in the Property inspector.

   When a user clicks the Submit button, the information in the form will be sent to the processing script.

4. Verify that "Submit" is the name in the Value text box and in the Button name text box in the Property inspector.

5. Click to the right of the Submit button on the form, insert a space, then click the **Button button** on the Insert panel, click the **No label tag option button** in the Input Tag Accessibility Attributes dialog box if necessary, click **OK**.

6. Click the **Reset form option button** in the Property inspector, verify that the Value text box and Button name text box are set to Reset, then compare your screen to Figure 29.

   When a user clicks the Reset button, the form removes any information typed by the viewer.

7. Save your work.

You added a Submit button and a Reset button to the form.

Test and PROCESS A FORM

What You'll Do

In this lesson, you will check the spelling on the feedback page and create a link to the feedback page on the about_us page. You will then open the about_us page in your browser, click the feedback link, then test the form and reset it.

Creating User-Friendly Forms

After you create a form, you should test it to make sure that it works correctly and is easy to use. Verify that the fields are arranged to provide a logical flow of information, so the user is not confused about where to go next when completing the form. Make sure that there is enough contrast between the form text and the table background so the text is readable.

When a form contains several required fields (fields that must be filled out before the form can be processed), it is a good idea to provide visual clues such as a different font color or other notation that label these fields as required fields. Often, you see an asterisk next to a required field with a corresponding note at either the top or the bottom of the form explaining that all fields marked with asterisks are required fields. This encourages users to initially complete these fields rather than attempt to submit the form and then receive an error message asking them to complete required fields that have been left blank. Using a different font color for the asterisks and notes is an easy way to call attention to them and make them stand out on the page.

When you are finished with your form, you should always have several people test it before you publish it. Then make any necessary changes based on any testing feedback that you receive and test it one final time.

Understanding Jump Menus

If your website contains many pages, you can add a jump menu to make it easier for users to navigate the site. **Jump menus** are menus that let users go directly from the current web page to another page in the site with two clicks. You can also use jump menus to provide links to other websites. To create a jump menu, use the Jump Menu button on the Insert panel to open the Insert Jump Menu dialog box. For each menu item, enter text and a URL, then select the options that determine how you want the menu and target pages to appear to the user.

Collecting Data with Forms

Figure 30: *Adding visual clues for required fields*

To request further information, please complete this form.	
🗒 First Name*	
Last Name*	
Email*	
I am interested in information about:	☐ Fishing ☐ Cruises
I would like to receive your newsletters.	○ Yes ○ No
I learned about you from:	Select from list: ▾
Comments:	
	Submit Reset
*Required field	

Copyright 2002 – 2013
Last updated on March 6, 2010

Hint for user   *Asterisks added after labels*

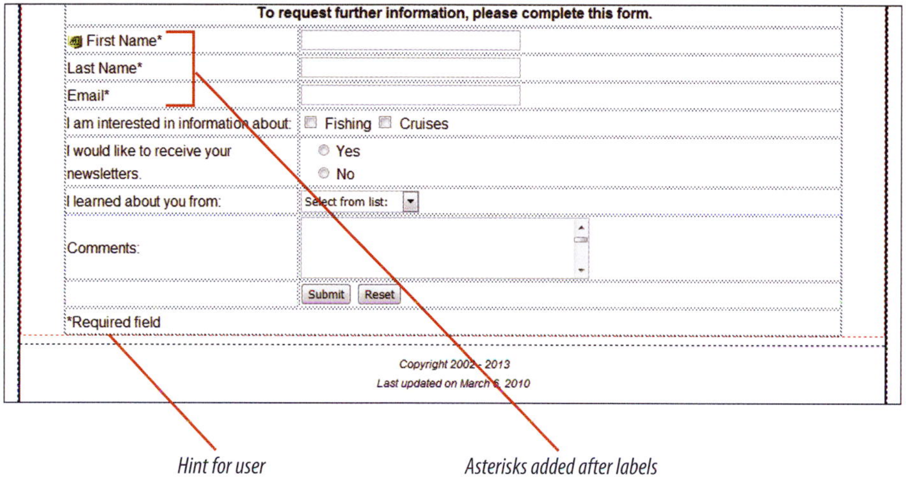

Using a Testing Server and Live View to Test Dynamic Content

When a web page contains content that allows the user to interact with the page by clicking or typing, and then responds to this input in some way, the page is said to contain **dynamic content**. A form is an excellent example of dynamic content, because as the user fills out the form, feedback can be returned, such as the availability of window seats on a particular airplane flight or whether or not certain colors or sizes of clothing items are available for purchase. This exchange of information is made possible through the use of a database, as you learned in Lesson 1. Once a form is developed and a database is tied to it, you should set up a **testing server** to evaluate how the form works and the data is processed. Your local computer or your remote server can serve as a testing server. You set up a testing server by filling out the relevant information in the Testing Server section of the Site Definition dialog box. You can also test your dynamic data in Design view by using Live View. **Live View** is a choice on the View menu that lets you add, edit, or delete dynamic content or server behaviors. You can use the Switch Design View to Live View button on the document toolbar to change to Live View. The opposite of dynamic content is static content. **Static content** refers to page content that does not change or allow user interaction.

Check spelling and create visual clues for required fields

1. Click **Commands** on the Application bar (Win) or Menu bar (Mac), click **Check Spelling** to check the spelling on the form.

2. Correct any spelling errors you find, then close the Check Spelling dialog box.

3. Click after the text First Name, then type * (an **asterisk**).

   The asterisk gives users a clue that this is a required field.

4. Repeat Step 3 after the words "Last Name" and "Email."

5. Merge the two cells in the last row, then type *Required field** in the merged field.

6. Compare your screen to Figure 30, then save and close the feedback page.

You checked the spelling on the feedback page, then added asterisks to the required fields on the page. Next, you typed text explaining what the asterisks mean and formatted the text with the body_text rule.

Link a file

1. Open the **about_us** page and click to place the insertion point to the right of the map at the bottom of the page.

TIP The insertion point may appear partially hidden, but you can continue with the steps. If you have difficulty placing it outside the link, go to Code view and place the insertion point right after the closing <p> tag.

2. Enter a paragraph break then type **Please give us your feedback so that we may make your next stay the best vacation ever!**

3. If necessary, select the text you typed in Step 2, then format it with the **body_text** rule.

4. Select the word "feedback," then use the **Point to File icon** ⊕ on the HTML Property inspector to link the feedback text to the feedback page.

5. Compare your screen with Figure 31, save your work, then preview the page in the browser.

(continued)

Figure 31 *Viewing the feedback link*

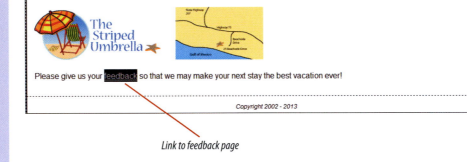

Link to feedback page

Using Spry Data Sets

One of the ways you can display data in a form is with a Spry data set. A **Spry data set** is a JavaScript object that stores data in rows and columns. You create a Spry data set in Dreamweaver and then write instructions to load the data from another source where the data is stored, such as an XML or HTML file. You can format the data to appear on a web page to your specifications. You create a Spry data set by using the Insert, Spry, Spry Data Set command on the Application bar (Win) or Menu bar (Mac). This command opens the Spry Data Set dialog box, where you then specify the Data Type, Data Set Name, which tags to detect, and the Data File name and location.

Collecting Data with Forms

Figure 32 *Testing the feedback page*

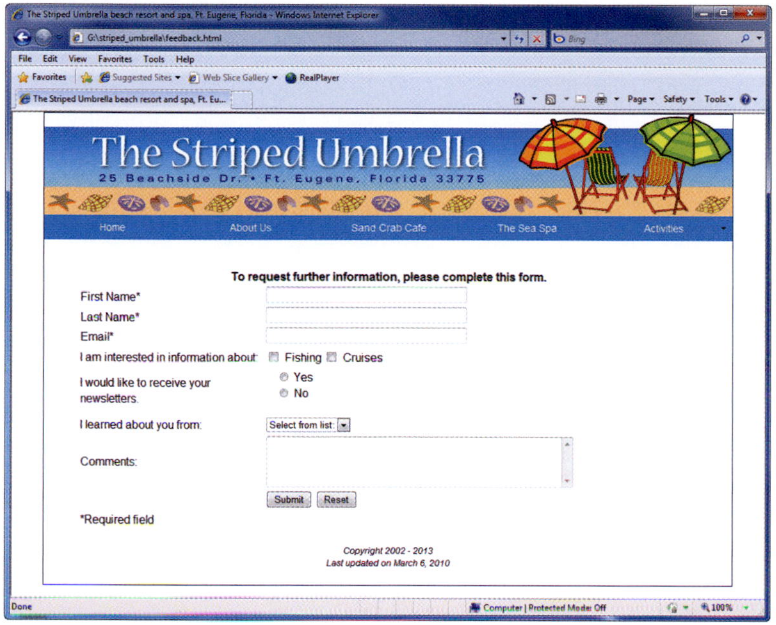

6. Click the **feedback link** to test it.

   The feedback page opens in a new window, as shown in Figure 32.

7. Test the form by filling it out, then clicking the **Reset button**.

   The Reset button clears the form, but the Submit button does not work because this form has not been set up to send information to a database. Linking to a database is beyond the scope of this book, but you can refer to the information on pages 9–5 and 9–7 to learn more about CGI scripts.

8. Close the browser and close all open pages.

You created a link on the about_us page to link to the feedback form, and tested it in your browser.

Using Spry Validation Field Widgets

A **Spry widget** is a page element that enables user interaction on a web page. Spry widgets are stored within the **Spry framework**, a JavaScript library that provides access to reusable widgets that you can add to your pages. Some of the Spry widgets are fields that can be added to a form. These form fields are called **Spry Validation Field widgets**. These are fields that display valid or invalid states when text is being entered in a form on a web page. This instant feedback provides users the opportunity to correct their form before they try to submit it. Sometimes the widgets provide hints, such as the correct date format to use or the minimum number of characters required in a field. When a user does not enter the data correctly, an error message is returned. To add a Spry Validation Field widget to a form, use the Insert, Spry, Spry Validation (field name) command, or select a button in the Spry category on the Insert panel. Spry widgets use a combination of CSS and JavaScript that work within the HTML code. The CSS code formats the widget and the JavaScript code makes it work.

Plan and create a form.

1. Open the Blooms & Bulbs website.
2. Open the tips page.
3. Scroll to the bottom of the page, insert two paragraph breaks to end the ordered list after the last line of text, then insert a form.
4. Set the Method to POST in the Property inspector if necessary.
5. Name the form **submit_tips**.
6. Set the Target to _self.
7. Save your work.

Edit and format a form.

1. Insert a table within the form that contains **9** rows and **2** columns. Set the Table width to **75%**, set the Border thickness to **0**, the Cell padding to **2**, and the Cell spacing to **1**.
2. Choose the Top row header icon, then include an appropriate table summary that indicates that the table will be used for form layout purposes.
3. Merge the cells in the top row and type **Submit Your Favorite Gardening Tip** in the newly merged cell.
4. Type **Email** in the first cell in the second row.
5. Type **Category** in the first cell in the third row.
6. Type **Subject** in the first cell in the fourth row.
7. Type **Description** in the first cell in the fifth row.
8. Apply the paragraph_text style to the table.
9. Merge both cells in the sixth row of the table, then insert the label **How long have you been gardening?** in the resulting merged cell.
10. Merge both cells in the seventh row of the table, then insert the label **Receive notification when new tips are submitted?** in the resulting merged cell.
11. Save your work.

Work with form objects.

1. Click in the second cell of the second row. Insert a text field with no label tag, naming it **email**. Set the Char width property to **30** and the Max chars property to **150**. (*Hint*: The Image Tag Accessibility Attributes dialog box will not appear if you do not have the accessibility preference set for adding form objects.)
2. Click in the second cell of the fourth row, then insert a text field with no label tag and the name **subject**. Set the Char width to **30** and the Max chars to **150**.
3. Click in the second cell of the fifth row, then insert a textarea with no label tag and the name **description**. Set the Char width to **40** and the Num lines to **5**.
4. To the right of the "Receive notification when new tips are submitted?" label, insert a space and a check box with no label tag. Set the name of the check box to **receive_tips**, enter **yes** in the Checked value text box, then verify that the initial state is Unchecked.
5. To the right of the text "How long have you been gardening?" insert a radio group named **years_gardening**, that uses line breaks. It should contain the labels **1 - 5 years**, **5 - 10 years**, **Over 10 years** and the following corresponding values for each label: **1+**, **5+**, and **10+**.
6. Insert a Select (list/menu) named **category** in the empty cell to the right of Category. Set the Type to List and the Height to 2. Use the List Values dialog box to add the following item labels: **Weed control**, **General growth**, and **Pest control**, and set the corresponding values for each to **weeds**, **growth**, and **pests**.
7. Insert a hidden field named **required** in the first cell of the eighth row that has the value **email**.
8. Insert a Submit button named **submit** in the second cell of the eighth row.
9. With your insertion point to the right of the Submit button, insert a Reset button named **reset** with the Reset form action.
10. Save your work.

Test and process a form.

1. Check the spelling on the form and correct any errors you find.

2. Type *(an asterisk) after the label Email.

3. Merge the cells in the last row, then type *Required field in the last row.

4. Insert a horizontal rule at the top and bottom of the table.

5. Center the table on the page.

6. Save your work.

7. Preview the page in your browser, compare your form to Figure 33, then test the form by filling it out and using the Reset button.

8. Close your browser, then close all open pages.

Figure 33 *Completed Skills Review*

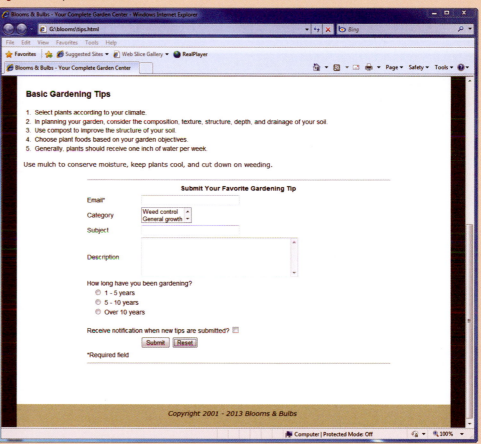

In this exercise, you continue your work on the TripSmart website you created in Chapters 1 through 8. The owner, Thomas Howard, wants you to create a form to collect information from users who are interested in receiving more information on one or more of the featured trips.

1. Open the TripSmart website.
2. Open the tours page.
3. Insert a form named **information** after the last paragraph on the page.
4. Specify the Method as POST, if necessary.
5. Insert a table in the form that contains **11** rows, **2** columns, a Table width of **75%**, a Border thickness of **0**, Cell padding of **1**, Cell spacing of **1**, a top Header, and an appropriate table summary.
6. Merge the cells in the top row, type **Please complete this form for additional information on these tours.**, apply the reverse_text rule, then change the cell background color to **#666633**.
7. Beginning in the second row, type the following labels in the cells in the first column: **First Name**, **Last Name**, **Street**, **City**, **State**, **Zip Code**, **Phone**, **Email**, and **I am interested in:**, then apply the paragraph_text rule to all of them.
8. Insert single-line text fields in the eight cells in the second column beginning with row 2 and assign the following names: **first_name**, **last_name**, **street**, **city**, **state**, **zip**, **phone**, and **email**.
9. Set the Char width to **30** and the Max chars to **100** for each of these text fields.
10. In the second cell of the tenth row, insert a check box with the label **Spain**, the name **spain**, and a Checked value of **yes**.
11. Repeat Step 10 to add another check box in the same cell next to the Spain check box with the label **China**, the name **china**, and a Checked Value of **yes**.

12. Apply the paragraph_text rule to the Spain and China labels.

13. Set the vertical alignment for each cell except the top cell to Top.

14. Insert a Submit button and a Reset button in the second cell of the 11th row.

15. Center the table in the form.

16. Click in the last cell in the first column and set the column width to 25%.

17. Save your work, preview the page in your browser, test the form, compare your screen to Figure 34, close your browser, then close the tours page.

Figure 34 *Completed Project Builder 1*

some of Spain's most picqueresque cities. Granada features the 13-century palace Alhambra with its beautiful gardens. Jerez, the home of the Andalusioan School of Equestrian Art, is our next stop. You will view a performance of the "dancing stallions" and visit a bodega. Next is Seville, where you will have a change to attend a traditional flamenco show. You may decide to splurge on an authentic flamenco dress! We end the visit with Barcelona where you will stay near the Barcelona Olympic Port. You will view the work of Spain's most famous architect: Gaudi, as you visit the unfinished Sagrada Familia Basilica along with the Parc Guell, a UNESCO World Heritage Site.

The second trip we are featuring is to China. We will depart on June 20 and arrive in Shanghai to stay three nights at the Shanghai Four Seasons Hotel.Shanghai sights will include a visit to the Bund, the Shanghai Museum, and a performace of the Shanghai Acrobats. From Shanghai we will depart for our three-day voyage down the Yangtze River on the River Dancer, where we will visit The Three Gorges. Upon disembarking, we will travel to Xian to view the Terra Cotta Warriors and explore the Shaanxi Museum. Our tour ends in Beijing with the Forbidden City, Tiananmen Square, and a day trip to the Great Wall of China.Our experienced guides all speak fluent English. Our team includes ornithologist JoAnne Rife, zoologist Jenny Williams, anthropologist Christina Elizabeth, and naturalist Richard Newland. Private air transport will whisk us to more distant game reserves with an opportunity to see the native Pandas. This is truly a trip of a lifetime. Make your reservations now!

Please complete this form for additional information on these tours.

First Name

Last Name

Street

City

State

Zip Code

Phone

Email

I am interested in: ☐ Spain ☐ China

Submit   Reset

TripSmart Copyright 2002 - 2013

Use Figure 35 as a guide to continue your work on the Carolyne's Catering website you created in Project Builder 2 in Chapters 1 through 8. Chef Carolyne asked you to place a simple form on the catering page that allows customers to fill in and fax lunch orders.

1. Open the Carolyne's Catering website.
2. Open the catering page.
3. Insert a form called **orders** under the table with POST as the method.
4. Insert a table in the form that contains **8** rows, **2** columns, and your choice of table width, border thickness, cell padding, and cell spacing. Use a top header and specify an appropriate table summary and header.
5. Merge the cells in the top row and type **Lunch Order**.
6. In the first column of cells, type the following labels under the table header: **Please select from the following:**, **Drink choice:**, **Desired pick-up time:**, **First Name:**, **Last Name:**, **Phone Number:**.
7. In the second cell of the second row, insert a radio group named **box_lunches** with the following labels and values: **Southwest Club Sandwich**, sandwich; **Chipotle Chicken Wrap**, wrap; **Pecan Chicken Salad**, salad.
8. In the second cell in the third row, insert a radio group called **drinks** with the following labels and values: **Raspberry tea**, **tea**; **Berry smoothie**, **smoothie**.
9. In the second cell of the fourth row, insert a single line text field named **time** with a character width and maximum characters of **10**.
10. In the second cell of the fifth, sixth, and seventh rows, insert single-line text fields named **first_name**, **last_name**, and **phone** using character widths of **30** and maximum characters of **100**.

11. Merge the cells in the last row and type **Fax order by 10:00 a.m. to 555-963-5938**.
12. Since they are going to fax the form, there is no need for a Submit button. You may add a Reset button if you like.
13. Format the text in the form with styles of your choice.
14. Set the cell alignment of each cell to top.
15. Select all of the cells in the first column except the cell in the last row, and set the Horizontal alignment to Right.
16. Center-align the first cell in the last row, then add a horizontal rule above the form.
17. Add any additional formatting of your choice to the page, table, or form properties.
18. Save your work, preview the page in a browser, test the form, compare your screen to Figure 35, close your browser, then close the catering page.

Figure 35 *Completed Project Builder 2*

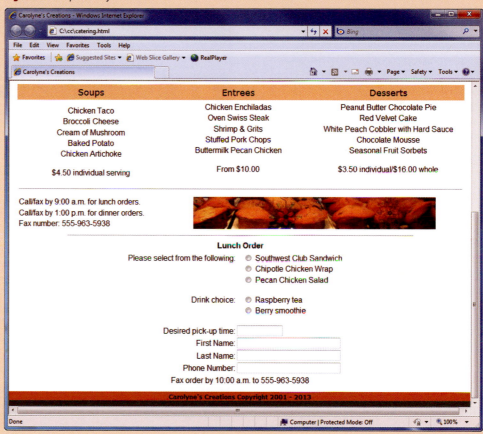

Websites use many form objects to collect information from users. The form shown in Figure 36 is well organized and requests information that most people are comfortable giving over the Internet, such as name, address, and phone number. There are several helpful explanations that guide the viewer in filling out the form correctly to report an environmental violation.

1. Connect to the Internet, then navigate to the U.S. Environmental Protection Agency website, pictured in Figure 36, www.epa.gov. (The page in Figure 36 is at www.epa.gov/compliance/complaints/index.html.)

2. Does this site use forms to collect information? If so, identify each of the form objects used to create the form.

3. Is the form organized logically? Explain why or why not.

4. What CGI script is being used to process the form? And where is that script located? Remember the name of the processing CGI script is included in the Action attribute of your form tag. (*Hint*: To view the code of a page in a browser, click View on the menu bar of your browser, then click Source or Page Source.)

5. Do you see any hidden fields?

6. Is this form secure?

7. Could the information in this form be collected with different types of form objects? If so, which form objects would you use?

8. Does the form use tables for page layout?

9. Does the form use labels for its fields? If so, were the labels created using the <label> element or with text labels in table cells? (*Hint*: Search the code for the form to look for <label> tags.)

Figure 36 *Design Project*

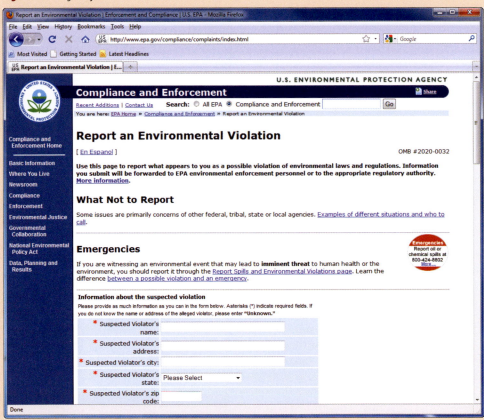

U. S. Environmental Protection Agency – www.epa.gov

In this project, you continue to work on the website that you have been developing since Chapter 1.

You continue building your site by designing and completing a page that contains a form to collect visitor information as it relates to the topic of your site.

1. Review your wireframes. Choose a page to develop that will use a form to collect information. Choose another page that you already developed on which you will place a jump menu.
2. Plan the content for the new page by making a list of the information that you will collect and the types of form objects you will use to collect that information. Plan to include at least one of every type of form object you learned about in the chapter. Be sure to specify how you will organize the form on the page.
3. Create the form and its contents.
4. Run a report that checks for broken links in the site. Correct any broken links that appear in the report.
5. Test the form by previewing it in a browser, entering information into it, and resetting it. Check to make sure the information gets to its specified location, whether that is a database or an email address.
6. Preview all the pages in a browser, then test all menus and links. Evaluate the pages for both content and layout.
7. Review the checklist shown in Figure 37. Make any modifications necessary to improve the form, the jump menu, or the page containing the form.
8. Close all open pages.

Figure 37 *Portfolio Project*

Website Checklist
1. Do all navigation links work?
2. Do all images appear correctly?
3. Do all form objects align correctly with their form labels?
4. Does the placement of the form objects appear in a logical order?
5. Does the most important information appear at the top of the form?
6. Did you test the form?
7. Are you happy with the overall appearance of each page?

CHAPTER 10 POSITIONING OBJECTS
WITH AP DIVS

1. Insert an AP div
2. Set the position and size of an AP element
3. Add content to an AP element
4. Set AP element properties

CHAPTER 10

POSITIONING OBJECTS WITH AP DIVS

Introduction

You have learned how to control the position of text and graphic elements with precision on your web pages using CSS layout blocks. With **CSS layout blocks**, you use containers formatted with CSS styles to place content on web pages. These containers can hold images, blocks of text, Flash movies, or any other page elements. You set the appearance and position of these containers using HTML tags known as **div tags**. With div tags, you can position elements next to each other, as well as on top of each other, in a stack. In this chapter, you will use another type of div called an AP div to place text and graphics on a page. AP stands for absolutely positioned. An **AP div tag** creates a div with a fixed position on a web page. When you create an AP div, Dreamweaver automatically creates a style for it. The name of the style begins with a pound sign (#) rather than a period. It is an ID type, not a class type.

Using AP Divs

AP divs let you control the appearance of elements on your web page. AP divs allow you to stack your information in a vertical pile, allowing for just one piece of information to be visible at a time. Browsers display AP divs as independent elements so you can easily change their contents without affecting the page flow. This makes them a good choice for page content that changes frequently or is based on certain conditions. AP divs do not disturb the position of other page elements so they are easy to add and remove without affecting the overall design.

You can add behaviors to your AP divs with JavaScript. **JavaScript** is a program that is used to add interactivity to web pages. It is a **client-side script**, in which, as you learned in Chapter 9, the commands from the program are executed on the user's computer. This is the opposite of **server-side scripts**, which are executed on the web server. **Behaviors** are preset pieces of JavaScript code that you can attach to page elements, such as an AP div. A behavior instructs the page element to respond in a specific way when an event occurs, such as when the mouse pointer is positioned over the element. Behaviors are attached to page elements using **ActionScript**, a Flash scripting language developers use to add interactivity to movies, control objects, exchange data, and to create complex animations.

TOOLS YOU'LL USE

CSS STYLES	AP ELEMENTS		▾≡
	☐ Prevent overlaps		

👁	ID	Z	
👁	noodles	3	
👁	granddad	2	
	children	1	

CSS Rule definition for #children

Category
Type
Background
Block
Box
Border
List
Positioning
Extensions

Type

Font-family: Arial, Helvetica, sans-serif ▾

Font-size: small ▾ px ▾   Font-weight: bold ▾

Font-style: ▾   Font-variant: ▾

Line-height: ▾ px ▾   Text-transform: ▾

Text-decoration: ☐ underline   Color: ☐ #FFF
☐ overline
☐ line-through
☐ blink
☐ none

[Help]   [OK]   [Cancel]   [Apply]

Insert
AN AP DIV

What You'll Do

In this lesson, you will draw an AP div on The Striped Umbrella home page and set its properties using the Property inspector.

Understanding AP Elements

AP elements are page elements that are absolutely positioned, or assigned a fixed position on a web page. The most common AP element is an AP div. AP divs are created with AP div tags. In this chapter, we will use the term "AP element" when speaking in general about AP elements and "AP div" when specifically referring to AP divs. Using AP div tags, you can stack AP divs on top of each other and specify that only certain elements be visible at certain times or under conditions you specify. You can use AP divs to create special effects on a web page. For instance, you can use AP divs to build a whole image from individual pieces. You can then add code that will allow you to slide the pieces into their positions one at a time. You can also use AP divs to create dynamic pages that contain moving parts or objects that become visible or invisible, based on selections made by website users.

Using AP divs to lay out a web page is like working with a stack of transparency sheets that you can stack on top of each other. The National Parks Service page shown in Figure 1 uses AP divs to create interactive page content. Each graphic in the Find by Category section is an AP div. As you place the pointer over a div, it becomes selected and the spinner points to it. As you move it away from the div, the div becomes deselected and the pointer moves away from it.

To insert an AP div, you can use the Draw AP Div button in the Layout Category on the Insert panel and drag to draw a rectangular shape anywhere on your page. You can also insert an AP div using the Layout Objects, AP Div command on the Insert menu. Specify the exact dimensions, color, and other attributes of a new AP div by changing the settings in the Preferences dialog box for all AP divs, or in the Property inspector for a specific AP div. After the AP div is in place, you can drag it to a different location on the page or edit the values in the L (left) or T (top) text boxes to change its position.

As you work with AP divs, it is often helpful to use guides to help you place and align the divs in consistent locations. A guide is a horizontal or vertical line that is used to position page content. Guides do not appear in the browser. You can add as many guides as you need to your web pages. To place a guide, drag the pointer from the horizontal or vertical ruler and release the mouse button when the guide is positioned in the correct location. A ScreenTip appears, telling you the exact position of the guide. You can use a guide to emulate a **fold line**, a term borrowed from newspapers. The fold line indicates where the paper is folded in half. The most important newspaper stories appear above the fold line. Similarly, you want the most important information on your page to appear above the "fold line," the portion of the screen that users can see without scrolling.

Using HTML Tags to Create AP Divs

Dreamweaver uses the <div> tag to create an AP div. The default value for the first AP div on a page appears as <div id="apDiv1">. Dreamweaver assigns each additional AP div the next number in sequence. You can use either the Property inspector or the AP Elements panel to rename each AP div with a name that is relevant to its content. The styles for AP divs reside in the head content as part of the CSS code.

Understanding AP Div Content

An AP div is like a separate HTML document within a web page. It can contain the same types of elements that a page can, such as background colors, images, links, tables, and text. You can also set the contents of an AP div to work directly with a specified Dreamweaver behavior to make the page interact with a viewer in a certain way.

Using Advanced Formatting

In using AP divs, it's best to use only as much content as fits in the container. If you add more information than the div can display

at one time, you will need to use advanced formatting controls to tell Dreamweaver how to handle the overflow. You can control the appearance of a selected AP div by changing the Clip, Visibility, and Overflow properties in the Property inspector.

The **Clip property** identifies the portion of an AP div's content that is visible in a web browser. By default, the clipping region matches the outside borders of the AP div, but you can change the amount that is visible by clipping one or all sides. For instance, if you set the L (left) Clip property to 10 pixels, then everything from the eleventh pixel to the right will appear in the browser. If you clip off 10 pixels from the right side, you will need to subtract 10 from the total width of the AP div and then type this value in the Clip R text box in the Property

inspector. The clip setting can be applied only to AP divs that have an Overflow attribute set to a value other than visible.

The **Vis property** lets you control whether the selected AP div is visible. You can set the Vis property to default, visible, hidden, or **inherit**, which means that the visibility of the AP div is automatically inherited from its parent AP div or page.

The **Overflow property** specifies how to treat excess content that does not fit inside an AP div. You can make the content visible, hide the content, specify that scroll bars appear, or let the current AP div automatically deal with the extra content in the same manner as its parent AP div or page. However, some browsers do not support the overflow property.

Figure 1 *Using AP divs for placing interactive content*

National Park Service website – www.nps.

Draw an AP div

1. Open The Striped Umbrella website, open the index page, click **View** on the Application bar (Win) or Menu bar (Mac), point to **Rulers**, then click **Show** to select this option if necessary.

   Rulers appear along the top and left side of the page and will help guide placement of page elements.

2. Place the mouse pointer on the horizontal ruler, then drag down to position a horizontal guide at the **460 pixel mark** on the vertical ruler.

3. Select the Layout category on the Insert panel, then click the **Draw AP Div button**.

4. Using Figure 2 as a guide, drag a **rectangle** in the middle of the home page, and under the guide, that is approximately 250 pixels wide and 150 pixels tall.

   A new AP div appears on the page, but it is not selected. An AP div icon [icon] appears above the upper-left corner of the AP div.

TIP You can also insert an AP div by clicking Insert on the Application bar (Win) or Menu bar (Mac), pointing to Layout Objects, and then clicking AP Div.

5. Click the **AP div icon** [icon] above the AP div to select it.

TIP You can also select an AP div by clicking one of its borders.

You drew an AP div on the home page, then selected it.

Figure 2 *New AP div added to the home page*

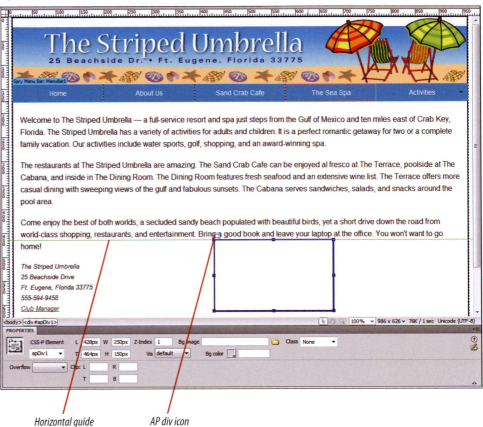

Horizontal guide   *AP div icon*

Figure 3 *Property inspector showing properties of selected AP div*

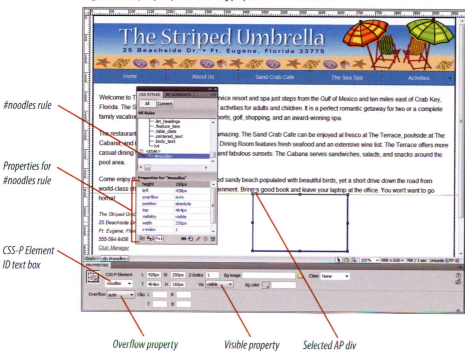

#noodles rule

Properties for #noodles rule

CSS-P Element ID text box

Overflow property　　*Visible property*　　*Selected AP div*

Define an AP div

1. With the AP div selected, select **apDiv1** in the CSS-P Element text box in the Property inspector, type **noodles**, then press **[Enter]** (Win) or **[return]** (Mac).

TIP If the AP div is not selected, click the <div#apDiv1> tag in the tag selector.

2. Verify that <div#noodles> is selected in the Tag selector.

3. Click the **Overflow list arrow** in the Property inspector, then click **auto**.

4. Click the **Vis list arrow**, then click **visible**.

5. Compare your screen to Figure 3.

The L, T, W, and H settings in the Property inspector specify the position and size of the AP div. Your settings will probably differ from those shown in the figure because you probably drew your AP div with slightly different measurements.

6. Scroll down to view the new rule that has been defined in the CSS Styles panel called #noodles.

When you draw an AP div, Dreamweaver automatically creates a rule for it. As you make changes to the element properties, they appear in the Properties pane, when the rule is selected.

TIP You may see two different <style> sheets listed: one for the AP div styles and one for the rest of the embedded styles.

7. Save your work.

You specified a name and other properties for the selected AP element. You viewed the new style in the CSS Styles panel.

Set the Position
AND SIZE OF AN AP ELEMENT

What You'll Do

Welcome to The Striped Umbrella — a full-service resort and spa just steps from the Gulf of Mexico and ten miles east of Crab Key, Florida. The Striped Umbrella has a variety of activities for adults and children. It is a perfect romantic getaway for two or a complete family vacation. Our activities include water sports, golf, shopping, and an award-winning spa.

The restaurants at The Striped Umbrella are amazing. The Sand Crab Cafe can be enjoyed al fresco at The Terrace, poolside at The Cabana, and inside in The Dining Room. The Dining Room features fresh seafood and an extensive wine list. The Terrace offers more casual dining with sweeping views of the gulf and fabulous sunsets. The Cabana serves sandwiches, salads, and snacks around the pool area.

Come enjoy the best of both worlds, a secluded sandy beach populated with beautiful birds, yet a short drive down the road from world-class shopping, restaurants, and entertainment. Bring a good book and leave your laptop at the office. You won't want to go home!

The Striped Umbrella
25 Beachside Drive
Ft. Eugene, Florida 33775
555-594-9458
Club Manager

Copyright 2002 - 2012
Last updated on March 17, 2010

▶ *In this lesson, you will use the Property inspector to position and size AP elements on the home page of The Striped Umbrella website.*

Understanding Absolute Positioning

To use AP elements, you must understand **absolute positioning**. The term "absolute" in this context means that the AP element will be locked in a fixed position on the page regardless of the size of the browser window. You position an AP element absolutely by specifying the distance between the upper-left corner of the AP element and the upper-left corner of the page or parent AP element in which it is contained. Figure 4 illustrates how an AP element keeps its position relative to the top left corner of a page as the page is scrolled. Because a browser treats AP elements as if they are separate HTML documents contained within a page, they do not interrupt the flow of content on the page or parent AP element in which they are contained. This means that AP elements placed on top of a page can hide the contents on the page.

AP elements have no impact on the location of other AP elements. In other words, if you insert an AP element, the page elements that follow it within the code will continue with the flow of the page, ignoring the presence of the AP element. This means you can create overlapping AP elements to create dynamic effects on a web page. To do this, you use JavaScript or CGI script to change the attributes associated with each AP element in response to actions by the viewer. For instance, an AP element could move or change its size when a viewer clicks or moves the mouse over a link on the page or in the AP element.

Setting Positioning Attributes

You can control the placement of AP elements by setting their attributes in the Property inspector. These attributes work together to create an AP element that will hold its position on a page.

The **Left property (L)** in the Property inspector specifies the distance between the left edge of an AP element and the left edge of the page or parent AP element that contains it. The **Top property (T)** in the Property inspector specifies the distance between the top edge of your AP element and the top edge of the page or the AP element that contains it.

The **Width (W)** and **Height (H) properties** specify the dimensions of the AP element, usually in pixels, although the AP element can be specified as a percentage of your screen dimension. For instance, you can specify that your AP element be 250 pixels by 250 pixels, or you can set it to 25% by 25%, which will create an AP element that is roughly 200 by 150 in a web browser on an 800×600 resolution monitor.

Use the **Z-Index property** in the Property inspector to specify the vertical stacking order of AP elements on a page. If you think of the page itself as AP element 0, then any number higher than that will appear on top of the page. For instance, if you have three AP elements with the Z-Index values of 1, 2, and 3, then 1 will appear below 2 and 3, while 3 will always appear above 1 and 2. You can create a dynamic website by changing the Z-Index settings dynamically, as the user is viewing the page, using Dreamweaver's built-in JavaScript behaviors.

QUICK TIP

You cannot set Z-Index values below 0.

Figure 4 *Scrolling a page containing an AP element*

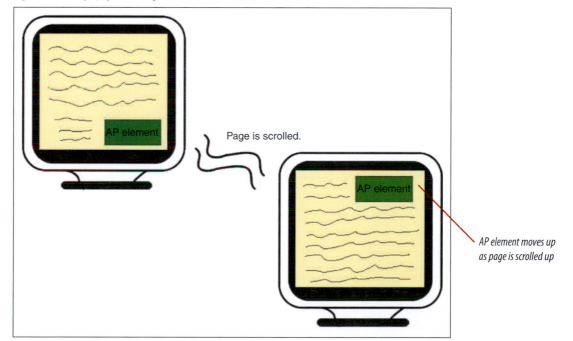

Set the Left and Top position of an AP div

1. Click the **AP div border** to select the AP div (if necessary).

2. Type **490px** in the L text box in the CSS-P Element section of the Property inspector, then press **[Tab]** (Win) or **[return]** (Mac).

   The AP div moves automatically to the position you specified.

3. Type **450px** in the T text box, then press **[Enter]** (Win) or **[return]** (Mac).

4. Save your work, then compare your screen to Figure 5.

TIP The AP div may appear in a different position on your screen, depending on your screen size.

You adjusted the upper-left corner position of the AP div.

Figure 5 *AP div moved up and to the left on the page*

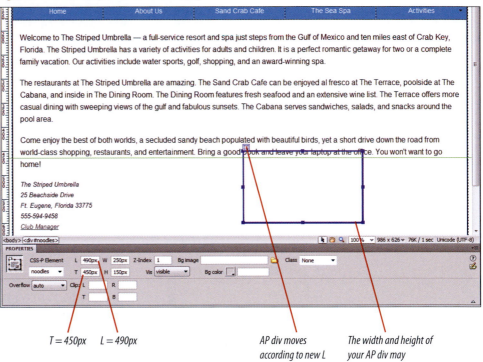

T = 450px   L = 490px

AP div moves according to new L and T properties

The width and height of your AP div may vary at this point

Figure 6 *AP div with width and height adjusted*

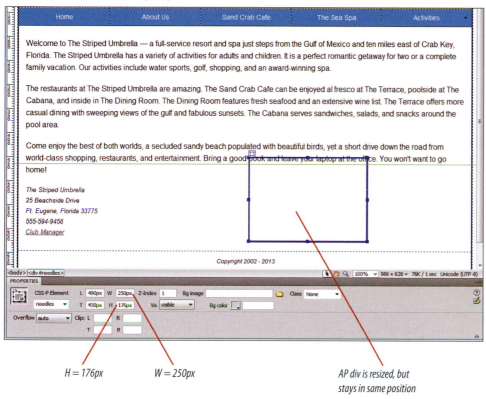

H = 176px

W = 250px

AP div is resized, but
stays in same position

Set AP div height and width

1. Click the **AP div border** to select the AP div (if necessary).

2. Type **250px** in the W text box, then press **[Tab]**.

   The AP div automatically adjusts its width to the dimension you specified.

3. Type **176px** in the H text box, then press **[Tab]**.

   The AP div automatically adjusts to the height you specified. Notice that the upper-left corner stays in the same position.

4. Save your work, then compare your screen to Figure 6.

You adjusted the height and width of the AP div.

Set the Z-Index value for AP divs

1. Draw another AP div anywhere on the page, select it, then name it **granddad**.

2. Select the granddad AP div (if necessary), then adjust its size and position by setting the following properties in the Property inspector: L: **280px**, T: **475px**, W: **250px**, and H: **165px**.

   The new AP div is now positioned on top of the noodles AP div, temporarily blocking all but its right and top borders.

3. Change the Z-Index value of the granddad AP div to **2** in the Property inspector, if necessary, as shown in Figure 7.

4. Repeat steps 1 and 2 to draw another AP div on the page to the right of the noodles AP div named **two_children** with the following properties: L: **710px**, T: **440px**, W: **200px**, and H: **250px**.

(continued)

Figure 7 *New granddad AP div overlaps noodles AP div*

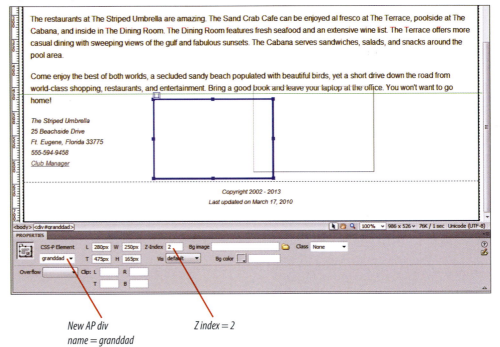

New AP div
name = granddad

Z index = 2

Figure 8 *noodles AP div moved on top of other two AP divs*

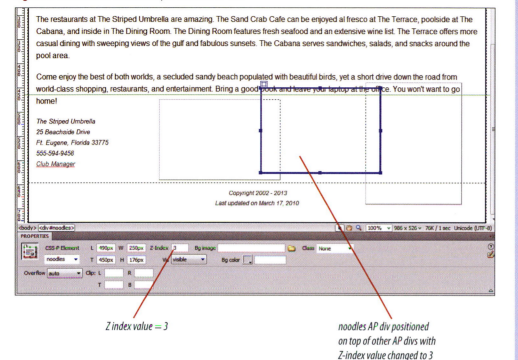

Z index value = 3

noodles AP div positioned
on top of other AP divs with
Z-index value changed to 3

5. Click the **noodles AP div** to select it, by clicking its border or the AP div icon ▢.

6. Change the Z-Index value of the noodles AP div to **3**.

7. Select the two_children AP div.

8. Change the Z-Index value of the two_children AP div to **1** in the Property inspector, then save your work.

   When an AP div is selected, it appears above other AP divs, regardless of the stacking order.

9. Select the **noodles AP div**, then compare your screen to Figure 8.

   The three AP divs are placed in position on the page, as shown in Figure 8. None of the AP divs has content yet. You can only see the outlines of each AP div and their stacking order on the page. The noodles and two_children AP divs look like they will appear on top of the paragraph text, but in the browser window they will appear slightly below the text.

You added two new AP divs named granddad and two_children to the home page, and specified their dimensions and position on the page using the Property inspector. You then adjusted their vertical stacking order.

Add Content
TO AN AP ELEMENT

What You'll Do

 ▶ *In this lesson, you will add a background image to an AP element. You will also insert an image on the other two AP elements and type text on an AP element.*

Understanding AP Element Content

As you learned in Lesson 1, an AP element is like a separate document within a web page. It contains the same types of elements that any page would, such as background colors, images, links, tables, and text. If you want to add an image to an AP element, insert the image just as you would insert one on a page using the Insert panel. Figure 9 shows an AP element with an image placed inside it. If you want to be able to type on top of the image, insert the image as a background image for the AP element, as shown in Figure 10.

If you add more content than the preset image size, the AP element will expand to display the content on your page in Dreamweaver. However, when you preview the page in the browser, the amount displayed will depend on how you set your Overflow settings.

As on a web page, if you specify both a background color and a background image, the background image will override the background color. As the page is loading, the AP element background color may appear until the AP element background image finishes loading.

Also, as with formatting text on a web page, you should use CSS to format your text on an AP element. You can also add all other AP element properties such as text indent, padding, margins, and background color with your styles.

Figure 9 *AP element with an inserted image*

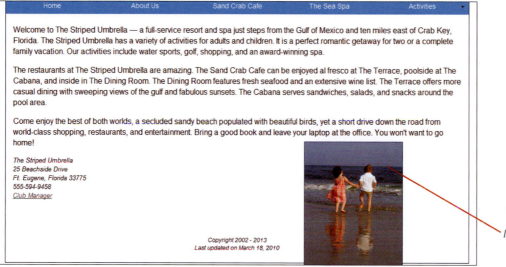

Inserted image

Figure 10 *AP element with an image inserted as a background image*

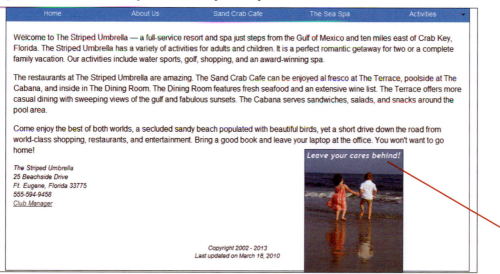

AP element with a
background image
and type added

Add an image to an AP div

1. Click inside the granddad AP div to place the insertion point there, click **Insert** on the Menu bar (Win) or Application bar (Mac), click **Image**, browse to the drive and folder where you store your Data Files, open the assets folder, then double-click **looking_at_birds.jpg**.

TIP Use care to place the insertion point inside the AP Div. It may take several attempts. You will see a long insertion point the height of the AP Div if you set it correctly.

2. Add the alternate text **Granddad and child looking at birds** as the alternate text, then click **OK**.

   The image is inserted onto the AP div, as shown in Figure 11.

3. Select the granddad AP div.

   The image exceeds the height of the AP div. The part of the image below the horizontal line is the overflow, as shown in Figure 12. To set the AP div properties to keep it from hiding the overflow in the browser or making the user use scroll bars to see the overflow, you set the Vis property to visible.

4. Change the Vis property to **visible**, compare your screen to Figure 12, then save your file.

5. Preview the page in your web browser, then close the browser.

TIP Remember you can also use Live View to preview your pages.

   The entire image is visible in the browser, but the bottom of the AP element overlaps the copyright information. You will adjust for this after you finish formatting each AP element.

(continued)

Figure 11 *Image inserted onto an AP div*

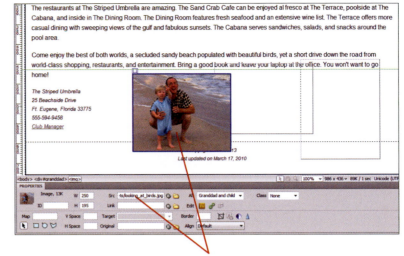

looking_at_birds.jpg inserted into the AP div

Figure 12 *Setting Vis properties for overflow*

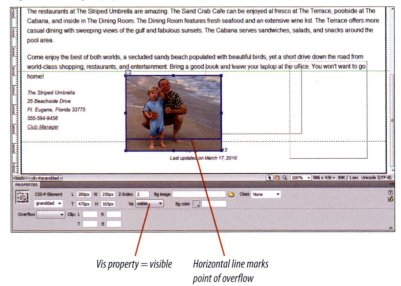

Vis property = visible *Horizontal line marks point of overflow*

Figure 13 *Second AP div with image inserted*

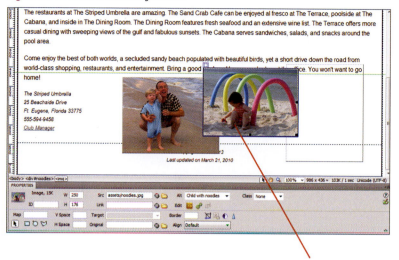

Image placed in noodles AP element

Figure 14 *AP divs as they appear in a browser window*

6. Click inside the noodles AP div to set the insertion point.

7. Select the Common category on the Insert panel, click the **Images list arrow**, then click **Image**.

8. Navigate to the drive and folder where you store your Data Files, open the assets folder, then double-click **noodles.jpg**.

9. Type **Child with noodles** in the Alternate text text box in the Image Tag Accessibility Attributes dialog box, click **OK**, then compare your screen to Figure 13.

10. Click to place the insertion point right after the last paragraph ending with "You won't want to go home!", then insert a paragraph break.

11. Insert a paragraph break after the email link, save your work, preview the page in your web browser, compare your screen to Figure 14, then close the browser.

TIP If your browser window is not resized to the width of the window shown in Figure 14, your AP divs will not be positioned as shown.

You inserted images onto two AP divs and changed the Vis property to visible for the first one to allow for overflow. You added white space at the bottom of the page to prevent the AP divs from hiding the copyright statement.

Set a background image

1. Select the two_children AP div then click the **Browse for File icon** 📁 next to the Bg image text box in the Property inspector to open the Select Image Source dialog box.

   Using the Bg image text box instead of the Insert panel inserts the image as a background on which you can easily enter text.

2. Navigate to the drive and folder where you store your Data Files, open the assets folder, then click **two_children_on_beach.jpg**.

3. Click **OK** (Win) or **Choose** (Mac), then compare your screen to Figure 15.

4. Refresh the Files panel to verify that two_children_on_beach.jpg was copied to the assets folder of the website.

You added a background image to the two_children AP div.

Figure 15 *Inserting a background image for an AP div*

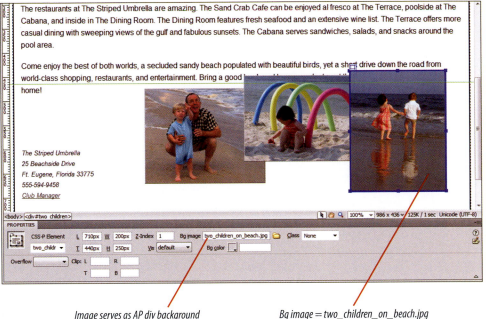

Image serves as AP div background

Bg image = two_children_on_beach.jpg

Figure 16 *Editing the #two_children rule*

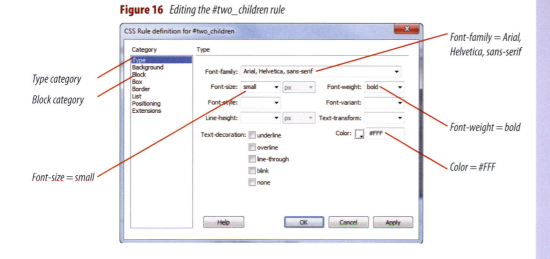

Type category

Block category

Font-size = small

Font-family = Arial, Helvetica, sans-serif

Font-weight = bold

Color = #FFF

Figure 17 *Index page with the formatted AP divs*

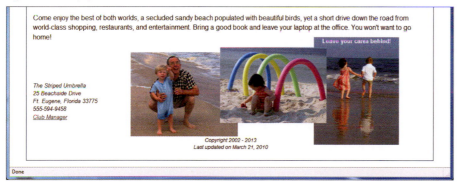

Add and format text on an AP div

1. Click inside the two_children AP div to set the insertion point.

2. Type **Leave your cares behind!**.

3. Click the **#two_children rule** in the CSS Styles panel, then click the **Edit Rule** button ✎.

4. Click the **Type category**, as shown in Figure 16, change Font-family to **Arial, Helvetica, sans-serif**; Font-size to **small**; Font-weight to **bold**; and Color to **#FFF**.

5. Click the **Block category**, change the Text-align setting to **center**, then click **OK**.

   The text changes to reflect the properties you have added to the two_children rule. It is white and centered on the AP div. When you have text on an AP div, you should format the text using the AP div tag rule in the CSS Styles panel, rather than using the Property inspector, or the Property inspector will create an additional rule. It is more efficient to have all rule properties for a div tag in one rule.

6. Save your work, preview the page in your web browser, then close your browser.

   The noodles AP div is obstructing the text on the two_children AP div. You lower its position on the page.

7. Drag the **noodles AP div icon** 🔲 down slightly to keep it from obstructing the text on the two_children AP div, save your file, preview it again in the browser, compare your screen to Figure 17, then close the browser.

You added text to the AP Div, and formatted it using the CSS Styles panel.

Set AP Element
PROPERTIES

What You'll Do

In this lesson, you will use the AP Elements panel to change the name of an AP element, view and hide an AP element, and edit the rule properties.

Use the AP Elements Panel

You can use the **AP Elements panel** to control the visibility, name, and Z-Index order of all the AP elements on a web page. You can also use the AP Elements panel to see how an AP element is nested within the page structure and to change the nesting status of an AP element. **Nested AP elements** are those whose HTML code is included within another AP element's code. Nested AP elements can share common styles, with the child AP element inheriting the styles from the parent AP element. To change the nesting status of an AP element, drag it to a new location in the AP Elements panel. You can open the AP Elements panel using the Window menu, or click its tab in the CSS Styles tab group. The AP Elements panel is handy when you are trying to select an AP element on the bottom of a stack. Clicking the AP element name selects the AP element on the page. You can

access the same information that is available in the AP Elements panel by selecting the AP element and viewing its settings in the Property inspector.

Using the AP Elements panel is the easiest way to change a series of AP element names, control AP element visibility while testing a site, and control the visible stacking order. The AP Elements panel also keeps track of all the AP elements on a page, making it easy to review the settings for each.

Set AP Elements Relative to Containers

When you insert an AP div on a web page, its position is relative to the top left corner of the browser window. A problem arises when the page is viewed in different browser window sizes. Figures 18 and 19 compare what happens when default settings are used and a page is viewed in a wide and a narrower browser window. The AP elements shift to the right when the browser window is resized to a narrower width since the left value for the AP elements are relative to the top left corner of the browser window. To prevent this shifting, you can make the AP elements' positions relative to a parent container, such as a CSS div tag, rather than relative to the page in the browser window. This is a two-step process. First, set the Positioning property of the div tag you wish to use as the parent container to relative. Second, cut and paste the code for the AP elements after the beginning tag for the parent container. The AP elements are then placed on the page relative to the top left corner of the parent container and will remain in a fixed position no matter how wide or narrow the browser window.

Figure 18 *AP elements in browser window*   **Figure 19** *AP elements in wider browser window*

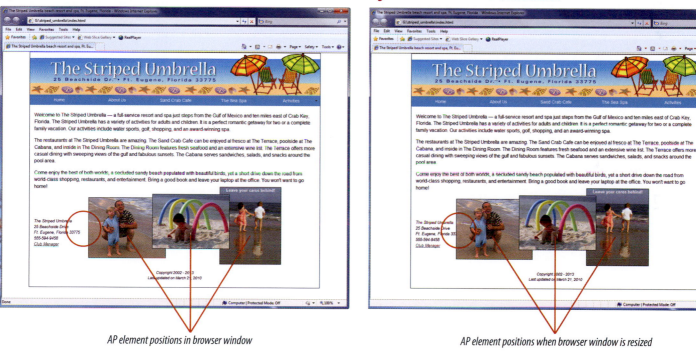

AP element positions in browser window   *AP element positions when browser window is resized*

Change the name of an AP element

1. Click **Window** on the Application bar (Win) or Menu bar (Mac), then click **AP Elements,** or click **AP Elements** in the CSS Styles Tab group.

   The AP Elements panel appears in the CSS Styles Tab group.

2. Click **two_children** on the AP Elements panel to select the two_children AP element.

3. Double-click **two_children** on the AP Elements panel to select its name.

4. Type **children**, press **[Enter]** (Win) or **[return]** (Mac), then compare your screen to Figure 20.

   The AP element is renamed.

TIP With the children AP div selected, it appears to be in front of the noodles AP div, but it is really behind it. When it is not selected, it appears in its actual position in back of the noodles AP div.

You used the AP Elements panel to change the name of one of the AP elements on the home page.

Figure 20 *Using the AP Elements panel to change an AP element name*

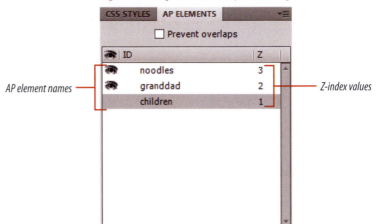

AP element names

Z-index values

Positioning Objects with AP Divs

Figure 21 *Using the AP Elements panel to hide the granddad AP element*

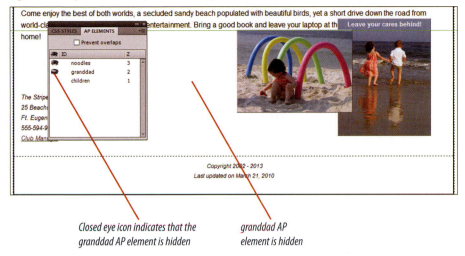

Closed eye icon indicates that the
granddad AP element is hidden

granddad AP
element is hidden

Figure 22 *Using the AP Elements panel to make the granddad AP element visible*

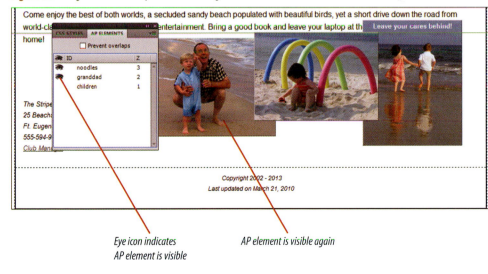

Eye icon indicates
AP element is visible

AP element is visible again

Control AP element visibility

1. Click the **visibility column** twice for the granddad AP element in the AP Elements panel, then compare your screen with Figure 21.

   The Closed eye icon appears, indicating that the granddad AP element no longer appears in the document window.

2. Click the **Closed eye icon** 👁 on the granddad AP element.

   Clicking the Closed eye icon makes the AP element visible, as shown in Figure 22. The Eye icon appears next to the granddad element in the AP Elements panel.

3. Click the **Open eye icon** 👁 on the granddad AP element.

   Clicking the Open eye icon makes the AP element inherit the visibility status of its parent objects. In this case, the parent object of the granddad AP element is the index page. Because the home page is visible, the granddad AP element is visible, too.

You used the AP Elements panel to change the visibility status of the granddad AP element.

Adjust the position of AP elements relative to a CSS container

1. Select the embedded .container rule in the CSS Styles panel, click the **Edit rule button** , click the **Positioning category**, click the **Position list arrow**, then click **relative**.

2. Compare your screen to Figure 23, then click **OK**.

   To force your AP elements to remain in a fixed position in all sizes of browser windows, set a parent container to a relative position, and then move the AP element tags below the opening rule for that parent container.

3. Switch to Code view, then locate and select the three lines of code for the three AP elements right under the opening body tag, as shown in Figure 24.

4. Cut the lines of code, paste them under the opening tag for the container rule, as shown in Figure 25, then refresh Code view.

5. Save your work, preview the page in your browser, then experiment by changing the width of your browser window.

   The AP elements remain in a fixed position on the page, rather than shifting as the window is resized.

You changed the position value for the container rule to relative. You then moved the code for the three AP elements to place them under the container tag so they will not shift their positions on the page when the browser window is resized.

Figure 23 *Changing the Positioning value for the container rule*

Positioning category

Position = relative

Figure 24 *Selecting the code for the three AP elements*

Code for the three AP elements

Figure 25 *Moving the code for the three AP elements*

The code for the three AP elements is moved under the container opening tag

Positioning Objects with AP Divs

Figure 26 *Adding a border to an AP element*

CSS Rule definition for #granddad

Category	Border
Type	
Background	
Block	
Box	
Border	
List	
Positioning	
Extensions	

Style — ☑ Same for all

Top:	solid		
Right:	solid		
Bottom:	solid		
Left:	solid		

Width — ☑ Same for all

thin	px
thin	px
thin	px
thin	px

Color — ☑ Same for all

#000
#000
#000
#000

Figure 27 *The AP elements with borders*

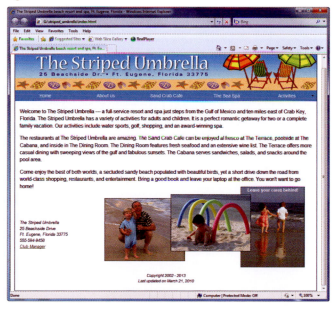

Add borders to AP elements

1. Close the browser, return to Design view, then click **#granddad** in the CSS Styles panel.

2. Click the **Edit Rule button** , click the **Border** category, click the **Top list arrow** in the Style column, click **solid**, click the **Top list arrow** in the Width column, click **thin**, click in the top Color text box, then type **#000**.

   You leave each "Same for all" check box checked so the border will be consistent for each side.

3. Compare your screen to Figure 26, then click **OK**.

4. Repeat Steps 1 and 2 to add a border to the other two AP elements.

   Since the granddad AP element has overflow, the border will not surround the entire image. You increase the size of the AP div to match the size of the image to prevent overflow.

5. Select the granddad AP element, then change the H value in the Property inspector from 165 px to 195 px.

6. Save your work, preview the index page in the browser again and compare your screen to Figure 27, close all open pages, then exit Dreamweaver.

You added borders to each AP element, then resized the granddad AP element to remove the overflow.

Insert an AP div.

1. Open the Blooms & Bulbs website, then open the index page.
2. Use the Draw AP Div button to draw a rectangle about 1 inch tall by 1 inch wide on the bottom half of your page.
3. Name this AP div **bloom**.

Set the position and size of an AP element.

1. Select the bloom AP div if necessary, then set the Left property to **650px**.
2. Set the Top property to **350px**.
3. Set the Width property to **250px**.
4. Set the Height property to **160px**.
5. Set the Z-Index property to **1** (if necessary).
6. Create another AP div anywhere on the page about 200 pixels wide and 100 pixels high, select it, then name it **spring_is_here**.

7. Select the spring_is_here AP div if necessary, then adjust the size with the following settings: Left to **550px**; Top to **380px**; Width to **175px**; and Height to **80px**.
8. Change the background color of the spring_is_here AP div to a light tan.
9. Change the Z-Index value of the spring_is_here AP div to **2** if necessary.
10. Save your work.

Add content to an AP element.

1. Place the insertion point in the bloom AP div, then insert the image spring_bloom.jpg from the drive and folder where you store your Data Files, adding **Spring bloom** as the alternate text.
2. Set the bloom AP div tag Vis property to default if necessary.
3. Set the bloom AP div tag Overflow property to visible.

4. Place the insertion point in the spring_is_here AP div, then type **Spring is here!**
5. Insert a line break, then type **Come see our new arrivals!**
6. Edit the #spring_is_here rule to set the Font-family to Arial, Helvetica, sans-serif, the Font-size to medium, the Font-weight to bold, the Color to #333, and the Text-align to center.
7. Save your work.

Set AP element properties.

1. Open the AP Elements panel (if necessary).
2. Use the AP Elements panel to change the spring_is_here AP div's name to **spring**.
3. Set the Vis property to visible.
4. On the web page, add a paragraph return after the email link.

5. Save your work.
6. Select the #container rule in the CSS Styles panel and change the Position value to relative.
7. Switch to Code view and cut the code for the two AP div tags under the body tag.
8. Paste the code for the two AP div tags under the opening tag for the container rule, refresh Code view, then save your work and return to Design view.
9. Preview the page in your browser, compare your screen to Figure 28, close your browser, adjust the AP element positions (if necessary), then save and close the index page.

Figure 28 *Completed Skills Review*

In this exercise, you will continue your work on the TripSmart website. The owner, Thomas Howard, wants you to create a small advertisement on the index page that showcases a fall tour to San Francisco.

1. Open the TripSmart website, then open the index page.
2. Delete the first horizontal rule on the page.
3. Draw an AP div that is approximately one inch tall and three inches wide on the bottom of the page, then name it **tour**.
4. Set the Left property of the tour AP div tag to **625px** and the Top property to **325px**.
5. Set the Width property of the tour AP div tag to **325px**, the height to **150px**, and the Z-Index property to **1** if necessary.
6. Insert the image sea_lions.jpg from the drive and folder where your chapter_10 data files are stored into the tour AP div, adding appropriate alternate text.
7. Use the Property inspector to compare the dimensions of the sea_lions image and the dimensions of the tour AP div, then adjust the width and height of the tour AP div so it fits the size of the sea_lions.jpg image.
8. Draw another AP div that is approximately 1 inch wide by one-half inches tall. Name it **san_francisco** and assign it a background color of your choice.
9. In the new AP div, enter the text **San Francisco this fall!**, enter a line break, type **Call today!**, then refer to Figure 29 to adjust text properties in the san_francisco element and the placement of the two AP elements on the page.
10. Use the CSS Styles panel to add borders of your choice to the #san_francisco rule and the #tours rule.
11. Use the CSS Styles panel to set the position of the #container rule to relative.
12. Move the code for the two AP div tags below the opening tag for the container rule.
13. Save your work, preview the page in your browser, compare your screen to Figure 29, close your browser, make any spacing adjustments to improve the position or sizes of the AP elements, then save and close the index page.

Figure 29 *Sample Project Builder 1*

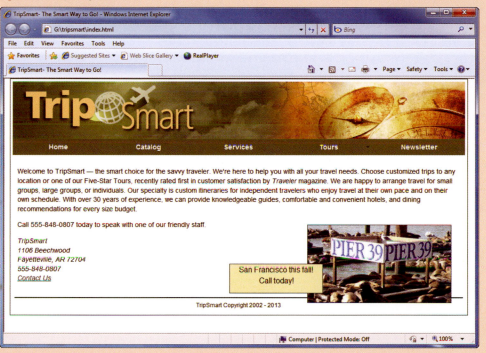

Use Figure 30 as a guide to continue your work on the Carolyne's Creations website.

1. Open the Carolyne's Creations website, then open the index page.
2. Create an AP div on the page, then insert the file cream_cheese_eggs.jpg from the drive and folder where you store your Data Files folder in the AP div, adding appropriate alternate text.

3. Name the AP div **cream_cheese_eggs**.
4. Adjust the size and position of the AP div with settings of your choice.
5. Add another AP div tag that displays the text **We would like to cater your next event!** and name it **cater**.
6. Set the font properties for the new AP div to settings of your choice and then set the Z indexes for each AP div to correctly display the text over the photo.

7. Add a paragraph break after the email link, then make the appropriate adjustments to lock the position of the two AP elements on the page in any size browser window.
8. Save your work, preview the page in your browser, close your browser, then close the index page.

Positioning Objects with AP Divs

Figure 30 *Completed Project Builder 2*

Gwen Gresham has recently been asked to redesign a website for a small business. She has decided to use CSS divs for her page layout. Because she has never developed a website with these features before, she decides to look at some other websites for ideas and inspiration.

1. Connect to the Internet, then go to the Weather Channel website at www.weather.com, as shown in Figure 31.
2. View the source code for the page and use the Edit, Find feature to locate div tags used in this site. (*Hint:* Use "div id" as the search string.)
3. View the source code for the page and locate the HTML tags that control the CSS page elements. (*Hint:* Use a CSS property such as "padding" as a search string.)
4. Do you see some div tags with either the dimensions or positions specified?

Figure 31 *Design Project*

This image was provided by the Weather Channel – www.weather.com

For this assignment, you will continue to work on the portfolio project that you have been developing since Chapter 1. There will be no Data Files supplied. You are building this website from chapter to chapter, so you must do each Portfolio Project assignment in each chapter to complete your website.

You will continue building your site by placing at least one AP div on a page.

1. Consult your wireframes to decide which page to develop for this chapter. Add a sketch to the wireframe to show how you will use an AP div on the page you have chosen.

2. Open the page and add the appropriate number of AP Divs to the page and configure them appropriately, making sure to name them and set the properties for each.

3. Add text, background images, and background colors to the AP divs.

4. Check to ensure that all AP divs are properly stacked using the Z-Index property.

5. Make the coding adjustments to lock the position of each AP div on the page when it is viewed with different browser sizes.

6. Review the checklist in Figure 32 and make any necessary modifications.

7. Save your work, preview the page in your browser, make any necessary modifications to make the page look good, close your browser, then close all open pages.

Figure 32 *Portfolio Project Checklist*

Website Checklist

1. Are all AP elements properly stacked with Z-index values assigned correctly?
2. Do all pages have page titles?
3. Do all navigation links work correctly?
4. Do your pages look acceptable in at least two different browsers and browser window sizes?
5. Do the AP elements hide any information on your pages?
6. Are you happy with the overall appearance of each page?

CHAPTER **11**

ADDING MEDIA AND
INTERACTIVITY WITH FLASH AND SPRY

1. Add and modify Flash objects

2. Add rollover images

3. Add behaviors

4. Add Flash video

ADDING MEDIA AND
INTERACTIVITY WITH
FLASH AND SPRY

Introduction

While a web site with text and static images is adequate for presenting information, you can create a much richer user experience by adding movement and interactive elements. You can use Dreamweaver to add media objects created in other programs to the pages of your website. Some of the external media file types include Adobe Fireworks menu bars, rollover images, and buttons; Flash video, sound, and animation; Flash Paper; Director and Shockwave movies and presentations; Java applets; ActiveX controls; server-side controls; and a variety of plug-ins. A **plug-in** (also called an **add-on**) is a small computer program that works with a host application such as a web browser to allow it to perform certain functions. For example, older web browsers usually don't come with the ability to play animations. So to play a Flash SWF file in a web browser, you would need to install the Adobe Flash Player plug-in. Newer browsers come with Flash Player preinstalled. To read Adobe PDF files, you need to install the Adobe Reader plug-in. Other players include Windows Media Player and RealPlayer by RealNetworks. Plug-ins allow you to extend the capabilities of the browser to display content, letting you create complex, interactive websites with media effects that can be viewed within the pages themselves. Then the pages don't have to load an external document player. In this chapter, you will use Dreamweaver to add Flash objects to The Striped Umbrella website and the means to allow them to play.

Understanding Media Objects

The term "media objects" has different meanings, depending on who you are talking to, and the industry in which they work. For our purposes, **media objects** are combinations of visual and audio effects and text to create a fully engaging experience with a website. Although this might be an open-ended definition, it is the experience you are striving for when you add video and audio elements to a web page. Think about the experience of watching a movie. You are engaged not just by the actors, but also by the sounds and special effects you experience. You want to create this same type of experience for your website users by adding media elements to your pages.

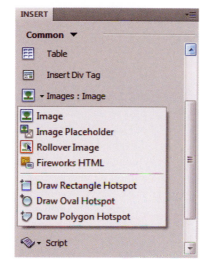

Add and Modify
FLASH OBJECTS

What You'll Do

▶ *In this lesson, you will insert and modify a Flash movie on the cafe page, and then play the movie both in Dreamweaver and in a browser.*

Understanding Adobe Flash

Flash is a software program that allows you to create low-bandwidth, high-quality animations and interactive elements that you can place on your web pages. **Low-bandwidth** animations are animations that don't require a fast connection to work properly. These animations use a series of vector-based graphics that load quickly and merge with other graphics and sounds to create short movies. **Vector-based graphics** are scalable graphics that are built using mathematical formulas, rather than built with pixels. Figure 1 shows a web page that contains several Flash objects. Figure 2 shows the Flash program used to create Flash objects.

Once you create these short movies, you can place them on your web pages. Flash movies require Flash Player, a plug-in that is included in the latest versions of Internet Explorer, Mozilla Firefox, Safari, and Opera,

to view them. If you are using an older browser that does not support the version of Flash used to create your movie, you can download the latest Flash Player from the Adobe website, located at www.adobe.com. Almost all Internet browsers worldwide use Flash Player. In addition, other tools, such as some cell phones and handheld devices, contain rich Flash content. **Rich content** is a general term that can mean visually stimulating, useful, or interactive content on a web page.

Inserting Flash Content

When you use the Insert panel to add Flash content to a web page, the code that links and runs the content (such as detecting the presence of Flash Player on the computer and directing the user to download the player if it is not found) is embedded into the page code. The original Flash file is stored as a separate file in the website root folder. There are several types of Flash content that you can incorporate to enhance your users' experience as they view and interact with your website. A **Flash button** is a button made from a small, predefined Flash movie that you can insert on a web page to provide site navigation, either in place of or in addition to other types of hyperlinks, such as plain text links. You can assign Flash buttons a variety of behaviors in response to user actions, such as opening a different page in the browser when the mouse pointer is placed over it. Like all Flash objects, Flash buttons have the .swf file extension.

Using Flash, you can also create Flash movies that include multimedia elements, such as audio files (both music and voiceovers), animated objects, scripted objects, clickable links, and just about any other animated or clickable object imaginable. You can use Flash movies to add content to your existing website or to create an entire website. To add a Flash movie to a web page, click SWF from the Media menu in the Common category on the Insert panel to open the Select SWF dialog box, and then choose the Flash movie you want to insert. As with images, always add a title tag when inserting Flash

content to provide accessibility. You also need to include code that will instruct the browser to check for and load Flash Player so the user can view the Flash content on the page. To view your Flash movies, you can either use Live view or preview them in a browser window. It is a kindness to your users to turn off the loop option for Flash movies unless you want the Flash content to play continuously while the page is being viewed. Content that plays continuously can be irritating to users when they do not have the controls to stop it.

Figure 1 *Website based on Flash*

NASA website – www.nasa.gov

Figure 2 *Adobe Flash CS5 workspace*

Insert Flash movies

1. Open the cafe page in The Striped Umbrella website.

2. Select the cafe logo on the left side of the page below the menu bar, then press **[Delete]** (Win) or **[delete]** (Mac).

3. Click the **Media button list arrow** on the Common category of the Insert panel, then click **SWF**.

4. Navigate to the drive and folder where you store your Data Files, click **crabdance.swf**, click **OK** (Win) or **Choose** (Mac), click **Yes** and then click **Save** to save the movie in the site root folder of the website, type **Crab logo animation** in the Title text box in the Object Tag Accessibility Attributes dialog box, then click **OK**. A Flash movie placeholder appears on the page, as shown in Figure 3.

TIP If you already have a Flash file in your site root folder, you can drag and drop it from the Assets panel or Files panel instead of using the Insert panel or Insert menu.

5. Click the **Loop check box** on the Property inspector to deselect it.

   By removing the Loop option, the file will play once in the browser, then stop.

You inserted a Flash movie on the cafe page of The Striped Umbrella website.

Figure 3 *Flash movie placeholder on the cafe page*

Properties of selected Flash movie

Loop check box

Flash movie placeholder

Collecting Flash Objects

Adobe and their devoted product users provide you with a variety of downloadable Flash objects that are available on the Adobe Exchange website, located at www.adobe.com/cfusion/exchange. At this site, you can find collections of menus, transitions, image galleries, and just about anything else you might want. If you can't find exactly what you want, you can download a trial version of Flash to experiment with creating your own Flash objects. If you find that you will want to create Flash objects regularly, you can purchase the licensed version either as a separate program or as part of a suite of programs. There are many other websites that offer downloadable Flash objects; some of the objects are free and some are for purchase.

Adding Media and Interactivity with Flash and Spry

Figure 4 *Flash movie playing in Dreamweaver*

Flash movie playing   Click to stop movie

Figure 5 *Flash movie playing in the browser*

Play a Flash movie in Dreamweaver and in a browser

1. With the placeholder selected, click the **Play button** in the Property inspector to view the crab.swf movie, as shown in Figure 4, then click **Stop**.

2. Save your work, then click **OK** to close the Copy Dependent Files dialog box.

   Two supporting files, expressInstall.swf and swfobject_modified.js, are copied to a new Scripts folder. These files are necessary for the video to play in the browser correctly.

3. Preview the page in your browser, compare your screen to Figure 5, then close your browser.

TIP If the movie did not play in Internet Explorer, click Tools on the menu bar, click Internet Options, click the Advanced tab, then click the Allow active content to run in files on My Computer check box on the Security tab. If you are using a different browser or a version of Internet Explorer that is earlier than 8.0, look for a similar setting.

You played a Flash movie on the cafe page in The Striped Umbrella website in Dreamweaver and in your browser.

Lesson 1   Add and Modify Flash Objects

Modify a Flash file from Dreamweaver

1. To complete the steps in this lesson, you need the full Flash program (not Flash Player). If you don't have the full Flash program installed on your computer, you can go to the Adobe web site at www.adobe.com to download a trial version or skip to Lesson 2 on page 11-10.

2. Use Explorer (Win) or Finder (Mac) to copy the crabdance.fla source file from the Data Files folder to the site root folder of The Striped Umbrella website.

   Even though you have the crabdance.swf file in your site root folder, you must copy the crabdance.fla source file to that location so you can make changes to it. After you change it, you have to republish it to recreate the .swf file to include your changes.

3. Close Explorer (Win) or Finder (Mac), then return to Dreamweaver.

4. With the Flash placeholder selected, click **Edit** in the Property inspector.

5. Click **crabdance.fla** in the striped_umbrella site root folder in the Locate FLA File dialog box, as shown in Figure 6, then click **Open**.

   The .swf file is a Flash Player file and cannot be edited. The .fla file is the editable Flash file. You must have this source file to edit the movie. After you select the .fla file, the file opens in Flash if Flash is installed on your computer.

TIP If you receive a warning that one or more fonts used for this movie are not available, click Choose Substitute, then choose another font.

(continued)

Figure 6 *Selecting the crab.fla file*

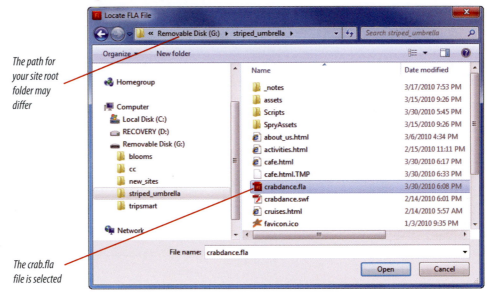

The path for your site root folder may differ

The crab.fla file is selected

Adding Media and Interactivity with Flash and Spry

Figure 7 *Editing the Flash movie and returning to Dreamweaver*

Click Done to save the file
and return to Dreamweaver

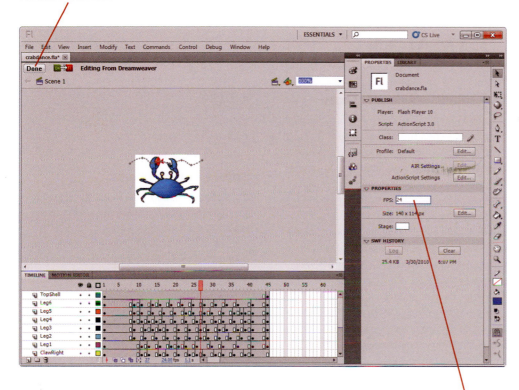

FPS text box

6. Click **12** next to FPS in the Properties panel, change the frame rate from 12 to **24** fps (frames per second) in the FPS text box, as shown in Figure 7, then click **Done**.

   Flash automatically saves both the crabdance.fla file and the crabdance.swf file, then closes. (If the crabdance.fla file opens with an element selected, click in the gray area of the screen to deselect it. If an element is selected, you will not see the FPS text box.)

7. Switch back to Dreamweaver, preview the page in your browser, then close the browser, close Flash, and close the cafe page.

   Notice that the movie plays a little faster now. You changed the frames per second to a larger number, which had the effect of the movie playing faster.

You used the Edit button in the Property inspector to find and modify the Flash movie in Flash, then returned to Dreamweaver.

Add Rollover
IMAGES

What You'll Do

▶ *In this lesson, you will add two rollover images to the activities page of The Striped Umbrella website.*

Understanding Rollover Images

A **rollover image** is an image that changes its appearance when the mouse pointer is placed over it in a browser. A rollover image actually consists of two images. The first image is the one that appears when the mouse pointer is not positioned over it, and the second image is the one that appears when the mouse pointer is positioned over it. Rollover images are often used to help create a feeling of action and excitement on a web page. For instance, suppose you are creating a website that promotes a series of dance classes. You could create a rollover image using two images of a dancer in two different poses. When a viewer places the mouse pointer over the image of the dancer in the first pose, the image would change to show the dancer in a different pose, creating a feeling of movement.

QUICK **TIP**

You can also add a link to a rollover image, so that the image will change only when the image is clicked.

Adding Rollover Images

You add rollover images to a web page using the Rollover Image command on the Images menu in the Common category shown in Figure 8. You specify both the original image and the rollover image in the Insert Rollover Image dialog box. The rollover image is the image that appears when the user moves (rolls) the mouse pointer over the original image. To prevent one of the images from being resized during the rollover, both images should be the same height and width. Another way to create a rollover image, button, or menu bar is to insert it as a Fireworks HTML file. After you create and export the file from Fireworks, the code for the rollover is automatically inserted in the web page file. The Fireworks HTML command is also on the Images menu, as shown in Figure 8.

QUICK TIP

It's a good idea to select the Preload rollover image check box in the Insert Rollover Image dialog box to ensure that the rollover image appears without a delay.

You can also use rollover images to display an image associated with a text link. For instance, suppose you are creating a website for an upcoming election. You could create a web page that contains a list of candidates for the election and add a rollover image for each candidate's name that would result in a photograph of the candidate appearing when the mouse is placed over his or her name. You can also use this effect to make appropriate images appear when you point to different menu options. For instance,

Figure 9 shows the Snapfish by HP website, which uses rollover images to highlight each menu option on its home page. When a rollover image is inserted onto a page, Dreamweaver automatically adds two behaviors; a Swap Image behavior and a Swap Image Restore behavior. A **Swap Image behavior** is JavaScript code that directs the browser to display a different image when the mouse is rolled over an image on the page. A **Swap Image Restore** behavior restores the swapped image back to the original image.

Figure 8 *Images menu on the Insert panel*

Images menu

Rollover Image command

Fireworks HTML command

Figure 9 *Snapfish by HP website with rollover images*

Rollover images change when mouse is positioned over new menu item

Add a rollover image

1. Close the cafe page if necessary, then open the activities page of The Striped Umbrella website.

2. Scroll down to find the image of the two dolphins, then delete it.

3. Click the **Images list arrow** in the Common group on the Insert panel, then click **Rollover Image**.

4. Type **dolphins** in the Image name text box.

5. Click **Browse** next to the Original image text box, browse to the drive and folder where you store your Data Files, open the assets folder, then double-click **one_dolphin.jpg**.

6. Click **Browse** next to the Rollover image text box, then double-click the **two_dolphins.jpg** file from the drive and folder where you store your Data Files for the Rollover image text box.

7. Type **Dolphins riding the surf** in the Alternate text text box, compare your screen to Figure 10, then click **OK**.

8. Select the image, set the Alignment to **Right**, add a **1-pixel** border to the image, add a **10-pixel** Horizontal space on the sides of the image, save your work, preview the page in your browser, move your mouse pointer over the dolphin image, then compare your screen to Figure 11.

   When you point to the image, the one_dolphin image is "swapped" with the two_dolphin image.

   TIP Remember to direct your browser to allow blocked content if the rollover does not work.

   (continued)

Figure 10 *Browsing to find the source files for the rollover image*

Figure 11 *Viewing the rollover image in the browser*

Image is swapped when the mouse pointer rolls over it

Figure 12 *Swap behavior code for rollover image*

```
156    <div class="content">
157        <p><span class="body_text"><br />
158        We have many activities for you to choose from, here at the  resort and in the surrounding area. </span></p>
159        <p class="body_text"><img src="assets/heron_waiting_small.jpg" alt="Ralph waiting patiently" width="350" height="219" hspace=
       "5" vspace="5" border="1" align="left" />Some of our visitors enjoy local fishing trips. We have a  small fleet of boats that will
       take you out for either a half or a full day. Or  you can surf cast, right from the beach. But beware of Ralph, our resident blue
       heron. He knows what you fishermen have in your coolers and if you aren't  careful, he'll take your catch off your hands and make a
       quick getaway!</p>
160        <p><a href="#" onmouseout="MM_swapImgRestore()" onmouseover="MM_swapImage('dolphins','','assets/two_dolphins.jpg',1)"><img src=
       "assets/one_dolphin.jpg" alt="Dolphins riding the surf" name="dolphins" width="252" height="180" hspace="10" border="1" align=
       "right" id="dolphins" /></a><span class="body_text">And don&rsquo;t forget our dolphin cruises. We have a unique  approach &mdash;
       two boats speed along, side by side, about 50 yards apart. The  dolphins love it because it generates a huge wake. You'll see them
       jumping  right between the boats! You can arrange for tickets for <a href="fishing.html">fishing excursions</a> or <a href=
       "cruises.html">dolphin cruises</a> at The Club House desk.</span></p>
161        <p class="body_text">Check out these links for kid-friendly attractions in the  area: </p>
162        <p class="body_text">The famous <a href="http://www.blueangels.navy.mil">Blue Angels</a>, the nation&rsquo;s oldest flying
       aerobatic  team, are stationed at the Naval Air Station Pensacola, less than a one-hour  drive from The Striped Umbrella. You can
       watch the team practice at the Museum  of Naval Aviation viewing area, an unforgettable experience for all ages. Information  on
       dates and times is posted on their website, or you can call The Club House desk.</p>
163        <p class="body_text">It's a short ride over the Alabama border to see the <a href="http://www.ussalabama.com">USS  Alabama</a>,
       one of America's most decorated battleships. The &quot;Mighty A&quot;  is docked at Battleship Memorial Park in Mobile Bay,
       Alabama. There you can  take a two-hour self-guided tour that is rich in history. Hours, directions,  and prices are posted on
       their website, or call The Club House desk.</p>
164        <!-- end .content -->
```

Code for rollover image

9. Close the browser.

10. Switch to Code view, then locate the code for the swap image behavior, shown in Figure 12.

   The code directs the browser to display the image with one dolphin "onmouseout"— when the mouse is not over the image. It directs the browser to display the image with two dolphins "onmouseover"—when the mouse is over the image.

TIP If your code is selected in Code view, that means the image is selected in Design view.

11. Return to Design view, then click the **Switch Design View to Live View button** `Live View` and place your pointer over the dolphin image.

   Live view allows you to preview the swap image behavior as it will appear in the browser.

12. Click `Live View` to turn off Live view.

You replaced an image with a rollover image on the activities page of The Striped Umbrella website, viewed the rollover in the browser and in Live view.

Add BEHAVIORS

What You'll Do

In this lesson, you will add an action that opens a browser window from the activities page of The Striped Umbrella website. You will then change the event for that action.

Adding Interactive Elements

You can make your web pages come alive by adding interactive elements to them. For instance, if you are creating a page about your favorite animals, you could attach an action to each picture that would result in a pop-up message with a description of the animal when the user rolls the mouse over it. You can add actions like this to elements by attaching behaviors to them. **Behaviors** are sets of instructions that you can attach to page elements that tell the page element to respond in a specific way when an event occurs, such as when the mouse pointer is positioned over the element. When you attach a behavior to an element, Dreamweaver generates the JavaScript code for the behavior and inserts it into your page code.

Using the Behaviors Panel

You can use the Behaviors panel located in the Tag panel group to insert a variety of JavaScript-based behaviors on a page. For instance, using the Behaviors panel, you can automate tasks, respond to user selections and mouse movements with pop-up menus, create games, go to a different URL, or add automatic dynamic effects to a web page. To insert a behavior, click the Add behavior button on the Behaviors panel to open the Actions menu, as shown in Figure 13, then click a behavior from the menu.

Understanding Actions and Events

Actions are triggered by events. For instance, if you want the user to see a page element slide across the page when the element is clicked, you would attach the Slide action using the onClick event to trigger the action. Other examples of events are onMouseOver and onLoad. The onMouseOver event will trigger an action when the mouse is placed over an object. The onLoad event will trigger an action when the page is first loaded in the browser window.

Using the Spry Framework

Some of the behaviors that you can add to web pages use a JavaScript library called the **Spry framework for AJAX**. **Asynchronous JavaScript and XML (AJAX)** is a method for developing interactive web pages that respond quickly to user input, such as clicking a map. In the library, you will find **spry widgets**, which are prebuilt components for adding interactivity to pages; and **spry effects**, which are screen effects such as fading and enlarging page elements. When you add a spry effect to a page element, Dreamweaver automatically adds a SpryAssets folder to the site root folder with the supporting files inside the folder.

Figure 13 *Behaviors panel with the Actions menu displayed*

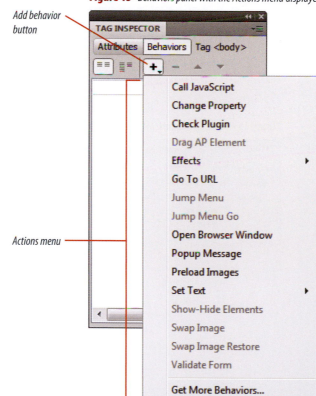

Add behavior button

Actions menu

Add a behavior

1. Open the file dw11_1.html from the drive and folder where you store your Data Files, then save it in the site root folder as **wildlife_message.html**, without updating links. Close the dw11_1.html page.

2. Select the fishing image on the activities page, click **Window** on the Application bar (Win) or Menu bar (Mac), then click **Behaviors** to open the Behaviors panel.

3. Click the **Add behavior button** ✚ on the Behaviors panel toolbar to open the Actions menu, as shown in Figure 14, then click **Open Browser Window** to open the Open Browser Window dialog box.

4. Click **Browse** next to the URL to display text box to open the Select File dialog box, navigate to the site root folder if necessary, then double-click **wildlife_message.html**.

5. Type **300** in the Window width text box, type **300** in the Window height text box, type **message** in the Window name text box, compare your screen to Figure 15, then click **OK**.

6. Save your work, preview the page in your browser, test the Open Browser Window effect by clicking the fishing image, as shown in Figure 16, then close both browser windows.

TIP The pop-up window will not work if pop-up blocking is enabled in your browser. To disable pop-up blocking in Internet Explorer 8, click Tools on the Command Bar, point to Pop-up Blocker, then click Turn Off Pop-up Blocker. In Firefox, click the Options button to tell the browser to display the wildlife_message page. If you are using the Google toolbar, you may also have to allow pop-ups.

You added an Open Browser Window effect to an image on the activities page of The Striped Umbrella website.

Figure 14 *Adding the Open Browser Window behavior to the fishing image*

Select fishing image

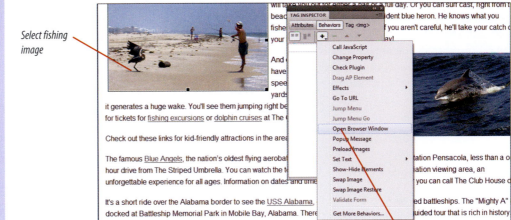

Click Open Browser Window

Figure 15 *Setting Open Browser Window options*

Figure 16 *Viewing the wildlife message in a browser*

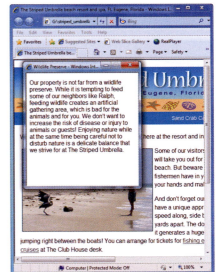

Adding Media and Interactivity with Flash and Spry

Figure 17 *Viewing the edited window size for the behavior*

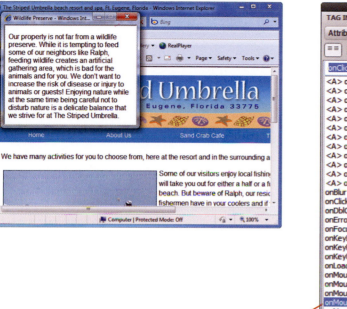

Figure 18 *Viewing the edited behavior*

onMouseOver
action

Edit a behavior

1. Right-click (Win) or [control]-click (Mac) the **right column** of the Open Browser Window action in the Behaviors panel, then click **Edit Behavior**.

   The Open Browser Window dialog box opens.

2. Change the window height to **225**, save your changes, preview the page in your browser, then click the **fishing image**.

   The browser window with the wildlife message is shorter in height, as shown in Figure 17.

3. Close the browser windows.

4. Click the **left column** of the Open Browser Window action in the Behaviors panel to display the events list arrow, click the **list arrow**, then click **onMouseOver**, as shown in Figure 18.

   This will change the event that triggers the action from clicking the image to simply placing the mouse over the image.

5. Save your work, open the page in the browser, then move the mouse over the fishing image.

   Now, simply placing the mouse over the image triggers the Open Browser Window event. (*Hint*: If you don't see the new window, disable the Google toolbar, or press [ctrl] and click to view the image.)

6. Close the browser windows, close the Behaviors panel, then close the wildlife_message page. Leave the activities page open.

You edited the behavior in the Behaviors panel.

Comparing the Behaviors and the Server Behaviors Panels

In addition to the Behaviors panel, Dreamweaver also features a Server Behaviors panel. Although the names are similar, the functions are not. You use the Behaviors panel to add JavaScript behaviors to page elements; use the Server Behaviors panel to add server behaviors, such as creating a login page or a page that is password protected. Building search pages to enable viewers to search a website for specific content is another server behavior that you can add with the Server Behaviors panel. After you have created a server behavior and enabled Dreamweaver to display live data, you can add, edit, or delete the server behavior while you are in Design view, but viewing the page in Live view. The Server Behaviors panel is in the Dynamic Content Tab group with the Databases, Bindings, and Components panels. The Databases panel is used to select the data source for dynamic data used with a page. The Bindings panel is used to define and edit dynamic content on a page. The Components panel is used to display information with ColdFusion components.

Lesson 3   Add Behaviors

Add Flash
VIDEO

What You'll Do

 *In this lesson, you will insert a Flash video on the activities page.*

Inserting Flash Video

Another way to add rich media content to your web pages is to insert video files. Of the several available video formats, one of the most popular is the Flash video format. **Flash video files** are files that can include both video and audio and have an .flv file extension. As with the Flash .swf file, you play the Flash video file using Flash Player. Since most users have Flash Player installed on their computers, you don't have to worry about losing users when you include video on your site. You have two choices for showing a Flash movie on your site:

using a progressive video download or a streaming video download. A **progressive video download** will download the video to the user's computer, then allow the video to play before it has completely downloaded. It will finish the download as the video plays, but the user will not notice that this is taking place. A **streaming video download** is similar to a progressive download, except streaming video uses buffers to gather the content as it downloads to ensure a smoother playback. A **buffer** is a temporary storage area on your hard drive that acts as a holding area for the Flash content as it is being played.

Other video formats that you can link or embed on a web page include **AVI (Audio Visual Interleave)**, the Microsoft standard for digital video, or **MPEG (Motion Picture Experts Group)** files.

Figure 19 shows a page on the Federal Aviation Administration website that allows visitors to view educational videos on a number of topics. Users can start and stop the video using on-screen controls,

use audio controls to mute the sound, and toggle a closed caption button to display the script. Used sparingly, video can be an effective way to add interest and depth to your web pages.

Figure 19 *Viewing a Flash video in a browser*

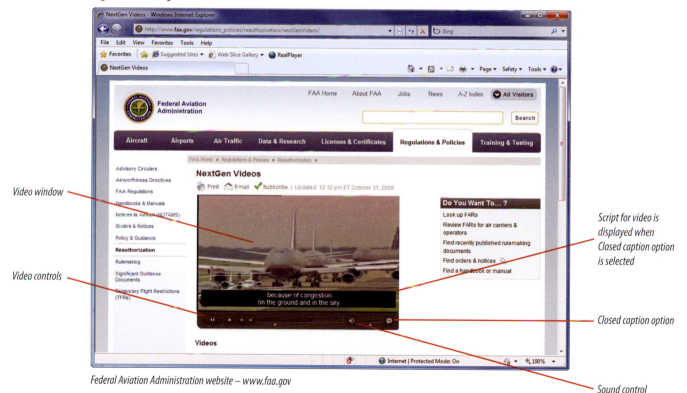

Video window

Video controls

Script for video is displayed when Closed caption option is selected

Closed caption option

Sound control

Federal Aviation Administration website – www.faa.gov

Add Flash video

1. Using Windows Explorer (Win) or Finder (Mac), copy the file **umbrella_anchor_movie.flv** from the drive and folder where you store your Data Files, paste it into your Striped Umbrella site root folder, then close Windows Explorer (Win) or Finder (Mac).

2. Click to place the insertion point under the last paragraph on the activities page.

   TIP You may not see the insertion point as clearly as you usually do.

3. Click the **Media list arrow** on the Insert panel, then click **FLV** to open the Insert FLV dialog box.

4. Verify that the Video type list menu shows Progressive Download Video as the type for the video.

5. Click the **Browse button** next to the URL text box, browse to your site root folder if necessary, then double-click **umbrella_anchor_movie.flv**.

6. Choose the **Halo Skin 1 (min width: 180) option** in the Skin menu (if necessary).

   The skin is the bar at the bottom of the video with the control buttons.

7. Type **180** in the Width text box, **180** in the Height text box, verify that the Constrain check box is checked, compare your screen to Figure 20, then click **OK**.

   A placeholder for the movie appears on the page. You can only view the video in the browser or in Live view.

   (continued)

Figure 20 *The Insert FLV settings for the umbrella anchor movie*

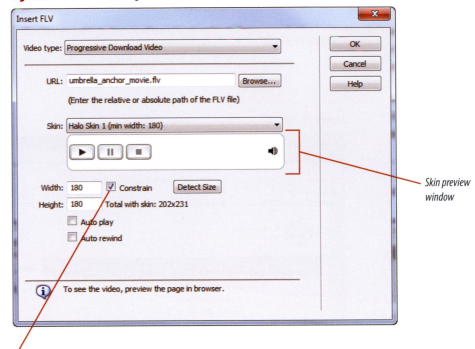

Skin preview window

Constrain check box

Figure 21 *Viewing the video in the browser*

It's a short ride over the Alabama border to see the USS Alabama, one of America's most decorated battleships. The "Mighty A" is docked at Battleship Memorial Park in Mobile Bay, Alabama. There you can take a two-hour self-guided tour that is rich in history. Hours, directions, and prices are posted on their website, or call The Club House desk.

See us to pick up your complimentary Umbrella Anchor!

Copyright 2002 - 2013
Last updated on April 2, 2010

Play button on skin

Figure 22 *Supporting video files added*

Two files added

Flash video file

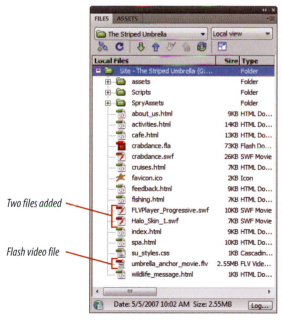

8. Place the insertion point to the right of the video placeholder image, then type **See us to pick up your complimentary Umbrella Anchor!**

9. Select the sentence and apply the feature_item rule to it, select the video placeholder, click the left arrow to place the insertion point to the left of the placeholder, then click the **Blockquote button** ⊞ nine times to indent both the video placeholder and the sentence.

10. Save your work, preview the page in the browser, then compare your screen to Figure 21.

    You click the Play button ▶ to play the movie and the Stop button ■ to stop the movie.

11. Play the movie, then close the browser window.

12. Notice the two files, in addition to the umbrella_anchor_movie.flv file, that have been added to the Files panel: Halo_Skin_1.swf and FLVPlayer_Progressive.swf, as shown in Figure 22.

    These two files instruct the skin to appear and function, and for the movie to start playing in the browser before it is completely downloaded.

13. Close all open pages and close Dreamweaver.

You inserted a Flash video on the page, then viewed the additional files added to the website as supporting files by Dreamweaver.

Add and modify Flash objects.

1. Open the Blooms & Bulbs website, then open the workshops page.
2. Add a paragraph break after the last paragraph, then insert the garden_quote.swf Flash movie from the drive and folder where you store your Data Files at the insertion point.
3. Type **Garden quote** in the Object Tag Accessibility Attributes dialog box, then add nine block quotes in front of the Flash object.
4. Play the garden_quote.swf movie in Dreamweaver, save your work, click OK to close the Dependent Files dialog box, preview the page in your browser, compare your screen to Figure 23, then close your browser.
5. Close the workshops page.

Add rollover images.

1. Open the tips page, then delete the butterfly graphic at the top of the page.
2. Verify that your insertion point is still at the beginning of the paragraph.
3. Insert a rollover image from the drive and folder where you store your Data Files by using the Images list arrow in the Common category on the Insert panel. Enter **butterfly_rollover** as the name, insert butterfly1.jpg from the drive and folder where you store your Data Files as the original image, butterfly2.jpg from the same location as the rollover image, then enter **Butterflies** as the alternate text.
4. Left-align the rollover image, then add a horizontal space of 10 pixels around the image.
5. Save your work, preview the page in the browser to test the rollover, then close the tips page.

Add behaviors.

1. Open the water_plants page.
2. Select the water lily image, then use the Behaviors panel to add the Appear/Fade effect that will fade from 100% to 50%, then select the Toggle Effect check box.
3. Edit the behavior to use the onMouseOver action, then save your work. (*Hint*: Dreamweaver adds a new SpryAssets folder in the site with the SpryEffects.js supporting file.)
4. Preview the page in the browser or with Live view. (*Hint*: Place the mouse over the image to test the

Figure 23 *Completed Skills Review*

Adding Media and Interactivity with Flash and Spry

behavior. The image will alternate between 100% and 50% opacity each time you place the mouse over it.)

5. Close the browser or return to Design view, then close the water_plants page.

Add Flash video.

1. Open the plants page, click right after the last sentence on the page (after "just arrived."), then insert a paragraph break.

2. In Windows Explorer (Win) or Finder (Mac), copy the hanging_baskets.flv file from the drive and folder where you store your Data Files to the Blooms and Bulbs site root folder.

3. In Dreamweaver, insert the hanging_baskets.flv file at the insertion point location using the following settings: Video Type: Progressive Download Video, URL: hanging_baskets.flv, Skin: Clear Skin1 (min width: 140), Width: 150, Height: 150. (*Hint*: Remember to copy the file to your site root folder first.)

4. Insert a line break after the video placeholder, type **Join us Saturday at 9:00 for a demonstration on hanging baskets.** with a line break after the word "for".

5. Create a new class rule named **.video** in the blooms_styles.css style sheet and set Text-align to center.

6. Click to place the insertion point to the right of the video placeholder and apply the video rule.

7. Save all files, preview the page and play the movie either in Live view or in the browser, then compare your screen to Figure 24.

8. Close the browser or return to Design view, then close all open pages.

Figure 24 *Completed Skills Review*

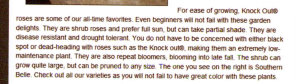

For ease of growing, Knock Out® roses are some of our all-time favorites. Even beginners will not fail with these garden delights. They are shrub roses and prefer full sun, but can take partial shade. They are disease resistant and drought tolerant. You do not have to be concerned with either black spot or dead-heading with roses such as the Knock out®, making them an extremely low-maintenance plant. They are also repeat bloomers, blooming into late fall. The shrub can grow quite large, but can be pruned to any size. The one you see on the right is Southern Belle. Check out all our varieties as you will not fail to have great color with these plants.

The Candy Cane Floribunda shown on the left is a beautiful rose with cream, pink, and red stripes and swirls. They have a heavy scent that will remind you of the roses you received on your most special occasions. These blooms are approximately four inches in diameter. They bloom continuously from early summer to early fall. The plants grow up to four feet tall and three feet wide. They are shipped bare root in February. You must see a close-up of these beauties! Click the image on the left to enlarge them.

In addition to these marvelous roses, we have many annuals, perennials, and water plants that have just arrived.

Join us Saturday at 9:00 for
a demonstration on hanging baskets.

Copyright 2001 - 2013 Blooms & Bulbs

In this exercise, you will continue your work on the TripSmart website. The owner of TripSmart would like you to change the catalog page to show each catalog item one at a time on the page. You create a Flash movie using the three featured items and place it on the page in place of the table.

1. Open the TripSmart website, then open the catalog page.
2. Delete the table, then type **Our products are backed by a 100% guarantee**.
3. Add a paragraph break, then insert the catalog.swf file from the drive and folder where you store your Data Files, then add the text **Catalog featured items** in the Object Tag Accessibly Attributes dialog box.
4. Add another paragraph break, type **Call today! 555-848-0807**, apply the list_headings rule to both lines of text, place the insertion point above the first sentence, use the CSS Property inspector to center the two sentences and the Flash placeholder, then save the file. Click OK to close the Dependent Files dialog box.
5. Preview the catalog page in the browser, then compare your screen to Figure 25. (Watch for a few seconds to see the images change.)
6. Close the browser, then close the catalog page.
7. Open the file dw11_2.html from the drive and folder where you store your Data Files, then save it in the TripSmart site root folder as **spain_trip.html**. Do not update links.

8. Attach the tripsmart_styles.css file to the page, then apply the **paragraph_text** style to the text.
9. Close the dw11_2.html page, then save and close the spain_trip.html page.
10. Open the spain page, then attach a behavior to the banner image that will open a new browser window when the banner image loads that displays the spain_trip.html file. Use 300 for the window width and 100 for the window height. Name the window **soldout**.
11. Save your work, preview the page in the browser to test the behavior, close the browser, then close all open pages.

Figure 25 *Completed Project Builder 1*

Adding Media and Interactivity with Flash and Spry

Use Figures 26 and 27 as a guide to continue your work on the Carolyne's Creations website. You have decided to add a video demonstrating how to sugar flowers for decoration.

1. Open the Carolyne's Creations website.
2. Open the index page.
3. Select the cater AP element on the right side of the page, then attach a behavior and an action of your choice to it.

4. Switch to Live view to preview the behavior, turn off Live view, save and close the index page, then open the adults page.
5. Place the insertion point under the last paragraph, insert a new paragraph, then insert the Flash video sugared_flowers.flv from the drive and folder where you store your Data Files using settings of your choice for the video.

6. Refer to the text in Figure 27 to add short descriptive text under the video, then format the text with the body_text rule.
7. Make any other adjustments you wish, save your page, then preview the page in the browser.
8. Close the browser, then close all open pages.

Figure 26 *Completed Project Builder 2*

Figure 27 *Completed Project Builder 2*

Chef Carolyne demonstrates
sugaring flowers for garnish

DESIGN PROJECT

Angie Wolf is an astronomer. She would like to design a website about planets, like the example shown in Figure 28. She would like her website to incorporate Flash elements, rollovers, and video and would like to use Dreamweaver to build the site.

1. Connect to the Internet and go to www.nasa.gov.
2. View the source code on several pages for the words "Flash" or "swf" to see if you see references to the use of Flash.
3. Which objects in the site are made with rollover images?
4. How has adding the Flash effects improved the appearance of this site?
5. Create a sketch of Angie's site that contains at least five pages. Indicate in your sketch what media elements you would insert in the site, including where you would add Flash objects, rollover images, and video.

Figure 28 *Design Project*

NASA website – www.nasa.gov

In this assignment, you will continue to work on the group website that you started in Chapter 1. There will be no Data Files supplied. You are building this site from chapter to chapter, so you must do each Portfolio Project assignment in each chapter to complete your site.

You will continue building your site by designing and completing a page that contains rich media content or by adding media content to existing pages. After completing your site, be sure to run appropriate reports to test the site.

1. Evaluate your wireframes, then choose a page, or series of pages, to develop in which you will include Flash objects as well as other media content, such as rollover images, video, and behaviors.
2. Plan the content for your new page so that the layout works well with both the new and old pages in your site. Sketch a plan for your wireframes for the media content you wish to add, showing which media elements you will use and where you will place them.

3. Create or find the media you identified in your sketch, choosing appropriate formatting.
4. Add the rollover images to the page.
5. Add a video, if possible, to the page.
6. Add a behavior to an AP element, then specify the action you would like to use with it.
7. Run a report on your new page(s) to ensure that all links work correctly.

8. Preview the new page (or pages) in your browser and test all links. Evaluate your pages for content and layout. Use the checklist in Figure 29 to make sure your website is complete.
9. Make any modifications that are necessary to improve the page.

Figure 29 *Portfolio Project checklist*

Website Checklist

1. Do your pages flow well together?
2. Do all Flash movies play properly in the browser?
3. Do all links work?
4. Do all rollover images display properly?
5. Do your Flash video files load quickly and play correctly?
6. Does the behavior assigned to an AP element respond correctly to the action assigned to it?

CHAPTER 12 CREATING AND
USING TEMPLATES

1. Create templates with editable regions

2. Use templates to create pages

3. Use templates to update a site

4. Use advanced template options

12

CREATING AND
USING TEMPLATES

Introduction

When you create a website, it's important to make sure that each page has a unified look so that users know they are in your site, no matter what page they are viewing. For instance, you should make sure that common elements such as the menu bar and company banner appear in the same place on every page and that every page has the same background. You have been using styles to provide continuity in your sites in previous chapters. Another way to make sure that every page in your site has a consistent appearance is by creating pages based on templates. A **template** is a special kind of page that contains both **locked regions**, which are areas on the page that cannot be modified by page authors (content contributors), as well as other types of regions that they can change or edit. For instance, an **optional region** is an area in the template that users can choose to show or hide, and an **editable region** is an area where template users can add or change content.

Using templates not only ensures a consistent appearance throughout a website, but also saves considerable development time. Templates are especially helpful if you are working with a team to create the pages in your site. In this chapter, you will create a template from an existing page in The Striped Umbrella website and define editable regions in it.

Understanding How to Use Templates

The ideal process for using templates is for one person (the template author) to create a template that has locked regions containing the design elements common to every page in the site, as well as regions with content that content contributors can add or change. Once the template is fully developed, other team members can use it to create other site pages, adding appropriate content to the editable regions of each page. If the template author makes changes to the template, all pages to which the template is attached can be automatically updated to reflect those changes.

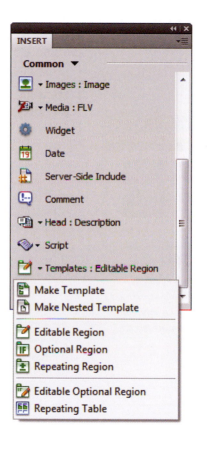

Create Templates with
EDITABLE REGIONS

What You'll Do

 *In this lesson, you will create a template based on the cruises page of The Striped Umbrella website. You will then define editable regions in the template, edit one of the CSS divs, and add links to the cruises and fishing pages. Finally, you will delete the template page title.*

Creating a Template from an Existing Page

If you have already created and designed a page that you think looks great, and you want to use the layout and design for other pages in your site, you can save the page as a template using the Save as Template command. Templates are saved with a .dwt extension and are stored in the Templates folder in the site root folder for your website. If your site does not have a Templates folder, Dreamweaver automatically creates one for you the first time you save a template. To view a list of templates in your site, open the Templates folder in the Files panel. To preview a template before opening it, open the Assets panel, click the Templates button on the Assets panel toolbar, and then click a template in the list. The template appears in the preview window above the templates list, as shown in Figure 1.

Defining Editable Regions

By default, when you save a template, all content on the page is locked, which means that no one else can add content or modify any part of the template to create new pages.

If your template is going to be used effectively, you must have at least one editable region in it so that other users can add content. You can specify a name for the region using the New Editable Region dialog box. Editable regions are outlined in blue on the template page, and the names of the editable regions appear in blue shaded boxes, as shown in Figure 2.

Defining Optional Regions

In addition to editable regions, you can also add optional regions to a template. An optional region is an area in a template that users can choose to either show or hide. For instance, you could place an image in an optional region, so that users of the template can decide whether or not to show it on the page they are creating. An optional region's visibility is controlled by the conditional statement **if**. You can specify a page element as an optional region using the New Optional Region dialog box. You can name the region and specify whether to show or hide it by default. The Editable and Optional Region dialog boxes are both accessed by clicking the Templates list arrow in the Common category of the Insert panel.

Defining Editable Optional Regions

If you want to give users the ability to show or hide a page element, as well as make modifications to it, then you can define the element as an **editable optional region**. For instance, you might want to make an advertisement an editable optional region so that users of the template can change its text and specify whether to show or hide it. Using the New Optional Region dialog box, you can name the region and specify whether to show or hide it by default.

Figure 1 *Template in Assets panel*

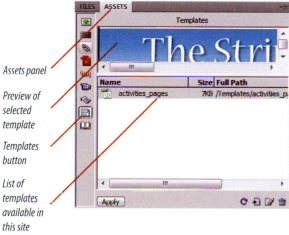

Assets panel

Preview of selected template

Templates button

List of templates available in this site

Figure 2 *Template with locked and editable regions*

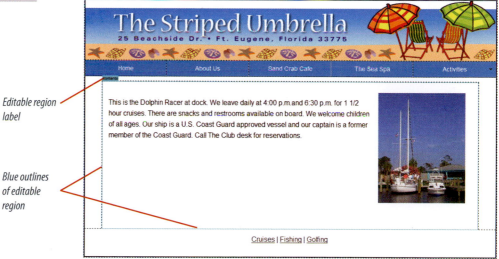

Editable region label

Blue outlines of editable region

Create a template from an existing page

1. Open Dreamweaver, open The Striped Umbrella website, then open the cruises page.

2. Click **File** on the Application bar (Win) or menu bar (Mac), then click **Save as Template** to open the Save As Template dialog box.

3. Verify that The Striped Umbrella is displayed in the Site text box, type **activities_pages** in the Save as text box, compare your screen to Figure 3, click **Save**, update the links, then click the **Refresh button** ⟳ on the Files panel toolbar.

   The Templates folder, which contains the activities_pages template, appears in the Files panel.

4. Click the **plus sign** next to the Templates folder to display the activities_pages.dwt file.

5. Display the Assets panel, click the **Templates button** 📄 to view the list of templates in the site, then compare your Assets panel to Figure 4. Click the **Refresh button** ⟳ if you don't see the template listed.

TIP To create a template from scratch, click File on the Application bar (Win) or Menu bar (Mac), click New to open the New Document dialog box, click Blank Template, click the type of template you want to create in the Template Type list, choose a layout from the Layout list, then click Create.

You created a template from the cruises page of The Striped Umbrella website.

Figure 3 *Save As Template dialog box*

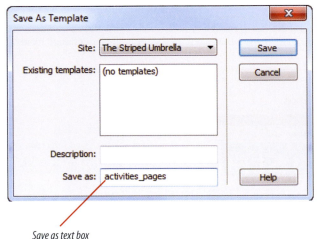

Save as text box

Figure 4 *Assets panel showing saved template in The Striped Umbrella website*

Preview of activities_pages template

Templates button

activities_pages template

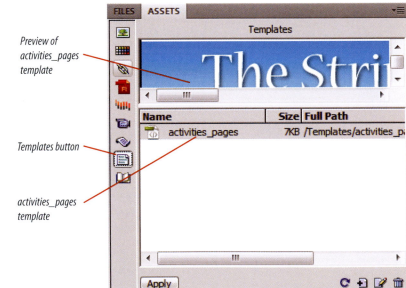

Figure 5 *New Editable Region dialog box*

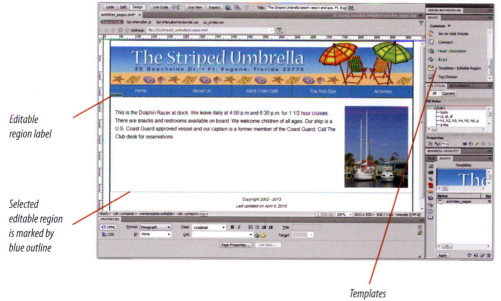

Name of new Editable Region

Figure 6 *activities_pages template with editable region added*

Editable region label

Selected editable region is marked by blue outline

Templates list arrow

Create an editable region

1. Click to place the insertion point in the div with the boat graphic, then click the **<div.content> tag** in the tag selector to select all of the content in the div.

2. Click the **Common category** on the Insert panel, if necessary.

3. Click the **Templates list arrow** in the Common category, then click **Editable Region** to open the New Editable Region dialog box.

TIP You can also press [Ctrl][Alt][V] (Win) or ⌘ [option][V] (Mac) to open the New Editable Region dialog box.

4. Type **contents** in the Name text box, as shown in Figure 5, click **OK**, click on the page to deselect the content, then compare your screen to Figure 6.

   A blue shaded box with the label "contents" appears above the top left corner of the div.

TIP You must have Invisible Elements turned on to see the blue shaded box.

5. Save your work.

TIP To remove an editable region from a template, select the editable region in the document window, click Modify on the Application bar (Win) or Menu bar (Mac), point to Templates, then click Remove Template Markup.

You created one editable region in the activities_pages template.

Modify a template

1. Click to place the insertion point inside the paragraph, then select the **<div.content> tag** on the tag selector.

   The content div is selected on the page in Design view.

2. Click the **.content rule** in the CSS Styles panel, then click the **Edit Rule button** to open the CSS Rule definition for .content dialog box.

3. Click the **Box category**, deselect the "Same for all" checkbox under the Margins settings, type **10** in the Top Margin text box, then, if necessary, click the list arrow next to the Top margin unit of measure text box and click **px**.

4. Clear the Bottom margin text box if necessary, repeat Step 3 to add a Right Margin of **40 px** and a Left Margin of **40 px**, then compare your screen to Figure 7.

5. Click **OK** to close the CSS Rule definition for the .content dialog box.

   Since there is not much content on these pages, changing these settings brings the page content more into the center of the page.

6. Delete the copyright statement and last updated statement in the page footer, then type **Cruises**.

   Since this area of the page is not designated as an Editable Area, users will not be able to change this content on pages based on this template unless they open the template itself.

   (continued)

Figure 7 *Editing the activities_page template*

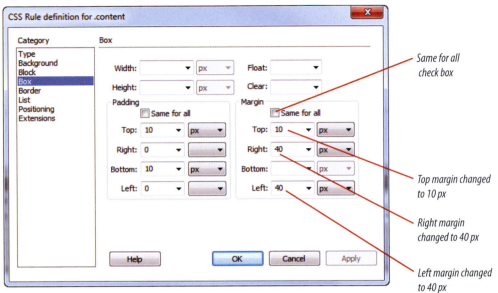

Same for all check box

Top margin changed to 10 px

Right margin changed to 40 px

Left margin changed to 40 px

Figure 8 *Links added to the activities_pages template*

Two links added
to the template

7. Press [**Spacebar**], insert a **Split Vertical bar** (the shift of the backslash key), press [**Spacebar**], type **Fishing**, then apply the centered_text rule to the two words.

8. Change to the CSS Property inspector, then remove the italic setting from the text.

9. Change to the HTML Property inspector, link the **Cruises text** to cruises.html, then link the **Fishing text** to fishing.html.

    Don't be concerned with the leading periods before the link in the Link text box. They simply indicate that the template file is in a different folder from the CSS file.

10. Add an additional paragraph break after the paragraph, click **File** on the Application bar (Win) or Menu bar (Mac), click **Save All**, then compare your screen to Figure 8.

11. Close the activities_pages template.

You edited the div tag rule, then added links to the cruises and fishing pages. Last, you added an additional paragraph break after the paragraph.

Using InContext Editing

Another way to allow users to modify web pages is through InContext Editing (ICE). **InContext Editing** is an online service that users can log into and be allowed to make changes to designated editable regions on a page while viewing it in a browser. This requires little knowledge of HTML or Dreamweaver. The commands to create editable regions are found in the InContext Editing category on the Insert panel. For more information, search either the Adobe Help files or the Adobe website at www.adobe.com.

Use Templates
TO CREATE PAGES

What You'll Do

 *In this lesson, you will use the activities_pages template to create a new page in The Striped Umbrella website. You will add content to the editable region, then apply the template to two existing pages in the website.*

Creating Pages with Templates

There are many advantages to using a template to create a page. First, it saves a lot of time, because part of the content and format of your page is already set. Second, it ensures that the page you create matches the look and format of other pages in the site. You can create a page based on a template using many different methods. One way is to click File on the Application bar (Win) or Menu bar (Mac), click New to open the New Document dialog box, click Page from Template, select the template you want to use, and then click Create. Templates can be used only in the website that contains them.

QUICK **TIP**

You can also create a new page based on a template by right-clicking (Win) or [control]-clicking (Mac) a template in the Assets panel, and then clicking New from Template.

Modifying Editable Regions

When you create a new page that is based on a template, certain areas of the new page are locked. You can tell which areas are locked by the appearance of the mouse pointer. When positioned over a locked region, the mouse pointer appears in the shape of a circle with a line cutting through it, as shown in Figure 9. Editable regions are outlined in blue and marked with a shaded blue label.

Editing, deleting, or adding content in editable regions of a template-based page works just like it does on any other page. Simply select the element you want to modify and make your changes, or click in the editable region and insert the new content.

Creating Links in Template-Based Pages

When you add a link to a page that is based on a template, it is important to use document-relative links; otherwise, they will not work. The path to a link actually goes from the template file (not from the template-based page) to the linked page. To ensure that all of your links are document-relative, select the page element to which you want to add a link, and then drag the Point to File icon from the Property inspector to the page you want to link to in the Files panel, as shown in Figure 10.

Figure 9 *Working with a template-based page*

Notation that this page is based on the activities_pages template

Pointer positioned over a locked region

Attaching a Template to an Existing Page

Sometimes you need to apply a template to a page that you have already created. For example, suppose you create a page for your department in your company's website, and then your manager tells you that it must be based on the template created by the marketing department. Before you attach a template to an existing page, you should delete any elements from your page that also appear in the template. For instance, if both your page and the template have a company logo, you should delete the logo on your page. If you don't delete it, the logo appears twice. Once you delete the duplicate content on your page, attach the template by opening your page, selecting the template in the Assets panel, and clicking the Apply button in the Assets panel. When you do this, the Inconsistent Region Names dialog box opens, allowing you to specify in which regions of the template to place the document head and body content from your page. To detach a template from a page, open the page you want to detach from the template, click Modify on the Application bar (Win) or Menu bar (Mac), point to Templates, then click Detach from Template.

QUICK TIP

You can also attach a template to an open page by dragging the template from the Assets panel to the Document window.

Figure 10 *Using the Point to File icon to specify a document-relative link*

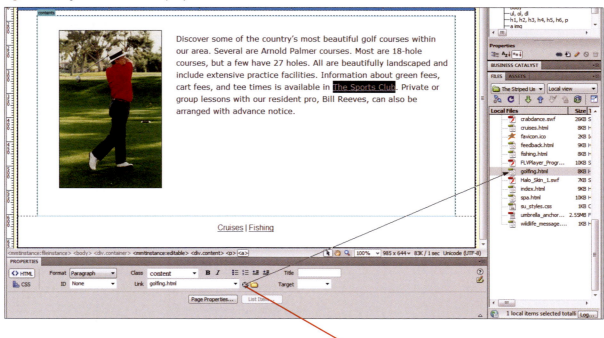

Point to File icon

Figure 11 *New Document dialog box*

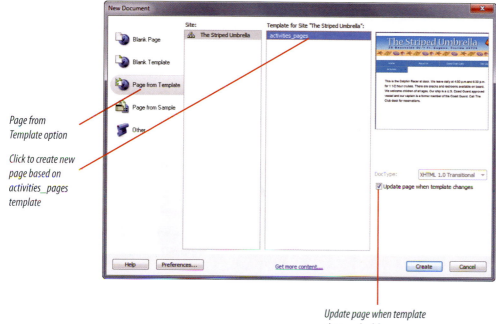

Page from Template option

Click to create new page based on activities_pages template

Update page when template changes check box

Create a new page based on a template

1. Click **File** on the Application bar (Win) or Menu bar (Mac), click **New** to open the New Document dialog box, then click **Page from Template**.

2. Click **The Striped Umbrella** in the Site list box (if necessary), click **activities_pages** in the Template for Site "The Striped Umbrella" list box (if necessary), verify that the **Update page when template changes check box** is selected, compare your screen to Figure 11, then click **Create**.

TIP You don't have to select the template name if there is only one listed. It will be automatically selected.

A new untitled page opens with the activities_pages template applied to it. The current content serves as placeholder content.

3. Click **File** on the Application bar (Win) or Menu bar (Mac), click **Save As** to open the Save As dialog box, type **golfing.html** in the File name text box, then click **Save**.

You created a new page in The Striped Umbrella website that is based on the activities_pages template. You then saved this page as golfing.html.

Modify editable regions in a template

1. Select the boats image, delete it, then insert golfer.jpg from the drive and folder where you store your Data Files at the insertion point, adding **Golfer swinging a club** as the alternate text.

2. Select and delete the existing text, then use the File, Import, Word Document command to import **golf.doc** (Win) from the drive and folder where you store your Data Files.

TIP If you are using a Macintosh, you'll need to copy and paste the text into Dreamweaver.

3. Enter a paragraph break, then insert the image ladies_group from the drive and folder where you store your Data Files, adding **Ladies' group** as the alternate text.

4. Select the golfer image, then apply Horizontal spacing of **30**, Vertical spacing of **20**, Border of **1**, and Alignment to **left**.

5. Select the ladies_group image, apply Horizontal spacing of **50**, a Border of **1**, deselect the image, then compare your screen to Figure 12.

You deleted content from the editable region of a new golf page based on the activities_pages template. You then replaced and formatted the image and imported text to replace the text in the content editable region.

Add a link

1. Select the text "The Sports Club" in the paragraph, then link the file **about_us.html** to the selected text, as shown in Figure 13.

2. Save and close the golfing.html page.

You linked a file to selected text.

Figure 12 *Golfing page with revised content in editable region*

Figure 13 *Linking to the about_us.html page*

Linked text

Link to about_us.html page

Figure 14 *New fishing page based on a template*

Convert existing pages to template-based pages

1. Open the fishing page.

2. Copy the paragraph of text on the left side of the page, then close the fishing page.

3. Create a new page based on the activities_pages template, replace the paragraph in the template with the paragraph you copied from the fishing page, then save the page as **fishing.html**, overwriting the original fishing.html page.

4. Delete the boat image and replace it with the **heron_small.jpg** image by dragging it from the assets folder into the contents editable region, then add **Ralph and his "catch"** for the alternate text.

5. Select the heron image, add Vertical spacing of **20**, Horizontal spacing of **30**, Border of **1**, and Alignment to **Left**.

6. Save the file, compare your screen with Figure 14, then close the page.

7. Create a new page based on the activities_pages template, then save it as **cruises.html**, overwriting the original cruises page. You do not have to replace any of the content because this is the page that was used for the template.

8. Select the boat image, change the Vertical spacing to **20**, the Horizontal spacing to **30**, the Border to **1**, the Alignment to **Left**, then save and close the cruises page.

You created a new HTML page based on a template and replaced text and images in the page. You then made an existing page into a template-based page.

Use Templates
TO UPDATE A SITE

What You'll Do

▶ *In this lesson, you will make a change to the activities_pages template, then update the site so that all pages based on the template reflect the change.*

Making Changes to a Template

If you create a successful site that draws large numbers of faithful users, your site will probably enjoy a long life. However, a good website should be updated frequently to keep the content fresh and timely. Your company might decide to make new products or offer new services. After a relatively short time, a website can look dated, even with no changes in the company. When changes occur in your company, on a large or small scale, you will need to make changes to your site's appearance and functionality. If your pages are based on a template or group of templates,

you will have a much easier time making those changes.

You use the same skills to make changes to a template as you would when creating a template. Start by opening the template from the Files panel or Assets panel, then add, delete, or edit content as you would on any non-template-based page. You can turn locked regions into editable regions using the New Editable Region command. To change an editable region back into a locked region, select the region, click Modify on the Application bar (Win) or Menu bar (Mac), point to Templates, and then click Remove Template Markup.

Finding Downloadable Templates

It is not necessary to create all of your templates from scratch or from existing pages. You can also use templates from outside sources, such as the Internet. A wide range of templates is available for web page components, such as buttons, Flash intros, and logos, as well as entire websites. These can include sites for businesses, charities, events, and many other venues. Some websites offer free templates for downloading and some offer them for sale. Go to your favorite search engine and type website templates in the Search text box. For example, www.yahootemplates.com offers many types of templates, both free and for sale.

Updating All Pages Based on a Template

One of the greatest benefits of working with templates is that any change you make to a template can be made automatically to all nested templates and pages that are based on the template. When you save a template that you have modified, the Update Template Files dialog box opens, asking if you want to update all the files in your site that are based on that template, as shown in Figure 15. When you click Update, the Update Pages dialog box opens and provides a summary of all the files that were updated.

Figure 15 *Update Template Files dialog box*

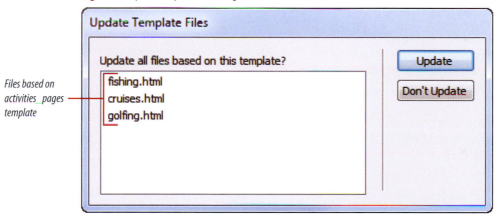

Files based on activities_pages template

Make changes to a template

1. Open the activities_pages template from the Templates folder. (*Hint*: You may have to click the plus sign to expand the Templates folder first.)

2. Click to place the insertion point after the second link, add a space, type a **split vertical bar**, then add another space.

3. Create a third link using the word **Golfing**, link it to the golfing page, then compare your screen to Figure 16.

4. Select the **Spry Menu bar**, select the **Activities menu item** in the first column in the Property Inspector, click the **Add menu item button** ✚ above the second column, then type **Golfing** in the Text text box.

5. Use the **Browse for file button** next to the Link text box, then link the new Golfing menu item to the golfing page, as shown in Figure 17.

6. Open the fishing page.

    The new link does not appear because you have not yet saved the template and updated the site.

7. Close the fishing page.

You opened the activities_pages template, added a new link, then modified the Spry Menu bar to include the golfing page in the Activities submenu.

Update all template-based pages in a site

1. Return to the activities_pages template (if necessary), click **File** on the Application bar (Win) or Menu bar (Mac), then click **Save All**.

    The Update Template Files dialog box opens, as shown in Figure 18.

(continued)

Figure 16 *activities_pages template with new link added*

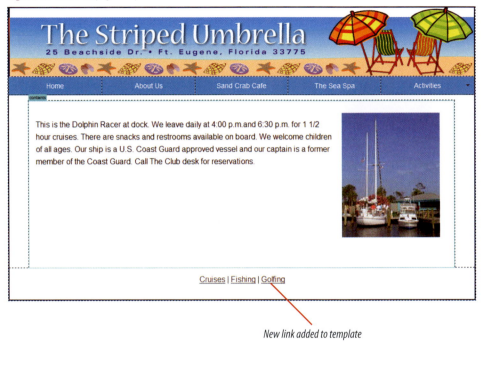

New link added to template

Figure 17 *Updating the Spry Menu bar*

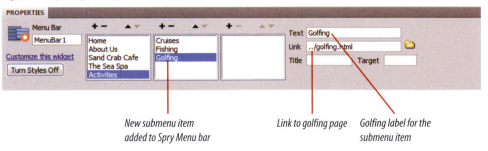

New submenu item added to Spry Menu bar

Link to golfing page

Golfing label for the submenu item

Figure 18 *Update Template Files dialog box*

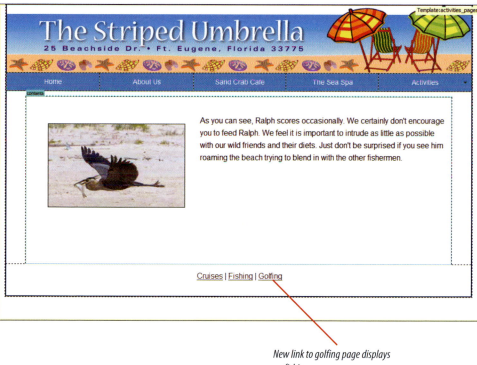

Figure 19 *Fishing page with template changes incorporated*

New link to golfing page displays
on fishing page

2. Click **Update** to open the Update Pages dialog box, then click **Close** after it has finishing updating the pages. (*Note*: This may take several seconds.)

3. Open the fishing page, then compare your screen to Figure 19.

   The fishing page, the cruises page, and the golfing page in the website now show the new link. The Activities link in the menu bar has three submenu items now.

4. Close the fishing page and the activities_pages template.

5. Open the activities page, click to place the insertion point at the end of the paragraph with the links to the cruises and fishing pages, press [spacebar], then type **We can also arrange tee times for you at area golf courses**.

   This new sentence provides text for a link to the golfing page.

6. Link the text **tee times** to golfing.html, then save and close the activities page.

7. Open the activities, about_us, cafe, index, feedback, and spa pages, repeat Steps 4 and 5 on the previous page to add the golfing submenu item to each menu bar, then save and close each page. (*Hint*: You can also just modify one menu bar, then use it to replace each of the other menu bars.)

You saved the activities_pages template and used the Update Template Files dialog box and the Update Pages dialog box to specify that all pages in the site based on the template be updated to reflect the template modifications. You also added text to the activities page that was used to provide a link to the golfing page. You then opened each of the other pages in the site that are not based on a template and modified each of their menu bars.

Use Advanced TEMPLATE OPTIONS

What You'll Do

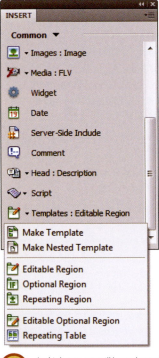

In this lesson, you will learn about advanced template settings that can be used for more complex templates.

Setting Parameters for Optional Regions

If your template will be used by many people, it might be a good idea to include several optional regions in it so that template users can pick and choose from a wide range of content elements. For example, on a retail site, you might have an optional region for each department to advertise a sale promotion. You would display the optional region for the department you want to feature during the time that department is having its sale. When the sale is over, you would hide that optional region. You might also want to set parameters for optional regions, specifying that they are displayed or hidden based on specific conditions. For instance, let's say you have two optional regions named shoe_sale_text and shoe_images. You could set the shoe_images optional region parameter to shoe_sale_text so that the shoe_images optional region would appear only when the shoe_sale_text optional region is showing, and would be hidden only when the shoe_sale_text optional region is hidden. Use the Advanced settings in the New Optional Region dialog box to set the parameters of an optional region. You can also write a conditional expression based on JavaScript. For instance, you could write the expression red == false to specify that a blue optional region appear only when a red optional region is hidden.

Nesting Templates

If you are working on a complex website that has many different pages used by different people or departments, you might need to create **nested templates**, which are templates that are based on another template. Nested templates are helpful when you want to define a page or parts of a page in greater detail. An advantage of using nested templates is that any changes made to the original template can be automatically updated in the nested template.

To create a nested template, create a new page based on the original template, then use the Save as Template command to save the page as a nested template. You can then make changes to the nested template by adding or deleting content and defining new editable regions. Note that editable regions in the original template are passed on as editable regions to the nested template.

Creating and Using Templates

However, if you add a new editable or optional region to an editable region that was passed on from the original template, the original editable region changes to a locked region in the nested template.

Creating Editable Attributes

There might be times when you want users of your template to be able to change certain attributes of an element in a locked region. For instance, perhaps you want to give users the ability to change the cell background color of the top row in a repeating table, or change the source file for an image in a locked area of the template. You can use the Editable Tag Attributes dialog box, shown in Figure 20, to specify that certain attributes of locked regions be editable. To do this, choose an attribute of a selected element, specify to make it editable, assign it a label, and specify its type and its default setting. For instance, in Figure 20, a link was first selected in a template. Then, the Editable Tag Attributes dialog box was opened by clicking Modify on the Application bar (Win) or Menu bar (Mac), pointing to Templates, and then clicking Make Attribute Editable. From that dialog box, you can choose the attribute and settings that you want to make editable. When you define editable attributes of elements in locked regions, template users can make changes to the element's attributes using the Template Properties dialog box.

Figure 20 *Editable Tag Attributes dialog box*

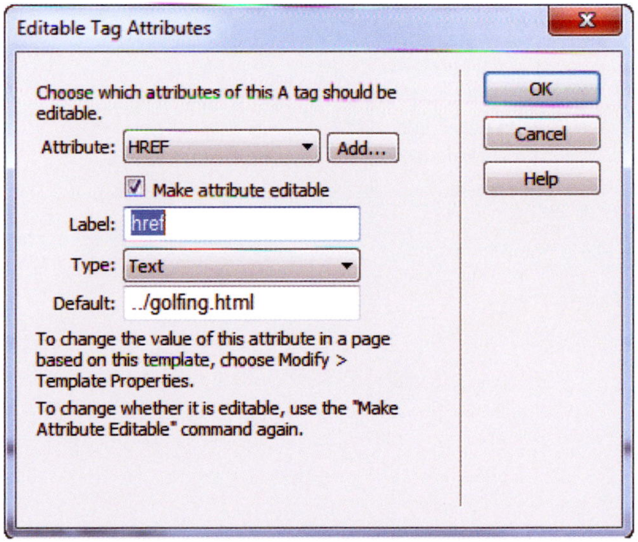

Create templates with editable regions.

1. Open the Blooms & Bulbs website, then open the plants page.
2. Save the plants page as a template called **plant_categories** and update the links.
3. Delete the heading, text, horizontal rule, video, and images in the content container. You should have only the banner, menu bar, and copyright statement left on the page. (*Note*: Go to code view and delete any leftover code that is not needed, but leave the H3 tags and the break tag.)
4. Delete the copyright statement at the bottom of the page, then type **Annuals - Perennials - Water Plants**. (*Note*: Make sure there is a space before and after each dash.)
5. Link the Annuals text to the annuals.html page, the Perennials text to the perennials.html page, and the Water Plants text to the water_plants.html page.
6. Use the Tag Selector to select the content div, then create an editable region with it named **descriptions**.
7. Save and close the plant_categories template.

Use templates to create pages.

1. Create a new page from the plant_categories template, then save it as **annuals.html**, overwriting the existing file.
2. Drag the coleus.jpg file from the website assets folder into the content div and type **Coleus** as the alternate text.
3. Deselect the image, import the file annuals.doc from the drive and folder where you store your Chapter 12 data files and place the text to the right side of the image, or use a word processing progam to copy and paste the text onto the page. (*Note*: The text appears below the image until you set the image alignment in the next step.)
4. Set the image alignment to left, then add V Space of 10 and H Space of 20.
5. Apply the Heading 3 format to the Annuals heading, then save and close the page.
6. Repeat Steps 1 through 5 to create a new page based on the plant_categories template, then save it as **perennials**, overwriting the existing page and using the ruby_grass.jpg file and the perennials.doc text. Format the text and graphics consistently based on the annuals.html page.
7. Repeat Steps 1 through 5 to create a new **water_plants** page based on the plant_categories template, using the water_lily.jpg file and the water_plants.doc text, formatting the text and graphics consistently to match the other pages based on the template.
8. Save and close all open pages.
9. Close the Word files and the word processing program if necessary.

Use templates to update a site.

1. Open the plant_categories template, then delete the two hyphens and the spaces between the three links in the footer div, replacing them with three non-breaking spaces. (*Hint*: Use the Insert, HTML, Special Characters, Non-Breaking Space command or the keyboard shortcut [Shift][Ctrl][Spacebar](Win) or [Shift][command][Spacebar](Mac).)

2. Save the template and the style sheet file, then update all files in the site that are based on the template.

3. Preview the annuals.html, perennials.html, and water_plants.html pages in your browser, compare your perennials page to Figure 21, close the browser, then close all open pages.

Figure 21 *Completed Skills Review*

In this Project Builder, you use a template to enhance the TripSmart website. Use Figure 22 as a guide as you work with the template.

1. Open the TripSmart website.
2. Open the catalog page, save it as a template named **catalog_pages**, and update the links.
3. Select the content div and create an editable region named **catalog_items**.
4. Delete the placeholder for the Flash file, then save and close the template.
5. Create a new page based on the catalog_pages template and save it as **clothing.html**.
6. Insert the Flash file catalog.swf under the statement of guarantee, then enter **Catalog Featured Clothing Items** in the Object Tag Accessibility Attributes dialog box for the title and type **clothing_items** in the Id text box on the Property inspector.
7. Enter a line break before the guarantee statement, then type **These are our featured clothing items this week.** above the guarantee statement.
8. Save and close the clothing.html page.
9. Create a new page based on the catalog_pages template and save it as **accessories.html**.
10. Enter a line break before the guarantee statement, then type **These are our featured accessories this week.** above the guarantee statement.
11. Insert the Flash file catalog2.swf from the drive and folder where you store your Data Files under the statement of guarantee. In the Object Tag Accessibility Attributes dialog box, enter **Catalog Featured Accessory Items** as the title, then enter **accessory_items** in the Id text box on the Property inspector.
12. Save and close the accessories page.
13. Create a new page based on the **catalog_pages** template, then save it as **catalog.html**, overwriting the original catalog.html page.
14. Insert the file two_customers.jpg from the drive and folder where your store your Chapter 12 Data Files after the guarantee statement and add appropriate alternate text.
15. Add a 1-pixel border to the image, then replace the guarantee statement with **Send us your travel photos that show our clothing or accessories. If we use one on our website, you'll get 25% off of your next order!** Use a line break between the two lines.
16. Save and close the catalog page.
17. Open the catalog_pages template.

18. Edit the Spry Menu bar to include two child menus under the Catalog menu: one named **Accessories** that links to the accessories.html page and one named **Clothing** that links to the clothing.html page.

19. Save the catalog_pages template, updating the pages based on the template. Verify that the pages have been updated.

20. Open each page in the site that is not based on the catalog_pages template and modify the menu bar to include the two child menus under the catalog menu. If you see a message warning you of JavaScript code that is no longer needed, you can either delete the referenced code, comment it out, or ignore it. It will not cause the page to be displayed incorrectly.

21. Save all pages and preview them in the browser, testing each link.

Figure 22 *Sample Project Builder 1*

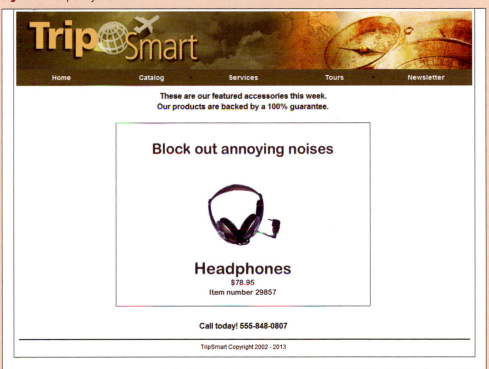

In this Project Builder, you continue your work on the Carolyne's Creations website. Carolyne would like to make sure that the pages in the site have a consistent appearance. She has asked you to create a template based on the recipes page to use for adding new recipes on the website.

1. Open the Carolyne's Creations website, then create a new template from the recipes page named **recipes** and update the links.
2. Select the Caramel Coconut Pie heading and the paragraph below it and create an editable region from it named **name_description**.
3. Select the photo and list of ingredients, and create an editable region named **photo_ingredients**.
4. Select the directions heading and text and create an editable region named **directions**.
5. Add a paragraph return right below the banner (select the banner, switch to Code view, place the insertion point right after the closing map tag, return to Design view, then press [Enter]) and type **Featured Recipes: Caramel Coconut Pie - Fried Green Tomatoes**, then insert a horizontal rule below the text.

6. Compare your screen to Figure 23, then save and close the template. (*Hint*: If the last ingredient does not appear in the bulleted list, it will on the pages based on the template when viewed in Live View or in a browser.)
7. Create a new file based on the recipes template and name it **recipes.html**, overwriting the original recipes.html file.
8. Close the new recipes page.
9. Create another new page based on the recipes template, and name it **fried_green_tomatoes.html**.
10. Using fried_green_tomatoes.doc from the drive and folder where you store your Data Files, replace the editable regions text in the fried_green_tomatoes.html file with the fried_green_tomatoes text from the Word file.
11. Replace the coconut_pie.jpg image with the fried_green_tomatoes.jpg image from the Chapter 12 Data Files, set the alignment to left if necessary, then change the alternate text to **Fried Green Tomatoes**.

12. Save your work, preview the page in either Live View or your browser, make any alignment, style, and spacing adjustments of your choice, then save your work.
13. Open the recipes template and link the text under the menu bar as follows: Caramel Coconut pie to recipes.html, and Fried Green Tomatoes to fried_green_tomatoes.html.
14. Save and close the template, updating the pages based on the template.
15. Save all files, preview the fried_green_tomatoes page in the browser, then compare your screen to Figure 24.
16. Test all links, close the browser, then close any open files.

Figure 23 *Completed Project Builder 2*

Featured Recipes: Caramel coconut Pie - Fried Green Tomatoes

name_description

Caramel Coconut Pie

This is one of our most requested desserts. It is simple, elegant, and refreshing. It is easy to make in advance, because you keep it frozen until just before serving. It makes two pies — one to eat and one to give away!

photo_ingredients

Ingredients:

- ¼ cup butter
- 7 oz. dried coconut
- ½ cup chopped pecans
- 1 package (8 oz.) cream cheese, softened
- 1 can (14 oz.) sweetened condensed milk
- 1 container (16 oz.) whipped topping, thawed
- 1 jar (12 oz.) caramel ice cream topping

2 pie shells (9 in.), baked

directions

Directions:

Melt butter in large skillet. Add coconut & pecans; cook until golden brown, stirring frequently. Set aside. Combine cream cheese & milk. Beat until smooth, then fold in whipped topping. Layer ¼ of cream cheese mixture into each pie shell. Drizzle ¼ of caramel topping on each pie. Sprinkle ¼ of coconut & pecan mixture evenly on each pie. Repeat layers. Cover & freeze until firm. Let stand at room temperature for 5 minutes before serving.

This recipe was contributed by Cosie Simmons.

Carolyne's Creations Copyright 2001 - 2013

Figure 24 *Completed Project Builder 2*

Featured Recipes: Caramel Coconut Pie - Fried Green Tomatoes

Fried Green Tomatoes

This recipe is one of our most popular brunch dishes. It is based on a traditional southern fried green tomato recipe with an upscale twist in the addition of goat cheese. We serve them on a pool of marinara sauce, garnished with chopped basil.

Ingredients:

- ¼ t kosher salt
- ¼ t freshly ground pepper
- ¼ t sugar
- 1 cup finely crushed crackers
- 1 egg
- ½ cup goat cheese
- 4 large green tomatoes, sliced
- Vegetable oil

Directions:

Combine the first four ingredients in a shallow bowl. Beat the egg until frothy in a smaller bowl. To assemble: spread a small amount of goat cheese on the top side of one tomato slice; dip the tomato in the egg, then roll both sides in the cracker crumbs. Place on waxed paper until ready to fry.

Heat the oil in a cast-iron skillet, and then fry the tomatoes about 3 minutes on each side or until brown. Drain on paper towels and serve.

Carolyne's Creations Copyright 2001 - 2013

There are many web sources for Dreamweaver page templates. Many of them are free and many are available for nominal fees. One such site is Yahoo!. The website pictured in Figure 25 was built from a template downloaded from the Yahoo! website.

1. Connect to the Internet, then go to www.yahootemplates.com.

2. Spend some time exploring the templates on this site by previewing several of them.

3. Think of an idea for a new site that you would like to create. The site can be for a club, organization, event, or any topic or person that interests you. Draw an outline and a sketch of the site, including the content that will be on each page.

4. After you have completed your sketch, look through the Yahoo! templates available, then choose an appropriate template for your site.

5. Explain why you chose this particular template.

6. Search for other sites on the Internet that offer templates for downloading.

7. List three sites that you found and the prices listed for downloading each template.

Figure 25 *Design Project*

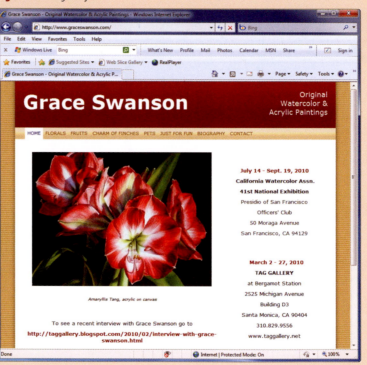

Grace Swanson website used with permission from Grace Swanson – www.graceswanson.com

In this assignment, you continue to work on the website that you created in earlier chapters, enhancing it by using templates. You first create a template from one of your existing pages and define editable regions in it. You then apply the template to a page and add content to the editable regions.

1. Consult your wireframes and decide which page you would like to use as a template. You will use the template to create at least one other page in your site.
2. Create a sketch of the template page you will create. Mark the page elements that will be in locked regions. Identify and mark at least one area that will be an editable region.
3. Create a new template, then define the editable regions in the template.
4. Make any necessary formatting adjustments to make sure it looks attractive, and then save the template. Create a new page based on the template, using the same name as the page on which the template is based, so that the earlier version of the page is overwritten.
5. Apply the template to another existing page in the site, making sure to delete all repeating elements contained in the template.
6. Review the template(s) and the template-based pages, and decide if you need to make improvements. Use the checklist in Figure 26 to make sure you completed everything according to the assignment.
7. Make any necessary changes.
8. Save your work, then close all open pages.

Figure 26 *Portfolio Project checklist*

Website Checklist

1. Does your template include at least one editable region?
2. Are all links on templates-based pages document-relative?
3. Do all editable regions have appropriate names?
4. Do all links work correctly?
5. Do all pages look good using at least two different browsers?
6. Are you happy with the overall appearance of each page?

CHAPTER

13

WORKING WITH LIBRARY
ITEMS AND SNIPPETS

1. Create and modify library items
2. Add library items to pages
3. Add and modify snippets

13

WORKING WITH LIBRARY
ITEMS AND SNIPPETS

Introduction

When creating a website, chances are good that you will want certain graphics or text blocks to appear in more than one place in the site. For instance, you might want the company contact information in several different places, or a footer containing links to the main pages of the site at the bottom of every page. Library items and snippets can help you work with these repeating elements more efficiently.

Understanding Library Items

If you want an element to appear repeatedly, then it's a good idea to save it as a library item. A **library item** is content that can contain text or graphics that you plan to use multiple times in your website and that is saved in a separate file in the Library folder of your website. When you need to use a library item on a web page, you can easily select it from the list of available library items in the Library category in the Assets panel. In addition to being readily available, another advantage of using library items is that when you make a change to the library item and then update the site, all instances of that item throughout the website will be updated to reflect the change.

Understanding Snippets

Another way to use the same content repeatedly throughout a site is to insert code snippets. **Code snippets** are ready-made, reusable pieces of code you can insert on a page. Dreamweaver provides a variety of code snippets you can use to create footers, drop-down menus, headers, and other page elements. Code snippets are stored in the Snippets panel and can be used on any open page in any website.

In this chapter, you will work with library items and code snippets to enhance The Striped Umbrella website.

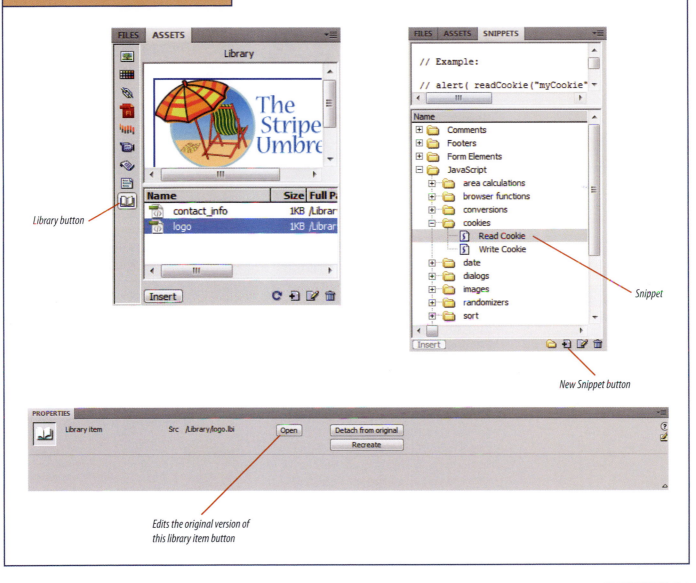

Library button

Snippet

New Snippet button

Edits the original version of this library item button

Create and Modify
LIBRARY ITEMS

What You'll Do

▶ *In this lesson, you will create a text-based library item. You will also create a library item that contains an image in the activities_pages template. You will then edit both library items and update the site to reflect those edits.*

Understanding the Benefits of Library Items

Using library items for repetitive elements—especially those that need to be updated frequently—can save you considerable time. For instance, suppose you want to feature an employee of the month photograph on every page in your site. You could create a library item named employee_photo and add it to every page. Then, when you need to update the site to show a new employee photo, simply replace the photo contained in the library item, and the photo would be updated throughout the site. Library items can contain a wide range of content, including text, images, tables, Flash files, and audio files.

Viewing and Creating Library Items

To view library items, open the Assets panel, then click the Library button. The library items appear in a list, and a preview of the selected library item appears above the list, as shown in Figure 1. To save text or an

image as a library item, select the item in the Document window, and then drag it to the Library on the Assets panel. You can also click Modify on the Application bar (Win) or Menu bar (Mac), point to Library, and then click Add Object to Library. The item that you added will appear in the preview window on the Assets panel and in the library item list with the temporary name Untitled assigned to it. Type a new name, and then press [Enter] (Win) or [return] (Mac) to give the library item a meaningful name. Library items on a web page appear in shaded yellow in the Document window, but not in the browser. When you click a library item in the Document window, the entire item becomes selected and the Property inspector changes to display three buttons that you can use to work with the library item, as shown in Figure 2.

QUICK TIP

You can also view a list of available library items by expanding the Library folder in the Files panel.

Modifying Library Items

You cannot edit library items on the web pages in which they appear. To make changes to a library item, you have to open it. To open a library item, select the item in the Document window, and then click Open in the Property inspector. The library item will appear in the Document window, where you can make edits or add content to it. When you are satisfied with your edits, save the library item using the Save command on the File menu. When you do this, the Update Library Items dialog box will appear, asking if you want to update all instances of the library item throughout the site.

Figure 1 *Library items in Assets panel*

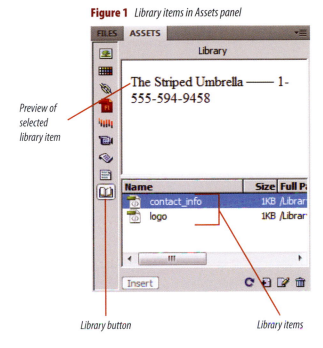

Preview of selected library item

Library button

Library items

Figure 2 *Web page containing library item*

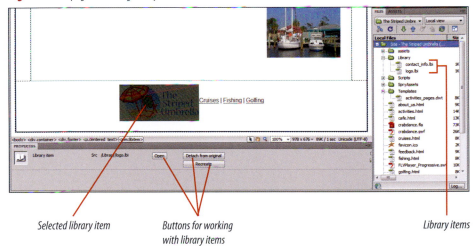

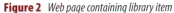

Selected library item

Buttons for working with library items

Library items

Create a text-based library item

1. Open The Striped Umbrella website, then open the index page.

2. Create a new class rule in the su_styles.css file called **contact_number** with the following settings: Font-family = **Arial**, **Helvetica**, **sans-serif**, Font-size = **small**, Font-weight = **bold**, color = **#006**, Text-align = **center**.

3. Move the copyright and last updated statements under the contact information, as shown in Figure 3, then apply the **contact_info rule** if necessary.

4. Type **The Striped Umbrella 555-594-9458** in their previous position in the footer, then apply the **contact_number rule**.

   Although the italic font-style was not used in the contact_number rule, the text displays in italics because it inherits the italic font-style from the footer rule.

5. Click to place the insertion point before the telephone number, change to the Text category on the Insert panel, click the **Characters list arrow**, click the **Em Dash button**, then add a space after the Em dash, as shown in Figure 3. (You want a space both before and after the Em dash.)

TIP You can also insert an Em dash by clicking Insert on the Application bar (Win) or Menu bar (Mac), pointing to HTML, pointing to Special Characters, and clicking Em-Dash.

6. Display the Assets panel, then click the **Library button** .

7. Select the line of text with the telephone number, then drag it to the Assets panel.

(continued)

Figure 3 *Inserting an Em dash*

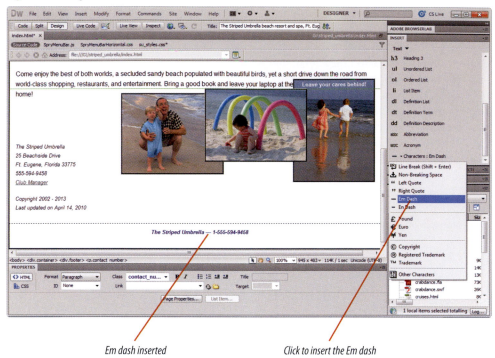

Em dash inserted   Click to insert the Em dash

Working with Library Items and Snippets

Figure 4 *Assets panel showing contact_info library item*

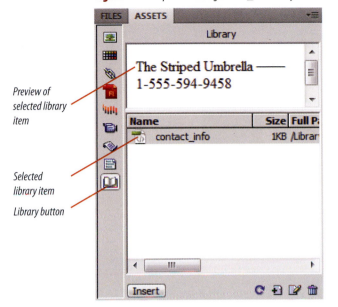

Preview of selected library item

Selected library item

Library button

Figure 5 *Viewing the contact_info library item in Code view*

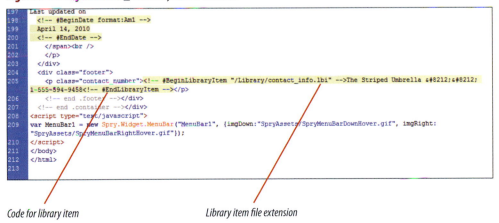

Code for library item

Library item file extension

8. Click **OK** to close the dialog box warning you that the library item will be saved without the style information.

   The text that you dragged is now an untitled library item on the Assets panel.

9. Type **contact_info** in the Name text box to replace "Untitled," press **[Enter]** (Win) or **[return]** (Mac) to name the library item, deselect the library item on the page, refresh the Assets panel if necessary, then compare your Assets panel to Figure 4.

   The text formatting appears on the page but not in the Assets panel. If you look closely, you will see that the contact information now has a lightly shaded yellow background on the page behind the text, indicating it is a library item.

TIP If you don't see the shading, make sure that Invisible Elements is checked on your View, Visual Aids submenu.

10. Switch to Code view to view the library item, as shown in Figure 5, then return to Design view.

    The library item file has the file extension .lbi. The yellow shading is easier to see in Code view.

11. Save and close the index.html page and the style sheet file.

You created a text-based library item from text on the index page.

Create an image-based library item

1. Click the **Templates button** 📄 on the Assets panel, then double-click the **activities_pages template** to open it.

2. Click the **Library button** 📖 on the Assets panel to display the library item.

3. Place the insertion point in the uneditable region to the left of the Cruises link, go to Code view, click between the end of the opening <p> tag and the beginning of the cruises link tag.

4. Insert the **su_logo.gif** from the website assets folder using the menu or the Insert panel (do not drag it), add **The Striped Umbrella logo** as the alternate text, set the alignment to Middle, deselect the logo, return to Design view, then compare your screen to Figure 6.

5. Select the logo and drag the selection to the Library on the Assets panel, then click **OK** to close the dialog box warning you that the style was not copied.

   The image is stored as a library item and appears in the preview window at the top of the Assets panel. A new untitled library item appears selected in the library item list. (Refresh the Assets panel if it does not appear.)

6. Type **logo** to replace "Untitled," press **[Enter]** (Win) or **[return]** (Mac) to name the library item on the Assets panel, then compare your screen to Figure 7.

7. Save your changes, then click **Update** in the Update Template Files dialog box to open the Update Pages dialog box.

(continued)

Figure 6 *Viewing the Striped Umbrella logo on the activities_pages template*

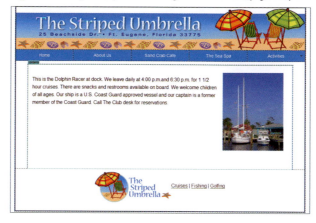

Figure 7 *logo library item added to Assets panel*

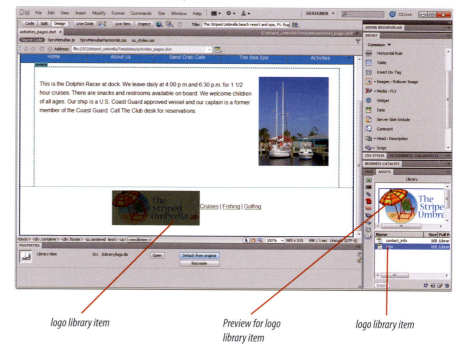

logo library item

Preview for logo library item

logo library item

Figure 8 *Update Pages dialog box with Library items and Templates check boxes checked*

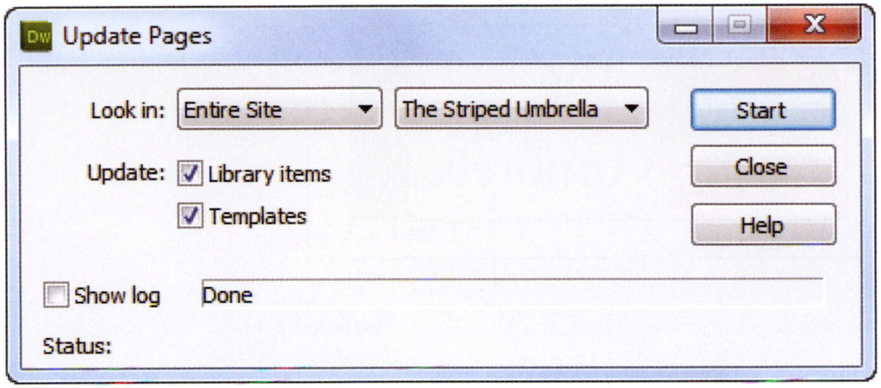

8. Click the **Look in list arrow**, click **Entire Site**, check the **Library items** and **Templates** check boxes, as shown in Figure 8, then click **Start**.

   Dreamweaver updates your files based on the changes made to the library item. If you select the Show log check box, you will see a list of the items that were updated.

9. Click **Close**, then open the cruises page to view the library item on the page. Because the cruises page was based on the activities_pages template, the page was updated to include the new logo library item.

10. Save all files, preview the cruises page in the browser, click the fishing and golfing links to view the logo on each of the pages, close your browser, and close all open pages except the activities_pages template.

You created a library item named logo that contains the resort logo in the activities_pages template. You then saved the template and updated all pages in the site that are based on the template.

Edit an image-based library item

1. Click the **logo library item** at the bottom of the activities_pages template.

2. Click **Open** in the Property inspector, as shown in Figure 9, to open the logo library item.

   The image appears in the Document window. The page tab displays the filename logo.lbi. The file extension .lbi denotes a library file.

TIP You can also open a library item by double-clicking it on the Assets panel.

(continued)

Figure 9 *Opening a library item*

Click to open a library item

3. Click the image in the Document window, then click the **Crop button** 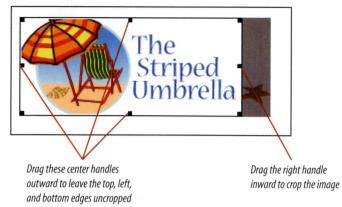 in the Property inspector.

4. Click **OK** to the message warning "The action you are about to perform will permanently alter the selected image."

An outline surrounds the image. The resizing handles on the outline let you crop the image.

5. Drag the right edge toward the center of the image to crop off the starfish on the right edge of the graphic, then drag the other three edges outward so the rest of the image is not cropped, as shown in Figure 10.

6. When you are satisfied with the crop, double-click the logo to execute the crop, then compare your screen to Figure 11.

TIP   You can also press [Enter](Win) or [return](Mac) to execute a crop.

You opened the logo library item, then cropped the image.

Figure 10 *Cropping the logo*

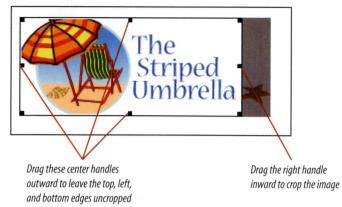

Drag these center handles
outward to leave the top, left,
and bottom edges uncropped

Drag the right handle
inward to crop the image

Figure 11 *Viewing the cropped logo*

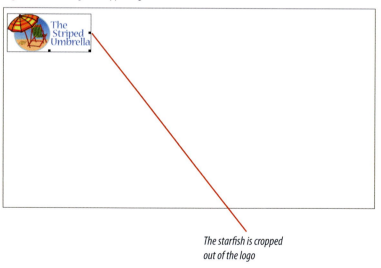

The starfish is cropped
out of the logo

Working with Library Items and Snippets

Figure 12 *Activities_page template showing the updated logo library item*

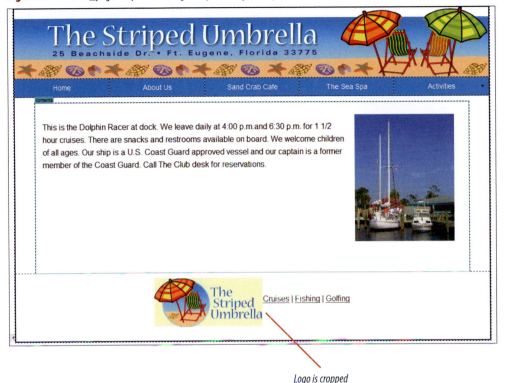

Logo is cropped

Update library items

1. Click **File** on the Application bar (Win) or Menu bar (Mac), then click **Save** to open the Update Library Items dialog box.

   The dialog box asks if you want to update the library item on the pages shown.

2. Click **Update** to open the Update Pages dialog box.

3. Click the **Look in list arrow**, click **Entire Site**, check the **Library items** and **Templates** check boxes, then click **Start**.

   Dreamweaver updates the cruises, fishing, golfing, and activities_pages files based on the changes you made to the library item.

4. Click **Close**, then close the logo.lbi file.

   The activities_pages template page reflects the change you made to the logo library item.

5. Compare your screen to Figure 12.

6. Save and close the activities_pages template, updating the pages in the site again.

You saved the logo library item and updated all pages in the site to incorporate the changes you made.

Edit a text-based library item

1. Open the index page, then click the **telephone text** to select the contact_info library item.

2. Click **Open** in the Property inspector to open the contact_info library item.

3. Edit the telephone number to read **555-594-9458 or 888-594-9458 toll free**, then compare your screen to Figure 13.

(continued)

Figure 13 *Contact_info library item after editing*

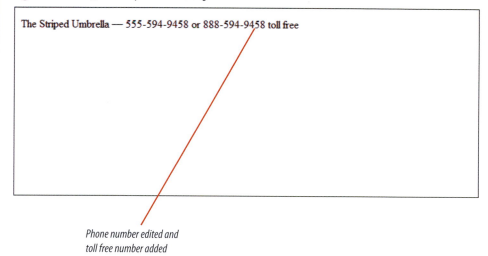

The Striped Umbrella — 555-594-9458 or 888-594-9458 toll free

Phone number edited and toll free number added

Figure 14 *Activities_pages template showing the updated logo library item*

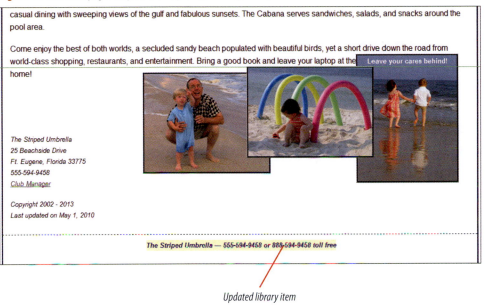

casual dining with sweeping views of the gulf and fabulous sunsets. The Cabana serves sandwiches, salads, and snacks around the pool area.

Come enjoy the best of both worlds, a secluded sandy beach populated with beautiful birds, yet a short drive down the road from world-class shopping, restaurants, and entertainment. Bring a good book and leave your laptop at the home!

Leave your cares behind!

The Striped Umbrella
25 Beachside Drive
Ft. Eugene, Florida 33775
555-594-9458
Club Manager

Copyright 2002 - 2013
Last updated on May 1, 2010

The Striped Umbrella — 555-594-9458 or 888-594-9458 toll free

Updated library item

4. Save your changes, update the site, then close the contact_info library item.
5. Compare your index page to Figure 14.

   The text reflects the edits you made to the contact_info library item.
6. Save and close the index page.

You edited the text in the contact_info library item, then saved the changes and updated the site.

Add Library
ITEMS TO PAGES

What You'll Do

 In this lesson, you will add the text-based library item you created to the about_us, activities, cafe, feedback, and spa pages. You will detach the library item on the index page and edit it. You will then delete one of the library items and restore the deleted item using the Recreate command.

Adding Library Items to a Page

Once you create a library item, it's easy to add it to any page in a website. All you do is drag the library item from the Assets panel to the desired location on the page. When you insert a library item, the actual content and a reference to the library item are copied into the code. The inserted library item is shaded in yellow in the Document window and is automatically updated to reflect any changes you make to the library item.

> **QUICK TIP**
>
> You can also insert a library item on a page by selecting the item on the Assets panel, then clicking Insert.

There may be times when you don't want content to be updated when you update the library item. For instance, suppose you want one of your pages to include photos of all past employees of the month. You would insert content from the current library item, but you do not want the photo to change when the library item is updated to reflect next month's employee photo. To achieve this, you would insert the content of a library item on a page, then click the Detach from original button in the Property inspector. The content from the library item will be inserted on the page, but it will not be linked to the library item.

Making Library Items Editable on a Page

There may be times when you would like to make changes to a particular instance of a library item on one page, without making those changes to other instances of the library item in the site. You can make a library item editable on a page by breaking its link to the library item. To do this, select the library item, and then click Detach from original in the Property inspector. Once you have detached the library item, you can edit the content like you would any other element on the page. Keep in mind, though, that this edited content will not be updated when you make changes to the library item.

Deleting and Recreating Library Items

If you know that you will never need to use a library item again, you probably want to delete it. To delete a library item, select it on the Assets panel, and then click the Delete button. Deleting a library item only removes it from the Library folder; it does not change the contents of the pages that contain that library item. All instances of

the deleted library item will still appear in shaded yellow in the site unless you detach them from the original. Be aware that you cannot use the Undo command to restore a library item. However, you can restore a library item by selecting any instance of the item in the site and clicking Recreate in the Property inspector. You can also recreate a

library item after you have exited and started Dreamweaver again, provided a deleted library item still has an instance remaining on a page. After you recreate a library item, it reappears on the Assets panel and you can make changes to it and update all pages in the site again. Figure 15 shows the Property inspector with Library item settings.

Figure 15 *Property inspector with Library item settings*

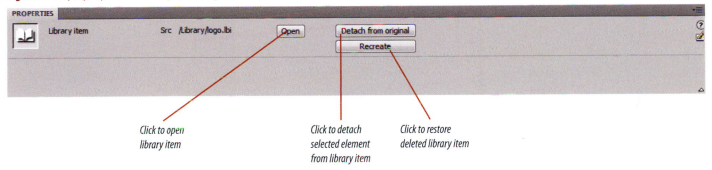

Click to open library item

Click to detach selected element from library item

Click to restore deleted library item

Add a library item to a page

1. Open the about_us page.

2. Delete the copyright and last updated statements at the bottom of the page.

3. Open the Assets panel, drag the **contact_info library item** from the Assets panel to the location from where you deleted the copyright statement, then click to deselect the library item.

   The contact_info item now appears where you placed it. It is shaded in yellow, indicating it is a library item.

4. Click to the right of the library item, then apply the **contact_number rule**.

5. Deselect the text, then compare your screen to Figure 16.

6. Save and close the about_us page.

(continued)

(continued)

Figure 16 *About us page with library item added*

them. A lifeguard is on duty from 9:00 a.m. until sunset. Check the flag each time you head for the beach for the status of current swimming conditions and advisories. Jellyfish can be a problem at times, so be careful when you are walking along the beach, especially as the tide is retreating from high tide. We have beach chairs, umbrellas, and towels available to our guests. Check with the attendant on duty. Water, juices, and soft drinks are also available for purchase at the end of the boardwalk. Don't forget your sunglasses, hat, and sunscreen! A sunburn is sure way to ruin a nice vacation. The gift shop in The Club House is a convenient place to pick up any items that you may have forgotten to bring along, in addition to an extensive inventory of bathing suits, sandals, and other beachwear.

Click the map below to view a larger size image.

Please give us your feedback so that we may make your next stay the best vacation ever!

The Striped Umbrella — 555-594-9458 or 888-594-9458 toll free

Library item

Figure 17 *Activities page with library item added*

It's a short ride over the Alabama border to see the USS Alabama, one of America's most decorated battleships. The "Mighty A" is docked at Battleship Memorial Park in Mobile Bay, Alabama. There you can take a two-hour self-guided tour that is rich in history. Hours, directions, and prices are posted on their website, or call The Club House desk.

See us to pick up your complimentary Umbrella Anchor!

The Striped Umbrella — 555-594-9458 or 888-594-9458 toll free

Library item

7. Repeat Steps 2 through 4 to add the **contact_info** library item to the activities page, as shown in Figure 17, then continue with the cafe, feedback, and spa pages, as well as the activities_pages template.

   If the page has a copyright statement, delete it before you add the library item. On the activities_pages template, enter a line break after the set of three links, then place the library item under links.

   TIP If you have trouble dragging the library item on a page, use the Insert button on the Assets panel instead.

8. Save and preview all of the edited pages in the browser, then close the browser.

9. Close all open pages.

You added the contact_info library item to the about_us, activities, cafe, feedback, and spa pages and the activities_pages template.

Creating Library Items

Although you can create library items with images, text, or a combination of the two, you can use only items that are within the body tags. For instance, when editing a library item, the CSS Styles panel will be unavailable because style sheet code is embedded in the head section, rather than just the body section. Likewise, the Page Properties dialog box will be unavailable because library items cannot include a body tag attribute such as text color. You can apply a rule after you have placed the library item on the page.

Make a library item editable on a page

1. Open the index page, then click the **contact_info library item** in the page footer.

   The Property inspector displays three buttons relating to library items.

2. Click **Detach from original** in the Property inspector.

   A dialog box opens, warning you that the item will no longer be automatically updated when the original library item changes.

3. Click **OK**.

   Notice that the contact information no longer appears in shaded yellow, indicating it is no longer a library item.

4. Type **in Florida** after the first telephone number, then compare your screen to Figure 18.

   The contact information is edited on the page, and the library item and all the uses of it on other pages are unaffected.

5. Save and close the index page.

You detached the contact information from the contact_info library item to make the text editable on the index page. You then added two words to the contact information.

Figure 18 *Editing a library item on a page*

The restaurants at The Striped Umbrella are amazing. The Sand Crab Cafe can be enjoyed al fresco at The Terrace, poolside at The Cabana, and inside in The Dining Room. The Dining Room features fresh seafood and an extensive wine list. The Terrace offers more casual dining with sweeping views of the gulf and fabulous sunsets. The Cabana serves sandwiches, salads, and snacks around the pool area.

Come enjoy the best of both worlds, a secluded sandy beach populated with beautiful birds, yet a short drive down the road from world-class shopping, restaurants, and entertainment. Bring a good book and leave your laptop at the home!

Leave your cares behind!

The Striped Umbrella
25 Beachside Drive
Ft. Eugene, Florida 33775
555-594-9458
Club Manager

Copyright 2002 - 2013
Last updated on May 1, 2010

The Striped Umbrella — 555-594-9458 in Florida or 888-594-9458 toll free

"in Florida" added to text

Figure 19 *Assets panel after deleting the logo library item*

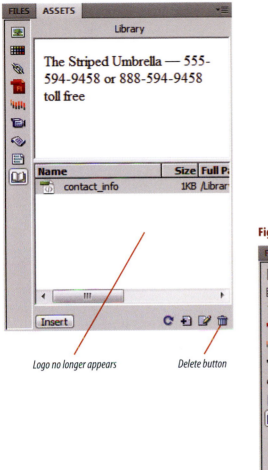

Logo no longer appears

Delete button

Figure 20 *Assets panel after recreating the logo library item*

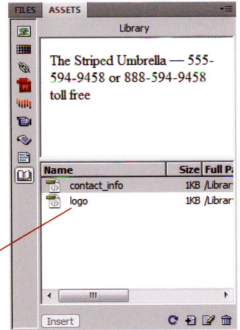

Recreated logo
library item

Delete a library item

1. Select the logo library item on the Assets panel.
2. Click the **Delete button** 🗑 on the Assets panel.

   A dialog box opens, asking if you are sure you want to delete the library item.
3. Click **Yes**, then compare your screen to Figure 19.

   The logo library item no longer appears on the Assets panel. Macintosh users may need to select the contact_info library item to see the change.

You deleted the logo library item on the Assets panel.

Recreate a library item

1. Open the activities_pages template.

   The logo still appears in shaded yellow, indicating it is still a library item, even though you deleted the library item to which it is attached.
2. Click the **logo** to select it.
3. Click **Recreate** in the Property inspector, then compare your screen to Figure 20.

   The logo library item is added to the Assets panel.

   If you do not see the logo library item, refresh the Assets panel.
4. Close the activities_pages template.

You recreated the logo library item that you deleted in the previous set of steps.

Add and Modify
SNIPPETS

What You'll Do

▶ In this lesson, you will add a predefined snippet from the Snippets panel to create a new footer for the index page. You will then replace the placeholder text and links in the snippet with appropriate text and links. Finally, you will save the modified snippet as a new snippet and add it to other pages.

Using the Snippets Panel

Creating a website is a huge task, so it's nice to know that you can save time by using ready-made code snippets to create various elements in your site. The Snippets panel, located in the Files panel group, contains a large collection of reusable code snippets organized in folders and named by element type. The Snippets panel contains two panes, as shown in Figure 21. The lower pane contains folders that can be expanded to view the snippets. The upper pane displays a preview of the selected snippet. Use the buttons at the bottom of the Snippets panel to insert a snippet, create a new folder in the Snippets panel, create a new snippet, edit a snippet, or remove a snippet.

Inserting and Modifying Snippets

Adding a snippet to a page is an easy task; simply drag the snippet from the Snippets panel to the desired location on the page. Once you position a snippet, you will need to replace the placeholder text, links, and images with appropriate content.

QUICK TIP

You can also add a snippet to a page by selecting the snippet in the Snippets panel, then clicking the Insert button on the Snippets panel.

Creating New Snippets

Once you've modified a snippet so that it contains text and graphics appropriate for your site, you might want to save it with a new name. Doing this will save time when using this snippet on other pages. To save a modified snippet as a new snippet, select the snippet content in the Document window, and then click the New Snippet button in the Snippets panel to open the Snippet dialog box. Use this dialog box to name the snippet and give it a description. Because the Snippet dialog box displays the snippet code, you can make edits to the code here if you wish. Any new snippets you create will appear in the Snippets panel.

Figure 21 *Snippets panel*

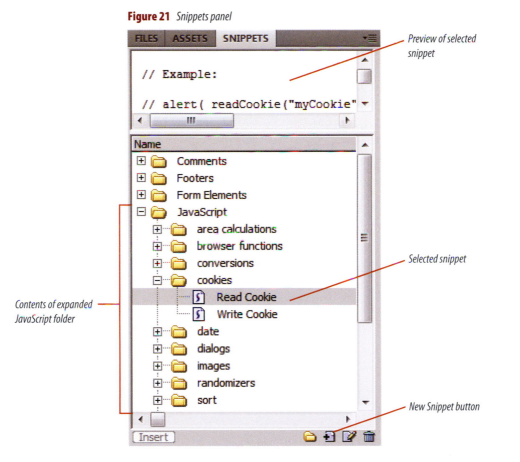

Preview of selected snippet

Selected snippet

Contents of expanded JavaScript folder

New Snippet button

Add a predefined snippet to a page

1. Open the index page.

2. Scroll to the bottom of the page, click to the right of the contact telephone numbers, then add a paragraph break.

3. Click **Window** on the Application bar (Win) or Menu bar (Mac), then click **Snippets** to open the Snippets panel.

4. Click the **plus sign (+)** (Win) or the **triangle** (Mac) next to the Footers folder in the Snippets panel to display the contents of the Footers folder.

5. Drag **Basic: Text Block** in the Footer folder to the bottom of the index page, under the contact telephone numbers, as shown in Figure 22.

   This text will serve as placeholder text until you replace it with the appropriate links for The Striped Umbrella website.

TIP Having a navigation bar with plain text links on each main page of a website ensures maximum accessibility for users.

6. Save your changes.

You added a predefined navigation bar and text block from the Snippets panel.

Figure 22 *Index page after inserting snippet*

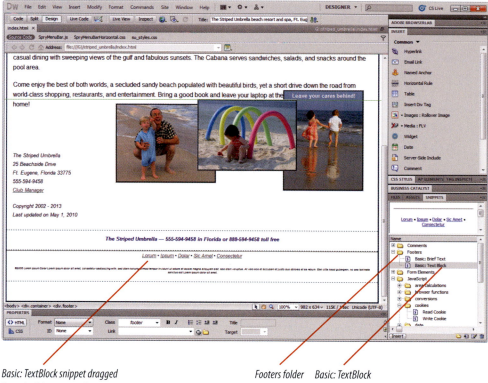

Basic: TextBlock snippet dragged from the Snippets panel

Footers folder   Basic: TextBlock snippet

Figure 23 *Index page after editing snippet placeholder text*

The restaurants at The Striped Umbrella are amazing. The Sand Crab Cafe can be enjoyed al fresco at The Terrace, poolside at The Cabana, and inside in The Dining Room. The Dining Room features fresh seafood and an extensive wine list. The Terrace offers more casual dining with sweeping views of the gulf and fabulous sunsets. The Cabana serves sandwiches, salads, and snacks around the pool area.

Come enjoy the best of both worlds, a secluded sandy beach populated with beautiful birds, yet a short drive down the road from world-class shopping, restaurants, and entertainment. Bring a good book and leave your laptop at home!

Leave your cares behind!

The Striped Umbrella
25 Beachside Drive
Ft. Eugene, Florida 33775
555-594-9458
Club Manager

Last updated on May 1, 2010

The Striped Umbrella — 555-594-9458 in Florida or 888-594-9458 toll free

Lorum • Ipsum • Dolar • Sic Amet • Consectetur
Copyright 2002 - 2013

Move the copyright statement from this location

Placeholder text is replaced with current copyright statement

Modify snippet text

1. Select the placeholder paragraph under the placeholder links, including the paragraph break after "consectetur," then press **[Delete]**.

   You will use the current copyright statement rather than the placeholder text.

2. Cut the current copyright statement (which is under the Club Manager email link), add a line break after the Snippet placeholder links, then paste the copyright statement under the Snippet placeholder links, as shown in Figure 23.

3. Save your work, then preview the page in the browser to make sure the contact_info library item is not behind the first AP div.

4. Close the browser, make any spacing corrections necessary, compare your screen to Figure 23, then save any changes made.

You edited the placeholder text contained in the navigation snippet on the index page.

Modify snippet links

1. Select the Lorum placeholder link, then type **Home**.

2. Replace the Ipsum placeholder link with **About Us**, replace the Dolor placeholder link with **Sand Crab Cafe**, replace the Sic Amet placeholder link with **The Spa**, then replace the Consectetur placeholder link with **Activities**.

3. Select all of the text in the snippet (including the copyright statement if necessary) and apply the **contact_info** rule.

4. Display the Files panel, select the **Home link text** in the footer at the bottom of the home page, then use the Point to File icon ⊕ in the Property inspector to set the Link property to the index page, as shown in Figure 24.

5. Use the Point to File icon ⊕ to set the Link property for the About Us, Sand Crab Cafe, The Spa, and Activities links.

6. Save your changes.

7. Preview the index page in your browser, test all the new navigation links, then close your browser.

You changed the names of the placeholder links and used the Point to File icon to create links to the five main pages in The Striped Umbrella website.

Create a new snippet

1. Select the **navigation footer** on the index page in Code view, as shown in Figure 25, being sure to select the entire div tag code so both lines of text and their formatting are selected.

(continued)

Figure 24 *Using the Point to File icon to create document-relative links in the new navigation links*

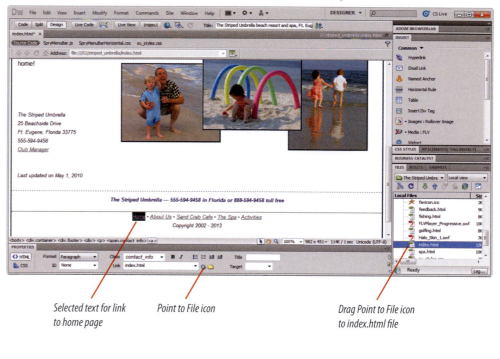

Selected text for link to home page

Point to File icon

Drag Point to File icon to index.html file

Figure 25 *Selecting the code for the snippet*

Select beginning div tag code

Include ending div tag code

Figure 26 *Snippet dialog box*

Name text box

Description text box

Code starts with <div

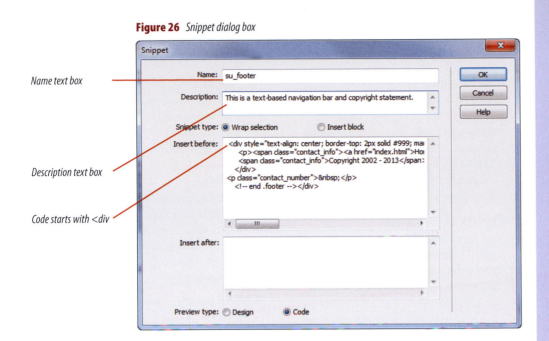

2. Select the Footers folder in the Snippets panel, then click the **New Snippet button** 🔁 to open the Snippet dialog box.

3. Type **su_footer** in the Name text box.

4. Type **This is a text-based navigation bar and copyright statement**. In the Description text box, compare your screen to Figure 26, then click **OK**.

 The new snippet is added to the Snippets panel.

5. Open the about_us page, change to Design view, place the insertion point to the right of the telephone contact information, insert a line break, then drag the **su_footer** from the Snippets panel to the page.

TIP You can also double-click a snippet to insert it on a page.

6. Repeat Step 5 to insert the **su_footer snippet** on all pages in the website, including the activities_pages template, except reset the links in the footer on the activities_pages template.

7. Save and preview all site pages in the browser, close the browser, make any necessary spacing adjustments, then close all open pages.

8. Recreate the site cache, run reports for Untitled Documents, Missing Alt Text, Broken Links, and Orphaned Files; then correct any errors.

 Cafe_logo.gif and two_dolphins_small.jpg are listed as orphaned files. You may also see the crabdance.fla file if you completed the Flash editing steps. These files are no longer needed, so you can move them, delete them, or leave them in the site.

9. Publish your site, then exit Dreamweaver.

You copied the text-based navigation bar from the index page and saved it as a snippet called su_footer. You then copied it to the rest of the main pages.

Create and modify library items.

1. Open the Blooms & Bulbs website, then open the index page.
2. Create a new class rule in the blooms_styles.css file called **telephone** with the following settings: Font-family: Verdana, Geneva, sans-serif; Font-size: 14 pixels; Font-weight: normal; Font-style: normal; Color: #000; Text-align: center.
3. Insert a new paragraph above the copyright statement, type **Blooms & Bulbs (555) 248-0806**, then apply the telephone rule to the text.
4. Select the text you typed in Step 3 if necessary, drag it to the Assets panel with the Library category displayed to create a new library item, then name it **telephone**.
5. Select the copyright statement, then create a new library item named **copyright**.
6. Edit the telephone library item to remove the parentheses around the area code and add a hyphen, then save the library item, update the index page, save the index page, then close the library item.
7. Open the newsletter page, insert blooms_logo.jpg from the drive and folder the drive and folder where you store your Data Files right after the email link near the bottom of the page, then type **Blooms & Bulbs logo** as the alternate text.
8. Right-align the logo, then drag it to the Assets panel to create a new library item, then name it **logo**.
9. Save and close the newsletter page.

Add library items to pages.

1. Open the workshops page, then delete the copyright statement.
2. Insert the telephone library item where you just deleted the copyright statement, click to the right of the library item, then apply the telephone rule to it.
3. Enter a paragraph break, then insert the copyright library item under the telephone library item then apply the footer rule.
4. Repeat Steps 1, 2, and 3 to add the telephone and copyright library items to the newsletter, plants, tips, pages and to the plant_categories template under the set of three links, then apply the telephone style and the footer rules to the library items on each page. Delete any existing copyright statements and update the template-based files after you add the library items to the template page.
5. Save all pages.
6. Delete the telephone library item from the Assets panel.
7. Switch to the index page, select the telephone library item on the page, then re-create it.
8. Save your work and preview all pages in the browser, then make any necessary adjustments to improve spacing.

Add and modify snippets.

1. At the bottom of the index page, insert a paragraph break before the telephone library item.
2. Insert the Basic: Text Block snippet in the new line using the Insert button on the Snippets panel.

3. Replace the placeholder links in the footer with text to link to the home, newsletter, plants, tips, and workshops pages.

4. Create a link for each link in the navigation bar to the appropriate page.

5. Delete the paragraph under the links in the snippet along with the paragraph return above the paragraph.

6. Create a new snippet from the footer you just inserted. Place it in the footer folder. Name the snippet **blooms_nav_footer**, give it an appropriate description, then apply the telephone rule to the footer.

7. Insert the new footer at the bottom of the newsletter, plants, tips, and workshops pages above the telephone library item, and apply the telephone rule to each of them.

8. Insert the footer at the bottom of the plant_categories.dwt page (you may need to use the Insert button instead of dragging), replacing the set of three links to the individual plant pages, apply the telephone rule, reset the links in the footer, then update all pages based on the template.

9. Save all pages, then preview each page in the browser to test the links in the footer to make sure they work. See Figure 27.

10. Close the browser, then close all open pages.

11. Run reports for Missing Alt Text, Untitled Documents, Broken Links, Orphaned Files; then correct any errors that you find. The butterfly.jpg file is listed as an orphaned file. You can delete it, move it to another folder, or leave it in the website if you wish. It is not needed at this time. It was replaced with two new images used in a rollover.

12. Publish your completed site, then exit Dreamweaver.

Figure 27 *Completed Skills Review*

In this Project Builder, you will continue your work on the TripSmart website. You have been given the TripSmart logo to use in the website and decide to create a library item from the logo combined with the copyright statement.

1. Open the TripSmart website, then open the index page.
2. Place the insertion point after the copyright statement, then enter a paragraph break.
3. Insert the file tripsmart_logo.jpg from the drive and folder where you store your Data Files onto the page, adding **TripSmart logo** for the alternate text.
4. Drag the copyright statement to the right of the logo, then delete the word "TripSmart".
5. Create a new class rule named **contact** in the tripsmart_styles.css style sheet with the following settings: Font-family: Arial, Helvetica, sans-serif; Font-size: 12 pixels; Font-weight: bold; Color: #330.
6. Apply the contact rule to the copyright statement.
7. Select both the logo and copyright statement, then use them to create a new library item named **logo**.
8. Save all files, preview the index page in the browser, make any necessary spacing adjustments to improve the page appearance, compare your screen to Figure 28, then close the browser.
9. Open the services page, replace the existing copyright statement with the logo library item, then apply the contact rule.
10. Repeat Step 9 to add the logo library item to the rest of the pages in the website. (*Hint*: To add the logo library item to the accessories, catalog, and clothing

pages, add it to the catalog_pages.dwt file, replacing the existing copyright statement.)
11. Save all files, then preview the pages in the browser.
12. Close the browser, then make any necessary adjustments to improve the page appearance.
13. Close all files, run reports for Missing Alt Text, Untitled Documents, Broken Links, Orphaned Files,

and non-Websafe Colors, then correct any errors that you find. The hats.jpg, pants.jpg, and vest.jpg files are listed as orphaned files. You can delete them, move them to another folder, or leave them in the website if you wish. They are not needed at this time, as they were replaced with a Flash file.
14. Publish your completed site, then exit Dreamweaver.

Figure 28 *Completed Project Builder 1*

In this Project Builder, you will continue your work on the Carolyne's Creations website. Chef Carolyne has asked you to add some plain text links at the bottom of each page to provide viewers with more accessible links that do not depend on the image map at the top of each page.

1. Open the Carolyne's Creations website.
2. Open the index page.
3. Insert two paragraph breaks after the email link in the content div.
4. Create a snippet of your choice to serve as a text-based menu bar at the bottom of the content div, then save the snippet as **cc_footer**.
5. Apply the content rule to the text then compare your screen to Figure 29.
6. Save your work, then preview the page in the browser.
7. Close the browser, then insert the navigation bar snippet at the bottom of the adults, children, classes, catering, fried_green_tomatoes, recipes template, and shop pages. (Remember to reset your links in the footer in the recipes template.)
8. Make any adjustments to the pages to improve the appearance, save your work, then preview each page in the browser.
9. Close the browser, then close all open pages.
10. Run reports for Untitled Documents, Missing Alt Text, Broken Links, and Orphaned Files; then correct any errors.
11. Publish your completed site, then exit Dreamweaver.

Figure 29 *Completed Project Builder 2*

Library items and snippets are commonly used in websites to ensure that repetitive information is updated quickly and accurately.

1. Connect to the Internet, then go to www.usa.gov as shown in Figure 30.
2. Spend some time exploring the pages of this site to become familiar with its elements. Do you see many repeating elements?
3. If you were developing this site, which images or text would you convert into library items? Print two pages from this website and write a list of some of the text and visual elements from these pages that you would make into library items.

Figure 30 *Design Project*

USA.gov website – www.usa.gov

In this project, you will continue to work on the website that you created in Chapter 1.

You will continue to enhance your website by using library items and snippets.

1. Consult your wireframes and decide which text and graphic elements in the site should be converted into library items. Write a list of these items.
2. Discuss what content to include in a footer that you will add to each page of the site using a snippet.
3. Convert all the text elements you identified in your list into library items.
4. Insert the library items that you created in Step 3 in appropriate places in the website.
5. Convert all the graphic elements you identified in Step 1 into library items.
6. Insert the graphic library items that you created in Step 5 in appropriate places in the website.
7. Edit two of the library items that you created, then save and update all instances of the library item in the site.
8. Add a footer to the website using one of the snippets in the Footers folder of the Snippets panel. Replace all placeholder links with appropriate links to each major page in the site and replace placeholder text with text that is suitable for your site.
9. Create a new snippet from the footer that was created in Step 8. Insert this snippet on the other pages of the site.
10. Save your work, preview all pages in a browser, then test all the links. Use the checklist in Figure 31 to make sure your website is complete.
11. Make any necessary changes, then save and close all open pages.
12. Run reports for Untitled Documents, Missing Alt Text, Broken Links, Orphaned Files, and non-Websafe Colors; then correct any errors that you find.
13. Publish your completed site, then exit Dreamweaver.

Figure 31 *Portfolio Project*

Website Checklist
1. Have you converted all repeating text elements into library items?
2. Have you converted all repeating graphic elements, such as logos, into library items?
3. Did you save and update the library items after making edits to them?
4. Do all links work correctly?
5. Did you add a footer to all pages in the website?
6. Did you run the appropriate reports and correct any errors that you found?

ACE CERTIFICATION GRID FOR ADOBE DREAMWEAVER CS5

Topic	Objectives	Chapter(s)
1.0 Understanding Web technologies	1.1 List and describe the infrastructure required to implement and deploy Web sites.	1 (p.1-20, 1-25)
	1.2 Given a scenario, explain the requirements for supporting videos and the SWF format.	11 (p. 11-2, 11-4, 11-5, 11-18, 11-19)
	1.3 Explain how to mitigate page weight.	2 (p. 2-2, 2-32)
	1.4 Describe techniques for making pages accessible.	2 (p. 2-4, 2-5, 2-6, 2-19) 4 (p. 4-13, 4-23) 5 (p. 5-30) 9 (p. 9-18)
2.0 Managing sites	2.1 Given a scenario, create a site. (Scenarios include: using the Site menu bar and Files panel)	1 (p. 1-24, 1-25, 1-29)
	2.2 Manage files associated with a Dreamweaver site. (Including: moving, deleting, renaming, copying)	1 (p. 1-26, 1-27, 1-32, 1-33) 4 (p. 4-19, 4-22)
	2.3 List and describe the methods available for connecting to a remote server. (Methods include: ftp, WebDAV, and local server)	7 (p. 7-16)
	2.4 Use get, put, check-in, and check-out to transfer files.	7 (p. 7-14, 7-26)
	2.5 Configure local, testing, and remote servers.	1 (p. 1-20, 1-21, 1-24, 1-25) 7 (p. 7-14, 7-21)
3.0 Working in Design view	3.1 Describe options available for positioning objects. (Options include: CSS and tables)	6 (p. 6-4, 6-6, 6-24)
	3.2 Given a visual aid, explain the purpose of and/or when to use that visual aid. (Visual aids include: Table borders, CSS layout box model, AP element outlines)	5 (p. 5-12) 6 (p. 6-22, 6-24, 6-25, 6-36, 6-37) 8 (p. 8-23)

CERTIFICATION GRID

(CONTINUED)

ACE CERTIFICATION GRID FOR ADOBE DREAMWEAVER CS5		
Topic	**Objectives**	**Chapter(s)**
	3.3 Work with the Property inspector in Design view.	1 (p. 1-6, 1-31) 2 (p. 2-6, 2-11, 2-13, 2-14, 2-16, 2-21, 2-23, 2-26) 3 (p.3-6 to 3-9, 3-19) 4 (p. 4-6, 4-9, 4-16, 4-26) 5 (p. 5-6, 5-7, 5-8, 5-13, 5-14, 5-19, 5-20) 12 (p. 12-12, 12-18)
	3.4 List and describe the panels and options available when using Design view.	1 (p. 1-4, 1-5, 1-6) 12 (p. 12-6)
4.0 Working in Code view	4.1 Configure preferences for Code view.	3 (p. 3-26, 3-27)
	4.2 Manage code by using Code view. (Options include: Collapsing, word wrap, highlighting invalid code, and formatting)	2 (p. 2-27) 3 (p. 3-26 to 3-29)
	4.3 Find and replace code in Code view. (Options include: entire site and current page)	7 (p. 7-7, 7-8)
	4.4 Explain how to select blocks of code in Code view.	3 (p. 3-30)
5.0 Working with assets	5.1 Create editable areas in templates.	12 (p. 12-4, 12-5, 12-7)
	5.2 Apply a template to a page. (Options include: applying a template to a new page, applying a template to an existing page)	12 (p.12-12, 12-13, 12-15)
	5.3 Create and use editable attributes.	12 (p. 12-20, 12-21)
	5.4 Create and use library items.	Chapter 13

Topic	Objectives	Chapter(s)
	ACE CERTIFICATION GRID FOR ADOBE DREAMWEAVER CS5	
	5.5 Manage assets by using the Assets panel.	1 (p. 1-10) 2 (p. 2-23) 4 (p. 4-7, 4-18, 4-19, 4-22, 4-23) 5 (p. 5-9, 5-31) 12 (p. 12-3 to 12-6)
	5.6 Given a media type, insert and deploy that media type into a page. (Media types include: SWF, FLV, images)	4 (p. 4-6, 4-7, 4-9, 4-10) Chapter 11
6.0 Designing pages with CSS	6.1 Create and work with AP elements.	Chapter 10
	6.2 Create styles for typography and positioning by using the CSS Property inspector.	3 (p. 3-10 to 3-12, 3-22)
	6.3 Describe the Box model.	6 (p. 6-5, 6-16)
	6.4 Create and attach style sheets to pages.	3 (p. 3-12, 3-13, 3-14, 3-24) 5 (p. 5-6)
	6.5 Explain the behavior of inheritance with respect to styles and style sheets.	6 (p. 6-17, 6-38, 6-39, 6-40) 8 (p. 8-22) 10 (p. 10-5, 10-20, 10-23)
	6.6 Explain the meaning of cascading and specificity with respect to CSS.	3 (p. 3-2, 3-10, 3-20, 3-21) 8 (8-22)
	6.7 Explain when and why you would use Inspect mode.	8 (p. 8-23)
7.0 Testing Web pages and sites	7.1 Identify attributes and reports used to ensure that pages and sites conform to accessibility standards.	4 (4-13, 4-23) 7 (p. 7-2 to 7-9)
	7.2 Describe the HTML reports that are available for testing.	7 (p. 7-4, 7-9)
	7.3 Identify and fix broken links.	5 (p. 5-30, 5-31)

CERTIFICATION GRID

(CONTINUED)

ACE CERTIFICATION GRID FOR ADOBE DREAMWEAVER CS5		
Topic	**Objectives**	**Chapter(s)**
8.0 Working with dynamic content	8.1 Given a scenario, describe the infrastructure required to support application servers. (Scenarios include: ColdFusion, ASP, JSP)	9 (p. 9-4, 9-5, 9-6)
	8.2 Describe the functionality provided by the Server Behaviors panel and Bindings panel.	11 (p. 11-17)
	8.3 Explain when and why you would use Live View.	1 (p. 1-4, 1-11) 9 (p. 9-31) 11 (p. 11-5, 11-13)
	8.4 Explain when and why you would use Live Code.	1 (p. 1-11)

(ACA) ADOBE WEB COMMUNICATION USING DREAMWEAVER CS5 OBJECTIVES—DREAMWEAVER CS5 REVEALED		
Topic	**Objective**	**Chapter(s)**
Domain 1.0 Setting Project Requirements	1.1 Identify the purpose, audience, and audience needs for a website.	
	1.1a Identify information that determines purpose, audience, and audience needs for a website.	1 (p. 1-19) 2 (p. 2-6)
	1.2 Identify web page content that is relevant to the website purpose and appropriate for the target audience.	
	1.2a Identify criteria for determining whether content is relevant to the website purpose.	1 (p. 1-19) 2 (p. 2-6)
	1.2b Identify criteria for determining whether content is appropriate for the target audience.	1 (p. 1-19) 2 (p. 2-6)
	1.3 Demonstrate knowledge of standard copyright rules (related terms, obtaining permission, and citing copyrighted material).	
	1.3a Use copyright terms correctly, such as "copyrighted," "fair use doctrine," "intellectual property," and "derivative works."	7 (p. 7-36, 7-39)
	1.3b Identify when permission must be obtained to use copyrighted material.	7 (p. 7-36, 7-39)
	1.3c Identify methods used to indicate content as copyrighted.	7 (p. 7-36, 7-39)
	1.3d Recognize proper methods for citing websites, images, sounds, video, and text from the Internet.	7 (p. 7-39)
	1.4a Define website accessibility.	2 (p. 2-5)
	1.4b Demonstrate knowledge of W3C Priority 1 Checkpoints and the W3C Priority 2 POUR principles for making a website accessible.	2 (p. 2-5, 2-19) 4 (p. 4-13, 4-23)

(ACA) ADOBE WEB COMMUNICATION USING DREAMWEAVER CS5 OBJECTIVES—DREAMWEAVER CS5 REVEALED		
Topic	**Objective**	**Chapter(s)**
	1.4c Explain why including accessibility in website design matters to clients and the target audience.	2 (p. 2-5, 2-6, 2-19) 7 (p. 7-9) 13 (p. 13-29)
	1.4d Identify elements of an HTML page that can be read by screen readers.	2 (p. 2-4) 4 (p. 4-13) 9 (p. 9-18)
	1.5 Make website development decisions based on your analysis and interpretation of design specifications.	
	1.5a Demonstrate knowledge of the relationship between end-user requirements and design and development decisions.	2 (p. 2-6) 7 (p. 7-5, 7-40, 7-41)
	1.5b Identify page elements that are affected by end-user technical factors such as download speed, screen resolution, operating system, and browser type.	2 (p. 2-2, 2-5, 2-6, 2-10, 2-11, 2-30, 2-31, 2-33) 4 (p. 4-2) 7 (p. 7-5)
	1.6 Understand project management tasks and responsibilities.	
	1.6a Identify items that might appear on a project plan.	1 (p. 1-18 to 1-21)
	1.6b Identify phases that might appear on a project plan.	1 (p. 1-18)
	1.6c Identify deliverables that might be produced during the project.	1 (p. 1-19)
	1.6d Identify common problems and issues in project management.	1 (p. 1-21) 7 (p. 7-5, 7-11, 7-22)

(ACA) ADOBE WEB COMMUNICATION USING DREAMWEAVER CS5 OBJECTIVES—DREAMWEAVER CS5 REVEALED		
Topic	**Objective**	**Chapter(s)**
Domain 2.0 Planning Site Design and Page Layout	2.1 Demonstrate general and Dreamweaver-specific knowledge of best practices for designing a website, such as maintaining consistency, separating content from design, using standard fonts, and utilizing visual hierarchy.	
	2.1a Identify attributes of a website that demonstrate consistency.	1 (p. 1-26) 2 (p. 2-2, 2-5, 2-6) 3 (p. 3-2, 3-6, 3-10, 3-11)
	2.1b Identify techniques used to maintain consistency.	1 (p. 1-26) 2 (p. 2-2, 2-6, 2-10, 2-11) 3 (p. 3-2, 3-11, 3-20) 8 (p. 8-2, 8-4) Chapter 12
	2.1c Identify the benefits of consistency.	2 (p. 2-2) 3 (p. 3-2) 8 (p. 8-2, 8-4)
	2.1d Identify benefits of using CSS styles.	2 (p. 2-10, 2-11) 3 (p. 3-2, 3-6, 3-11, 3-20) 8 (p. 8-2, 8-4, 8-5)
	2.1e Identify features used to maintain page structure and content hierarchy.	3 (p. 3-2, 3-7 to 3-9, 3-13)
	2.1f Demonstrate knowledge of fixed and flexible page sizing.	6 (p. 6-4, 6-6, 6-24)
	2.1g Demonstrate knowledge of page layout and CSS design decisions that affect how a web page will print.	6 (p. 6-24) 8 (p. 8-25)
	2.1h Demonstrate knowledge of CSS best practices.	8 (p. 8-2, 8-4, 8-5, 8-22 to 8-25) 10 (p. 10-14, 10-19)

(ACA) ADOBE WEB COMMUNICATION USING DREAMWEAVER CS5 OBJECTIVES—DREAMWEAVER CS5 REVEALED		
Topic	Objective	Chapter(s)
	2.2 Produce website designs that work equally well on various operating systems and browser versions/configurations.	
	2.2a Identify website elements that display differently on various operating systems and browser versions/configurations.	2 (p. 2-5, 2-10) 3 (p. 3-13)
	2.2b Demonstrate knowledge of page elements that may not appear the same in different browsers.	7 (p. 7-5) 8 (p. 8-23)
	2.2c Demonstrate knowledge of BrowserLab online service for cross-browser compatibility testing.	7 (p. 7-5)
	2.3 Demonstrate knowledge of page layout design concepts and principles.	
	2.3a Demonstrate knowledge of graphic design elements and principles.	2 (p. 2-2, 2-5, 2-32) 4 (p. 4-23) 9 (p. 9-4)
	2.3b Identify examples of horizontal symmetry, vertical symmetry, diagonal symmetry, radial symmetry, and asymmetric layout.	2 (p. 2-32) Glossary
	2.3c Recognize examples of page designs that violate design principles or best practices.	2 (p. 2-2, 2-6) 4 (p. 4-2, 4-23)
	2.4 Identify basic principles of website usability, readability, and accessibility.	
	2.4a List elements used to improve website usability.	1 (p. 1-26) 2 (p. 2-2) 3 (p. 3-13) 4 (p. 4-23) 5 (p. 5-30) 9 (p. 9-4) 11 (p. 11-4)

(ACA) ADOBE WEB COMMUNICATION USING DREAMWEAVER CS5 OBJECTIVES—DREAMWEAVER CS5 REVEALED

Topic	Objective	Chapter(s)
	2.4b Demonstrate knowledge of text formatting guidelines that improve readability.	2 (p. 2-5) 3 (p. 3-2, 3-4 to 3-9, 3-13) 4 (p. 4-23) 9 (p. 9-4)
	2.4c Identify specific techniques used to make a website accessible to viewers with visual and motor impairments.	4 (p. 4-13, 4-23) 6 (p. 6-23) 9 (p. 9-13) 11 (p. 11-4) 13 (p. 13-29)
	2.4d Identify elements of a website that by default are not read by screen readers.	4 (p. 4-13)
	2.5 Demonstrate knowledge of flowcharts, storyboards, and wireframes to create web pages and a site map (site index) that maintain the planned website hierarchy.	
	2.5a Demonstrate knowledge of flowcharts.	1 (p. 1-19, 1-20)
	2.5b Demonstrate knowledge of storyboards.	1 (p. 1-19, 1-20)
	2.5c List items that appear on a website design storyboard.	1 (p. 1-19, 1-20)
	2.5d Demonstrate knowledge of wireframes.	1 (p. 1-19, 1-20) 5 (p. 5-32) 6 (p. 6-22)
	2.5e Recognize a website that follows the planned website hierarchy.	1 (p. 1-20) 5 (p. 5-32) 7 (p. 7-40)
	2.6 Communicate with others (such as peers and clients) about design and content plans.	7 (p. 7-22)

(ACA) ADOBE WEB COMMUNICATION USING DREAMWEAVER CS5 OBJECTIVES—DREAMWEAVER CS5 REVEALED

Topic	Objective	Chapter(s)
Domain 3.0 Understanding the Adobe Dreamweaver CS5 Interface	3.1 Identify elements of the Dreamweaver interface.	
	3.1a Identify and label elements of the Dreamweaver interface.	1 (p. 1-4 to 1-6)
	3.1b Demonstrate knowledge of the differences between Design view, Code view, Split view, and Live mode.	1 (p. 1-6, 1-9, 1-11, 1-15) 8 (p. 8-13)
	3.1c Demonstrate knowledge of the Workspace Switcher.	1 (p. 1-10)
	3.1d Demonstrate knowledge of working with related files and the Code Navigator.	1 (p. 1-5) 3 (p. 3-16, 3-17, 3-18, 3-21, 3-25)
	3.2 Use the Insert bar.	
	3.2a Identify types of content that can be created or inserted by using the Insert bar.	1 (p. 1-4) 2 (p. 2-7, 2-8, 2-16, 2-20, 2-22, 2-29) 4 (p. 4-6, 4-8) 9 (p. 9-8, 9-12, 9-14, 9-19 to 9-24, 9-26, 9-28, 9-29) 10 (p. 10-4, 10-17) 11 (p. 11-4, 11-6, 11-10, 11-12,11-20)

Topic	Objective	Chapter(s)
(ACA) ADOBE WEB COMMUNICATION USING DREAMWEAVER CS5 OBJECTIVES—DREAMWEAVER CS5 REVEALED		
	3.2b Demonstrate knowledge of how to change between the categories on the Insert bar.	1 (p. 1-4) 2 (p. 2-7, 2-8, 2-16, 2-20, 2-22, 2-29) 11 (p. 11-6, 11-10, 11-12, 11-20) 12 (p. 12-7, 12-20) 13 (p. 13-6)
	3.3 Use the Property inspector.	
	3.3a Demonstrate knowledge of the various functions of the Property inspector.	1 (p. 1-6, 1-31) 2 (p. 2-6, 2-11, 2-13, 2-14, 2-16, 2-21, 2-26) 3 (p. 3-6 to 3-9, 3-12, 3-14) 4 (p. 4-6, 4-9, 4-16, 4-26) 5 (p. 5-6, 5-7, 5-8, 5-13, 5-14, 5-19, 5-20) 8 (p. 8-9) 9 (p. 9-6, 9-9, 9-19, 9-21, 9-22, 9-26, 9-28, 9-29) 10 (p. 10-7 to 10-13, 10-16, 10-18) 12 (p. 12-9, 12-18) 13 (p. 13-15)

(ACA) ADOBE WEB COMMUNICATION USING DREAMWEAVER CS5 OBJECTIVES—DREAMWEAVER CS5 REVEALED

Topic	Objective	Chapter(s)
	3.4 Use the Assets panel.	
	3.4a Demonstrate knowledge of the Site and Favorites lists on the Assets panel.	4 (p. 4-4, 4-5, 4-7, 4-19, 4-22, 4-23)
	3.4b Identify types of content that can be accessed by using the Assets panel.	2 (p. 2-23) 4 (p. 4-4, 4-5, 4-7, 4-23) 5 (p. 5-9, 5-31) 12 (p. 12-3, 12-5, 12-6, 12-15)
	3.4c Demonstrate knowledge of how to apply assets from the Assets panel to a web page.	4 (p. 4-5) 12 (p. 12-15)
	3.5 Use the Files panel.	
	3.5a Identify uses of the Files panel.	1 (p. 1-2, 1-5, 1-6, 1-10, 1-22, 1-23, 1-27, 1-28, 1-32, 1-33) 2 (p. 2-14, 2-16) 4 (p. 4-19, 4-22) 5 (p. 5-6) 8 (p. 8-6) 11 (p. 11-21)
	3.6 Customize the workspace	
	3.6a Demonstrate how to open, minimize, collapse, close, resize, dock, and undock panels; how to access preset workspaces; how to change document views; how to save a custom workspace.	1 (p. 1-9, 1-10)

(ACA) ADOBE WEB COMMUNICATION USING DREAMWEAVER CS5 OBJECTIVES—DREAMWEAVER CS5 REVEALED

Topic	Objective	Chapter(s)
Domain 4.0 Adding Content by Using Dreamweaver CS5	4.1 Define a Dreamweaver site.	
	4.1a Demonstrate knowledge of the terms "local site," "remote site/folder," "web server," and "root folder."	1 (p. 1-20, 1-21, 1-24, 1-25)
	4.1b Demonstrate knowledge of the steps for defining a new Dreamweaver site.	1 (p. 1-24, 1-25, 1-29)
	4.2 Create, title, name, and save a web page.	
	4.2a Demonstrate knowledge of the steps used to create, save, and name a new HTML page.	1 (p. 1-30, 1-32, 1-33) 6 (p. 6-8)
	4.2b Demonstrate knowledge of rules for naming HTML files.	2 (p. 2-15)
	4.2c Demonstrate knowledge of best practices for naming HTML files.	2 (p. 2-15)
	4.2d Identify the result of naming an HTML file "index.htm(l)" or "default.htm(l)."	1 (p. 1-27) 2 (p. 2-15)
	4.2e Differentiate between document filenames and document or page titles.	1 (p. 1-32) 2 (p. 2-4)
	4.2f Demonstrate knowledge of how to assign a document or page title.	2 (p. 2-6)
	4.3 Add text to a web page.	
	4.3a Demonstrate knowledge of how to add text to an HTML page.	2 (p. 2-10, 2-12, 2-15, 2-16, 2-20) 6 (p. 6-10, 6-11, 6-38)
	4.3b Demonstrate knowledge of the effect of a Return key press and a Shift-Return key press when typing text on an HTML page.	2 (p. 2-12) 5 (p. 5-18)

CERTIFICATION GRID
(CONTINUED)

(ACA) ADOBE WEB COMMUNICATION USING DREAMWEAVER CS5 OBJECTIVES—DREAMWEAVER CS5 REVEALED		
Topic	**Objective**	**Chapter(s)**
	4.4 Insert images and apply alternative text on a web page.	
	4.4a Demonstrate knowledge of the steps for inserting images.	1 (p. 1-31) 2 (p. 2-14) 4 (p. 4-6, 4-7, 4-9, 4-10) 12 (p. 12-14, 12-15)
	4.4b Demonstrate knowledge of how to add alternative text to images by using the Image Tag Accessibility Attributes dialog box or the Property inspector.	4 (p. 4-6, 4-8, 4-10, 4-13, 4-17) 12 (p. 12-14, 12-15)
	4.4c Identify image file types that can be viewed in all browsers.	4 (p. 4-2, 4-4)
	4.4d Demonstrate knowledge of image file types and their uses.	4 (p. 4-4)
	4.4e Demonstrate knowledge of using Photoshop Smart Objects.	4 (p. 4-15)
	4.4f Identify purpose and benefits to using In Context Editing.	6 (p. 6-6) 12 (p. 12-9)
	4.5 Link web content, using hyperlinks, e-mail links, and named anchors.	
	4.5a Demonstrate knowledge of terms "hyperlink," "e-mail link," and "named anchor."	1 (p. 1-12) 2 (p. 2-18) 5 (p. 5-2)
	4.5b Demonstrate knowledge of hyperlinks, including the differences between absolute, site-root-relative, and document-relative hyperlinks.	5 (p. 5-4, 5-5)

Topic	Objective	Chapter(s)
(ACA) ADOBE WEB COMMUNICATION USING DREAMWEAVER CS5 OBJECTIVES—DREAMWEAVER CS5 REVEALED		
	4.5c Demonstrate knowledge of how to link text and images to another web page of the same site.	2 (p. 2-21, 2-22) 4 (p. 4-24, 4-26) 5 (p. 5-8, 5-16, 5-19, 5-20, 5-29, 5-32) 9 (p. 9-32) 12 (p. 12-9, 12-11, 12-12, 12-14)
	4.5d Demonstrate knowledge of how to link text and images to another website.	5 (p. 5-6, 5-7)
	4.5e Demonstrate knowledge of how to link text or images to an e-mail address.	2 (p. 2-18, 2-22)
	4.5f Demonstrate knowledge of how to create and link to a named anchor.	5 (p. 5-10 to 5-15)
	4.5g Demonstrate knowledge of how to target links.	5 (p. 5-28)
	4.6 Insert rich media, such as video, sound, and animation in Flash format.	
	4.6a Demonstrate knowledge of best practices when incorporating Adobe Flash elements into a web page such as embedding, player detection, and alt tags.	11 (p. 11-4, 11-5)
	4.6b Demonstrate knowledge of how to add SWF and Flash video files to a web page.	11 (p. 11-5, 11-6, 11-20, 11-21)
	4.6c Demonstrate knowledge of how to view SWF and Flash video files in Live Mode.	9 (p. 9-31) 11 (p. 11-13, 11-20, 11-23)
	4.7 Insert navigation bars, rollover images, and buttons created in Fireworks on a web page.	
	4.7a Demonstrate knowledge of how to insert navigation bars, rollover images, and buttons created in Fireworks.	5 (p. 5-18) 11 (p. 11-10, 11-11)

(ACA) ADOBE WEB COMMUNICATION USING DREAMWEAVER CS5 OBJECTIVES—DREAMWEAVER CS5 REVEALED		
Topic	**Objective**	**Chapter(s)**
	4.8 Build image maps.	
	4.8a Demonstrate knowledge of the terms "hotspot" and "image map" as used in web page design.	5 (p. 5-26 to 5-29)
	4.8b Demonstrate knowledge of how to create an image map.	5 (p. 5-26 to 5-29)
	4.8c Identify best practices when creating image maps.	5 (p. 5-26)
	4.8d Demonstrate knowledge of how to set properties for a hotspot by using the Property inspector.	5 (p. 5-28, 5-29)
	4.9 Import tabular data to a web page.	
	4.9a Demonstrate knowledge of how to import tabular data.	2 (p. 2-16) 6 (p. 6-36, 6-38)
	4.9b Demonstrate knowledge of table, cell, row, and column properties.	6 (p. 6-22, 6-24, 6-25, 6-36, 6-37)
	4.9c Demonstrate knowledge of how to set and change table, cell, row, and column properties.	6 (p. 6-22 to 6-30, 6-36, 6-37)
	4.9d Demonstrate knowledge of sizing methods used for tables.	6 (p. 6-24, 6-25)
	4.9e Demonstrate knowledge of how to insert and delete columns and rows.	6 (p. 6-26)
	4.9f Demonstrate knowledge of how to merge and split cells.	6 (p. 6-27, 6-30, 6-31)
	4.10 Import and display a Microsoft Word or Microsoft Excel document to a web page.	
	4.10a Demonstrate knowledge of how to add Word or Excel content to a web page.	2 (p. 2-15, 2-16) 6 (p. 6-10) 12 (p. 12-14)

(ACA) ADOBE WEB COMMUNICATION USING DREAMWEAVER CS5 OBJECTIVES—DREAMWEAVER CS5 REVEALED		
Topic	**Objective**	**Chapter(s)**
	4.10b Demonstrate knowledge of the correct settings to use when importing a Word document, based on the content in the document.	2 (p. 2-10, 2-16)
	4.10c Demonstrate knowledge of how to link to a Word or Excel document from a web page.	2 (p. 2-16) 6 (p. 6-38)
	4.11 Create forms.	
	4.11a Demonstrate knowledge of which form inputs are appropriate for collecting various types of information.	9 (p. 9-16 to 9-18)
	4.11b Demonstrate knowledge of how to use Dreamweaver to insert various form elements on a page.	9 (p. 9-13 to 9-29)
	4.11c Demonstrate knowledge of methods used to transmit form data.	9 (p. 9-4 to 9-7)
Domain 5.0 Organizing Content by Using Dreamweaver CS5	5.1 Set and modify document properties.	
	5.1a Identify document properties that can be set or edited globally by using the Page Properties dialog box.	2 (p. 2-4, 2-9) 4 (p. 4-18, 4-20, 4-21)
	5.1b Demonstrate knowledge of how to set or modify global page properties, and global CSS styles, including those for text, links, and background.	2 (p. 2-4, 2-9) 4 (p. 4-18, 4-20, 4-21) 8 (p. 8-2, 8-4, 8-16) 10 (p. 10-19)
	5.1c Differentiate the uses of global CSS rules and CSS rules for div tags.	8 (p. 8-4, 8-5, 8-16)

(ACA) ADOBE WEB COMMUNICATION USING DREAMWEAVER CS5 OBJECTIVES—DREAMWEAVER CS5 REVEALED		
Topic	**Objective**	**Chapter(s)**
	5.2 Organize web page layout with relative and absolutely-positioned div tags and CSS styles.	
	5.2a Demonstrate knowledge of how to insert a div tag in standard mode.	10 (p. 10-4, 10-6)
	5.2b Demonstrate knowledge of the advantages of using div tags instead of tables for page layout.	6 (p. 6-2)
	5.2c Demonstrate knowledge of the distinctions among absolute, relative, fixed, and static positioning.	10 (p. 10-2, 10-9)
	5.2d Demonstrate knowledge of div tag attributes such as height, width, margin, and padding.	10 (p. 10-5, 10-7, 10-14)
	5.2e Demonstrate knowledge of how to modify div tag attributes.	10 (p. 10-5, 10-7, 10-10, 10-12, 10-16, 10-22, 10-25)
	5.2f Demonstrate knowledge of how to display overlapping content on a web page using div tags.	10 (p. 10-2, 10-4,10-12, 10-13)
	5.2g Demonstrate knowledge of how to use external style sheets.	3 (p. 3-20, 3-21, 3-22, 3-23) 8 (p. 8-2, 8-16 to 8-20)
	5.2h Demonstrate knowledge of how to create CSS rules in the property inspector.	8 (p. 8-10)
	5.2i Demonstrate knowledge of how to define, modify, and check CSS rules.	3 (p. 3-15) 6 (p. 6-4, 6-5, 6-15) 8 (p. 8-4, 8-5, 8-8 to 8-15, 8-23, 8-25)
	5.3 Modify text and text properties.	

(ACA) ADOBE WEB COMMUNICATION USING DREAMWEAVER CS5 OBJECTIVES—DREAMWEAVER CS5 REVEALED

Topic	Objective	Chapter(s)
	5.3a Demonstrate knowledge of fonts, including what viewers see if they do not have the selected font installed or if "Default Font" is selected as the font type.	2 (p. 2-10, 2-11)
	5.3b Demonstrate knowledge of how to change font, font size, and color.	3 (p. 3-13, 3-15, 3-18, 3-19, 3-22)
	5.3c Demonstrate knowledge of how to apply a paragraph style to a paragraph of text.	2 (p. 2-16)
	5.3d Demonstrate knowledge of how to indent text to set off a block quotation.	3 (p. 3-9) 5 (p. 5-15) 6 (p. 6-36)
	5.3e Demonstrate knowledge of how to align paragraphs.	2 (p. 2-11)
	5.3f Demonstrate knowledge of ordered, unordered, and definition lists.	3 (p. 3-2, 3-4 to 3-9)
	5.3g Demonstrate knowledge of how to create unordered and ordered lists and how to set properties for a list by using the List Item button in the Property inspector.	3 (p. 3-4 to 3-9)
	5.3h Demonstrate knowledge of how to create definition lists.	3 (p. 3-2, 3-4)
	5.3i Demonstrate knowledge of how to apply emphasis to text by using the Insert menu or the Property inspector.	2 (p. 2-13)
	5.3j Demonstrate knowledge of how to create a custom font stack using the Edit Font list command in the Properties Inspector or for the font-family property in the CSS rule definition dialog box.	2 (p. 2-11) 3 (p. 3-13)
	5.4 Modify images and image properties.	
	5.4a Demonstrate knowledge of the capabilities and limitations of editing or modifying images in Dreamweaver.	4 (p. 4-12, 4-15)
	5.4b Demonstrate knowledge of how to scale an image.	13 (p. 13-10, 13-11)

(ACA) ADOBE WEB COMMUNICATION USING DREAMWEAVER CS5 OBJECTIVES—DREAMWEAVER CS5 REVEALED

Topic	Objective	Chapter(s)
	5.4c Demonstrate knowledge of editing static and interactive assets with Fireworks, Photoshop, and Flash from inside Dreamweaver.	4 (p. 4-15) 11 (p. 11-8, 11-9)
	5.5 Create web page templates.	
	5.5a Demonstrate knowledge of Dreamweaver templates.	2 (p. 2-6) 6 (p. 6-8) Chapter 12
	5.5b Demonstrate knowledge of how to create a new Dreamweaver template.	12 (p. 12-4, 12-6, 12-10)
	5.5c Demonstrate knowledge of how to save an existing HTML file as a Dreamweaver template.	12 (p. 12-4)
	5.5d Demonstrate knowledge of how to create and edit editable regions on a template.	12 (p. 12-7, 12-10)
	5.5e Demonstrate knowledge of how to apply or build pages from templates, and how to detach a template from a page.	12 (p. 12-10, 12-11, 12-12)
	5.6 Use basic HTML tags to set up an HTML document, format text, add links, create tables, and build ordered and unordered lists.	
	5.6a Demonstrate knowledge of HTML tags, including HTML, HEAD, TITLE, BODY, H1–H6, P, EM, STRONG, A HREF, TABLE, TR, TD, OL, LI, UL.	3 (p. 3-7, 3-11, 3-16, 3-27) 4 (p. 4-21) 6 (p. 6-25, 6-29)
	5.7 Add head content to make a web page visible to search engines.	
	5.7a Demonstrate knowledge of head content, meta tags, and tag selector.	2 (p. 2-4, 2-6, 2-7, 2-8) 6 (p. 6-21)
	5.7b Demonstrate knowledge of how to add and edit head content using the Common category in the Insert bar.	2 (p. 2-7, 2-8)

Topic	Objective	Chapter(s)
	5.8 Use CSS to implement a reusable design.	
	5.8a Demonstrate knowledge of how to create inline styles and external style sheets.	3 (p. 3-10, 3-11, 3-12 to 3-15, 3-20)
	5.8b Demonstrate knowledge of how to use CSS to set properties for text and HTML tags.	8 (p. 8-2, 8-4, 8-5, 8-8 to 8-20)
	5.8c Demonstrate knowledge of the advantages of using CSS for design.	6 (p. 6-4) 8 (p. 8-2, 8-4, 8-5)
	5.8d Demonstrate knowledge of how to use CSS Starter Layouts.	6 (p. 6-2, 6-4 to 6-8)
	5.8e Demonstrate knowledge of how to use different selector types such as descendent selectors, classes, the tag selector, pseudo class selectors, and group selectors.	8 (p. 8-22, 8-24)
	5.8f Demonstrate knowledge of how to troubleshoot CSS issues using tools such as CSS layout backgrounds.	6 (p. 6-4, 6-5, 6-15, 6-16)
Domain 6.0 Evaluating and Maintaining a Site by Using Dreamweaver CS5	6.1 Conduct technical tests.	
	6.1a Demonstrate knowledge of how to check spelling on a web page.	2 (p. 2-17) 9 (p. 9-31)
	6.1b Demonstrate knowledge of how to test links by using the Check Links Sitewide command.	5 (p. 5-30, 5-31) 7 (p. 7-2, 7-4, 7-6)
	6.1c Demonstrate knowledge of how to preview a web page in a browser.	2 (p. 2-30, 2-31, 2-33) 7 (p. 7-5)
	6.1d Demonstrate knowledge of how to test a website against a storyboard.	5 (p. 5-32) 7 (p. 7-40)

**(ACA) ADOBE WEB COMMUNICATION USING DREAMWEAVER CS5 OBJECTIVES—DREAMWEAVER CS5 REVEALED**

CERTIFICATION GRID
(CONTINUED)

(ACA) ADOBE WEB COMMUNICATION USING DREAMWEAVER CS5 OBJECTIVES—DREAMWEAVER CS5 REVEALED

Topic	Objective	Chapter(s)
	6.1e Demonstrate knowledge of how to test CSS layouts across web browsers.	6 (p. 6-4, 6-15, 6-16, 6-41) 7 (p. 7-5) 8 (p. 8-23)
	6.2 Identify techniques for basic usability tests.	
	6.2a Demonstrate knowledge of elements involved in conducting a website usability test, such as observation and interviews.	7 (p. 7-18)
	6.3 Identify methods for collecting site feedback.	
	6.3a Demonstrate knowledge of methods for collecting viewer feedback and site evaluation information to determine if the site meets intended goals and user needs.	2 (p. 2-7, 2-18) 7 (p. 7-5, 7-18) 8 (p. 8-23, 8-25) 9 (p. 9-2, 9-4, 9-30, 9-32, 9-33)
	6.4 Present web pages to others (such as team members and clients) for feedback and evaluation.	7 (p. 7-5, 7-19, 7-40, 7-41)
	6.5 Manage assets, links, and files for a site.	
	6.5a Demonstrate knowledge of how to delete files by using the Files panel.	4 (p. 4-19, 4-22) 7 (p. 7-4)
	6.5b Demonstrate knowledge of how to rename files and update links by using the Files panel.	1 (p. 1-27)
	6.5c Demonstrate knowledge of how to link files by dragging, using the Point-to-File icon in the Property inspector and the Files panel.	2 (p. 2-21) 5 (p. 5-14)
	6.5d Demonstrate knowledge of the terms "Get," "Put," "Check In," "Check Out," "Publish," and "Remote Server" as they apply to managing files and publishing a website.	7 (p. 7-14 to 7-26)

(ACA) ADOBE WEB COMMUNICATION USING DREAMWEAVER CS5 OBJECTIVES—DREAMWEAVER CS5 REVEALED

Topic	Objective	Chapter(s)
	6.5e Demonstrate knowledge of expanding and collapsing the Files panel to access features such as the site map, get and put, check in and out, and refreshing the Files panel.	7 (p. 7-20, 7-22 to 7-25)
	6.5f Demonstrate knowledge of using file management techniques such as Subversion control and check-in/check-out when working in teams.	7 (p. 7-22 to 7-25, 7-26 to 7-29)
	6.5g Demonstrate knowledge of using the Related Files toolbar.	1 (p. 1-5) 3 (p. 3-21, 3-25)
	6.5h Demonstrate knowledge of FTP server and Web server relationships to a Dreamweaver site.	1 (p. 1-21, 1-24) 7 (p. 7-14 to 7-21)
	6.6 Publish and update site files to a remote server.	
	6.6a Demonstrate knowledge of how to set up a connection to a remote server.	1 (p. 1-21, 1-24, 1-25) 7 (p. 7-17 to 7-21)
	6.6b Demonstrate knowledge of how to publish files to a remote server.	1 (p. 1-21, 1- 24) 7 (p. 7-14 to 7-21)
	6.6c Demonstrate knowledge of how to use the Files panel to connect to and disconnect from a remote site, how to upload files to a remote site, and how to download files from a remote site.	1 (p. 1-21, 1-24) 7 (p. 7-15, 7-20)

Read the following information carefully.

Find out from your instructor the location where you will store your files.

- To complete many of the chapters in this book, you need to use the Data Files provided on the CD at the back of this book.
- Your instructor will tell you whether you will be working from the CD or copying the files to a drive on your computer or on a server. Your instructor will also tell you where you will store the files you create and modify.
- All the Data Files are organized in folders named after the chapter in which they are used. For instance, all Chapter 1 Data Files are stored in the chapter_1 folder. You should leave all the Data Files in these folders; do not move any Data File out of the folder in which it is originally stored.

Copy and organize your Data Files.

- Copy the folders that contain the Data Files to a USB storage device, network folder, hard drive, or other storage device if you will not be working from the CD.
- As you build each website, the exercises in this book will guide you to copy the Data Files you need from the appropriate Data Files folder to the folder where you are storing the website. Your Data Files should always remain intact because you are copying (and not moving) them to the website.
- Because you will be building a website from one chapter to the next, sometimes you will need to use a Data File that is already contained in the website you are working on.

Find and keep track of your Data Files and completed files.

- Use the **Data File Supplied** column to make sure you have the files you need before starting the chapter or exercise indicated in the **Chapter** column.
- Use the **Student Creates File** column to find out the filename you use when saving your new file for the exercise.

ADOBE DREAMWEAVER CS5			
Chapter	**Data File Supplied**	**Student Creates File**	**Used In**
Chapter 1	dw1_1.html		Lesson 2
	assets/pool.jpg		
	assets/su_banner.gif		
	dw1_2.html	about_us.html	Lesson 4
	assets/su_banner.gif	activities.html	
		cafe.html	
		cruises.html	
		fishing.html	
		index.html	
		spa.html	
	dw1_3.html	annuals.html	Skills Review
	dw1_4.html	index.html	
	assets/blooms_banner.jpg	newsletter.html	
	assets/tulips.jpg	perennials.html	
		plants.html	
		tips.html	
		water_plants.html	
		workshops.html	
	dw1_5.html	catalog.html	Project Builder 1
	assets/tripsmart_banner.jpg	china.html	
		index.html	

ADOBE DREAMWEAVER CS5			
Chapter	**Data File Supplied**	**Student Creates File**	**Used In**
Chapter 1, continued		newsletter.html	
		services.html	
		spain.html	
		tours.html	
	dw1_6.html	adults.html	Project Builder 2
	assets/cc_banner.jpg	catering.html	
		children.html	
		classes.html	
		index.html	
		recipes.html	
		shop.html	
			Design Project
			Portfolio Project
Chapter 2	dw2_1.html		Lesson 2
	spa.doc		
	assets/sea_spa_logo.jpg		
	assets/su_banner.gif		
	dw2_2.html		Skills Review
	gardening_tips.doc		
	assets/blooms_banner.jpg		
	assets/butterfly.jpg		

ADOBE DREAMWEAVER CS5			
Chapter	**Data File Supplied**	**Student Creates File**	**Used In**
Chapter 2, continued			Project Builder 1
			Project Builder 2
			Design Project
			Portfolio Project
Chapter 3	questions.doc		Lesson 1
		su_styles.css	Lesson 2
		blooms_styles.css	Skills Review
	dw3_1.html		Project Builder 1
		tripsmart_styles.css	
	assets/tripsmart_banner.jpg		
	dw3_2.html	cc_styles.css	Project Builder 2
	assets/cc_banner.jpg		
	assets/pie.jpg		
			Design Project
			Portfolio Project
Chapter 4	dw4_1.html		Lesson 1
	assets/boardwalk.png		
	assets/club_house.jpg		
	assets/stripes_back.gif		Lesson 3
	assets/su_banner.gif		
	assets/su_logo.gif		
	assets/umbrella_back.gif		

ADOBE DREAMWEAVER CS5			
Chapter	**Data File Supplied**	**Student Creates File**	**Used In**
Chapter 4, continued	favicon.ico		Lesson 4
	assets/map_large.jpg		
	assets/map_small.jpg		
	dw4_2.html		Skills Review
	flower.ico		
	assets/blooms_banner.jpg		
	assets/daisies.jpg		
	assets/rose_bloom.jpg		
	assets/rose_bud.jpg		
	assets/two_roses.jpg		
	assets/two_roses_large.jpg		
	dw4_3.html		Project Builder 1
	airplane.ico		
	assets/bull_fighter.jpg		
	assets/stallion.jpg		
	assets/tripsmart_banner.jpg		
	dw4_4.html		Project Builder 2
	assets/cc_banner.jpg		
	assets/paella.jpg		
	assets/paella_pan.jpg		
			Design Project
			Portfolio Project

ADOBE DREAMWEAVER CS5			
Chapter	**Data File Supplied**	**Student Creates File**	**Used In**
Chapter 5	dw5_1.html		Lesson 1
	assets/su_banner.gif		
	assets/herron_waiting_small.jpg		
	assets/two_dolphins_small.jpg		
	SpryAssets/SpryMenuBar.js	SpryAssets/SpryMenuBar.js	Lesson 3
	SpryAssets/SpryMenuBarDown.gif	SpryAssets/SpryMenuBarDown.gif	
	SpryAssets/SpryMenuBarDownHover.gif	SpryAssets/SpryMenuBarDownHover.gif	
	SpryAssets/SpryMenuBarHorizontal.css	SpryAssets/SpryMenuBarHorizontal.css	
	SpryAssets/SpryMenuBarRight.gif	SpryAssets/SpryMenuBarRight.gif	
	SpryAssets/SpryMenuBarRightHover.gif	SpryAssets/SpryMenuBarRightHover.gif	
	dw5_2.html		Lesson 5
	dw5_3.html		
	assets/boats.jpg		
	assets/heron_small.jpg		
	dw5_4.html		Skills Review
	dw5_5.html		
	dw5_6.html		
	dw5_7.html		
	assets/blooms_banner.jpg		

Data Files List

ADOBE DREAMWEAVER CS5			
Chapter	**Data File Supplied**	**Student Creates File**	**Used In**
Chapter 5, continued	assets/coleus.jpg		
	assets/grass.jpg		
	assets/plants.jpg		
	assets/ruby__grass.jpg		
	assets/trees.jpg		
	assets/water_lily.jpg		
	SpryAssets/SpryMenuBar.js	SpryAssets/SpryMenuBar.js	
	SpryAssets/SpryMenuBarDown.gif	SpryAssets/SpryMenuBarDown.gif	
	SpryAssets/SpryMenuBarDownHover.gif	SpryAssets/SpryMenuBarDownHover.gif	
	SpryAssets/SpryMenuBarHorizontal.css	SpryAssets/SpryMenuBarHorizontal.css	
	SpryAssets/SpryMenuBarRight.gif	SpryAssets/SpryMenuBarRight.gif	
	SpryAssets/SpryMenuBarRightHover.gif	SpryAssets/SpryMenuBarRightHover.gif	
	dw5_8.html		Project Builder 1
	dw5_9.html		
	dw5_10.html		
	assets/gaudi_dragon.jpg		
	assets/great_wall.jpg		
	assets/panda.jpg		
	assets/tripsmart_banner.jpg		

ADOBE DREAMWEAVER CS5			
Chapter	**Data File Supplied**	**Student Creates File**	**Used In**
Chapter 5, continued	assets/warriors.jpg		
	SpryAssets/SpryMenuBar.js	SpryAssets/SpryMenuBar.js	
	SpryAssets/SpryMenuBarDown.gif	SpryAssets/SpryMenuBarDown.gif	
	SpryAssets/SpryMenuBarDownHover.gif	SpryAssets/SpryMenuBarDownHover.gif	
	SpryAssets/SpryMenuBarHorizontal.css	SpryAssets/SpryMenuBarHorizontal.css	
	SpryAssets/SpryMenuBarRight.gif	SpryAssets/SpryMenuBarRight.gif	
	SpryAssets/SpryMenuBarRightHover.gif	SpryAssets/SpryMenuBarRightHover.gif	
	dw5_11.html		Project Builder 2
	dw5_12.html		
	dw5_13.html		
	assets/cc_banner_with_text.jpg		
	assets/children_cooking.jpg		
	assets/cookies_oven.jpg		
	assets/dumplings1.jpg		
	assets/dumplings2.jpg		
	assets/dumplings3.jpg		
	assets/fish.jpg		
			Design Project
			Portfolio Project

ADOBE DREAMWEAVER CS5			
Chapter	**Data File Supplied**	**Student Creates File**	**Used In**
Chapter 6	cafe.doc		Lesson 2
	assets/cafe_logo.gif		
	assets/cafe_photo.jpg		
	assets/chocolate_cake.jpg		Lesson 6
	composting.doc		Skills Review
	assets/chives.jpg		
	assets/gardening_gloves.gif		
	assets/hat.jpg		Project Builder 1
	assets/pants.jpg		
	assets/vest.jpg		
	menu_items.doc		Project Builder 2
	assets/muffins.jpg		
			Design Project
			Portfolio Project
Chapter 7		The Striped Umbrella.ste	Lesson 5
		Blooms & Bulbs.ste	Skills Review
		TripSmart.ste	Project Builder 1
		Carolyne's Creations.ste	Project Builder 2
			Design Project
			Portfolio Project

ADOBE DREAMWEAVER CS5			
Chapter	**Data File Supplied**	**Student Creates File**	**Used In**
Chapter 8	striped_umbrella folder with new website files		Lesson 1
	blooms folder with new website files		Skills Review
	tripsmart folder with new website files		Project Builder 1
	cc folder with new website files		Project Builder 2
Chapter 9	dw9_1.html	feedback.html	Lesson 1
	assets/su_banner.gif		
Chapter 10	assets/looking_at_birds.jpg		Lesson 3
	assets/noodles.jpg		
	assets/two_children_on_beach.jpg		
	assets/spring_bloom.jpg		Skills Review
	assets/sea_lions.jpg		Project Builder 1
	assets/cream_cheese_eggs.jpg		Project Builder 2
Chapter 11	crabdance.fla		Lesson 1
	crabdance.swf		
	assets/one_dolphin.jpg		Lesson 2
	assets/two_dolphins.jpg		
	dw11_1.html	wildlife_message.html	Lesson 3
	umbrella_anchor_movie.flv		Lesson 4

Data Files List

ADOBE DREAMWEAVER CS5			
Chapter	Data File Supplied	Student Creates File	Used In
Chapter 11, continued	garden_quote.swf		Skills Review
	hanging_baskets.flv		
	assets/butterfly1.jpg		
	assets/butterfly2.jpg		
	catalog.fla		Project Builder 1
	dw11_2.html	spain_trip.html	
	catalog.swf		
	sugared_flowers.flv		Project Builder 2
Chapter 12		activities_pages.dwt	Lesson 1
	golf.doc	golfing.html	Lesson 2
	assets/golfer.jpg		
	assets/ladies_group.jpg		
	annuals.doc	plant_categories.dwt	Skills Review
	perennials.doc	water_plants.html	
	water_plants.doc		
	catalog2.fla	catalog_items.dwt	Project Builder 1
	catalog2.html	accessories.html	
	catalog2.swf	clothing.html	
	assets/two_customers.jpg		
	fried_green_tomatoes.doc	fried_green_tomatoes.html	Project Builder 2
	assets/fried_green_tomatoes.jpg	recipes.dwt	

ADOBE DREAMWEAVER CS5			
Chapter	**Data File Supplied**	**Student Creates File**	**Used In**
Chapter 12, continued			Project Builder 2
			Design Project
			Portfolio Project
Chapter 13	assets/blooms_logo.jpg		Skills Review
	assets/tripsmart_logo.gif		Project Builder 1

GLOSSARY

A

Absolute path
A path containing an external link that references a link on a web page outside of the current website, and includes the protocol "http" and the URL, or address, of the web page.

Absolute positioning
Refers to the way that a page element, such as an AP element, is locked in a fixed position on a page.

Action property
A form property that specifies the application or script that will process the data in a form.

ActionScript
A Flash scripting language developers use to add interactivity to movies, control objects, exchange data, and create complex animations.

Active Server Pages (ASP)
Server-side application used for processing data in a form.

Add-ons
Program extensions that add features to an existing application. Also called plug-ins.

Adobe AIR
An Adobe product used for developing content that can be delivered with a browser or as a desktop application.

Adobe Bridge
A standalone application that serves as the hub for the Adobe Create Suite 5. Can be used for file management tasks such as opening, viewing, sorting, and rating files.

Adobe BrowserLab
An Adobe online service for cross-browser and cross-platform compatibility testing.

Adobe Community Help
A collection of materials such as tutorials, published articles, or blogs, which is part of the Adobe Help content.

Adobe CSS Advisor
A part of the Adobe website that offers solutions for resolving issues with your web pages.

Aligning an image
Positioning an image on a web page in relation to other elements on the page.

All Rules pane
The top half of the CSS Styles panel that displays a list of the style sheets and rules for the open page when the Switch to All (document) Mode button is selected.

Alternate text
Descriptive text that can be set to appear in place of an image while the image is downloading. Alternate text is used by screen readers to describe images to users with visual impairment.

AP div
A div that is assigned a fixed position on a web page; the term AP stands for absolute position.

AP div tag
A div that creates a container with a fixed position on a web page.

AP element
The resulting container that an AP div tag creates on a page.

AP Elements panel
Panel in the CSS panel group that is used to control the visibility, name, and Z-Index stacking order of AP elements on a web page.

Apache web server
A public domain, open source web server that is available using several different operating systems including UNIX and Windows.

Application bar (Win)
The toolbar located above the Document window which includes menu names, a Workspace switcher, and other application commands.

Assets
Files that are not web pages, such as images, Flash files, and video clips.

Assets folder
A subfolder in the local site root folder in which you store most of the files that are not web pages, such as images, Flash files, and video clips. This folder is often named images, but can be assigned any name.

Assets panel
A panel that contains nine categories of assets, such as images, used in a website. Clicking a category button displays a list of those assets.

Asymmetrical balance
A design principle in which page elements are placed unevenly on either side of an imaginary vertical line in the center of the page to create a feeling of tension or express a feeling or mood.

Asynchronous JavaScript and XML (AJAX)
Method for developing interactive web pages that respond quickly to user input, such as clicking a map.

AVI (Audio visual Interleave)
The Microsoft standard for digital video format.

─────── **B** ───────

Background color
A color that fills an entire web page, frame, table, cell, or CSS layout block.

Background image
A graphic file used in place of a background color.

Banner
Image that generally appears across the top or down the side of a web page and can incorporate a company's logo, contact information, and links to the other pages in the site.

BaseCamp
A web-based project collaboration tool.

Behavior
Simple action scripts that let you incorporate interactivity by modifying content based on variables like user actions. A behavior tells a page object to respond in a specific way when an event occurs, such as when the mouse pointer is positioned over the object.

Blog
A website where the website owner regularly posts commentaries and opinions on various topics.

Body
The part of a web page that appears in a browser window. It contains all of the page content that is visible to users, such as text, images, and links.

Border
An outline that surrounds a cell, a table, or a CSS layout block.

Breadcrumbs trail
A list of links that provides a path from the initial page opened in a website to the page being currently viewed.

Broken links
Links that cannot find the intended destination file for the link.

Browser
Software used to display web pages, such as Microsoft Internet Explorer, Mozilla Firefox, Google Chrome, or Apple Safari.

Browser Compatibility Check (BCC)
A Dreamweaver feature that checks for problems in the HTML code that might present a CSS rendering issue in some browsers by underlining questionable code in green.

Browser Navigation toolbar
A toolbar that contains navigation buttons you use when you are following links on your pages in Live view.

Buffer
A temporary storage area on your hard drive that acts as a holding area for Flash content as it is being played.

Bullet
A small dot or similar icon preceding unordered list items.

Bulleted list
An unordered list that uses bullets.

─────── **C** ───────

Camera raw files
Camera raw file formats are files that contain unprocessed data and are not yet ready to be printed, similar to a negative from a film camera.

Cascading
The way styles are ranked in order of precedence as they are applied to page elements.

Cascading Style Sheets (CSS)
Sets of formatting attributes used to format web pages to provide a consistent presentation for content across the site.

Cell padding
The distance between the cell content and the cell walls in a table.

Cell spacing
The distance between cells in a table.

Cell walls
The edges surrounding a cell in a table.

Cells
Small boxes within a table that are used to hold text or graphics. Cells are arranged horizontally in rows and vertically in columns.

Check box
A form object used to create a list of options from which users can make multiple selections.

Check in files

A Dreamweaver feature that is used in a team environment to allow access to a file by team members when another team member has completed work on it.

Check out files

A Dreamweaver feature that is used in a team environment to restrict access to a file by team members when it is currently being edited by another team member.

Child container

A container created with HTML tags whose code resides inside a parent container. Its properties are inherited from its parent container unless otherwise specified.

Child page

A page at a lower level in a web hierarchy that links to page at a higher level called a parent page.

Class style

A combination of formatting attributes that can be applied to a block of text or other page elements; a class style name begins with a period. Also called custom style.

Class type

See Custom type.

Clean HTML code

HTML code that performs its function without using unnecessary instructions, which take up memory.

Client-side scripting

The user's computer processes a form, rather than a web server.

Clip property

A property that determines the portion of a AP div's content that will be visible when displayed in a web browser.

Cloak

To mark a file, folder, or file type for exclusion from several commands, including Put, Get, Synchronize, Check In, and Check Out.

Cloaked file

A file that is marked to be excluded from certain processes, such as being transferred to the remote site.

Code hints

An auto-complete feature that displays lists of tags that appear as you type in Code view.

Code Inspector

A separate floating window that displays the current page in Code view.

Code snippets

Ready-made, reusable pieces of code you can insert on a web page.

Code view

Code view shows the underlying HTML code for the page; use this view to read or edit the **code.**

Coding toolbar

A toolbar that contains buttons that are used when working in Code view.

Cold Fusion

Server-side application used for processing data in a form.

Columns

Table cells arranged vertically.

Comments

Helpful text describing portions of the HTML code, such as a JavaScript function. Comments are inserted in the code and are not visible in the browser window.

Common Gateway Interface (CGI)

Server-side application used for processing data in a form.

Compound type

A type of style that is used to format a selection.

Copyright

A legal protection for the particular and tangible expression of an idea. The right of an author or creator of a work to copy, distribute, and modify a thing, idea, or image; a type of intellectual property.

CS Live

A management feature of the Adobe Creative Suite that can be used to organize your work whether you work in groups or by yourself; it is accessed through the CS Live list arrow on the Application bar or through the Window, Extensions, Access CS Live command.

CSS block

See CSS Layout block

CSS layout block

A section of a web page defined and formatted using a Cascading Style Sheet. Also called CSS block.

CSS Layout Box Model

CSS layout blocks defined as rectangular boxes of content with margins, padding, and borders.

CSS page layout
A method of positioning objects on web pages through the use of containers formatted with CSS.

Custom button
In a form, a button that triggers action that you specify on the page.

Custom style
See Class style.

Custom type
A type of style that can contain a combination of formatting attributes that can be applied to a block of text or other page elements. Custom style names begin with a period (.). Also known as a class type.

D

Debug
To find and correct coding errors.

Declaration
The property and value of a style in a Cascading Style Sheet.

Default base font
Size 3 (Dreamweaver). The default font that is applied to any text without an assigned size on a web page.

Default font color
The color the browser uses to display text if no other color is assigned.

Default link color
The color the browser uses to display links if no other color is assigned.

Defining a website
Specifying a website's name and the location of the local site root folder using the Dreamweaver Site Setup dialog box.

Definition lists
Lists made up of terms with indented descriptions or definitions.

Delimited files
Database, word processing, or spreadsheet files that have been saved as text files with data separated with delimiters.

Delimiter
A comma, tab, colon, semicolon, or similar character that separates tabular data.

Deliverables
Products that will be provided to the client at the product completion such as pages or graphic elements created.

Dependent file
File that another file needs to be complete, such as an image or style sheet.

Derivative work
An adaptation of another work, such as a movie version of a book. A new, original product that includes content from a previously existing work.

Description
A short summary that resides in the head section of a web page and describes the website content.

Design notes
Separate files in a website that contain additional information about a file and are not displayed in a browser.

Design view
Design view shows the page as it would appear in a browser and is primarily used for creating and designing a web page.

Diagonal symmetry
A design principle in which page elements are balanced along the invisible diagonal line of the page.

Div tag
An HTML tag that is used to format and position web page elements.

Dock
A collection of panels or panel groups.

Document toolbar
A toolbar that contains buttons and drop-down menus for changing the current work mode, checking browser compatibility, previewing web pages, debugging web pages, choosing visual aids, and viewing file management options.

Document window
The large area under the document toolbar in the Dreamweaver workspace where you create and edit web pages.

Document-relative path
A path referenced in relation to the web page that is currently displayed.

Domain name
An IP address expressed in letters instead of numbers, usually reflecting the name of the business represented by the website. Also referred to as a URL.

Down Image state
The state of a page element when the element has been clicked with the mouse pointer.

Download
The process of transferring files from a remote site to a local site.

Download time
The time it takes to transfer a file to another computer.

Dreamweaver workspace
The Dreamweaver program screen that includes all of the menus, panels, buttons, inspectors, and panes that you use to create and maintain websites.

Drop zone
A heavy blue line that indicates where a palette or panel can be docked.

DSL
Digital Subscriber Line. A type of high-speed Internet connection.

Dual Screen layout
A layout that utilizes two monitors while working in Dreamweaver.

Dynamic content
Content that allows the user to interact with the page by clicking or typing, and then responds to this input in some way.

E

Editable optional region
An area on a template where users can add or change content, and that users can also choose to show or hide.

Editable region
An area in a template where users of the template can add or change content.

Embedded style
Styles that are part of an HTML page rather than comprising a separate file. Also called internal styles, internal CSS, or embedded CSS.

Expanded Tables Mode
A Dreamweaver mode that displays tables with temporary cell padding and spacing to make it easier to see the individual table cells.

Export data
To save data that was created in Dreamweaver in a special file format so that you can open it in another software program.

External links
Links that connect to web pages in other websites or to an e-mail address.

External Style Sheet
Collection of styles stored in a separate file that control the formatting of content on a web page. External style sheets have a .css file extension. Also called external styles or external CSS.

F

Facebook
A social networking site. *See also* Social networking.

Fair use
Allows a user to make a copy of all or part of a work, even if permission *has not* been granted.

Favicon
Short for favorites icon. A small icon that represents your site, similar to a logo, that appears next to the title of a web page in a browser.

Favorites
Assets that are used repeatedly in a website and are included in their own category in the assets panel.

Fieldset
An HTML tag used to group related form elements together.

File field
Form object that allows users to upload files to a web server.

File Transfer Protocol
See FTP.

Files panel
A window similar to Windows Explorer (Windows) or Finder (Macintosh), where Dreamweaver stores and manages files and folders. The Files panel contains a list of all the folders and files in a website.

Fixed layout
A fixed page layout that expresses all container widths in pixels and remains the same size regardless of the size of the browser window.

Flash button
A button made from a small, predefined Flash movie.

Flash Player
A free Adobe program that allows Flash movies (.swf and .exe formats) to be viewed on a computer.

Flash video files
Files created in Flash that can include both video and audio and area saved with the .flv file extension.

Floating workspace
A feature of Adobe products that allows each document and panel to appear in its own window.

Focus group
A focus group is a marketing tool that asks a group of people for feedback about a product, such as the impact of a television ad or the effectiveness of a website design.

Font combination
A set of three font choices that specify which fonts a browser should use to display text on your screen; if one font is not available, the browser will use the next one specified in the font combination. Also called font-family.

Font-family
See Font combination.

Form control
See Form object.

Form element
See Form object.

Form field
See Form object.

Form input
See Form object.

Form label
A label that identifies a form object by its function.

Form name property
A form property that specifies a unique name for the form.

Form object
An object on a web page, such as a text box, radio button, or check box, that collects information from users. Also referred to as form element, form control, or form field.

Frameset
Multiple web pages displayed together using more than one frame or window.

FTP
File Transfer Protocol. The process of uploading and downloading files to and from a remote site.

—————— **G** ——————

GET method
A form property that specifies that ASCII data collected in the form will be sent to the server appended to the URL or to the file included in the Action property.

GIF file
Graphics Interchange Format file. A GIF is a type of file format used for images placed on web pages that can support both transparency and animation.

Global CSS rule
A rule that affects all website content.

Google Video Chat
A free application program that you can use to communicate live with other people through video conferencing.

GPS
Global Positioning System. Devices are used to track your position through a global satellite navigation system.

Graphic
Picture or design element that adds visual interest to a page.

Grids
Horizontal and vertical lines that fill the page and are used to place page elements.

Guides
Horizontal and vertical lines that you drag from the rulers onto the page to help you align objects.

—————— **H** ——————

Head content
The part of a web page that includes the page title that appears in the title bar of the browser and meta tags, which are HTML codes that include information about the page, such as keywords and descriptions, and are not visible in the browser.

Headings
Six different formats that can be applied to text: Heading 1 (the largest size) through Heading 6 (the smallest size).

Height (H) property
A property that specifies the height of an AP div either in pixels or as a percentage of the screen height.

Hex triplet
An RGB value in hexadecimal format. *See also* Hexadecimal RGB value.

Hexadecimal RGB value
A value that represents the amount of red, green, and blue in a color and is based on the Base 16 number system.

Hidden field
Form object that makes it possible to provide information to the web server and form-processing script without the user knowing that the information is being sent.

History panel

Contains a record of each action performed during an editing session. Up to 1000 levels of Undo are available through the History panel (20 levels by default).

Home page

The first page that is displayed when users go to a website.

Horizontal and vertical space

Blank space above, below, and on the sides of an image that separates the image from the text or other elements on the page.

Horizontal symmetry

A design principle in which page elements are balanced side-to-side across the page.

Hotspot

A clickable area on an image that, when clicked, links to a different location on the page or to another web page.

HTML

Hypertext Markup Language. A language web developers use to create web pages.

HTTP

The set of rules that determines how web pages are formatted and transmitted over the World Wide Web.

Hyperlinks

Image or text elements on a web page that users click to display another location on the page, another web page on the same website, or a web page on a different website. Also called links.

Hypertext Transfer Protocol Secure (HTTPS)

The set of rules (protocol) for transferring secure information over the Internet.

I

ID type

A type of CSS rule that is used to redefine an HTML tag.

If statement

A statement that checks to see if a condition is true for an optional region in a template, then either displays or hides the optional region based on the results.

Image

A graphic such as a photograph or a piece of artwork on a web page. Images in a website are known as assets.

Image form field

A form field that contains an image; can use them to create buttons that contain custom graphics.

Image map

An image that has been divided up into sections, each of which serves as a link.

Image placeholder

An image placeholder is a graphic the size of an image you plan to use that holds the position on the page until the image is placed.

Import data

To bring data created in one software application into another application.

InContext Editing (ICE)

An online service that users can log into and be allowed to make changes to designated editable regions on a page while viewing it in a browser.

index.html

The filename of a website's home page.

Inheritance

The CSS governing principle that allows for the properties of a parent container to be used to format the content in a child container.

Inline style

A style whose code is placed within the body tags of a web page.

Insert panel

The Insert panel includes eight categories of buttons for creating and inserting objects displayed as a drop-down menu: Common, Layout, Forms, Data, Spry, InContext Editing, Text, and Favorites.

Inspect mode

Works together with Live View to help you identify HTML elements and their associated CSS styles.

Intellectual Property

An image or idea that is owned and retained by legal control.

Interactivity

Allows visitors to your website to interact with and affect content by moving or clicking the mouse or using the keyboard.

Internal links

Links to web pages within the same website.

Internet Service Provider

See ISP.

IP address

An assigned series of numbers, separated by periods, that designates an address on the Internet.

ISP

Internet Service Provider. A service to which you subscribe to be able to connect to the Internet with your computer.

Item

An individual link in a Spry menu bar.

J

Java Server Page (JSP)
Server-side application used for processing data in a form.

JavaScript
A web-scripting code that interacts with HTML code to create dynamic content, such as rollovers or interactive forms on a web page. Also called Jscript.

JPEG file
Joint Photographic Experts Group file. A JPEG is a type of file format used for images that appear on web pages. Many photographs are saved with the JPEG file format.

Jump menu
Navigation menu that lets users go quickly to different pages in a site or to different sites on the Internet.

K

Keywords
Words that relate to the content of a website and reside in the head section of a web page.

L

Label tag
A form attribute that assigns a descriptive label to a form object.

LAN
A local area network.

Left property
The property that specifies the distance between the left edge of an AP div and the left edge of the page or parent AP div that contains it.

Library item
Content that can contain text or graphics that you plan to use multiple times in your website and is saved in a separate file in the Library folder of your website.

Licensing agreement
The permission given by a copyright holder that conveys the right to use the copyright holder's work.

Link
See Hyperlink.

Liquid layout
A page layout that expresses all container widths in percents and changes size depending on the size of the browser window.

List form object
A form object that lets users select one or more options from a list of choices.

Live view
Live view displays an open document as if you were viewing it in a browser, with interactive elements active and functioning.

Local site
The location of your local site root folder where your website files are stored while being developed.

Local site folder
A folder on a hard drive, flash drive, or floppy disk that holds all the files and folders for a website. Also called local root folder or local site root folder.

Locked region
An area on a template that cannot be changed by users of the template.

Low-bandwidth animations
Animations that don't require a fast connection to work properly.

M

Mailto: link
An e-mail address formatted as a link that opens the default mail program with a blank, addressed message.

Media object
A combination of visual and audio effects and text to create a fully engaging experience with a website.

Media-dependent style sheet
A style sheet tool for identifying the device being used and formatting the page appropriately.

Menu bar
An area on a web page that contains links to the main pages of a website. Also called a navigation bar.

Menu bar (Mac)
In Dreamweaver, the area located above the Document window that includes menu names, a Workspace switcher, and other application commands.

Menu form object
A form object that lets users select a single option from a list of choices.

Merge cells
To combine multiple adjacent cells in a table into one cell.

Meta data
Information about a file, such as keywords, descriptions, and copyright information.

Meta tags
HTML codes that reside in the head section of a web page and include information about the page such as keywords and descriptions.

Method property
A form property that specifies the HyperText Transfer Protocol (HTTP) used to send the form data to a web server.

MPEG (Motion Picture Experts Group)
A digital video format.

MySpace
A social networking site. *See also* Social networking.

——————— **N** ———————

Named anchor
A specific location on a web page that is used to link to that portion of the web page.

Navigation bar
A set of text or graphic links usually organized in rows or columns that viewers can use to navigate between pages of a website. *See* Menu bar.

Navigation structure
The way that menu bars and other internal links are organized in websites for users to navigate from page to page within the website.

Nested AP element
An AP div whose HTML code is included within another AP div's code.

Nested table
A table within a table.

Nested template
A template that is based on another template.

No right-click script
JavaScript code that will block users from displaying the shortcut menu when they right-click an image on a web page.

Non-breaking space
A space that is left on the page by a browser.

Non-web safe colors
Colors that might not be displayed uniformly across computer platforms.

Numbered lists
Lists of items that are presented in a specific order and preceded by numbers or letters in sequence. Also called ordered lists.

——————— **O** ———————

Online communities
Online communities, or virtual communities, are social websites you can join, such as Facebook and Twitter, where you can communicate with others by posting messages or media content such as images or videos.

Optional region
Region in a template that template users can choose to either show or hide.

Ordered lists
Lists of items that are placed in a specific order and preceded by numbers or letters. Sometimes called numbered lists.

Orphaned files
Files that are not linked to any pages in the website.

Over Image state
The state of a page element when the mouse pointer is over the element.

Over While Down Image state
The state of a page element when the mouse pointer is clicked and held over the element.

Overflow property
A property that specifies how to handle excess content that does not fit inside an AP div.

——————— **P** ———————

Panel
A tabbed window in Dreamweaver that displays information on a particular topic or contains related commands.

Panel groups
Sets of related panels that are grouped together and are displayed through the Window menu. Also known as Tab groups.

Parent container
A container created with HTML tags with other containers falling between its opening and closing tags.

Parent page
A page at a higher level in a web hierarchy that links to other pages on a lower level called child pages.

Path (file location)
The location of an open file in relation to its place in the folder structure of the website.

Permissions process
The process of obtaining permission to legally use content (such text, photos, music, trademarks, and merchandise) in a work such as a website or book.

Plug-in

A computer program that works with a host application such as a web browser to allow it to perform certain functions. *See also* Add-on.

PNG file

Portable Network Graphics file. PNG is a file format used for images placed on web pages that is capable of showing millions of colors but is small in file size. The native file format in Fireworks.

Podcasts

Digitally broadcasted files users can download and play using devices such as computers or MP3 players; POD stands for Programming On Demand.

Point of contact

A place on a web page that provides users with a means of contacting the company.

POST method

A form property that specifies that the form data should be sent to the processing script as a binary or encrypted file, allowing you to send data securely.

POWDER

The acronym for Protocol for Web Description Resources. This is an evaluation system for web pages developed with the World Wide Web Consortium (W3C) that provides summary information about a website.

Progressive video download

A download type that will download a video to a user's computer, and then allow the video to play before it has completely downloaded.

Properties pane

The bottom half of the CSS Styles panel that lists a selected rule's properties.

Property inspector

In Dreamweaver, a panel that displays the properties of a selected web page object. The contents of the Property inspector vary according to the object currently selected.

Pseudo class style

A style that determines the appearance of a page element when a certain condition from information external to the HTML source is met.

Public domain

Work that is no longer protected by copyright. Anyone can use it for any purpose.

Publish a website

To make a website available for viewing on the Internet or on an intranet by transferring the files to a web server.

—————— **R** ——————

Radial symmetry

A design principle in which page elements are balanced from the center of the page outward, like the petals of a flower.

Radio button

A form object that provides an option for selecting a form item; displays as a small circle in a form.

Radio group

A group of radio buttons used to provide a list of options from which only one selection can be made.

RDS

Remote Development Services. A connection type for transferring files used with web servers using Cold Fusion.

Reference panel

A panel used to find answers to coding questions, covering topics such as HTML, JavaScript, and Accessibility.

Regular expressions

Combinations of characters, such as a phrase that begins or ends with a particular word or tag.

Related files

Files that are linked to a document and are necessary for the document to display and function correctly.

Related Files toolbar

A toolbar located below an open document's filename tab that displays the names of any related files.

Relative path

A path used with an internal link to reference a web page or graphic file within the website.

Remote server

A web server that hosts websites and is not directly connected to the computer housing the local site.

Remote site

A website that has been published to a remote server.

Render

To draw on a computer screen; Macintosh and Windows computers render fonts on the screen differently.

Reset button

A button, that, when clicked, will clear data from a form and reset it to its default values.

Rich content

Attractive and engaging images, interactive elements, video, or animations. Also called rich media content.

Rollover

A special effect that changes the appearance of an object when the mouse moves over it.

Rollover image

An image that changes its appearance when the mouse pointer is placed over it in a browser.

Root folder

See Local site folder.

Root-relative path

A path referenced from a website's root folder.

Rows

Table cells arranged horizontally.

RSS

Really Simple Syndication; a way of distributing regularly released information. *See also* RSS feeds.

RSS feeds

A method that websites use, utilizing RSS (Really Simple Syndication), to distribute news stories, information about upcoming events, and announcements.

Rule of thirds

A design principle that entails dividing a page into nine squares and then placing the page elements of most interest on the intersections of the grid lines.

Rules

Sets of formatting attributes that define styles in a Cascading Style Sheet.

Rules pane

The middle pane of the CSS Styles panel that displays the location of the current selected rule in the open document.

S

Sans serif fonts

Fonts with block-style characters; commonly used for headings and subheadings.

Scope creep

Making impromptu changes or additions to a project without corresponding increases in the schedule or budget.

Screen reader

A device used by users with a visual impairment to convert written text on a computer monitor to spoken words.

Seamless image

A tiled image that is blurred at the edges so that it appears to be all one image.

Secure FTP (SFTP)

An FTP option that lets you encrypt file transfers to protect your files, user names, and passwords; in Dreamweaver set this in the Site Setup dialog box.

Secure Socket Layer (SSL)

The industry standard for viewing and sending confidential information over the Internet by encrypting the data.

Selector

The name of the tag to which style declarations have been assigned.

Semantic markup

Coding to emphasize meaning.

Semantic web

Refers to the way web page content such as paragraph text or list items can be coded to emphasize their meaning to users.

Serif fonts

Ornate fonts that have a tail, or stroke, at the end of some characters. These tails lead the eye from one character to the next, making it easier to recognize words; therefore, serif fonts are generally used in text passages.

Server-side scripting

A method used to process information a form collects and uses applications that reside on the web server.

Show Code and Design views

A combination of Code view and Design view. The best view for correcting errors.

Site definition

The site definition for a website contains important information about the site, including its URL, preferences that you've specified, and other secure information, such as login and password information.

Site map

A graphical representation or a directory listing of how web pages relate to each other within a website.

Skype

A free application program that you can use to communicate live with other people through video conferencing.

Slider

The small indicator on the left side of the History panel that you can drag to undo or redo an action.

Smart object

An image layer that stores image data from raster or vector images.

Snippet

See Code snippets.

Social networking
The grouping of individual web users who connect and interact with other users in online communities.

Soft return
A shortcut key combination that forces text to a new line without creating a new paragraph by creating a <br> tag. Also called a line break.

Split cells
To divide cells into multiple cells.

Spry
Open source code developed by Adobe Systems to help designers quickly incorporate dynamic content on their web pages. Also known as Spry framework.

Spry data set
A JavaScript object that stores data in rows and columns.

Spry effect
Screen effects such as fading and enlarging page elements.

Spry framework for AJAX
A JavaScript library that provides access to reusable widgets that you can add to web pages.

Spry menu bar
One of the pre-set widgets available in Dreamweaver that creates a dynamic, user-friendly menu bar that is easy to insert and customize.

Spry Validation Field widgets
Form fields that display valid or invalid states when text is being entered in a form on a web page.

Spry widget
A page element that enables user interaction on a web page.

Standard Mode
A Dreamweaver mode that is used when you insert a table using the Insert Table button or command.

Standard toolbar
A toolbar that contains buttons you use to execute frequently used commands that are also available on the File and Edit menus.

State
In a browser, the condition of an item in a Spry menu bar in relation to the mouse pointer.

Static content
Page content that does not change or allow user interaction.

Status bar
The area located at the bottom of the program window (Win) or the image window (Mac) that displays information such as the file size of the active window and a description of the active tool. In Dreamweaver, a bar that appears at the bottom of the Dreamweaver document window. The left end of the status bar displays the tag selector, which shows the HTML tags being used at the insertion point location. The right end displays the window size and estimated download time for the page displayed.

Step
Each task performed in the History panel.

Storyboard
A small sketch that represents each page in a website or screen in an application. Like a flowchart, a storyboard shows the relationship of each page or screen to the other pages in the site or screens. Similar to a wireframe.

Streaming video download
Similar to a progressive video download, except streaming video downloads use buffers to gather the content as it is downloading to ensure a smoother playback.

String
A series of characters or words.

Style Rendering toolbar
A toolbar that contains buttons that allow you to display a web page as different media types (e.g., handheld).

Submit button
A button which, when clicked, will send the data from a form on a web page to a web server to be processed.

Summary for Selection pane
The top half of the CSS Styles panel that displays the selected rule's properties when the Switch to Current Selection Mode button is selected.

Swap image behavior
JavaScript code that directs the browser to display a different image when the mouse is rolled over an image on a web page.

Swap image restore behavior
JavaScript code that directs the browser to restore a swapped image back to the original image.

Synchronize files
A Dreamweaver command that compares the names, dates, and times on all files on a local and remote site, then transfers only the files that have changed since the last upload.

T

Tab groups
Sets of related panels that are grouped together. Also known as panel groups.

Table header
Text placed at the top or sides of a table on a web page that is read by screen readers to help provide accessibility for table content.

Tables
Grids of rows and columns that can be used either to hold tabular data on a web page or as a basic design tool for data placement.

Tabular data
Data arranged in columns and rows and separated by a delimiter.

Tag selector
The left side of the status bar that displays HTML tags used at the insertion point location.

Tag type
A classification by type of style used to redefine an HTML tag.

Tags (HTML)
HTML tags are the parts of the code that specify the appearance for all page content when viewed in a browser.

Target
The location on a web page that the browser displays when users click an internal link.

Target property
In a form, the property that lets you specify the window in which you want the form data to be processed, such as _blank, which opens a form in a separate browser window.

Templates
Web pages that contain the basic layout for each page in the site, including the location of a company logo, banner, or navigation links.

Terms of use
The rules that a copyright owner uses to establish use of his or her work.

Testing server
A server that is used to evaluate how a web site is functioning before it is published.

Text area field
A text field that can store several lines of text.

Text field
A form object used for collecting a string of characters such as a name.

Thumbnail
A small version of a larger image. Also called thumbnail image.

Tiled image
A small graphic that repeats across and down a web page, appearing as individual squares or rectangles.

Tools panel
A panel separated into categories containing tools and their options.

Top property
The property that specifies the distance between the top edge of an AP div and the top edge of the page or a parent AP div.

Tracing image
An image that is placed in the background of a web page as a guide to create page elements on top of it, similar to the way tracing paper is used.

Trademark
Protects an image, word, slogan, symbol, or design used to identify goods or services.

Tweet
A short message posted on the Twitter website that is no more than 140 characters.

Twitter
A website where viewers can post short messages, called "tweets."

U

Unordered lists
Lists of items that do not need to be placed in a specific order and are usually preceded by bullets.

Unvisited links
Links that have not been clicked by the user. The default color for unvisited links is blue.

Upload
The process of transferring files from a local drive to a web server.

URL
Uniform Resource Locator. An address that determines a route on the Internet or to a web page. *See* Domain name.

V

Validate markup
A Dreamweaver command that searches through the HTML code to flag code that could cause errors to occur with different language versions, such as XHTML or XML.

Vector-based graphics
Scaleable graphics that are built using mathematical formulas, rather than with pixels.

Vertical symmetry
A design principle in which page elements are balanced up and down the page.

Vidcast
Another name for video podcast. Also called vodcast.

View
A choice for displaying page content in the Document window. Dreamweaver has three working views: Design view, Code view, and Show Code and Design views.

Vis property
A property that lets you control whether a selected AP div is visible or hidden.

Visited links
Links that have been previously clicked, or visited. The default color for visited links is purple.

Vodcasts
Video podcasts. Also called vidcasts.

VSS
Microsoft Office Visual SafeSource. A connection type for transferring files with the Windows operating system.

— W —

W3C
World Wide Web Consortium; an international group of companies that develops standards for the World Wide Web. *See also* WCAG.

WCAG
Web Content Accessibility Guidelines, Version 2.0 developed by the World Wide Web Consortium (W3C); contains guidelines for website development, including accessibility guidelines.

Web 2.0
The evolution of web applications that facilitate and promote information sharing among Internet users.

Web browser
A program, such as Microsoft Internet Explorer, Apple Safari, Google Chrome, or Mozilla Firefox, that lets you display HTML-developed web pages.

Web cam
A camera used for video web conferencing.

Web design program
A program for creating interactive web pages containing text, images, hyperlinks, animation, sound, and video.

Web server
A computer dedicated to hosting websites that is connected to the Internet and configured with software to handle requests from browsers.

WebDav
Web-based Distributed Authoring and Versioning. A type of connection used with the WebDav protocol, such as a website residing on an Apache web server.

Web-safe colors
Colors that display consistently in all browsers and on Macintosh, Windows, and Unix platforms.

Website
A website is a group of related web pages that are linked together and share a common interface and design.

White space
An area on a web page that is not filled with text or graphics; may or may not be white.

Widget
A widget is a piece of code that allows a user to interact with a program, such as clicking a menu item to open a page.

Width (W) property
The property that specifies the width of an AP div, either in pixels or as a percentage of the screen width.

Wiki
Refers to a site where a user can use simple editing tools to contribute and edit the page content in a site. Named for the Hawaiian word for "quick."

Wikipedia
An online encyclopedia that allows users to contribute to site content.

Wireframe
A prototype that represents every page and its contents in a website. Like a flowchart or storyboard, a wireframe shows the relationship of each page in the site to all the other pages.

Workspace
The entire window, from the Application bar (Win) or Menu bar (Mac) at the top of the window, to the status bar at the bottom border of the program window. The area in the Dreamweaver program window that includes all of the menus, panels, buttons, inspectors, and panes that you use to create and maintain websites.

Workspace switcher
A drop-down menu located in the top right corner on the Application bar (Win) or Menu bar (Mac) that allows you to change the workspace layout.

WYSIWYG
An acronym for What You See Is What You Get, meaning that your web page should look the same in the browser as it does in the web editor.

X

XHTML

XHTML is the acronym for eXtensible HyperText Markup Language, the current standard language used to create web pages.

XML

XML stands for Extensible Markup Language, a type of file that is used to develop customized tags to store information.

XSL

Extensible Stylesheet Language. Similar to CSS; the XSL style sheet information formats containers created with XML.

XSLT

Extensible Stylesheet Language Transformations. XSLT interprets the code in the XSL file to transform an XML document, much like style sheet files transform HTML files.

Y

YouTube

A website where you can upload and share videos.

Z

Z-Index property

A property that specifies the vertical stacking order of AP divs on a page.

Index